THE
ESSENTIAL
SANTAYANA

THE ESSENTIAL SANTAYANA

Selected Writings

edited by The Santayana Edition

compiled and with an introduction
by Martin A. Coleman

*Indiana
University
Press*

BLOOMINGTON AND INDIANAPOLIS

This book is a publication of

Indiana University Press
601 North Morton Street
Bloomington, IN 47404-3797 USA

http://iupress.indiana.edu

Telephone orders   800-842-6796
Fax orders   812-855-7931
Orders by e-mail   iuporder@indiana.edu

Cataloging information is available from the Library of Congress.

ISBN 978-0-253-35348-1 (cl.)
ISBN 978-0-253-22105-6 (pbk.)

This book is dedicated to

ANGUS KERR-LAWSON

whose editorial work and scholarship

have enriched and enlivened Santayana studies.

"[T]he spirit . . . has perceived that . . . it is in the hands of some alien and inscrutable power. . . . I stand before [this power] simply receptive, somewhat as, in Rome I might stand before the great fountain of Trevi. There I see jets and cascades flowing in separate streams and in divers directions. I am not sure that a single Pontifex Maximus designed it all, and led all those musical waters into just those channels. Some streams may have dried up or been diverted since the creation; some rills may have been added today by fresh rains from heaven; behind one of those artificial rocks some little demon, of his own free will, may even now be playing havoc with the conduits; and who knows how many details, in my image, may not have been misplaced or multiplied by optical tricks of my own? Yet here, for the spirit, is one total marvellous impression, one thunderous force, confronting me with this theatrical but admirable spectacle."

"Ultimate Religion" (*Essential Santayana*, 340–41; originally appeared in *Obiter Scripta*, 284–86). Photograph courtesy of Herman J. Saatkamp Jr.

Contents

Acknowledgments

The editors of the Santayana Edition would like to thank the people who helped in the production of *The Essential Santayana*.

John Lachs, Herman J. Saatkamp Jr., William G. Holzberger, and Angus Kerr-Lawson laid the foundation for *The Essential Santayana* through many years of documentary research, editorial work, critical scholarship, and conversations with publishers.

We are grateful to the many scholars who answered our requests for suggestions for and comments on the content and organization of *The Essential Santayana,* including Thomas Alexander, Michael Brodrick, James Campbell, Matthew Caleb Flamm, James Gouinlock, Larry Hickman, Nathan Houser, Till Kinzel, Tom Kirby-Smith, Marta Kunecka, Henry Samuel Levinson, Richard C. Lyon, John McDermott, Daniel Moreno-Moreno, Richard M. Rubin, Krzysztof Skowroñski, John J. Stuhr, Glenn Tiller, and Jessica Wahman.

We appreciate the efforts of our graduate student interns, including Geoffery E. Gagen, who copied and scanned text selections; Christine McNulty, who compiled and calculated survey results; Carrie Torrella-McCord, who proofread; Christine Sego-Caldwell, who proofread and helped research information for the headnotes; and Jay Perry, who researched publication information.

The Santayana Edition
Marianne S. Wokeck, Editor
Martin A. Coleman, Associate Editor
Kristine W. Frost, Associate Editor
Johanna E. Resler, Assistant Editor
David E. Spiech, Assistant Textual Editor

http://www.iupui.edu/~santedit/

Chronology of the Life and Work of George Santayana

Adapted and abridged from William G. Holzberger, "Chronology," *Letters of George Santayana*, 1:443–60

1849 Josefina Borrás (c. 1826–1912), George Santayana's mother, marries George Sturgis (1817–57) of Boston, aboard British warship in Manila Bay.

1857 George Sturgis dies in Manila at age forty.

1862 Josefina Borrás Sturgis marries Agustín Santayana (1814–93) in Madrid.

1863 George Santayana born on 16 December at No. 69, Calle Ancha de San Bernardo, Madrid.

1864 Santayana christened Jorge Agustín Nicolás on 1 January in parish church of San Marcos, Madrid.

1868 (or **1869**) Santayana's mother, with daughters Susana and Josephine, moves to Boston to honor first husband's wish that children be raised in America; Santayana remains with father in Spain.

1872 Santayana and father travel to America in June; father returns to Ávila several months later.

1882 Santayana graduates from Boston Latin School; attends Harvard College in autumn.

1883 Santayana visits father in Spain for first time since coming to America. Advised by William James at Harvard not to pursue philosophy.

1885 Meets John Francis ("Frank") Stanley, 2d Earl Russell and elder brother of Bertrand Russell, who becomes close friend.

1886 Santayana's Bachelor of Arts degree is awarded *summa cum laude* and *in absentia*. Begins study in Germany.

1889 Santayana completes dissertation on "Lotze's System of Philosophy" under direction of Josiah Royce; awarded Master of Arts and Doctor of Philosophy degrees by Harvard University; begins as Instructor in Philosophy at Harvard.

1893 Santayana's father dies at age 79 during summer in Ávila; Santayana's student and friend Warwick Potter dies in October; at end of this year Santayana undergoes his *metanoia* or fundamental change of heart resulting in renunciation of the world.

1896 Santayana's first book-length philosophical work is published by Scribner's: *The Sense of Beauty: Being the Outlines of Aesthetic Theory*. Spends year at Cambridge University; appears in court in October to testify on behalf of Frank Russell, defending against charges of estranged wife.

1897 Santayana resumes teaching at Harvard; lives with mother.

1898 Santayana promoted from instructor to assistant professor.

1899 Santayana's *Lucifer: A Theological Tragedy* published.

1900 *Interpretations of Poetry and Religion* published.

1904 Santayana sails from New York to Plymouth, England, in mid-July; visits Paris, Rome, Venice, Naples, Pompeii, Sicily, and Greece.

1905 Visits Egypt, Palestine, Tel Aviv, Jerusalem, Damascus, Baalbeck, Beirut, Athens, Constantinople, Budapest, and Vienna. While still abroad, Santayana invited by Harvard to become Hyde Lecturer at the Sorbonne for 1905–6. First four volumes of *The Life of Reason; or, the Phases of Human Progress* published.

1906 Fifth volume of *The Life of Reason* published. Santayana returns to America in September; resumes teaching at Harvard.

1907 Santayana promoted from assistant professor to full professor.

1911 In April Santayana delivers final lecture at Harvard. Travels to Wisconsin and California.

1912 Santayana departs America for last time on 24 January. Mother dies on 5 February.

1913 *Winds of Doctrine: Studies in Contemporary Opinion* published.

1914 World War I breaks out; Santayana remains in Oxford until April 1919.

1916 *Egotism in German Philosophy* published.

1920 Santayana begins spending winters in Rome; continues to summer in Paris, Ávila, Glion, at Lake Geneva, or Cortina d'Ampezzo.

1923 *Scepticism and Animal Faith* and last collection of Santayana's poetry to appear during his lifetime, *Poems: Selected by the Author and Revised,* published.

1925 *Dialogues in Limbo* published.

1927 Santayana meets Daniel Cory, age 22, who will become his assistant and friend. *The Realm of Essence: Book First of Realms of Being* published.

1928 Santayana declines offer of the Norton Chair of Poetry at Harvard for 1928–29. Half sister Susana dies in Ávila, on 10 February, at age 77.

1930 Half sister Josephine dies in Ávila, on 15 October, at age 77. *The Realm of Matter: Book Second of Realms of Being* published.

1931 *The Genteel Tradition at Bay* published. In December Santayana declines offer to become William James Professor of Philosophy at Harvard.

1932 Santayana attends philosophical congress commemorating tercentenary of Spinoza's birth, held at The Hague on 6–10 September; delivers a lecture on "Ultimate Religion." Attends meeting in London to commemorate tercentenary of John Locke's birth; on 19 October delivers address on "Locke and the Frontiers of Common Sense."

1933 *Some Turns of Thought in Modern Philosophy* published.

1935 *The Last Puritan: A Memoir in the Form of a Novel* published in London (published in New York the next year).

1936 *The Last Puritan* becomes Book-of-the-Month Club bestseller.

1937 *The Realm of Truth: Book Third of Realms of Being* published in London (published in New York the next year).

1938 The first book-length biography, *George Santayana,* by George Washburne Howgate published.

1939 World War II breaks out in Europe; Santayana denied regular long-term visa by Swiss officials, decides to remain in Italy.

1940 *The Realm of Spirit: Book Fourth of Realms of Being* published. *The Philosophy of George Santayana* published.

1941 Santayana moves into nursing home operated by Blue Sisters of the Little Company of Mary, an order of Roman Catholic Irish nuns.

1944 *Persons and Places* published; becomes bestseller.

1945 *The Middle Span* published. Santayana awarded Nicholas Murray Butler Medal by Columbia University.

1946 *The Idea of Christ in the Gospels; or, God in Man: A Critical Essay* published.

1948 *Dialogues in Limbo, With Three New Dialogues* published.

1951 *Dominations and Powers: Reflections on Liberty, Society, and Government* published.

1952 On 4 June Santayana falls on the steps of the Spanish Consulate in Rome; injuries include three broken ribs, bleeding head wound, and patches of pneumonia on lungs; physician is amazed by Santayana's recovery. Santayana continues working until increasing blindness and illness make further labor impossible. On 26 September Santayana dies of stomach cancer. On 30 September his body is interred in the Tomb of the Spaniards.

1953 *My Host the World* published. *The Posthumous Poems,* together with two early plays, published as *The Poet's Testament: Poems and Two Plays.*

1955 *The Letters of George Santayana,* a selection of two hundred and ninety-six letters to eighty-six recipients, edited by Daniel Cory, published.

Bibliographical Abbreviations

The following is a list of abbreviations and bibliographical references to Santayana's works and secondary source materials. The abbreviations are used for books cited in the introductions and head notes. Citations from the current work are referenced by (*ES,* page number).

Primary Sources

BR   *Birth of Reason & Other Essays.* Edited by Daniel Cory. New York and London: Columbia University Press, 1968.

COUS   *Character and Opinion in the United States: With Reminiscences of William James and Josiah Royce and Academic Life in America.* New York: Charles Scribner's Sons; London: Constable and Co. Ltd.; Toronto: McLeod, 1920. Volume eleven of the critical edition of *The Works of George Santayana* (*WGS*).

CP   *The Complete Poems of George Santayana: A Critical Edition.* Edited by William G. Holzberger. Lewisburg, PA: Bucknell University Press; London: Associated University Presses, 1979.

DL   *Dialogues in Limbo.* London: Constable and Co. Ltd., 1925; New York: Charles Scribner's Sons, 1926. Volume fourteen of the critical edition (*WGS*).

DP   *Dominations and Powers: Reflections on Liberty, Society, and Government.* New York: Charles Scribner's Sons; London: Constable and Co. Ltd., 1951. Volume nineteen of the critical edition (*WGS*).

EGP   *Egotism in German Philosophy.* New York: Charles Scribner's Sons; London and Toronto: J. M. Dent & Sons Ltd., 1916. Volume ten of the critical edition (*WGS*).

GTB   *The Genteel Tradition at Bay.* New York: Charles Scribner's Sons; London: "The Adelphi," 1931. Volume seventeen of the critical edition (*WGS*).

HC   *A Hermit of Carmel and Other Poems.* New York: Charles Scribner's Sons, 1901; London: R. Brimley Johnson, 1902.

ICG   *The Idea of Christ in the Gospels; or, God in Man: A Critical Essay.* New York: Charles Scribner's Sons; Toronto: Saunders, 1946. Volume eighteen of the critical edition (*WGS*).

IPR   *Interpretations of Poetry and Religion.* New York: Charles Scribner's Sons; London: Black, 1900. Volume three of the critical edition (*WGS*) edited by William G. Holzberger and Herman J. Saatkamp Jr., with an introduction by Joel Porte. Cambridge, MA: The MIT Press, 1989. (Citations refer to critical edition page numbers.)

LP   *The Last Puritan: A Memoir in the Form of a Novel.* London: Constable and Co. Ltd., 1935; New York: Charles Scribner's Sons, 1936; Volume four of the critical edition (*WGS*) edited by William G. Holzberger and Herman J. Saatkamp Jr., with an introduction by Irving Singer. Cambridge, MA: The MIT Press, 1994. (Citations refer to critical edition page numbers.)

LGS   *The Letters of George Santayana.* Volume Five (in eight books) of the critical edition (*WGS*) edited by William G. Holzberger, Herman J. Saatkamp Jr., and Marianne S. Wokeck, with an introduction by William G. Holzberger. Cambridge, MA: The MIT Press, 2000–2008. (Citations in the notes refer to book and page number; i.e., *LGS*, 8:150 is page 150 of Book Eight.)

LR   *The Life of Reason: or, the Phases of Human Progress.* Five volumes. New York: Charles Scribner's Sons; London: Constable and Co. Ltd., 1905–06. Volume seven of the critical edition of *WGS* edited by Martin Coleman and Marianne Wokeck, with an introduction by James Gouinlock.

   LR1   *Introduction and Reason in Common Sense.* Volume 1, 1905.

   LR2   *Reason in Society.* Volume 2, 1905.

   LR3   *Reason in Religion.* Volume 3, 1905.

   LR4   *Reason in Art.* Volume 4, 1905.

   LR5   *Reason in Science.* Volume 5, 1906.

LE   *Little Essays: Drawn From the Writings of George Santayana by Logan Pearsall Smith, With the Collaboration of the Author.* New York: Charles Scribner's Sons; London: Constable and Co. Ltd., 1920.

LUC   *Lucifer: A Theological Tragedy.* Chicago and New York: Herbert S. Stone, 1899.

LHT   Revised limited second edition published as *Lucifer, or the Heavenly Truce: A Theological Tragedy.* Cambridge, MA: Dunster House; London: W. Jackson, 1924.

OB   *Obiter Scripta: Lectures, Essays and Reviews.* Edited by Justus Buchler and Benjamin Schwartz. New York: Charles Scribner's Sons; London: Constable and Co. Ltd., 1936.

PP   *Persons and Places: Fragments of Autobiography.* Volume one of the critical edition (*WGS*) edited by William G. Holzberger and Herman J. Saatkamp Jr., with an introduction by Richard C. Lyon. Cambridge,

MA: The MIT Press, 1986. (Citations refer to critical edition page numbers.)

PP1   *Persons and Places: The Background of My Life.* New York: Charles Scribner's Sons; London: Constable and Co. Ltd., 1944.

PP2   *The Middle Span.* New York: Charles Scribner's Sons, 1945; London: Constable and Co. Ltd., 1947.

PP3   *My Host the World.* New York: Charles Scribner's Sons; London: Cresset Press, 1953.

POML *Physical Order and Moral Liberty.* Edited by John Lachs. Nashville, TN: Vanderbilt University Press, 1969.

PSL   *Platonism and the Spiritual Life.* New York: Charles Scribner's Sons; London: Constable and Co. Ltd., 1927. Volume fifteen of the critical edition (*WGS*).

PSA   *Poems: Selected by the Author and Revised.* London: Constable and Co. Ltd., 1922; New York: Charles Scribner's Sons, 1923.

PT   *The Poet's Testament: Poems and Two Plays.* New York: Charles Scribner's Sons, 1953.

RB   *Realms of Being.* Four volumes. New York: Charles Scribner's Sons; London: Constable and Co. Ltd., 1927–40. Volume sixteen of the critical edition (*WGS*).

    RE   *The Realm of Essence: Book First of Realms of Being,* 1927.

    RM   *The Realm of Matter: Book Second of Realms of Being,* 1930.

    RT   *The Realm of Truth: Book Third of Realms of Being.* London: Constable; Toronto: Macmillan Company, 1937; New York: Charles Scribner's Sons, 1938.

    RS   *The Realm of Spirit: Book Fourth of Realms of Being,* 1940.

RB1 *Realms of Being.* One-volume edition, with a new introduction by the author. New York: Charles Scribner's Sons, 1942.

SAF   *Scepticism and Animal Faith: Introduction to a System of Philosophy.* New York: Charles Scribner's Sons; London: Constable and Co. Ltd., 1923. Volume thirteen of the critical edition (*WGS*).

SB   *The Sense of Beauty: Being the Outlines of Aesthetic Theory.* New York: Charles Scribner's Sons; London: A. and C. Black, 1896. Volume two of the critical edition (*WGS*) edited by William G. Holzberger and Herman J. Saatkamp Jr., with an introduction by Arthur C. Danto. Cambridge, MA: The MIT Press, 1988. (Citations refer to critical edition page numbers.)

SE   *Soliloquies in England and Later Soliloquies.* New York: Charles Scribner's Sons; London: Constable and Co. Ltd., 1922. Volume twelve of the critical edition (*WGS*).

SOV   *Sonnets and Other Verses.* Cambridge and Chicago: Stone and Kimball, 1894.

TTMP   *Some Turns of Thought in Modern Philosophy: Five Essays.* New York: Charles Scribner's Sons; Cambridge: Cambridge University Press, 1933. Volume seventeen of the critical edition (*WGS*).

TPP   *Three Philosophical Poets: Lucretius, Dante, and Goethe.* Cambridge, MA: Harvard University Press; London: Oxford University Press, 1910. Volume eight of the critical edition (*WGS*) edited by Martin Coleman and Marianne Wokeck, with an introduction by James Seaton.

WD   *Winds of Doctrine: Studies in Contemporary Opinion.* New York: Charles Scribner's Sons; London: J. M. Dent & Sons Ltd., 1913. Volume nine of the critical edition (*WGS*).

Secondary Sources

WAGS   Arnett, Willard. *George Santayana.* New York: Washington Square Press, 1968.

LY   Cory, Daniel. *Santayana: The Later Years: A Portrait with Letters.* New York: George Braziller, 1963.

UAS   Flamm, Matthew Caleb, and Krzysztof Piotr Skowroñski, editors. *Under Any Sky: Contemporary Readings of George Santayana.* Newcastle upon Tyne, United Kingdom: Cambridge Scholars Publishing, 2007.

AFSL   Lachs, John, editor. *Animal Faith and the Spiritual Life.* New York: Appleton-Century-Crofts, 1967.

JLGS   Lachs, John. *George Santayana.* Boston: Twayne Publishers, 1988.

OnS   Lachs, John. *On Santayana.* Belmont, CA; London: Wadsworth, 2001.

SPSL   Levinson, Henry S. *Santayana, Pragmatism, and the Spiritual Life.* Chapel Hill: University of North Carolina Press, 1992.

GSB   McCormick, John. *George Santayana: A Biography.* New York: Alfred A. Knopf, 1987.

BSS   *Overheard in Seville: Bulletin of the Santayana Society.* Edited by Angus Kerr-Lawson.

<http://indiamond6.ulib.iupui.edu/Santayana/>

PGS   Schilpp, Paul Arthur, editor. *The Philosophy of George Santayana.*
Volume II of *The Library of Living Philosophers.* Evanston and Chicago:
Northwestern University Press, 1940.

TRS   Singer, Beth. *The Rational Society: A Critical Study of Santayana's Thought.*
Cleveland, OH: Press of Case Western Reserve University, 1970.

SAEP   Sprigge, Timothy L. S. *Santayana.* London and Boston: Routledge,
1995. Second edition of *Santayana: An Examination of his Philosophy,*
with a new introduction, select bibliography, and a foreword by Angus
Kerr-Lawson.

LITE   Woodward, Anthony. *Living in the Eternal: A Study of George Santayana.*
Nashville, TN: Vanderbilt University Press, 1988.

About This Book

Given George Santayana's exquisite style and prolific output, it was difficult to condense his important writings into a single volume. But this wealth of material ensures that everything included in *The Essential Santayana* is a significant piece of work by an extraordinary thinker.

In consultation with the other editors of the Santayana Edition, I composed an initial list of essays and chapters to include in *The Essential Santayana*. We selected works based on their traditional influence and popularity, their representativeness with respect to Santayana's philosophical vision, or their importance according to Santayana's comments in his correspondence. I grouped the selected titles under thematic heads corresponding to his philosophical and literary interests to produce a provisional table of contents, which I then shared with an international group of Santayana scholars. Based on the comments and recommendations of these scholars, I refined the table of contents and began working with the other editors of the Santayana Edition to compile texts for the volume.

The texts of the selections in *The Essential Santayana* were taken, when possible, from *The Works of George Santayana* (The MIT Press, Cambridge, Mass., and London), an unmodernized, critical edition of the philosopher's published and unpublished writings. An "unmodernized" edition retains outdated and idiosyncratic punctuation, spelling, capitalization, and word division in order to reflect the full intent of the author as well as the initial texture of the work. A "critical" edition allows the exercise of editorial judgment in making corrections, changes, and choices among authoritative readings. The goal of the editors of the criticial edition is to produce texts that accurately represent Santayana's final intentions regarding his works, and to record all evidence (in textual apparatus that lists all variants and emendations) on which editorial decisions have been based.

In case a selected text had not yet been published in the critical edition, it was typically drawn from a first edition. The source text was then scanned and the transcription was proofread against the original. Details of the source of each text are provided in an accompanying head note and the bibliography at the front of this book.

The editorial approach in this volume takes Santayana's philosophical writing to be the heart of his work, and the heart of this book consists of three sections addressed to traditionally philosophical themes. The contents of the first and last sections treat personal origins and cultural prospects respectively, but they are not detached from Santayana's philosophy. He claimed that he stood "in philosophy exactly where [he stood] in daily life;" to do otherwise, he thought, would be dishonest (*ES*, 51). The five sections of *The Essential Santayana*–I. Autobiography; II. Skepticism and Ontology; III. Rational Life in Art, Religion, and Spirituality; IV. Ethics and Politics; V. Literature, Culture, and Criticism–reflect the range of Santayana's thought.

Martin A. Coleman

Introduction: The Essential Santayana

There is little hope of evoking *the* essence of Santayana.

Certainly there is such an essence, at least according to Santayana. As certainly as Santayana existed, there is a particular character that distinguishes him as the individual he was and not Charles Peirce or John Dewey. And as certainly as he had a philosophy made up of thoughts which were "events in the world" (*RB1*, 131), there is an essence that distinguishes his philosophy from all others. Santayana maintained that any thing, in virtue of existing, embodies a definite character, and that is its eternal, unchanging essence (*PGS*, 525).

And essences are, on Santayana's view, just what humans intuit if they intuit anything: "they are precisely that which is clearest and most indubitably present in the brightest light. They are, in any 'idea,' all that can be observed, retained, recalled, or communicated" (*PGS*, 500). In fact, he thought that *only* essences are present to us; it is material existences that cannot be directly intuited. Matter is on a different plane of being than essences: both are real, but only matter exists and it is not immediately accessible to the human mind. We intuit essences, and these essences we take as representative of what their existing objects are like.

This suggests why there is little hope of grasping the essence of Santayana: one may intuit an essence, say of a living person, but how can one be sure that it is identical to the essence embodied in the existing individual? Or one may intuit the essence of Santayana's philosophy, but how can one be sure that it is identical to the essence embodied in his actual cogitations? Since one has no direct access to matter, one cannot compare the material existence to the intuited essence.

But this is no difficulty. Santayana wrote: "Our worst difficulties arise from the assumption that knowledge of existences ought to be literal" (*ES*, 83). We make trouble for ourselves when we assume that the essence we intuit (which is a *term* of knowledge) should be somehow identical with the existing thing (which is the *object* of knowledge). Santayana held that such an assumption is incompatible with a naturalistic understanding of the human intellect: It entails an unrealistic standard of certainty for knowledge, which breeds superstition and belief in immaterial powers. Because we never have certainty in fact, we are tempted to posit some undetectable realm or medium of true knowledge that somehow influences the sensible world of matter; or we claim that an immaterial mind mysteriously becomes a factor in the material world registering and directing objects of knowledge. Once this assumption is rejected, the inability to evoke the essence of Santayana is no longer a difficulty. Literal knowledge of existences is seen to be neither necessary nor possible.

Literal knowledge is not necessary because symbolic knowledge meets human needs quite well (*ES*, 83–84). An intuited essence may function as a symbol for an existing object; we can take an essence as standing for the nature or the sum of the properties of an existing thing. This is perfectly adequate for us to realize our natural goods–from avoiding dangers and securing safety to cultivating human consciousness. Taking intuited essences as symbols is a function of the imagination, and the test of fitness for symbols is action in a material environment existing independently of human aims and desires. Santayana emphasized the importance of imagination without ever losing faith in an independent reality of material existences, entailed in every action and intention. Together, imagination and action contribute to human knowledge.

Literal knowledge, in the sense of an exact copy of material existences, is not possible because intuited essences and embodied essences result from different natural processes. According to Santayana, it may be possible for an intuited essence to be identical to an essence embodied in an existing object but he thought it highly unlikely. To expect human ideas to mirror nature is egotistical because it privileges the human intellect over the rest of nature. Human ideas express the activity of the human organism; they do not reproduce intrinsic essences of existing objects. Santayana pointed out that nature "has embodied, from indefinite past time, whatever essences she has embodied without asking our leave or conforming beforehand (as philosophers seem to expect) to the economy and logic of our thoughts" (*RB1*, 136).

This is not to claim that human ideas are irrelevant to nature. Nature produces them in human consciousness at definite points in the course of natural events; they are manifestations of nature in consciousness. Hence, they are relevant symbols of material existences. However, the character of the relevance varies with the conscious human organism and the situation, and intuited essences as symbols often reveal more about the organism intuiting them than about the objects for which they might stand.

A reader's intuited essence of Santayana, then, is a symbol for the man or his philosophy; and though it may reveal something about Santayana, it probably reveals more about the maker of the symbol. Santayana had a favorite image he used to express this inevitable variance between the essence intuited by a reader or observer and the object of inspection: "The idea Paul has of Peter, Spinoza observes, expresses the nature of Peter less than it betrays that of Paul" (*WD*, 77).[1] If an idea of Santayana expresses the nature of the one with that idea, then *The Essential Santayana*, as an expression of the editor's idea of Santayana, shows that the editor has a background in philosophy and reads Santayana primarily as a philosopher, though Santayana was an accomplished writer in several genres. And certainly the selections and their classifications within the five sections of this volume demonstrate editorial tendencies that are accidental rather than essential to the philosophy of Santayana. But the volume is not worthless for not evoking *the* essence of Santayana.

While *The Essential Santayana* will evoke a different idea in the mind of the reader than, say, Santayana's 1923 work *Scepticism and Animal Faith* or an earlier edited collection of Santayana's writings, none of these essences can be said to be essential to Santayana's philosophy because "expressiveness is a most accidental matter. What a line suggests at one reading, it may never suggest again even to the same person" (*LR4*, 91). The symbolic essences evoked by expressions are

---

[1] See also *LGS,* 6:58, 6:187; *SAF,* 247; *RB1,* 141. The text in Spinoza is found in *Ethics,* Part II, Prop. XVII, Scolium.

not permanently related to the essences of an author's intentions. A reader's intuited essence of Santayana's philosophy, whether intuited after reading every last word he wrote or after reading a one-volume selection of texts, always will vary from the essence embodied by Santayana's philosophy.

Santayana wrote, "I am sorry for my critics if they think they must read and classify the numerous books I have written, if they are to gain a fair view of my philosophy. They will feel obliged to distinguish periods, and tendencies and inconsistent positions. But that is all insignificant, extraneous, accidental."[2] He considered the vital part of his thought to be "the living thread, still squirming and ignited," and not found in "the cold old academic printed stuff" or some complete set of expressions.

This comment suggests what *The Essential Santayana* is not: Santayana's living inspiration captured on the page, the absolute truth of Santayana's philosophy, the last word on Santayana's most important writings. The first, human discourse cannot express; the second, like any "essences embodied . . . in the human body and total human career," is "not such as human imagination can easily conceive" (*RB1,* 131); and the third will come with Santayana's last reader but will be no more or less authoritative than the present volume, at least under the aspect of eternity.

But none of this is to suggest that thorough reading, edited volumes, and intellectual activity are meaningless and vain. Such a conclusion would indicate a lingering reverence for literal knowledge: to believe that the rejection of literal knowledge entails the rejection of all knowledge betrays the assumption that knowledge can be only literal. Symbolic knowledge as Santayana understood it does not reduce all to vanity. It serves moral enlightenment, and this suggests an interpretation of Santayana's comments that points to what *The Essential Santayana* may be if it is a fruitful symbol of Santayana's philosophy: an invitation to self-understanding. In this, *The Essential Santayana* would come closest to reviving the living thread of Santayana's philosophy.

The inevitable gap between the essence evoked in a reader by the present volume and the embodied essence of Santayana's actual thoughts is no obstacle to human understanding if the aim of that understanding is moral. Symbolic knowledge serves the moral aim by inviting clearer understanding of the symbolizing organism; it can reveal the framer of ideas to himself. Santayana thought that "[i]n nature, as in a book, we can discover only such thoughts as we are capable of framing" (*RB1,* 593). The essences one assigns to existences reveal one's capacities; and these in turn indicate one's goods, that is, the tendencies of one's perfection or what one is good for. This self-knowledge can be pursued through learning and reflection, and aided by the works of others, including books.

This does not entail that the truth about a thinker or his works is up for grabs depending on the interpreter's constitution, or that a reader's self-knowledge is proof of a sound interpretation of Santayana. While Santayana acknowledged the thoughts of a critic or commentator seldom if ever match those of the author of the text being critiqued, he also believed that one might come closer to the

---

[2] George Santayana, "An Introduction," *Cronos,* 1:2 (1947), 1.

author's thoughts according to the degree of "likeness between the capacities of the writer and the reader" (*RB1*, 593). One ought not let this revive hopes for literal knowledge. His point was that interpretations can be better or worse as determined by actual capacities, that is, by abilities to function and perform certain activities. Action in an independently existing universe, and not some standard of literal knowledge, is the check on imagination.

If *The Essential Santayana* expresses a just and suitable symbol, then it ought to appeal to readers who value the awareness of essence and a refined human consciousness, as Santayana did. In other words, this volume of writings, if well selected, should appeal to those inclined to intellectual activities similar to Santayana's. This book will serve its intended aim if, rather than eliciting any particular essence, it encourages reflection and a deeper appreciation of the intuition of essences as the highest function of human life.

But even if the volume is wisely selected and well edited, there remain questions about the contemporary value of any book about George Santayana.

Why Santayana? Why Now?

To the questions "Why Santayana? Why now?" I answer that Santayana's work offers a philosophical vision of human values without superstition. This vision reveres truth with courage and sincerity. These values diverge from—without condemning—the love of celebrity, possessions, and power prominent in popular alternative visions of human life. Santayana's prized values arise from the potentials and capacities of human reason and spirituality, and his understanding of human spirituality is always rooted in nature, in the larger universe. Hence, Santayana's vision is broad but not shallow and human but not anthropocentric. Accordingly, he conceived of science without arrogance; religion without fanaticism; pluralism without coercion; and disillusion without nihilism.

I answer further that Santayana the best-selling novelist, cultural critic, poet, playwright, and author of unconventional philosophical works was among the most intellectual of public intellectuals. He rejected academic professionalism but never aspired to punditry. He wrote for those who would read him, neither excluding readers through intentional obscurity nor pandering to popular sensibilities. In 1936 *Time* magazine acknowledged his prominence with his portrait on its cover. After World War II American soldiers and civilians in Rome sought out the philosopher for autographs, photographs, and conversation, which he provided with grace and good humor. He lived a relaxed and simple (almost ascetic) life of "Epicurean contentment," as he called it (*LGS*, 5:297), devoted to contemplation, writing, and quietly generous friendship. He was a retiring though visible exemplar of the human life he articulated in his works.

The contemporary cultural relevance of Santayana's outlook becomes clearer if one chooses reason and intelligence in response to popular notions of post-modernism, to social fragmentation, and to globalization. Santayana's broadly humanistic philosophy not only respects but draws heavily on established cultural traditions while denying the universal hegemony of any one tradition. His outlook is unmistakably grounded in European culture, the English language, the

Greek philosophical tradition, and the Roman Catholic religious tradition. But his thought also displays a deep appreciation for Asian philosophical and religious traditions both as contrast and complement to his European roots. Furthermore, Santayana was undenably influenced by his American experience–an experience of conflicted allegiances that often provoked his best literary and philosophical writing. Out of this cultural material Santayana created a philosophy that is both open to the variety of human experience and faithful to the concrete individual.

In his autobiography, he wrote,

> The full grown human soul should respect all traditions and understand all passions; at the same time it should possess and embody a particular culture, without any unmanly relaxation or mystical neutrality. Justice is one thing, indecision is another, and weak. If you allow all men to live according to their genuine natures, you must assert your own genuine nature and live up to it (*PP*, 464).

In times of rapid social and technological change and accompanying cultural uncertainty, Santayana's philosophy is a serious and cheerful alternative to various forms of irrationalism such as the fundamentalism, fanaticism, or shallow relativism that seem to threaten intellectual life from all sides. Santayana's philosophy values the richest fruits of social life such as religion, art, and science; but it never ignores the tragic nature of individual human existence and the unavoidable limitations and losses of being mortal. He acknowledged the conflicted nature of human experience, but also imagined in detail the harmony of the Life of Reason and the unassailable freedom available to the human spirit. Santayana's philosophy is materialism without reductionism and idealism without superstition.

Materialism, Morality, and Lay Religion

This sort of summary response to questions about Santayana's importance might need qualification if it is not to tempt the false impression that Santayana was a cultural savior or missionary. Such a portrait of Santayana is ruled out by his own words: "My philosophy is not urgent or 'militant': you can manage perfectly without it, but you will find a quiet solidity in it at the end" (*LGS*, 8:127). He made no claims for the necessity of his views and did not try to impose them on others. Even when writing as a cultural critic he never intended to reform society, nor did he seek followers or converts. He was especially sensitive to coercive philosophies and avoided them.

Santayana was suspicious of moralistic philosophers who read their particular human interests into the structure of the universe and then justified the imposition of their values on others by devising a metaphysics preloaded with the very values they promoted. This sort of philosophical legerdemain was a perennial target of Santayana's philosophical critique. Against it he offered his naturalism or, as he often preferred to call it, his materialism, by which he viewed the universe as vast beyond human comprehension and indifferent to human interests (*PGS*, 508).

On Santayana's view the universe consists of matter, which is dynamic and in flux, making existence thoroughly contingent. The material universe has produced living creatures with sensitivities that can be employed to satisfy natural impulses. All impulses are originally innocent, and from its own standpoint each one has an equal right to fulfillment. But collections of impulses manifested in living organisms inevitably conflict—both internally to the organism and externally with those of other creatures. Reason is the harmony of impulses and moral values are the ends of impulses preserved as ideals and deemed good. Certain moral values, those of a dominant culture perhaps, may be hypostatized and taken as superior to other aims of equally legitimate impulses. In this process of hypostatizing traditional and cultural values lies the source of the moralistic metaphysics that Santayana criticized.

Santayana rejected *a priori* values and held that understanding morality consists in self-knowledge, that is, in understanding the perfections of one's individual nature. Each individual has a perfect form, a fulfillment of the natural impulses arising in the living organism; but an individual's particular perfection cannot be legislated ahead of time by an institution or government. Hence, social reform schemes and rigid cultural standards jeopardize recognition and respect for an individual's moral perfection.

Santayana keenly felt the reality of the individual and thought it false and ultimately pointless to dictate a philosophy to another. He wrote, "I think . . . that lectures, like sermons, are usually unprofitable. Philosophy can be communicated only by being evoked; the pupil's mind must be engaged dialectically in the discussion. Otherwise all that can be taught is the literary history of philosophy, that is, the *phrases* that various philosophers have rendered famous" (*PP,* 391). Santayana himself did not fully escaped the fate of being reduced to a famous phrase or two, but he understood that a genuine philosophy was much more. He saw that the communication of a philosophy is the result of a spiritual kinship rather than the conveyance of a body of facts. Accordingly Santayana characterized his philosophy as "a discipline of the mind and heart, a lay religion" (*RB1,* 827) rather than a set of propositions or arguments.

Santayana was explicit that he did not intend his philosophy to be the basis of any school of thought or movement. His work was "not intended to found a sect" (*PP,* 393). He wrote, "I never wished to be a professional or public man. Nor do I want disciples: I want only a few sympathetic friends, and I have them" (*LGS,* 8:264–65). But his conception of his work as a spiritual discipline or a religion without disciples suggests a tension in how to regard his writings. That is, his comments might suggest his work to be idiosyncratic to the point of inaccessibility to any but the author. Indeed, in a letter to his nephew he wrote, "[m]y father used to say that every old man had his own rhetoric: and that is probably my case; and you must study Santayanese as a special language" (*LGS,* 3:118–19). But, as the quotation indicates, he believed that the problem was no greater with him than with any old man. And though he did not wish to lead a sect neither did he intend his lay religion to be merely personal.

A Common Sense Philosophy

Santayana intended his philosophy to be consistent with the circumstances in which all humans find themselves, and he aimed to bracket as far as possible the accidental influences that shaped his own understanding. He observed that the facts and interests by which any philosophical theory may be judged are public and accessible to all; they "are known . . . in the daily process of living" (*RB1,* 827). His goal was "to enlighten this process morally, and to define its ultimate issues" (*RB1,* 827). His philosophy is, among other things, an attempt to articulate the inescapable conditions imposed by a material universe on creatures capable of consciousness and contemplation, and so of spirituality. These principles are deeply embedded in everyday opinions, though they might be poorly expressed and inconsistently understood. Santayana sought to express these ideas clearly; to enlighten human living, not revolutionize it.

In this way, Santayana's philosophy is one of common sense, though perhaps the phrase is used here in an uncommon way. The point is that Santayana's characterization of his philosophy as a spiritual discipline in a special language need not be understood as negating the present effort at assembling his writings for a broad audience. The example of his own philosophical work makes this point in two ways: First, philosophically, in an explanation of how one mind can conceive another mind; and, second, practically, in the way Santayana himself engaged the works of other philosophers. This second point is taken up in the next two sections of this introductory essay.

The opacity of the thought of another is, on Santayana's view, universal and not a problem specific to reading highly individualistic philosophers. He wrote, "[a] sense for alien thought is . . . at its inception a complete illusion. The thought is one's own, it is associated with an image moving in space, and is uncritically supposed to be a hidden part of that image" (*LR1,* 148). I indulge in an illusion when I assign a thought or feeling to another because the thought is really my own projected onto someone else. To assign one's own thoughts or feelings to another is called the pathetic fallacy.[3] Santayana characterized this fallacy as "a return to that early habit of thought by which our ancestors peopled the world with benevolent and malevolent spirits; what they felt in the presence of objects they took to be a part of the objects themselves" (*ES,* 271). This is the habit of animism, of the poet personifying nature; it is the confusing of an intuited idea with the existing object of the idea.

Yet there is a case in which this is not a fallacy, namely when "the object observed happens to be an animal similar to the observer and similarly affected, as for instance when a flock or herd are swayed by panic fear" (*LR1,* 149). This projection of feeling and thought is the only way to divine the feelings and thoughts of creatures like one's self. This is the escape from the paralysis of solipsism, and on Santayana's view humans are compelled to follow this way by their animal natures. The condition of being material creatures includes a prerational and undeniable expectation that objects exist independently in a field of mutual

---

[3] For the importance of the pathetic fallacy in Santayana's philosophy, see Daniel Moreno's "The Pathetic Fallacy in Santayana," *Overheard in Seville: Bulletin of the Santayana Society* 22 (2004), 16–22.

influence. This expectation is not an argument but is made explicit in the movements and activities of the living animal.

As sensitive and rational creatures we have a brute faith that we are in the
presence of others who think and feel as we do in similar circumstances. This
is an instance of Santayana's notion of *animal faith*. This "is a faith not founded
on reason but precipitated in action, and in that intent, which is virtual action,
involved in perception" (*ES,* 86). Beyond this faith, sympathetic imagination
gives insight into the minds of others though it "extends only so far as does the
analogy between the object and the instrument of perception" (*LR1,* 152). We can
understand each other only insofar as we share a common physical structure and
common conditions and activities.

The commonality required for understanding can be achieved by means
manufactured and adaptable, namely by language. On Santayana's view, symbols, phrases, and gestures can elicit in an observer an attitude corresponding to
the idea the speaker had when employing the means of communication; having
exactly the same attitude as the speaker had is to understand exactly. In this
way, Santayana's philosophy indicates how understanding is possible and how
his readers could understand a collection of his writings.

But the possibility of comprehension is accompanied by the possibility of accidental influences, which make an attitude familiar to one person almost impossible for another to adopt. If my environment varies widely from that of another,
if our constitutions have been modified in some way, or if our interests diverge
radically, it will be more difficult for sympathetic imagination to bridge the gap
of comprehension between us. This led Santayana to observe that all particular
philosophies embraced by people, all languages of logic, all categories of sense
are "accidental paraphernalia," something fitted to the particular circumstances
of different people (*PP,* 392). In fact, he held that each philosophical system is
limited, perspectival, and "a personal work of art" (*ES,* 47).

This relativity gives the lie to philosophical systems presented as systems of
the universe. Systems with such grand pretensions seize on one aspect of human
experience and refine, exaggerate, and emphasize it to the exclusion of all else,
resulting in what Santayana called "philosophical heresy." It is a heresy relative
to the orthodoxy of prerational assumptions that comprises the background of all
philosophizing. This background consists of the traditions, conventions, and fundamental beliefs of humankind founded on animal faith; it is the often erroneous
network of unreflective assumptions that are practically efficient and potentially
self-correcting. Philosophical heresies neglect this background of orthodoxy and
treat artistic creations of selective emphasis as literal truths, denying their partial
and illusory natures.

But neither this human tendency to heresy nor the perspectival nature of
philosophical systems was for Santayana a reason to reject all philosophies as
worthless. Such a response would betray a romantic despair and a lingering if
unacknowledged desire for omniscience, universal fixity, or comforting illusions;
and Santayana was, as he wrote, "never afraid of disillusion and [chose] it" (*ES,* 7).

This meant that Santayana studied philosophy honestly, without pining for an idealized past or holding false hopes of a universally applicable system.

Engaging Philosophies

Santayana's continued engagement with philosophy may be instructive for those who would read him for enlightenment; his practice may serve as an example of how and why to read philosophy. According to Santayana, a philosophy is a "distinct vision of the universe and definite convictions about human destiny" (*ES*, 526). So the study of philosophies examines these expressions of the meanings that make human life livable, understandable, and beautiful. Particular systems may be the work of individuals, but enduring philosophies, like great works of art, express the meanings of a life shared across space and often across time, that is, the meanings and values that animate a culture. Santayana held the study of philosophical systems, accidental and partial though they may be, to be an important part of the humanities, distinct from scientific pursuits or paths to eternal salvation. This sort of study he thought of as "initiating us into the history of human life and mind" (*PP*, 392) with the purpose of understanding the capacities and potentials of a human life.

As a student of philosophy, Santayana was a close and careful reader, as evidenced by the extensive marginal notes in the volumes of his personal library.[4] His reading and his written work reveal a broad range of influences from the history of philosophy, including Plato, Aristotle, Democritus, Lucretius, Aquinas, Leibniz, Spinoza, Hume, Kant, Fichte, Hegel, and Schopenhauer. He also attended to the work of his contemporaries: he read and criticized Bergson, Dewey, Royce, James, Nietzsche, and Freud; he credited conversations with Bertrand Russell and G. E. Moore with helping him refine his theory of essences; and he read and commented on Whitehead, Husserl, Heidegger, and others in published writings and letters. But Santayana was explicit about the thinkers who influenced him the most: the Greeks and Spinoza; and his discussion of their influences is helpful in understanding Santayana's approach to philosophy.

Early in his career Santayana read the Greeks as exemplars of rational life and claimed that they had "drawn for us the outlines of an ideal culture" (*ES*, 288, 296). He acknowledged that even as a student he exhibited "Hellenism in morals," that is, the view that happiness lay not in a collection of miscellaneous pleasures but rather in imagination and judgment (*PP*, 259). Given this early affinity it is not surprising that he sought and found in Greek philosophy a point of departure for his own philosophy. In 1896–97 he undertook a systematic study of Plato and Aristotle at Cambridge University while on leave from teaching at Harvard. He wrote that "by that study and change of scene my mind was greatly enriched; and the composition of *The Life of Reason* was the consequence" (*ES*, 11). This five-

---

[4] Paul Grimley Kuntz, "Appendix: Santayana's Reading of Lotze's *Logik* and *Metaphysik* Revealed in Marginalia," in *Lotze's System of Philosophy* (Bloomington and London: Indiana University Press, 1971), 95; *PP*, xvii; see also Richard Rubin, "The Philosophical and Interpretative Import of Santayana's Marginalia," *Overheard in Seville: Bulletin of the Santayana Society* 24 (2006), 12–18.

volume work was the first great articulation of Santayana's philosophical system and in large part it owed its themes and emphases to the Greeks.

Heraclitus and Democritus were, for Santayana, the two great philosophers of physical being. Heraclitus was "the honest prophet of immediacy" who discarded convention and recovered intellectual innocence (ES, 288). Democritus, by contrast, pursued intelligibility and sought not merely experience but understanding of experience. Santayana saw in Democritus the very principles of explanation, if explanation be understood as discovering origins, changes, and regularities. On such a view mechanism cannot be dismissed as one explanation among others; rather it is explanation. Socrates' accomplishment was the deliverance of logic and ethics from authority, giving them human dimensions. Plato provided the ultimate expression of Socratic ethics by articulating the ideals that lay at the foundations of Greek conscience. Aristotle gave the philosophy of human nature a natural basis, and Santayana thought that "[t]he Life of Reason finds [in Aristotle's ethics] its classic explication" (ES, 291).

Though he acknowledged the success of Aristotle, Santayana did not think it superfluous to again examine the Life of Reason, his name for "that part of experience which perceives and pursues ideals" (ES, 283). He regarded his attempt as a needed response to changing times: "though the principles of reason remain the same the facts of human life and of human conscience alter" (ES, 291). The Greeks could provide a pattern of rational development, but what actually was valued had changed. The impulses to be harmonized and the ideals pursued were not the same as for the Greeks. New conditions, both physical and moral, resulted in new ideals and this prompted Santayana to reexamine the Life of Reason.

Another reason for revision lay in intellectual developments since the time Aristotle wrote. Experience had clarified aspects of Aristotle's metaphysics, and made possible a better understanding of reason in nature. While Santayana admired Aristotle's metaphysics for its acknowledgment of the reality of ideas, he recognized that Aristotle's high regard for ideas had led him ultimately to make "the whole material universe gravitate around them and feel their influence, though in a metaphysical and magic fashion to which a more advanced natural science need no longer appeal" (LR1, 171). Even though Aristotle had rejected the metaphysics of Plato and his substantial ideals, Aristotle still held essences to exert influence in the material world as final causes. For Santayana, an essence, as the character of a thing, has ideal status but cannot contribute to physical explanations. Essences or ideals are fully natural but are not factors in the realm of matter. Such a view, in rejecting a universe of ends that direct the material flux, entails a new expression of the life that perceives and pursues ideals. Santayana expressed this human life of ideals for the age of modern science.

Santayana drew further support from the Greeks in articulating his relationship to American culture. He wrote in a letter to William James in 1900 that his study of Plato and Aristotle had given him the confidence to acknowledge as rational his dislike and discomfort regarding "an unintelligible sanctimonious and often disingenuous Protestantism" (LGS, 1:214) that dominated intellectual life in America. Previously he had assumed his irritation arose from clashing preferences or a difference in personal sympathies. But he came to see in American culture a deep conflict between the American will and the American intellect; in other words, an absence of the harmony of natural impulses that is reason. This observation resulted in several works of cultural critique, including the famous 1911 essay, "The Genteel Tradition in American Philosophy."

Spinoza was perhaps the only philosopher who could rival the Greeks for influence on Santayana's work. Santayana wrote that Spinoza "in several respects laid the foundation of my philosophy" (*PP*, 233–34), and he recognized Spinoza as his "master and model" in naturalistic morality. In both the Greeks and Spinoza, Santayana found a combination of "the two insights that for me were essential: naturalism as to the origin and history of mankind, and fidelity, in moral sentiment, to the inspiration of reason, by which the human mind conceives truth and eternity, and participates in them ideally" (*PP*, 257–58). This "spontaneous agreement" between two different traditions was not, of course, thoroughgoing, and the Greeks and Spinoza were in some respects complementary influences on Santayana's thought, compensating for each other's deficiencies.

Spinoza continued the tradition of what Santayana called "orthodox physics," which began with Thales and culminated for the Greeks in Democritus. Hence, Spinoza's naturalism corrected for Aristotle's metaphysical excesses. But Spinoza was deficient in his humanism: "He had no ideal of human greatness and no sympathy with human sorrow" (*PP*, 235). For Santayana the Greeks made up for Spinoza's deficit because their ethics included "a virile, military, organic view of human life" and they "knew what it was to have a country, a native religion, a beautiful noble way of living, to be defended to the death" (*PP*, 257). The Greeks, unlike Spinoza, displayed a heroic, rather than a merely descriptive, recognition of the infinite power of nature to dominate any of its parts.

Self-Knowledge Is the Aim of Philosophy

But rooting out technical shortcomings was not the primary end of Santayana's inquiry. His "happiness lay in understanding . . . rather than in contradicting" philosophers who had come before him (*RB1*, 827–28). Obviously this did not mean that he suspended judgment and made no criticisms. He had definite ideas about the function and value of the philosopher: the ideal philosopher would be one who, after mastering human opinion, could construct a broad and even-handed system of ideas that would deepen human understanding. This would be someone with an extensive understanding like Aristotle, but without a sectarian tendency toward metaphysics, and an expansive vision like Dante, but without a mystical tendency toward supernaturalism. Santayana's conception of the ideal philosopher converged with his idea of the rational poet: both would deepen understanding by prompting human imagination to systematic expression of meanings, ideals, and beliefs about the universe (*OB*, 98–99).

This conception of the ideal philosopher provided a standard by which Santayana could discover biases, prejudices, and false steps in the history of philosophy. Such a reflective inquiry might be characterized as "a laborious sympathetic progress through all human illusions" with the intention of "looking deep and looking straight" and "making belief a direct expression of instinct and perception."[5] The laborious survey of human thought was not, for Santayana at least, a catalogue of facts or a collection of details. His interest was in persons and ideas. He wrote that he "wished to rethink the thoughts of those philosophers, to understand why they took the direction they took, and then to consider the consequences and implications of taking that direction" (*PP*, 391). But rethinking the thoughts of past philosophers was for Santayana not an intellectual dress-up game. He did not approach philosophy aiming to relive the past.

Despite a stated preference for antiquity as a model of rational human life, Santayana was not nostalgic. That label more accurately applies to an under-graduate professor of Santayana's at Harvard, Charles Eliot Norton (1827–1908), whom Santayana remembered as a sweetly sad teacher "shaking his head with a slight sigh" and telling his students that the Greeks never played football and that America had no French cathedrals, no Shakespeare, and no gentlemen (*ES*, 555–56). In contrast Santayana accepted that the time of the Greeks had passed and was not coming back; and he even acknowledged that his earlier rever-ence had been too extreme in identifying Greek culture with *the* Life of Reason. His "Hellas [had been] a mere dream," representing one possible harmony of impulses among others (*PGS*, 560). But this was neither a reason to jettison the past philosophies nor to lament the present. For him philosophy remained rel-evant because of its potential to aid present enlightenment. He wrote, "I am not guided by any urgent desire to recover the past, but by an impulse to understand myself and to achieve integrity" (*PGS*, 520). On Santayana's view the goal of inquiry into human illusion is moral; it is self-knowledge.

Hence, disagreement was not condemnation of others' views but rather expression of one's own. Santayana regarded criticism as dependent on crite-ria that are ultimately "spontaneous and sanctioned only by the material and moral consequences" (*PGS*, 551), and the activity of criticism itself counters the risk of subjectivism. Criticism keeps the critic honest by taking up public sub-ject matter, acknowledging other minds, and testing one's judgments against others'. Criticism not only wards off absolutism but simultaneously serves self-knowledge. According to Santayana, criticism "sharpens our wits and clarifies our allegiances, and it makes a beginning in putting our own principles, as well as those we are criticising, where they respectively belong in the family of possible principles" (*PGS*, 549).

This view of criticism lends a background of rigor to Santayana's admission that he "treated Plato (and all other philosophers) somewhat cavalierly, not at all from disrespect or quarrelsomeness or lack of delight in their speculations, but because my interest has seldom been strictly philological or historical. I have studied very little except for pleasure, and have made my authors a quarry or a touchstone for my own thoughts" (*PGS*, 543). Santayana was not admitting to playing fast and loose with the history of philosophy; rather he was stating that he never intended to be an expositor. His aim had been to clarify the place of

---

[5] George Santayana, "Emerson the Poet," in *Santayana on America*, edited by Richard C. Lyon (New York: Harcourt, Brace & World, 1968), 270–71.

other philosophies "within the frame of [his] naturalism" (*PGS,* 550). He sought to understand others' principles of criticism and interpretations of experience not in order to vanquish or adopt them but to better understand himself. Hence he wrote, "[m]y criticism is criticism of my self" (*SAF,* 305).

Of course, what underlies all of this is Santayana's animal faith, the brute sense of the existence of matter. "Knowledge of this common world, and of the human passions that govern it, is presupposed in all criticism" (*PGS,* 550). This is Santayana's basic dogma, what he calls his materialism: "a humble philosophy [that] cannot wish to dictate to matter, like rationalism, what it shall be and what it shall do" (*PGS,* 550). Santayana did not impose his philosophical principles on the universe, rather he sought to understand it. In criticism, he did not impose his opinions on those who disagreed. Since critical principles are spontaneous and emerge out of natural conditions, he was no more inclined to dictate his opinions to others than to the universe.

But despite, or rather because of, Santayana's anti-dictatorial approach he was criticized, especially in America, by those who would make morals into metaphysics and would assert "the actual dominance of reason or goodness over the universe at large" (*PGS,* 503). His lack of moralism seemed to his critics to be morally objectionable. The historian Bruce Kuklick attributed this opinion to Santayana's Harvard colleagues, who seemed to keep him around as a cautionary example for students of what one would become without religion.[6] There was at Harvard an "official freedom" to think as one pleased, but it was a kind of tamed pluralism that served the goal of diversity or miscellany for its own sake. And it was maintained by the assumption that everyone was to be encouraged and aided. There was, on Santayana's view, neither genuine criticism nor an intelligent harmony—only a universal duty (*COUS,* 59).

Santayana recognized the futility of engaging such critics directly. They were justified according to their lights as much as he was justified from his perspective, and he saw the endless back-and-forth that would characterize direct debate. Echoing James' idea that to understand a man's philosophy, one must place oneself "at the center of a man's philosophic vision,"[7] Santayana thought "the better way is to approach any system, as well as the criticisms of it, from within, beginning with what was their vital foundation, and proceeding to its corollaries" (*PGS,* 503).

And indeed this is how Santayana approached other philosophers, whom he sought to understand rather than contradict, and whose thoughts he wanted to rethink not in order to relive other lives but as a means to understanding his own life and integrating his own vital impulses. In his response to criticism he often took the opportunity to express and clarify his own foundational principles. This approach made his critical writings consistent with the basic motives that lay behind his career as a philosopher. He wrote:

---

[6] Bruce Kuklick, *The Rise of American Philosophy* (New Haven and London: Yale University Press, 1977), 366.

[7] William James, *A Pluralistic Universe,* vol. 4, *The Works of William James,* edited by Fredson Bowers and Ignas K. Skrupskelis (Cambridge, MA and London: Harvard University Press, 1977), 117.

> When I had to choose a profession, the prospect of a quiet academic existence seemed the least of evils. I was fond of reading and observation, and I liked young men; but I have never been a diligent student either of science or art, nor at all ambitious to be learned. . . . My pleasure was rather in expression, in reflection, in irony. . . . My naturalism or materialism is no academic opinion: . . . it is an everyday conviction which came to me, as it came to my father, from experience and observation of the world at large, and especially of my own feelings and passions. (*ES*, 10–11)

Santayana wanted not academic disputation, philological subtleties, or professional success, but the pleasures of reflection on the most basic conditions of his existence—the indomitable material world—and on the feelings and passions it registered in him, and sincere and honest expression of what he found. He did not intend his resulting system of philosophy to be the basis of a school or sect; rather "[i]t aspires to be only a contribution to the humanities, the expression of a reflective, selective, and free mind" (*PP*, 393).

Self-Expression Is the Activity of Philosophy

Expression as Santayana conceived it was not an anything-goes, spontaneous venting of emotion. Far from a self-indulgent release of immediate feeling, he aimed to express "a certain shrewd orthodoxy which the sentiment and practice of laymen maintain everywhere" (*ES*, 51). He acknowledged that "expression" is an ambiguous term. It can refer to self-manifestation, a blundering and sterile explosion that goes no further than its immediate appearance, or to rational art, which is pregnant and "capable of reproducing in representation the experience from which it sprang" (*LR4*, 94). Representations change and drift from the author's intention, but this is limited when there is "some external object or some recurring human situation [that] gives them a constant standard" (*LR4*, 96). This is the material world of animal faith, and this is what Santayana believed could keep his expressions in check.

Expression as artistic representation, on Santayana's view, is perfectly consistent with his goal of self-knowledge. "Any deep interpretation of oneself, or indeed of anything, has . . . a largely representative truth. Other men, if they look closely, will make the same discovery for themselves" (*ES*, 326). This is because human nature, though variable, retains an invariable core, just as the human body retains a fundamental structure without which it would cease to be human. Hence, any deep interpretation of oneself inevitably points toward the basic conditions of human life, and for Santayana these led ultimately to the material world implicated in all action and perception.[8] This is why Santayana, in describing Collingwood's definition of metaphysics as "the history of the various ultimate presuppositions made unconsciously by people at various times," could identify his own metaphysics with self-criticism or self-knowledge (*PGS*, 519–20).

---

[8] For a detailed discussion of self-knowledge in Santayana's philosophy and its relevance to knowledge of the material world, see Jessica Wahman's "The Meaning of Self-Knowledge in Santayana's Philosophy," *Overheard in Seville: Bulletin of the Santayana Society* 19 (2001), 1–7; and Glenn Tiller's response in the same issue, "Self-Knowledge and Psychology: Literary, Dialectical, and Scientific," 8–9.

Philosophy after this manner will not yield a system of the universe. Any human production, no matter how penetrating and honest, will be partial relative to the vastness of the universe. A philosophy may acknowledge absolute truth, an objective material world, and an ideal of breadth and depth of insight; but, as already noted, it will be "a personal work of art which gives a specious unity to some chance vista in the cosmic labyrinth" (*ES*, 47). For Santayana, honest philosophy requires acknowledgment of its idiosyncrasy; it aims at sincerity rather than omniscience.

In eschewing universal pronouncements, disputation, and proof, Santayana's writing style reflects his understanding of philosophy as grounded in personal experience. He wrote with a rhetorical grace that he himself characterized as "spontaneous and inevitable" (*PGS*, 604). In other words, it is a style most suited to the particular organism, environment, and history of the author; and Santayana's style in particular is consistent with his poetic sensibilities and talents.[9] His work is well known for its elegance and aphoristic appeal, but the literary character of his work has regularly drawn criticism for its apparent lack of argument and scholarly apparatus and its seeming lack of precision.

Certainly Santayana did not write in the prevailing scholarly idiom, and even his doctoral dissertation lacked the expected references to secondary sources.[10] Not only did he forgo footnotes, he also never adopted the pseudoscientific jargon or ugly technical language that have plagued much of twentieth-century philosophy. He claimed to resist professional pressures in refusing to become a specialist, and it appears he resisted the pressures of academic fashion in refusing to alter his preferred style of expression (*PP*, 395).

But this should not be interpreted as a rejection of careful scholarship. Santayana observed that "[a] supreme work presupposes minute study, sympathy with varied passions, many experiments in expression; but these preliminary things are submerged in it and are not displayed side by side with it, like the foot-notes to a learned work, so that the ignorant may know they have existed" (*ES*, 326). He was discussing Virgil and Dante when he made this claim, and this apparently is the tradition that Santayana attempted to follow in his work. Santayana's biographer contends that Santayana's work may omit the apparatus but proves the critical and learned character of his mind (*GSB*, 82).[11]

---

[9] For insight into Santayana's style and especially his irony and drama, see Morris Grossman, "Interpreting Intepretations," *Overheard in Seville: Bulletin of the Santayana Society* 8 (1990), 18–28; and Henry Samuel Levinson's response in the same issue, "What Good is Irony?" 29–34.

[10] Paul Grimley Kuntz, "Introduction: Rudolf Herman Lotze, Philosopher and Critic," in *Lotze's System of Philosophy* (Bloomington and London: Indiana University Press, 1971), 95–96.

[11] John Dewey, in a review of the first two volumes of Santayana's *Life of Reason*, would seem to agree with McCormick. Dewey noted approvingly that in Santayana's books "the ordinary logical machinery is kept out of sight. But Dr. Santayana has not only swallowed logical formulae; he has digested them. There are many books with much pretense of system and coherent argumentation that have not a fraction of the inevitableness and coherency of these chapters. In the main, Emerson's demand for a logic, so long that it may remain unspoken, is fulfilled" (John Dewey, "Review of *The Life of Reason, or the Phases of Human Progress*" in *The Middle Works, 1899–1924*, edited by Jo Ann Boydston [Carbondale and Edwardsville: Southern Illinois University Press, 1977], 321).

Not only was Santayana a close reader who made careful notes on what inter-ested him, he was also a careful writer and revealed in his letters the method behind his flowing prose. He claimed to follow the advice of the French critic, poet, and proponent of classicism, Nicolas Boileau-Despréaux (1636–1711): "Polish it continually, repolish it; add occasionally, and delete often" (*LGS,* 8:218).

Santayana's attention to style aimed not at entertainment or diversion but rather served his philosophical outlook. Because he believed the material world was known by faith and only immaterial essences were intuited directly, matters of fact could not be captured directly in language. The material world that is the object of language is always in flux, intuited essences are symbols of some portion of the flux, and language communicates such symbols. Hence, Santayana wrote, "[l]iteral views, to my mind, cannot be cognitive of matters of fact: therefore, . . . the looseness and variety of my language indicated my sense of the seriousness of my subject, and my respect for it. . . . When on the contrary I choose to be literal . . . I am . . . laughing up my sleeve" (*PGS,* 576). His well-crafted and poetic style is an acknowledgment of both the limitation of the human intellect in rela-tion to nature and the creative potential of human imagination.

Contemporary Relevance

Santayana's rejection of fashionable idiom and academic disputation does not entail irrelevance to persistent philosophical questions. He did not reject phi-losophy, only the affectations of the academy. He concerned himself with ques-tions about the nature of reality, consciousness, and truth; and there are indeed connections between Santayana's thought and other philosophical conversa-tions.[12] For example, in contemporary debates about naturalism and pragmatism Santayana's work remains relevant, especially his response to skepticism and his notion of animal faith.

In the twentieth century Donald Davidson, Hilary Putnam, and Richard Rorty were concerned with questions of realism, and naturalism has been the back-drop of these speculations. But Joseph Margolis has argued that naturalism in American philosophy, which had been mainly a rejection of the supernatural, gave way during the twentieth century to "naturalizing," which fosters reduc-tionisms, physicalisms, and eliminativisms.[13] Such an approach, he thinks, brings with it an attenuated Cartesianism.[14] He adopts this term, from the seventeenth-century French philosopher René Descartes, to mark philosophical doctrines that support, at the least, the idea that human knowers may realize a true account of the world uncolored by human inquiry, in other words, the idea of literal knowl-

---

[12] Santayana's ideas may be relevant because of their distinction from contemporary debates. Glenn Tiller's article "Distance from the Truth" (*UAS,* 22–33) discusses Santayana's notion of truth and contends that it stands out for its lack of affinity with much of contemporary speculation. He finds that Santayana's theory of truth bears little resemblance to coherence, correspondence, pragmatic, and deflationary theories (*UAS,* 23). In its difference Santayana's philosophy may find relevance as the source of new insights.

[13] Joseph Margolis, *Reinventing Pragmatism* (Ithaca, NY, and London: Cornell University Press, 2002), 6–7.

[14] Ibid., 13.

edge. This Cartesianism may also entail, seemingly paradoxically for naturalism, the strong separation of human knowers and the world we know.[15] Margolis thinks that Cartesian realism and its attendant dualism have been disastrous for establishing a viable realism, and he argues that Davidson, Putnam, and Rorty have retained some form or another of Cartesian realism.

Margolis looks with good reason to a reinvented pragmatism as a response to persistent Cartesianism. Santayana's philosophy is relevant to the project because in response to Cartesianism it offers a realism that rejects literal knowledge and maintains a naturalism without reductionism, and it also suggests a helpful corrective to reductionist tendencies in the pragmatic tradition.

Santayana's response to Cartesianism can be found in his book *Scepticism and Animal Faith,* where he reconsidered skepticism and challenged its centuries-old conception descended from Descartes to arrive at a realism rooted in the notion of animal faith. Descartes wanted to establish a solid foundation for knowledge by doubting everything until he found one certain and indubitable piece of information—namely that he existed as a thinking thing, a fact supposedly entailed by the very act of doubting. Santayana found Cartesian skepticism disingenuous and lacking in rigor. Skepticism in this tradition leaves favored conventions untouched by doubt. For example, the romantic solipsist retains "personal history and destiny" and a mystic retains "the feeling of existence" (*ES,* 67).

The result of this dishonest or wayward skepticism is an abstracted conception of knowledge, a conception that ignores actual experience in favor of unavowed presumptions. This gives rise to a wildly implausible conception of knowledge as something certain and impervious to doubt, an example of which can be had only by smuggling in something already given a free pass from skeptical scrutiny.

To show the inadequacy of this conception of knowledge, Santayana took skepticism to its honest conclusion. The thoroughgoing skeptic would have no occasion to notice a self or history and no knowledge of existences. Santayana wrote, "[s]cepticism may thus be carried to the point of denying change and memory, and the reality of all facts" (*ES,* 71). Yet even this conclusion taken as fact would be struck down. One is left with ambiguity and contradiction.

Santayana's point was not to destroy all intellectual life but rather to demonstrate that the traditional philosophical conception of knowledge is insincere in its establishment and impossible in practice. This results from a deceptive employment of skepticism. Skepticism, wrote Santayana, "is an exercise, not a life" (*ES,* 77). It eradicates prejudices, including those that declare knowledge must be literal and certain. We cannot actually live with such a conception of knowledge, and we do not. Actual living is impervious to skepticism and can discount skepticism's philosophical products. This counter to skepticism is animal faith or honest acknowledgment of the basic beliefs that underlie our daily activities. Animal faith does not eliminate skepticism but rather restores the roots of actual life after their denial by modern epistemology.

Santayana's notion of animal faith is, according to John Lachs, equally as important as any philosophical method introduced by Descartes or Kant; and

---

[15] Ibid., 38.

Lachs wonders, in light of Kant's reputation, whether Santayana might have achieved greater academic regard had he couched his method in obscure terminology (*OnS*, 93). Furthermore, Lachs contends that employing the method of animal faith and determining the ideas implicated in action is far more likely than analyzing propositions or describing experience phenomenologically to lead to sensible philosophical judgments (*OnS*, 93). The importance of the notion goes beyond a response to Descartes and may suggest an improvement of an important aspect of pragmatism.

Santayana's thought, according to Angus Kerr-Lawson, may provide a needed corrective for the pragmatic analysis of ideas.[16] Santayana employed pragmatic criteria in his understanding of ideas not as literal pictures of existence but as perspectival symbols whose value depends on their success in action. But for him this did not exhaust valuable or true ideas; the pragmatic criteria have a limited range. Pragmatic analysis is helpful for knowledge about the natural world, but fuller understanding of human action requires ideas that cannot be justified in pragmatic terms. Santayana's corrective is animal faith in material existence and the further categories of absolute truth and essence.

Santayana's faith in material existence—his materialism—and the further categories of reality he distinguished provide a setting for understanding action and employing pragmatic analysis. This appeal to animal faith guards against the reductionist tendencies to which pragmatism is vulnerable because of its empiricist heritage. Empiricist traditions reduce knowledge to knowledge of ideas, sensations, or analyzed bits of experience and thereby dissolve the natural world into private dreams. Animal faith restores knowledge to knowledge of existing objects.

For Santayana, knowledge is rooted in material interaction, not intuition. Knowledge is not intuition of ideas but faith in existing objects *and* intuited essences that function as better or worse symbols of those objects. His posited categories of matter, truth, and essence follow from animal faith and check the tendencies of empiricism to reduce knowledge to a play of subjective fancy. Pragmatic analysis unchecked by these categories, Kerr-Lawson suggests, risks falling into the empiricist reduction of knowledge to ideas and forsaking material existence. Animal faith provides the context for fruitful pragmatic analysis.

While the present discussion intends to suggest the relevance to contemporary debates of Santayana's philosophy, the fact of its relevance is in a sense incidental to its character. Santayana wrote to William James: "philosophy seems to me to be its own reward, and its justification lies in the delight and dignity of the art itself" (*LGS*, 1:90). While many claim to recognize that intellectual pursuits have their own attraction, intellectual activity often is taken to be justified by its potential for discovering new solutions to problems, new techniques of control, new products, or new markets. The joy of intellectual activity then seems incidental, like a pleasant accompaniment to serious business or a reward for work. On this view, thinking is harnessed for the benefit of an established morality,

---

[16] Angus Kerr-Lawson, "Santayana's Limited Pragmatism," *Overheard in Seville: Bulletin of the Santayana Society* 25 (2007): 31–37.

some agenda dictated by bodily needs or wants. But Santayana believed that the human capacity for thought, while always dependent on the body in its origins, has its own end independent of animal nature.

Philosophy as Celebration

On Santayana's view, a philosophy is a sense of the universe and the ways of human living. Philosophy as an activity articulates this sense and attempts to understand the particular situation we find ourselves in as conscious beings in a material universe. This understanding, a good for creatures with the impulse to think, is self-knowledge; and it differs from (even as it is made possible by) well-adjusted interaction with the material environment that enables animals to thrive. Philosophical understanding is not a means to mastering the universe and cannot deliver us from human fatalities such as loss, disease, and death; nor is it the elimination of disagreement, because philosophy does not aim at a final doctrine or complete statement of the nature of things. Indeed, philosophy as understanding is an ongoing activity, a continuing realization of the human capacity to intuit essences and in that way behold a timeless and unchanging realm. In this way, philosophy is celebration; it celebrates consciousness and cherishes the phenomenon of spirituality in a material universe.

Celebrating consciousness entails release of awareness from the demands of the body. Consciousness then focuses on what is immediately intuited and escapes, if only for the moment, the contingency of material flux and the anxiety of existence. When practiced honestly such focused awareness is not denial, but rather it is refinement of consciousness for the joy of it. This appreciation of the immediate is appreciation of something valuable in itself. It is absorption in the moment and release from the binding relations of regrets about the past and anxieties for the future. The present moment, as John Lachs has characterized it, then displays "the sheer joy of conscious existence independently of what happened and what may come."[17] We might recognize this appreciation, this joy, this celebration as the essence of Santayana's philosophy. Then we can understand better Santayana's dismissal of "the cold old academic printed stuff," and why no book could capture such an essence. In fact, there is no need to communicate the experience of the present moment because, as Lachs explains, it is shared.[18] Each of us is in the present moment and can enjoy it as we will; no text can deliver it or direct the attention of those who ignore it.

Though the immediate is open to all, few experience it with regularity; and contemplating immediate objects is deadly as a way of life since life is a material phenomenon. However, contemplation of the immediate remains an important human experience because it is the perfection of natural impulses—namely, the impulses that give rise to consciousness. For Santayana, cultivation of consciousness sets the philosopher apart. One no longer distracted by that which is incidental to consciousness and whose intuitions and emotions flow easily through

[17] John Lachs, "The Past, the Future and the Immediate," *The Transactions of the Charles S. Peirce Society* 39:2 (2003), 160.

[18] Ibid., 161.

harmonized habits is "a real <u>philosopher</u> and not . . . [as the rest of us may be] <u>professors</u> of the philosophy of other people, or of our own opinions" (*LGS,* 5:120).

The celebration of consciousness may be better understood by an analogy that Santayana suggested in an essay about athletics. If the athlete refines and celebrates the abilities of the human body, then the philosopher may do the same for consciousness.

Athletics, according to Santayana, are not ultimately justified by their utility for health. The excessive training or hard contact threaten health more than they help it; and if health were the primary aim, then gentle exercise such as moderate walking or swimming would be enough. Santayana contended that athletics "are a response to a natural impulse and exist only as an end in themselves."[19] Likewise, philosophy is a response to sensitive impulses and a refinement of consciousness for its own sake. It is no reliable aid to fitness in practical, everyday matters; instinct would be a more dependable guide to assured action. This is not to deny that philosophical reflection and athletics may bestow some benefit on action and health, but these benefits are secondary on Santayana's view and cannot be the genuine motives.

Santayana also rejected the notion that athletics can be justified as preparation for war. While he acknowledged an intimate relation between athletics and war, it is not a relation of means to ends. Rather, athletics result when the need for war has disappeared and those freed impulses can be directed to something else, more beautiful and refined than war. He wrote that "[w]ar can thus become a luxury and flower into artistic forms, whenever the circumstances of life no longer drain all the energy native to the character."[20] Similarly, when one escapes the concerns of nourishing the body, defending against threats, and pursuing physical comforts, consciousness is free to contemplate ideas, to trace the realm of essence, and forget the cares for which essences are taken as symbols. The activity becomes an art, detached from the chaos of the realm of matter.

The suggestion that athletics grow out of war liberated from the need for it reflects Santayana's views on the origin of consciousness in the animal struggle for survival. Material welfare is the province of the self-preserving organization of an organism that Santayana called *psyche;* consciousness or awareness he called *spirit.* "The psyche needs to prepare for all things that may chance in its life: it needs to be universally vigilant, universally retentive. In satisfying this need it forms the spirit, which therefore initially tends to look, to remember, to understand" (*ES,* 352–353). Although spirit shares the destiny of psyche and is sympathetic to psyche in its "tragic confusion," spirit's sympathy is not due to a concern with survival. Rather spirit "craves to see [psyche and her world] everywhere well-ordered and beautiful. . . . This is the specific function of spirit, which it lives by fulfilling, and dies if it cannot somehow fulfil" (*ES,* 353). The function of

---

[19] George Santayana, "Philosophy on the Bleachers," in *George Santayana's America,* edited by James Ballowe (Urbana, Chicago, and London: University of Illinois Press, 1967), 123.

[20] Ibid., 124.

spirit is to observe and understand. Spirit depends on psyche and is generated by psyche, but "in its intellectual vocation, infinitely transcends" psyche (*RB1*, 613).

But few can answer the call of spirit and escape the cares that beset the psyche; and similarly, few people have the opportunity to dedicate themselves to developing physical skills to the level of world-class athletes. For most people, spirit is distracted "from the spontaneous exercise of its liberty, . . . [held] down to the rack of care, doubt, pain, hatred, and vice" (*RB1*, 673); and would-be athletes are distracted by other concerns or obligations, or they simply lack the necessary talent. Santayana described athletics as "an art in which only the few, the exceptionally gifted, can worthily succeed."[21] The gift of the philosopher, as of the poet and the mystic, is the "trick of arresting the immediate" (*RB1*, 156): consciousness is absorbed in intuition and "belief in existence has turned into contemplation of essence" (*PGS*, 542). Santayana wrote, "I happen to be able to do this trick and to enjoy doing it, which by no means implies that I refuse ever to trust perception or to believe in facts, when the facts really impose and justify such belief, which is not always" (*PGS*, 542). This gift or trick is a human one and does not endow divinity on practitioners; flights of spirit cannot abolish the realm of matter. Santayana acknowledged limits on spirituality and wrote of his "personal attitude towards the ambition of those who aspire to be pure spirits. I do not share it" (*LGS*, 3:351). Just as the godlike athlete remains mortal, so the philosopher too cannot escape the claims of the body.

The divine likeness, however temporary it may be, appeals powerfully not only to the direct participant but also to those taking part vicariously. Of the rare achievement Santayana wrote that, "we all participate through the imagination in the delight and meaning of what lies beyond our power of accomplishment. A few moments of enjoyment and intuition, scattered throughout our lives, are what lift the whole of it from vulgarity."[22] Outstanding athletic achievements seize the imagination because they represent fundamental human virtues and enact a "sort of physical drama, a drama in which all moral and emotional interest are in a manner involved."[23] Athletic contests display "the essence of physical conflict" and stir the whole soul.

The greatest appeal of athletics, according to Santayana, lies in its spontaneity and vitality. He wrote that, "[t]he curse of our time is industrial supremacy, the sacrifice of every spontaneous faculty and liberal art to the demands of an overgrown material civilization. Our labour is servile and our play frivolous."[24] These conditions, thought Santayana, stunt imagination and enslave wills to the point that play is subsumed to the habits of work (so that it can be enjoyed only as it increases productivity or serves health). Athletics defies these constraints, and in this Santayana saw the sign of rebellion against conformity and industrialism.

Athletics seemed to Santayana "fruits of that spontaneous life, of which the higher manifestations are not suffered to appear. Perhaps it is well that the body

---

[21] Ibid.

[22] Ibid., 125.

[23] Ibid., 127.

[24] Ibid., 128.

should take the lead, since that is the true and safe order of nature. The rest, if it comes, will then rest on a sound basis."[25] Here the connection to philosophy is explicit. Santayana suggested that perhaps a physical culture that allows impulses to bloom and flourish could eventually recognize and cultivate impulses that reach for ideas, that delight in the intuition of essences, and that celebrate consciousness. He was not suggesting that the one follows the other automatically, but as favorable conditions for one form of life suggest the possibility of other forms of life, so too a free physical life might portend a free spiritual life.

The hope is not unreasonable: where celebration is valued, additional activities could conceivably be celebrated. The exceptional athlete celebrates refined bodily motions and intensified competitive impulses that in their basic phases are shared by most human beings. The philosopher celebrates the life of the spirit, which is, claimed Santayana, "intimately natural to all of us" (*PGS*, 569). He observed that spirit "breaks out momentarily in the shabbiest surroundings, in laughter, understanding, and small surrenders of folly to reason. . . . Such moments . . . often . . . come to ne'er-do-wells, poets, actors, or rakes" (*ES*, 363). The philosopher differs by adding constancy to the light shed by such moments on the human condition and gaining understanding of consciousness and appreciation of essence so that the material circumstances of such outbreaks of spirit become "almost indifferent occasions." Hence Santayana's claim that "[p]hilosophy is a more intense sort of experience than common life is" (*TPP*, 124).

The Essential Santayana is intended to be a celebration of an extraordinary thinker and writer, but in the spirit of Santayana it is not meant to be a commemorative celebration but rather one that actively engages the gift of consciousness that he celebrated. This volume is not only an opportunity to "participate through the imagination in the delight and meaning" of the achievements of a philosopher; it is offered also as an inspiration to live more intensely, more humanely, and more consciously. Sincerity requires the acknowledgment that this volume could never be essential to the exercise of spirit; but it could contribute to efforts to become more aware of the occasions on which spirit might break out. And its appearance might conceivably indicate a growing freedom in spiritual life.

Martin A. Coleman

---

[25] Ibid., 129.

THE
ESSENTIAL
SANTAYANA

I

Autobiography

Santayana enjoyed the role of detached observer and outsider. In his autobiography, he wrote "I like to be a stranger . . . , it was my destiny; but I wish to be the only stranger. For this reason I have been happiest among people of all nationalities who were not of my own age, class, or family circle; for then I was a single exceptional personage in their world, and they a complete harmonious milieu for me to drop into and live with for a season" (*PP,* 528).

The preference seems to reflect the estrangement and dislocation that marked Santayana's childhood. Santayana was born in Madrid, Spain, on 16 December 1863, the only child of his mother's second marriage. The first had produced five children, of whom two daughters and one son survived childhood. In 1869 Santayana's mother departed Spain for her first husband's hometown, Boston, Massachusetts, with her two daughters. Her other son had already moved there for schooling. Santayana remained in Spain with his father until 1872, when they joined the family in America. His father returned to Spain the next year, and Santayana was raised by his mother and sister in Boston.

Santayana graduated from the Boston Public Latin School, and in the fall of 1882 he entered Harvard, where he studied philosophy with William James and Josiah Royce. He graduated *summa cum laude* with his Bachelor of Arts in 1886 and received the Walker Travelling Fellowship to study philosophy in Germany for two years. In 1889 he finished his dissertation, *Lotze's System of Philosophy,* under the direction of Josiah Royce and received his Master of Arts and Doctor of Philosophy from Harvard. That fall he began teaching philosophy at Harvard.

Santayana taught at Harvard for twenty-two years and during that time regularly made summer trips to Europe, usually visiting England and Spain. Beginning in the summer of 1904, he used his year of leave from Harvard to travel in Europe, Egypt, present-day Turkey, and the Middle East. He extended his stay abroad a second year by accepting the James Hazen Hyde Lectureship from Harvard, which supported a faculty member for one academic year as he lectured in French universities.

In 1912 Santayana moved to Europe to take up writing full-time. He resigned from Harvard and never returned to the United States. He had no permanent residence in Europe, though during World War I he was forced to reside in England. In 1919 he resumed his travels in Europe and established a pattern of movement he would maintain until 1939 and the outbreak of war in Europe. He usually lived in hotels and traveled with the seasons: he would live in Rome or Nice in the winter, and Paris or Cortina d'Ampezzo in northern Italy in the summer, followed by a visit to family in Spain on his way back south for the winter.

In 1939 Santayana wintered in Venice because his usual hotel in Rome was closed for renovation. He returned to Rome in 1940, and in 1941 after being denied permission to go to Spain he moved into the Clinica della Piccola Compagna di Maria (Clinic of the Little Company of Mary, known popularly as the Blue Nuns for the color of their habits), where he lived during World War II and died in 1952.

While this life of travel and detachment may reflect the early influence of separation and immigration, some have suggested that these influences shaped Santayana's entire philosophy. One commentator speculates that the shock of the move from Spain to Boston instilled in Santayana his lifelong sense of the contingency of the material world and its arbitrary imposition of circumstances on an observing but impotent self (Richard C. Lyon, "Introduction: George Santayana [1863–1952]" in *Santayana in America* [New York: Harcourt Brace and World, 1968], xv). Another argues that his detachment was a strategy for coping with the despair of being abandoned by his mother, whom he portrayed as cold and distant even when she was present (Lois Hughson, "The Uses of Despair: The Source of Creative Energy in George Santayana," *American Quarterly* 23:5 [1971]: 725–37; *PP*, 42–43). The authors of a prominent history of American philosophy find it difficult to "repress the conviction that his subsequent pessimism and fatalism about life must have had roots in" the events of his childhood (Elizabeth Flower and Murray G. Murphey, *A History of Philosophy in America* [New York: G. P. Putnam's Sons, 1977], 774). Santayana's biographer locates "one source of his philosophical scepticism" in the experience of being uprooted from Spain and replaced in New England (*GSB*, 19).

But Santayana was wary of such explanations; he doubted their accuracy and their relevance for his philosophy. In "A General Confession" he wrote, "I do not assert that [my family background] was actually the origin of my system; in any case its truth would be another question. I propose simply to describe as best I can the influences under which I have lived, and leave it for the reader, if he cares, to consider how far my philosophy may be an expression of them" (*ES*, 5). For his part Santayana maintained that the influence of his particular circumstances, while certainly affecting his language, mode of expression, and the illustrating facts in his writing, did not influence his philosophy; and he declared that "under whatever sky I had been born, since it is the same sky, I should have had the same philosophy" (*ES*, 54).

Santayana admitted that his chance circumstances of being a foreign student threw into relief the distinction between spirit and matter. Being unable to unconsciously absorb the outlook of his classmates and neighbors—an outlook Santayana took to be optimistic and egotistical with respect to the material universe—he understood that "[t]he world was My Host; I was a temporary guest in his busy and animated establishment. . . . My Host and I could become friends diplomatically; but we were not akin in either our interests or our powers" (*ES*, 32). But his philosophical formulations of this relationship between spirit and world were intended to be expressions of conditions more than personal, no matter how personally distinctively the style of expression.

The pieces chosen for the first section of *The Essential Santayana*, "Autobiography," each exhibit the double awareness of "the feeling of being a stranger and an exile by nature as well as by accident" (*ES*, 32). But each is consistent with Santayana's attempt to situate his life in the universe rather than the universe in his life; hence he wrote that "accidents are accidents only to ignorance; in reality all physical events flow out of one another by a continuous intertwined derivation" (*ES*, 24). These selections are undeniably philosophical, but what can be discounted as merely personal is left to the reader to decide according to his or her own concerns.

A General Confession

The Philosophy of George Santayana. Edited by Paul Arthur Schilpp. Evanston and Chicago: Northwestern University Press, 1940, 3–30.

This three-part autobiographical essay appeared in its present form in The Philosophy of George Santayana, *the second volume in* The Library of Living Philosophers. *The format of the series, which continues today under the editorship of Randall E. Auxier, includes a collection of articles about a particular philosopher, responses by that philosopher, a bibliography of the philosopher's works, and an intellectual autobiography. Santayana's autobiographical essay consists of reworked material from three earlier publications. Part I first appeared as "A Brief History of My Opinions" in* Contemporary American Philosophy, *volume 2 (edited by George Plimpton Adams and William Pepperell Montague [New York: The Macmillan Company, 1930], 237–57). Part II derives from the "Preface" to* The Works of George Santayana *(Triton Edition, volume 1 [New York: Scribner's, 1936], vii–xi). Part III appeared as the "Preface" to* The Works of George Santayana *(Triton Edition, volume 7 [New York: Scribner's, 1937], vii–xv). Writing to Schilpp about the title of this selection, Santayana remarked that "it is the phrase used by Catholics when, on great festive occasions, they make review of all their past sins" (LGS, 6:229).*

I

How came a child born in Spain of Spanish parents to be educated in Boston and to write in the English language? The case of my family was unusual. We were not emigrants; none of us ever changed his country, his class, or his religion. But special circumstances had given us hereditary points of attachment in opposite quarters, moral and geographical; and now that we are almost extinct—I mean those of us who had these mixed associations—I may say that we proved remarkably staunch in our complex allegiances, combining them as well as logic allowed, without at heart ever disowning anything. My philosophy in particular may be regarded as a synthesis of these various traditions, or as an attempt

---

Part I of "A General Confession" appeared originally as "Brief History of My Opinions," in *Contemporary American Philosophy,* edited by G. P. Adams and William P. Montague (1930), II, 237–257, and is reprinted by permission of The Macmillan Company, New York. Part II is an excerpt from Mr. Santayana's Preface to volume I of the Triton Edition of *The Works of George Santayana* (1936), and is reprinted by permission of Charles Scribner's Sons, New York. Part III is the Preface to Volume VII of the Triton Edition (1936), also reprinted by permission of Charles Scribner's Sons.

Whatever minor changes from the original articles appear in the above text were made by Mr. Santayana himself. The new title for this newly combined autobiography was also furnished by Mr. Santayana.–Ed.

to view them from a level from which their several deliverances may be justly understood. I do not assert that such was actually the origin of my system; in any case its truth would be another question. I propose simply to describe as best I can the influences under which I have lived, and leave it for the reader, if he cares, to consider how far my philosophy may be an expression of them.

In the first place, we must go much farther afield than Boston or Spain, into the tropics, almost to the antipodes. Both my father and my mother's father were officials in the Spanish civil service in the Philippine Islands. This was in the 1840's and 1850's, long before my birth; for my parents were not married until later in life, in Spain, when my mother was a widow. But the tradition of the many years which each of them separately had spent in the East was always alive in our household. Those had been, for both, their more romantic and prosperous days. My father had studied the country and the natives, and had written a little book about the Island of Mindanao; he had been three times round the world in the sailing-ships of the period, and had incidentally visited England and the United States, and been immensely impressed by the energy and order prevalent in those nations. His respect for material greatness was profound, yet not unmixed with a secret irony or even repulsion. He had a seasoned and incredulous mind, trained to see other sorts of excellence also: in his boyhood he had worked in the studio of a professional painter of the school of Goya, and had translated the tragedies of Seneca into Spanish verse. His transmarine experiences, therefore, did not rattle, as so often happens, in an empty head. The sea itself, in those days, was still vast and blue, and the lands beyond it full of lessons and wonders. From childhood I have lived in the imaginative presence of interminable ocean spaces, coconut islands, blameless Malays, and immense continents swarming with Chinamen, polished and industrious, obscene and philosophical. It was habitual with me to think of scenes and customs pleasanter than those about me. My own travels have never carried me far from the frontiers of Christendom or of respectability, and chiefly back and forth across the North Atlantic—thirty-eight fussy voyages; but in mind I have always seen these things on an ironical background enormously empty, or breaking out in spots, like Polynesia, into nests of innocent particoloured humanity.

My mother's figure belonged to the same broad and somewhat exotic landscape; she had spent her youth in the same places; but the moral note resounding in her was somewhat different. Her father, José Borrás, of Reus in Catalonia, had been a disciple of Rousseau, an enthusiast and a wanderer: he taught her to revere pure reason and republican virtue and to abhor the vices of a corrupt world. But her own temper was cool and stoical, rather than ardent, and her disdain of corruption had in it a touch of elegance. At Manila, during the time of her first marriage, she had been rather the grand lady, in a style half Creole, half early Victorian. Virtue, beside those tropical seas, might stoop to be indolent. She had given a silver dollar every morning to her native major-domo, with which to provide for the family and the twelve servants, and keep the change for his wages. Meantime she bathed, arranged the flowers, received visits, and did embroidery. It had been a spacious life; and in our narrower circumstances in later years the sense of it never forsook her.

Her first husband, an American merchant established in Manila, had been the ninth child of Nathaniel Russell Sturgis, of Boston (1779–1856). In Boston, accordingly, her three Sturgis children had numerous relations and a little property, and there she had promised their father to bring them up in case of his death. When this occurred, in 1857, she therefore established herself in Boston; and this fact, by a sort of prenatal or pre-established destiny, was the cause of my connection with the Sturgis family, with Boston, and with America.

It was in Madrid in 1862, where my mother had gone on a visit intended to be temporary, that my father and she were married. He had been an old friend of hers and of her first husband's, and was well aware of her settled plan to educate her children in America, and recognized the propriety of that arrangement. Various projects and combinations were mooted: but the matter eventually ended in a separation, friendly, if not altogether pleasant to either party. My mother returned with her Sturgis children to live in the United States and my father and I remained in Spain. Soon, however, this compromise proved unsatisfactory. The education and prospects which my father, in his modest retirement, could offer me in Spain were far from brilliant; and in 1872 he decided to take me to Boston, where, after remaining for one cold winter, he left me in my mother's care and went back to Spain.

I was then in my ninth year, having been born on December 16, 1863, and I did not know one word of English. Nor was I likely to learn the language at home, where the family always continued to speak a Spanish more or less pure. But by a happy thought I was sent during my first winter in Boston to a Kindergarten, among much younger children, where there were no books, so that I picked up English by ear before knowing how it was written: a circumstance to which I probably owe speaking the language without a marked foreign accent. The Brimmer School, the Boston Latin School, and Harvard College then followed in order: but apart from the taste for English poetry which I first imbibed from our excellent English master, Mr. Byron Groce, the most decisive influences over my mind in boyhood continued to come from my family, where, with my grown-up brother and sisters, I was the only child. I played no games, but sat at home all the afternoon and evening reading or drawing; especially devouring anything I could find that regarded religion, architecture, or geography.

In the summer of 1883, after my Freshman year, I returned for the first time to Spain to see my father. Then, and during many subsequent holidays which I spent in his company, we naturally discussed the various careers that might be open to me. We should both of us have liked the Spanish army or diplomatic service: but for the first I was already too old, and our means and our social relations hardly sufficed for the second. Moreover, by that time I felt like a foreigner in Spain, more acutely so than in America, although for more trivial reasons: my Yankee manners seemed outlandish there, and I could not do myself justice in the language. Nor was I inclined to overcome this handicap, as perhaps I might have done with a little effort: nothing in Spanish life or literature at that time particularly attracted me. English had become my only possible instrument, and I deliberately put away everything that might confuse me in that medium. English, and the whole Anglo-Saxon tradition in literature and philosophy, have always been a medium to me rather than a source. My natural affinities were elsewhere. Moreover, scholarship and learning of any sort seemed to me a means, not an end. I always hated to be a professor. Latin and Greek, French, Italian, and German, although I can read them, were languages which I never learned well. It seemed an accident to me if the matters which interested me came clothed in the rhetoric of one or another of these nations: I was not without a certain temperamental rhetoric of my own in which to recast what I adopted. Thus in renouncing everything else for the sake of English letters I might be said to have been guilty, quite unintentionally, of a little stratagem, as if I had set out to say plausibly in English as many un-English things as possible.

This brings me to religion, which is the head and front of everything. Like my parents, I have always set myself down officially as a Catholic: but this is a matter of sympathy and traditional allegiance, not of philosophy. In my adolescence, religion on its doctrinal and emotional side occupied me much more than it does now. I was more unhappy and unsettled; but I have never had any unquestioning faith in any dogma, and have never been what is called a practising Catholic. Indeed, it would hardly have been possible. My mother, like her father before her, was a Deist: she was sure there was a God, for who else could have made the world? But God was too great to take special thought for man: sacrifices, prayers, churches, and tales of immortality were invented by rascally priests in order to dominate the foolish. My father, except for the Deism, was emphatically of the same opinion. Thus, although I learned my prayers and catechism by rote, as was then inevitable in Spain, I knew that my parents regarded all religion as a work of human imagination: and I agreed, and still agree, with them there. But this carried an implication in their minds against which every instinct in me rebelled, namely that the works of human imagination are bad. No, said I to myself even as a boy: they are good, they alone are good; and the rest—the whole real world—is ashes in the mouth. My sympathies were entirely with those other members of my family who were devout believers. I loved the Christian epic, and all those doctrines and observances which bring it down into daily life: I thought how glorious it would have been to be a Dominican friar, preaching that epic eloquently, and solving afresh all the knottiest and sublimest mysteries of theology. I was delighted with anything, like Mallock's *Is Life Worth Living?,* which seemed to rebuke the fatuity of that age. For my own part, I was quite sure that life was not worth living; for if religion was false everything was worthless, and almost everything, if religion was true. In this youthful pessimism I was hardly more foolish than so many amateur mediævalists and religious æsthetes of my generation. I saw the same alternative between Catholicism and complete disillusion: but I was never afraid of disillusion, and I have chosen it.

Since those early years my feelings on this subject have become less strident. Does not modern philosophy teach that our idea of the so-called real world is also a work of imagination? A religion—for there are other religions than the Christian—simply offers a system of faith different from the vulgar one, or extending beyond it. The question is which imaginative system you will trust. My matured conclusion has been that no system is to be trusted, not even that of science in any literal or pictorial sense; but all systems may be used and, up to a certain point, trusted as symbols. Science expresses in human terms our dynamic relation to surrounding reality. Philosophies and religions, where they do not misrepresent these same dynamic relations and do not contradict science, express destiny in moral dimensions, in obviously mythical and poetical images: but how else should these moral truths be expressed at all in a traditional or popular fashion? Religions are the great fairy-tales of the conscience.

When I began the formal study of philosophy as an undergraduate at Harvard, I was already alive to the fundamental questions, and even had a certain dialectical nimbleness, due to familiarity with the fine points of theology: the arguments for and against free will and the proofs of the existence of God were warm and clear in my mind. I accordingly heard James and Royce with more wonder than serious agreement: my scholastic logic would have wished to reduce James at once to a materialist and Royce to a solipsist, and it seemed strangely irrational in them to resist such simplification. I had heard many Unitarian sermons (being taken to hear them lest I should become too Catholic), and had been interested in them so far as they were rationalistic and informative, or even amusingly irreligious, as I often thought them to be: but neither in those discourses nor in Harvard philosophy was it easy for me to understand the Protestant combination of earnestness with waywardness. I was used to see water flowing from fountains, architectural and above ground: it puzzled me to see it drawn painfully in bucketfuls from the subjective well, muddied, and half spilt over.

There was one lesson, however, which I was readier to learn, not only at Harvard from Professor Palmer and afterwards at Berlin from Paulsen, but from the general temper of that age well represented for me by the *Revue Des Deux Mondes* (which I habitually read from cover to cover) and by the works of Taine and of Matthew Arnold—I refer to the historical spirit of the nineteenth century, and to that splendid panorama of nations and religions, literatures and arts, which it unrolled before the imagination. These picturesque vistas into the past came to fill in circumstantially that geographical and moral vastness to which my imagination was already accustomed. Professor Palmer was especially skilful in bending the mind to a suave and sympathetic participation in the views of all philosophers in turn: were they not all great men, and must not the aspects of things which seemed persuasive to them be really persuasive? Yet even this form of romanticism, amiable as it is, could not altogether put to sleep my scholastic dogmatism. The historian of philosophy may be as sympathetic and as self-effacing as he likes: the philosopher in him must still ask whether any of those successive views were true, or whether the later ones were necessarily truer than the earlier: he cannot, unless he is a shameless sophist, rest content with a truth *pro tem*. In reality the sympathetic reconstruction of history is a literary art, and it depends for its plausibility as well as for its materials on a conventional belief in the natural world. Without this belief no history and no science would be anything but a poetic fiction, like a classification of the angelic choirs. The necessity of naturalism as a foundation for all further serious opinions was clear to me from the beginning. Naturalism might indeed be criticized–and I was myself intellectually and emotionally predisposed to criticize it, and to oscillate between supernaturalism and solipsism–but if naturalism was condemned, supernaturalism itself could have no point of application in the world of fact; and the whole edifice of human knowledge would crumble, since no perception would then be a report and no judgment would have a transcendent object. Hence historical reconstruction seemed to me more honestly and solidly practised by Taine, who was a professed naturalist, than by Hegel and his school, whose naturalism, though presupposed at every stage, was disguised and distorted by a dialectic imposed on it by the historian and useful at best only in simplifying his dramatic perspectives and lending them a false absoluteness and moralistic veneer.

The influence of Royce over me, though less important in the end than that of James, was at first much more active. Royce was the better dialectician, and traversed subjects in which I was naturally more interested. The point that particularly exercised me was Royce's Theodicy or justification for the existence of evil. It would be hard to exaggerate the ire which his arguments on this subject aroused in my youthful breast. Why that emotion? Romantic sentiment that could find happiness only in tears and virtue only in heroic agonies was something familiar to me and not unsympathetic: a poetic play of mine, called *Lucifer,* conceived in those days, is a clear proof of it. I knew Leopardi and Musset largely by heart; Schopenhauer was soon to become, for a brief period, one of my favourite authors. I carried Lucretius in my pocket: and although the spirit of the poet in that case was not romantic, the picture of human existence which he drew glorified the same vanity. Spinoza, too, whom I was reading under Royce himself, filled me with joy and enthusiasm:

I gathered at once from him a doctrine which has remained axiomatic with me ever since, namely that good and evil are relative to the natures of animals, irreversible in that relation, but indifferent to the march of cosmic events, since the force of the universe infinitely exceeds the force of any one of its parts. Had I found, then, in Royce only a romantic view of life, or only pessimism, or only stoical courage and pantheistic piety, I should have taken no offence, but readily recognized the poetic truth or the moral legitimacy of those positions. Conformity with fate, as I afterwards came to see, belongs to post-rational morality, which is a normal though optional development of human sentiment: Spinoza's "intellectual love of God" was a shining instance of it.

But in Royce these attitudes, in themselves so honest and noble, seemed to be somehow embroiled and rendered sophistical: nor was he alone in this, for the same moral equivocation seemed to pervade Hegel, Browning, and Nietzsche. That which repelled me in all these men was the survival of a sort of forced optimism and pulpit unction, by which a cruel and nasty world, painted by them in the most lurid colours, was nevertheless set up as the model and standard of what ought to be. The duty of an honest moralist would have been rather to distinguish, in this bad or mixed reality, the part, however small, that could be loved and chosen from the remainder, however large, which was to be rejected and renounced. Certainly the universe was in flux and dynamically single: but this fatal flux could very well take care of itself; and it was not so fluid that no islands of a relative permanence and beauty might not be formed in it. Ascetic conformity was itself one of these islands: a scarcely inhabitable peak from which almost all human passions and activities were excluded. And the Greeks, whose deliberate ethics was rational, never denied the vague early Gods and the environing chaos, which perhaps would return in the end: but meantime they built their cities bravely on the hill-tops, as we all carry on pleasantly our temporal affairs, although we know that to-morrow we die. Life itself exists only by a modicum of organization, achieved and transmitted through a world of change: the momentum of such organization first creates a difference between good and evil, or gives them a meaning at all. Thus the core of life is always hereditary, steadfast, and classical; the margin of barbarism and blind adventure round it may be as wide as you will, and in some wild hearts the love of this fluid margin may be keen, as might be any other loose passion. But to *preach* barbarism as the only good, in ignorance or hatred of the possible perfection of every natural thing, was a scandal: a belated Calvinism that remained fanatical after ceasing to be Christian. And there was a further circumstance which made this attitude particularly odious to me. This romantic love of evil was not thoroughgoing: wilfulness and disorder were to reign only in spiritual matters; in government and industry, even in natural science, all was to be order and mechanical progress. Thus the absence of a positive religion and of a legislation, like that of the ancients, intended to be rational and final, was very far from liberating the spirit for higher flights: on the contrary, it opened the door to the pervasive tyranny of the world over the soul. And no wonder: a soul rebellious to its moral heritage is too weak to reach any firm definition of its inner life. It will feel lost and empty unless it summons the random labours of the contemporary world to fill and to enslave it. It must let mechanical and civic achievements reconcile it to its own moral confusion and triviality.

It was in this state of mind that I went to Germany to continue the study of philosophy—interested in all religious or metaphysical systems, but sceptical about them and scornful of any romantic worship or idealization of the real world. The life of a wandering student, like those of the Middle Ages, had an immense natural attraction for me—so great, that I have never willingly led any other. When I had to choose a profession, the prospect of a quiet academic existence seemed the least of evils. I was fond of reading and observation, and I liked young men; but I have never been a diligent student either of science or art, nor at all ambitious to be learned. I have been willing to let cosmological problems and technical questions solve themselves as they would or as the authorities agreed for the moment that they should be solved. My pleasure was rather in expression, in reflection, in irony: my spirit was content to intervene, in whatever world it might seem to find itself, in order to disentangle the intimate moral and intellectual echoes audible to it in that world. My naturalism or materialism is no academic opinion: it is not a survival of the alleged materialism of the nineteenth century, when all the professors of philosophy were idealists: it is an everyday conviction which came to me, as it came to my father, from experience and observation of the world at large, and especially of my own feelings and passions. It seems to me that those who are not materialists cannot be good observers of themselves: they may hear themselves thinking, but they cannot have watched themselves acting and feeling; for feeling and action are evidently accidents of matter. If a Democritus or Lucretius or Spinoza or Darwin works within the lines of nature, and clarifies some part of that familiar object, that fact is the ground of my attachment to them: they have the savour of truth; but what the savour of truth is, I know very well without their help. Consequently there is no opposition in my mind between materialism and a Platonic or even Indian discipline of the spirit. The recognition of the material world and of the conditions of existence in it merely enlightens the spirit concerning the source of its troubles and the means to its happiness or deliverance: and it was happiness or deliverance, the supervening supreme expression of human will and imagination, that alone really concerned me. This alone was genuine philosophy: this alone was the life of reason.

Had the life of reason ever been cultivated in the world by people with a sane imagination? Yes, once, by the Greeks. Of the Greeks, however, I knew very little: the philosophical and political departments at Harvard had not yet discovered Plato and Aristotle. It was with the greater pleasure that I heard Paulsen in Berlin expounding Greek ethics with a sweet reasonableness altogether worthy of the subject: here at last was a vindication of order and beauty in the institutions of men and in their ideas. Here, through the pleasant medium of transparent myths or of summary scientific images, like the water of Thales, nature was essentially understood and honestly described; and here, for that very reason, the free mind could disentangle its true good, and could express it in art, in manners, and even in the most refined or the most austere spiritual discipline. Yet, although I knew henceforth that in the Greeks I should find the natural support and point of attachment for my own philosophy, I was not then collected or mature enough to pursue the matter; not until ten years later, in 1896–1897, did I take the opportunity of a year's leave of absence to go to England and begin a systematic reading of Plato and Aristotle under Dr. Henry Jackson of Trinity College, Cambridge. I am not conscious of any change of opinion supervening, nor of any having occurred earlier; but by that study and change of scene my mind was greatly enriched; and the composition of *The Life of Reason* was the consequence.

This book was intended to be a summary history of the human imagination, expressly distinguishing those phases of it which showed what Herbert Spencer called an adjustment of inner to outer relations; in other words, an adaptation of fancy and habit to material facts and opportunities. On the one hand, then, my subject being the imagination, I was never called on to step beyond the subjective sphere. I set out to describe, not nature or God, but the ideas of God or nature bred in the human mind. On the other hand, I was not concerned with these ideas for their own sake, as in a work of pure poetry or erudition, but I meant to consider them in their natural genesis and significance; for I assumed throughout that the whole life of reason was generated and controlled by the animal life of man in the bosom of nature. Human ideas had, accordingly, a symptomatic, expressive, and symbolic value: they were the inner notes sounded by man's passions and by his arts: and they became rational partly by their vital and inward harmony—for reason is a harmony of the passions—and partly by their adjustment to external facts and possibilities—for reason is a harmony of the inner life with truth and with fate. I was accordingly concerned to discover what wisdom is possible to an animal whose mind, from beginning to end, is poetical: and I found that this could not lie in discarding poetry in favour of a science supposed to be clairvoyant and literally true. Wisdom lay rather in taking everything good-humouredly, with a grain of salt. In science there was an element of poetry, pervasive, inevitable, and variable: it was strictly scientific and true only in so far as it involved a close and prosperous adjustment to the surrounding world, at first by its origin in observation and at last by its application in action. Science was the mental accompaniment of art.

Here was a sort of pragmatism: the same which I have again expressed, I hope more clearly, in one of the *Dialogues in Limbo* entitled "Normal Madness." The human mind is a faculty of dreaming awake, and its dreams are kept relevant to its environment and to its fate only by the external control exercised over them by Punishment, when the accompanying conduct brings ruin, or by Agreement, when it brings prosperity. In the latter case it is possible to establish correspondences between one part of a dream and another, or between the dreams of separate minds, and so create the world of literature, or the life of reason. I am not sure whether this notion, that thought is a controlled and consistent madness, appears among the thirteen pragmatisms which have been distinguished, but I have reason to think that I came to it under the influence of William James; nevertheless, when his book on *Pragmatism* appeared, about the same time as my *Life of Reason,* it gave me a rude shock. I could not stomach that way of speaking about truth; and the continual substitution of human psychology—normal madness, in my view—for the universe, in which man is but one distracted and befuddled animal, seemed to me a confused remnant of idealism, and not serious.

The William James who had been my master was not this William James of the later years, whose pragmatism and pure empiricism and romantic metaphysics have made such a stir in the world. It was rather the puzzled but brilliant doctor, impatient of metaphysics, whom I had known in my undergraduate days, one of whose maxims was that to study the abnormal was the best way of understanding the normal; or it was the genial author of *The Principles of Psychology,* chapters of which he read from the manuscript and discussed with a small class of us in 1889. Even then what I learned from him was perhaps chiefly things which explicitly he never taught, but which I imbibed from the spirit and background of his teaching. Chief of these, I should say, was a sense for the immediate: for the unadulterated, unexplained, instant fact of experience. Actual experience, for William James, however varied or rich its assault might be, was always and altogether of the nature of a sensation: it possessed a vital, leaping, globular unity which made the only fact, the flying fact, of our being. Whatever continuities of quality might be traced in it, its existence was always momentary and self-warranted. A man's life or soul borrowed its reality and imputed wholeness from the intrinsic actuality of its successive parts; existence was a perpetual rebirth, a travelling light to which the past was lost and the future uncertain. The element of indetermination which James felt so strongly in this flood of existence was precisely the pulse of fresh unpredictable sensation, summoning attention hither and thither to unexpected facts. Apprehension in him being impressionistic—that was the age of impressionism in painting too—and marvellously free from intellectual assumptions or presumptions, he felt intensely the fact of contingency, or the contingency of fact. This seemed to me not merely a peculiarity of temperament in him, but a profound insight into existence, in its inmost irrational essence. Existence, I learned to see, is intrinsically dispersed, seated in its distributed moments, and arbitrary not only as a whole, but in the character and place of each of its parts. Change the bits, and you change the mosaic: nor can we count or limit the elements, as in a little closed kaleidoscope, which may be shaken together into the next picture. Many of them, such as pleasure and pain, or the total picture itself, cannot possibly have pre-existed.

But, said I to myself, were these novelties for that reason unconditioned? Was not sensation, by continually surprising us, a continual warning to us of fatal conjunctions occurring outside? And would not the same conjunctions, but for memory and habit, always produce the same surprises? Experience of indetermination was no proof of indeterminism; and when James proceeded to turn immediate experience into ultimate physics, his thought seemed to me to lose itself in words or in confused superstitions. Free will, a deep moral power contrary to a romantic indetermination in being, he endeavoured to pack into the bias of attention—the most temperamental of accidents. He insisted passionately on the efficacy of consciousness, and invoked Darwinian arguments for its utility—arguments which assumed that consciousness was a material engine absorbing and transmitting energy: so that it was no wonder that presently he doubted whether consciousness existed at all. He suggested a new physics or metaphysics in which the essences given in immediate experience should be deployed and hypostatized into the constituents of nature: but this pictorial cosmology had the disadvantage of abolishing the human imagination, with all the pathos and poetry of its animal status. James thus renounced that gift for literary psychology, that romantic insight, in which alone he excelled; and indeed his followers are without it. I pride myself on remaining a disciple of his earlier unsophisticated self, when he was an agnostic about the universe, but in his diagnosis of the heart an impulsive poet: a master in the art of recording or divining the lyric quality of experience as it actually came to him or to me.

Lyric experience and literary psychology, as I have learned to conceive them, are chapters in the life of one race of animals, in one corner of the natural world. But before relegating them to that modest station (which takes nothing away from their spiritual prerogatives) I was compelled to face the terrible problem which arises when, as in modern philosophy, literary psychology and lyric experience are made the fulcrum or the stuff of the universe. Has this experience any external conditions? If it has, are they knowable? And if it has not, on what principle are its qualities generated or its episodes distributed? Nay, how can literary psychology or universal experience have any seat save the present fancy of the psychologist or the historian? Although James had been bothered and confused by these questions, and Royce had enthroned his philosophy upon them, neither of these my principal teachers seemed to have come to clearness on the subject: it was only afterwards, when I read Fichte and Schopenhauer, that I began to see my way to a solution. We must oscillate between a radical transcendentalism, frankly reduced to a solipsism of the living moment, and a materialism posited as a presupposition of conventional sanity. There was no contradiction in joining together a scepticism which was not a dogmatic negation of anything and an animal faith which avowedly was a mere assumption in action and description. Yet such oscillation, if it was to be justified and rendered coherent, still demanded some understanding of two further points: what, starting from immediate experience, was the *causa cognoscendi* of the natural world; and what, starting from the natural world, was the *causa fiendi* of immediate experience?

On this second point (in spite of the speculations of my friend Strong) I have not seen much new light. I am constrained merely to register as a brute fact the emergence of consciousness in animal bodies. A psyche, or nucleus of hereditary organization, gathers and governs these bodies, and at the same time breeds within them a dreaming, suffering, and watching mind. Such investigations as those of Fraser and of Freud have shown how rich and how mad a thing the mind is fundamentally, how pervasively it plays about animal life, and how remote its first and deepest intuitions are from any understanding of their true occasions. An interesting and consistent complement to these discoveries is furnished by behaviourism, which I heartily accept on its positive biological side: the hereditary life of the body, modified by accident or training, forms a closed cycle of habits and actions. Of this the mind is a concomitant spiritual expression, invisible, imponderable, and epiphenomenal, or, as I prefer to say, hypostatic: for in it the moving unities and tensions of animal life are synthesized on quite another plane of being, into actual intuitions and feelings. This spiritual fertility in living bodies is the most natural of things. It is unintelligible only as all existence, change, or genesis is unintelligible; but it might be better understood, that is, better assimilated to other natural miracles, if we understood better the life of matter everywhere, and that of its different aggregates.

On the other point raised by my naturalism, namely on the grounds of faith in the natural world, I have reached more positive conclusions. Criticism, I think, must first be invited to do its worst: nothing is more dangerous here than timidity or convention. A pure and radical transcendentalism will disclaim all knowledge of fact. Nature, history, the self become ghostly presences, mere notions of such things; and the being of these images becomes purely internal to them; they exist in no environing space or time; they possess no substance or hidden parts, but are all surface, all appearance. Such a being, or quality of being, I call an essence; and to the consideration of essences, composing of themselves an eternal and infinite realm, I have lately devoted much attention. To that sphere I transpose the familiar pictures painted by the senses, or by traditional science and religion. Taken as essences, all ideas are compatible and supplementary to one another, like the various arts of expression; it is possible to perceive, up to a certain point, the symbolic burden of each of them, and to profit by the spiritual criticism of experience which it may embody. In particular, I recognize this spiritual truth in the Neo-Platonic and Indian systems, without admitting their fabulous side: after all, it is an old maxim with me that many ideas may be convergent as poetry which would be divergent as dogmas. This applies, in quite another quarter, to that revolution in physics which is now loudly announced, sometimes as the bankruptcy of science, sometimes as the breakdown of materialism. This revolution becomes, in my view, simply a change in notation. Matter may be called gravity or an electric charge or a tension in an ether; mathematics may readjust its equations to more accurate observations; any fresh description of nature which may result will still be a product of human wit, like the Ptolemaic and the Newtonian systems, and nothing but an intellectual symbol for man's contacts with matter, in so far as they have gone or as he has become distinctly sensitive to them. The real matter, within him and without, will meantime continue to rejoice in its ancient ways, or to adopt new ones, and incidentally to create these successive notions of it in his head.

When all the data of immediate experience and all the constructions of thought have thus been purified and reduced to what they are intrinsically, that is, to eternal essences, by a sort of counterblast the sense of existence, of action, of ambushed reality everywhere about us, becomes all the clearer and more imperious. This assurance of the not-given is involved in action, in expectation, in fear, hope, or want: I call it animal faith. The object of this faith is the substantial energetic thing encountered in action, whatever this thing may be in itself; by moving, devouring, or transforming this thing I assure myself of its existence; and at the same time my respect for it becomes enlightened and proportionate to its definite powers. But throughout, for the description of it in fancy, I have only the essences which my senses or thought may evoke in its presence; these are my inevitable signs and names for that object. Thus the whole sensuous and intellectual furniture of the mind becomes a store whence I may fetch terms for the description of nature, and may compose the silly home-poetry in which I talk to myself about everything. All is a tale told, if not by an idiot, at least by a dreamer; but it is far from signifying nothing. Sensations are rapid dreams: perceptions are dreams sustained and developed at will; sciences are dreams abstracted, controlled, measured, and rendered scrupulously proportional to their occasions. Knowledge accordingly always remains a part of imagination in its terms and in its seat; yet by virtue of its origin and intent it becomes a memorial and a guide to the fortunes of man in nature.

In the foregoing I have said nothing about my sentiments concerning æsthetics or the fine arts; yet I have devoted two volumes to those subjects, and I believe that to some people my whole philosophy seems to be little but rhetoric or prose poetry. I must frankly confess that I have written some verses; and at one time I had thoughts of becoming an architect or even a painter. The decorative and poetic aspects of art and nature have always fascinated me and held my attention above everything else. But in philosophy I recognize no separable thing called æsthetics; and what has gone by the name of the philosophy of art, like the so-called philosophy of history, seems to me sheer verbiage. There is in art nothing but manual knack and professional tradition on the practical side, and on the contemplative side pure intuition of essence, with the inevitable intellectual or luxurious pleasure which pure intuition involves. I can draw no distinction—save for academic programmes—between moral and æsthetic values: beauty, being a good, is a moral good; and the practice and enjoyment of art, like all practice and all enjoyment, fall within the sphere of morals—at least if by morals we understand moral economy and not moral superstition. On the other hand, the good, when actually realized and not merely pursued from afar, is a joy in the immediate; it is possessed with wonder and is in that sense æsthetic. Such pure joy when blind is called pleasure, when centred in some sensible image is called beauty, and when diffused over the thought of ulterior propitious things is called happiness, love, or religious rapture. But where all is manifest, as it is in intuition, classifications are pedantic. Harmony, which might be called an æsthetic principle, is also the principle of health, of justice, and of happiness. Every impulse, not the æsthetic mood alone, is innocent and irresponsible in its origin and precious in its own eyes; but every impulse or indulgence, including the æsthetic, is evil in its effect, when it renders harmony impossible in the general tenor of life, or produces in the soul division and ruin. There is no lack of folly in the arts; they are full of inertia and affectation and of what must seem ugliness to a cultivated taste; yet there is no need of bringing the catapult of criticism against it: indifference is enough. A society will breed the art which it is capable of, and which it deserves; but even in its own eyes this art will hardly be important or beautiful unless it engages deeply the resources of the soul. The arts may die of triviality, as they were born of enthusiasm. On the other hand, there will always be beauty, or a transport akin to the sense of beauty, in any high contemplative moment. And it is only in contemplative moments that life is truly vital, when routine gives place to intuition, and experience is synthesized and brought before the spirit in its sweep and truth. The intention of my philosophy has certainly been to attain, if possible, such wide intuitions, and to celebrate the emotions with which they fill the mind. If this object be æsthetic and merely poetical, well and good: but it is a poetry or æstheticism which shines by disillusion and is simply intent on the unvarnished truth.

II

The liberal age in which I was born and the liberal circles in which I was educated flowed contentedly towards intellectual dissolution and anarchy. No atmosphere could have been more unfavourable to that solidity and singleness of conviction to which by nature I was addressed. I suffered from a slack education, conflicting traditions, deadening social pressure, academic lumber, and partisan heat about false problems. The pure philosophy to which, in spirit, I was wedded from the beginning, the orthodox human philosophy in which I ought to have been brought up, has never had time to break through and show all its native force, pathos, and simplicity. I ought to have begun where I have ended.

Would it be possible to indicate, in a page or two, what I conceive orthodox human philosophy to be? Perhaps: because the thing is not unknown. The ancients came innocently upon it in various fields. Yet not even Aristotle, much less the moderns, ever conceived it in its entirety, with a just balance of its parts. I seem to recognise three orthodox schools of philosophy, each humanly right in its own sphere, but wrong in ignoring or denying the equal human rightness of the other two.

The Indians are orthodox in transcendental reflection. They take systematically the point of view of the spirit. For there is an invisible and inevitable moral witness to everything, not a physical or psychological self, but a higher centre of observation to which this world, or any world, or any God, is an imposed and questionable accident. Being morally inspired, being the voice of a living soul, this spirit has dramatic relations with the world which it encounters. The encounter may occasionally turn into a passionate embrace in which the spirit and all things seem merged in utterable unity. But that is a dramatic episode like any other: the tragic spirit revives and recovers its solitude. It would not be an actual spirit at all if it were not a personal moral being subject to fortune and needing to be saved. Spiritual philosophy would therefore not be orthodox if it were not ascetic and detached from the world.

The Greeks before Socrates reached orthodoxy in natural philosophy, which was re-established later in Spinoza and in modern science. Natural philosophers quarrel among themselves just because they are engaged in a common task with the issue undetermined. Yet they are all conspiring to trace and conceive the structure and history of this natural world in which everyone finds himself living.

The Greeks after Socrates founded orthodoxy in morals. I have endeavoured to retrace this theme in *The Life of Reason* and in my entire criticism of literature and religion. The principles of orthodoxy here were most clearly laid down by Plato in the *Philebus* and in the First Book of the *Republic;* but unfortunately, contrary to the modesty of Socrates himself, these principles were turned instinctively into a new mythology, in the effort to lend power and cosmic ascendency to the good: a good which is *good* only because, at each point, life and aspiration are spontaneously directed upon it. Ethics, as Aristotle said, is a part of politics, the foundation of this art being human nature, and its criterion harmony in living. But how should harmony be achieved in living if the inward spirit is distracted and the outer conditions of existence are unknown? Soundness in natural and in spiritual philosophy therefore seems requisite to soundness in politics.

That is all my message: that morality and religion are expressions of human nature; that human nature is a biological growth; and finally that spirit, fascinated and tortured, is involved in the process, and asks to be saved. What is salvation? Some organic harmony in forms and movements is requisite for life; but physical life is blind and groping and runs up continually against hostile forces, disease and death. It is therefore in the interests of life to become more intelligent and to establish a harmony also with the environment and the future. But life enlightened is spirit: the voice of life, and therefore aspiring to all the perfections to which life aspires, and loving all the beauties that life loves; yet at the same time spirit is the voice of truth and of destiny, bidding life renounce beauty and perfection and life itself, whenever and wherever these are impossible.

III

In *Winds of Doctrine* and my subsequent books, a reader of my earlier writings may notice a certain change of climate. There were natural causes for this change. I was weathering the age of fifty. My nearer relations were dead or dispersed. I had resigned my professorship at Harvard, and no longer crossed and re-crossed the Atlantic. I have explained the effect of these changes in the Preface to the later edition of the *Life of Reason,* and in what has already preceded here. My *Soliloquies in England* contain clear indications that, in spite of the war then raging, fancy in me had taken a new lease of life. I felt myself nearer than ever before to rural nature and to the perennial animal roots of human society. It was not my technical philosophy that was principally affected, but rather the meaning and status of philosophy for my inner man. The humanism characteristic of the *Sense of Beauty* and *Life of Reason* remained standing; but foundations were now supplied for that humanism by a more explicit and vigorous natural philosophy; a natural philosophy which, without being otherwise changed than as the growth of natural science might suggest, was itself destined to be enveloped later by the ontology contained in *Realms of Being.* These additions are buttresses and supports: the ontology justifies materialism, and the materialism justifies rational ethics and an æsthetic view of the mind.

Certainly materialism cannot justify moral ideals *morally.* Morally a sentiment can be confirmed only by another sentiment, for whatever that may be worth. But materialism justifies the life of reason martially, as a fighting organisation, and explains its possible strength and dominance. What from the moral point of view we call the instruments of reason are primarily the ground and cause of reason: and reason can control matter only because reason is matter organised, and assuming a form at once distinctive, plastic, and opportune. Unity of direction is thus imposed on our impulses; the impulses remain and continue to work and to take themselves most seriously; things tempt and hurt us as much as ever. Yet this very synthesis imposed upon the passions has brought steadiness and scope into the mind. The passions seem less absolute than before: we see them in a more tragic or comic light; and we see that even our noble and civilised life of reason is bought at a price. As there were wild animal joys that it has banished, so there may be divine insights that it cannot heed.

I had begun philosophising quite normally, by bleating like any young lamb: agitated by religion, passionately laying down the law for art and politics, and even bubbling over into conventional verses, which I felt to be oracular and irresistible. But my vocation was clear: my earliest speculation was at once intimate and universal, and philosophically religious, as it has always remained; yet not exclusively on the lines of that complete Christian system which first offered itself to my imagination. I was always aware of alternatives; nor did these alternatives seem utterly hostile and terrible. My enthusiasm was largely dramatic; I recited my Lucretius with as much gusto as my Saint Augustine; and gradually Lucretius sank deeper and became more satisfying. What I demanded unconditionally was dramatic wholeness. I wanted to articulate each possible system, to make it consistent, radical, and all-embracing. Hesitation and heresy were odious to me in any quarter; and I cared more for the internal religious force of each faith than for such external reasons as might be urged to prove that faith or to disprove it. What indeed could such external reasons be but corollaries to some different system, itself needing to be believed?

A judicial comparison of various systems of life and morals was therefore not possible for me until I had found a sure foothold for criticism, other than the histrionic convictions between which my youthful sentiment could so easily oscillate. This foothold was supplied to me by human nature, as each man after due Socratic self-questioning might find it in himself, and as Plato and Aristotle express it for mankind at large in their rational ethics. There is nothing unalterably fixed in this moral physiognomy of man, any more than in his bodily structure; but both are sufficiently recognisable and constant for the purposes of medicine and politics. The point of chief speculative interest is that morality, like health, is determined by the existing constitution of our animal nature, and the opportunities or denials that materially confront us; so that we are much deeper and more deeply bound to physical reality than our wayward thoughts and wishes might suggest. The potential, in an organic being developing through time, is necessarily richer and more important than the actual. The actual is superficial, occasional, ephemeral; present will and present consciousness are never the true self. They are phenomena elicited by circumstances from a psyche that remains largely unexpressed. Yet this psyche, this inherited nature or seed, flowers in those manifestations, filling them as they pass with beauty and passion: and nothing will be moral or personal in ideas except what they borrow by a secret circulation from the enduring heart. There, and not in any superstitious precepts, lies the root of duty and the criterion of perfection.

In saying this I am far from wishing to attribute a metaphysical fixity or unity to the psyche, or to claim for my own person an absolute singleness and consistency. Some passive drifting and some fundamental vagueness there must be in every animal mind; and the best-knit psyche still participates in the indefinite flux of matter, is self-forgetful in part, and is mortal. But this only proves that no man can be wholly a philosopher or an artist, or wholly himself. We are moral individuals, we exist as persons, only imperfectly, by grace of certain essences kindly imputed to us by our own thoughts or by the thoughts of others. There is always a moral chaos, though it be a dynamic mathematical order, beneath our rationalised memory or criticism: a chaos which is an indispensable support and continual peril to the spirit, as the sea is to a ship. Yet in our nautical housekeeping we may disregard the background. The deluge keeps our rational ark afloat, and our thoughts follow our treasures.

Yet not necessarily all our thoughts. The need of keeping a look-out may generate a disinterested interest in the winds and tides, and we may end by smiling at the moral reasons which we first assigned for the deluge. In my later writings I speak of something called the spiritual life; of a certain *disintoxication* clarifying those passions which the life of reason endeavours to harmonise. Is spirit then hostile to reason? Is reason hostile to spirit? Neither: but within the life of reason there is incidental rivalry in the types of organisation attempted, in their range, and in the direction in which the inevitable sacrifices are accepted. Spirit and reason, as I use the words, spring from the same root in organic life, namely, from the power of active adaptation possessed by animals, so that the external world and the future are regarded in their action. Being regarded in action, absent things are then regarded in thought; and this is intelligence. But intelligence and reason are often merely potential, as in habit, memory, institutions, and books: they become spirit only when they flower into actual consciousness. Spirit is essentially simpler, less troubled, more lyrical than reason: it is not specifically human. It may exist in animals, perhaps in plants, as it certainly exists in children; and in its outlook, far from being absorbed in tasks and cares, like reason, it is initially universal and addressed to anything and everything that there may happen to be.

Between the spiritual life and the life of reason there is accordingly no contradiction: they are concomitant: yet there is a difference of temper and level, as there is between agriculture and music. The ploughman may sing, and the fiddler at times may dig potatoes; but the vocations pull in different ways. Being ready for everything, and a product of vital harmony, spirit finds an initial delight in art and contrivance, in adventure and discovery, for these are forms of order and enlarged harmony: yet in the midst of business, spirit suspends business, and begins to wonder, to laugh, or to pray. A family quarrel may easily arise between these mental faculties; a philosopher sympathises naturally with speculation; but the ethics of this conflict are the same as in other conflicts: to know oneself, and to impose on oneself or on others only the sacrifices requisite to bring one's chosen life to perfection.

I have always disliked mystics who were not definite in their logic and orthodox in their religion. Spirit is not a power: it comes to fulfil, not to destroy. By understanding the world we may in a certain ideal sense transcend it; but we do not transcend it by misunderstanding it: on the contrary, we remain in that case dupes of our own flesh and our own egotism. Every temperament and every vocation, even the highest, engages us in a special course that imposes sweeping renunciations in other directions. But these renunciations would not be true sacrifices if the things sacrificed were not admittedly good. Marriage and wealth, sport and adventure, dominion and war are not condemned by the spiritual man in being renounced. They are left benevolently or sadly for the natural man, who is generously and inevitably engaged in them. The passions are the elements of life; nevertheless they are deceptive and tragic. They fade from the mind of the old man who can survey their full course; unless indeed he makes himself a shrill and emasculated echo of them, forgetting the dignity of years. Sometimes these passions shock and repel a young soul even at their first assault: and then we have the saint or seer by nature, who can transcend common experience without having tasted it; but this is a rare faculty, abnormal and not to be expected or even desired. Thus there is a certain option and practical incompatibility between spirituality and humanism, between poetry and business, between sheer logic and sound sense; but the conflict is only marginal, the things are concentric, and spirit merely heightens and universalises the synthesis which reason makes partially, as occasion requires, in the service of natural interests. To make this synthesis is itself a natural interest, as the child loves to look and to explore: and spirit, the conscience of nature that sees the truth of nature, is the most natural of things.

My later philosophy, then, on the moral side, merely develops certain ultimate themes of the inner life which had run in my head from the beginning: they had dominated my verse, and had reappeared in my early accounts of poetry and religion, of Platonic love, and post-rational morality. The developments in no way disturb the biological basis assigned to all life; they do not make my naturalistic ethics dogmatic. They are proposed merely as optional. They are confessions of the sentiment with which the spectacle of things and the discipline of experience can fill a reflective mind.

Within the same naturalistic frame my later philosophy has also elaborated the analysis of perception, of belief, and of "ideas" in general; and in this direction I have come to discriminate something which seems strangely to irritate my critics: I mean, what I call essence and the realm of essence. These words, and my whole presentation of this subject, were perhaps unfortunate. I have advanced an emancipating doctrine in traditional terms; the terms excite immediate scorn in modern radical quarters, while the emancipating doctrine horrifies those conservatives to whom the terms might not give offense. I am sorry: but this accident after all is of little consequence, especially as the same doctrine—loaded, no doubt, with other accidental lumber—is being propagated by various influential writers in uglier and more timely terms. The point is to reduce evidence to the actually evident, and to relegate all the rest to hypothesis, presumption, and animal faith. What I call essence is not something alleged to exist or subsist in some higher sphere: it is the last residuum of scepticism and analysis. Whatsoever existing fact we may think we encounter, there will be obvious features distinguishing that alleged fact from any dissimilar fact and from nothing. All such features, discernible in sense, thought, or fancy, are essences; and the realm of essence which they compose is simply the catalogue, infinitely extensible, of all characters logically distinct and ideally possible. Apart from the events they may figure in, these essences have no existence; and since the realm of essence, by definition, is infinitely comprehensive and without bias, it can exercise no control over the existing world, nor determine what features shall occur in events, or in what order.

Indeed, it might seem idle to have mentioned these pure essences at all, which living thought traverses unwittingly, as speech does the words of one's native language; yet the study of grammar is enlightening, and there is a clarifying and satiric force in the discrimination of essences. For the irony of fate will have it that these ghosts are the only realities we ever actually can find: and it is rather the thought-castles of science and the dramatic vistas of history that, for instant experience, are ghostly and merely imagined. What should mind be, if it were not a poetic cry? Mind does not come to repeat the world but to celebrate it. The essences evoked in sensation and thought are naturally original, graphic, and morally coloured. Consciousness was created by the muses; but meantime industrious nature, in our bodily organisation, takes good care to keep our actions moderately sane, in spite of our poetic genius.

Thus as in my younger days in respect to religions, so now in respect to all experience and all science, critical reflection has emancipated me from the horrid claim of ideas to literal truth. And just as religion, when seen to be poetry, ceases to be deceptive and therefore odious, and becomes humanly more significant than it seemed before; so experience and science, when seen to be woven out of essences and wholly symbolic, gain in moral colour and spirituality what they lose in dead weight. The dead weight falls back from sensuous images and intellectual myths to the material fatality that breeds and sustains them.

This fatality itself, in proving wholly arbitrary, seems to oppress us less; it inspires courage and good humour, rather than supplications and fears. Perhaps what the realm of essence, in its mute eternity, chiefly adds to our notion of nature is the proof that nature is contingent. An infinite canvas is spread before us on which any world might have been painted. The actuality of things is sharpened and the possibilities of things are enlarged. We cease to be surprised or distressed at finding existence unstable and transitory. Why should it have been otherwise? Not only must our own lives be insecure, as earthly seasons change, but perhaps all existence is in flux, even down to its first principles. *Dum vivimus vivamus.* Everything, so long as it recognisably endures, is free to deploy its accidental nature; and we may lead the life of reason with a good grace, harmonising as well as possible our various impulses and opportunities, and exploring the realm of essence as our genius may prompt.

The exposition of my philosophy is still incomplete, and in many directions, as for instance in mathematical physics, the development of it is beyond my powers. Yet virtually the whole system was latent in me from the beginning. When in adolescence I oscillated between solipsism and the Catholic faith, that was an accidental dramatic way of doing honour both to rigour and to abundance. But the oscillation was frivolous and the two alternate positions were self-indulgent. A self-indulgent faith sets up its casual myths and rashly clings to them as to literal truths; while a self-indulgent scepticism pretends to escape all dogma, forgetting its own presuppositions. With time it was natural that oscillation should give place to equilibrium; not, let us hope, to a compromise, which of all things is the most unstable and unphilosophical; but to a radical criticism putting each thing where it belongs. Without forgetting or disowning anything, myth might then be corrected by disillusion, and scepticism by sincerity. So transformed, my earliest affections can survive in my latest.

My Place, Time, and Ancestry

Persons and Places: Fragments of Autobiography. Volume one of the critical edition of *The Works of George Santayana.* Edited by William G. Holzberger and Herman J. Saatkamp Jr., with an Introduction by Richard C. Lyon. Cambridge, MA: The MIT Press, 1986, 3–10.

This is the first chapter in the first volume of Santayana's three-volume work Persons and Places: Fragments of Autobiography. *Santayana finished the first volume,* The Background of My Life, *in 1941, while forced by the war to remain in Rome. Italian wartime regulations prevented transmission of the manuscript by post to his publisher, Charles Scribner's Sons, in New York; but the manuscript finally reached New York through diplomatic channels in July 1942 and was published in 1944. Portions of the present selection were first published as "Persons and Places: Time, Place, and Parents" in* The Atlantic Monthly *(171 [March 1943]: 45–54). According to Santayana, the first five chapters of his autobiography "all describe chiefly things that happened before I was born, but given as I heard about them, so that I am the narrator, though not the theme" (LGS, 7:8). He characterized his autobiographical project as "a complete rambling, endless, philosophical and satirical stream of recollections" (LGS, 7:46), and "the true subject is the impressions left in me by the various persons and places I came across" (LGS, 7:129).*

A document in my possession testifies that in the parish church of San Marcos in Madrid, on the first of January, 1864, a male child, born on the sixteenth of the previous December, at nine o'clock in the evening, at No. 69 Calle Ancha de San Bernardo, was solemnly christened; being the legitimate son of Don Agustín Ruiz de Santayana, native of Zamora, and of Doña Josefina Borrás, native of Glasgow; his paternal grandparents being Don Nicolás, native of Badumès, in the province of Santander, and Doña María Antonia Reboiro, native of Zamora; and his maternal grandparents being Don José, native of Reus, Catalonia, and Doña Teresa Carbonell, native of Barcelona. The names given him were Jorge Agustín Nicolás, his godparents being Don Nicolás Ruiz de Santayana, and Doña Susana Sturgis; "whom I admonished", writes Don Joaquín Carrasco, who signs the certificate with his legal *rúbrica* or flourish, "of their spiritual relationship and duties."*

---

*Don Paulino Corrales Diaz, Presbítero, Licenciado en Sagrada Teología y Cura Proprio de la Parroquia de San Marcos de esta Corte, y en su nombre D. Prudencio M. Gil y Arguso, encargado accidentalmente del Despacho.

Certifico: Que en el libro décimo de Bautismos que se guarda en este archivo al folio setenta y cinco se halla inscripta la siguiente partida, que copiada literalmente dice así:
En San Marcos de Madrid a primero de Enero de mil ochocientos sesenta y cuatro, yo Don Joaquín Carrasco, Teniente Mayor de Cura de la misma bauticé solemnemente en ella a un niño que nació el diez y seis de Diciembre del año último, a las nueve de la noche, en la Calle Ancha de San Bernardo, Nº 69, cᵗᵒ 2º, hijo legítimo de Dⁿ Agustín Ruiz de Santayana, natural de Zamora, y de Dᵃ Josefina

A shrewd fortune-teller would have spotted at once, in this densely Spanish document, the two English names, Glasgow and Sturgis. Where did they come from, what did they forebode? Might not seeds of my whole future lie buried there? And if the diviner had had preternatural powers, he might even have sniffed something important in those last, apparently so effete and perfunctory words, that Doña Susana Sturgis, who was my mother's daughter by a former marriage and then twelve years of age, had been forewarned of her spiritual relationship and duties: not that she should forbear marrying my godfather, my uncle Nicolás, who was a major in the Spanish army, with a wife and child, and forty-five years old; that was canonical red-tape nothing to the purpose; but that she was called by Providence to be really my spiritual mother and to catechise my young mind. It was she that initiated me into theology, architecture and polite society.

With parents evidently Catalans of the Catalonians, how did my mother come to be born in Glasgow, and how did she ever marry a Bostonian named Sturgis? These facts, taken separately, were accidents of travel, or rather of exile and of colonial life; but accidents are accidents only to ignorance; in reality all physical events flow out of one another by a continuous intertwined derivation; and those odd foreign names, Sturgis and Glasgow. They were in fact secretly allied and their presence here had a common source in my grandfather's character and circumstances and in the general thaw, so to speak, of that age: incongruous wreckage of a great inundation.

Not that I would nail the flag of fatalism to the mast at the beginning of this retrospective voyage. What we call the laws of nature are hasty generalisations; and even if some of them actually prevailed without exception or alloy, the fact that these laws and not others (or none) were found to be dominant would itself be groundless; so that nothing could be at bottom more arbitrary than what always happens, or more fatal than what happens but once or by absolute chance. Yet

---

Borrás, natural de Glasgow (Escocia); abuelos Paternos, Dⁿ Nicolás, natural de Badumes (Santander) y Dª Maria Antonia Reboiro, natural de Zamora, Maternos, Dⁿ José, natural de Reus (Tarragona) y Dª Teresa Carbonell, natural de Barcelona: Se le puso por nombre Jorge, Agustín, Nicolás, y fueron Padrinos Dⁿ Nicolás Ruiz de Santayana y Dª Susana Sturgis, a quienes advertí el parentesco espiritual y obligaciones, y lo firmé Joaquin Carrasco = Rubricado.

Concuerda con su original. (San Marcos de Madrid a tres de Septiembre de mil novecientos diez y nueve)

Prudencio M. Gil Arguso
(rubricado)

sello
de S. Marcos

Vᵒ Bᵒ

Sello de la Vicaría
General, Madrid-Alcalá

El Provisor interino
Dⁿ Bernardo Barbajero

(rubricado)

in the turbid stream of nature there are clear stretches, and traceable currents; and it is interesting to follow the beginnings and the developments of a run here and a whirlpool there, and to watch the silent glassy volume of water slip faster and faster towards the edge of some precipice. Now my little cockle-shell and the cockle-shells of the rest of my family, and of the whole middle and upper class (except the unsinkable politicians) were being borne along more or less merrily on the surface-currents of a treacherous social revolution; and the things that happened to us, and the things we did, with their pleasant and their hopeless sides, all belong to that general moral migration.

My grandfather, José Borrás y Bufurull, belonged to a well-established family of Reus, of the sort that possess a house in the town and a farm in the country. In this as in other ways many old towns near the Mediterranean preserve the character of ancient cities or *civitates,* and Reus in particular is a place of great dignity in the eyes of its inhabitants, who are reputed to speak habitually of "Reus, Paris, and London". But José was a younger son, and the law of entail or *mayorazgo* still prevailed at that time in Catalonia, so that the house and land and an almost Roman authority as head of the family fell to his eldest brother. Yet dignity to the classic mind does not involve great wealth or much *Lebensraum,* and younger sons, even in Reus, had to seek their fortunes away from home. They might indeed expect hospitality or a little aid from their families in time of stress, but were well aware that in the ancestral estate and community there was no place or occupation for more than one household at a time. There was the Church always tempting them, if it tempted them; there were the other professions, and there was the New World, or at least Cuba and the Philippines. One of my grandfather's brothers had actually combined these opportunities, become a monk, and later been established as a parish priest in Montevideo or in Buenos Aires.* The ultimate resource, among all my Spanish acquaintance and relations, was some post under the government; and my grandfather might very well have sought his fortunes no further afield than Barcelona, or at most Madrid; but he went much further. Economic considerations were probably not uppermost in his mind; if they were, his career must have disheartened him. Those were unsettled and unsettling times, the repercussions of the French Revolution had not spent themselves, and emancipation of mind was sure to follow, if it had not preceded, being cast loose upon the world. In any case we know that my grandfather, far from becoming a monk like his brother, became a Deist, an ardent disciple of Rousseau, and I suspect a Free-mason; and when a French army entered Spain, in 1823, to restore the shaken authority of Ferdinand VII and the absolute monarchy, José Borrás was compelled, or thought it advisable, to leave the country. The story goes that he fled first to Las Palmas, in the Balearic Islands, where he saw and wooed Teresa Carbonell, a stout blonde with very blue eyes (my mother's

---

*A history of the Borrás family of Reus has been published, but it contains hardly any information about my grandfather and none about my mother. In some respects the traditions recorded there diverge from those that my mother handed down; they may be more accurate, as my mother had no great interest or respect for the past. The exact facts in any case are not important, and I report the impressions that I have gathered.

eyes were also blue and large); and that after a romantic marriage he persuaded her to follow him in his wanderings. In my certificate of baptism, however, Teresa Carbonell is set down as a native of Barcelona, which is not strictly incompatible with her living later at Las Palmas, or her family belonging there; but she and her whole history are wrapped in some obscurity, and suggest various problems that I have no means of solving.

One of these problems is why my grandfather should have chosen Glasgow for a place of refuge, and what he did there. Mahon, in the neighbouring Minorca, had long been in British occupation, and occasions may have presented themselves to sail from there to Scotland, or perhaps to Lancashire; and he seems to have remained in these parts for some years, probably giving Spanish lessons and in any case learning English. This exile in poverty and obscurity, in so remote, cheerless, and industrial a scene, may not have been altogether unwelcome to him. Catalans are industrially and economically minded; novelty and distance allure them; and who knows how many utopias and ideologies, and what reflections on the missed opportunities of human government and art may not have kept his brain and his heart warm in that chilly climate. All I can say is that his thirst for exploration or his longing for a simpler and more ideal society carried him eventually across the Atlantic, to rural, republican, distinguished, Jeffersonian Virginia. Here, if anywhere, mankind had turned over a new leaf, and in a clean new world, free from all absurd traditions and tyrant mortgages, was beginning to lead a pure life of reason and virtue. With slavery? Perhaps that was only a temporary necessity, a kindly apprenticeship to instil into the simple negro a love of labour and of civilised arts; and as the protection of industries might be justified provisionally, until they could become well-rooted, so domestic servitude might be justified provisionally, until the slaves were ripe for freedom. Be that as it may, José Borrás either came well recommended or ingratiated himself easily into the democracy of Winchester, Virginia, becoming (as a florid testimonial averred) one of its most honoured and beloved citizens; so much so that as the years revolved, and a change of government in the liberal direction had occurred in Spain, his Winchester friends induced Andrew Jackson, then President of the United States, to appoint him American consul at Barcelona. Thus his cordial attachments in exile enabled him eventually to return home, not only safely but gloriously, and with some prospect of bread and butter.*

---

*The President of the United States of America

to all who shall see these presents, greeting.

No ye, that reposing special trust and confidence in the abilities and the integrity of Joseph Borras of Spain, I have nominated and by and with the advice and consent of the Senate do appoint him consul of the United States of America for the Port of Barcelona, in Spain, and for such other parts as shall be nearer thereto than the residence of any other consul or vice-consul of the United States within the same allegiance,–and do authorize and empower him to have and to hold the said office and to exercise and enjoy all the rights, preeminences, privileges, and authorities to the same of right appertaining, during the pleasure of the President of the United States for the time being; HE demanding and receiving no fees or perquisites of office whatever, which shall not be expressly established by some law of the United States. And I do hereby enjoin all captains, masters, and commanders of ships and other vessels, armed or un-armed, sailing under the flag of the United States as well as all

An element of mystery or mystification hangs about this home-coming. The date of my mother's birth, according to her official papers, was 1828, but there is reason to believe that in reality it was 1826. When she was brought to Spain in 1835 the shocking fact appeared that she had never been christened. Was there no Catholic priest in Glasgow in those days, and none in Winchester, Virginia? Had no travelling ecclesiastic been met with in all those wanderings? No doubt her father's enlightened principles made him regard all religious practices, morally and philosophically, as indifferent, while socially it was advisable that everyone should be affiliated to the religious customs prevalent in his country. But what was to be my mother's country? If it were to be Scotland or Virginia, she ought to be christened and brought up a Protestant; if it were to be Spain, it was imperative that she should be a Catholic. The matter therefore had to be suspended until the question of final residence was settled; although it may seem singular that my grandmother should have wholly acquiesced in this view and allowed her daughter to grow up, as they say in Spain, a Moor. Now, however, the matter had to be patched up as expeditiously and quietly as possible. Friends and relations, even clerical advisers, are very accommodating in Spain and very ingenious. The age of seven, the canonical age of reason, when one begins to sin of one's own accord, was the right age for confirmation; young Josefina was small for her age; let her official age be reduced to seven years, let a private christening, to supply the place of the missing documents, be smuggled in before the confirmation, and then the child would be launched quite legally and becomingly in her religious career, with confession and communion to follow immediately. This wealth of sacraments, raining down on her unprepared and extraordinarily self-reliant little soul, seems not to have left much hunger for further means of grace; my mother always spoke of such things as of troublesome and empty social requirements; and even ordinary social requirements, like visiting, rather annoyed her, as if they interfered with her liberty and interrupted her peace. On

---

others of their citizens, to acknowledge and consider him the said Joseph Borras accordingly. And I do hereby pray and request Her Majesty, the Queen of Spain, Her governors and officers to permit the said Joseph Borras fully and peaceably to enjoy and exercise the said office without giving or suffering to be given un to him any molestation or trouble, but on the contrary to afford him all proper countenance and assistance; I offering to do the same for all those who shall in like manner be recommended to me by Her said Majesty.

In testimoney whereof I have caused these letters to be made patent, and the seal of the United States be hereunto affixed.

Given under my hand at the City of Washington, the third day of March in the year of our Lord one thousand eight hundred and thirty-five, and of the Independence of the United States of America the fifty-ninth.

    (Signed)Andrew Jackson
By the President
(SEAL)
John Forsyth, Secretary of State.

the whole, however, her ten years or more of girlhood in Barcelona seem to have been gay and happy–the only frankly happy period of her life. Without being robust, her health was perfect, her needlework exquisite, her temper equable and calm; she loved and was loved by her girl-friends; she read romantic verses and select novels; above all, she danced. That was the greatest pleasure in life for her: not for the sake of her partners, those were surely only round dances, and the partners didn't count; what counted was the joy of motion, the sense of treading lightly, in perfect time, a sylph in spotless muslin, enriched with a ribbon or a flower, playing discreetly with her fan, and sailing through the air with feet that seemed scarcely to touch the ground. Even in her old age my mother never walked, she stepped. And she would say, in her quaint, perhaps Virginian, English: "Will you step in?" She was not beautiful, and prematurely regarded herself as an old woman, and put on a white lace cap; but she had good points and made a favourable ideal impression, even if she did not positively attract. I can imagine her in her young days, agile of foot and hand, silent and enigmatic behind her large sunken blue eyes, thin lips, and brown corkscrew curls, three on a side, setting off her white complexion. If men did not often make love to her, especially not the men who care specifically for women, she amply took her revenge. Her real attachments, apart from her devotion to her father, were to her women friends, not to crowds of them, but to two or three and for life. To men as men, even to her two husbands, she seems to have been cold, critical and sad, as if conscious of yielding to some inevitable but disappointing fatality.

I will translate a letter written to her by my father, dated Jan. 28, 1888, when I was in my second year at the University of Berlin, and it began to seem clear that I should drift into an academic life in America.

"My dear Josefina; I have had much pleasure in taking note of your kind letter and of the verses which, while thinking of me, you wrote twenty-five years ago. A volume would be requisite for me to recount the memories I have of our relations during now little less than half a century. When we were married I felt as if it were written that I should be united with you, yielding to the force of destiny, although I saw plainly the difficulties that then surrounded such a union, apart from those that would not fail to arise later. Strange marriage, this of ours! So you say, and so it is in fact. I love you very much, and you too have cared for me, yet we do not live together. But it is necessary to keep in mind the circumstances peculiar to our case. I have always believed that the place in which it would be natural for you to live was Boston, in consequence of your first marriage which determined the course of your whole life. My position has offered and now offers no inducement, none, to balance the propriety or necessity of that arrangement. On my side, I could not then or later leave my own country for good, in order to live in Boston, when in view of my age and impediments it was impossible for me to learn to speak English well and to mix in that society. Here I have been a help to my family, and there I should only have been an encumbrance.

"I should have wished that Jorge should not have been separated from me, but I found myself compelled to take him in person and leave him in your charge and in that of his brother and sisters. Unhappy compulsion! Yet it was much better for him to be with you than with me, and I prefer his good to my pleasure."

How much in this was clearness of vision, how much was modesty, how much was love of quietness and independence? It is not a question for me to decide, but there was certainly something of all those motives. Education such as I received in Boston was steadier and my associations more regular and calmer than they would have been in Spain; but there was a terrible moral disinheritance involved, an emotional and intellectual chill, a pettiness and practicality of outlook and ambition, which I should not have encountered amid the complex passions and intrigues of a Spanish environment. From the point of view of learning, my education at the Boston Latin School and at Harvard College was not solid or thorough; it would not have been solid or thorough in Spain; yet what scraps of learning or ideas I might have gathered there would have been vital, the wind of politics and of poetry would have swelled them, and allied them with notions of honour. But then I should have become a different man; so that my father's decision was all for my good, if I was to be the person that I am now.

Epilogue on *My Host, The World*

Persons and Places: Fragments of Autobiography. Volume one of the critical edition of *The Works of George Santayana.* Edited by William G. Holzberger and Herman J. Saatkamp Jr., with an Introduction by Richard C. Lyon. Cambridge, MA: The MIT Press, 1986, 537–47.

This is the final chapter of the third and final volume of Santayana's autobiography (Chapter XXXII in the one-volume edition). Santayana completed the third volume in 1945 but wished it to be published posthumously. He permitted excerpts (with minor changes) to appear in The Atlantic Monthly *prior to his death, including the present selection (*The Atlantic Monthly, *183 [January 1949]: 26–30). In 1953, the year following Santayana's death, the third volume was published. Santayana had originally titled it* In the Old World, *but he reportedly changed it to* Seeking Places for a Chosen Life. *The publisher disliked this title and prevailed on Santayana's literary executor, Daniel Cory, to change the title to* My Host the World, *after the title of the final chapter; the critical edition title,* My Host, The World, *matches Santayana's final manuscript. In calling the world his host, Santayana explained that the world is "not meant for man, but habitable by him, and possible to exploit, with prudence, in innumerable ways" (ES, 30–31). Santayana had intended his three-volume work eventually to be published as one volume under the title* Persons and Places: Fragments of Autobiography, *as it was in 1963 and again in 1986, when it appeared as volume one of the critical edition of* The Works of George Santayana.

Persons and places people the world; they individuate its parts; and I have devoted this book to recording some of them that remain alive in my memory. Mine are

Private poetical character of these reminiscences.
insignificant recollections: for even when the themes happen to have some importance as persons and places in the great world, it is not at all in that capacity that I prize and describe them. I keep only some old miniature or some little perspective that

caught my eye in passing, when the persons perhaps were young and the places empty and not dressed up to receive visitors, as are museums, libraries, ball-rooms and dinner-tables. Those were free glimpses of the world that I could love and could carry away. They were my consolations.

Yet the very contrast between these glimpses, all picturesque and aerial, and the vast obscure inexorable world from which they came, forced me gradually to form some notion of that material world also. We were a blue-sea

Yet I loved land and sea in their inhumanity.
family; our world was that of colonial officials and great merchants. From the beginning I learned to think of the earth as a globe with its surface chiefly salt water, a barren treacherous and intractable waste for mankind, yet tempting and beautiful and

swarming with primitive animals not possible to tame or humanise but sometimes good to eat. In fine, I opened my eyes on the world with the conviction that it was inhuman: not meant for man, but habitable by him, and possible to exploit, with prudence, in innumerable ways: a conviction that everything ever since has confirmed.

One peculiarity was common to all these possible satisfactions: they brought something perfect, consummate, final. The sea, after no matter what storms, returned to its equilibrium and placidity; its gamut was definite. Voyages all led to some port. The vastness and violence of nature, in challenging and often decimating mankind, by no means tend to dehumanise it. The quality of attainable goods may change, and also the conditions for attaining them; but the way is always open, at the right time, for the right sort of animal and for the right sort of mind. Dogs have their day; arts have their dates; and the great question is not what age you live in or what art you pursue, but what perfection you can achieve in that art under those circumstances.

The great master of sympathy with nature, in my education, was Lucretius. Romantic poets and philosophers, when they talk of nature, mean only landscape or other impressions due to aerial perspectives, sensuous harmonies of colour or form, or vital intoxications, such as those of riding, sea-faring, or mountain-climbing. Nature is loved for heightening self-consciousness and prized for ministering to human comfort and luxury, but is otherwise ignored as contemptible, dead, or non-existent. Or when people's temper is hardy and pugnacious, they may require nature as a buffer on which to rain their mighty blows and carve their important initials. Where human strength comes from or what ends human existence might serve, they neither know nor care.

The spirit in me felt itself cast upon this social and political world somewhat like Robinson Crusoe upon his island. We were both creatures of the same Great Nature; but my world, in its geography and astronomy, like Robinson Crusoe's island, had much more massive and ancient foundations than the small utterly insecure waif that had been wrecked upon it. In its social and political structure, however, my world was more like Crusoe's energetic person; for my **My own person an annoying part of my world.** island was densely inhabited; an ugly town, a stinted family, a common school; and the most troublesome and inescapable of its denizens was the particular body in which my spirit found itself rooted; so rooted that it became doubtful whether that body with its feelings and actions was not my true self, rather than this invisible spirit which they oppressed. I seemed to be both; and yet this compulsive and self-tormenting creature called "Me" was more odious and cruel to the "I" within than were the sea and sky, the woods and mountains or the very cities and crowds of people that this animal "Me" moved among: for the spirit in me was happy and free ranging through that world, but troubled and captive in its close biological integument.

This is the double conflict, the social opposition and the moral **Yet spirit must be incarnate.** agony, that spirit suffers by being incarnate; and yet if it were not incarnate it could not be individual, with a station in space and time, a language and special perspectives over nature and history: indeed, if not incarnate, spirit could not *exist* at all or be the inner light and perpetual witness of a *life* in its dramatic vicissitudes.

If it be the fate of all spirit to live in a special body and a special age, and yet, for its vocation and proper life, to be addressed from that centre to all life and to all being, I can understand why I have been more sensible to this plight and to this mission than were most of my contemporaries. For by chance I was a foreigner where I was educated; and although the new language and customs interested me and gave me no serious trouble, yet speculatively and emotionally, especially in regard to religion, the world around me was utterly undigestible. The times also were moving, rapidly and exultingly, towards what for me was chaos and universal triviality. At first these discords sounded like distant thunder. Externally they were not yet violent; the world smiled in my eyes as I came to manhood, and the beauties and dignity of the past made the present unimportant. And as the feeling of being a stranger and an exile by nature as well as by accident grew upon me in time, it came to be almost a point of pride; some people may have thought it an affectation. It was not that; I have always admired the normal child of his age and country. My case was humanly unfortunate, and involved many defects; yet it opened to me another vocation, not better (I admit no absolute standards) but more speculative, freer, juster, and for me happier.

My accidental foreignness favoured my spiritual freedom.

I had always dreamt of travel, and it was oftenest in the voluntary, interested, appreciative rôle of the traveller that I felt myself most honest in my dealings with my environment. The world was My Host; I was a temporary guest in his busy and animated establishment. We met as strangers; yet each had generic and well-grounded ideas of what could be expected of the other. First impressions made these expectations more precise; the inn was habitable; the guest was presumably solvent. We might prove mutually useful. My Host and I could become friends diplomatically; but we were not akin in either our interests or our powers. The normal economy of an innkeeper, though incidentally and in a measure it supplies the wants of his guests, knows nothing of their private moral economy. Their tastes in wines, in service, or in music may entirely outrun or contradict his long-established practice, which he will impose on his guests with all the authority of a landlord; and there may not be another inn in the place, or only worse ones. The guest has no right to demand what is not provided. He must be thankful for any little concessions that may be made to his personal tastes, if he is tactful and moderate in his requirements, pays his bills promptly and gives decent tips.

Landlord and guest.

Such at least was the case in the nineteenth century when the world made itself pleasant to the traveller; and not to rich travellers only but to the most modest, and even to the very poor in their little purchases and popular feasts. Personal freedom produced a certain dignity and good humour even in bargaining; for to buy and sell, to patronise a shop or a boarding-house, was an act of kindness; and bills, at least in civilly commercial England, were always receipted "with thanks". Having lived a peaceful independent life, free from hardship or misfortune, I have found it easy to conform externally with the mechanism of society. Matter has been kind to me, and I am a lover of matter. Not only aesthetically but

Virtues of a commercial age and country.

dynamically, as felt by Lucretius, nature to me is a welcome presence; and modern progress in mechanical invention and industrial luxury has excited joyously my materialistic imagination, as it did prophetically that of Bacon. Moreover, I inherited from my father a bond with matter which Bacon and Lucretius probably did not feel: the love of employing leisure in small mechanical occupations. I should never have read and written so much if the physical side of these employments had not been congenial to me and rich with a quiet happiness. Any common surroundings and any commonplace people pleased me well enough; it was only when sugary rapture was demanded about them or by them, as happened almost everywhere in my youth, that my stomach rose in radical protest. Then I discovered how much the human world of my time had become the enemy of spirit and therefore of its own light and peace.

How had this happened? Not at all as lovers of antiquity or of the middle ages seem to think, because of mechanical inventions or natural sciences or loss of Christian faith. These transformations might all have occurred in the normal growth of society. Variety in cultures is not due to aberrations any more than is the variety of animal species. But there may be aberration in any species or any culture when it **Radical disease of Western civilisation.** becomes *vicious;* that is, when it forms habits destructive of its health and of its ability to prosper in its environment. Now modern sciences and inventions are not vicious in this sense; on the contrary, they bring notable additions to human *virtù.* And I think that the Renaissance, with the historical learning and humanism which it fostered, was also a great gain for human happiness and self-knowledge. Of this the surface of the modern world during my youth gave continual evidence, in spite of an undercurrent of unrest and disaffection sometimes heard rumbling below. "My Host's" establishment made a brave appearance; and I was particularly conscious of many new facilities of travel, breadth of information, and cosmopolitan convenience and luxury. Though there was no longer any dignity in manners, or much distinction in costume, fashion had not lost all its charm. In literature and the fine arts talent could give pleasure by its expertness, if not by its taste or savour. I have described how in Boston and in England I sometimes sipped the rim of the plutocratic cup; and this was a real pleasure, because beneath the delicacy of the material feast there was a lot of shrewd experience in that society, and of placid kindness.

There was another cosmopolitan circle, less select and less worldly, but no less entertaining and no less subject to fashion and to ironical gossip, the Intellectuals, into whose company I was sometimes drawn. I was officially one of them, yet they felt in their bones that I might be secretly a traitor. "Ah, yes," cried a distinguished Jesuit recently when I was **I displease other intellectuals.** casually mentioned, "he is the *poetical* atheist." And an Italian professor, also a Catholic but tinged with German idealism, remarked of me: "The trouble with him is that he has never succeeded in outgrowing materialism." Finally a faithful diehard of British psychologism, asked why I was overlooked among contemporary philosophers, replied: "Because he has no originality. Everything in him is drawn from Plato and Leibniz." This critical band is democratic in that it recognises no official authority and lets a fluid public opinion carry the day; yet it is, on principle, in each man, private and independent in judgment. Few, however, have much time to read originals or to study facts. Leaders and busybodies must obey their momentum. A personal reaction on what other people say is socially sufficient; it will do for the press; and it will corroborate the critic's opinion in his own eyes.

I cannot overcome a settled distrust of merely intellectual accomplishment, militant in the void. I prefer common virtues and current beliefs, even if intellectually prejudiced and simple, when the great generative order of nature has bred them, and lent them its weight and honesty. For I do not rebel in the least at political and moral mutations when this same generative order brings them about

Fatuity militant. spontaneously; for it is then on the side of change that clear intelligence discerns the lesser danger and the wider interests. I should have loved the Gracchi; but not the belated Cato or the belated Brutus. All four were martyrs; but the first two spoke for the poor, for the suffering half of the people, oppressed by a shortsighted power that neglected its responsibilities; while the last two were conceited ideologues, jealous of their traditional rights, and utterly blind to destiny. If I were not too old and could venture to write in French, I should compose a short history of *Les Faux Pas de la Philosophie;* by which title I should not refer to *innocent* errors, with which all human speculation must be infected, nor to the symbolic or mythological form of the wisest wisdom, but only to militant heresies and self-contradictions due to wilful conceit, individual or tribal, verbal or moral; and there is little in European philosophy that is not infected with these *unnecessary* errors. Let the reader compose his own catalogue of these blind alleys explored by the ancients and by the moderns; since this is a biographical book, I will limit myself to the first and principal *Faux Pas* that the world has seemed to me to have taken in my time.

The contemporary world has turned its back on the attempt and even on the desire to live reasonably. The two great wars (so far) of the twentieth century were adventures in enthusiastic unreason. They were inspired by

Two chief demands of rational morals. unnecessary and impracticable ambitions; and the "League" and the "United Nations" feebly set up by the victors, were so irrationally conceived that they at once reduced their victory to a stalemate. What is requisite for living rationally? I think the conditions may be reduced to two: First, self-knowledge, the Socratic key to wisdom; and second, sufficient knowledge of the world to perceive what alternatives are open to you and which of them are favourable to your true interests.

Now the contemporary world has plenty of knowledge of nature for its purposes, but its purposes show a positively insane abandonment of its true interests.

The modern world has plenty of mechanical science, but no self-knowledge. You may say that the proletariat knows its interests perfectly; they are to work less and to earn more. Those are indeed its interests so long as it remains a proletariat: but to be a proletariat is an inhuman condition. Proletarians are human beings, and their first interest is to have a home, a family, a chosen trade, and freedom in practising it. And more particularly a man's true interest may exceptionally be not to have those things, but to wander alone like the rhinoceros; or perhaps to have a very special kind of home, family, and occupation. There must be freedom of movement and vocation. There must be *Lebensraum* for the spirit.

There have always been beggars and paupers in the world, because there is bound to be a margin of the unfit—too bad or too good to keep in step with any well organised society: but that the great body of mankind should sink into a proletariat has been an unhappy effect of the monstrous growth of cities, made possible by the concentration of trade and the multiplication of industries, mechanised, and swelling into monopolies.

Simpler societies know better their place in nature.

The natural state of mankind, before foreign conquerors dominate it or native ideologues reform it, is full of incidental evils; prophets have ample cause for special denunciations and warnings; yet there is, as in all animal economy, a certain nucleus of self-preserving instincts and habits, a normal constitution of society. Nature with its gods is their landlord of whose fields and woods they are local and temporary tenants; and with this invincible power they make prudent and far-seeing covenants. They know what is for their good, and by what arts it might be secured. They live by agriculture, the hunting and breeding of animals, and such domestic arts as their climate and taste lead them to cultivate; and when a quarrel arises among them, or with strangers, they battle to preserve or to restore their free life, without more ambitious intentions. They are materially and morally rooted in the earth, bred in one land and one city. They are *civilised*. Wandering nations, with nothing of their own and working havoc wherever they go, are *barbarians*. Such "barbarians" were the proletariat of antiquity. When they occupied some civilised region without exterminating the natives, and established in the old strongholds a permanent foreign domination, they became half-civilised themselves, without shedding altogether the predatory and adventurous practices of their ancestors. This is the compound origin and nature of modern Western governments.

Varied, picturesque, and romantic mixtures of civilisation beneath and barbarism above have filled the history of Christendom, and produced beautiful transient arts, in which there was too little wisdom and too much fancy and fashion: think of Gothic architecture, or of manners, dress, poetry, and philosophy from the middle ages to our day. Civilisation had become more enterprising, plastic, and irresponsible, while barbarism seemed to retreat into sports, and into legal extravagances in thought and action. Intellectual

Barbarism in the romantic mind coexists with civilisation in mechanical arts.

chaos and political folly could thus come to coexist strangely with an irresistible dominance of mechanical industry. The science that served this industrial progress by no means brought moral enlightenment. It merely enlarged acquaintance with phenomena and enabled clever inventors to construct all sorts of useful or superfluous machines. At first perhaps it was expected that science would make all mankind both rich and free from material cares (two contradictory hopes) and would at the same time enlighten them at last about the nature of things, including their own nature, so that adequate practical wisdom would be secured together with fabulous material well-being.

This is the dream of the moderns, on which I found My Host boastfully running his establishment. He expected his guests also to act accordingly and to befuddle and jollify one another, so that all should convince themselves that they were perfectly happy and should advertise their Host's business wherever they went. Such forced enterprise, forced confidence, and forced satisfaction would never have sprung from domestic arts or common knowledge spontaneously extended. It was all artificial and strained, marking the inhuman domination of some militant class or sect. This society lacked altogether that essential trait of rational living, to have a clear, sanctioned, ultimate aim. The cry was for vacant freedom and indeterminate progress: *Vorwärts! Avanti! Onward! Full speed ahead!* without asking whether directly before you was not a bottomless pit.

Deluded optimism of the Great Merchants.

This has been the peculiar malady of my own times. I saw the outbreak of it in my boyhood, and I have lived to see what seem clear symptoms of its end. The Great Merchants of my parents' youth had known nothing of it on their blue-sea voyages round Cape Horn or the Cape of Good Hope. Their good hope had been to amass a great fortune in fifteen or twenty years, and return home to bring up a blooming family in splendour and peace. They foresaw an orderly diffused well-being spreading out from them over all mankind. The fountains of happiness were ready to flow in every heart and mind if only people were suffered to have their own way materially and socially. That the masses would crowd out, exclude, indoctrinate, enslave, and destroy one another could not cross their genial and innocent minds, as they skimmed those immense oceans in their tight, strictly disciplined, white-sailed little craft.

Alas! The healthy growth of science and commerce had been crossed, long before the rise of the Great Merchants, by an insidious moral and political revolution. From the earliest times there have been militant spirits not content with inevitable changes and with occasional wars between neighbouring states, not usually wars of conquest or eternal hatred, but collisions in readjusting the political equilibrium between nations when their actual relations were no longer the same. Indeed, the tragic causes of conflict and ruin in civilisations are fundamentally internal to each society. A whole city or state may sometimes be destroyed, like Carthage; but history, then, comes to an end for that particular society, and the others continue their course as if their vanished rival had never existed. This course may be cut short, however, by internal disruption and suicidal revolutions. Every generation is born as ignorant and wilful as the first man; and when tradition has lost its obvious fitness or numinous authority, eager minds will revert without knowing it to every false hope and blind alley that had tempted their predecessors long since buried under layer upon layer of ruins. And these eager minds may easily become leaders; for society is never perfect; grievances and misfortunes perpetually breed rebellion in the oppressed heart; and the eloquent imagination of youth and of indignation will find the right words to blow

Perverse militancy in politics.

the discontent, always smouldering, into sudden flame. Often things as they are become intolerable; there must be insurrection at any cost, as when the established order is not only casually oppressive, but ideally perverse and due to some previous epidemic of militant madness become constitutional. Against that domination, established in wilful indifference to the true good of man and to his possibilities, any political nostrum, proposed with the same rashness, will be accepted with the same faith. Thus the blind in extirpating the mad may plant a new madness.

That this is the present state of the world everyone can see by looking about him, or reading the newspapers; but I think that the elements in this crisis have been working in the body-politic for ages; ever since the Reformation, not to say since the age of the Greek Sophists and of Socrates. For the virulent cause of this long fever is subjectivism, egotism, conceit of mind. Not that culture of the conscience and even the logical refinements of dialectic are anything but good for the mind itself and for moral self-knowledge, which is one of the two conditions that I have assigned to political sanity; but the same logical arts are fatal if they are used to construct, by way of a moral fable, an anthropomorphic picture of the universe given out for scientific truth and imposed on mankind by propaganda, by threats, and by persecution. And this militant method of reforming mankind by misrepresenting their capacities and their place in the universe is no merely ancient or mediaeval delusion. It is the official and intolerant method of our most zealous contemporary prophets and reformers. Barbarism has adopted the weapons of flattery and prophecy. Merciless irrational ambition has borrowed the language of brotherly love.

Present free fight of egotistical follies.

The very fact, however, that these evils have deep roots, and have long existed without destroying Western civilisation, but on the contrary, have stimulated its contrary virtues and confused arts,—this very fact seems to me to counsel calmness in contemplating the future. Those who look for a panacea will not find it. Those who advise resignation to a life of industrial slavery (because spiritual virtues may be cultivated by a slave, like Epictetus, more easily perhaps than by rich men) are surrendering the political future to an artificial militant regime that cannot last unaltered for a decade anywhere, and could hardly last a day, if by military force it were ever made universal. The fanaticism of all parties must be allowed to burn down to ashes, like a fire out of control. If it survives, it will be only because it will have humanised itself, reduced its dogmas to harmless metaphors, and sunk down a tap-root, to feed it, into the dark damp depths of mother earth. The economy of nature includes all particular movements, combines and transforms them all, but never diverts its wider processes, to render them obedient to the prescriptions of human rhetoric. Things have their day, and their beauties in that day. It would be preposterous to expect any one civilisation to last for ever.

But earthquakes do not destroy the earth.

Had it happened in my time (as by chance it did happen) that my landlord should give me notice that he was about to pull down his roof over my head, I might have been a little troubled for a moment; but presently I should have begun to look for other lodgings not without a certain curious pleasure, and probably should have found some (as I did, and better ones) in which to end my days. So, I am confident, will the travelling Spirit do,—this ever-renewed witness, victim, and judge of existence, divine yet born of woman. Obediently it will learn other affections in other places, unite other friends, and divide other peoples; and the failure of over-exact hopes and overweening ambitions will not prevent Spirit from continually turning the passing virtues and sorrows of nature into glimpses of eternal truth.

II

Skepticism and Ontology

When Santayana claimed that skepticism is an exercise, not a life, he certainly was not diminishing the importance of skepticism. He described it as "the chastity of the intellect" which allows the speculative philosopher "to view all experience simply, in the precision and distinctness which all its parts acquire when not referred to any substance which they might present confusedly" (*ES*, 78). Skepticism frees the thinker from the commitment of belief and is a means to clarity. This speculative vantage point promotes awareness of essences and suggests an understanding of being that recognizes a non-epistemological basis of belief. This understanding acknowledges that the body cannot live according to the skeptical intellect and is committed before any reflection to the existence of a material environment; and this stubborn faith of the body—this animal faith—is the source of belief in material existence.

Skepticism shows the distinctive activity of the intellect to be intuiting essences rather than determining beliefs, and it suggests the instinctive roots of belief in matter. In this way, the exercise of skepticism led Santayana to his realms of being, namely the realms of essence, matter, truth, and spirit. These comprise his ontology, that is, his understanding of the nature of being. The selected essays and chapters in this second part of *The Essential Santayana* explain the character and consequences of Santayana's skepticism, his notion of animal faith, and the development of his ontology.

Santayana's ontological system, which he claimed is "*no system of the universe*" (*ES*, 51), is consistent with his philosophy of philosophy found in "Philosophical Heresy." He attempted in his ontology to think clearly about reality, to eliminate arbitrary conventions, conflicting opinions, and subjective perspectives as far as possible, while acknowledging that the effort could not achieve any ideal objectivity. In his book *Scepticism and Animal Faith,* Santayana acknowledged the limits of his system when he stated that the realms of being are "not parts of a cosmos, nor one great cosmos together: they are only kinds or categories of things which I find conspicuously different and worth distinguishing, at least in my own thoughts" (*ES*, 51–52).

Awareness of limits is evident in Santayana's skepticism, which rejects the quest for certain knowledge. Skepticism may arise when experience disappoints dogma, but it cannot eliminate all unreliable dogma. Santayana observed that skepticism historically has been used disingenuously to affirm some favored dogma and so has been artificial and incomplete. He attempted an honest and thoroughgoing skepticism and discovered that suspending all belief reveals essence—the real though non-existent character or quality given in intuition and shorn of all significance, whether moral or epistemological.

Actual belief in existence is rooted in animal faith, "a sort of expectation and open-mouthedness, [which] is earlier than intuition; intuitions come to help it out and lend it something to posit" (*ES,* 86). No object of animal faith is ever intuited; rather intuited essences are taken to stand for that which is believed to exist. In this way knowledge is faith mediated by symbols, that is, essences taken symbolically.

Essences taken literally as revealing the nature of particular existences would be illusory, but such illusions are vital to how we understand other minds. We have no direct intuition of other minds, but we can explain the thoughts and feelings of others by ascribing to them our own intuited essence. This method may be reliable when the observer and the subject are engaged in the same activity. This sort of explanation Santayana called literary psychology, an act of imagination that stands in contrast to scientific psychology, which explains human mental activity in terms of bodily processes and physical interactions.

The inevitability of literary psychology does not entail that human interaction is a matter of arbitrary imagination, and in fact Santayana credited a particular kind of interaction with waking one up to the reality of truth. Being lied to by someone leads one to reflect on the discrepancy between the report and the facts of the matter or "what everybody spontaneously means by" the word 'truth' (*ES,* 113).

In elucidating his ideas, Santayana used the history of philosophy both as a starting point and a target for criticism. Though he found "sophistry . . . and limping scepticism" in modern philosophy (*ES,* 120), he also appreciated the criticism of knowledge that came out of the tradition of Hume and Kant. He accepted their disintegration of illusion but rejected their condemnation of belief because of its human origins. His conception of knowledge in terms of animal faith and essences was an attempt to restore "the notions of substance, soul, nature, and discourse. . . . without forgetting the assumptions on which they rest" (*ES,* 124).

Santayana's disillusioned philosophy acknowledges the place of illusion in human life with the phrase "Normal Madness." He wrote that "life is at once the quintessence and the sum of madness" (*ES,* 128) in its disposition toward permanence when the entire natural order is in flux. Thinking is the expression in consciousness of this madness with ideas defying the perpetual change of the material universe, and we succumb when we believe in the ideas that appear to us and wrap "the naked atoms in a veil of dreams" (*ES,* 131). Wisdom, thought Santayana, is "evanescent madness, when the dream still continues but no longer deceives" (*ES,* 132).

Santayana could enjoy the dream and the essences, but he did not wish to be deceived and so sought to understand the nature of being, which led to his considerations in "Some Meanings of the Word 'Is'." In this preliminary survey of his ontology he noted seven meanings of the word "is," by which he elaborated the distinction between existence and essence.

Santayana further refined the distinction between existence and essence in his four-volume *Realms of Being,* in which his central question was the nature of the free life of the mind. Each volume examines in detail one of the realms, and this inquiry into reality, thought Santayana, served to clarify how mind can exercise its function, escape its troubles, and find joy. "The great characteristic of the human spirit," he wrote, "is its helplessness and misery, most miserable and helpless when it fancies itself dominant and independent; and the great problem for it is salvation, purification, rebirth into a humble recognition of the powers on which it depends, and into a sane enjoyment of its appropriate virtues" (*RB1*, xxxii). Understanding the realms of being could situate the mind, bringing it peace and restoring its native excellence.

The proper home of mind or spirit is the Realm of Essence, but this is not a supernatural heaven. Santayana was explicit that essence is natural, has no intrinsic moral value or significance, and is impotent in the material realm. An essence is what it is and nothing else. It is the character exemplified in an existing material object or an intuition. It is inalienably individual, independent, and free from any spatial or temporal reference. Hence, each essence is an eternal universal and retains perfect identity with itself. Essences are infinitely various, ideal, and non-existent, but Santayana insisted that they are most real and "have being in an eminent degree" (*ES*, 160).

Acquaintance with essence Santayana called intuition, which is the actualization of spirit. Even though spirit arises in the animal due to material pressures to notice and foresee events, spirit picks out only essences. This means that essences are not abstracted from existences. Essences give importance to facts, not the other way round: things are instruments, essences are essential.

Santayana had observed that his theory of essence met with strong disapproval and remarked that critics laid greater emphasis on the theory than he did. According to Santayana, "almost everybody" missed "the vital foundation of [his] philosophy": The Realm of Matter (*PGS*, 503).

Santayana preferred to call his philosophy materialism rather than naturalism, because the latter term seemed to him open to "worse equivocations" than the former: "The term materialism seems," he wrote, "safer, precisely because more disliked; and the cruder notions of it are so crude that they may be easily distinguished and discarded" (*PGS*, 508). He thought the word captured the assumption of animal faith: the belief in an environing natural world that includes other creatures thinking pretty much the same things, or the sense of an irrational flux moving the creature along without reason from past to future.

Santayana's materialism was his attempt to take seriously both the brute fact of the contingency of matter and the wonder of the human capacity to reason. The pressing question became that of the role of human understanding in a universe in which knowledge rested on an inevitable faith. Taking seriously the belief in material nature entails rejecting idealism and the view that nature is illusory, and this belief led Santayana to distinguish five indispensable properties of substance and to reject teleology as a "form of mock explanation" (*ES*, 188). Yet, he retained the notion of final causes understood as "moral perspectives superposed on natural causation" (*ES*, 194). They are materially impotent but spiritually valuable.

To understand the relation of matter to spirit it is helpful to understand the relation of psyche to consciousness. Psyche is the system of patterns or "specific form of physical life" embodied in any living organism (*ES*, 200). Though psyche is not a substance, it is a mode of substance; hence psychic events occur in the realm of matter. By contrast, consciousness and all mental life are part of the realm of spirit. Consciousness or spirit is "an overtone of psychic strains, mutations, and harmonies" (*ES*, 209) and "a spiritual synthesis of organic movements" (*ES*, 210). The images produced by the sensitive psyche generate perception and mental life, and so the spirit has its basis in the material flux. Though spirit contemplates the various forms that matter might take, it has no power over the flux of matter out of which it arises.

Like spirit, truth is faithful to its basis in the material flux, being "the complete ideal description of existence" (*ES*, 222). Ontologically truth is secondary to essence and matter, and Santayana wrote in *The Realm of Truth* that the eternity of truth "is but the wake of the ship of time, a furrow which matter must plough upon the face of essence" (*RB1*, 405).

The basis of truth in contingent matter means there are no necessary truths. Santayana explained that because essences or terms of thought are infinite, every particular fact is arbitrary. "Infinite alternatives were open to existence" when matter embodied some particular essence (*ES*, 214); and since it is the embodiment of essence in matter that determines what is true, truth as the description of arbitrary existence is itself arbitrary. Santayana illustrated his position by reviewing four claims often regarded as necessary truths and explaining why they are not.

The material flux that renders no truth necessary also makes facts arbitrary. Santayana thought that an assertion of necessity regarding facts betrays an enfeebled imagination, and he pointed out that spirit arose in order to escape such limitations on imagination imposed by the realm of matter. In surveying the infinite realm of essence spirit sees the contingency of facts as well as alternative forms that matter could have assumed, thereby undercutting claims of physical necessity. Logical necessity may remain, but Santayana denied that it expresses any truth. Logic is ideal and expresses a system among essences. Such a system expresses truth only when that truth can be discovered by means other than that system; that is, when essences are embodied in matter. "Truth will then domesticate our logic in the world" (*ES*, 221).

Though Santayana distinguished truth and logic, he acknowledged a sense in which a faithful mathematical or logical analysis of some accepted idea could, through its fidelity, be called true. But such fidelity in human thought is difficult to maintain because of a thinker's inevitable "drift of ideation," and Santayana warned against giving the name "logic" to the resulting dialectic (*ES*, 226). To do so is to abandon serious thinking for the notion that there is no truth beyond one's own subjective experience, a notion he labeled romantic idealism. Rather than abandon objectivity, one can acknowledge that existence is objective and irrational and cannot be elucidated fully in terms of essence; but since we must always resort to essences to describe facts, all description is to some extent partial and unstable. By acknowledging this we can avoid fallacies that lead philosophy astray; namely that terms of discourse are responsible for relativity and subjectivism, and that matter is somehow deficient for not meeting human expectations.

To eliminate the human element from thought, Santayana regarded as both impossible and undesirable. Impossible because consciousness has a material basis, and this entails passional influences that introduce into experience "expectation, partiality, superstition, hyperbole, rage, and enthusiasm" (*ES,* 232); undesirable because passion introduces interest and relevance lacking in a mere mechanical notation of details. The resulting dramatic reading of events disregards many facts in favor of expressing the movement and ultimate issue of some controlling passion; and such "dramatic truth" as expressed in myths and epics is accordingly a fiction. But dramatic fictions express principles of action otherwise undetectable and indicate "the gist of existence" or the point of an action (*ES,* 233). They are fancies when regarded as descriptions of fact, but in expressing the push and aim of action they reveal the truth about material relations and human passions.

Moral passions may also express truth. Santayana acknowledged the apparent meaninglessness of calling a moral judgment true, because the judgment appears to refer to no object or reality; yet a moral judgment could be true or false to the fundamental needs of the agent. He wrote, "truth and error may be possible in morals, in so far as they are truths or errors in self-knowledge" (*ES,* 237). He rejected, however, any "morality in general" (*ES,* 243) and thought it a piece of dogmatism to extend moral truths beyond the natural organization asserting them. One can neither legitimately impose one's moral truths on others, nor beneficially forsake one's own animal bias for the sake of harmony on a broad scale. The honest and healthy nature admits the reality of good and evil even when it conflicts with the moral judgments of others. "Moral truth . . . signifies only complete, enlightened, ultimate sincerity" in acknowledging and respecting one's own preferences and biases (*ES,* 242).

Complete and sincere self-knowledge is, of course, difficult to achieve; and, according to Santayana, a lack of self-knowledge may account for a common aversion to truth. He observed that we often quite innocently take the human being as the standard of all things, but this false understanding of the place and significance of the self leads to hostility toward the truth of a material universe that vastly exceeds the human scale. Love of truth comes with realizing the nature of spirit as "a child of truth" (*ES,* 248), that is, as the result of matter exhibiting patterns and cohering in organisms. These embodiments of essence belong to the realm of truth and give birth to spirit. Spirit finds its joy in surveying the realm of truth, showing how love of truth is natural to the spirit.

In spite of this natural love, one can be tempted to deny truth by despair and disappointment at not knowing the entire truth. Knowledge of the entire truth is beyond the capacity of any human knower, whose limited perspective results in knowledge that is partial, biased, and relative. But relativism does not entail a denial of truth. Santayana held that "the truth has a superhuman status: so that an absence of true opinions or criteria would not in the least abolish it" (*ES,* 255). Hence, any denial of truth is better understood as a denial of the knowledge of truth. He wrote, "the denial of truth is due to palpable confusions between truth and knowledge of truth, between essence and existence, between the ideal and the actual" (*ES,* 259).

Philosophical Heresy

Obiter Scripta: Lectures, Essays and Reviews. Edited by Justus Buchler and Benjamin Schwartz. New York: Charles Scribner's Sons; London: Constable and Co. Ltd., 1936, 94–107.

First intended as a lecture, this article was published in the Journal of Philosophy, Psychology, and Scientific Methods *(12 [1915]: 113–16). Santayana wrote from Oxford, England, to the editor of the journal that he had "read the first part of this paper to the Ox. Phil. Soc." (LGS, 2:220). The article was later collected in* Obiter Scripta. *It gives a concise account of Santayana's philosophy of philosophy. He observed philosophical systems that emphasized some aspect of common sense to the exclusion of other parts and thereby departed from "the current imagination and good sense of mankind" (ES, 44), which he took as the standard of orthodoxy. He believed it heretical to elevate such a partial philosophy to the status of a universal system and thought it more prudent and honest to confess that a philosophical system is a personal work of art.*

Systems of philosophy are the work of individuals. Even when a school is formed it prevails only in certain nations for a certain time, and unless the expression of dissent is suppressed by force, the dominant school even then is challenged by other schools no less plausible and sincere. Viewed from a sufficient distance, all systems of philosophy are seen to be personal, temperamental, accidental, and premature. They treat partial knowledge as if it were total knowledge: they take peripheral facts for central and typical facts: they confuse the grammar of human expression, in language, logic, or moral estimation, with the substantial structure of things. In a word, they are human heresies.

But if all philosophies are heresies, with what orthodoxy shall we contrast them? Evidently not with any philosophical or religious system, since it is just these systems that we are calling heretical. Much less with the collection of the critic's casual opinions. The more general the folly of mankind, the more likely is the critic himself to share it, especially as folly is a thing that folly is prone to impute. As the drunkard mutters, "you are drunk," so the philosopher scans the assemblage of his fellow-creatures and murmurs, "you are wrong." If we laugh at him for this, how shall we set up our personal opinions as a criterion by which the errors of mankind are to be judged?

The background of philosophical systems, the orthodoxy round which their heresies play, is no private or closed body of doctrine. It is merely the current imagination and good sense of mankind—something traditional, conventional, incoherent, and largely erroneous, like the assumptions of a man who has never reflected, yet something ingenuous, practically acceptable, fundamentally sound, and capable of correcting its own innocent errors. There is a knowledge which common life brings even to savages and which study, exploration, and the arts can clarify and make more precise; and this all men share in proportion to their competence and intelligence, no matter what philosophies or religions may fill their heads at the same time.

Heresies are systems that inherit all the claims of orthodoxy with only a part of its resources. In developing their chosen theme *à outrance,* they override the rest, though based on a quite similar authority. Heresy is thus no mere innocent error or native partiality, such as all natural beings are condemned to by their limited experience and faculties: it is rather an unnecessary error, a rebellious partisanship, a deliberate attachment to something the evidence against which is public and obvious; it is a sin against the light. This is none the less true because it is the excess of light at one point that produces and seems to justify this residual blindness. Philosophic systems are heretical because they abound in their own sense to the extent of denying or artificially transforming perfectly well-known matters, parts of that human orthodoxy to which they themselves must appeal for their foundations and for their plausibility.

The great misfortune of human orthodoxy is the natural apathy of reason. The beauty of truth is not great enough to attract the eye for its own sake. The truth is often ugly or terrible, and almost always less simple and unqualified than our love of eloquence would wish it to be. Discourse instinctively deviates from the truth, to set forth instead something more manageable, more rhythmical, more flattering. But the products of imagination sometimes strain it too much: the accumulated illusion suddenly collapses, and then for the first time we rub our eyes, and notice and express literally what we see and think. It is commonly at such times only that human orthodoxy makes much progress in articulation. A consequence of this is that its tenets are not arranged in an order appropriate to them or appropriate to their object. They do not form a logical hierarchy nor a clear natural history of the world. For they have not been reached by a gentle and continuous study of the truth, but rather by fits and starts, when some scandalous error exhausted people's patience and stung them into an eloquence and clearness they never knew before. Human orthodoxy is in its Apostolic Age; it has not yet had its Fathers or its Councils. Like early Christianity, it possesses instinct and tradition enough to exclude heresy after heresy as they arise, but it lacks a calm and adequate fund of doctrine that should not so much rebuke heresy as render heresy superfluous by solving beforehand the dark problems that provoke it.

Hence even when human orthodoxy has acquired a certain consistency, such that, for instance, an "Encyclopedia Britannica" can be compiled, older and collateral ideas have not disappeared. There are always at hand, for any meditative individual, a good many suggestions of experience which human orthodoxy has neither assimilated nor extirpated; and he may, if his genius so inclines, prefer one of these unreclaimed or unreclaimable notions to orthodoxy as a whole, or he may try to combine it with a human orthodoxy modified or unhinged to suit it.

These backslidings, these reversions to the initial illogical wealth of the mind, produce various superstitious, mystical, or atavistic heresies. These mark the fact that, side by side with the waking life of reason, many animal illusions survive in the mind, many dramatic fancies and pre-rational habits of thought. Religious revelations and philosophies, when they do not express the deliverance of reason poetically, as they often do, but traverse reason altogether and undermine it mystically, belong to this atavistic class of heresies. They may run very deep, lifting the whole fabric of vulgar reason from its centre, and reducing it to an illusion. We call them heresies retrospectively, in view of the orthodoxy we have achieved, but in themselves they are a forest of potential orthodoxies, elder rivals to that which public human life has accepted.

Another sort of heresy is peripheral and due to exclusive interest and confidence in some province of orthodoxy. This chosen part—sometimes the part last discovered—is taken for the key to the whole. Such heresy is sectarian. The scout assumes the role of the general. Excited by some little fact he has discerned, he shouts back his orders to the whole army, of whose extent and situation he has no notion. Hence the whole plague of little dogmatisms, that would harp universal harmonies on a single string. Yet these philosophies, being founded on the intent perception of something given and loved, are likely to supply a true description, or at least an appropriate symbol, of that particular object. When neutralized by further knowledge and reduced to their proper scope and importance, these sects can contribute their special vista to the orthodox landscape: they can leave, as they retire, a sediment of science.

It would seem that a philosopher should not willingly be either mystical or sectarian. He will inevitably try to explain his mystical experience in the light of his clear knowledge, and so graft his favourite insights and bold hypotheses upon the stem of common sense. He will also wish not to be unfair to any element of the truth. Yet, as things stand, he can hardly remain a mere spokesman of human orthodoxy. That is a body of beliefs and appreciations far too chaotic to satisfy a reflective mind. Must, then, every philosopher, in proportion to the coherence and technical strength of his thought, be a heretic in spite of himself? Not inevitably. I think I see two ways in which philosophy might be achieved without heterodoxy. One is a very hard way indeed, that of comprehensive synthesis; a speculation so evenly inspired and broadly based that it should report the system or the medley of known things without twisting any of them. Such a philosophy would be to human orthodoxy what the Fathers of the Church were to the Apostles, or the Doctors to the Fathers. This is a feat which no philosopher has accomplished, or is likely ever to succeed in. Those who have attempted it may have been the least deluded of philosophers, but they were also the least philosophical. They have not satisfied the critical mind almost at any point; they have recorded human opinion rather than mastered and deepened it, as a philosopher should. If, on the contrary, the pupil of common sense is masterful and systematic, he is sure to leave, in spite of himself, a large part of human orthodoxy out of account, and to become a sectarian. Aristotle, for instance, who is as normal a philosopher as possible, nevertheless upsets or ignores the whole of genuine physics—certainly half of human knowledge—in respect to which he is a humanist turned metaphysician, and casting the universe in the moulds of grammar and ethics. Yet it is this heresy that gives his philosophy its character and its grandeur. A philosopher who was quite conventional and safe in every sphere of knowledge could hardly make such a great impression. He would bleat with the flock, and would be rightly regarded as an amateur in philosophy, like Cicero or Bacon. His eclecticism would remain incoherent, literary, and, as Nietzsche would say, human, all-too-human. Either way, therefore, there is little hope of reaching an orthodox philosophy by the synthetic method.

The other method by which I can imagine a man becoming a philosopher without being a heretic is far more modest, far easier, if only one has a temperament humble and sceptical enough. It lies in confessing that a system of philosophy is a personal work of art which gives a specious unity to some chance vista in the cosmic labyrinth. To confess this is to confess a notorious truth; yet it would be something novel if a philosopher should confess it, and should substitute the pursuit of sincerity for the pursuit of omniscience.

The first requisite of such a philosophy would be to renounce all claim to be a system of the universe. It would leave the theory of the universe to science, to human orthodoxy, or to religious revelation. It would concentrate all its attention on personal experience, personal perspectives, personal ideals. And in expressing these private views, it would not become heretical, or conflict in the least with human orthodoxy; for human orthodoxy does not ignore the fact that men have different sorts of imagination and emotion, that their affections and apprehensions are various, and that they do not approach by the same paths even those points on which they agree. A philosopher setting forth his cognitive and moral experience in his own way would, therefore, not be more heterodox than a poet with an original vision, so long as he abstained from regarding so interesting an idiosyncrasy as the measure of all things.

Several great philosophers, like Socrates and Hume, have come very near to avoiding heresy after this fashion. But they have not quite avoided it, for they have assigned to their introspection a public value which it did not have, and have denied the validity of some of the sciences, or of all of them. Had they reported ingenuously what they perceived (as sometimes they affected to do), had the psychology of Hume not been malicious or the ethics of Socrates intolerant, all their profound radicalism might have left them orthodox. If given out for merely personal perspectives, all scepticism, all transcendentalism, all possible moral ideals, might be taken up into the life of reason. If the inevitable play and normal illusions of the senses continue to interest the artist without confusing his practical and scientific knowledge, why should the normal illusions of partial acquaintance with things, and the inevitable play of private interests, confuse a philosopher about the nature of the great world beyond?

I am well aware that this mode of avoiding heresy, by living in one's own house, while leaving the universe to manage its own affairs, is something repugnant to philosophers. They crave totality in their views and authority in their sentiments. Nevertheless, their views have no totality. They touch the hem of nature's garment, as science does; and if science feels some virtue pass into it at that contact, it cannot fathom the source of that influence, nor map out the realities that may lie beyond. How should a complete chart of the universe descend into the twilight of an animal mind, served by quite special senses, swayed by profound passions, subject to the epidemic delusions of the race, and lost in the perhaps infinite world that bred it? And the moral sentiments of philosophers, however worthy of respect they may be for their sincerity or for their humanity (or in exceptional cases, for both), have no authority. Vehement as they may be, no other man's sentiment is obliged to conform to them. Their sense of value is a fact, it is a fact interesting to the historian, and fundamental in their own ethics; but in the life of nature it is a peripheral thing, a surface phenomenon, the expression of a profound subterranean ferment; and while nothing could be of greater moment in poetry or politics, nothing could be a worse or more heretical foundation for a system of physics, or even for a theory of human society.

If, however, by way of exception, a philosophical heresy could lose its venom and recognize that it was a myth, a graphic way of rendering and lighting up some group of facts or observations, lending them a certain specious unity and rhythm,–then the greatest incentive to envenomed heresy would be removed in minds of an opposite cast. For heresy is often stimulated by the hatred of error, if not by the love of truth. It arises very largely by reaction against other heresies. A man sees how false another man's system is in some particular by which he himself happens to be otherwise impressed; and he hastens, in his hatred of error at that particular point, to construct a system contradicting his opponent there, while perhaps following him in everything else. But as the critic is conscious of being a purist in this one place, and exposing a fable, he never suspects that what he has not examined, but retained, and even what he has substituted, may be fabulous as well. Proud of being a radical, he cannot imagine that he is a dupe. But if his opponent had presented his objectionable view as a personal impression, as the expression of a private experience by which the divergent experiences of other people were in no way denied or rebuked, the spur to lie for the pleasure of giving the lie to others would never prick him, and the self-expression of his own mind might proceed in sincerity, in peace, and in good humour.

Such are the hazards of human opinion and such the possibilities of an orthodox philosophy, as I conceive that human orthodoxy would itself represent them. There is, however, a well-known philosophy of philosophy that would discard all these distinctions. It would maintain that human thought was an absolute thing, that it existed and developed on its own internal principles and resources, without any environment. What this philosophy starts from and calls knowledge is, according to its description, not knowledge at all, but only absolute imagination, a self-generated experience expressing no prior existence and regarding no external object, either material or ideal. Such absolute imagination, since its development could not be affected by anything outside (there being nothing outside), would evidently require all those variations and ingredients which I have called heresies; they would all express its initial pregnancy more or less completely, and would be taken up and carried on in the next phase of its life. All the parts of orthodoxy might thus, in isolation, be called heretical, while the sum total and infinite life of heresy would be orthodoxy, or rather would be reality itself. We are in a world of romantic soliloquy, peopled by subjective lights and subjective assurances; and it is easy to see how well such a discovery might serve

Protestant theologians to justify their past and idealize their future.

This assimilation of heresy and orthodoxy would be harmless enough if it confessed that it was merely the composition of an historical artist, the autobiography, as it were, of a groping speculation that likes to imagine itself to be the whole life and experience of a solitary god. An interesting cross vista of the world may be thus opened up, as by an egotistical poet; and if we are more interested in ourselves than in things, we may well be delighted with such a synthesis of our experiences and of our preferences, as if these made up the sum of existence.

From this point of view, which some modern idealists identify with philosophic method, it is evident that Columbus brought America into existence by bringing it into consciousness, and that geography in general cannot express the disposition of the earth's surface, but only the disposition or will of certain spirits to cultivate geography. Similarly, mathematics would lack an articulate and eternal subject-matter. It would not describe the essential relations of ideal terms, about which insight must always be insight and confusion confusion. No: it would rather, at each stage of its history, express the genius of a race, a state of society, and an individual, in expressing which no error is ever possible, since the will to square the circle cannot misrepresent itself, but perfectly displays the vital impulse, singular and precious, of somebody in some place and at some moment. What superficial people call madness would thus have nothing wasteful and tragic about it. It would give the exact measure of life in one of its most intimate outflowings. If you rashly took the madness out of people, perhaps they might have nothing left that they could call their own. Nay, universal reason itself would have nothing to work upon.

This romantic philosophy of philosophy is itself a good instance of heresy, both mystical and sectarian. The idealist takes the subjective point of view because he likes it, because his doubts or his dogmas are in that way dissolved deliciously; and that is legitimate. He adds, however, that this subjective point of view is the only right and ultimate one, which is a sectarian heresy; and that it opens to him the substance and the plan of the universe, which is a heresy of the mystical and atavistic kind. As becomes a heretic, he is rather fierce about all this, and rather persistent; but in the long run he cannot prevent the world from retaining its happy orthodoxy, and putting him and his private persuasions where they belong.

Indeed, the paradox that human thought is absolute, and therefore neither true nor false, neither orthodox nor heretical, is so extraordinary that many who call themselves idealists are far from maintaining it in its purity. They might practically admit what the unphilosophical imagine, that madness creates images that are personal, temporary, and useless; that geography studies an earth that existed before all geographers, and brought them forth; that mathematics describes ideal objects which are eternal and impersonal. All this they might admit under cover of the doctrine that the whole truth is already present to the mind of God, parts of the same being revealed to us *seriatim,* as our knowledge increases. Truth would here be the logician's substitute for reality, and the mind of God the psychologist's substitute for the truth. The external standards of orthodoxy, under these idealistic names, would in either case be restored. We should need only to ask what this truth described, or what this mind of God thought about, to behold the natural, historical, and mathematical worlds reinstated, as every one instinctively believes them to subsist. Opinions would no longer have a share in the truth simply because they had a place in evolution. Madness would again be madness, error error, and heresy heresy. We should cease to hear of the absolute life of thought, in which everything was thoroughly significant and thoroughly pathological. Knowledge might really advance and accumulate, because there would be a world for it to discover, and progress might be real just because, in view of its fixed and natural goal, it would not be inevitable, constant, or endless. The naturalistic conception of what philosophy is and can be, of how it strays and how it is tested, would then be restored by general consent, as indeed it should be; for it is the plain deliverance of a long and general experience.

Preface *[Scepticism and Animal Faith]*

Scepticism and Animal Faith: Introduction to a System of Philosophy. New York: Charles Scribner's Sons; London: Constable and Co. Ltd., 1923, v–x. Volume thirteen of the critical edition of *The Works of George Santayana.*

This preface appeared in Scepticism and Animal Faith, *the book title exhibiting Santayana's preference for British spelling. The book is an introduction to Santayana's system of philosophy subsequently presented in his four-volume* Realms of Being. *In this preface Santayana claimed that his system is neither his nor new, and he denied that it is universal, metaphysical, or part of any contemporary movement of philosophy. "For good or ill," he wrote, "I am an ignorant man, almost a poet, and I can only spread a feast of what everybody knows" (E.S, 53). He was emphasizing the intended fidelity of his system to orthodoxy, that is, its aim to express clearly and honestly the partial and human outlook he has inherited.*

Here is one more system of philosophy. If the reader is tempted to smile, I can assure him that I smile with him, and that my system—to which this volume is a critical introduction—differs widely in spirit and pretensions from what usually goes by that name. In the first place, *my system is not mine, nor new.* I am merely attempting to express for the reader the principles to which he appeals when he smiles. There are convictions in the depths of his soul, beneath all his overt parrot beliefs, on which I would build our friendship. I have a great respect for orthodoxy; not for those orthodoxies which prevail in particular schools or nations, and which vary from age to age, but for a certain shrewd orthodoxy which the sentiment and practice of laymen maintain everywhere. I think that common sense, in a rough dogged way, is technically sounder than the special schools of philosophy, each of which squints and overlooks half the facts and half the difficulties in its eagerness to find in some detail the key to the whole. I am animated by distrust of all high guesses, and by sympathy with the old prejudices and workaday opinions of man-kind: they are ill expressed, but they are well grounded. What novelty my version of things may possess is meant simply to obviate occasions for sophistry by giving to everyday beliefs a more accurate and circumspect form. I do not pretend to place myself at the heart of the universe nor at its origin, nor to draw its periphery. I would lay siege to the truth only as animal exploration and fancy may do so, first from one quarter and then from another, expecting the reality to be not simpler than my experience of it, but far more extensive and complex. I stand in philosophy exactly where I stand in daily life; I should not be honest otherwise. I accept the same miscellaneous witnesses, bow to the same obvious facts, make conjectures no less instinctively, and admit the same encircling ignorance.

My system, accordingly, is *no system of the universe.* The Realms of Being of which I speak are not parts of a cosmos, nor one great cosmos together: they are only kinds or categories of things which I find conspicuously different and worth distinguishing, at least in my own thoughts. I do not know how many things in the universe at large may fall under each of these classes, nor what other Realms of Being may not exist, to which I have no approach or which I have not happened to distinguish in my personal observation of the world. Logic, like language, is partly a free construction and partly a means of symbolising and harnessing in expression the existing diversities of things; and whilst some languages, given a man's constitution and habits, may seem more beautiful and convenient to him than others, it is a foolish heat in a patriot to insist that only his native language is intelligible or right. No language or logic is right in the sense of being identical with the facts it is used to express, but each may be right by being faithful to these facts, as a translation may be faithful. My endeavour is to think straight in such terms as are offered to me, to clear my mind of cant and free it from the cramp of artificial traditions; but I do not ask any one to think in my terms if he prefers others. Let him clean better, if he can, the windows of his soul, that the variety and beauty of the prospect may spread more brightly before him.

Moreover, my system, save in the mocking literary sense of the word, is *not metaphysical*. It contains much criticism of metaphysics, and some refinements in speculation, like the doctrine of essence, which are not familiar to the public; and I do not disclaim being metaphysical because I at all dislike dialectic or disdain immaterial things: indeed, it is of immaterial things, essence, truth, and spirit that I speak chiefly. But logic and mathematics and literary psychology (when frankly literary) are not metaphysical, although their subject-matter is immaterial, and their application to existing things is often questionable. Metaphysics, in the proper sense of the word, is dialectical physics, or an attempt to determine matters of fact by means of logical or moral or rhetorical constructions. It arises by a confusion of those Realms of Being which it is my special care to distinguish. It is neither physical speculation nor pure logic nor honest literature, but (as in the treatise of Aristotle first called by that name) a hybrid of the three, materialising ideal entities, turning harmonies into forces, and dissolving natural things into terms of discourse. Speculations about the natural world, such as those of the Ionian philosophers, are not metaphysics, but simply cosmology or natural philosophy. Now in natural philosophy I am a decided materialist–apparently the only one living; and I am well aware that idealists are fond of calling materialism, too, metaphysics, in rather an angry tone, so as to cast discredit upon it by assimilating it to their own systems. But my materialism, for all that, is not metaphysical. I do not profess to know what matter is in itself, and feel no confidence in the divination of those *esprits forts* who, leading a life of vice, thought the universe must be composed of nothing but dice and billiard-balls. I wait for the men of science to tell me what matter is, in so far as they can discover it, and am not at all surprised or troubled at the abstractness and vagueness of their ultimate conceptions: how should our notions of things so remote from the scale and scope of our senses be anything but schematic? But whatever matter may be, I call it matter boldly, as I call my acquaintances Smith and Jones without knowing their secrets: whatever it may be, it must present the aspects and undergo the motions of the gross objects that fill the world: and if belief in the existence of hidden parts and movements in nature be metaphysics, then the kitchen-maid is a metaphysician whenever she peels a potato.

My system, finally, though, of course, formed under the fire of contemporary discussions, is *no phase of any current movement.* I cannot take at all seriously the present flutter of the image-lovers against intelligence. I love images as much as they do, but images must be discounted in our waking life, when we come to business. I also appreciate the other reforms and rebellions that have made up the history of philosophy. I prize their sharp criticism of one another and their several discoveries; the trouble is that each in turn has denied or forgotten a much more important truth than it has asserted. The first philosophers, the original observers of life and nature, were the best; and I think only the Indians and the Greek naturalists, together with Spinoza, have been right on the chief issue, the relation of man and of his spirit to the universe. It is not unwillingness to be a disciple that prompts me to look beyond the modern scramble of philosophies: I should gladly learn of them all, if they had learned more of one another. Even as it is, I endeavour to retain the positive insight of each, reducing it to the scale of nature and keeping it in its place; thus I am a Platonist in logic and morals, and a transcendentalist in romantic soliloquy, when I choose to indulge in it. Nor is it necessary, in being teachable by any master, to become eclectic. All these vistas give glimpses of the same wood, and a fair and true map of it must be drawn to a single scale, by one method of projection, and in one style of calligraphy. All known truth can be rendered in any language, although the accent and poetry of each may be incommunicable; and as I am content to write in English, although it was not my mother-tongue, and although in speculative matters I have not much sympathy with the English mind, so I am content to follow the European tradition in philosophy, little as I respect its rhetorical metaphysics, its humanism, and its worldliness.

There is one point, indeed, in which I am truly sorry not to be able to profit by the guidance of my contemporaries. There is now a great ferment in natural and mathematical philosophy and the times seem ripe for a new system of nature, at once ingenuous and comprehensive, such as has not appeared since the earlier days of Greece. We may soon be all believing in an honest cosmology, comparable with that of Heraclitus, Pythagoras, or Democritus. I wish such scientific systems joy, and if I were competent to follow or to forecast their procedure, I should gladly avail myself of their results, which are bound to be no less picturesque than instructive. But what exists to-day is so tentative, obscure, and confused by bad philosophy, that there is no knowing what parts may be sound and what parts merely personal and scatter-brained. If I were a mathematician I should no doubt regale myself, if not the reader, with an electric or logistic system of the universe expressed in algebraic symbols. For good or ill, I am an ignorant man, almost a poet, and I can only spread a feast of what everybody knows. Fortunately exact science and the books of the learned are not necessary to establish my essential doctrine, nor can any of them claim a higher warrant than it has in itself: for it rests on public experience. It needs, to prove it, only the stars, the seasons, the swarm of animals, the spectacle of birth and death, of cities and wars. My philosophy is justified, and has been justified in all ages and countries, by the facts before every man's eyes; and no great wit is requisite to discover it, only (what is rarer than wit) candour and courage. Learning does not liberate men from superstition when their souls are cowed or perplexed; and, without learning, clear eyes and honest reflection can discern the hang of the world, and distinguish the edge of truth from the might of imagination. In the past or in the future, my language and my borrowed knowledge would have been different, but under whatever sky I had been born, since it is the same sky, I should have had the same philosophy.

There Is No First Principle of Criticism

Scepticism and Animal Faith: Introduction to a System of Philosophy. New York: Charles Scribner's Sons; London: Constable and Co. Ltd., 1923, 1–5. Volume thirteen of the critical edition of *The Works of George Santayana.*

This selection appeared as Chapter I of Scepticism and Animal Faith *and announces that the philosopher must begin* in medias res. *There are no first principles of reasoning; rather there are long-established habits that become apparent only after they are represented in mind as principles. The sorts of reasoning actually carried out include two sorts of criticism: empirical and transcendental. Empirical criticism distinguishes compulsory facts from conventional beliefs, but as it is carried out one wonders what led to those conventional interpretations of plain facts. Transcendental criticism seeks these principles of interpretation, and in the hands of the skeptic it pushes empiricism to justify knowledge of fact. Failing to do so, empiricism reveals its own unacknowledged principles of interpretation or "tendencies to feign."*

A philosopher is compelled to follow the maxim of epic poets and to plunge *in medias res*. The origin of things, if things have an origin, cannot be revealed to me, if revealed at all, until I have travelled very far from it, and many revolutions of the sun must precede my first dawn. The light as it appears hides the candle. Perhaps there is no source of things at all, no simpler form from which they are evolved, but only an endless succession of different complexities. In that case nothing would be lost by joining the procession wherever one happens to come upon it, and following it as long as one's legs hold out. Every one might still observe a typical bit of it; he would not have understood anything better if he had seen more things; he would only have had more to explain. The very notion of understanding or explaining anything would then be absurd; yet this notion is drawn from a current presumption or experience to the effect that in some directions at least things do grow out of simpler things: bread can be baked, and dough and fire and an oven are conjoined in baking it. Such an episode is enough to establish the notion of origins and explanations, without at all implying that the dough and the hot oven are themselves primary facts. A philosopher may accordingly perfectly well undertake to find *episodes of evolution* in the world: parents with children, storms with shipwrecks, passions with tragedies. If he begins in the middle he will still begin at the beginning of something, and perhaps as much at the beginning of things as he could possibly begin.

On the other hand, this whole supposition may be wrong. Things may have had some simpler origin, or may contain simpler elements. In that case it will be incumbent on the philosopher to prove this fact; that is, to find in the complex present objects evidence of their composition out of simples. But in this proof also he would be beginning in the middle; and he would reach origins or elements only at the end of his analysis.

The case is similar with respect to first principles of discourse. They can never be discovered, if discovered at all, until they have been long taken for granted, and employed in the very investigation which reveals them. The more cogent a logic is, the fewer and simpler its first principles will turn out to have been; but in discovering them, and deducing the rest from them, they must first be employed unawares, if they are the principles lending cogency to actual discourse; so that the mind must trust current presumptions no less in discovering that they are logical—that is, justified by more general unquestioned presumptions—than in discovering that they are arbitrary and merely instinctive.

It is true that, quite apart from living discourse, a set of axioms and postulates, as simple as we like, may be posited in the air, and deductions drawn from them *ad libitum;* but such pure logic is otiose, unless we find or assume that discourse or nature actually follows it; and it is not by deduction from first principles, arbitrarily chosen, that human reasoning actually proceeds, but by loose habits of mental evocation which such principles at best may exhibit afterwards in an idealised form. Moreover, if we could strip our thought for the arena of a perfect logic, we should be performing, perhaps, a remarkable dialectical feat; but this feat would be a mere addition to the complexities of nature, and no simplification. This motley world, besides its other antics, would then contain logicians and their sports. If by chance, on turning to the flowing facts, we found by analysis that they obeyed that ideal logic, we should again be beginning with things as we find them in the gross, and not with first principles.

It may be observed in passing that no logic to which empire over nature or over human discourse has ever been ascribed has been a cogent logic; it has been, in proportion to its exemplification in existence, a mere description, psychological or historical, of an actual procedure; whereas pure logic, when at last, quite recently, it was clearly conceived, turned out instantly to have no necessary application to anything, and to be merely a parabolic excursion into the realm of essence.

In the tangle of human beliefs, as conventionally expressed in talk and in literature, it is easy to distinguish a compulsory factor called facts or things from a more optional and argumentative factor called suggestion or interpretation; not that what we call facts are at all indubitable, or composed of immediate data, but that in the direction of fact we come much sooner to a stand, and feel that we are safe from criticism. To reduce conventional beliefs to the facts they rest on—however questionable those facts themselves may be in other ways—is to clear our intellectual conscience of voluntary or avoidable delusion. If what we call a fact still deceives us, we feel we are not to blame; we should not call it a fact, did we see any way of eluding the recognition of it. To reduce conventional belief to the recognition of matters of fact is empirical criticism of knowledge.

The more drastic this criticism is, and the more revolutionary the view to which it reduces me, the clearer will be the contrast between what I find I know and what I thought I knew. But if these plain facts were all I had to go on, how did I reach those strange conclusions? What principles of interpretation, what tendencies to feign, what habits of inference were at work in me? For if nothing in the facts justified my beliefs, something in me must have suggested them. To disentangle and formulate these subjective principles of interpretation is transcendental criticism of knowledge.

Transcendental criticism in the hands of Kant and his followers was a sceptical instrument used by persons who were not sceptics. They accordingly imported into their argument many uncritical assumptions, such as that these tendencies to feign must be the same in everybody, that the notions of nature, history, or mind which they led people to adopt were the right or standard notions on these subjects, and that it was glorious, rather than ignominious or sophistical, to build on these principles an encyclopædia of false sciences and to call it knowledge. A true sceptic will begin by throwing over all those academic conventions as so much confessed fiction; and he will ask rather if, when all that these arbitrary tendencies to feign import into experience has been removed, any factual element remains at all. The only critical function of transcendentalism is to drive empiricism home, and challenge it to produce any knowledge of fact whatsoever. And empirical criticism will not be able to do so. Just as inattention leads ordinary people to assume as part of the given facts all that their unconscious transcendental logic has added to them, so inattention, at a deeper level, leads the empiricist to assume an existence in his radical facts which does not belong to them. In standing helpless and resigned before them he is, for all his assurance, obeying his illusion rather than their evidence. Thus transcendental criticism, used by a thorough sceptic, may compel empirical criticism to show its hand. It had mistaken its cards, and was bluffing without knowing it.

Dogma and Doubt

Scepticism and Animal Faith: Introduction to a System of Philosophy. New York: Charles Scribner's Sons; London: Constable and Co. Ltd., 1923, 6–10. Volume thirteen of the critical edition of *The Works of George Santayana.*

In this selection, Chapter II of Scepticism and Animal Faith, *Santayana observed that dogma is automatic and variable, and this guarantees that conflicts run deeply through the mass of our opinions. When shocks of experience make these conflicts actual, doubt arises, skepticism grows, and criticism becomes possible. In suspecting some error about facts, skepticism presupposes facts. When facts are presupposed and the possibility of error recognized, one may become aware of the "tendencies to feign"—the dogmas and deceptions—operating in oneself. These dogmas are necessary and compulsory, but necessity of belief is not justification of belief. In response to this situation Santayana proposed to strain "his dogmas through the utmost rigours of scepticism" (*ES, 60). *Even though it may not achieve truth, this extreme skepticism is at least not dishonorable. One may not eliminate these dogmas, but one can refuse to be taken in by their claims to be true.*

Custom does not breed understanding, but takes its place, teaching people to make their way contentedly through the world without knowing what the world is, nor what they think of it, nor what they are. When their attention is attracted to some remarkable thing, say to the rainbow, this thing is not analysed nor examined from various points of view, but all the casual resources of the fancy are called forth in conceiving it, and this total reaction of the mind precipitates a dogma; the rainbow is taken for an omen of fair weather, or for a trace left in the sky by the passage of some beautiful and elusive goddess. Such a dogma, far from being an interpenetration or identification of thought with the truth of the object, is a fresh and additional object in itself. The original passive perception remains unchanged; the thing remains unfathomed; and as its diffuse influence has by chance bred one dogma to-day, it may breed a different dogma to-morrow. We have therefore, as we progress in our acquaintance with the world, an always greater confusion. Besides the original fantastic inadequacy of our perceptions, we have now rival clarifications of them, and a new uncertainty as to whether these dogmas are relevant to the original object, or are themselves really clear, or if so, which of them is true.

A prosperous dogmatism is indeed not impossible. We may have such determinate minds that the suggestions of experience always issue there in the same dogmas; and these orthodox dogmas, perpetually revived by the stimulus of things, may become our dominant or even our sole apprehension of them. We shall really have moved to another level of mental discourse; we shall be living on ideas. In the gardens of Seville I once heard, coming through the tangle of palms and orange trees, the treble voice of a pupil in the theological seminary, crying to his playmate: "You booby! of course angels have a more perfect nature than

men." With his black and red cassock that child had put on dialectic; he was playing the game of dogma and dreaming in words, and was insensible to the scent
of violets that filled the air. How long would that last? Hardly, I suspect, until the
next spring; and the troubled awakening which puberty would presently bring
to that little dogmatist, sooner or later overtakes all elder dogmatists in the press
of the world. The more perfect the dogmatism, the more insecure. A great high
topsail that can never be reefed nor furled is the first carried away by the gale.

To me the opinions of mankind, taken without any contrary prejudice (since
I have no rival opinions to propose) but simply contrasted with the course of
nature, seem surprising fictions; and the marvel is how they can be maintained.
What strange religions, what ferocious moralities, what slavish fashions, what
sham interests! I can explain it all only by saying to myself that intelligence is
naturally forthright; it forges ahead; it piles fiction on fiction; and the fact that
the dogmatic structure, for the time being, stands and grows, passes for a proof
of its rightness. Right indeed it is in one sense, as vegetation is right; it is vital;
it has plasticity and warmth, and a certain indirect correspondence with its soil
and climate. Many obviously fabulous dogmas, like those of religion, might for
ever dominate the most active minds, except for one circumstance. In the jungle
one tree strangles another, and luxuriance itself is murderous. So is luxuriance in
the human mind. What kills spontaneous fictions, what recalls the impassioned
fancy from its improvisation, is the angry voice of some contrary fancy. Nature,
silently making fools of us all our lives, never would bring us to our senses; but
the maddest assertions of the mind may do so, when they challenge one another.
Criticism arises out of the conflict of dogmas.

May I escape this predicament and criticise without a dogmatic criterion?
Hardly; for though the criticism may be expressed hypothetically, as for instance
in saying that if any child knew his own father he would be a wise child, yet the
point on which doubt is thrown is a point of fact, and that there are fathers and
children is assumed dogmatically. If not, however obscure the essential relation
between fathers and children might be ideally, no one could be wise or foolish in
assigning it in any particular instance, since no such terms would exist in nature
at all. Scepticism is a suspicion of error about facts, and to suspect error about
facts is to share the enterprise of knowledge, in which facts are presupposed and
error is possible. The sceptic thinks himself shrewd, and often is so; his intellect, like the intellect he criticises, may have some inkling of the true hang and
connection of things; he may have pierced to a truth of nature behind current
illusions. Since his criticism may thus be true and his doubt well grounded, they
are certainly assertions; and if he is sincerely a sceptic, they are assertions which
he is ready to maintain stoutly. Scepticism is accordingly a form of belief. Dogma
cannot be abandoned; it can only be revised in view of some more elementary
dogma which it has not yet occurred to the sceptic to doubt; and he may be right
in every point of his criticism, except in fancying that his criticism is radical and
that he is altogether a sceptic.

This vital compulsion to posit and to believe something, even in the act of
doubting, would nevertheless be ignominious, if the beliefs which life and intel-

ligence forced upon me were always false. I should then be obliged to honour the sceptic for his heroic though hopeless effort to eschew belief, and I should despise the dogmatist for his willing subservience to illusion. The sequel will show, I trust, that this is not the case; that intelligence is by nature veridical, and that its ambition to reach the truth is sane and capable of satisfaction, even if each of its efforts actually fails. To convince me of this fact, however, I must first justify my faith in many subsidiary beliefs concerning animal economy and the human mind and the world they flourish in.

That scepticism should intervene in philosophy at all is an accident of human history, due to much unhappy experience of perplexity and error. If all had gone well, assertions would be made spontaneously in dogmatic innocence, and the very notion of a *right* to make them would seem as gratuitous as in fact it is; because all the realms of being lie open to a spirit plastic enough to conceive them, and those that have ears to hear, may hear. Nevertheless, in the confused state of human speculation this embarrassment obtrudes itself automatically, and a philosopher to-day would be ridiculous and negligible who had not strained his dogmas through the utmost rigours of scepticism, and who did not approach every opinion, whatever his own ultimate faith, with the courtesy and smile of the sceptic.

The brute necessity of believing something so long as life lasts does not justify any belief in particular; nor does it assure me that not to live would not, for this very reason, be far safer and saner. To be dead and have no opinions would certainly not be to discover the truth; but if all opinions are necessarily false, it would at least be not to sin against intellectual honour. Let me then push scepticism as far as I logically can, and endeavour to clear my mind of illusion, even at the price of intellectual suicide.

Wayward Scepticism

Scepticism and Animal Faith: Introduction to a System of Philosophy. New York: Charles Scribner's Sons; London: Constable and Co. Ltd., 1923, 11–20. Volume thirteen of the critical edition of *The Works of George Santayana.*

In this selection, Chapter III of Scepticism and Animal Faith, *Santayana pursued his skeptical inquiry and called into doubt religious beliefs, history, science, perception, and memory, until he arrived at "solipsism of the present moment" (ES, 63), in which the skeptic is an unbelieving observer of the immediate show. He thought this position honest though impossible to maintain in the face of human experience. He noticed that past philosophers employed solipsism of the present moment in order "to cast away everything that is not present in their prevalent mood, or in their deepest thought, and to set up this chosen object as the absolute" (ES, 65). Like philosophical heretics who emphasize one aspect of experience to the exclusion of all else, these skeptics preserved some pet notion even as criticism stripped away all other dogmas. These sorts of skepticism do not deny affirmation but intensify it on behalf of some favored notion held beyond criticism.*

Criticism surprises the soul in the arms of convention. Children insensibly accept all the suggestions of sense and language, the only initiative they show being a certain wilfulness in the extension of these notions, a certain impulse towards private superstition. This is soon corrected by education or broken off rudely, like the nails of a tender hand, by hard contact with custom, fact, or derision. Belief then settles down in sullenness and apathy to a narrow circle of vague assumptions, to none of which the mind need have any deep affinity, none of which it need really understand, but which nevertheless it clings to for lack of other footing. The philosophy of the common man is an old wife that gives him no pleasure, yet he cannot live without her, and resents any aspersions that strangers may cast on her character.

Of this homely philosophy the tender cuticle is religious belief; really the least vital and most arbitrary part of human opinion, the outer ring, as it were, of the fortifications of prejudice, but for that very reason the most jealously defended; since it is on being attacked there, at the least defensible point, that rage and alarm at being attacked at all are first aroused in the citadel. People are not naturally sceptics, wondering if a single one of their intellectual habits can be reasonably preserved; they are dogmatists angrily confident of maintaining them all. Integral minds, pupils of a single coherent tradition, regard their religion, whatever it may be, as certain, as sublime, and as the only rational basis of morality and policy. Yet in fact religious belief is terribly precarious, partly because it is arbitrary, so that in the next tribe or in the next century it will wear quite a different form; and partly because, when genuine, it is spontaneous and continually remodelled, like poetry, in the heart that gives it birth. A man of the world soon learns to discredit established religions on account of their variety and absurdity, although he may good-naturedly continue to conform to his own; and a mystic before long begins fervently to condemn current dogmas, on account of his own different inspiration. Without philosophical criticism, therefore, mere experience and good sense suggest that all positive religions are false, or at least (which is enough for my present purpose) that they are all fantastic and insecure.

Closely allied with religious beliefs there are usually legends and histories, dramatic if not miraculous; and a man who knows anything of literature and has observed how histories are written, even in the most enlightened times, needs no satirist to remind him that all histories, in so far as they contain a system, a drama, or a moral, are so much literary fiction, and probably disingenuous. Common sense, however, will still admit that there are recorded facts not to be doubted, as it will admit that there are obvious physical facts; and it is here, when popular philosophy has been reduced to a kind of positivism, that the speculative critic may well step upon the scene.

Criticism, I have said, has no first principle, and its desultory character may be clearly exhibited at this point by asking whether the evidence of science or that of history should be questioned first. I might impugn the belief in physical facts reported by the senses and by natural science, such as the existence of a ring of Saturn, reducing them to appearances, which are facts reported by personal remembrance; and this is actually the choice made by British and German critics of knowledge, who, relying on memory and history, have denied the existence of anything but experience. Yet the opposite procedure would seem more judicious; knowledge of the facts reported by history is mediated by documents which are physical facts; and these documents must first be discovered and believed to have subsisted unknown and to have had a more or less remote origin in time and place, before they can be taken as evidence for any mental events; for if I did not believe that there had been any men in Athens I should not imagine they had had any thoughts. Even personal memory, when it professes to record any distant experience, can recognise and place this experience only by first reconstructing the material scene in which it occurred. Memory records moral events in terms of their physical occasions; and if the latter are merely imaginary, the former must be doubly so, like the thoughts of a personage in a novel. My remembrance of the past is a novel I am constantly recomposing; and it would not be a historical novel, but sheer fiction, if the material events which mark and ballast my career had not their public dates and characters scientifically discoverable.

Romantic solipsism, in which the self making up the universe is a moral person endowed with memory and vanity, is accordingly untenable. Not that it is unthinkable or self-contradictory; because all the complementary objects which might be requisite to give point and body to the idea of oneself might be only ideas and not facts; and a solitary deity imagining a world or remembering his own past constitutes a perfectly conceivable universe. But this imagination would have no truth and this remembrance no control; so that the fond belief of such a deity that he knew his own past would be the most groundless of dogmas; and while by chance the dogma might be true, that deity would have no reason to think it so. At the first touch of criticism he would be obliged to confess that his alleged past was merely a picture now before him, and that he had no reason to suppose that this picture had had any constancy in successive moments, or that he had lived through previous moments at all; nor could any new experience ever lend any colour or corroboration to such a pathological conviction. This is obvious; so that romantic solipsism, although perhaps an interesting state of mind, is not a position capable of defence; and any solipsism which is not a solipsism of the present moment is logically contemptible.

The postulates on which empirical knowledge and inductive science are based—namely, that there has been a past, that it was such as it is now thought to be, that there will be a future and that it must, for some inconceivable reason, resemble the past and obey the same laws—these are all gratuitous dogmas. The sceptic in his honest retreat knows nothing of a future, and has no need of such an unwarrantable idea. He may perhaps have images before him of scenes somehow not in the foreground, with a sense of before and after running through the texture of them; and he may call this background of his sentiency the past; but the relative obscurity and evanescence of these phantoms will not prompt him to suppose that they have retreated to obscurity from the light of day. They will be to him simply what he experiences them as being, denizens of the twilight. It would be a vain fancy to imagine that these ghosts had once been men; they are simply nether gods, native to the Erebus they inhabit. The world present to the sceptic may continue to fade into these opposite abysses, the past and the future; but having renounced all prejudice and checked all customary faith, he will regard both as painted abysses only, like the opposite exits to the country and to the city on the ancient stage. He will see the masked actors (and he will invent a reason) rushing frantically out on one side and in at the other; but he knows that the moment they are out of sight the play is over for them; those outlying regions and those reported events which the messengers narrate so impressively are pure fancy; and there is nothing for him but to sit in his seat and lend his mind to the tragic illusion.

The solipsist thus becomes an incredulous spectator of his own romance, thinks his own adventures fictions, and accepts a solipsism of the present moment. This is an honest position, and certain attempts to refute it as self-contradictory are based on a misunderstanding. For example, it is irrelevant to urge that the present moment cannot comprise the whole of existence because the phrase "a present moment" implies a chain of moments; or that the mind that calls any moment the present moment virtually transcends it and posits a past and a future beyond it. These arguments confuse the convictions of the solipsist with those of a spectator describing him from outside. The sceptic is not committed to the implications of other men's language; nor can he be convicted out of his own mouth by the names he is obliged to bestow on the details of his momentary vision. There may be long vistas in it; there may be many figures of men and beasts, many legends and apocalypses depicted on his canvas; there may even be a shadowy frame about it, or the suggestion of a gigantic ghostly something on the hither side of it which he may call himself. All this wealth of objects is not inconsistent with solipsism, although the implication of the conventional terms in which those objects are described may render it difficult for the solipsist always to remember his solitude. Yet when he reflects, he perceives it; and all his heroic efforts are concentrated on *not* asserting and *not* implying anything, but simply noticing what he finds. Scepticism is not concerned to abolish ideas; it can relish the variety and order of a pictured world, or of any number of them in succession, without any of the qualms and exclusions proper to dogmatism. Its case is simply not to credit these ideas, not to posit any of these fancied worlds, nor this ghostly mind imagined as viewing them. The attitude of the sceptic is not inconsistent; it is merely difficult, because it is hard for the greedy intellect to keep its cake without eating it. Very voracious dogmatists like Spinoza even assert that it is impossible, but the impossibility is only psychological, and due to their voracity; they no doubt speak truly for themselves when they say that the idea of a horse, if not contradicted by some other idea, *is* a belief that the horse exists; but this would not be the case if they felt no impulse to ride that imagined horse, or to get out of its way. Ideas become beliefs only when by precipitating tendencies to action they persuade me that they are signs of things; and these things are not those ideas simply hypostatised, but are believed to be compacted of many parts, and full of ambushed powers, entirely absent from the ideas. The belief is imposed on me surreptitiously by a latent mechanical reaction of my body on the object producing the idea; it is by no means implied in any qualities obvious in that idea. Such a latent reaction, being mechanical, can hardly be avoided, but it may be discounted in reflection, if a man has experience and the poise of a philosopher; and scepticism is not the less honourable for being difficult, when it is inspired by a firm determination to probe this confused and terrible apparition of life to the bottom.

So far is solipsism of the present moment from being self-contradictory that it might, under other circumstances, be the normal and invincible attitude of the spirit; and I suspect it may be that of many animals. The difficulties I find in maintaining it consistently come from the social and laborious character of human life. A creature whose whole existence was passed under a hard shell, or was spent in a free flight, might find nothing paradoxical or acrobatic in solipsism; nor would he feel the anguish which men feel in doubt, because doubt leaves them defenceless and undecided in the presence of on-coming events. A creature whose actions were pre-determined might have a clearer mind. He might keenly enjoy the momentary scene, never conceiving himself as a separate body or as anything but the unity of that scene, nor his enjoyment as anything but its beauty: nor would he harbour the least suspicion that it would change or perish, nor any objection to its doing so if it chose. Solipsism would then be selflessness and scepticism simplicity. They would not be open to disruption from within. The ephemeral insect would accept the evidence of his ephemeral object, whatever quality this might chance to have; he would not suppose, as Descartes did, that in thinking anything his own existence was involved. Being new-born himself, with only this one innate (and also experimental) idea, he would bring to his single experience no extraneous habits of interpretation or inference; and he would not be troubled by doubts, because he would believe nothing.

For men, however, who are long-lived and teachable animals, solipsism of the present moment is a violent pose, permitted only to the young philosopher, in his first intellectual despair; and even he often cheats himself when he thinks he assumes it, and professing to stand on his head really, like a clumsy acrobat, rests on his hands also. The very terms "solipsism" and "present moment" betray this impurity. An actual intuition, which by hypothesis is fresh, absolute, and not to be repeated, is called and is perhaps conceived as an *ipse,* a self-same man. But identity (as I shall have occasion to observe in discussing identity in essences) implies two moments, two instances, or two intuitions, between which it obtains. Similarly, a "present moment" suggests other moments, and an adventitious limitation either in duration or in scope; but the solipsist and his world (which are not distinguishable) have by hypothesis no environment whatsoever, and nothing limits them save the fact that there is nothing more. These irrelevances and side glances are imported into the mind of the sceptic because in fact he is retreating into solipsism from a far more ambitious philosophy. A thought naturally momentary would be immune from them.

A perfect solipsist, therefore, hardly is found amongst men; but some men are zealous in bringing their criticism down to solipsism of the present moment just because this attitude enables them to cast away everything that is not present in their prevalent mood, or in their deepest thought, and to set up this chosen object as the absolute. Such a compensatory dogma is itself not critical; but criticism may help to raise it to a specious eminence by lopping off everything else. What remains will be different in different persons: some say it is Brahma, some that it is Pure Being, some that it is the Idea or Law of the moral world. Each of these absolutes is the sacred residuum which the temperament of different philosophers or of different nations clings to, and will not criticise, and in each case it is contrasted with the world in which the vulgar believe, as something deeper, simpler, and more real. Perhaps when solipsism of the present moment is reached by a philosopher trained in abstraction and inclined to ecstasy, his experience, at this depth of concentration, will be that of an extreme tension which is also liberty, an emptiness which is intensest light; and his denial of all natural facts and events, which he will call illusions, will culminate in the fervent assertion that all is One, and that One is Brahma, or the breath of life. On the other hand, a scientific observer and reasoner, who has pried into substance, and has learned that all the aspects of nature are relative and variable, may still not deny the existence of matter in every object; and this element of mere intensity, drawn from the sense of mere actuality in himself, may lead him to assert that pure Being is, and everything else is not. Finally, a secondary mind fed on books may drop the natural emphasis which objects of sense have for the living animal, and may retain, as the sole filling of its present moment, nothing but the sciences. The philosopher will then balance his denial of material facts by asserting the absolute reality of his knowledge of them. This reality, however, will extend no farther than his information, as some intensest moment of recollection may gather it together; and his personal idea of the world, so composed and so limited, will seem to him the sole existence. His universe will be the after-image of his learning.

We may notice that in these three instances scepticism has not suspended affirmation but has rather intensified it, pouring it all on the devoted head of one chosen object. There is a tireless and deafening vehemence about these sceptical prophets; it betrays the poor old human Psyche labouring desperately within them in the shipwreck of her native hopes, and refusing to die. Her sacrifice, she believes, will be her salvation, and she passionately identifies what remains to her with all she has lost and by an audacious falsehood persuades herself she has lost nothing. Thus the temper of these sceptics is not at all sceptical. They take their revenge on the world, which eluded them when they tried to prove its existence, by asserting the existence of the remnant which they have still by them, insisting that this, and this only, is the true and perfect world, and a much better one than that false world in which the heathen trust. Such infatuation in the solipsist, however, is not inevitable; no such exorbitant credit need be given to the object, perhaps a miserable one, which still fills the sceptical mind, and a more dispassionate scepticism, while contemplating that object, may disallow it.

Ultimate Scepticism

Scepticism and Animal Faith: Introduction to a System of Philosophy. New York: Charles Scribner's Sons; London: Constable and Co. Ltd., 1923, 33–41. Volume thirteen of the critical edition of *The Works of George Santayana.*

In this selection, Chapter VI of Scepticism and Animal Faith, *Santayana pursued skepticism beyond the conclusions of skeptics who imported hidden presumptions into their systems. In order to understand what remains for intuition after a more thorough-going skepticism, he distinguished reality and existence. The immediate datum of the present moment is real, thought Santayana, but it cannot exist. No datum can exist because existence entails external relations and change; but the datum of intuition has only internal relations and a fixed character. Hence, ultimate skepticism leaves untouched the reality of the immediate datum but denies its existence. Any sense of existence comes from an aspect of experience other than intuition of the datum. Ultimate skepticism, then, doubts all existence, but any skeptical dogma denying existence could not attain the status of fact since that dogma would necessarily become an existing fact. Though it appears epistemologically inadequate, ultimate skepticism can be a helpful spiritual discipline.*

Why should the mystic, in proportion as he dismisses the miscellany of experience as so much illusion, feel that he becomes one with reality and attains to absolute existence? I think that the same survival of vulgar presumptions which leads the romantic solipsist to retain his belief in his personal history and destiny, leads the mystic to retain, and fondly to embrace, the feeling of existence. His speculation is indeed inspired by the love of security: his grand objection to the natural world, and to mortal life, is that they are deceptive, that they cheat the soul that loves them, and prove to be illusions: the assumption apparently being that reality must be permanent, and that he who has hold on reality is safe for ever. In this the mystic, who so hates illusions, is the victim of an illusion himself: for the reality he has hold of is but the burden of a single moment, which in its solipsism thinks itself absolute. What is reality? As I should like to use the term, reality is being of any sort. If it means character or essence, illusions have it as much as substance, and more richly. If it means substance, then sceptical concentration upon inner experience, or ecstatic abstraction, seems to me the last place in which we should look for it. The immediate and the visionary are at the opposite pole from substance; they are on the surface or, if you like, at the top; whereas substance if it is anywhere is at the bottom. The realm of immediate illusion is as real as any other, and very attractive; many would wish it to be the only reality, and hate substance; but if substance exists (which I am not yet ready to assert) they have no reason to hate it, since it is the basis of those immediate feelings which fill them with satisfaction. Finally, if reality means existence, certainly the mystic and his meditation may exist, but not more truly than any other natural fact; and what would exist in them would be a pulse of animal being, kindling that momentary ecstasy, as animal life at certain intensities is wont to do. The theme of that meditation, its visionary object, need not exist at all; it may be incapable of existing if it is essentially timeless and dialectical. The animal mind treats its data as facts, or as signs of facts, but the animal mind is full of the rashest presumptions, positing time, change, a particular station in the midst of events yielding a particular perspective of those events, and the flux of all nature pre-cipitating that experience at that place. None of these posited objects is a datum in which a sceptic could rest. Indeed, existence or fact, in the sense which I give to these words, cannot be a datum at all, because existence involves external rela-tions and actual (not merely specious) flux: whereas, however complex a datum may be, with no matter what perspectives opening within it, it must be embraced in a single stroke of apperception, and nothing outside it can belong to it at all. The datum is a pure image; it is essentially illusory and unsubstantial, however thunderous its sound or keen its edge, or however normal and significant its pres-ence may be. When the mystic asserts enthusiastically the existence of his imme-diate, ideal, unutterable object, Absolute Being, he is peculiarly unfortunate in his faith: it would be impossible to choose an image less relevant to the agencies that actually bring that image before him. The burden and glow of existence which he is conscious of come entirely from himself; his object is eminently empty, impo-tent, non-existent; but the heat and labour of his own soul suffuse that emptiness with light, and the very hum of change within him, accelerated almost beyond endurance and quite beyond discrimination, sounds that piercing note.

The last step in scepticism is now before me. It will lead me to deny exis-tence to any datum, whatever it may be; and as the datum, by hypothesis, is the whole of what solicits my attention at any moment, I shall deny the existence of everything, and abolish that category of thought altogether. If I could not do this, I should be a tyro in scepticism. Belief in the existence of anything, includ-ing myself, is something radically incapable of proof, and resting, like all belief, on some irrational persuasion or prompting of life. Certainly, as a matter of fact, when I deny existence I exist; but doubtless many of the other facts I have been denying, because I found no evidence for them, were true also. To bring me evi-dence of their existence is no duty imposed on facts, nor a habit of theirs: I must employ private detectives. The point is, in this task of criticism, to discard every belief that is a belief merely; and the belief in existence, in the nature of the case, can be a belief only. The datum is an idea, a description; I may contemplate it without belief; but when I assert that such a thing exists I am hypostatising this datum, placing it in presumptive relations which are not internal to it, and wor-shipping it as an idol or thing. Neither its existence nor mine nor that of my belief can be given in any datum. These things are incidents involved in that order of nature which I have thrown over; they are no part of what remains before me.

Assurance of existence expresses animal watchfulness: it posits, within me and round me, hidden and imminent events. The sceptic can easily cast a doubt on the remoter objects of this belief; and nothing but a certain obduracy and want of agility prevents him from doubting present existence itself. For what could present existence mean, if the imminent events for which animal sense is watching failed altogether, failed at the very roots, so to speak, of the tree of intuition, and left nothing but its branches flowering *in vacuo?* Expectation is admittedly the most hazardous of beliefs: yet what is watchfulness but expectation? Memory is notoriously full of illusion; yet what would experience of the present be if the veracity of primary memory were denied, and if I no longer believed that anything had just happened, or that I had ever been in the state from which I suppose myself to have passed into this my present condition?

It will not do for the sceptic to take refuge in the confused notion that expectation *possesses* the future, or memory the past. As a matter of fact, expectation is like hunger; it opens its mouth, and something probably drops into it, more or less, very often, the sort of thing it expected; but sometimes a surprise comes, and sometimes nothing. Life involves expectation, but does not prevent death: and expectation is never so thoroughly stultified as when it is not undeceived, but cancelled. The open mouth does not then so much as close upon nothing. It is buried open. Nor is memory in a better case. As the whole world might collapse and cease at any moment, nullifying all expectation, so it might at any moment have sprung out of nothing: for it is thoroughly contingent, and might have begun to-day, with this degree of complexity and illusive memory, as well as long ago, with whatever energy or momentum it was first endowed with. The backward perspective of time is perhaps really an inverted expectation; but for the momentum of life forward, we might not be able to space the elements active in the present so as to assign to them a longer or a shorter history; for we should not attempt to discriminate amongst these elements such as we could still count on in the immediate future, and such as we might safely ignore: so that our conception of the past implies, perhaps, a distinction between the living and the dead. This distinction is itself practical, and looks to the future. In the absolute present all is specious; and to pure intuition the living are as ghostly as the dead, and the dead as present as the living.

In the sense of existence there is accordingly something more than the obvious character of that which is alleged to exist. What is this complement? It cannot be a feature in the datum, since the datum by definition is the whole of what is found. Nor can it be, in my sense at least of the word existence, the intrinsic constitution or specific being of this object, since existence comports external relations, variable, contingent, and not discoverable in a given being when taken alone: for there is nothing that may not lose its existence, or the existence of which might not be conceivably denied. The complement added to the datum when it is alleged to exist seems, then, to be added by *me;* it is the finding, the occurrence, the assault, the impact of that being here and now; it is the experience of it. But what can experience be, if I take away from it the whole of what is experienced? And what meaning can I give to such words as impact, assault, occurrence, or finding, when I have banished and denied my body, my past, my residual present being, and everything except the datum which I find? The sense of existence evidently belongs to the intoxication, to the *Rausch,* of existence itself; it is the strain of life within me, prior to all intuition, that in its precipitation and terror, passing as it continually must from one untenable condition to another, stretches my attention absurdly over what is not given, over the lost and the unattained, the before and after which are wrapped in darkness, and confuses my breathless apprehension of the clear presence of all I can ever truly behold.

Indeed, so much am I a creature of movement, and of the ceaseless metabolism of matter, that I should never catch even these glimpses of the light, if there were not rhythms, pauses, repetitions, and nodes in my physical progress, to absorb and reflect it here and there: as the traveller, hurried in a cloud of smoke and dust through tunnel after tunnel in the Italian Riviera, catches and loses momentary visions of blue sea and sky, which he would like to arrest, but cannot; yet if he had not been rushed and whistled along these particular tunnels, even those snatches, in the form in which they come to him, would have been denied him. So it is the rush of life that, at its open moments, floods me with intuitions, partial and confused, but still revelations; the landscape is wrapped in the smoke of my little engine, and turned into a tantalising incident of my hot journey. What appears (which is an ideal object and not an event) is thus confused with the event of its appearance; the picture is identified with the kindling or distraction of my attention falling by chance upon it; and the strain of my material existence, battling with material accidents, turns the ideal object too into a temporal fact, and makes it seem substantial. But this fugitive existence which I egotistically attach to it, as if its fate was that of my glimpses of it, is no part of its true being, as even my intuition discerns it; it is a practical dignity or potency attributed to it by the irrelevant momentum of my animal life. Animals, being by nature hounded and hungry creatures, spy out and take alarm at any datum of sense or fancy, supposing that there is something substantial there, something that will count and work in the world. The notion of a moving world is brought implicitly with them; they fetch it out of the depths of their vegetating psyche, which is a small dark cosmos, silently revolving within. By being noticed, and treated as a signal for I know not what material opportunity or danger, the given image is taken up into the business world, and puts on the garment of existence. Remove this frame, strip off all suggestion of a time when this image was not yet present, or a time when it shall be past, and the very notion of existence is removed. The datum ceases to be an appearance, in the proper and pregnant sense of this word, since it ceases to imply any substance that appears or any mind to which it appears. It is an appearance only in the sense that its nature is wholly manifest, that it is a specific being, which may be mentioned, thought of, seen, or defined, if any one has the wit to do so. But its own nature says nothing of any hidden circumstances that shall bring it to light, or any adventitious mind that shall discover it. It lies simply in its own category. If a colour, it is just this colour; if a pain, just this pain. Its appearance is not an event: its presence is not an experience; for there is no surrounding world in which it can arise, and no watchful spirit to appropriate it. The sceptic has here withdrawn into the intuition of a surface form, without roots, without origin or environment, without a seat or a locus; a little universe, an immaterial absolute theme, rejoicing merely in its own quality. This theme, being out of all adventitious relations and not in the least threatened with not being the theme it is, has not the contingency nor the fortunes proper to an existence; it is simply that which it inherently, logically, and unchangeably is.

Existence, then, not being included in any immediate datum, is a fact always open to doubt. I call it a fact notwithstanding, because in talking about the sceptic I am positing his existence. If he has any intuition, however little the theme of that intuition may have to do with any actual world, certainly I who think of his intuition, or he himself thinking of it afterwards, see that this intuition of his must have been an event, and his existence at that time a fact; but like all facts and events, this one can be known only by an affirmation which posits it, which may be suspended or reversed, and which is subject to error. Hence all this business of intuition may perfectly well be doubted by the sceptic: the existence of his own doubt (however confidently I may assert it for him) is not given to him then: all that is given is some ambiguity or contradiction in images; and if afterwards he is sure that he has doubted, the sole cogent evidence which that fact can claim lies in the psychological impossibility that, so long as he believes he has doubted, he should not believe it. But he may be wrong in harbouring this belief, and he may rescind it. For all an ultimate scepticism can see, therefore, there may be no facts at all, and perhaps nothing has ever existed.

Scepticism may thus be carried to the point of denying change and memory, and the reality of all facts. Such a sceptical dogma would certainly be false, because this dogma itself would have to be entertained, and that event would be a fact and an existence: and the sceptic in framing that dogma discourses, vacillates, and lives in the act of contrasting one assertion with another—all of which is to exist with a vengeance. Yet this false dogma that nothing exists is tenable intuitively and, while it prevails, is irrefutable. There are certain motives (to be discussed later) which render ultimate scepticism precious to a spiritual mind, as a sanctuary from grosser illusions. For the wayward sceptic, who regards it as no truer than any other view, it also has some utility: it accustoms him to discard the dogma which an introspective critic might be tempted to think self-evident, namely, that he himself lives and thinks. That he does so is true; but to establish that truth he must appeal to animal faith. If he is too proud for that, and simply stares at the datum, the last thing he will see is himself.

Nothing Given Exists

Scepticism and Animal Faith: Introduction to a System of Philosophy. New York: Charles Scribner's Sons; London: Constable and Co. Ltd., 1923, 42–48. Volume thirteen of the critical edition of *The Works of George Santayana.*

Acknowledging that skepticism is doubt about existence, Santayana in this selection, Chapter VII of Scepticism and Animal Faith, *examined in more detail the concept of existence and its denial. Existence is, wrote Santayana, "such being as is in flux, determined by external relations, and jostled by irrelevant events" (ES, 72). The good skeptic would see that the immediate datum is not existence but may consider whether the flux of appearances constitutes existence. But then all the doubts about existence that first prompted inquiry and skepticism resurface: how many appearances exist? What kind exist? In what order do they appear? Hence, existence is hardly immediate and remains the same problem it was before skeptical inquiry began. The immediate datum taken in itself and without reference to anything further is unproblematical; problems arise only when referring an appearance to something supposed to exist beyond it. Santayana deployed a* reductio ad absurdum *argument to dismiss the idea that presence to intuition is sufficient to establish existence. He then proposed to use the word "existence" only for events or facts occurring in nature and not images or ideas. So the act of intuiting an idea, but not the intuited idea, is an existent fact.*

Scepticism is not sleep, and in casting a doubt on any belief, or proving the absurdity of any idea, the sceptic is by no means losing his sense of what is proposed. He is merely doubting or denying the *existence* of any such object. In scepticism, therefore, everything turns on the meaning of the word existence, and it will be worth while to stop a moment here to consider it further.

I have already indicated roughly how I am using the word existence, namely, to designate such being as is in flux, determined by external relations, and jostled by irrelevant events. Of course this is no definition. The term existence is only a name. In using it I am merely pointing out to the reader, as if by a gesture, what this word designates in my habits of speech, as if in saying Cæsar I pointed to my dog, lest some one should suppose I meant the Roman emperor. The Roman emperor, the dog, and the sound Cæsar are all indefinable; but they might be described more particularly, by using other indicative and indefinable names, to mark their characteristics or the events in which they figured. So the whole realm of being which I point to when I say existence might be described more fully; the description of it would be physics or perhaps psychology; but the exploration of that realm, which is open only to animal faith, would not concern the sceptic.

The sceptic turns from such indefinite confusing objects to the immediate, to the datum; and perhaps for a moment he may fancy he has found true existence there; but if he is a good sceptic he will soon be undeceived. Certainly in the immediate he will find freedom from the struggle of assertion and counter-assertion: no report there, no hypothesis, no ghostly reduplication of the obvious, no ghostly imminence of the not-given. Is not the obvious, he might ask, the truly existent? Yet the obvious is only the apparent; and this in both senses of this ambiguous word. The datum is apparent in the sense of being self-evident and luminous; and it is apparent also in the sense of merely appearing and being unsubstantial. In this latter sense, the apparent threatens to become the non-existent. Does not the existent profess to be more than apparent: to be not so much the self-evident as that which I am seeking evidence for, in the sense of testimony? Is not the existent, then (which from its own point of view, or physically, is more than the apparent), cognitively and from my point of view less than the apparent? Does it not need witnesses to bear testimony to its being? And what can recommend those witnesses to me except their intrinsic eloquence? I shall prove no sceptic if I do not immediately transfer all my trust from the existence reported to the appearance reporting it, and substitute the evidence of my senses for all lawyer's evidence. I shall forget the murders and embroglios talked about in the court, and gaze at the judge in his scarlet and ermine, with the pale features of an old fox under his grey wig; at the jury in their stolidity; at the witness stammering; at the counsel, officially insolent, not thinking of what he is saying mechanically, but whispering something that really interests him in an aside, almost yawning, and looking at the clock to see if it is time for luncheon; and at the flood of hazy light falling aslant on the whole scene from the high windows. Is not the floating picture, in my waking trance, the actual reality, and the whole world of existence and business but a perpetual fable, which this trance sustains?

The theory that the universe is nothing but a flux of appearances is plausible to the sceptic; he thinks he is not believing much in believing it. Yet the residuum of dogma is very remarkable in this view; and the question at once will assail him how many appearances he shall assert to exist, of what sort, and in what order, if in any, he shall assert them to arise; and the various hypotheses that may be suggested concerning the character and distribution of appearances will become fresh data in his thought; and he will find it impossible to decide whether any such appearances, beyond the one now passing before him, are ever actual, or whether any of the suggested systems of appearances actually exists. Thus existence will loom again before him, as something problematical, at a distance from that immediacy into which he thought he had fled.

Existence thus seems to re-establish itself in the very world of appearances, so soon as these are regarded as facts and events occurring side by side or one after the other. In each datum taken separately there would be no occasion to speak of existence. It would be an obvious appearance; whatever appeared there would be simply and wholly apparent, and the fact that it appeared (which would be the only fact involved) would not appear in it at all. This fact, the existence of the intuition, would not be asserted until the appearance ceased to be actual, and was viewed from the outside, as something that presumably had occurred, or would occur, or was occurring elsewhere. In such an external view there might be truth or error; not so in each appearance taken in itself, because in itself and as a whole each is a pure appearance and bears witness to nothing further. Nevertheless, when some term within this given appearance comes to be regarded as a sign of some other appearance not now given, the question is pertinent whether that other appearance exists or not. Thus existence and non-existence seem to be relevant to appearances in so far as they are problematical and posited from outside, not in so far as they are certain and given.

Hence an important conclusion which at first seems paradoxical but which reflection will support; namely, that the notion that the datum exists is un-meaning, and if insisted upon is false. That which exists is the fact that the datum is given at that particular moment and crisis in the universe; the intuition, not the datum, is the fact which occurs; and this fact, if known at all, must be asserted at some other moment by an adventurous belief which may be true or false. That which is certain and given, on the contrary, is something of which existence cannot be predicated, and which, until it is used as a description of something else, cannot be either false or true.

I see here how halting is the scepticism of those modern philosophers who have supposed that to exist is to be an idea in the mind, or an object of consciousness, or a fact of experience, if by these phrases no more is meant than to be a datum of intuition. If there is any existence at all, presence to consciousness is neither necessary nor sufficient to render it an existence. Imagine a novelist whose entire life was spent in conceiving a novel, or a deity whose only function was to think a world. That world would not exist, any more than the novel would comprise the feelings and actions of existing persons. If that novelist, in the heat of invention, believed his personages real, he would be deceived: and so would that deity if he supposed his world to exist merely because he thought of it. Before the creation could be actual, or the novel historical, it would have to be enacted elsewhere than in the mind of its author. And if it was so enacted, it would evidently not be requisite to its existence that any imaginative person, falsely conceiving himself to be its author, should form an image of it in his mind. If he did so, that remarkable clairvoyance would be a fact requiring explanation; but it would be an added harmony in the world, not the ground of its existence.

If for the sake of argument I accept the notion that presence to intuition is existence, I may easily disprove it by a *reductio ad absurdum*. If nothing not given in intuition can exist, then all those beliefs in existing facts beyond my intuition, by which thought is diversified when it is intelligent, would be necessarily false, and all intelligence would be illusion. This implication might be welcome to me, if I wished not to entertain any opinions which might conceivably be wrong. But the next implication is more disconcerting, namely, that the intuitions in which such illusion appears can have no existence themselves: for being instances of intuition they could not be data for any intuition. At one moment I may *believe* that there are or have been or will be other moments; but evidently they would not be *other* moments, if they were data to me now, and nothing more. If presence to intuition were necessary to existence, intuition itself would not exist; that is, no other intuition would be right in positing it; and as this absence of transcendence would be mutual, nothing would exist at all. And yet, since presence to intuition would be sufficient for existence, everything mentionable would exist without question, the non-existent could never be thought of, to deny anything (if I knew what I was denying) would be impossible, and there would be no such thing as fancy, hallucination, illusion, or error.

I think it is evidently necessary to revise a vocabulary which lends itself to such equivocation, and if I keep the words existence and intuition at all, to lend them meanings which can apply to something possible and credible. I therefore propose to use the word existence (in a way consonant, on the whole, with ordinary usage) to designate not data of intuition but facts or events believed to occur in nature. These facts or events will include, *first,* intuitions themselves, or instances of consciousness, like pains and pleasures and all remembered experiences and mental discourse; and *second,* physical things and events, having a transcendent relation to the data of intuition which, in belief, may be used as signs for them; the same transcendent relation which objects of desire have to desire, or objects of pursuit to pursuit; for example, such a relation as the fact of my birth (which I cannot even remember) has to my present persuasion that I was once born, or the event of my death (which I conceive only abstractly) to my present expectation of some day dying. If an angel visits me, I may intelligibly debate the question whether he exists or not. On the one hand, I may affirm that he came in through the door, that is, that he existed before I saw him; and I may continue in perception, memory, theory, and expectation to assert that he was a fact of nature: in that case I believe in his existence. On the other hand, I may suspect that he was only an event in me, called a dream; an event not at all included in the angel as I saw him, nor at all like an angel in the conditions of its existence; and in this case I disbelieve in my vision: for visiting angels cannot honestly be said to exist if I entertain them only in idea.

Existences, then, from the point of view of knowledge, are facts or events affirmed, not images seen or topics merely entertained. Existence is accordingly not only doubtful to the sceptic, but odious to the logician. To him it seems a truly monstrous excrescence and superfluity in being, since anything existent is more than the description of it, having suffered an unintelligible emphasis or materialisation to fall upon it, which is logically inane and morally comic. At the same time, existence suffers from defect of being and obscuration; any ideal nature, such as might be exhaustively given in intuition, when it is materialised loses the intangibility and eternity proper to it in its own sphere; so that existence doubly injures the forms of being it embodies, by ravishing them first and betraying them afterwards.

Such is existence as approached by belief and affirmed in animal experience; but I shall find in the sequel that considered physically, as it is unrolled amidst the other realms of being, existence is a conjunction of natures in adventitious and variable relations. According to this definition, it is evident that existence can never be given in intuition; since no matter how complex a datum may be, and no matter how many specious changes it may picture, its specious order and unity are just what they are: they can neither suffer mutation nor acquire new relations: which is another way of saying that they cannot exist. If this whole evolving world were merely given in idea, and were not an external object posited in belief and in action, it could not exist nor evolve. In order to exist it must enact itself ignorantly and successively, and carry down all ideas of it in its own current.

The Discovery of Essence

Scepticism and Animal Faith: Introduction to a System of Philosophy. New York: Charles Scribner's Sons; London: Constable and Co. Ltd., 1923, 67–76. Volume thirteen of the critical edition of *The Works of George Santayana.*

Santayana undertook skeptical inquiry not to find epistemological certainty, but rather to free his mind from the prejudices, expectations, and meanings assigned to immediate appearances. In this selection, Chapter IX of Scepticism and Animal Faith, *Santayana discussed how "[t]he sceptic . . . finds himself in the presence of more luminous and less equivocal objects than does the working and believing mind; only these objects are without meaning, they are only what they are obviously, all surface" (ES, 78). In other words, skepticism may introduce one to essences, already familiar appearances untethered from any beliefs in existence. Since skepticism was prompted originally by a fear of error or illusion, Santayana considered responses to that fear: first, death, which erases doubt but brings no understanding; second, correction of error and substitution of belief, which can satisfy animal demands but is speculatively unsatisfying due to there being no criterion of truth; and third, enjoying the essence without being taken in by any illusory claim to existence. This third response affords a broader acquaintance with form and the infinite realm of essences, the only thing that makes life interesting for a creature endowed with consciousness.*

The loss of faith, as I have already observed, has no tendency to banish ideas; on the contrary, since doubt arises on reflection, it tends to keep the imagination on the stretch, and lends to the whole spectacle of things a certain immediacy, suavity, and humour. All that is sordid or tragic falls away, and everything acquires a lyric purity, as if the die had not yet been cast and the ominous choice of creation had not been made. Often the richest philosophies are the most sceptical; the mind is not then tethered in its home paddock, but ranges at will over the wilderness of being. The Indians, who deny the existence of the world, have a keen sense for its infinity and its variegated colours; they play with the monstrous and miraculous in the grand manner, as in the *Arabian Nights.* No critic has had a sharper eye for the outlines of ideas than Hume, who found it impossible seriously to believe that they revealed anything. In the critic, as in the painter, suspension of belief and of practical understanding is favourable to vision; the arrested eye renders every image limpid and unequivocal. And this is not merely an effect of physiological compensation, in that perhaps the nervous energy withdrawn from preparations for action is allowed to intensify the process of mere sensation. There ensues a logical clarification as well; because so long as belief, interpretation, and significance entered in, the object in hand was ambiguous; in seeking the fact the mind overlooked or confused the datum. Yet each element in this eager investigation–including its very eagerness–is precisely what it is; and if I renounce for the moment all transitive intelligence, and give to each of these elements its due definition, I shall have a much richer as well as clearer collection of terms and relations before me, than when I was clumsily attempting to make up m mind. Living beings dwell in their expectations rather than in their senses. If they are ever to *see* what they see, they must first in a manner stop living; they must suspend the will, as Schopenhauer put it; they must photograph the idea that is flying past, veiled in its very swiftness. This swiftness is not its own fault, but that of my haste and inattention; my hold is loose on it, as in a dream; or else perhaps those veils and that swiftness are the truth of the picture; and it is they that the true artist should be concerned to catch and to eternalise, restoring to all that the practical intellect calls vague its own specious definition. Nothing is vague in itself, or other than just what it is. Symbols are vague only in respect to their signification, when this remains ambiguous.

It is accordingly an inapt criticism often passed upon Berkeley and Hume that they overlooked vagueness in ideas, although almost every human idea is scandalously vague. No, their intuition of ideas, at least initially, was quite direct and honest. The ambiguity they overlooked lay in the relation of ideas to physical things, which they wished to reduce to groups or series of these pellucid ideas—a chimerical physics. Had they abstained altogether from identifying ideas with objects of natural knowledge (which are events and facts), and from trying to construct material things out of optical and tactile images, they might have much enriched the philosophy of specious reality, and discerned the innocent realm of ideas as directly as Plato did, but more accurately. In this they need not have confused or undermined faith in natural things. Perception *is* faith; more perception may extend this faith or reform it, but can never recant it except by sophistry. These virgin philosophers were like the cubists or futurists in the painting of to-day. They might have brought to light curious and neglected forms of direct intuition. They could not justly have been charged with absurdity for seeing what they actually saw. But they lapse into absurdity, and that irremediably, if they pretend to be the first and only masters of anatomy and topography.

Far from being vague or abstract the obvious ideas remaining to a complete sceptic may prove too absorbing, too multitudinous, or too sweet. A moral reprobation of them is no less intelligible than is the scientific criticism which rejects them as illusions and as no constituents of the existing world. Conscience no less than business may blame the sceptic for a sort of luxurious idleness; he may call himself a lotus-eater, may heave a sigh of fatigue at doing nothing, and may even feel a touch of the vertigo and wish to close the eyes on all these images that entertain him to no purpose. But scepticism is an exercise, not a life; it is a discipline fit to purify the mind of prejudice and render it all the more apt, when the time comes, to believe and to act wisely; and meantime the pure sceptic need take no offence at the multiplicity of images that crowd upon him, if he is scrupulous not to trust them and to assert nothing at their prompting. Scepticism is the chastity of the intellect, and it is shameful to surrender it too soon or to the first comer: there is nobility in preserving it coolly and proudly through a long youth, until at last, in the ripeness of instinct and discretion, it can be safely exchanged for fidelity and happiness. But the philosopher, when he is speculative only, is a sort of perpetual celibate; he is bent on not being betrayed, rather than on being annexed or inspired; and although if he is at all wise he must see that the true marriage of the mind is with nature and science and the practical arts, yet in his special theoretic vocation, it will be a boon to him to view all experience simply, in the precision and distinctness which all its parts acquire when not referred to any substance which they might present confusedly, nor to any hypothesis or action which they might suggest.

The sceptic, then, as a consequence of carrying his scepticism to the greatest lengths, finds himself in the presence of more luminous and less equivocal objects than does the working and believing mind; only these objects are without meaning, they are only what they are obviously, all surface. They show him everything thinkable with the greatest clearness and force; but he can no longer imagine that he sees in these objects anything save their instant presence and their face-value. Scepticism therefore suspends all knowledge worthy of the name, all that transitive and presumptive knowledge of facts which is a form of belief; and instead it bestows intuition of ideas, contemplative, æsthetic, dialectical, arbitrary. But whereas transitive knowledge, though important if true, may always be challenged, intuition, on the contrary, which neither has nor professes to have any ulterior object or truth, runs no risks of error, because it claims no jurisdiction over anything alien or eventual.

In this lucidity and calmness of intuition there is something preternatural. Imagine a child accustomed to see clothes only on living persons and hardly distinguishing them from the magical strong bodies that agitate them, and suddenly carry this child into a costumer's shop, where he will see all sorts of garments hung in rows upon manikins, with hollow breasts all of visible wire, and little wooden nobs instead of heads: he might be seriously shocked or even frightened. How should it be possible for clothes standing up like this not to be people? Such abstractions, he might say to himself, are metaphysically impossible. Either these figures must be secretly alive and ready, when he least expects it, to begin to dance, or else they are not real at all, and he can only fancy that he sees them. Just as the spectacle of all these gaunt clothes without bodies might make the child cry, so later might the whole spectacle of nature, if ever he became a sceptic. The little word *is* has its tragedies; it marries and identifies different things with the greatest innocence; and yet no two are ever identical, and if therein lies the charm of wedding them and calling them one, therein too lies the danger. Whenever I use the word *is*, except in sheer tautology, I deeply misuse it; and when I discover my error, the world seems to fall asunder and the members of my family no longer know one another. Existence is the strong body and familiar motion which the young mind expects to find in every dummy. The oldest of us are sometimes no less recalcitrant to the spectacle of the garments of existence—which is all we ever saw of it—when the existence is taken away. Yet it is to these actual and familiar, but now disembowelled objects, that scepticism introduces us, as if to a strange world; a vast costumer's gallery of ideas where all sorts of patterns and models are on exhibition, without bodies to wear them, and where no human habits of motion distract the eye from the curious cut and precise embroideries of every article. This display, so complete in its spectacular reality, not a button nor a feather wanting or unobserved, is not the living crowd that it ought to be, but a mockery of it, like the palace of the Sleeping Beauty. To my conventional mind, clothes without bodies are no less improper than bodies without clothes; yet the conjunction of these things is but human. All nature runs about naked, and quite happy; and I am not so remote from nature as not to revert on occasion to that nakedness—which is unconsciousness—with profound relief. But ideas without things and apparel without wearers seem to me a stranger condition; I think the garments were made to fit the limbs, and should collapse without them. Yet, like the fig leaves of Eden, they are not garments essentially. They become such by accident, when one or another of them is appropriated by the providential buyer—not necessarily human—whose instinct may choose it; or else it is perfectly content to miss its chance, and to lie stacked for ever among its motley neighbours in this great store of neglected finery.

It was the fear of illusion that originally disquieted the honest mind, congenitally dogmatic, and drove it in the direction of scepticism; and it may find three ways, not equally satisfying to its honesty, in which that fear of illusion may be dispelled. One is death, in which illusion vanishes and is forgotten; but although anxiety about error, and even positive error, are thus destroyed, no solution is offered to the previous doubt: no explanation of what could have called forth that illusion or what could have dissipated it. Another way out is by correcting the error, and substituting a new belief for it: but while in animal life this is the satisfying solution, and the old habit of dogmatism may be resumed in consequence without practical inconvenience, speculatively the case is not at all advanced; because no criterion of truth is afforded except custom, comfort, and the accidental absence of doubt; and what is absent by chance may return at any time unbidden. The third way, at which I have now arrived, is to entertain the illusion without succumbing to it, accepting it openly as an illusion, and forbidding it to claim any sort of being but that which it obviously has; and then, whether it profits me or not, it will not deceive me. What will remain of this non-deceptive illusion will then be a truth, and a truth the being of which requires no explanation, since it is utterly impossible that it should have been otherwise. Of course I may still ask why the identity of this particular thing with itself should have occurred to *me;* a question which could only be answered by plunging into a realm of existence and natural history every part and principle of which would be just as contingent, just as uncalled-for, and just as inexplicable as this accident of my being; but that this particular thing, or any other which might have occurred to me instead, should be constituted as it is raises no problem; for how could *it* have been constituted otherwise? Nor is there any moral offence any longer in the contingency of my view of it, since my view of it involves no error. The error came from a wild belief about it; and the possibility of error came from a wild propensity to belief. Relieve now the pressure of that animal haste and that hungry presumption; the error is washed out of the illusion; it is no illusion now, but an idea. Just as food would cease to be food, and poison poison, if you removed the stomach and the blood that they might nourish or infect; and just as beautiful things would cease to be beautiful if you removed the wonder and the welcome of living souls, so if you eliminate your anxiety, deceit itself becomes entertainment, and every illusion but so much added acquaintance with the realm of form. For the unintelligible accident of existence will cease to appear to lurk in this manifest being, weighting and crowding it, and threatening it with being swallowed up by nondescript neighbours. It will appear dwelling in its own world, and shining by its own light, however brief may be my glimpse of it: for no date will be written on it, no frame of full or of empty time will shut it in; nothing in it will be addressed to me, nor suggestive of any spectator. It will seem an event in no world, an incident in no experience. The quality of it will have ceased to exist: it will be merely the quality which it inherently, logically, and inalienably is. It will be an ESSENCE.

Retrenchment has its rewards. When by a difficult suspension of judgement I have deprived a given image of all adventitious significance, when it is taken neither for the manifestation of a substance nor for an idea in a mind nor for an event in a world, but simply if a colour for that colour and if music for that music, and if a face for that face, then an immense cognitive certitude comes to compensate me for so much cognitive abstention. My scepticism at last has touched bottom, and my doubt has found honourable rest in the absolutely indubitable. Whatever essence I find and note, that essence and no other is established before me. I cannot be mistaken about it, since I now have no object of intent other than the object of intuition. If for some private reason I am dissatisfied, and wish to change my entertainment, nothing prevents; but the change leaves the thing I first saw possessed of all its quality, for the sake of which I perhaps disliked or disowned it. That, while one essence is before me, some one else may be talking of another, which he calls by the same name, is nothing to the purpose; and if I myself change and correct myself, choosing a new essence in place of the old, my life indeed may have shifted its visions and its interests, but the characters they had when I harboured them are theirs without change. Indeed, only because each essence is the essence defined by instant apprehension can I truly be said to have changed my mind; for I can have discarded any one of them only by substituting something different. This new essence could not be different from the former one, if each was not unchangeably itself.

There is, then, a sort of play with the non-existent, or game of thought, which intervenes in all alleged knowledge of matters of fact, and survives that knowledge, if this is ever questioned or disproved. To this mirage of the non-existent, or intuition of essence, the pure sceptic is confined; and confined is hardly the word; because though without faith and risk he can never leave that thin and bodiless plane of being, this plane in its tenuity is infinite; and there is nothing possible elsewhere that, as a shadow and a pattern, is not prefigured there. To consider an essence is, from a spiritual point of view, to enlarge acquaintance with true being; but it is not even to broach knowledge of fact; and the ideal object so defined may have no natural significance, though it has æsthetic immediacy and logical definition. The modest scope of this speculative acquaintance with essence renders it infallible, whilst the logical and æsthetic ideality of its object renders that object eternal. Thus the most radical sceptic may be consoled, without being rebuked nor refuted; he may leap at one bound over the whole human tangle of beliefs and dogmatic claims, elude human incapacity and bias, and take hold of the quite sufficient assurance that any essence or ideal quality of being which he may be intuiting has just the characters he is finding in it, and has them eternally.

This is no idle assurance. After all, the only thing that can ultimately interest me in other men's experience or, apart from animal egotism, in my own, is just this character of the essences which at any time have swum into our ken; not at all the length of time through which we may have beheld them, nor the circumstances that produced that vision; unless these circumstances in turn, when considered, place before the mind the essences which it delights to entertain. Of course, the choice and the interest of essences come entirely from the bent of the animal that elicits the vision of them from his own soul and its adventures; and nothing but affinity with my animal life lends the essences I am able to discern their moral colour, so that to my mind they are beautiful, horrible, trivial, or vulgar. The good essences are such as accompany and express a good life. In them, whether good or bad, that life has its eternity. Certainly when I cease to exist and to think, I shall lose hold on this assurance; but the theme in which for a moment I found the fulfilment of my expressive impulses will remain, as it always was, a theme fit for consideration, even if no one else should consider it, and I should never consider it again.

Nor is this all. Not only is the character of each essence inalienable, and, so long as it is open to intuition, indubitable, but the realm of essences is infinite. Since any essence I happen to have hit upon is independent of me and would possess its precise character if I had never been born, or had never been led by the circumstances of my life and temperament to apprehend that particular essence, evidently all other essences, which I have not been led to think of, rejoice in the same sort of impalpable being–impalpable, yet the only sort of being that the most rugged experience can ever actually find. Thus a mind enlightened by scepticism and cured of noisy dogma, a mind discounting all reports, and free from all tormenting anxiety about its own fortunes or existence, finds in the wilderness of essence a very sweet and marvellous solitude. The ultimate reaches of doubt and renunciation open out for it, by an easy transition, into fields of endless variety and peace, as if through the gorges of death it had passed into a paradise where all things are crystallised into the image of themselves, and have lost their urgency and their venom.

The Watershed of Criticism

Scepticism and Animal Faith: Introduction to a System of Philosophy. New York: Charles Scribner's Sons; London: Constable and Co. Ltd., 1923, 99–108. Volume thirteen of the critical edition of *The Works of George Santayana.*

*Part of this selection first appeared in the essay "Literal and Symbolic Knowledge" (*Journal of Philosophy, Psychology, and Scientific Methods, *15 [1918], 421–44), which subsequently appeared in* Obiter Scripta *in 1936. This selection, Chapter XI of* Scepticism and Animal Faith, *brings together the two elements of the book title. Considering skepticism, Santayana saw that it left intuition deprived of any existing thing, and hence any intuitions taken as knowledge are always illusory. Considering animal faith, he observed that the extreme unease of doubt that prompts skeptical inquiry is irrelevant to the natural function of the mind. Discouragement about the ability to discern error from fact does not result from failure but rather from a misconception about what counts as success. To make its way through the natural world, the animal requires only symbols of material existence, not direct intuition; and essences—illusory as they may be—perform this symbolic function successfully enough. Perception and science are not means to omniscience; rather, they bring dignity to the animal by harmonizing it with nature. "Complete scepticism is accordingly not inconsistent with animal faith; the admission that nothing given exists is not incompatible with belief in things not given" (ES, 85). Skepticism prevents one from assenting to illusions, and animal faith guides one by means of habit. Skepticism is an analysis of experience, while animal faith is an instinctive attitude in action.*

I have now reached the culminating point of my survey of evidence, and the entanglements I have left behind me and the habitable regions I am looking for lie spread out before me like opposite valleys. On the one hand I see now a sweeping reason for scepticism, over and above all particular contradictions or fancifulness of dogma. Nothing is ever present to me except some essence; so that nothing that I possess in intuition, or actually see, is ever *there;* it can never exist bodily, nor lie in that place or exert that power which belongs to the objects encountered in action. Therefore, if I regard my intuitions as knowledge of facts, all my experience is illusion, and life is a dream. At the same time I am now able to give a clearer meaning to this old adage; for life would not be a dream, and all experience would not be illusion, if I abstained from believing in them. The evidence of data is only obviousness; they give no evidence of anything else; they are not witnesses. If I am content to recognise them for pure essences, they cannot deceive me; they will be like works of literary fiction, more or less coherent, but without any claim to exist on their own account. If I hypostatise an essence into a fact, instinctively placing it in relations which are not given within it, I am putting my trust in animal faith, not in any evidence or implication of my actual experience. I turn to an assumed world about me, because I have organs for turning, just as I expect a future to reel itself out without interruption because I am wound up to go on myself. To such ulterior things no manifest essence can bear any testimony. They must justify themselves. If the ulterior fact is some intuition elsewhere, its existence, if it happens to exist, will justify that belief; but the fulfilment of my prophecy, in taking my present dream for testimony to that ulterior experience, will be found only in the realm of truth—a realm which is itself an object of belief, never by any possibility of intuition, human or divine. So too when the supposed fact is thought of as a substance, its existence, if it is found in the realm of nature, will justify that supposition; but the realm of nature is of course only another object of belief, more remote if possible from intuition than even the realm of truth. Intuition of essence, to which positive experience and certitude are confined, is therefore always illusion, if we allow our hypostatising impulse to take it for evidence of anything else.

In adopting this conclusion of so many great philosophers, that all is illusion, I do so, however, with two qualifications. One is emotional and moral only, in that I do not mourn over this fatality, but on the contrary rather prefer speculation in the realm of essence—if it can be indulged without practical inconvenience—to alleged information about hard facts. It does not seem to me ignominious to be a poet, if nature has made one a poet unexpectedly. Unexpectedly nature lent us existence, and if she has made it a condition that we should be poets, she has not forbidden us to enjoy that art, or even to be proud of it. The other qualification is more austere: it consists in not allowing exceptions. I cannot admit that some particular essence—water, fire, being, atoms, or Brahma—is the intrinsic essence of all things, so that if I narrow my imagination to that one intuition I shall have intuited the heart and the whole of existence. Of course I do not deny that there is water and that there is being, the former in most things on earth, and the latter in everything anywhere; but these images or words of mine are not the things they designate, but only names for them. Desultory and partial propriety these names may have, but no metaphysical privilege. No more has the expedient of some modern critics who would take illusion as a whole and call it the universe; for in the first place they are probably reverting to belief in discourse, as conventionally conceived, so that their scepticism is halting; and in the second place, even if human experience could be admitted as known and vouched for, there would be an incredible arrogance in positing it as the whole of being, or as itself confined to the forms and limits which the critic assigns to it. The life of reason as I conceive it is a mere romance, and the life of nature a mere fable; such pictures have no metaphysical value, even if as sympathetic fictions they had some psychological truth.

The doctrine of essence thus renders my scepticism invincible and complete, while reconciling me with it emotionally.

If now I turn my face in the other direction and consider the prospect open to animal faith, I see that all this insecurity and inadequacy of alleged knowledge are almost irrelevant to the natural effort of the mind to describe natural things. The discouragement we may feel in science does not come from failure; it comes from a false conception of what would be success. Our worst difficulties arise from the assumption that knowledge of existences ought to be literal, whereas knowledge of existences has no need, no propensity, and no fitness to be literal. It is symbolic initially, when a sound, a smell, an indescribable feeling are signals to the animal of his dangers or chances; and it fulfils its function perfectly—I mean its moral function of enlightening us about our natural good—if it remains symbolic to the end. Can anything be more evident than that religion, language, patriotism, love, science itself speak in symbols? Given essences unify for intuition, in entirely adventitious human terms, the diffuse processes of nature; the æsthetic image—the sound, the colour, the expanse of space, the scent, taste, and sweet or cruel pressure of bodies—wears an aspect altogether unlike the mechanisms it stands for. Sensation and thought (between which there is no essential difference) work in a conventional medium, as do literature and music. The experience of essence is direct; the expression of natural facts through that medium is indirect. But this indirection is no obstacle to expression, rather its condition; and this vehicular manifestation of things may be knowledge of them, which intuition of essence is not. The theatre, for all its artifices, depicts life in a sense more truly than history, because the medium has a kindred movement to that of real life, though an artificial setting and form; and much in the same way the human medium of knowledge can perform its pertinent synthesis and make its pertinent report all the better when it frankly abandons the plane of its object and expresses in symbols what we need to know of it. The arts of expression would be impossible if they were not extensions of normal human perception. The Greeks recognised that astronomy and history were presided over by Muses, sisters of those of tragic and comic poetry; had they been as psychological as modern reflection has become, they might have had Muses of sight, hearing, and speech. I think they honoured, if they did not express, this complementary fact also, that all the Muses, even the most playful are witnesses to the nature of things. The arts are evidences of wisdom, and sources of it; they include science. No Muse would be a humane influence, nor worthy of honour, if she did not studiously express the truth of nature with the liberty and grace appropriate to her special genius.

Philosophers would not have overlooked the fact that knowledge is, and ought to be, symbolical, if intuition did not exist also, giving them a taste of something which perhaps they think higher and more satisfying. Intuition, when it is placid and masterful enough to stand alone, free from anxiety or delusion about matters of fact, is a delightful exercise, like play; it employs our imaginative faculty without warping it, and lets us live without responsibility. The playful and godlike mind of philosophers has always been fascinated by intuition; philosophers—I mean the great ones—are the infant prodigies of reflection. They often take intuition of essence for their single ideal, and wish to impose it on the workaday thoughts of men; they make a play-world for themselves which it is glorious to dominate, much as other men of genius, prolonging the masterfulness of childhood, continue to play at this or at that in their politics and their religion. But knowledge of existence has an entirely different method and an entirely different ideal. It is playful too, because its terms are intuitive and its grammar or logic often very subjective. Perception, theory, hypothesis are rapid, pregnant, often humorous; they seize a fact by its skirts from some unexpected quarter, and give it a nickname which it might be surprised to hear, such as the rainbow or the Great Bear. Yet in the investigation of facts all this play of mind is merely instrumental and indicative: the intent is practical, the watchfulness earnest, the spirit humble. The mind here knows that it is at school; and even its fancies are docile. Its nicknames for things and for their odd ways of behaving are like those which country people give to flowers; they often pointedly describe how things look or what they do to us. The ideas we have of things are not fair portraits; they are political caricatures made in the human interest; but in their partial way they may be masterpieces of characterisation and insight. Above all, they are obtained by labour, by investigating what is not given, and by correcting one impression by another, drawn from the same object—a thing impossible in the intuition of essences. They therefore conduce to wisdom, and in their perpetual tentativeness have a cumulative truth.

Consider the reason why, instead of cultivating congenial intuitions, a man may be drawn to the study of nature at all. It is because things, by their impact, startle him into attention and a new thought. Such external objects interest him for what they do, not for what they are; and knowledge of them is significant, not for the essence it displays to intuition (beautiful as this may be) but for the events it expresses or foreshadows. It matters little therefore to the pertinent knowledge of nature that the substance of things should remain recondite or unintelligible, if their movement and operation can be rightly determined on the plane of human perception. It matters little if their very existence is vouched for only by animal faith and presumption, so long as this faith posits existence where existence is, and this presumption expresses a prophetic preadaptation of animal instincts to the forces of the environment. The function of perception and natural science is, not to flatter the sense of omniscience in an absolute mind, but to dignify animal life by harmonising it, in action and in thought, with its conditions. It matters little if the news these methods can bring us of the world is fragmentary and is expressed rhetorically; what matters is that science should be integrated with art, and that the arts should substitute the dominion of man over circumstances, as far as this is possible, for the dominion of chance. In this there is no sacrifice of truth to utility; there is rather a wise direction of curiosity upon things on the human scale, and within the range of art. Speculation beyond those limits cannot be controlled, and is irresponsible; and the symbolic terms in which it must be carried on, even at close quarters, are the best possible indications for the facts in question. All these inadequacies and imperfections are proper to perfect signs, which should be brief and sharply distinguished.

Complete scepticism is accordingly not inconsistent with animal faith; the admission that nothing given exists is not incompatible with belief in things not given. I may yield to the suasion of instinct, and practise the arts with a humble confidence, without in the least disavowing the most rigorous criticism of knowledge or hypostatising any of the data of sense or fancy. And I need not do this with a bad conscience, as Parmenides and Plato and the Indians seem to have done, when they admitted illusion or opinion as an epilogue to their tight metaphysics, on the ground that otherwise they would miss their way home. It is precisely by *not* yielding to opinion and illusion, and by *not* delegating any favourite essences to be the substance of things, that I aspire to keep my cognitive conscience pure and my practical judgement sane; because in order to find my way home I am by no means compelled to yield ignominiously to any animal illusion; what guides me there is not illusion but habit; and the intuitions which accompany habit are normal signs for the circle of objects and forces by which that habit is sustained. The images of sense and science will not delude me if instead of hypostatising them, as those philosophers did the terms of their dialectic, I regard them as graphic symbols for home and for the way there. That such external things exist, that I exist myself, and live more or less prosperously in the midst of them, is a faith not founded on reason but precipitated in action, and in that intent, which is virtual action, involved in perception. This faith, which it would be dishonest not to confess that I share, does no violence to a sceptical analysis of experience; on the contrary, it takes advantage of that analysis to interpret this volatile experience as all animals do and must, as a set of symbols for existences that cannot enter experience, and which, since they are not elements in knowledge, no analysis of knowledge can touch—they are in another realm of being.

I propose now to consider what objects animal faith requires me to posit, and in what order; without for a moment forgetting that my assurance of their existence is only instinctive, and my description of their nature only symbolic. I may know them by intent, based on bodily reaction; I know them initially as whatever confronts me, whatever it may turn out to be, just as I know the future initially as whatever is coming, without knowing what will come. That something confronts me here, now, and from a specific quarter, is in itself a momentous discovery. The aspect this thing wears, as it first attracts my attention, though it may deceive me in some particulars, can hardly fail to be, in some respects, a telling indication of its nature in its relation to me. Signs identify their objects for discourse, and show us where to look for their undiscovered qualities. Further signs, catching other aspects of the same object, may help me to lay siege to it from all sides; but signs will never lead me into the citadel, and if its inner chambers are ever opened to me, it must be through sympathetic imagination. I might, by some happy unison between my imagination and its generative principles, intuit the essence which is actually the essence of that thing. In that case (which may often occur when the object is a sympathetic mind) knowledge of existence, without ceasing to be instinctive faith, will be as complete and adequate as knowledge can possibly be. The given essence will be the essence of the object meant; but knowledge will remain a claim, since the intuition is not satisfied to observe the given essence passively as a disembodied essence, but instinctively affirms it to be the essence of an existence confronting me, and beyond the range of my possible apprehension. Therefore the most perfect knowledge of fact is perfect only pictorially, not evidentially, and remains subject to the end to the insecurity inseparable from animal faith, and from life itself.

Animal faith being a sort of expectation and open-mouthedness, is earlier than intuition; intuitions come to help it out and lend it something to posit. It is more than ready to swallow any suggestion of sense or fancy; and perhaps primitive credulity, as in a dream, makes no bones of any contradiction or incongruity in successive convictions, but yields its whole soul to every image. Faith then hangs like a pendulum at rest; but when perplexity has caused that pendulum to swing more and more madly, it may for a moment stop quivering at a point of unstable equilibrium at the top; and this vertical station may be likened to universal scepticism. It is a more wonderful and a more promising equilibrium than the other, because it cannot be maintained; but before declining from the zenith and desisting from pointing vertically at zero, the pendulum of faith may hesitate for an instant which way to fall, if at that uncomfortable height it has really lost all animal momentum and all ancient prejudice. Before giving my reasons—which are but prejudices and human—for believing in events, in substances, and in the variegated truths which they involve, it may be well to have halted for breath at the apex of scepticism, and felt all the negative privileges of that position. The mere possibility of it in its purity is full of instruction; and although I have, for my own part, dwelt upon it only ironically, by a scruple of method, and intending presently to abandon it for common sense, many a greater philosopher has sought to maintain himself acrobatically at that altitude. They have not succeeded; but an impossible dwelling-place may afford, like a mountain-top, a good point of view in clear weather from which to map the land and choose a habitation.

Knowledge Is Faith Mediated by Symbols

Scepticism and Animal Faith: Introduction to a System of Philosophy. New York: Charles Scribner's Sons; London: Constable and Co. Ltd., 1923, 164–81. Volume thirteen of the critical edition of *The Works of George Santayana.*

Part of this selection first appeared as the second part of "Three Proofs of Realism" in Essays in Critical Realism: A Cooperative Study of the Problem of Knowledge *(Durant Drake, Arthur O. Lovejoy, James Bissett Pratt, Arthur K. Rogers, George Santayana, Roy Wood Sellars, C. A. Strong [London: Macmillan] 1920, 163–84). In this selection, Chapter XVIII of* Scepticism and Animal Faith, *Santayana explains his conception of knowledge as faith. A knower is a natural creature, and knowledge consists of the effects of the environment on the creature in so far as they guide action, support further living, and contribute to beneficial adjustment. The living organization or psyche of a creature creates consciousness or spirit, and as psyche directs the creature it creates intent in the spirit. Spirit with intent takes intuited essences as descriptions of the objects that occupy psyche. Yet it is not spirit or intuition that distinguishes objects in action; that is accomplished by faith or "animal presumption, positing whatsoever object instinct is materially predisposed to cope with, as in hunger, love, fighting, or the expectation of a future" (ES, 90). No object of this animal faith can ever be intuited; there is no direct perception of existence. Instinctive reactions focus attention on some existing object and experience modifies these reactions. Santayana considered the distinction between essences of scientific data and essences of myths, and the relation of knowledge and belief. He contended that knowledge is true belief, and a true belief is adequate for, not identical to, its object.*

In the claims of memory I have a typical instance of what is called knowledge. In remembering I believe that I am taking cognisance not of a given essence but of a remote existence, so that, being myself here and now, I can consider and describe something going on at another place and time. This leap, which renders knowledge essentially faith, may come to seem paradoxical or impossible like the leap of physical being from place to place or from form to form which is called motion or change, and which some philosophers deny, as they deny knowledge. Is there such a leap in knowing? Am I really here and now when I apprehend some remote thing? Certainly, if by myself I understand the psyche within my body, which directs my outer organs, reacts on external things, and shapes the history and character of the individual animal that bears my name. In this sense I am a physical being in the midst of nature, and my knowledge is a name for the effects which surrounding things have upon me, in so far as I am quickened by them, and readjusted to them. I am certainly confined at each moment to a limited space and time, but may be quickened by the influence of things at any distance, and may be readjusting myself to them. For the naturalist there is accordingly no paradox in the leap of knowledge other than the general marvel of material interaction and animal life.

If by myself, however, I meant pure spirit, or the light of attention by which essences appear and intuitions are rendered actual, it would not be true that I am confined or even situated in a particular place and time, nor that in considering things remote from my body, my thoughts are taking any unnatural leap. The marvel, from the point of view of spirit, is rather that it should need to be planted at all in the sensorium of some living animal, and that, being rooted there, it should take that accidental station for its point of view in surveying all nature, and should dignify one momentary phase of that animal life with the titles of the Here and the Now. It is only spirit, be it observed, that can do this. In themselves all the points of space-time are equally central and palpitating, and every phase of every psyche is a focus for actual readjustments to the whole universe. How then can the spirit, which would seem to be the principle of universality and justice, take up its station in each of these atoms and fight its battles for it, and prostitute its own light in the service of that desperate blindness? Can reason do nothing better than supply the eloquence of prejudice? Such are the puzzles which spirit might find, I will not say in the leap of knowledge, but in the fatality which links the spirit to a material organ so that, in order to reach other things, it is obliged to leap; or rather can never reach other things, because it is tethered to its starting-point, except by its intent in leaping, and cannot even discover the stepping-stone on which it stands because its whole life is the act of leaping away from it. There is no reason, therefore, in so far as knowledge is an apanage of spirit, why knowledge should not bathe all time and all existence in an equal light, and see everything as it is, with an equal sympathy and immediacy. The problem for the spirit is how it could ever come to pick out one body or another for its cynosure and for its instrument, as if it could not see save through such a little eye-glass, and in such a violent perspective. This problem, I think, has a ready answer, but it is not one that spirit could ever find of itself, without a long and docile apprenticeship in the school of animal faith. This answer is that spirit, with knowledge and all its other prerogatives, is intrinsically and altogether a function of animal life; so that if it were not lodged in some body and expressive of its rhythms and relations, spirit would not exist at all. But this solution, even when spirit is humble enough to accept it, always seems to it a little disappointing and satirical.

Spirit, therefore, has no need to leap in order to know, because in its range as spirit it is omnipresent and omnimodal. Events which are past or future in relation to the phase of the psyche which spirit expresses in a particular instance, or events which are remote from that psyche in space, are not for that reason remote from spirit, or out of its cognitive range: they are merely hidden, or placed in a particular perspective for the moment, like the features of a landscape by the hedges and turns of a road. Just as all essences are equally near to spirit, and equally fit and easy to contemplate, if only a psyche with an affinity to those essences happens to arise; so all existing things, past, future, or infinitely distant, are equally within the range of knowledge, if only a psyche happens to be directed upon them, and to choose terms, however poor or fantastic, in which to describe them. In choosing these terms the psyche creates spirit, for they are essences given in intuition; and in directing her action or endeavour, backward or forward, upon those remote events, she creates intent in the spirit, so that the given essences become descriptions of the things with which the psyche is then busied.

But how, I may ask, can intent distinguish its hidden object, so that an image, distorted or faithful, may be truly or falsely projected *there*, or used to describe *it?* How does the spirit divine that there is such an object, or where it lies? And how can it appeal to a thing which is hidden, the object of mere intent, as to a touchstone or standard for its various descriptions of that object, and say to them, as they suggest themselves in turn: You are too vague, You are absurd, You are better, You are absolutely right?

I answer that it does so by animal presumption, positing whatsoever object instinct is materially pre-disposed to cope with, as in hunger, love, fighting, or the expectation of a future. But before developing this reply, let me make one observation. Since intuition of essence is not knowledge, knowledge can never lie in an overt comparison of one datum with another datum given at the same time; even in pure dialectic, the comparison is with a datum *believed* to have been given formerly. If both terms were simply given they would compose a complex essence, without the least signification. Only when one of the terms is indicated by intent, without being given exhaustively, can the other term serve to define the first more fully, or be linked with it in an assertion which is not mere tautology. An object of faith—and knowledge is one species of faith—can never, even in the most direct perception, come within the circle of intuition. Intuition of things is a contradiction in terms. If philosophers wish to abstain from faith, and reduce themselves to intuition of the obvious, they are free to do so, but they will thereby renounce all knowledge, and live on passive illusions. No fact, not even the fact that these illusions exist, would ever be, or would ever have been, anything but the false idea that they had existed. There would be nothing but the realm of essence, without any intuition of any part of it, nor of the whole: so that we should be driven back to a nihilism which only silence and death could express consistently; since the least actual assertion of it, by existing, would contradict it.

Even such acquaintance with the realm of essence as constitutes some science or recognisable art—like mathematics or music—lies in intending and positing great stretches of essence not now given, so that the essences now given acquire significance and become pregnant, to my vital feeling, with a thousand things which they do not present actually, but which I know where to look for eventually, and how to await. Suppose a moment ago I heard a clap of thunder, loud and prolonged, but that the physical shock has subsided and I am conscious of repose and silence. I may find some difficulty, although the thing was so recent, in *rehearsing* even now the exact volume, tone, and rumblings of that sound; yet I *know* the theme perfectly, in the sense that when it thunders again, I can say with assurance whether the second crash was longer, louder, or differently modulated. In such a case I have no longer an intuition of the first thunder-clap, but a memory of it which is knowledge; and I can define on occasion, up to a certain point and not without some error, the essence given in that particular past intuition. Thus even pure essences can become objects of intent and of tentative knowledge when they are not present in intuition but are approached and posited indirectly, as the essences given on another particular occasion or signified by some particular word. The word or the occasion are natural facts, and my knowledge is focussed upon them in the first instance by ordinary perception or conception of nature: and the essence I hope to recover is elicited gradually, imaginatively, perhaps incorrectly, at the suggestion of those assumed facts, according to my quickness of wit, or my familiarity with the conventions of that art or science. In this way it becomes possible and necessary to learn about essences as if they were things, not initially by a spontaneous and complete intuition, but by coaxing the mind until possibly, at the end, it beholds them clearly. This is the sort of intuition which is mediated by language and by works of fine art; also by logic and mathematics, as they are learned from teachers and out of books. It is not happy intuition of some casual datum: it is laborious recovery, up to a certain point, of the *sort* of essence somebody else may have intuited. Whereas intuition, which reveals an essence directly, is not knowledge, because it has no ulterior object, the designation of some essence by some sign does convey knowledge, to an intelligent pupil, of what that essence was. Obviously such divination of essences present elsewhere, so that they become present here also, in so far as it is knowledge, is trebly faith. Faith first in the document, as a genuine natural fact and not a vapid fancy of my own; for instance, belief that there is a book called the Bible, really handed down from the ancient Jews and the early Christians, and that I have not merely dreamt of such a book. Faith then in the significance of that document, that it means some essence which it is not; in this instance, belief that the sacred writers were not merely speaking with tongues but were signifying some intelligible points in history and philosophy. Faith finally in my success in interpreting that document correctly, so that the essences it suggests to me now are the very essences it expressed originally: in other words, the belief that when I read the Bible I understand it as it was meant, and not fantastically.

I revert now to the question how it is possible to posit an object which is not a datum, and how without knowing positively what this object is I can make it the criterion of truth in my ideas. How can I test the accuracy of descriptions by referring them to a subject-matter which is not only out of view now but which probably has never been more than an object of intent, an event which even while it was occurring was described by me only in terms native to my fancy? If I know a man only by reputation, how should I judge if the reputation is deserved? If I know things only by representations, are not the representations the only things I know?

This challenge is fundamental, and so long as the assumptions which it makes are not challenged in turn, it drives critics of knowledge inexorably to scepticism of a dogmatic sort, I mean to the assertion that the very notion of knowledge is absurd. One assumption is that knowledge should be intuition: but I have already come to the conclusion that intuition is not knowledge. So long as a knowledge is demanded that shall be intuition, the issue can only be laughter or despair; for if I attain intuition, I have only a phantom object, and if I spurn that and turn to the facts, I have renounced intuition. This assumption alone suffices, therefore, to disprove the possibility of knowledge. But in case the force of this disproof escaped us, another assumption is at hand to despatch the business, namely, the assumption that in a true description–if we grant knowledge by description–the terms should be identical with the constituents of the object, so that the idea should *look like* the thing that it knows. This assumption is derived from the other, or is a timid form of it: for it is supposed that I know by intuiting my idea, and that unless that idea resembled the object I wish to know, I could not even by courtesy be said to have discovered the latter. But the intuition of an idea, let me repeat, is not knowledge; and if a thing resembling that idea happened to exist, my intuition would still not be knowledge of it, but contemplation of the idea only.

Plato and many other philosophers, being in love with intuition (for which alone they were perhaps designed by nature), have identified science with certitude, and consequently entirely condemned what I call knowledge (which is a form of animal faith) or relegated it to an inferior position, as something merely necessary for life. I myself have no passionate attachment to existence, and value this world for the intuitions it can suggest, rather than for the wilderness of facts that compose it. To turn away from it may be the deepest wisdom in the end. What better than to blow out the candle, and to bed! But at noon this pleasure is premature. I can always hold it in reserve, and perhaps nihilism is a system–the simplest of all–on which we shall all agree in the end. But I seem to see very clearly now that in doing so we should all be missing the truth: not indeed by any false assertion, such as may separate us from the truth now, but by dumb ignorance–a dumb ignorance which, when proposed as a solution to actual doubts, is the most radical of errors, since it ignores and virtually denies the pressure of those doubts, and their living presence. Accordingly, so long as I remain awake and the light burning, that total dogmatic scepticism is evidently an impossible attitude. It requires me to deny what I assert, not to mean what I mean, and (in the sense in which seeing is believing) not to believe what I see. If I wish, therefore, to formulate in any way my actual claim to knowledge–a claim which life, and in particular memory, imposes upon me–I must revise the premises of this nihilism. For I have been led to it not by any accidental error, but by the logic of the assumption that knowledge should be intuition of fact. It is this presumption that must be revoked.

Knowledge is no such thing. It is not intramental nor internal to experience. Not only does it not require me to compare two given terms and to find them similar or identical, but it positively excludes any intuitive possession of its object. Intuition subsists beneath knowledge, as vegetative life subsists beneath animal life, and within it. Intuition may also supervene upon knowledge, when all I have learned of the universe, and all my concern for it, turn to a playful or a hypnotising phantom; and any poet or philosopher, like any flower, is free to prefer intuition to knowledge. But in preferring intuition he prefers ignorance. Knowledge is knowledge because it has compulsory objects that pre-exist. It is incidental to the predicaments and labour of life: also to its masterful explorations and satirical moods. It is reflected from events as light is reflected from bodies. It expresses in discourse the modified habits of an active being, plastic to experience, and capable of readjusting its organic attitude to other things on the same material plane of being with itself. The place and the pertinent functions of these several things are indicated by the very attitude of the animal who notices them; this attitude, physical and practical, determines the object of intent, which discourse is about.

When the proverbial child cries for the moon, is the object of his desire doubtful? He points at it unmistakably; yet the psychologist (not to speak of the child himself) would have some difficulty in recovering exactly the sensations and images, the gathering demands and fumbling efforts, that traverse the child's mind while he points. Fortunately all this fluid sentience, even if it could be described, is irrelevant to the question; for the child's sensuous experience is not his object. If it were, he would have attained it. What his object is, his fixed gaze and outstretched arm declare unequivocally. His elders may say that he doesn't know what he wants, which is probably true of them also: that is, he has only a ridiculously false and inconstant idea of what the moon may be in itself. But his attention is arrested in a particular direction, his appetition flows the same way; and if he may be said to know anything, he knows there is something there which he would like to reach, which he would like to know better. He is a little philosopher; and his knowledge, if less diversified and congealed, is exactly like science.

The attitude of his body in pointing to the moon, and his tears, fill full his little mind, which not only reverberates to this physical passion, but probably observes it: and this felt attitude *identifies the object* of his desire and knowledge *in the physical world.* It determines what particular thing, in the same space and time with the child's body, was the object of that particular passion. If the object which the body is after is identified, that which the soul is after is identified too: no one, I suppose, would carry dualism so far as to assert that when the mouth waters at the sight of one particular plum, the soul may be yearning for quite another.

The same bodily attitude of the child *identifies the object in the discourse of an observer.* In perceiving what his senses are excited by, and which way his endeavour is turned, I can see that the object of his desire is the moon, which I too am looking at. That I am looking at the same moon as he can be proved by a little triangulation: our glances converge upon it. If the child has reached the inquisitive age and asks "What is that?" I understand what he means by "that" and am able to reply sapiently "That is the moon," only because our respective bodies, in one common space, are discoverably turned towards one material object, which is stimulating them simultaneously. Knowledge of discourse in other people, or of myself at other times, is what I call literary psychology. It is, or may be, in its texture, the most literal and adequate sort of knowledge of which a mind is capable. If I am a lover of children, and a good psycho-analyst, I may feel for a moment exactly as the child feels in looking at the moon: and I may know that I know his feeling, and very likely he too will know that I know it, and we shall become fast friends. But this rare adequacy of knowledge, attained by dramatic sympathy, goes out to an object which in its existence is known very indirectly: because poets and religious visionaries feel this sort of sympathy with all sorts of imaginary persons, of whose existence and thoughts they have only intuition, not knowledge. If I ask for evidence that such an object exists, and is not an *alter ego* of my private invention, I must appeal to my faith in nature, and to my conventional assumption that this child and I are animals of the same species, in the same habitat, looking at the same moon, and likely to have the same feelings: and finally the psychology of the tribe and the crowd may enable me half to understand how we know that we have the same feelings at once, when we actually share them.

The attitude of the child's body also *identifies the object for him, in his own subsequent discourse.* He is not likely to forget a moon that he cried for. When in stretching his hand towards it he found he could not touch it, he learned that this bright good was not within his grasp, and he made a beginning in the experience of life. He also made a beginning in science, since he then added the absolutely true predicate "out of reach" to the rather questionable predicates "bright" and "good" (and perhaps "edible") with which his first glimpse had supplied him. That active and mysterious thing, co-ordinate with himself, since it lay in the same world with his body, and affected it—the thing that attracted his hand, was evidently the very thing that eluded it. His failure would have had no meaning and would have taught him nothing—that is, would not have corrected his instinctive reactions—if the object he saw and the object he failed to reach had not been identical; and certainly that object was not brightness nor goodness nor excitements in his brain or psyche, for these are not things he could ever have attempted or expected to touch. It is only things on the scale of the human senses and in the field of those instinctive reactions which sensation calls forth, that can be the primary objects of human knowledge: no other things can be discriminated at first by an animal mind, or can interest it, or can be meant and believed in by it. It is these instinctive reactions that select the objects of attention, designate their locus, and impose faith in their existence. But these reactions may be modified by experience, and the description the mind gives of the objects reacted upon can be revised, or the objects themselves discarded, and others discerned instead. Thus the child's instinct to touch the moon was as spontaneous and as confident at first as his instinct to look at it; and the object of both efforts was the same, because the same external agency aroused them, and with them the very heterogeneous sensations of light and of disappointment. These various terms of sense or of discourse, by which the child described the object under whose attractions and rebuffs he was living, were merely symbols to him, like words. An animal naturally has as many signs for an object as he has sensations or emotions in its presence. These signs are miscellaneous essences—sights, sounds, smells, contacts, tears, provocations— and they are alternative or supplementary to one another, like words in different languages. The most diverse senses, such as smell and sight, if summoned to the same point in the environment, and guiding a single action, will report upon a single object. Even when one sense brings all the news I have, its reports will change from moment to moment with the distance, variation, or suspension of the connection between the object and my body: and this without any relevant change in the object itself. Nay, often the very transformation of the sensation bears witness that the object is unchanged; as music and laughter, overheard as I pass a tavern, are felt and known to continue unabated, and to be no merriment of mine, just because they fade from my ears as I move away.

The object of knowledge being that designated in this way by my bodily attitude, the æsthetic qualities I attribute to it will depend on the particular sense it happens to affect at the moment, or on the sweep and nature of the reaction which it then calls forth on my part. This diversity in signs and descriptions for a single thing is a normal diversity. Diversity, when it is not contradiction, irritates only unreasonably dogmatic people; they are offended with nature for having a rich vocabulary, and sometimes speaking a language, or employing a syntax, which they never heard at home. It is an innocent prejudice, and it yields easily in a generous mind to pleasure at the wealth of alternatives which animal life affords. Even such contradictions as may arise in the description of things, and may truly demand a solution, reside in the implication of the terms, not in their sensuous or rhetorical diversity: they become contradictory only when they assign to the object contrary movements or contrary effects, not when they merely exhibit its various appearances. Looking at the moon, one man may call it simply a light in the sky; another, prone to dreaming awake, may call it a virgin goddess; a more observant person, remembering that this luminary is given to waxing and waning, may call it the crescent; and a fourth, a full-fledged astronomer, may say (taking the æsthetic essence before him merely for a sign) that it is an extinct and opaque spheroidal satellite of the earth, reflecting the light of the sun from a part of its surface. All these descriptions envisage the same object—otherwise no relevance, conflict, or progress could obtain among them. What that object is in its complete constitution and history will never be known by man; but that this object exists in a known space and time and has traceable physical relations with all other physical objects is a fact posited from the beginning; it was posited by the child when he pointed, and by me when I saw him point. If it did not so exist and (as sometimes happens) he and I were suffering from a hallucination, in thinking we were pointing at the moon we should be discoverably pointing at vacancy: exploration would eventually satisfy us of that fact, and any bystander would vouch for it. But if in pointing at it we were pointing to it, its identity would be fixed without more ado; disputes and discoveries concerning it would be pertinent and soluble, no matter what diversity there might be in the ideal essences—light, crescent, goddess, or satellite—which we used as rival descriptions of it while we pointed.

I find that the discrimination of essence brings a wonderful clearness into this subject. All data and descriptions—light, crescent, goddess, or satellite—are equally essences, terms of human discourse, in-existent in themselves. What exists in any instance, besides the moon and our various reactions upon it, is some intuition, expressing those reactions, evoking that essence, and lending it a specious actuality. The terms of astronomy are essences no less human and visionary than those of mythology; but they are the fruit of a better focussed, more chastened, and more prolonged attention turned upon what actually occurs; that is, they are kept closer to animal faith, and freer from pictorial elements and the infusion of reverie. In myth, on the contrary, intuition wanders idly and uncontrolled; it makes epicycles, as it were, upon the reflex arc of perception; the moonbeams bewitch some sleeping Endymion, and he dreams of a swift huntress in heaven. Myth is nevertheless a relevant fancy, and genuinely expressive; only instead of being guided by a perpetual fresh study of the object posited by animal faith and encountered in action, it runs into marginal comments, personal associations, and rhetorical asides; so that even if based originally on perception, it is built upon principles internal to human discourse, as are grammar, rhyme, music, and morals. It may be admirable as an expression of these principles, and yet be egregiously false if asserted of the object, without discounting the human medium in which it has taken form. Diana is an exquisite symbol for the moon, and for one sort of human loveliness; but she must not be credited with any existence over and above that of the moon, and of sundry short-skirted Dorian maidens. She is not other than they: she is an image of them, the best part of their essence distilled in a poet's mind. So with the description of the moon given by astronomers, which is not less fascinating; this, too, is no added object, but only a new image for the moon known even to the child and me. The space, matter, gravitation, time, and laws of motion conceived by astronomers are essences only, and mere symbols for the use of animal faith, when very enlightened: I mean in so far as they are alleged to constitute knowledge of a world which I must bow to and encounter in action; for if astronomy is content to be a mathematical exercise without any truth, an object of pure intuition, its terms and its laws will, of course, be ultimate realities, apart from what happens to exist: realities in the realm of essence. In the description of the natural world, however, they are mere symbols, mediating animal faith. Science at any moment may recast or correct its conceptions (as it is doing now) giving them a different colour; and the nerve of truth in them will be laid bare and made taut in proportion as the sensuous and rhetorical vesture of these notions is stripped off, and the dynamic relations of events, as found and posited by material exploration, are nakedly recorded.

Knowledge accordingly is belief: belief in a world of events, and especially of those parts of it which are near the self, tempting or threatening it. This belief is native to animals, and precedes all deliberate use of intuitions as signs or descriptions of things; as I turn my head to see who is there, before I see who it is. Furthermore, knowledge is true belief. It is such an enlightening of the self by intuitions arising there, that what the self imagines and asserts of the collateral thing, with which it wrestles in action, is actually true of that thing. Truth in such presumptions or conceptions does not imply adequacy, nor a pictorial identity between the essence in intuition and the constitution of the object. Discourse is a language, not a mirror. The images in sense are parts of discourse, not parts of nature: they are the babble of our innocent organs under the stimulus of things; but these spontaneous images, like the sounds of the voice, may acquire the function of names; they may become signs, if discourse is intelligent and can recapitulate its phases, for the things sought or encountered in the world. The truth which discourse can achieve is truth in its own terms, appropriate description: it is no incorporation or reproduction of the object in the mind. The mind notices and intends; it cannot incorporate or reproduce anything not an intention or an intuition. Its objects are no part of itself even when they are essences, much less when they are things. It thinks the essences, with that sort of immediate and self-forgetful attention which I have been calling intuition; and if it is animated, as it usually is, by some ulterior interest or pursuit, it takes the essences before it for messages, signs, or emanations sent forth to it from those objects of animal faith; and they become its evidences and its description for those objects. Therefore any degree of inadequacy and originality is tolerable in discourse, or even requisite, when the constitution of the objects which the animal encounters is out of scale with his organs, or quite heterogeneous from is possible images. A sensation or a theory, no matter how arbitrary its terms (and all language is perfectly arbitrary), will be true of the object, if it expresses some true relation in which that object stands to the self, so that these terms are not misleading as signs, however poetical they may be as sounds or as pictures.

Finally, knowledge is true belief grounded in experience, I mean, controlled by outer facts. It is not true by accident; it is not shot into the air on the chance that there may be something it may hit. It arises by a movement of the self sympathetic or responsive to surrounding beings, so that these beings become its intended objects, and at the same time an appropriate correspondence tends to be established between these objects and the beliefs generated under their influence.

In regard to the original articles of the animal creed—that there is a world, that there is a future, that things sought can be found, and things seen can be eaten—no guarantee can possibly be offered. I am sure these dogmas are often false; and perhaps the event will some day falsify them all, and they will lapse altogether. But while life lasts, in one form or another this faith must endure. It is the initial expression of animal vitality in the sphere of mind, the first announcement that anything is going on. It is involved in any pang of hunger, of fear, or of love. It launches the adventure of knowledge. The object of this tentative knowledge is things in general, whatsoever may be a work (as I am) to disturb me or awake my attention. The effort of knowledge is to discover what sort of world this disturbing world happens to be. Progress in knowledge lies open in various directions, now in the scope of its survey, now in its accuracy, now in its depth of local penetration. The ideal of knowledge is to become natural science: if it trespasses beyond that, it relapses into intuition, and ceases to be knowledge.

Belief in Substance

Scepticism and Animal Faith: Introduction to a System of Philosophy. New York: Charles Scribner's Sons; London: Constable and Co. Ltd., 1923, 182–91. Volume thirteen of the critical edition of *The Works of George Santayana.*

Unlike modern philosophers who "make substances out of the sensations or ideas which they regard as ultimate facts" (ES, 98), Santayana, in Chapter XIX of Scepticism and Animal Faith, *pointed to the "spontaneous quality" in animal responses to show the unavoidable belief in substance. He thought that belief in substance is prior to intuition; it is not a matter of proof and is "appetition before it is description" (ES, 101). He wrote, "[b]elief in substance . . . is the most irrational, animal, and primitive of beliefs: it is the voice of hunger. But when, as I must, I have yielded to this presumption, and proceeded to explore the world, I shall find in its constitution the most beautiful justification for my initial faith, and the proof of its secret rationality" (ES, 103). He explicitly acknowledged the pragmatic character of his view, although he considered that the apparent justification of faith might be "a bribe offered by fortune to confirm my illusions" (ES, 103).*

All knowledge, being faith in an object posited and partially described, is belief in substance, in the etymological sense of this word; it is belief in a thing or event subsisting in its own plane, and waiting for the light of knowledge to explore it eventually, and perhaps name or define it. In this way my whole past lies waiting for memory to review it, if I have this faculty; and the whole future of the world in the same manner is spread out for prophecy, scientific or visionary, to predict falsely or truly. Yet the future and the past are not ordinarily called substances; probably because the same material substance is assumed to run through both. Nevertheless, from the point of view of knowledge, every event, even if wholly psychological or phenomenal, is a substance. It is a self-existing fact, open to description from the point of view of other events, if in the bosom of these other events there is such plasticity and intent as are requisite for perception, prophecy, or memory.

When modern philosophers deny material substance, they make substances out of the sensations or ideas which they regard as ultimate facts. It is impossible to eliminate belief in substance so long as belief in existence is retained. A mistrust in existence, and therefore in substance, is not unphilosophical; but modern philosophers have not given full expression to this sceptical scruple. They have seldom been disinterested critics, but often advocates of some metaphysic that allured them, and whose rivals they wished to destroy. They deny substance in favour of phenomena, which are hypostatised essences, because phenomena are individually wholly open to intuition; but they forget that no phenomenon can intuit another, and that if it contains knowledge of that other, it must be animated by intent, and besides existing itself substantially must recognise its object as another substance, indifferent in its own being to the cognisance which other substances may take of it. In other words, although each phenomenon in passing is an object of intuition, all absent phenomena, and all their relations, are objects of faith; and this faith must be mediated by some feature in the present phenomenon which faith assumes to be a sign of the existence of other phenomena elsewhere, and of their order. So that in so far as the instinctive claims and transcendent scope of knowledge are concerned, phenomenalism fully retains the belief in substance. In order to get rid of this belief, which is certainly obnoxious to the sceptic, a disinterested critic would need to discard all claims to knowledge, and to deny his own existence and that of all absent phenomena.

For my own part, having admitted discourse (which involves time and existences deployed in time, but synthesised in retrospect), and having admitted shocks that interrupt discourse and lead it to regard itself as an experience, and having even admitted that such experience involves a self beneath discourse, with an existence and movement of its own—I need not be deterred by any *a priori* objections from believing in substance of any sort. For me it will be simply a question of good sense and circumstantial evidence how many substances I admit, and of what sort.

In the genesis of human knowledge (which I am not attempting to trace here) the substance first posited is doubtless matter, some alluring or threatening or tormenting thing. The ego, as Fichte tells us, unaware of itself, posits a non-ego, and then by reflection posits itself as the agent in that positing, or as the patient which the activity posited in the non-ego posits in its turn. But all this positing would be mere folly, unless it was an intelligent discovery of antecedent facts. Why should a non-existent ego be troubled with the delirious duty of positing anything at all? And, if nothing else exists, what difference could it make what sort of a world the ego posited, or whether it posited a thousand inconsequential worlds, at once or in succession? Fichte, however, was far from sharing that absolute freedom in madness which he attributes to the creative ego; he had a very tight tense mind, and posited a very tense tight world. His myths about the birth of knowledge (or rather of systematic imagination) out of unconscious egos, acts, and positings concealed some modest truths about nature. The actual datum has a background, and Fichte was too wise to ignore so tremendous a fact. Romantic philosophy, like romantic poetry, has its profound ways of recognising its own folly, and so turning it into tragic wisdom. As a matter of fact, the active ego is an animal living in a material world; both the ego and the non-ego exist substantially before acquiring this relation of positing and being posited. The instinct and ability to posit objects, and the occasion for doing so, are incidents in the development of animal life. Positing is a symptom of sensibility in an organism to the presence of other substances in its environment. The sceptic, like the sick man, is intent on the symptom; and positing is his name for felt plasticity in his animal responses. It is not a bad name; because plasticity, though it may seem a passive thing, is really a spontaneous quality. If the substance of the ego were not alive, it would not leap to meet its opportunities, it would not develop new organs to serve its old necessities, and it would not kindle itself to intuition of essences, nor concern itself to regard those essences as appearances of the substances with which it was wrestling. The whole life of imagination and knowledge comes from within, from the restlessness, eagerness, curiosity, and terror of the animal bent on hunting, feeding, and breeding; and the throb of being which he experiences at any moment is not proper to the datum in his mind's eye—a purely fantastic essence—but to himself. It is out of his organism or its central part, the psyche, that this datum has been bred. The living substance within him being bent, in the first instance, on pursuing or avoiding some agency in its environment, it projects whatever (in consequence of its reactions) reaches its consciousness into the locus whence it feels the stimulus to come, and it thus frames its description or knowledge of objects. In this way the ego really and sagaciously posits the non-ego: not absolutely, as Fichte imagined, nor by a gratuitous fiat, but on occasion and for the best of reasons, when the non-ego in its might shakes the ego out of its primitive somnolence.

Belief in substance is accordingly identical with the claim to knowledge, and so fundamental that no evidence can be adduced for it which does not pre-suppose it. In recognising any appearance as a witness to substance and in admitting (or even in rejecting) the validity of such testimony, I have already made a substance of the appearance; and if I admit other phenomena as well, I have placed that substance in a world of substances having a substantial unity. It is not to external pressure, through evidence or argument, that faith in substance is due. If the sceptic cannot find it in himself, he will never find it. I for one will honour him in his sincerity and in his solitude. But I will not honour him, nor think him a philosopher, if he is a sceptic only histrionically, in the wretched controversies of the schools, and believes in substance again when off the stage. I am not concerned about make-believe philosophies, but about my actual beliefs. It is only out of his own mouth, or rather out of his own heart, that I should care to convince the sceptic. Scepticism, if it could be sincere, would be the best of philosophies. But I suspect that other sceptics, as well as I, always believe in substance, and that their denial of it is sheer sophistry and the weaving of verbal arguments in which their most familiar and massive convictions are ignored.

It might seem ignominious to believe something on compulsion, because I can't help believing it; when reason awakes in a man it asks for reasons for everything. Yet this demand is unreasonable: there cannot be a reason for everything. It is mere automatic habit in the philosopher to make this demand, as it is in the common man not to make it. When once I have admitted the facts of nature, and taken for granted the character of animal life, and the incarnation of spirit in this animal life, then indeed many excellent reasons for the belief in substance will appear; and not only reasons for using the category of substance, and positing substance of some vague ambient sort, but reasons for believing in a substance rather elaborately defined and scientifically describable in many of its habits and properties. But I am not yet ready for that. Lest that investigation, when undertaken, should ignore its foundations or be impatient of its limits, I must insist here that trust in knowledge, and belief in anything to know, are merely instinctive and, in a manner, pathological. If philosophy were something prior to convention rather than (as it is) only convention made consistent and deliberate, philosophy ought to reject belief in substance and in knowledge, and to entrench itself in the sheer confession and analysis of this belief, as of all others, without assenting to any of them. But I have found that criticism has no first principle, that analysis involves belief in discourse, and that belief in discourse involves belief in substance; so that any pretensions which criticism might set up to being more profound than common sense would be false pretensions. Criticism is only an exercise of reflective fancy, on the plane of literary psychology, an after-image of that faith in nature which it denies; and in dwelling on criticism as if it were more than a subjective perspective or play of logical optics, I should be renouncing all serious philosophy. Philosophy is nothing if not honest; and the critical attitude, when it refuses to rest at some point upon vulgar faith, inhibits all belief, denies all claims to knowledge, and becomes dishonest; because it itself claims to know.

Does the process of experience, now that I trust my memory to report it truly, or does the existence of the self, now that I admit its substantial, dynamic, and obscure life underlying discourse, require me to posit any other substances? Certainly it does. Experience, for animal faith, begins by reporting what is not experience; and the life of the self, if I accept its endeavours as significant, implies an equally substantial, dynamic, ill-reported world around it, in whose movements it is implicated. In conveying this feeling, as in all else, experience *might* be pure illusion; but if I reject this initial and fundamental suasion of my cognitive life, it will be hard to find anything better to put in its place. I am unwilling to do myself so much useless violence as to deny the validity of primary memory, and assert that I have never, in fact, had any experience at all; and I should be doing myself even greater violence if I denied the validity of perception, and asserted that a thunder-clap, for instance, was only a musical chord, with no formidable event of any sort going on behind the sound. To be startled is to be aware that something sudden and mysterious has occurred not far from me in space. The thunder-clap is felt to be an event in the self and in the not-self, even before its nature as a sound—its æsthetic quality for the self—is recognised at all; I first know I am shaken horribly, and then note how loud and rumbling is the voice of the god that shakes me. That first feeling of something violent and resistless happening in the world at large, is accompanied by a hardly less primitive sense of something gently seething within me, a smouldering life which that alien energy blows upon and causes to start into flame.

If this be not the inmost texture of experience, I do not know what experience is. To me experience has not a string of sensations for its objects; what it brings me is not at all a picture-gallery of clear images, with nothing before, behind, or between them. What such a ridiculous psychology (made apparently by studying the dictionary and not by studying the mind) calls hypotheses, intellectual fictions, or tendencies to feign, is the solid body of experience, on which what it calls sensations or ideas hang like flimsy garments or trinkets, or play like a shifting light and shade. Experience brings belief in substance (as alertness) *before* it brings intuition of essences; it is appetition *before* it is description. Of course sensation would precede idea, if by sensation we understood contact with matter, and by idea pure reverie about ideal things; but if idea means expectation, or consciousness having intent, and if sensation means æsthetic contemplation of data without belief, then idea precedes sensation: because an animal is aware that something is happening long before he can say to himself what that something is, or what it looks like. The ultimate datum to which a sceptic may retreat, when he suspends all life and opinion, some essence, pure and non-existent and out of all relation to minds, bodies, or events—surely that is not the stuff out of which experience is woven: it is but the pattern or picture, the æsthetic image, which the tapestry may ultimately offer to the gazing eye, incurious of origins, and contemptuous of substance. The radical stuff of experience is much rather breathlessness, or pulsation, or as Locke said (correcting himself) a certain uneasiness; a lingering thrill, the resonance of that much-struck bell which I call my body, the continual assault of some masked enemy, masked perhaps in beauty, or of some strange sympathetic influence, like the cries and motions of other creatures; and also the hastening and rising of some impulse in me in response. Experience, at its very inception, is a revelation of *things;* and these things, before they are otherwise distinguished, are distinguishable into a here and a there, a now and a then, nature and myself in the midst of nature.

It is a mere prejudice of literary psychology, which uses the grammar of adult discourse, like a mythology, in which to render primitive experience—it is a mere prejudice to suppose that experience has only such categories as colour, sound, touch, and smell. These essences are distinguished eventually because the senses that present them can be separated at will, the element each happens to furnish being thus flashed on or cut off, like an electric light: but far more primitive in animal experience are such dichotomies as good and bad, near and far, coming and going, fast and slow, just now and very soon. The first thing experience reports is the existence of something, merely as existence, the weight, strain, danger, and lapse of being. If any one should tell me that this is an abstraction, I should reply that it would seem an abstraction to a parrot, who used human words without having human experience, but it is no abstraction to a man, whose language utters imperfectly, and by a superadded articulation, the life within him. Aristotle, who so often seems merely grammatical, was not merely grammatical when he chose substance to be the first of his categories. He was far more profoundly psychological in this than the British and German psychologists who discard the notion of substance because it is not the datum of any separate sense. None of the separate data of sense, which are only essences, would figure at all in an experience, or would become terms in knowledge, if a prior interest and faith did not apprehend them. Animal watchfulness, lying in wait for the signals of the special senses, lends them their significance, sets them in their places, and retains them, as descriptions of things, and as symbols in its own ulterior discourse.

This animal watchfulness carries the category of substance with it, asserts existence most vehemently, and in apprehension seizes and throws on the dark screen of substance every essence it may descry. To grope, to blink, to dodge a blow, or to return it, is to have very radical and specific experiences, but probably without one assignable image of the outer senses. Yet a nameless essence, the sense of a moving existence, is there most intensely present; and a man would be a shameless, because an insincere, sceptic, who should maintain that this experience exists *in vacuo,* and does not express, as it feels it does, the operation of a missile flying, and the reaction of a body threatened or hit: motions in substance anterior to the experience, and rich in properties and powers which no experience will ever fathom.

Belief in substance, taken transcendentally, as a critic of knowledge must take it, is the most irrational, animal, and primitive of beliefs: it is the voice of hunger. But when, as I must, I have yielded to this presumption, and proceeded to explore the world, I shall find in its constitution the most beautiful justification for my initial faith, and the proof of its secret rationality. This corroboration will not have any logical force, since it will be only pragmatic, based on begging the question, and perhaps only a bribe offered by fortune to confirm my illusions. The force of the corroboration will be merely moral, showing me how appropriate and harmonious with the nature of things such a blind belief was on my part. How else should the truth have been revealed to me at all? Truth and blindness, in such a case, are correlatives, since I am a sensitive creature surrounded by a universe utterly out of scale with my self: I must, therefore, address it questioningly but trustfully, and it must reply to me in my own terms, in symbols and parables, that only gradually enlarge my childish perceptions. It is as if Substance said to Knowledge: My child, there is a great world for thee to conquer, but it is a vast, an ancient, and a recalcitrant world. It yields wonderful treasures to courage, when courage is guided by art and respects the limits set to it by nature. I should not have been so cruel as to give thee birth, if there had been nothing for thee to master; but having first prepared the field, I set in thy heart the love of adventure.

Literary Psychology

Scepticism and Animal Faith: Introduction to a System of Philosophy. New York: Charles Scribner's Sons; London: Constable and Co. Ltd., 1923, 252–61. Volume thirteen of the critical edition of *The Works of George Santayana.*

In this selection, Chapter XXIV of Scepticism and Animal Faith, *Santayana distinguished two ways of interpreting the behavior of other animate creatures: "whereas scientific psychology is addressed to the bodies and the material events composing the animate world, literary psychology restores the essences intervening in the perception of those material events, and re-echoes the intuitions aroused in those bodies" (ES, 107). Understanding of the mental life of another is impossible through direct intuition; instead the observer imaginatively interprets the mind of another by ascribing his or her own essences to the other person. One who does this well may appear to read other minds directly, but accurate interpretation actually is a symptom of insight, "a poetic by-product of fineness in instinct and in perception" (ES, 106–7). In a letter he explained that "literary psychology, all sympathy and imagination on the human scale, . . . on occasion may be absolutely and literally true of 'experience', since, unlike physical science, it describes experience in the very terms native to experience itself" (LGS, 4:340).*

Scientific psychology is a part of physics, or the study of nature; it is the record of how animals act. Literary psychology is the art of imagining how they feel and think. Yet this art and that science are practised together, because one characteristic habit of man, namely speech, yields the chief terms in which he can express his thoughts and feelings. Still it is not the words, any more than the action and attitude which accompany them, that are his *understanding* of the words, or his *sense* of his attitude and action. These can evidently be apprehended only dramatically, by imitative sympathy; so that literary psychology, however far scientific psychology may push it back, always remains in possession of the moral field.

When nature was still regarded as a single animal, this confusion extended to science as a whole, and tinctured the observation of nature with some suggestion of how a being that so acts must be minded, and what thoughts and sentiments must animate it. Such myths cannot be true; not because nature or its parts may not be animate in fact, but because there is no vital analogy between the cosmos and the human organism; so that if nature is animate as a whole, or in her minute or gigantic cycles, animation there is sure not to resemble human discourse, which is all we can attribute to her. Myth and natural theology are accordingly fabulous essentially and irremediably. If literary psychology is to interpret the universe at large, it can be only very cautiously, after I have explored nature scientifically as far as I can, and am able to specify the degree of analogy and the process of concretion that connect my particular life with the universal flux.

Myth is now extinct (which is a pity) and theology discredited; but the same confusion subsists in the quarters where it is not fashionable to doubt. History, for instance, is partly a science, since it contains archæological and antiquarian lore and a study of documents; but it is also, in most historians, an essay in dramatic art, since it pretends to rehearse the ideas and feelings of dead men. These would not be recoverable even if the historian limited himself to quoting their recorded words, as he would if he was conscientious; because even these words are hard to interpret afterwards, so as to recover the living sentiment they expressed. At least authentic phrases, like authentic relics, have an odour of antiquity about them which helps us to feel transported out of ourselves, even if we are transported in fact only into a more romantic and visionary stratum of our own being. Classic historians, however, are not content with quoting recorded words: they compose speeches for their characters, under the avowed inspiration of Clio; or less honestly, in modern times, they explain how their heroes felt, or what influences were at work in the spirit of the age, or what dialectic drove public opinion from one sentiment to another. All this is shameless fiction; and the value of it, when it has a value, lies exclusively in the eloquence, wisdom, or incidental information found in the historian. Such history can with advantage be written in verse, or put upon the stage; its virtue is not at all to be true, but to be well invented.

Philosophy fell into the same snare when in modern times it ceased to be the art of thinking and tried to become that impossible thing, the science of thought. Thought can be found only by being enacted. I may therefore guide my thoughts according to some prudent rule, and appeal as often as I like to experience for a new starting-point or a controlling perception in my thinking; but I cannot by any possibility make experience or mental discourse at large the object of investigation: it is invisible, it is past, it is nowhere. I can only surmise what it might have been, and rehearse it imaginatively in my own fancy. It is an object of literary psychology. The whole of British and German philosophy is only literature. In its deepest reaches it simply appeals to what a man says to himself when he surveys his adventures, re-pictures his perspectives, analyses his curious ideas, guesses at their origin, and imagines the varied experience which he would like to possess, cumulative and dramatically unified. The universe is a novel of which the ego is the hero; and the sweep of the fiction (when the ego is learned and omnivorous) does not contradict its poetic essence. The composition is perhaps pedantic, or jejune, or overloaded; but on the other hand it is sometimes most honest and appealing, like the autobiography of a saint; and taken as the confessions of a romantic scepticism trying to shake itself loose from the harness of convention and of words, it may have a great dramatic interest and profundity. But not one term, not one conclusion in it has the least scientific value, and it is only when this philosophy is good literature that it is good for anything.

The literary character of such accounts of experience would perhaps have been more frankly avowed if the interest guiding them had been truly psychological, like that of pure dramatic poetry or fiction. What kept philosophers at this task—often quite unsuited to their powers—was anxiety about the validity of knowledge in physics or in theology. They thought that by imagining how their ideas might have grown up they could confirm themselves in their faith or in their scepticism. Practising literary psychology with this motive, they did not practise it freely or sympathetically; they missed, in particular, the decided dominance of the passions over the fancy, and the nebulous and volatile nature of fancy itself. For this reason the poets and novelists are often better psychologists than the philosophers. But the most pertinent effect of this appeal of science to a romantic psychology was the *hypostasis of an imagined experience,* as if experience could go on in a void without any material organs or occasions, and as if its entire course could be known by miracle, as the experiences of the characters in a novel are known to the author.

Criticism of knowledge is thus based on the amazing assumption that a man can have an experience which is past, or which was never his own. Although criticism can have no first principle, I have endeavoured in this book to show how, if genuinely and impartially sceptical, it may retreat to the actual datum and find there some obvious essence, necessarily without any given place, date, or inherence in any mind. But from such a datum it would not be easy to pass to belief in anything; and if the leap was finally taken, it would be confessedly at the instance of animal faith, and in the direction of vulgar and materialistic convictions. Modern critics of knowledge have had more romantic prepossessions. Often they were not really critics, saying *It seems,* but rebels saying *I find, I know,* or empiricists saying *Everybody finds, Everybody knows.* Their alleged criticism of science is pure literary psychology, gossip, and story-telling. They are miraculously informed that there are many minds, and that these all have a conventional experience. What this experience contains, they think is easily stated. You have but to ask a friend, or make an experiment, or imagine how you would feel in another man's place. So confident is this social convention, that the natural world in which these experiences are reported to occur, and the assumed existence of which renders them imaginable, may be theoretically resolved into a picture contained in them. Thus the ground is removed which sustained all this literary psychology and suggested the existence of minds and their known experience at all; yet the groundless belief in these minds, and in copious knowledge of their fortunes, is retained as obvious; and this novelesque universe is called the region of facts, or of immediate experience, or of radical empiricism. Literary psychology thus becomes a metaphysics for novelists. It supplies one of the many thinkable systems of the universe, though a fantastic one; and I shall return to it, under the name of psychologism, when considering the realm of matter. Here I am concerned only with the evidence that such masses of experience exist or are open to my inspection.

No inspection is competent to discover anything but an essence; what social intuition touches is therefore always a dramatic illusion of life in others or in myself, never the actual experience that may have unfolded itself elsewhere as a matter of fact. Yet this dramatic illusion, like any given essence, may be a true symbol for the material events upon which the psyche is then directed; in this case, the life of other people, or my own past life, as scientific psychology might describe it. A good literary psychologist, who can read people's minds intuitively, is likely to anticipate their conduct correctly. His psychological imagination is not a link in this practical sagacity but a symptom of it, a poetic by-product of fineness in instinct and in perception. Slight indications in the attitude or temper of the persons observed, much more than their words, will suggest to the sympathetic instinct of the observer what those persons are in the habit of doing, or are inclined to do; and the stock idea assigned to them, or the stock passion attributed to them, will be but a sign in the observer's discourse for that true observation. I watch a pair of lovers; and it requires no preternatural insight for me to see whether the love is genuine, whether it is mutual, whether it is waxing or waning, irritable or confident, sensual or friendly. I may make it the nucleus of a little novel in my own mind; and it will be a question of my private fancy and literary gift whether I can evolve language and turns of sentiment capable of expressing all the latent dispositions which the behaviour of those lovers, unconscious of my observation, suggested to me. Have I read their minds? Have I divined their fate? It is not probable; and yet it is infinitely probable that minds and fates were really evolving there, not generically far removed from those which I have imagined.

The only facts observable by the psychologist are physical facts, and the only events that can test the accuracy of his theories are material events; he is therefore in those respects simply a scientific psychologist, even if his studies are casual and desultory. Whence, then, his literary atmosphere? For there is not only the medium of words which intervenes in any science, but the ulterior sympathetic echo of feelings truly felt and thoughts truly rehearsed and intended. I reply that whereas scientific psychology is addressed to the bodies and the material events composing the animate world, literary psychology restores the essences intervening in the perception of those material events, and re-echoes the intuitions aroused in those bodies. This visionary stratum is the true immediate as well as the imagined ultimate. Even in the simplest perceptions on which scientific psychology, or any natural science, can be based, there is an essence present which only poetry can describe or sympathy conceive. Schoolroom experiments in optics, for instance, are initially a play of intuitions, and exciting in that capacity; I see, and am confident and pleased that others see with me, this colour of an after-image, this straight stick bent at the surface of the water, the spokes of this wheel vanishing as it turns. For science, these given essences are only stepping-stones to the conditions under which they arise, and their proper æsthetic nature, which is trivial in itself, is forgotten in the curious knowledge I may acquire concerning light and perspective and refraction and the structure of the eye. Yet in that vast, vibrating, merciless realm of matter I am, as it were, a stranger on his travels. The adventure is exhilarating, and may be profitable, but it is endless and, in a sense, disappointing; it takes me far from home. I may seem to myself to have gained the whole world and lost my own soul. Of course I am still at liberty to revert in a lyrical moment to the immediate, to the intuitions of my childish senses; yet for an intelligent being such a reversion is a sort of *gran rifiuto* in the life of mind, a collapse into lotus-eating and dreaming. It is here that the Muses come to the rescue, with their dramatic and epic poetry, their constructive music, and their literary psychology. Knowledge of nature and experience of life are presupposed; but as at first, in the beginnings of science, intuition was but a sign for material facts to be discovered, so now all material facts are but a pedestal for images of other intuitions. The poet feels the rush of emotion on the other side of the deployed events; he wraps them in an atmosphere of immediacy, luminous or thunderous; and his spirit, that piped so thin a treble in its solitude, begins to sing in chorus. Literary psychology pierces to the light, to the shimmer of passion and fancy, behind the body of nature, like Dante issuing from the bowels of the earth at the antipodes, and again seeing the stars.

Such a poetic interpretation of natural things has a double dignity not found in sensuous intuitions antecedent to any knowledge of the world. It has the dignity of virtual truth, because there are really intuitions in men and animals, varying with their fortunes, often much grander and sweeter than any that could come to me. The literary psychologist is like some antiquary rummaging in an old curiosity shop, who should find the score of some ancient composition, in its rude notation, and should sit down at a wheezy clavichord and spell out the melody, wondering at the depth of soul in that archaic art, so long buried, and now so feebly revealed. This curious music, he will say to himself, was mighty and glorious in its day; this moonlight was once noon. There is no illusion in this belief in life long past or far distant; on the contrary, the sentimentalist errs by defect of imagination, not by excess of it, and his pale water-colours do no justice to the rugged facts. The other merit that dignifies intuitions mediated by knowledge of things, is that they release capabilities in one's own soul which one's personal fortunes may have left undeveloped. This makes the mainspring of fiction, and its popular charm. The illusion of projecting one's own thoughts into remote or imaginary characters is only half an illusion: these thoughts were never there, but they were always here, or knocking at the gate; and there is an indirect victory in reaching and positing elsewhere, in an explicit form, the life which accident denied me, and thereby enjoying it *sub rosa* in spite of fate. And there are many experiences which are only tolerable in this dream-like form, when their consequences are negligible and their vehemence is relieved by the distance at which they appear, and by the show they make. Thus both the truth and the illusion of literary psychology are blessings: the truth by revealing the minds of others, and the illusion by expanding one's own mind.

These imaginative blessings, however, are sometimes despised, and philosophers, when they suspect that they have no evidence for their psychological facts, or become aware of their literary flavour, sometimes turn away from this conventional miscellany of experience, and ask what is the substantial texture of experience beneath. Suppose I strain my introspection in the hope of discovering it; the picture (for such a method can never yield anything but pictures) may be transformed in two ways, to which two schools of recent literary psychology are respectively wedded. One transformation turns experience, intensely gaped at, into a mere strain, a mere sense of duration or tension; the other transformation unravels experience into an endless labyrinth of dreams. In the one case, experience loses its articulation to the extent of becoming a dumb feeling; and it is hard to see how, if one dumb undifferentiated feeling is the only reality, the illusion of many events and the intuition of many pictures could be grafted upon it. In the other case experience increases its articulation to the extent of becoming a chaos;

and the sensitive psychology that dips into these subterranean dreams needs, and easily invents, guiding principles by which to classify them. Especially it reverts to sexual and other animal instincts, thus grafting literary psychology (which in this field is called psycho-analysis) again on natural substance and the life of animals, as scientific psychology may report it.

This natural setting restores literary psychology to its normal status; it is no longer a chimerical metaphysics, but an imaginative version, like a historical novel, of the animation that nature, in some particular regions, may actually have possessed. The fineness and complexity of mental discourse within us may well be greater than we can easily remember or describe; and there is piety as well as ingenuity in rescuing some part of it from oblivion. But here, as elsewhere, myth is at work. We make a romance of our incoherence, and compose new unities in the effort to disentangle those we are accustomed to, and find their elements. Discourse is not a chemical compound; its past formations are not embedded in its present one. It is a life with much iteration in it, much recapitulation, as well as much hopeless loss and forgetfulness. As the loom shifts, or gets out of order, the woof is recomposed or destroyed. It is a living, a perpetual creation; and the very fatality that forces me, in conceiving my own past or future, or the animation of nature at large, to imagine that object afresh, with my present vital resources and on the scale and in the style of my present discourse—this very fatality, I say, reveals to me the nature of discourse everywhere, that it is poetry. But it is poetry about facts, or means to be; and I need not fear to be too eloquent in expressing my forgotten sentiments, or the unknown sentiments of others. Very likely those sentiments, when living, were more eloquent than I am now.

The Implied Being of Truth

Scepticism and Animal Faith: Introduction to a System of Philosophy. New York: Charles Scribner's Sons; London: Constable and Co. Ltd., 1923, 262–71. Volume thirteen of the critical edition of *The Works of George Santayana.*

Truth, explained Santayana in Chapter XXV of Scepticism and Animal Faith, *is not an immediate concern of the active animal; faith is enough. He wrote, "[t]he active object posited alone interests the man of action; if he were interested in the rightness of the action, he would not be a man of action but a philosopher" (ES, 111). He thought that modern philosophers continued this instinctive neglect of truth, because in their view "only things as they seem from moment to moment" exist, making the contrast between opinion and truth meaningless (ES, 112). According to such thinkers, opinion is all. But this view cannot stand, thought Santayana, in the face of the "experience of other people lying," which leads the "man of action" to realize a difference between what is said and what is the case. The awareness that comes with disputation is of "[t]hat standard comprehensive description of any fact which neither I nor any man can ever wholly repeat" (ES, 112). This, thought Santayana, was "what everybody spontaneously means by" the word 'truth' (ES, 113).*

From the beginning of discourse there is a subtle reality posited which is not a thing: I mean the truth. If intuition of essence exists anywhere without discourse, the being of truth need not be posited there, because intuition of itself is intransitive, and having no object other than the datum, can be neither true nor false. Every essence picked up by intuition is equally real in its own sphere; and every degree of articulation reached in intuition defines one of a series of essences, each contained in or containing its neighbour, and each equally central in that infinite progression. The central one, for apprehension, is the one that happens to appear at that moment. Therefore in pure intuition there is no fear of picking up the wrong thing, as if the object were a designated existence in the natural world; and therefore the being of truth is not broached in pure intuition.

Truth is not broached even in pure dialectic, which is only the apprehension of a system of essences so complex and finely articulated, perhaps, as to tax human attention, or outrun it if unaided by some artifice of notation, but essentially only an essence like any other. Truth, therefore, is as irrelevant to dialectic as to merely æsthetic intuition. Logic and mathematics are not true inherently, however cogent or extensive. They are ideal constructions based on ideal axioms; and the question of truth or falsity does not arise in respect to them unless the dialectic is asserted to apply to the natural world, or perhaps when a dispute comes up as to the precise essence signified by some word, such as, for instance, infinity.

When men first invented language and other symbols, or fixed in reflection the master-images of their dreams and thoughts, it seemed to them that they were discovering parts of nature, and that even in those developments they must be either right or wrong. There was a *true* name for every object, a part of its nature.

There was a *true* logic, and a *true* ethics, and a *true* religion. Certainly in so far as these mixed disciplines were assertions about alleged facts, they were either right or wrong; but in so far as they were systems of essences, woven together in fancy to express the instincts of the mind, they were only more or less expressive and fortunate and harmonious, but not at all true or false. Dialectic, though so fine-spun and sustained, is really a more primitive, a more dream-like, exercise of intuition than are animal faith and natural science. It is more spontaneous and less responsible, less controlled by secondary considerations, as poetry is in contrast with prose. If only the animals had a language, or some other fixed symbols to develop in thought, I should be inclined to believe them the greatest of dialecticians and the greatest of poets. But as they seem not to speak, and there is no ground for supposing that they rehearse their feelings reflectively in discourse, I will suppose them to be very empty-headed when they are not very busy; but I may be doing them an injustice. In any case their dreams would not suggest to them the being of truth; and even their external experience may hardly do so.

It might seem, perhaps, that truth must be envisaged even by the animals in action, when things are posited; especially as uncertainty and change of tactics and purpose are often visible in their attitudes. Certainly truth is there, if the thing pursued is such as the animal presumes it to be; and in searching for it in the right quarter and finding it, he enacts a true belief and a true perception, even if he does not realise them spiritually. What he realises spiritually, I suppose, is the pressure of the situation in which he finds himself, and the changes in his object; but that his belief from moment to moment was right or wrong he probably never notices. Truth would then not come within his purview, nor be distinguished amongst his interests. He would want to be successful, not to be right.

So in a man, intent experience, when not reflective, need not disclose the being of truth. Sometimes, in a vivid dream, objects suffer a transformation to which I eagerly adapt myself, changing my feelings and actions with complete confidence in the new facts; and I never ask myself which view was true, and which action appropriate. I live on in perfect faith, never questioning the present circumstances as they appear, nor do I follow my present policy with less assurance than I did the opposite policy a moment before. This happens to me in dreams; but politicians do the same thing in real life, when the lives of nations are at stake. In general I think that the impulse of action is translated into a belief in changed things long before it reproaches itself with having made any error about them. The recognition of a truth to be discerned may thus be avoided; because although a belief in things must actually be either true or false, it is directed upon the present existence and character of these things, not upon its own truth. The active object posited alone interests the man of action; if he were interested in the rightness of the action, he would not be a man of action but a philosopher. So long as things continue to be perceived in one form or another, and can be posited accordingly, the active impulse is released, and the machine runs on prosperously until some hitch comes, or some catastrophe. It is then always the things that are supposed to have changed, not the forms of folly. Even the most pungent disappointment, as when a man loses a bet, is not regarded otherwise than as a misfortune. It is all the fault of the dice; they might and ought to have turned up differently. This, I say to myself, is an empirical world; all is novelty in it, and it is luck and free will that are to blame. My bet was really right when I made it; there was no error about the future then, for I acted according to the future my fancy painted, which was the only future there was. My act was a creative act of vitality and courage; but afterwards things accountably went wrong, and betrayed their own promise.

I am confirmed in this surmise about the psychology of action by the reasoning of empirical and romantic philosophers, who cling to this instinctive attitude and deny the being of truth. No substance exists, according to their view, but only things as they seem from moment to moment; so that it is idle to contrast opinion with truth, seeing that there is nothing, not even things, except in opinion. They can easily extend this view to the future of opinion or of experience, and maintain that the future does not exist except in expectation; and at a pinch, although the flesh may rebel against such heroic subjectivism, they may say that the past, too, exists only in memory, and that no other past can be thought of or talked about; so that there is no truth, other than current opinion, even about the past. If an opinion about the past, they say, seems problematical when it stands alone, we need but corroborate it by another opinion about the past in order to make it true. In other words, though the word truth is familiar to these philosophers, the idea of it is unintelligible to them, and absent altogether from their apprehension of the world.

The experience which perhaps makes even the empiricist awake to the being of truth, and brings it home to any energetic man, is the experience of other people lying. When I am falsely accused, or when I am represented as thinking what I do not think, I rebel against that contradiction to my evident self-knowledge; and as the other man asserts that the liar is myself, and a third person might very well entertain that hypothesis and decide against me, I learn that a report may fly in the face of the facts. There is, I then see clearly, a comprehensive standard description for every fact, which those who report it as it happened repeat in part, whereas on the contrary liars contradict it in some particular. And a little further reflection may convince me that even the liar must recognise the fact to some extent, else it would not be *that* fact that he was misrepresenting; and also that honest memory and belief, even when most unimpeachable, are not exhaustive and not themselves the standard for belief or for memory, since they are now clearer and now vaguer, and subject to error and correction. That standard comprehensive description of any fact which neither I nor any man can ever wholly repeat, is the truth about it.

The being of truth thus seems to be first clearly posited in disputation; and a consequence of this accident (for it is an accident from the point of view of the truth itself under what circumstances men most easily acknowledge its authority)—a consequence is that truth is often felt to be somehow inseparable from rival opinions; so that people say that if there was no mind and consequently no error there could be no truth. They mean, I suppose, that nothing can be correct or incorrect except some proposition or judgement regarding some specific fact; and that the same constitution of the fact which renders one description correct, renders any contradictory description erroneous. "Truth" is often used in this abstract sense for correctness, or the quality which all correct judgements have in common; and another word, perhaps "fact" or "reality," would then have to be used for that standard comprehensive description of the object to which correct judgements conform. But a fact is not a description of itself; and as to the word "reality," if it is understood to mean existence, it too cannot designate a description, which is an essence only. Facts are transitory, and any part of existence to which a definite judgement is addressed is transitory too; and when they have lapsed, it is only their essence that subsists and that, being partially recovered and assigned to them in a retrospective judgement, can render this judgement true. Opinions are true or false by repeating or contradicting some part of the truth about the facts which they envisage; and this truth about the facts is the standard comprehensive description of them—something in the realm of essence, but more than the essence of any fact present within the limits of time and space which that fact occupies; for a comprehensive description includes also all the radiations of that fact—I mean, all that perspective of the world of facts and of the realm of essence which is obtained by taking this fact as a centre and viewing everything else only in relation with it. The truth about any fact is therefore infinitely extended, although it grows thinner, so to speak, as you travel from it to further and further facts, or to less and less relevant ideas. It is the splash any fact makes, or the penumbra it spreads, by dropping through the realm of essence. Evidently no opinion can embrace it all, or identify itself with it; nor can it be identified with the facts to which it relates, since they are in flux, and it is eternal.

The word truth ought, I think, to be reserved for what everybody spontaneously means by it: the standard comprehensive description of any fact in all its relations. Truth is not an opinion, even an ideally true one; because besides the limitation in scope which human opinions, at least, can never escape, even the most complete and accurate opinion would give precedence to some terms, and have a direction of survey; and this direction might be changed or reversed without lapsing into error; so that the truth is the field which various true opinions traverse in various directions, and no opinion itself. An even more impressive difference between truth and any true discourse is that discourse is an event; it has a date not that of its subject-matter, even if the subject-matter be existential and roughly contemporary; and in human beings it is conversant almost entirely with the past only, whereas truth is dateless and absolutely identical whether the opinions which seek to reproduce it arise before or after the event which the truth describes.

The eternity of truth is inherent in it: all truths—not a few grand ones—are equally eternal. I am sorry that the word eternal should necessarily have an unction which prejudices dry minds against it, and leads fools to use it without understanding. This unction is not rhetorical, because the nature of truth is really sublime, and its name ought to mark its sublimity. Truth is one of the realities covered in the eclectic religion of our fathers by the idea of God. Awe very properly hangs about it, since it is the immovable standard and silent witness of all our memories and assertions; and the past and the future, which in our anxious life are so differently interesting and so differently dark, are one seamless garment for the truth, shining like the sun. It is not necessary to offer any evidence for this eternity of truth, because truth is not an existence that asks to be believed in, and that may be denied. It is an essence involved in positing any fact, in remembering, expecting, or asserting anything; and while no truth need be acknowledged if no existence is believed in, and none would obtain if there was no existence in fact, yet on the hypothesis that anything exists, truth has appeared, since this existence must have one character rather than another, so that only one description of it in terms of essence will be complete; and this complete description, covering all its relations, will be the truth about it. No one who understands what is meant by this eternal being of truth can possibly deny it; so that no argument is required to support it, but only enough intensity of attention to express what we already believe.

Inspired people, who are too hot to think, often identify the truth with their own tenets, to signify by a bold hyperbole how certain they feel in their faith; but the effect is rather that they lead foolish people, who may see that this faith may be false, to suppose that therefore the truth may be false also. Eternal truths, in the mouth of both parties, are then tenets which the remotest ancestors of man are reputed to have held, and which his remotest descendants are forbidden to abandon. Of course there are no eternal tenets: neither the opinions of men, nor mankind, nor anything existent can be eternal; eternity is a property of essences only. Even if all the spirits in heaven and earth had been so far unanimous on any point of doctrine, there is no reason, except the monotony and inertia of nature, why their logic or religion or morals should not change to-morrow from top to bottom, if they all suddenly grew wiser or differently foolish.

At the risk of being scholastic I will suggest the uses to which the word eternal and the terms akin to it might be confined if they were made exact.

A thing that occupied but one point of physical time would be *instantaneous*. No essence is instantaneous, because none occupies any part of physical time or space; and I doubt whether any existence is instantaneous either; for if the mathematicians decide that the continuous or extended must be composed of an infinite number of inextended and non-contiguous units, in bowing to their authority I should retain a suspicion that nothing actual is confined to any of these units, but that the smallest event has duration and contains an infinite number of such units; so that one event (though not one instant) can be contiguous to another.

A given essence containing no specious temporal progression or perspective between its parts would be *timeless*. Colour, for instance, or number, is timeless. The timeless often requires to be abstracted from the total datum, because round any essence as actually given there is an atmosphere of duration and persistence, suggesting the existential flux of nature behind the essence. Colour seems to shine, that is, to vibrate. Number seems to mount, and to be built up. The timeless is therefore better illustrated in objects like laws or equations or definitions, which though intent on things in time, select relations amongst them which are not temporal.

A being that should have no external temporal relations and no locus in physical time would be *dateless*. Thus every given essence and every specious present is dateless, internally considered, and taken transcendentally, that is, as a station for viewing other things or a unit framing them in. Though dateless, the specious present is not timeless, and an instant, though timeless, is not dateless.

Whatsoever, having once arisen, never perishes, would be *immortal*. I believe there is nothing immortal.

Whatsoever exists through a time infinite in both directions is *everlasting*. Matter, time, the life of God, souls as Plato conceived them, and the laws of nature are commonly believed to be everlasting. In the nature of the case this can be only a presumption.

That which without existing is contemporary with all times is *eternal*. Truth is dateless and eternal, but not timeless, because, being descriptive of existence, it is a picture of change. It is frozen history. As Plato said that time was a moving image of eternity, we might say that eternity was a synthetic image of time. But it is much more than that, because, besides the description of all temporal things in their temporal relations, it contains everything that is not temporal at all; in other words, the whole realm of essence, as well as the whole realm of truth.

Comparison with Other
Criticisms of Knowledge

Scepticism and Animal Faith: Introduction to a System of Philosophy. New York: Charles Scribner's Sons; London: Constable and Co. Ltd., 1923, 289–309. Volume thirteen of the critical edition of *The Works of George Santayana.*

This selection, Chapter XXVII of Scepticism and Animal Faith, *shows how Santayana employed the history of philosophy both as an object of critique and a background to clarify his own ideas. For example, he contrasts his own skeptical project with the halting skepticism of modern philosophy. He acknowledged Hume and Kant as insightful critics of knowledge, but he thought they offered nothing to replace what they rejected, and he criticized their "attempt to conceive experience divorced from its physical ground and from its natural objects" (*ES, 119*). Their rejection of old philosophical notions such as essence, substance, and spirit in the name of reason and experience concealed an elevation of ego that would later flourish in idealistic philosophies. By contrast, Santayana's notion of animal faith counters idealism's dissolution of nature. In his thorough-going naturalism Santayana believed he was following Spinoza, whom he thought the only genuinely modern philosopher.*

Descartes was the first to begin a system of philosophy with universal doubt, intended to be only provisional and methodical; but his mind was not plastic nor mystical enough to be profoundly sceptical, even histrionically. He could doubt any particular fact easily, with the shrewdness of a man of science who was also a man of the world; but this doubt was only a more penetrating use of intelligence, a sense that the alleged fact might be explained away. Descartes could not lend himself to the disintegration of reason, and never doubted his principles of explanation. For instance, in order to raise a doubt about the applicability of mathematics to existence (for their place in the realm of essence would remain the same in any case) he suggested that a malign demon might have been the adequate cause of our inability to doubt that science. He thus assumed the principle of sufficient reason, a principle for which there is no reason at all. If any idea or axiom were really *a priori* or spontaneous in the human mind, it would be infinitely improbable that it should apply to the facts of nature. Every genius, in this respect, is his own malign demon. Nor was this the worst; for Descartes was not content to assume that reason governs the world—a notion scandalously contrary to fact, and at bottom contrary to reason itself, which is but the grammar of human discourse and aspiration linking mere essences. He set accidental limits to his scepticism even about facts. "I think, therefore I am," if taken as an inference is sound because analytical, only repeating in the conclusion, for the sake of emphasis, something assumed in the premise. If taken as an attestation of fact, as I suppose it was meant, it is honest and richly indicative, all its terms being heavy with empirical connotations. What is "thinking," what is "I," what is "therefore," and what is "existence"? If there were no existence there would certainly be no persons and no thinking, and it may be doubted (as I have indicated above) that anything exists at all. That any being exists that may be called "I," so that I am not a mere essence, is a thousand times more doubtful, and is often denied by the keenest wits. The persuasion that in saying "I am" I have reached an indubitable fact, can only excite a smile in the genuine sceptic. No *fact* is self-evident; and what sort of fact is this "I," and in what sense do I "exist"? Existence does not belong to a mere datum, nor am I a datum to myself; I am a somewhat remote and extremely obscure object of belief. Doubtless what I *mean* by myself is an existence and even a substance; but the rudimentary phantoms that suggest that object, or that suggest the existence of anything, need to be trusted and followed out by a laborious empirical exploration, before I can make out at all what they signify. Variation alleged, strain endured, persistence assumed—notions which when taken on faith lead to the assertion of existence and of substance, if they remained merely notions would prove nothing, disclose nothing, and assert nothing. Yet such, I suppose, are the notions actually before me when I say "I am." As to myself, when I proceed to distinguish that object in the midst of the moving world, I am roughly my body, or more accurately, its living centre, master of its organs and seat of its passions; and this inner life of the body, I suspect, was the rock of vulgar belief which Descartes found at hand, easy to mount on, after his not very serious shipwreck. And the rock was well chosen; not because the existence of my inner man is a simpler or a surer fact than any other; to a true sceptic this alleged being so busily thinking and willing and fuming within my body is but a strange feature in the fantastic world that appears for the moment. Yet the choice of the inner man as the one certain existence was a happy one, because this sense of life within me is more constant than other perceptions, and not wholly to be shaken off except in profound contemplation or in some strange forms of madness. It was a suitable first postulate for the romantic psychologist. On this stepping-stone to idealism the father of modem philosophy, like another Columbus, set his foot with elegance. His new world, however, would be but an unexplored islet in the world of the ancients if all he discovered was himself thinking.

Thinking is another name for discourse; and perhaps Descartes, in noting his own existence, was really less interested in the substance of himself, or in the fact that he was alive, than in the play of terms in discourse, which seemed to him obvious. Discourse truly involves spirit, with its intuition and intent, surveying those terms. And the definition of the soul, that its essence is to think, being a definition of spirit and not of a man's self, supports this interpretation. But discourse, no less than the existence of a self, needs to be posited, and the readiness with which a philosopher may do so yields only a candid confession of personal credulity, not the proof of anything. The assumption that spirit discoursing exists, and is more evident than any other existence, leads by a slightly different path to the same conclusion as the assumption of the self as the fundamental fact. In the one case discourse will soon swallow up all existence, and in the other this chosen existence, myself, will evaporate into discourse: but it will remain an insoluble problem whether I am a transcendental spirit, not a substance, holding the whole imaginary universe in the frame of my thought, or whether I am an instance of thinking, a phase of that flux of sentience which will then be the substance of the world. It is only if we interpret and develop the Cartesian axiom in the former transcendental sense that it supplies an instrument for criticism. Understood in an empirical way, as the confident indication of a particular fact, it is merely a chance dogma, betraying the psychological bias of reflection in modern man, and suggesting a fantastic theory of the universe, conveniently called psychologism; a theory which fuses the two disparate substances posited by Descartes, and maintains that while the inner essence of substance everywhere is to think, or at least to feel, its distribution, movement, and aspect, seen from without, are those of matter.

In adopting the method of Descartes, I have sought to carry it further, suspending all conventional categories as well as all conventional beliefs; so that not only the material world but all facts and all existences have lost their status, and become simply the themes or topics which intrinsically they are. Neither myself nor pure spirit is at all more real in that realm of essence than any other mentionable thing. When it comes to assertion (which is belief) I follow Descartes in choosing discourse and (as an implication of discourse) my substantial existence as the objects of faith least open to reasonable doubt; not because they are the first objects asserted, nor because intrinsically they lend themselves to existence better than anything else, but simply because in taking note of anything whatever I find that I am assuming the validity of primary memory; in other words, that the method and the fact of observation are adventitious to the theme. But the fact that observation is involved in observing anything does not imply that observation is the only observed fact: yet in this gross sophism and insincerity the rest of psychologism is entangled.

Hume and Kant seemed sceptics in their day and were certainly great enemies of common sense, not through any perversity of temper (for both were men of wise judgement) but through sophistical scruples and criticism halting at unfortunate places. They disintegrated belief on particular points of scholastic philosophy, which was but common sense applied to revelation; and they made no attempt to build on the foundations so laid bare, but rather to comfort themselves with the assurance that what survived was practically sufficient, and far simpler, sounder, and purer than what they had demolished. After the manner of the eighteenth century, they felt that convention was a burden and an imposture, not because here and there it misinterpreted nature, but because it interpreted or defined nature at all; and in their criticism they ran for a fall. They had nothing to offer in the place of what they criticised, except the same cheque dishonoured. All their philosophy, where it was not simply a collapse into living without philosophy, was retrenchment; and they retrenched in that hand-to-mouth fashion which Protestantism had introduced and which liberalism was to follow. They never touched bottom, and nothing could be more gratuitous or more helpless than their residual dogmas. These consisted in making metaphysics out of literary psychology; not seeing that the discourse or experience to which they appealed was a social convention, roughly dramatising those very facts of the material world, and of animal life in it, which their criticism had denied.

Hume seems to have assumed that every perception perceived itself. He assumed further that these perceptions lay in time and formed certain sequences. Why a given perception belonged to one sequence rather than to another, and why all simultaneous perceptions were not in the same mind, he never considered; the questions were unanswerable, so long as he ignored or denied the existence of bodies. He asserted also that these perceptions were repeated, and that the repetitions were always fainter than the originals—two groundless assertions, unless the transitive force of memory is admitted, and impressions are distinguished from ideas externally, by calling an intuition an impression when caused by a present object, visible to a third person, and calling it an idea when not so caused. Furthermore, he invoked an alleged habit of perceptions always to follow one another in the same order—something flatly contrary to fact; but the notion was made plausible by confusion with the habits of the physical world, where similar events recur when the conditions are similar. Intuitions no doubt follow the same routine; but the conditions for an intuition are not the previous intuitions, but the whole present state of the psyche and of the environment, something of which the previous intuitions were at best prophetic symptoms, symptoms often falsified by the event.

All these haltings and incoherences arose in the attempt to conceive experience divorced from its physical ground and from its natural objects, as a dream going on *in vacuo.* So artificial an abstraction, however, is hard to maintain consistently, and Hume, by a happy exercise of worldly wit, often described the workings of the mind as our social imagination leads us all vaguely to conceive them. In these inspired moments he made those acute analyses of our notions of material things, of the soul, and of cause, which have given him his name as a sceptic. These analyses are bits of plausible literary psychology, essays on the origin of common sense. They are not accounts of what the notions analysed mean, much less scientific judgements of their truth. They are supposed, however, by Hume and by the whole modern school of idealists, to destroy both the meaning of these notions and the existence of their intended objects. Having explained how, perhaps, early man, or a hypothetical infant, might have reached his first glimmerings of knowledge that material things exist, or souls, or causes, we are supposed to have proved that no causes, no souls, and no material things can exist at all. We are not allowed to ask how, in that case, we have any evidence for the existence of early man, or of the hypothetical infant, or of any general characteristics of the human mind, and its tendencies to feign. The world of literature is sacred to these bookish minds; only the world of nature and science arouses their suspicion and their dislike. They think that "experience," with the habits of thought and language prevalent in all nations, from Adam down, needs only to be imagined in order to be known truly. All but this imagined experience seems to them the work of imagination. While their method of criticism ought evidently to establish not merely solipsism, but a sort of solipsism of the present datum, yet they never stop to doubt the whole comedy of human intercourse, just as the most uncritical instinct and the most fanciful history represent it to be. How can such a mass of ill-attested and boldly dogmatic assumptions fail to make the critics of science uncomfortable in their own house? Is it because the criticism of dogma in physics, without this dogma in psychology, could never so much as begin? Is not their criticism at bottom a work of edification or of malice, not of philosophic sincerity, so that they reject the claim to knowledge only in respect to certain physical, metaphysical, or religious objects which the modern mind has become suspicious of, and hopes to feel freer without? Meantime, they keep their conventional social assumptions without a qualm, because they need them to justify their moral precepts and to lend a false air of adequacy to their view of the world. Thus we are invited to believe that our notions of material things do not mean what they assert, but being illusions in their deliverance, really signify only the series of perceptions that have preceded them, or that, for some unfathomable reason, may be expected to ensue.

All this is sheer sophistry, and limping scepticism. Certainly the vulgar notions of nature, and even the scientific ones, are most questionable; and they may have grown up in the way these critics suggest; in any case they have grown up humanly. But they are not mere images; they are beliefs; and the truth of beliefs hangs on what they assert, not on their origin. The question is whether such an object as they describe lies in fact in the quarter where they assert it to lie; the genealogy of these assertions in the mind of the believer, though interesting, is irrelevant. *It is for science and further investigation of the object to pronounce on the truth of any belief.* It will remain a mere belief to the end, no matter how much corroborated and corrected; but the fact that it is a belief, far from proving that it must be false, renders it possibly true, as it could not be if it asserted nothing and had no object beyond itself which it pointed to and professed to describe. This whole school criticises knowledge, not by extending knowledge and testing it further, but by reviewing it maliciously, on the tacit assumption that knowledge is impossible. But in that case this review of knowledge and all this shrewd psychology are themselves worthless; and we are reduced, as Hume was in his deeper moments of insight, to a speechless wonder. So that whilst all the animals trust their senses and live, philosophy would persuade man alone not to trust them and, if he was consistent, to stop living.

This tragic conclusion might not have daunted a true philosopher, if like the Indians he had reached it by a massive moral experience rather than by incidental sophistries with no hold on the spirit. In that case the impossibility of knowledge would have seemed but one illustration of the vanity of life in general. That all is vanity was a theme sometimes developed by Christian preachers, and even in some late books of the Bible, with special reservations; but it is an insight contrary to Hebraic religion, which invokes supernatural or moral agencies only in the hope of securing earthly life and prosperity for ever. The wisdom demanded could, therefore, not be negative or merely liberating; and scepticism in Christian climes has always seemed demoralising. When it forced itself on the reluctant mind, people either dismissed it as a game not worth playing and sank back, like Hume, into common sense, though now with a bad conscience; or else they sought some subterfuge or equivocation by which knowledge, acknowledged to be worthless, was nevertheless officially countersigned and passed as legal tender, so that the earnest practice of orthodoxy, religious or worldly, or both at once, might go on without a qualm. Evidently, to secure this result, it was necessary to set up some oracle, independent of natural knowledge, that should represent some deeper reality than natural knowledge could profess to reach; and it was necessary that this oracle itself, by a pious or a wilful oversight, should escape criticism; for otherwise all was lost. It escaped criticism by virtue of the dramatic illusion which always fills the sails of argument, and renders the passing conviction the indignant voice of omniscience and justice. The principle invoked in criticism, whatever it might be, could not be criticised. It did not need to be defended: its credentials were the havoc it wrought among more explicit conventions. And yet, by a mocking fatality, those discredited conventions had to be maintained in practice, since they are inevitable for mankind, and the basis, even by their weaknesses, of the appeal to that higher principle which, in theory, was to revise and reject them. This higher principle was no alternative view of the world, no revelation of further facts or destinies; it was the thinking or dreaming spirit that posited those necessary conventions, and would itself die if it ceased to posit them. In discrediting the fictions of spirit we must, therefore, beware of suspending them. We are not asked to abolish our conception of the natural world, nor even, in our daily life, to cease to believe in it; we are to be idealists only north-north-west, or transcendentally; when the wind is southerly, we are to remain realists. The pronouncements of animal faith have no doubt been reversed in a higher court, but with this singular proviso, that the police and the executioner, while reverently acknowledging the authority of the higher tribunal, must unflinchingly carry out the original sentence passed by the lower. This escape from scepticism by ambiguity, and by introducing only cancelled dogmas, was chosen by German philosophy at the beginning of the nineteenth century, and by modernism and pragmatism at the end of it.

Kant was thought a sceptic in his day, and called his philosophy criticism; but his scepticism was very impure and his criticism, though laborious, was very uncritical. That he was regarded as a great philosopher in the nineteenth century is due to the same causes that made Locke seem a great philosopher in the eighteenth, not to any intrinsic greatness. He announced some revolutionary principles, which alarmed and excited the public, but he did not carry them out, so that the public was reassured. In his criticism of knowledge he assumed without question the Humian sequences of perceptions, although contrary to his doctrine of time; and, more wisely than Hume, he never abandoned the general sense that these perceptions had organs and objects beneath and beyond them; but having cut off, by his malicious criticism of knowledge, the organs and objects which perceptions notoriously have, he was forced to forge others, artificial and metaphysical. Instead of the body, he posited a transcendental ego, the categories of thought, and a disembodied law of duty; instead of natural substances he posited the unknowable. I shall revert to these subjects in discussing the realm of matter, which is where they belong. Here I am concerned only with the analysis of knowledge, which in Kant was most conscientious, and valuable in spite of its rationalistic bias and its mythical solutions.

Any intelligent mind comes upon data and takes them for signs of things. Empirical criticism consists in reverting from these objects of intent, the things of common sense and science, to the immediate data by which they are revealed. But since data are not vacantly stared at by an intelligent being, but are interpreted and combined, there is evidently a subtler element in knowledge of things than the data which empirical criticism reverts to: namely, the principles of interpretation, since the data are read and taken to be significant of existing objects, far richer and more persistent and more powerful than themselves. These principles I have summarily called animal faith, not being concerned to propose any analysis of them that should apply to all minds or to all objects; for I conceive, for instance, that the future, in other animals, may be a more frequent and vivid object of animal faith than the past or the material environment posited by human beings. But Kant, assuming that mind everywhere must have a single grammar, investigated very ingeniously what he conceived to be its recondite categories, and schemata, and forms of intuition: all pompous titles for what Hume had satirically called tendencies to feign. But Kant, in dishonouring the intellect, at least studied it devotedly, like an alienist discovering the logic of madness; and he gave it so elaborate an articulation, and imposed it so rigorously on all men for ever, that people supposed he was establishing the sciences on a solid foundation rather than prescribing for all men a gratuitous uniformity in error. Yet this was his true meaning: and in spite of its psychological prefaces and metaphysical epilogues, and in spite of this pedantry about the necessary forms of all the sciences, the heart of the Kantian system was the most terrible negation. Among transcendental principles he placed space, time, and causality; so that, if he had been consistent, he would have had to regard all multiple and successive existence as imagined only. Everything conceivable would have collapsed into the act of conceiving it, and this act itself would have lost its terms and its purpose, and evaporated into nothing. But not at all; as if aware that all his conclusions were but curiosities in speculation and academic humours, he continued to think of experience as progressing in time, trifled most earnestly with astronomy and geography, and even comforted the pious with a postulate of immortality, as if time existed otherwise than in imagination. In fact, these backslidings were his amiable side: he always retained a certain humanity and wisdom, being much more thoroughly saturated with his conventional presuppositions than with his extravagant conclusions.

A philosopher, however, must be taken at his best, or at his worst; in any case, his pure doctrine must be freed as far as possible from its personal alloy: and the pure doctrine of Kant was that knowledge is impossible. Anything I could perceive or think was *ipso facto* a creature of my sense or thought. Nature, history, God and the other world, even a man's outspread experience, could be things imagined only. Thought—for it was still assumed that there was thought—was a bubble, self-inflated at every moment, in an infinite void. All else was imaginary;

no world could be anything but the iridescence of that empty sphere. And this transcendental thought, so rich in false perspectives, could it be said to exist anywhere, or at any time, or for any reason?

Here we touch one of those ambiguities and mystifications in which German philosophy takes refuge when pressed; strong in the attack, it dissolves if driven to the defensive. Transcendentalism, in so far as it is critical, is a method only; the principles by which data are interpreted come into play whenever intelligence is at work. The occasions for this exercise, as a matter of fact, are found in animal life; and while every mind, at every moment, is the seat and measure of its own understanding, and creates its own knowledge (though, of course, not the objects on which animal life is directed and which it professes to know) yet the quality and degree of this intelligence may vary indefinitely from age to age and from animal to animal. Transcendental principles are accordingly only principles of local perspective, the grammar of fancy in this or that natural being quickened to imagination, and striving to understand what it endures and to utter what it deeply wills. The study of transcendental logic ought, therefore, to be one of the most humane, tender, tentative of studies: nothing but sympathetic poetry and insight into the hang and rhythm of various thoughts. It should be the finer part of literary psychology. But such is not the transcendentalism of the absolute transcendentalists. For them the grammar of thought is single and compulsory. It is the method of the creative fiat by which not this or that idea of the universe, but the universe itself, comes into being. The universe has only a specious existence; and the method by which specious existence is evoked in thought is divine and identical in all thinking.

But why divine, and why always identical? And why any thinking at all, or any process or variation in discourse, other than the given perspectives of the present vision? At this point vertigo seizes the transcendentalist, and he no longer knows what he means. On the one hand, phenomena cannot be produced by an agency prior to them, for his first principle is that all existence is phenomenal and exists only in being posited or discovered. Will, Life, Duty, or whatever he calls this transcendental agency, by which the illusions of nature and history are summoned from the vasty deep, cannot be a fact, since all facts are created by its incantations. On the other hand phenomena cannot be substantial on their own account, for then they would not be phenomena but things, and no transcendental magician, himself non-existent and non-phenomenal, would be needed to produce them.

Absolute transcendentalism—the only radical form of a psychological criticism of knowledge—is accordingly not a thinkable nor a stable doctrine. It is merely a habit of speaking ambiguously, with a just sense for the living movement of thought and a romantic contempt for its deliverance. Self-consciousness cannot be, as this school strove to make it, a first principle of criticism: it is far too complex and derivative for that. But transcendentalism is a legitimate attitude for a poet in his dramatic reflections and romantic soliloquies; it is the principle of perspective in thought, the scenic art of the mental theatre. The fully awakened soul, looking about it in this strange world, may well believe that it is dreaming. It may review its shifting memories, with a doubt whether they were ever anything in themselves. It may marshal all things in ideal perspectives about the present moment, and esteem them important and even real only in so far as they diversify the mental landscape. And to compensate it for the visionary character which the world takes on, it may cultivate the sense (by no means illusory) of some deep fountain of feeling and fancy within the self. Such wistful transcendentalism is akin to principles which in India long ago inspired very deep judgements upon life. It may be practised at will by any reflective person who is minded to treat the universe, for the time being, as so much furniture for his dreams.

Yet this attitude, seeing that man is not a solitary god but an animal in a material and social world, must be continually abandoned. It must be abandoned precisely when a man does or thinks anything important. Its own profundity is dreamful, and, so to speak, digestive: action, virtue, and wisdom sound another note. It is therefore no worthy philosophy; and in fact the Germans, whose philosophy it is, while so dutiful in their external discipline, are sentimental and immoral in their spiritual economy. If a learned and placid professor tells me he is creating the universe by positing it in his own mind according to eternal principles of logic and duty, I may smile and admire such an inimitable mixture of enthusiasm and pedantry, profundity and innocence. Yet there is something sinister in this transcendentalism, apparently so pure and blameless; it really expresses and sanctions the absoluteness of a barbarous soul, stubborn in its illusions, vulgar in its passions, and cruel in its zeal—cruel especially to itself, as barbarism always is, because it feeds and dilates its will as if its will were an absolute power, whereas it is nothing but a mass of foolish impulses and boasts ending in ignominy. Moreover, transcendentalism cannot even supply a thorough criticism of knowledge, which would demand that the ideas of self, of activity, and of consciousness should be disintegrated and reduced to the immediate. In the immediate, however, there is no transcendental force nor transcendental machinery, not even a set of perceptions nor an experience, but only some random essence, staring and groundless.

I hope I have taken to heart what the schools of Hume and Kant have to offer by way of disintegrating criticism of knowledge, and that in positing afresh the notions of substance, soul, nature, and discourse, I have done so with my eyes open. These notions are all subject to doubt; but so, also, are the notions proposed instead by psychological philosophers. None of these have reached the limit of possible doubt; yet the dogmas they have retained, being romantic prejudices, are incoherent and incapable of serving as the basis for any reasonable system: and in a moral sense they are the very opposite of philosophy. When pressed, their negations end in solipsism and their affirmations in rhapsody. Far from purging the mind and strengthening it, that it might gain a clearer and more stable vision of the world, these critics have bewildered it with a multitude of methods and vistas, the expression of the confusion reigning in their day between natural science and religious faith, and between psychology and scepticism.

My endeavour has been to restore these things to their natural places, without forgetting the assumptions on which they rest. But the chief difference between my criticism of knowledge and theirs lies in the conception of knowledge itself. The Germans call knowledge *Wissenschaft,* as if it were something to be found in books, a catalogue of information, and an encyclopædia of the sciences. But the question is whether all this *Wissenschaft* is knowledge or only learning. My criticism is criticism of myself: I am talking of what I believe in my active moments, as a living animal, when I am really believing something: for when I am reading books belief in me is at its lowest ebb; and I lend myself to the suasion of eloquence with the same pleasure (when the book is well written) whether it be the *Arabian Nights* or the latest philosophy. My criticism is not essentially a learned pursuit, though habit may sometimes make my language scholastic; it is not a choice between artificial theories; it is the discipline of my daily thoughts and the account I actually give to myself from moment to moment of my own being and of the world around me. I should be ashamed to countenance opinions which, when not arguing, I did not believe. It would seem to me dishonest and cowardly to militate under other colours than those under which I live. Merely learned views are not philosophy; and therefore no modern writer is altogether a philosopher in my eyes, except Spinoza; and the critics of knowledge in particular seem to me as feeble morally as they are technically.

I should like, therefore, to turn to the ancients and breathe again a clear atmosphere of frankness and honour; but in the present business they are not very helpful. The Indians were poets and mystics; and while they could easily throw off the conventions of vulgar reason, it was often only to surrender themselves to other conventions, far more misleading to a free spirit, such as the doctrine of transmigration of souls; and when, as in Buddhism, they almost vanquished that illusion, together with every other, their emasculated intellect had nothing to put in its place. The Greeks on the contrary were rhetoricians; they seldom or never reverted to the immediate for a foothold in thought, because the immediate lies below the level of language and of political convention. But they were disputatious, and in that sense no opinion escaped their criticism. In this criticism they simply pitted one plausible opinion against another, supporting each in turn by all conceivable arguments, based on no matter what prejudices or presumptions. The result of this forensic method was naturally a suspense of rational judgement, favourable now to frivolity and now to superstition. The frivolity appeared in the Sophists who, seeing that nothing was certain, impudently assumed as true whatever it was socially convenient to advocate. Protagoras seems to have reduced this bad habit to an honest system, when he taught that each occasion is, for itself, the ultimate judge of truth. This, taken psychologically, is evidently the case: a mind cannot judge on other subjects nor on other evidences than are open to it when judging. But the judging moment need not judge truly; and to maintain (as Protagoras does in Plato's *Dialogue* and as some pragmatists have done in our day) that all momentary opinions are equal in truth, though not equal in value, is to fail in radical scepticism: for it is to assume many moments, and knowledge (utterly inexplicable on these principles) of their several sequences and import; and to assume something even more wanton, a single standard of value by which to judge them all. Such incoherence is not surprising in sophists whose avowed purpose in philosophising is to survive and succeed in this world, or perhaps in the next. Worldly people will readily admit that some ideas are better than others, even if both sets are equally false. The interest in truth for its own sake is not a worldly interest, but the human soul is capable of it; and there might be spirits directed on the knowledge of truth as upon their only ultimate good, as there might be spirits addressed exclusively to music. Which arts and sciences are worth pursuing, and how far, is a question for the moralist, to be answered in each case in view of the faculties and genius of the persons concerned, and their opportunities. Socrates may humorously eschew all science that is useless to cobblers; he thereby expresses his plebeian hard sense, and his Hellenic joy in discourse and in moral apologues; but if he allows this pleasant prejudice to blind him to the possibility of physical discoveries, or of cogent mathematics, he becomes a simple sophist. The moralist needs true knowledge of nature–even a little astronomy–in order to practise the art of life in a becoming spirit; and an agnosticism which was not merely personal, provisional, and humble would be the worst of dogmas.

A sinking society, with its chaos of miscellaneous opinions, touches the bottom of scepticism in this sense, that it leaves no opinion unchallenged. But as a complete suspense of judgement is physically impossible in a living animal, every sceptic of the decadence has to accept some opinion or other. Which opinions he accepts, will depend on his personal character or his casual associations. His philosophy therefore deserts him at the threshold of life, just when it might cease to be a verbal accomplishment; in other words, he is at intervals a sophist, but at no time a philosopher. Nevertheless, among the Greek sceptics there were noble minds. They turned their scepticism into an expression of personal dignity and an argument for detachment. In such scepticism every one who practises philosophy must imitate them; for why should I pledge myself absolutely to what in fact is not certain? Physics and theology, to which most philosophies are confined, are dubious in their first principles: which is not to say that nothing in them is credible. If we assert that one thing is more probable than another, as did the sceptics of the Academy, we have adopted a definite belief, we profess to have some hold on the nature of things at large, a law seems to us to rule events, and the lust of scepticism in us is chastened. This belief in nature, with a little experience and good sense to fill in the picture, is almost enough by way of belief. Nor can a man honestly believe less. An active mind never really loses the conviction that it is scenting the way of the world.

Living when human faith is again in a state of dissolution, I have imitated the Greek sceptics in calling doubtful everything that, in spite of common sense, any one can possibly doubt. But since life and even discussion forces me to break away from a complete scepticism, I have determined not to do so surreptitiously nor at random, ignominiously taking cover now behind one prejudice and now behind another. Instead, I have frankly taken nature by the hand, accepting as a rule in my farthest speculations the animal faith I live by from day to day. There are many opinions which, though questionable, are inevitable to a thought attentive to appearance, and honestly expressive of action. These natural opinions are not miscellaneous, such as those which the Sophists embraced in disputation. They are superposed in a biological order, the stratification of the life of reason. In rising out of passive intuition, I pass, by a vital constitutional necessity, to belief in discourse, in experience, in substance, in truth, and in spirit. All these objects may conceivably be illusory. Belief in them, however, is not grounded on a prior probability, but all judgements of probability are grounded on them. They express a rational instinct or instinctive reason, the waxing faith of an animal living in a world which he can observe and sometimes remodel.

This natural faith opens to me various Realms of Being, having very different kinds of reality in themselves and a different status in respect to my knowledge of them. I hope soon to invite the friendly reader to accompany me in a further excursion through those tempting fields.

Normal Madness

Dialogues in Limbo. London: Constable and Co. Ltd., 1925; New York: Charles Scribner's Sons, 1925, 36–57. Volume fourteen of the critical edition of *The Works of George Santayana.*

This selection first appeared as Chapter III of Dialogues in Limbo. *The book collects imagined conversations between souls from the history of philosophy and the Spirit of a Stranger still living on Earth. Several dialogues appeared in slightly different form in 1924 and 1925 in the American journal* The Dial. *The book was reissued in 1948 with a new preface and three additional dialogues. Santayana wrote of the dialogues that "[t]hey are not . . . a work of erudition or even of retrospective fancy, and I am not at all sure that the extant sayings of Democritus and the rest will justify everything that I put in their mouths. . . . My Democritus is intended to establish between his 'atoms & void' on the one hand and his 'normal madness' on the other precisely the same opposition and connection that the Indians established between Brahma and Illusion" (LGS, 3:256). Santayana wrote to a correspondent that "you . . . have struck the bull's eye, as far as my heart is concerned, by saying that you especially like my* Dialogues in Limbo, *and the idea of 'Normal Madness'" (LGS, 8:58).*

Democritus. You reappear in season, inquisitive Pilgrim, and to-day you must take a seat beside me. These young men are compelling my hoary philosophy to disclose the cause of all the follies that they perpetrated when alive. They still wear, as you see, their youthful and lusty aspect; for when we enter these gates Minos and Rhadamanthus restore to each of us the semblance of that age at which his spirit on earth had been most vivid and masterful and least bent by tyrant circumstance out of its natural straightness. Therefore Alcibiades and Dionysius and Aristippus walk here in the flower of their youth, and I sit crowned with all the snows and wisdom of extreme old age; because their souls, though essentially noble, grew daily more distracted in the press of the world and more polluted, but mine by understanding the world grew daily purer and stronger. They are still ready for every folly, though luckily they lack the means; and the chronicle of vanity remains full of interest for them, because they are confident of shining in it. Yet the person whom this subject most nearly touches is you, since you are still living, and life is at once the quintessence and the sum of madness. Here our spirits can be mad only vicariously and at the second remove, as the verses in which Sophocles expresses the ravings of Ajax are themselves sanely composed, and a calm image of horror. But your thoughts, in the confusion and welter of existence, are still rebellious to metre; you cannot yet rehearse your allotted part, as we do here, with the pause and pomp of a posthumous self-knowledge. My discourse on madness, therefore, will not only celebrate your actions, but may open your eyes; and I assign to you on this occasion the place of honour, as nearest of kin to the goddess Mania, who to-day presides over our games.

There is little philosophy not contained in the distinction between things as they exist in nature, and things as they appear to opinion; yet both the substance and its appearance often bear the same name, to the confusion of discourse. So it is with the word madness, which sometimes designates a habit of action, sometimes an illusion of the mind, and sometimes only the opprobrium which a censorious bystander may wish to cast upon either.

Moralists and ignorant philosophers like Socrates—of whom women and young men often think so highly—do not distinguish nature from convention, and because madness is inconvenient to society they call it contrary to nature. But nothing can be contrary to nature; and that a man should shriek or see wild visions or talk to the air, or to a guardian genius at his elbow, or should kill his children and himself, when the thing actually occurs, is not contrary to nature, but only to the habit of the majority. The diseases which destroy a man are no less natural than the instincts which preserve him. Nature has no difficulty in doing what she does, however wonderful or horrible it may seem to a fancy furnished only with a few loose images and incapable of tracing the currents of substance; and she has no hostility to what she leaves undone and no longing to do it. You will find her in a thousand ways unmaking what she makes, trying again where failure is certain, and neglecting the fine feats which she once easily accomplished, as if she had forgotten their secret. How simple it was once to be a Greek and ingenuously human; yet nature suffered that honest humanity to exist only for a few doubtful years. It peeped once into being, like a weed amid the crevices of those Aegean mountains, and all the revolving aeons will not bring it back. Nature is not love-sick; she will move on; and if to the eye of passion her works seem full of conflict, vanity, and horror, these are not horrors, vanities, or conflicts to her. She is no less willing that we should be mad than that we should be sane. The fly that prefers sweetness to a long life may drown in honey; nor is an agony of sweetness forbidden by nature to those inclined to sing or to love.

Moral terms are caresses or insults and describe nothing; but they have a meaning to the heart, and are not forbidden. You may, therefore, without scientific error, praise madness or deride it. Your own disposition and habit will dictate these judgements. A weak and delicate animal like man could have arisen only in an equable climate, in which at all seasons he might hunt and play, and run naked or gaily clad according to his pleasure: he therefore at first regards the Hyperborean regions, where summer and winter are sharply contrasted, as cruel and uninhabitable; yet if by accident or necessity he becomes hardened to those changes, he begins to think his native forests pestiferous and fit only for snakes and monkeys. So it is also with the climates of the mind. Every nation thinks its own madness normal and requisite; more passion and more fancy it calls folly, less it calls imbecility. Of course, according to nature, to possess no fancy and no passion is not to possess too little, and a stone is no imbecile; while to have limitless passion and fancy is not to have too much, and a drone among bees or a poet among men is not a fool for being all raptures. In the moralist aspiration is free to look either way. If some gymnosophist sincerely declares that to move or to breathe or to think is vanity, and that to become insensible is the highest good, in that it abolishes illusion and all other evils, to him I object nothing; if starkness is his treasure, let him preserve it. If on the other hand Orpheus or Pythagoras or Plato, having a noble contempt for the body, aspire to soar in a perpetual ecstasy, and if with their eyes fixed on heaven they welcome any accidental fall from a throne or from a housetop as a precious liberation of their spirits, fluttering to be free, again I oppose nothing to their satisfaction: let them hug Icarian madness to their bosoms, as being the acme of bliss and glory.

What, Aristippus and Dionysius, are you so soon asleep? I confidently expected you at this point to applaud my oration. But sleep on, if you prefer dreams to an understanding of dreams.

Perhaps you others, whose wits are awake, may ask me how, if in nature there be nothing but atoms in motion, madness comes to exist at all. I will not reply that motion and division are themselves insanity, although wise men have said so; for if division and motion are the deepest nature of things, insanity would be rather the vain wish to impose upon them unity and rest. For by sanity I understand assurance and peace in being what one is, and in becoming what one must become; so that the void and the atoms, unruffled and ever ready, are eminently sane. Not so however, those closed systems which the atoms often form by their cyclical motion: these systems are automatic; they complete and repeat themselves by an inward virtue whenever circumstances permit; yet even when circumstances do not permit, they madly endeavour to do so. This mad endeavour, when only partially defeated, may restore and propagate itself with but slight variations, and it is then called life. Of life madness is an inseparable and sometimes a predominant part: every living body is mad in so far as it is inwardly disposed to permanence when things about it are unstable, or is inwardly disposed to change when, the circumstances being stable, there is no occasion for changing. That which is virtue in season is madness out of season, as when an old man makes love; and Prometheus or Alexander attempting incredible feats is a miracle of sanity, if he attempts them at the right moment.

So much for madness in action, inevitable whenever the impulses of bodies run counter to opportunity. But life, both in its virtue and in its folly, is also expressed in fancy, creating the world of appearance. In the eye of nature all appearance is vain and a mere dream, since it adds something to substance which substance is not; and it is no less idle to think what is true than to think what is false. If ever appearance should become ashamed of being so gratuitous and like an old gossip should seek to excuse its garrulity by alleging its truth, neither the void nor the atoms would heed that excuse or accept it. Are they, forsooth, insecure that they should call upon that sleepy witness to give testimony to their being? Their being is indomitable substance and motion and action, and to add thought, impalpable and ghostly, is to add madness. Indeed fancy as if aware of its vanity, makes holiday as long as it can; its joy is in fiction, and it would soon fade and grow weary if it had to tell the truth. The heroes in the *Iliad,* instead of doing a man's work in silence, like honest atoms, love to recite their past exploits and to threaten fresh deeds of blood: had they respected reality they would have been content to act, but they must prate and promise, because they live by imagination. If their boasts are lies, as is probable, they are all the more elated. These fools might almost have perceived their own idiocy, if they had merely described their true actions, saying, "I am standing on two legs; I am hurling a spear, I am running away, I am lying flat and dead on the ground." The truth, my friends, is not eloquent, except unspoken; its vast shadow lends eloquence to our sparks of thought as they die into it. After all there was some sense in that nonsense of Socrates about the sun and moon being governed by reason, for they go their rounds soberly, without talking or thinking.

That the intoxication of life is the first cause of appearance you have all observed and experienced when you have danced in a chorus, or performed your military exercises, stamping on the ground in unison and striking your swords together; ordered motion being naturally fertile in sound, in flashing light, and in gladness. Such appearances, in the safe and liberal life of a god, would not be deceptive, since a god need not be concerned about his own existence, which is secure, or that of other things, which is indifferent, and he is not tempted to assert falsely, as men do, that sound and splendour and gladness are the substance of those things or of himself. In him the intoxication of life in creating appearance would not create illusion, but only an innocent and divine joy. Accordingly, when the voice of a god traverses the air, the burden of it is neither true nor false; only the priest or the people, anxiously interpreting that oracle according to their fears and necessities, render false or true by their presumption such scraps of it as they may hear. The god, however, was not mindful of them but was singing to himself his own song. This divine simplicity of nature is ill understood by mortals, who address everything to their mean uses and vain advantage; whereby in the struggle to lengthen their days a little they fill them with distraction.

This is a third and most virulent form of madness, in which the dreams of the vegetative soul are turned into animal error and animal fury. For animals cannot wait for the slow ministrations of earth and air, but as you see in birds and kittens and young children, must be in a fidget to move; prying in all directions and touching and gobbling everything within reach. This is their only entertainment, for they have lost all fine inner sensibility, and their feelings and fancies arise only when their whole soul is addressed to external things of which they are necessarily ignorant—for what can a simpleton know of the streams of atoms actually coursing about him? His mind is furnished only with feelings and images generated within, but being distracted by the urgency of his lusts and fears, he takes those images and feelings for pleasant lures or fantastic and stalking enemies. Thus whereas locomotion by itself would be unconscious and fancy by itself would be innocent and free from error, fancy married with locomotion, as it must be in the strife of animals, begets false opinion and wraps the naked atoms in a veil of dreams.

Such is the origin of opinion; and as the chief endeavour of the animal body is to defend and propagate itself at all costs, so the chief and most lasting illusion of the mind is the illusion of its own importance. What madness to assert that one collocation of atoms or one conjunction of feelings is right or is better, and another is wrong or is worse! Yet this baseless opinion every living organism emits in its madness, contradicting the equal madness of all its rivals. They say the stars laugh at us for this, but what is their own case? The sun and the planets may seem to gaping observation to lead a sane life, having found paths of safety; yet to the sharp eye of science the ambush is visible into which they glide. If they think themselves immortal gods, and feast and laugh together as they revolve complacently, they are mad, because a sudden surprise awaits them, and the common doom. Had they been wise, like philosophers who know themselves mortal, they should have consented and made ready to die, seeing that they are not pure atoms or the pure void, and that in forming them nature was not in earnest but playing. They would have done well to laugh, if they had laughed at themselves; for those who will not laugh with nature in her mockery and playfulness, turn her sport first into delusion and then into anguish.

Such being the nature and causes of madness, is there no remedy for it? In answering this question I broach the second and kindlier part of my discourse, when having described the disease I bring hope of health and prescribe the cure. A radical cure, though it exists, I will not propose to you, for you are young and inquisitive and not ready to renounce all life and all knowledge. Only some great and heroic sage can begin by disowning madness altogether and felling the tree of opinion at the root; nor would he, by leaping into total salvation, attain to any understanding of his former distress. In abolishing illusion he would have forgotten its existence and virtually denied it; so that for the blatant errors of his lusty years he would have substituted one great mute and perpetual error: the total ignorance which besets the atoms regarding the patterns and the dreams which in fact they generate. Suddenly to renounce all madness is accordingly to miss the truth about madness, together with the whole comic rout of this world, which is marvellously fertile in comedy.

My physic accordingly will be more gentle; I will not prescribe instant death as the only medicine. Wisdom is an evanescent madness, when the dream still continues but no longer deceives. In all illusions there is some truth, since being products of nature they all have some relation to nature, and a prudent mind by lifting their masks may discover their true occasions. Doubtless the number and swiftness of the atoms, even in a little space, must always elude human discernment; but the more foolish images of sense may be disallowed in favour of others more faithful to the true rhythms and divisions of nature. Thus to the innocent eye the six stout spokes of a chariot-wheel revolving rapidly are merged and blurred in one whirling disc; but the philosopher, though no less subject than other men to this illusion, on seeing the disc will remember the spokes, and in all his fevers and griefs will be mindful of the atoms; his forced illusions will not deceive him altogether, since he knows their cause, and it is in his power, if the worst befall, by a draught of atoms artfully mingled, to dispel all his griefs and fevers for ever. Meantime, in the interests of human life, without inquiring into its ultimate vanity, a conventional distinction may be drawn between madness and sanity. Belief in the imaginary and desire for the impossible will justly be called madness; but those habits and ideas will be conventionally called sane which are sanctioned by tradition and which, when followed, do not lead directly to the destruction of oneself or of one's country. Such conventional sanity is a normal madness like that of images in sense, love in youth, and religion among nations.

Two protecting deities, indeed, like two sober friends supporting a drunkard, flank human folly and keep it within bounds. One of these deities is Punishment, and the other Agreement. The very mad man chokes, starves, runs into the sea, or having committed some fearful rape or murder is sentenced to death by the magistrate. Even if harmless, he is tied with a chain, and dies like a dog in his kennel. Punishment thus daily removes the maddest from the midst of mankind. The remnant, though their thoughts be in their homely way still dull or fantastic, then plod on in relative safety, while the unhappy souls whom Punishment has overtaken rest from their troubles. For no sooner has the system of atoms forming an animal body lost its equilibrium and been dispersed in death, than no pain or fancy or haggard hope subsists in that system any longer, and the peace of indifference and justice returns to the world; and if here or in the memory of men some echo of that life reverberates, it rings without anguish, the note once sounded repeating itself perpetually, pure and undisturbed. This is the good work which Punishment does daily, healing and harmonizing the worst of follies.

Yet before dying in the arms of Punishment madness may be mitigated and tamed by Agreement, like a young colt broken in and trained to gallop in harness. The automatism of life, which is necessarily spontaneous and blind, may by adjustment with its occasions become a principle of health and genius, the parent of noble actions and beautiful works. Fancy, too, in creating images which have no originals in nature—since in nature there is nothing but atoms and the void—may by union with the times and order of natural events become the mother of names, pleasant and familiar, by which those events are called in the language of sense. Thus the most diverse imaginations in various species of animals may be rendered compatible with sagacity and with a prosperous life. Migratory fowl do not record their voyages in books, like human geographers, yet they have appointed dreams and secret sensations which warn them of the season for flight, and they are well informed about Egypt without consulting Herodotus. If omens were observed scientifically and not superstitiously interpreted, augury might be a true art of substitution, like language. There are many false tales told both by Greeks and barbarians which at times are useful to the state, because by an artful disposition of signs and sounds they dispose the inner parts of men favourably for breasting labour or war. Thus the most deed-dyed illusion, if it be interwoven with good habits, may flourish in long amity with things, naming and saluting them, as we do the stars, or the gods, without understanding their nature.

Such amity can the god Agreement establish even between aliens, but between brothers he weaves a subtler and a sweeter bond. For when kindred bodies have the same habitat and the same arts they also have the same illusions; and their common madness gives to each a perfect knowledge of the other's mind. Whereas the images in the eye or the thoughts of the heart can agree but loosely and, as it were, politically with material things, they may agree exactly with the images in another eye, and the thoughts of another heart. This free unanimity was called friendship by the Greeks, who alone of all nations have understood the nature of friendship. Barbarians of course may fight faithfully in bands, and may live in tribes and in cities, hugging their wives and children to their bosom; but such instinctive love, which all animals manifest, is not friendship. It moves in the realm of nature, and concerns only action and fate, whereas friendship is agreement in madness, when the same free thoughts and the same fraternal joys visit two kindred spirits. It was not for fighting loyally side by side that the Spartan phalanx or the Theban band were incomparable in the annals of war, but for fighting side by side for the sake of the beautiful, and in order that the liberal madness of their friendship might not end, unless it ended in death. All the glories of Greece are the fruits of this friendship and belong to the realm of madness tempered by Agreement; for out of the very fountain of madness Apollo and the Muses drew that intoxication which they taught to flow in the paths of health and of harmony. The Greeks in the intervals between their wars, instead of sinking into luxury and sloth, or into a vain industry, instituted games, in which peace was made keen and glorious by a beautiful image of war. Actual war is a conflict of matter with matter, as blind as it is inevitable; but the images which it breeds survive in peace, as we survive in these removed spaces after the battle of existence. So even the wisest when alive play with images and interests, and the glitter of many rival opinions hides the deep harmony with nature by which these opinions live. There is sweetness and quaint reason in these frail thoughts of our after-life, as in the wisdom of children. What could be madder than a ghost? Yet by the harmony which each of us has long since attained with himself, and by the freedom and peace which we gladly grant to one another, we immortalize the life of friendship and share it with the gods.

Let such, then, be my discourse upon madness. Philosophers are unjust to the madness of the vulgar, and the vulgar to that of madmen and philosophers, not seeing how plausible a substitute it is for their own, because everybody thinks himself sane; wherein precisely shines his blinding illusion. I have wished in a manner to remove the mystery and the odium from this universal predicament of mortals, and to show it to be no anomaly. Madness is natural and, like all things natural, it loves itself, and often, by its innocence or by its signification, it lives in harmony with the rest of nature; otherwise, by the action it comports, it finds its quietus in punishment and death.

Alcibiades. Your discourse, indomitable Sage, has filled us all with wonder, and left us without the wish to speak. The Stranger, if he had dared, should have broken this silence rather than I, for you tell us that madness comes of being alive, and very likely he thinks that such an opinion comes of being dead.

Democritus. Very likely, but let him speak for himself.

The Stranger. I should not hesitate to do so if I had anything to object to so persuasive a discourse, but words on my part are superfluous, since I recognize the truth of every part of it. To show you, however, that the living are not always unwilling to confess their plight, I will repeat an old story of the sort which we compose for children. It seems curiously to confirm all that the noble Democritus has taught us.

Once upon a time, so the story runs, the whole world was a garden in which a tender fair-haired child, whose name was Autologos, played and babbled alone. There was, indeed, an old woman who tended the garden, a goddess in disguise; but she lived in a cave and came out only at night when the child was asleep, for like the bat and the astronomer she could see better in the dark. She had a sharp pruning-hook on a very long pole, with which she silently pruned every tree and shrub in the garden, even the highest branches, cutting off the dead twigs and shaking down the yellow leaves in showers; and often, muttering surly words to herself which were not intelligible, she would cut off some flower or some bud as well, so that when the child awoke he missed them and could not imagine what had become of them. Now the child in his play gave names to everything that he liked or disliked; and the rose he called Beauty, and the jasmin Pleasure, and the hyacinth Sweetness, and the violet Sadness, and the thistle Pain, and the olive Merit, and the laurel Triumph, and the vine Inspiration. He was highly pleased with all these names, and they made those flowers and plants so much more interesting to him, that he thought those names were their souls. But one day, having pricked himself with the thorns of a rose, he changed her name to Love; and this caused him to wonder why he had given those particular names to everything rather than quite different names; and the child began to feel older. As he sat brooding on this question, for he had stopped playing, a man in a black gown came into the garden who was a botanist, and said: "It matters little what names you give to flowers because they already have scientific names which indicate their true genera and species; the rose is only a rose, and is neither Beauty nor Love; and so with all the other flowers. They are flowers and plants merely, and they have no souls." Hearing this the child began to cry, very much to the botanist's annoyance, for being a busy man he disliked emotion. "After all," he added, "those names of yours will do no harm, and you may go on using them if you please; for they are prettier than those which truly describe the flowers, and much shorter; and if the word soul is particularly precious to you, you may even say that plants and flowers have souls: only, if you wish to be a man and not always a child, you must understand that the soul of each flower is only a name for its way of life, indicating how it spreads its petals in the morning and perhaps closes them at night, as you do your eyes. You must never suppose, because the flower has a soul, that this soul does anything but what you find the flower actually doing." But the child was not comforted, and when the wind had dried his tears, he answered: "If I cannot give beautiful names to the plants and flowers which shall be really their souls, and if I cannot tell myself true tales about them, I will not play in the garden any more. You may have it all to yourself and botanize in it, but I hate you." And the child went to sleep that night quite flushed and angry. Then, as silently as the creeping moonlight, the old woman came out of her cave and went directly to the place where the child was sleeping, and with a great stroke of her pruning-knife cut off his head; and she took him into her cave and buried him under the leaves which had fallen on that same night, which were many. When the botanist returned in the morning and found the child gone he was much perplexed. "To whom," said he to himself, "shall I now teach botany? There is nobody now to care for flowers, for I am only a professor, and if I can't teach anybody the right names for flowers, of what use are flowers to me?" This thought oppressed the poor man so much that he entirely collapsed, and as he was rather wizened to begin with, he was soon reduced to a few stiff tendons and bones, like the ribs of a dry leaf; and even these shreds soon crumbled, and he evaporated altogether. Only his black gown remained to delight the rag-picker. But the goddess in guise of that old woman went on pruning the garden, and it seemed to make no difference in her habits that the child and the botanist were dead.

I think we may surmise that the true name of this goddess must have been Dikè, the same that the wise Democritus was calling Punishment; and the botanist's name must have been Nomos, whom he was calling Agreement; and of course the child Autologos was that innocent illusion which was the theme of his whole discourse.

Aristippus. If this be the nature of madness, I propose that we immediately raise an altar to that deity, and worship him hereafter as the only beneficent god; and in order to avoid the protests of the vulgar, who think madness an evil, we will disguise our deity under the name of Autologos, borrowed from the Stranger's tale; and we will not identify him with the Furies or Harpies, but with Pan, Apollo, Orpheus, and Dionysus.

Dionysius. Agreed: and since my name is derived from that of Dionysus, who must have been my ancestor, I proclaim myself high priest of the new temple.

Democritus. You pay my speech a great tribute. I have celebrated the mad god so fitly that I have filled his votaries with a new frenzy of worship.

Alcibiades. Aristippus and Dionysius are enemies of science, and you, Democritus, are a believer in it. Being no judge in the matter, I will not pronounce between you, but I can conceive that a man who has spent his whole long life distilling herbs and grinding stones into powder should believe that he knows something of their substance. Nevertheless, intense study, too, is hypnotic, and might not the lucid theory of nature which you think partly awakens you out of the dream of life, be but a dream within a dream and the deepest of your illusions? My whole career seems a myth to me now in memory; yet when I interpret it in terms of your philosophy and imagine instead nothing but clouds of atoms drifting through a black sky, I seem to be descending into an even deeper cavern of reverie. Suppose I was dreaming of a chariot-race, hearing the shouting crowds, blushing to be myself the victor, and reining in my quivering steeds to receive the crown, and suppose that suddenly my dream was transformed, and Olympia and the sunshine and myself and my horses and my joy and the praises of the Athenians turned to atoms fatally combined—I am afraid that, like the child in the Stranger's tale, I should burst into tears at that change of dreams.

Democritus. Do you think I should blame you? Is the sublimity of truth impatient of error? I know well the shock that comes to innocence on discovering that the beautiful is unsubstantial. The soul, too, has her virginity and must bleed a little before bearing fruit. You misconceive my philosophy if you suppose that I deny the beautiful or would madly forbid it to appear. Has not my whole discourse been an apology for illusion and a proof of its necessity? When I discover that the substance of the beautiful is a certain rhythm and harmony in motion, as the atoms dance in circles through the void (and what else should the substance of the beautiful be if it has a substance at all?) far from destroying the beautiful in the realm of appearance my discovery raises its presence there to a double dignity; for its witchery, being a magic birth, is witchery indeed; and in it its parent nature, whose joy it is, proves her fertility. I deny nothing. Your Olympian victory and your trembling steeds, spattered with foam, and your strong lithe hand detaining them before the altar of Apollo, while you receive the crown—how should science delete these verses from the book of experience or prove that they were never sung? But where is their music now? What was it when passing? A waking dream. Yes, and grief also is a dream, which if it leaves a trace leaves not one of its own quality, but a transmuted and serene image of sorrow in this realm of memory and truth. As the grief of Priam in Homer and the grief of Achilles, springing from the dreadful madness of love and pride in their two bosoms, united in the divine ecstasy of the poet, so all the joys and griefs of illusion unite and become a strange ecstasy in a sane mind. What would you ask of philosophy? To feed you on sweets and lull you in your errors in the hope that death may overtake you before you understand anything? Ah, wisdom is sharper than death and only the brave can love her. When in the thick of passion the veil suddenly falls, it leaves us bereft of all we thought ours, smitten and consecrated to an unearthly revelation, walking dead among the living, not knowing what we seem to know, not loving what we seem to love, but already translated into an invisible paradise where none of these things are, but one only companion, smiling and silent, who by day and night stands beside us and shakes his head gently, bidding us say Nay, nay, to all our madness. Did you think, because I would not spare you, that I never felt the cold steel? Has not my own heart been pierced? Shed your tears, my son, shed your tears. The young man who has not wept is a savage, and the old man who will not laugh is a fool.

Some Meanings of the Word "Is"

Obiter Scripta: Lectures, Essays and Reviews. Edited by Justus Buchler and Benjamin Schwartz. New York: Charles Scribner's Sons; London: Constable and Co. Ltd., 1936, 189–212.

This selection first appeared in The Journal of Philosophy *(21 [1924]: 365–77). A shorter version with the same title was published in 1915 (*The Journal of Philosophy, Psychology, and Scientific Methods, *12 [1915]:66–68). As early as 1914 Santayana had intended the article as the first chapter of his* Realms of Being. *The 1924 article was republished in* Obiter Scripta, *and in a letter to the editors of that volume Santayana wrote: "I am also glad that you have rescued the 'Meanings of the Word "Is"'.' On re-reading that article, I feel that it contains my whole philosophy in a very clear and succinct form: I was dissuaded by a friend from putting it into 'The Realm of Essence', and also by my own feeling that it covered too much ground to go into that volume. Here [in* Obiter Scripta*] it is in its place." (LGS, 5:158). The seven meanings of the word "is" that Santayana distinguished demonstrate different realms of being that make up his ontological system.*

Language is Loose because Significant.–Words, as Bacon said, are wise men's counters, they mark some gain or some wager of thought. If they prejudice philosophy, they contain philosophy. The articulation of language, however, can never be the articulation of things. Language is a by-product of animal life which may eventually serve as a record or as an instrument; it helps to summarize, classify, and analyze man's contact with the world, reducing things to human perspectives on a human scale. Nor can language preserve the scope or movement even of thought, since it marks only certain terms or *termini*–boundary stones like statues at the end of vistas–on which attention is sharply arrested; the approach, the atmosphere, and the setting remain unnamed. A word cannot be adequate if it has a meaning at all: only whistling is adequate. Significant speech is a lasso thrown into the air, lucky if it catches some living thing by a leg or by a horn. It would be idle as well as ungrateful to quarrel with words when one must use them; but in venturing upon a long discourse it may be prudent to notice the degree to which some important term abbreviates the facts it stands for, or puts them under an alien category; and since I am about to distinguish various realms of being,* I will begin with some consideration of the word *"is,"* for this little word has many meanings.

First meaning of the word "is": Identity.–Of these meanings the most radical and proper is that in which I may say of any thing that it is what it is. This asseveration does not commit me to any description of the object nor to any assertion of its existence. I merely note its idiosyncrasy as a particular counter in the pile,

---

*This paper was intended to form the first chapter of *Realms of Being. *It has not appeared in its entirety, however, in *The Realm of Essence *or *The Realm of Matter, *the first two volumes of *Realms of Being. *The brief passages there reprinted are noted below.

something which, whatever it may be, is that object and no other. Its qualitative identity enables me to distinguish it, to study it, and to hold it fast in thought, so that I may eventually frame a definition of it, and perhaps assert or deny its existence. The copula properly denotes this singular and exclusive identity of each term with itself; not only in the abstract case of *A* is *A,* but also when the term (*e.g.,* the triangle) is specifically determined up to a certain degree of articulation (*e.g.,* as a plane enclosed by three straight lines); an articulation which the verb *"to be"* (when I say, Let *a, b, c* be a triangle) registers and posits, so as to permit me to identify the object in question; for if an object had no specific character, it would be meaningless to say that *it* was before me or was the theme of my discourse.

That what I see, I see, or what I am, I am, may seem a vain assertion; practical minds are not interested in any thing except for the sake of something else. They are camp-followers or heralds of the flux of nature, without self-possession. Yet if that which is actual and obvious at the moment never had a satisfying character, no satisfaction would ever be possible, and life would be what a romantic philosophy would make it—a wild-goose chase. In reality, to a simple or to a recollected spirit, the obvious often is enough.* Its identity may have a deep charm, like that of a jewel. I may long ruminate upon it, and impress it upon myself by repetitions, as when, fixing my mind's eye on some essence ideally determinate, I say to myself "No, no," or "Business is business." The repetition serves to detach and to render indubitable the essence meant, so that my judgment may recognize it to the exclusion of circumstances, which do not alter essences.

Identity the principle of essence.—This being the most radical intimate meaning of the word *"is,"* I have felt justified in usurping the term *"essence,"* derived from the same root, to designate any ideal or formal nature, any thing always necessarily identical with itself.† Essence so understood much more truly *is* than any substance or any experience or any event: for a substance, event, or experience may change its form or may exist only by changing it, so that all sorts of things that are proper to it in one phase will be absent from it in another. It will not be a unit at all, save by external delimitation. Perhaps some abstract constancy in quantity, energy, or continuity may be discovered to run through it, but this constant element will never be the actual experience, event, or substance in its living totality at any moment. Or perhaps all the phases of such an existence may be viewed together and synthesized into one historical picture; but this picture would again not be the existent substance, experience, or event unrolling itself in act. It would be only a description of that portion of the flux seen under the form of eternity; in other words, it would be an essence and not an existence. Essence is just that character which any existence wears in so far as it remains identical with itself and so long as it does so; the very character which it throws overboard by changing, and loses altogether when it becomes something else. To be able to become something else, to suffer change and yet endure, is the privilege of existence, be it in a substance, an event, or an experience; whereas

---

*The text from this point to the end of the paragraph is reprinted slightly modified in *The Realm of Essence,* p. 6.

†The rest of this paragraph and all of the next are reprinted in *The Realm of Essence,* pp. 23–24.

essences can be exchanged, but not changed. Existence at every step casts off one essence and picks up another: we call it the same existence when we are able to trace its continuity in change, by virtue of its locus and proportions; but often we are constrained to give up the count, and to speak of a new event, a new thing, or a new experience. The essences or forms traversed in mutation render this mutation possible and describable: without their eternal distinctness no part of the flux could differ in any respect from any other part, and the whole would collapse into a lump without order or quality. So much more profound is the eternal being of the essences traversed in change, than that of the matter or attention or discourse which plays with those essences at touch and go.

Notion of the Realm of Essence.–Nothing, then, more truly *is* than character. Without this wedding garment no guest is admitted to the feast of existence: whereas the unbidden essences do not require that invitation (with which very low characters are sometimes honoured) in order to preserve their proud identity out in the cold. There those few privileged revellers will soon have to rejoin them, not a whit fatter for their brief surfeit of being. After things lose their existence, as before they attain it, although it is true of them that they have existed or will exist, they have no internal being except their essences, quite as if they had never broached Existence at all: yet the identity of each essence with itself and difference from every other essence suffices to distinguish and define them all in eternity, where they form the Realm of Essence. True and false assertions may be made about any one of them, such, for instance, as that it does not exist; or that it includes or excludes some other essence, or is included or excluded by it.

Transition to Looser Meanings: Posited or Problematical Identities.–Nevertheless, the hypnotic charm of identity, or the dialectic pattern of essences, soon wearies a restive animal and seems to him idiotic. Having once observed and established the identity of every essence with itself, I may well turn to something else and put the word *"is"* to more pregnant uses. Identity itself will interest me more when, being that of a thing and not of an essence, it becomes problematical. I shall then be intent, not on some term directly present to intuition, but on some ulterior term signified by one or more different symbols themselves given immediately. The identity of things and persons is regularly masked in this way by their various names or appearances, so that their identity may be denied by the sceptic, and the assertion of it, far from being trivial, may be instructive, surprising or tragic. Thus pointing to a stranger in rags I may say: "This is Odysseus, the King"; or I may discover that XI is eleven, or that 11 is 7 + 4. Evidently such identifications do not intend to identify the two terms in their immediacy: the present aspect of Odysseus is not that of a king, those two Roman letters are not the English word "eleven," nor is one of those arithmetical symbols actually the other. So when I say "This is John," it would not be a very penetrating criticism of my poor human logic to argue that I was confusing a man with a sound, and pronouncing them identical. The identity is that of John with himself, an intended and existing object. The sound of his name and his image to sight are converging symbols, both signifying the same living person, with his ancestry and continuity in the material world. This term, posited as identical with itself, is removed from immediacy and belongs to a plane of being believed in by me, which if my animal faith misleads me need not exist at all: yet even in that case, I should be setting up a fixed theme of discourse, to which ulterior ideas might also be relevant; as when I point to a picture and say: "This is not Saint George but the Archangel Michael, because he has wings." I am content if the hints of sense, fused in the heat of recognition, lead me to some staunch ideal identity.

Second Meaning: Equivalence.–I may, however, be less concerned with the ulterior essence or thing through which two different symbols are identified than in the diversity of the symbols themselves. It is silly to urge that water is water, but interesting to not that *aqua* is *eau*. Where the native word carries the mind straight to the object, the foreign words interpose their own idiosyncrasy, and I not only notice their presence, but the fact that they have no resemblance whatever to the object they signify. They lead a life of their own, the life of sense or of language, in which touch may be sharpened into smell or sight, and a Latin word may become a French one which retains none of the original sounds, yet has exactly the same meaning. I thus learn that words and sensations may signify the same thing in endlessly different ways; and when some monoglot idiot balks at this wealth of synonyms (like Pierrot willing to touch a "dead man" but not a "corpse"), I can rebuke him by saying, "But it's the same thing!" The thing is indeed the same, but not the æsthetic essences that symbolize it to the fancy. So when Walt Whitman exclaims, "Alabama, Minnesota, Maryland, Vermont!" if his inspiration had not faltered and he had completed the list, the poetic essence of that catalogue would not be identical with the single cry, "The United States!" Attention forms individuals. When the parts are taken separately, each is at the centre of the world, and stops at its own boundary: when they are taken together, no boundaries are visible and many a feature found in one part may form a unit, like a river or a road, with a feature continuing it in another part. Sometimes, too, when two very different expressions are alleged to be equivalent, the identification of their objects seems doubtful or even shocking: as if instead of six square yards of carpet I am offered 7776 square inches of it, or a vote instead of freedom, or the most real of beings instead of God.

Equivalent terms coupled by the word *"is"* are, accordingly, far from identical; and even if the identity of the object meant be granted, the substitution of one term for the other may make an important difference to the lover of form, thought, or language. Even in matters of business, there is a choice of methods and manners; if you pay a bill in gold or in coppers, by cheque or in bank-notes, the sum may be the same, but the action and the experience are different. The medium in such a transaction may seem irrelevant, but some medium is indispensable, and the interest in the choice of that medium is ineradicable: because the immediate is always with us.

Now in philosophy there is a medium which plays a great part, namely, thought. Thought is an outsider in respect to the things, facts, events, and essences which it considers; for although thought is itself an event and has an essence, it cannot at the time consider that fact. Even that which it considers it cannot exhaust. It identifies, connects, and describes its objects not according to their intrinsic natures but according to their names or images in discourse, and to the dialectical relations of these names or images.

Third Meaning: Definition.—Hence the importance which some philosophers give to definition. They are always asking you to tell them *what* some natural object is—man, matter, time, God—as if any definition whatever which you might offer of such deep-lying realities would be likely to come nearer to the thing as it is than do current names, sundry indications, or even the sum total of your discourse on that subject. Man, they say, *is* a rational animal: a circle *is* a plane figure bounded by a curve every part of which is equally distant from a point within called the centre. These definitions may be correct; but if I had no independent knowledge of what a man or a circle was, I could not judge whether they were correct or not. Pure discourse likes to take the bit in its teeth; and a geometer might tell me that he need have no notion whatever of the circle save that which the definition gives him, and that all his deductions would follow just as well from that premise; indeed, it is only from that premise that they must follow if they are to be valid mathematically. The definition of the circle *is* the circle for the geometer. It would therefore be better, and worthier of the purity of deductive science, to drop such terms as circle, which suggests wheels, round eyes, and other vulgar objects, and to invent a symbol or formula to express the definition only, without any images borrowed from sense.

I believe this is the right method of dialectic; and if it is rigorously employed, it keeps discourse revolving about essences alone, and only about such essences as it has explicitly selected. But then, let it be remembered, these essences are not alleged to be the essences of anything existing. What follows from the algebraic formula for the circle is not alleged to hold good of hoops or rose-windows or the course of the planets. So that when any material, visible, or imagined circle is said to *be* a circle in the mathematical sense, the assertion is worse than false: it is irrelevant. Nothing can *be* the definition of it: at best the definition may be true of it. No definition, and no dialectic proceeding from the definition, can vouch for this natural truth. Only animal faith, trust in appearances, or experience in practical arts can justify such a presumption, or can even propose it. Definition is therefore perfectly useless for natural knowledge; but it is, when strictly adhered to, a fountain of deductions which are unimpeachable in themselves, although their relevance to matters of fact is problematical, and can only be asserted by one who knows those facts independently.

Definitions are complex names and they have the same function as names. They cannot repeat the essence of a thing, because its essence is its whole texture and character. An adequate definition of any existing thing would be as complicated as the thing itself, and true only of that individual, or of such others, if any, as were indistinguishable from it internally. Nevertheless, like names, definitions are sometimes useful. If I asked a man "Who are you?" he might not unreasonably think the question impertinent, seeing that I was in his presence, and he might reply "I am myself." So when I ask of a thing, "What is that?" if the thing could overhear me, it might justly retort, "I am that I am." If, however, the man I challenged was of a mild and affable temper, and explained that he was Jenkins, that name might not be unmeaning to me. I might instantly conclude that I had not heard of him before, and should probably not hear of him again. So if I learned that the tome before me was a work of poetry, although poetry is proverbially difficult to define, I should know that all further consideration of it on my part was optional. Definitions may inform me of the place in which conventional discourse puts the object before me, and if I trust the wisdom of the definer, I shall have a useful hint concerning the ways of that object. A card may suffice to tell me the sex, rank, and nationality of the person whose name it bears, and may even enable me to guess whether he comes to pay his compliments or to solicit a subscription. Though a name seems to report who a man is, and a definition what a thing is, yet the thing no more is its definition than the man is his name.

Fourth Meaning: Predication.—Most often, perhaps, in common speech, the word *"is"* marks some property in what presumably has other properties as well, as in the formula *A* is *B*. Such a formula would be self-contradictory if being always meant identity. Wine is wine, and red is red, but red is not wine nor (in the sense of identity) can wine be red. Yet this is the constant assertion made by the word *"is"* when it attributes qualities to substances or predicates adjectives of nouns.

How an adjective can belong to a substantive is best seen when the adjective is a mere epithet and grammatically redundant, as when Homer speaks of the wine-coloured sea. Predication is supplementary definition, and as definition is never adequate to facts, further definition of them is always possible. The word "sea" and the images it may call up are one complex symbol for that element on which Homer had so often been tossed; the essence "purple," now emerging in the same context, is an added symbol for the same object. Predication is an elaborate naming under pressure of sensation or shifts of thought: it is poetry. Intuition here mixes its pigments and lays them on, stroke by stroke. The whole composition, at each stage, will no doubt be imputed to some substance, as if it formed its essence; but the very multiplication of epithets shows how inexhaustible and external that substance is in its truth; the poet is enduring and celebrating a divine power, and singing its many names. His whole discourse is the modulation of one vast epithet. It does not transgress the sphere of essence, but touches in turn and brings to the focus of attention now one manifestation of the god and now another. In study, whether artistic or scientific, the originality of mind is by no means laid aside; study merely carries out with a greater volume and force the primary poetry of the senses, by which intuition arises in the beginning, when each organ, stimulated by the unimaginable currents of its substance, chooses the essences which shall symbolize that stimulus to consciousness. The essence which any particular organ or any particular poet shall evoke depends, of course, on the material conditions which, in creating intuition at all, create its language, according to the "genius" of that poet or of that organ. Every quality possibly found in any thing, or predicated of it, is a fundamental and separate essence evoked on that occasion. The circumstance that some essences are used as subjects in discourse and some as attributes is itself only rhetorical; but it corresponds to the fact that in nature some formal units are more constant than others; as, for instance, the mass of a body is more constant than its position; therefore, in discourse we call the mass the substance and the position the accident. In the realm of essence, however, all elements are simply juxtaposed, and the trick of predicating one essence of another is only a means of carrying attention from some whole to a feature included in it, or to some larger whole in which it is a feature; in other words a means of analysis or synthesis. The resulting term in both cases is simply an essence, all surface; and there is no meaning in calling an essence the substance or the attribute of any other. Animal faith, with the intent which expresses it intellectually, may use any or all essences as predicates of a substance posited beyond them; but these predicates are poetic epithets for that substance, not constituents of it. They vary with the senses and genius of the observer. A stained-glass window, after I have studied it for a moment, offers a vastly different essence to my intuition from that contained in my first glimpse of it; and the simplest natural object is far more complicated than any Gothic design.

Fifth Meaning: Existence.–When I assume that there is a substance perhaps without pretending to know what it is, save that I have this local and temporal encounter with it, I am using the word *"is"* in an entirely different sense in which it means existence. This assertion of existence is imposed on me antecedently by the actions or expectations in the midst of which intuition arises, and without which it would never arise; and to this underlying faith is due the habit of predication itself, and the function of giving names. Essences present to intuition would never be predicated of one another, or understood to signify anything but what they obviously are, were they not projected into a common place and time, the seat of a presumed substance, by confusion with which the given essences (in reality only terms for intuition) are reputed to exist too. I do not need to believe in what I actually see; if I could limit myself to seeing, such a belief would be superfluous and unmeaning; but I am compelled to believe in the butt of my actions or the objects of my fears or memories, substances on which my efforts converge, or from which influences radiate upon me. The vague light, without outline or colour, which may first come to me from the church window is certainly not the composition which I afterwards discover there, yet I call them perceptions of the same thing, because I am convinced *a priori*, by the persevering attitude of my body and other converging circumstances, that a common source existed for both images, namely, a single material window fixed in its place, designed by its particular architect and built by his particular masons and glaziers. If no such natural object existed, that vague light and that precise composition would have nothing to do with each other; and unless I surreptitiously assign a natural existence to myself and give dates to those intuitions in my personal history, the light and the composition would have no temporal or spatial relations, and would not belong to one world, or exist at all. For the realm of existence (as I understand the word) is that arena of action, conveniently called nature, of which animals are parts and to which they are addressed before they have intuitions, if they ever have them; and the meaning of intuitions, when they come, is to mark the salient points of this world of nature, in so far as the sensitive animal can cope with it or is affected by it. The terms of intuition, the given essences, come to him as signals; and they are names to him for what exists about him, long before he notices their æsthetic quality. It is a great misfortune, at least for philosophy, that the word *"is,"* which denotes the qualitative idiosyncrasy of any essence whatsoever, should also have been used to denote existence, something peculiar to the flux of nature, and only as actually flowing.*

Existence means being in external relations.—When the word *"is"* designates existence, it claims for the object of intent a place in this flux; an object of intent (such as I have when on being startled I cry, "what's that?") is sufficiently identified by the external relations through which I approach it. I may completely ignore or mistake its true nature—an error or indifference which would be impossible if that object were not distinguished already as the object I mean to regard. It is whatever is there now, in such a context, creating such a disturbance. Its hidden nature, whatever it may be, is embodied in existence, and turned from an eternal essence into a fact when it is caught somewhere in the net of time, space, evolution, derivation, and association. Lying myself in the same context, I can turn to it by groping; and on coming into material contact with it, I may have rapid and varied intuitions supplying me with various notes, in the terms of my personal senses and emotions, which are my comment on it; perhaps it appears to be something small, black, rapidly moving, and unpleasant. These miscellaneous characteristics, the essences present to my intuition, are its names in my discourse; of course they are not the essence of that object itself, which for all my description reveals might as well be a mouse as a mosquito; nor do I seriously suppose they form its essence, since I remain still curious and apprehensive of what that essence may secretly be; whether, for instance, it may be such as to render the thing poisonous. But since I have only my chance intuitions by which to describe that object, I am tempted to assign existence for the nonce to this accidental description, as if it were the true essence of the thing; the radical and perpetual occasion of human illusion, dogmatism, and error.

Whether the claim to existence made on behalf of any object is just or not is a question that can never be decided by analyzing the given description of what is said to exist, but only by exploring the flux of nature, by experience or testimony, until the region in which the existing thing is alleged to lie (for if it exists it must lie somewhere) is thoroughly explored, and I can judge whether my original description, granting my terms and my circumstances, was a fair description of what actually lies there. If it was a fair description, I may conclude that what I had in mind really existed; if not, I must admit that I was mistaken, since what really existed was something not fairly describable in that way, nor properly called by that name. A very inadequate designation of the object—for example, in the

---

*The Spanish language is comparatively discriminating in this matter, having three verbs for "to be" which cannot be used interchangeably. "To be or not to be" must be rendered by *existir*; "That is the question" requires *ser*; "There's the rub" demands *estar*. Existence, essence, and condition or position are thus distinguished instinctively; but idiom profits more by this nicety than does philosophy, and I must say despairingly "Sea lo que Dios quiera," "Be it [i.e., let it happen] as God will." Fortunately events have some English verbs to themselves—"occur," "happen," "arise"—and we need not say stupidly that they simply are. The phrase "there is" (like the German *ist da, es gibt, ist vorhanden*) also helps to distinguish existence from pure being.

case of the existence of God—may be perfectly correct and sufficient for human purposes; but the places and times (say the miracles or revelations or eschatological events) in which the existence of such an object would be unmistakably manifested must be definitely fixed; otherwise the *existence* of the object, the very point in question, would not be broached at all; for it is idle to say that a thing exists or does not exist, if I do not say when or where it is to be met with in the world of action.

Sixth Meaning: Actuality.—To this natural sphere the word "existence" may be confined with advantage; for even a living intuition, or bit of actual discourse, is generated at some particular point of space and time and expresses a material predicament of some animal. Had intuition no such root and status in nature, it could not be said to exist. Inwardly considered, each intuition is invisible, being the act of seeing something else; and it cannot run up against itself or find itself in any part of the landscape which it views, and to which it lends a specious unity and actuality. Moreover, if an intuition were not posited from the outside, as the thought of some particular person at some particular time, even its spiritual synthetic function would vanish; for it would be indistinguishable from the unity of the essence discerned—an eternal and non-existential object. A living intuition is, accordingly, a phase of animal life; and apart from such heats of nature the light of thought would never shine and no essence would ever appear. Nevertheless, considered in itself, an intuition is autonomous; it knows nothing of its organs or conditions, but single-mindedly greets whatever essence may appear, or borne onwards by animal faith, idolatrously regards that essence as a whole world, or as a chief part of a world, existing absolutely. Here, surely, is a very vivid and notable event, an existence possessing such unity, scope, and concentration as no other existence possesses; indeed scope, concentration, and unity have no other principle than intuition. Yet in this superlative existence proper to intuition there is something ironical. While it exists so positively that some philosophers admit no other reality, it is indiscoverable in the context of nature where existence must lie. Moreover, a chief characteristic of existence is flux, even conventionally static things, like houses, being composed by external and therefore reversible relations; but intuition (though externally considered it has a date and duration) is a synthesis, and therefore no flux. A flux which was all flux could never appear; in becoming a specious flux, it is caught in a unitary vista. Intuition is not a divisible event, like all events in nature. The separation and temporal order of its terms, like these terms themselves, are specious, an idea of succession and not a succession of facts; and there is no possibility whatever of placing various intuitions, apart from their organs and objects, in any relation of contiguity or succession.

Intuitions are therefore not existences in the same sense as natural things, nor events after the fashion of natural events; and yet we must say of them preeminently that they exist and arise, unless we are willing to banish spirit from nature altogether and to forget, when we do so, that spirit in us is then engaged in discovering nature and in banishing spirit. Why should philosophers wish to impoverish the world in order to describe it more curtly? Its exuberance will make it easier to describe, if they adapt their logic to its constitution. Intuition is an emanation of life, an intellectual response of the animal to his vicissitudes; it is an actualization or hypostasis of formal facts in nature, not an added existence on the same plane as its organ. If either the substance or the intuition were a phenomenon (which neither is), the relation of intuition to substance might be called epiphenomenal; for the two are not collateral, but the intuition is as completely dependent on the body for arising, as the body and nature at large are dependent on intuition for being imagined, loved, or described. This spiritual hypostasis of life into intuition is therefore less and more than natural existence and deserves a different name. I will call it actuality. *Is,* applied to spirit or to any of its modes, accordingly means is actual; in other words, exists not by virtue of inclusion in the dynamic, incessant, and infinitely divisible flux of nature, but by its intrinsic incandescence, which brings essences to light and creates the world of appearances.

Seventh Meaning: Derivation.—Belief in existence leads to still another use of the word *"is,"* the most misleading of all, by which one thing is said to be another because it is derived from it, or has the same substance. Suppose intuition presents me with a point of light; taking that essence instinctively for the sign of some existence, I may say to myself, "There is a spark." But in the world of nature, to which I am now addressed, a spark is no isolated fact; it has some origin, some substance, some consequences, and these probably interest me much more than my bare intuition of a point of light. But what origin, what substance, what consequences? It is conventionally known to me that a point of light may mean a spark from a horse's hoof, a burning cinder, a rocket, a distant lamp-post, a motor on the road, a revolving light-house, a ship at sea, or a blow in the eye. Nevertheless, ignoring those familiar possibilities, I may say to myself, "This spark is a firefly and not a star." I have thus travelled in search of explanation very far indeed from my datum. Instead of saying, "A point is a point," I first said, "A spark exists"; and then I said, "This spark is an insect." The word *"is"* has become a synonym of *"comes from";* it attributes to an alleged fact a source in another alleged fact, asserting that the two are continuous genetically, however different they may be in character.

If this license in the use of the word *"is"* be allowed (and it would be pedantic to forbid it), I may still ask which of various suggested things a particular thing is; and I may find myself traversing the whole flux of nature in search for the being of the simplest object. This search becomes more confusing, and at the same time more urgent, when a psychological world is interposed, or substituted for the world of matter; one school of philosophers will then maintain that everything physical is really mental, and another school that everything mental is really physical. A capital instance of this habit is found in the phrase, dear to critical philosophers, that something "is nothing but" something else. Thus we hear that a word is nothing but a *flatus vocis,* that a house is nothing but bricks and mortar, that a mind is nothing but a bundle of perceptions, that God is nothing but a tendency not ourselves that makes for righteousness, or that matter is nothing but a permanent possibility of sensation. The phrase "nothing but" claims adequacy for the definition that follows: but a definition can define adequately an essence only, it cannot pretend to exhaust a fact; therefore, if such assertions are taken strictly, they themselves become "nothing but" definitions of fresh terms, and not discoveries. If on the contrary we take them loosely, as indicating the partial origin of certain facts or ideas, they may be correct; every fact and idea has antecedents which might be discovered if our knowledge of nature and of dreams were sufficiently profound. But in practice this sort of naturalistic analysis is seldom thorough; in none of the five examples given above, for instance, is the origin of the facts or ideas in question assigned correctly. One element in their composition may be specified: but the radical phrase "nothing but," in excluding all other elements (not to speak of the resulting unities of form), turns a shrewd observation into a cheap error. Even if the derivation of any fact could be assigned adequately, that fact would not be identical with what brought it about; and to say that things *are* what they are made of is to use the verb "to be" in a confused and confusing way, although the poverty of language may render such speech inevitable.

Here are seven distinct meanings of the word *"is,"* which it will be well to distinguish if I wish to know what I am saying. In practice the ambiguities of language are neutralized by looseness and good sense in the interpretation of it; but a philosopher leads himself into foolish difficulties and more foolish dogmas if he assumes that words have fixed meanings to which single facts in nature must correspond. He ought, therefore, to use language more freely than the public rather than more strictly, since he professes to have a clearer view of things. My purpose is not to limit the uses of the word *"is,"* but to become and remain aware that these uses are various, and that no argument in which they figure has the least cogency, even within the sphere of dialectic, until these uses are discriminated.

Preface to *Realms of Being*

The Realm of Essence: Book First of Realms of Being. New York: Charles Scribner's Sons; London: Constable and Co. Ltd., 1927, v–xix. Volume sixteen of the critical edition of *The Works of George Santayana.*

This preface comes from the The Realm of Essence, *the first volume of the four-volume* Realms of Being. *It first appeared in slightly different form as "A Preface to a System of Philosophy" in the* Yale Review *(13 [1924]: 417–30). Santayana thought this preface less technical than other chapters of his book, and in a 1923 letter he recommended it to the editor of the* Yale Review, *writing that it is "comparatively comprehensible and will give those who care to read it a general idea of what I am after" (LGS, 3:175). Santayana had been planning* Realms of Being *since at least 1911 and originally conceived of three realms: Essence, Matter, and Consciousness (LGS, 2:37). Later the name of one realm was changed and another was added, to make four realms: Essence, Matter, Truth, and Spirit. Santayana wrote a book for each realm, and in 1942 they were published together in a one-volume (unabridged) edition as* Realms of Being.

The world is old, and can have changed but little since man arose in it, else man himself would have perished. Why, then, should he still live without a sure and sufficient philosophy? The equivalent of such a philosophy is probably hereditary in sundry animals not much older than man. They have had time to take the measure of life, and have settled down to a routine of preferences and habits which keeps their heads, as a race, above water; and they are presumably visited at appropriate seasons by magic images, which are symbols to them for the world or for the cycles of their destiny. Among groups of men an equilibrium of this moral sort has been sometimes approached—in India, in China, under the Moslem or the Catholic regimens; and if socialist or other panaceas now exercise such a strange influence over men's hearts, it is perhaps because they are impatient of being so long the sport of divers ignorant dogmas and chance adventures, and aspire to live in a stable harmony with nature.

In fact, beneath these various complete systems which have professed but failed to be universal, there is actually a dumb human philosophy, incomplete but solid, prevalent among all civilised peoples. They all practise agriculture, commerce, and mechanical arts, with artificial instruments lately very much complicated; and they necessarily possess, with these arts, a modicum of sanity, morality, and science requisite for carrying them on, and tested by success in doing so. Is not this human competence philosophy enough? Is it not at least the nucleus of all sound philosophy? In spite of the superficial confusion reigning in the world, is not the universal wisdom of the future actually gathering about this human competence in engineering, in chemistry, in medicine, in war?

It might seem so, since the sort of knowledge involved in the arts, though it may not go very far, is compulsory so far as it goes, and being sanctioned by success, it ought to be permanent and progressive. There is indeed a circle of material events called nature, to which all minds belonging to the same society are

The realm of matter.

responsive in common. Not to be responsive to these facts is simply to be stupid and backward in the arts; those who explore and master their environment cannot help learning what it is. In this direction competence involves enlightenment. Among minds forming a moral society, and able to compare their several opinions, this enlightenment in the expert is coercive over the layman also, because the same facts confront them both. Did not the same facts confront them, communication would be impossible between them, or if communication was reputed to exist by magic there would be no possible conflict or progress among their opinions, because they would not refer to the same events. Even if each declared himself competent and prosperous in his own world, he would know nothing of the world of his neighbours. Their several minds would simply be variously or similarly brilliant, like jewels, signifying nothing to one another.

If any mind hopes to address another (or even itself) persuasively, as I now wish to address the reader and my own thoughts, it must assume a single system of events to which both minds are responsive, and which includes their respective bodies and actions. Assuming such a common world, it is easy to see how animals may acquire knowledge of it and may communicate it. Material events will arouse in them intuitions conformable to their several stations, faculties, and passions; and their active nature (since they are animals, not plants) will compel them to regard many of the essences so given in intuition as signs for the environment in which they move, modifying this environment and affected by it. This assumption justifies itself at every turn in practice, and establishes in the habits of all men, in proportion to their competence, an appropriate adjustment to the *Realm of Matter,* and in their imagination a suitable picture of the same.

Nevertheless, since the station, faculties, and passions of all men are not identical, these pictures will not be similar. Different observers may be addressed to

The realm of essence.

different regions of nature, or sensitive to different elements in the same region; thus dwellers in distinct planets must evidently have distinct geographies, and the same battle in the clouds will be known to the deaf only as lightning and to the blind only as thunder, each responding to a different constituent of the total event, and not simultaneously. So an eclipse–itself but one aspect of a constellation of events in the heavens–may be known in various entirely different terms; by calculation before it occurs, by sense when it is occurring, by memory immediately afterwards, and by reports to posterity. All these indications are entirely inadequate to the facts they reveal in the realm of matter, and qualitatively unlike those facts; they are a set of variegated symbols by which sensitive animals can designate them. Of course, the existence and use of such languages is an added fact in nature–a fact so important and close to the egotism of the animals themselves as perhaps to obscure all else in their eyes. Their instinct, indeed, keeps their attention stretched upon the material world that actually surrounds them; but sometimes sensation and language, instead of being passed over like the ticking of the telegraph, may become objects in themselves, in all their absolute musical insignificance; and then animals become idealists. The terms in which they describe things, unlike the things they meant to describe, are purely specious, arbitrary, and ideal; whether visual, tactile, auditory, or conceptual these terms are essentially *words*. They possess intrinsically, in their own ontological plane, only logical or æsthetic being; and this contains no indication whatever of the material act of speaking, touching, or looking which causes them to appear. All possible terms in mental discourse are essences existing nowhere; visionary equally, whether the faculty that discovers them be sense or thought or the most fantastic fancy.

Such diversity in animal experience taken in itself exhibits sundry qualities or forms of being, a part of the infinite multitude of distinguishable ideal terms which (whether ever revealed to anybody or not) I call the *Realm of Essence*. Pure intuition, in its poetic ecstasy, would simply drink in such of these essences as happened to present themselves; but for a wakeful animal they are signals. They report to his spirit, in very summary and uncertain images, the material events which surround him and which concern his welfare. They may accordingly become terms in knowledge if interpreted judiciously, and if interpreted injudiciously they may become illusions.

The dumb philosophy of the human animal, by which he rears his family and practises the arts and finds his way home, might take definite shape and establish a healthy routine in all his dealings with matter (which includes society), and yet his imaginative experience might retain all its specious originality. The control which the environment exercises over the structure and conduct of animals is decidedly loose. They can live dragging a long chain of idle tricks, diseases, and obsolete organs; and even this loose control fails almost entirely in the case

All mental discourse is more or less significant poetry.

of alternative senses or languages, one of which may serve as well as another. Many species survive together, many rival endowments and customs and religions. And the same control fails altogether in regard to the immaterial essences which those senses or languages call up before the mind's eye. Adaptation is physical, and it is only the material operation in sensation or speech that can possibly be implicated in the clockwork of nature. The choice of those visionary essences which meantime visit the mind, though regular, is free; they are the transcript of life into discourse, the rhetorical and emotional rendering of existence, which when deepened and purified, becomes poetry or music. There can be no reason why differences in these spheres, even among men of the same race, should not be perpetual. It would be mere sluggishness and egotism to regret it. Such differences are not merely added like a vain luxury to a sane recognition, in other conscious terms, of the facts of nature. The "sane" response to nature is by action only and by an economy which nature can accept and weave into her own material economy; but as to the terms of sense and discourse, they are all from the very beginning equally arbitrary, poetical, and (if you choose) mad; yet all equally symptomatic. They vary initially and intangibly from mind to mind, even in expressing the same routine of nature. The imagination which eventually runs to fine art or religion is the same faculty which, under a more direct control of external events, yields vulgar perception. The promptings and the control exercised by matter are continuous in both cases; the dream requires a material dreamer as much as the waking sensation, and the latter is a transcript of his bodily condition just as directly as the dream. Poetic, creative, original fancy is not a secondary form of sensibility, but its first and only form. The same manual restlessness and knack which makes man a manufacturer of toys makes him, when by chance his toys prove useful, a manufacturer of implements. Fine art is thus older than servile labour, and the poetic quality of experience is more fundamental than its scientific value. Existence may revert at any moment to play, or may run down in idleness; but it is impossible that any work or discovery should ever come about without the accompaniment of pure contemplation, if there is consciousness at all; so that the inherent freedom of the spirit can never be stamped out, so long as spirit endures.

Nor is it safe to imagine that inspired people, because they dream awake in their philosophy, must come to grief in the real world. The great religious and

The realm of spirit. political systems which I mentioned above have had brilliant careers. Their adepts have been far from making worse soldiers than sceptics make, or worse workmen than materialists; nor have they committed suicide or been locked up in the madhouse more often than exact philosophers. Nature drives with a loose rein, and vitality of any sort, even if expressed in fancy, can blunder through many a predicament in which reason would despair. And if the mythical systems decline at last, it is not so much by virtue of the maladjustments underlying their speculative errors—for their myths as a whole are wisely contrived—as because imagination in its freedom abandons these errors for others simply because the prevalent mood of mankind has changed, and it begins dreaming in a different key. Spirit bloweth where it listeth, and continually undoes its own work. This world of free expression, this drift of sensations, passions, and ideas, perpetually kindled and fading in the light of consciousness, I call the *Realm of Spirit*. It is only for the sake of this free life that material competence and knowledge of fact are worth attaining. Facts for a living creature are only instruments; his play-life is his true life. On his working days, when he is attentive to matter, he is only his own servant, preparing the feast. He becomes his own master in his holidays and in his sportive passions. Among these must be counted literature and philosophy, and so much of love, religion, and patriotism as is not an effort to survive materially. In such enthusiasms there is much asseveration; but what they attest is really not the character of the external facts concerned, but only the spiritual uses to which the spirit turns them.

A philosopher cannot wish to be deceived. His philosophy is a declaration of policy in the presence of the facts; and therefore his first care must be to ascertain

The range of reasonable curiosity. and heartily to acknowledge all such facts as are relevant to his action or sentiment—not less, and not necessarily more. The pursuit of truth is a form of courage, and a philosopher may well love truth for its own sake, in that he is disposed to confront destiny, whatever it may be, with zest when possible, with resignation when necessary, and not seldom with amusement. The facts to which it is prudent and noble in him to bare his bosom are the morally relevant facts, such as touch his fortunes or his heart, or such as he can alter by his efforts; nor can he really discover other facts. Intuition, or absolute apprehension without media or doubt, is proper to spirit perusing essences; it is impossible to animals confronting facts. Animals know things by exploration, reaction, and prophetic fancy; they therefore can know only such parts and depths of nature as they explore materially and respond to vitally. The brave impulse to search may, indeed, become eager and may wish to recognise no limits; and there may be spirits so utterly practical and serious that the pursuit of material facts absorbs them altogether, to the exclusion of all play of mind. Yet such hectic exactitude is an expression of fear, and automatic rather than rational. Curiosity in an animal always has limits which it is foolish to transgress, because beyond them theory insensibly lapses into verbal myths, and if still taken for true knowledge defeats the honest curiosity that inspired it. What renders knowledge true is fidelity to the object; but in the conduct and fancy of an animal this fidelity can be only rough, summary, dramatic; too much refine-ment renders it subjective, as does too much haste. This is true of mathematical refinements no less than of verbal pedantries. The realm of matter can never be disclosed either to hypothesis or to sensation in its presumable inmost structure and ultimate extent: the garment of appearance must always fit it loosely and drape it in alien folds, because appearance is essentially an adaptation of facts to the scale and faculty of the observer.

There are also moral limits to seriousness and utter literalness in thought. The tragic compulsion to honour the facts is imposed on man by the destiny of his body, to which that of his mind is attached. But his destiny is not the only theme possible to his thought, nor the most congenial. The best part of this destiny is that he may often forget it; and existence would not be worth preserving if it had to be spent exclusively in anxiety about existence.

It follows from all this that knowledge of facts merely because they are facts cannot be the ultimate object of a philosopher, although he must wish to know the whole unvarnished truth about relevant matters. A liberal mind must live on its own terms, and think in them; it is not inferior to what sur-rounds it; fact-worship on its part would accordingly be a fault in taste and in morals. What is the function of philosophy? To dis- **Relativity of knowledge.** close the absolute truth? But is it credible that the absolute truth should descend into the thoughts of a mortal creature, equipped with a few special senses and with a biassed intellect, a man lost amidst millions of his fellows and a prey to the epidemic delusions of the race? Possession of the absolute truth is not merely by accident beyond the range of particular minds; it is incompatible with being alive, because it excludes any particular station, organ, interest, or date of survey: the absolute truth is undiscoverable just because it is not a perspective. Perspec-tives are essential to animal apprehension; an observer, himself a part of the world he observes, must have a particular station in it; he cannot be equally near to everything, nor internal to anything but himself; of the rest he can only take views, abstracted according to his sensibility and foreshortened according to his interests. Those animals which I was supposing endowed with an adequate philosophy surely do not possess the absolute truth. They read nature in their private idioms. Their imagination, like the human, is doubtless incapable of coping with all things at once, or even with the whole of anything natural. Mind was not created for the sake of discovering the absolute truth. The absolute truth has its own intangible reality, and scorns to be known. The function of mind is rather to increase the wealth of the universe in the spiritual dimension, by adding appearance to substance and passion to necessity, and by creating all those private perspectives, and those emotions of wonder, adventure, curiosity, and laughter which omniscience would exclude. If omniscience were alone respectable, creation would have been a mistake. The single duty of all creatures would then be to repair that creative error, by abolishing their several senses and desires and becoming indistinguishable from one another and from nothing at all; and if all creation could attain to this sort of salvation, the absolute substance, in whose honour all else had been abandoned, would become unconscious. The time will doubtless come for each of us, if not for the universe at large, to cease from care; but our passage through life will have added a marvellous episode to the tale of things; and our distinction and glory, as well as our sorrow, will have lain in being something in particular, and in knowing what it is.

Thus if there is a sense in which all special and separable existence is illusion, there is another sense in which illusion is itself a special and separable existence; and if this be condemned for not being absolute substance and for excluding knowledge of the absolute truth, it may also be prized for these very reasons. Sensation is true enough. All experience yields some acquaintance with the realm of essence, and some perspective of the material world; and this would always be a true perspective (since things seen at that angle and with that organ really look like that) if the appearance were not stretched to cover more than it covers in reality. Of such true perspectives the simplest and most violently foreshortened may be as good as the most complicated, the most poetical or pictorial as good as the most scientific, not only æsthetically but even cognitively; because it may report the things concerned on that human scale on which we need to measure them, and in this relation may report them correctly. Nor is the error which such very partial knowledge may breed, when inflated by precipitate judgements and vanity, altogether unavoidable. The variety of senses in man, the precarious rule of his instincts, and the range of his memory and fancy, give rise in him eventually to some sense of error and even of humour. He is almost able to pierce the illusions of his animal dogmatism, to surrender the claim to inspiration, and in one sense to transcend the relativity of his knowledge and the flightiness of his passions by acknowledging them with a good grace.

This relativity does not imply that there is no absolute truth. On the contrary, if there were no absolute truth, all-inclusive and eternal, the desultory views taken from time to time by individuals would themselves be absolute. They would be irrelevant to one another, and incomparable in point of truth, each being without any object but the essence which appeared in it. If views can be more or less correct, and perhaps complementary to one another, it is because they refer to the same system of

The realm of truth.

nature, the complete description of which, covering the whole past and the whole future, would be the absolute truth. This absolute truth is no living view, no actual judgement, but merely that segment of the realm of essence which happens to be illustrated in existence. The question whether a given essence belongs to this segment or not—that is, whether a suggested idea is or is not true—has a tragic importance for an animal intent on discovering and describing what exists, or has existed, or is destined to exist in his world. He seldom has leisure to dwell on essences apart from their presumable truth; even their beauty and dialectical pattern seem to him rather trivial, unless they are significant of facts in the realm of matter, controlling human destiny. I therefore give a special name to this tragic segment of the realms of essence and call it the *Realm of Truth.*

The knowledge of relevant truth, while it has this fundamental moral importance, is far from being our only concern in the life of reason. It comes in only incidentally, in so far as a staunch and comprehensive knowledge of things makes a man master of things, and independent of them in a great measure. The business of a philosopher is rather to be a good shepherd of his thoughts. The share of attention and weight **Human values of knowledge.** which he gives to physical speculation or to history or to psychology will express his race and disposition, or the spirit of his times; everyone is free to decide how far material arts and sciences are worth pursuing, and with what free creations they shall be surrounded. Young and ardent minds, and races without accumulated possessions, tend to poetry and metaphysics; they neglect or falsify the truth in the heat of their imaginative passion. Old men, and old nations, incline to mix their wine with larger dilutions of reality; and they prefer history, biography, politics, and humorous fictions; because in all these, while the facts are neither conceived nor tested scientifically, the savour of earth and of experience remains dominant.

By the philosopher, however, both the homeliest brew and the most meticulous science are only relished as food for the spirit. Even if defeated in the pursuit of truth, the spirit may be victorious in self-expression and self-knowledge; and if a philosopher could be nothing else, he might still be a moralist and a poet. He will do well to endow his vision of things with all the force, colour, and scope of which his soul is capable. Then if he misses the truth of nature, as in many things is probable, he will at least have achieved a work of imagination. In such a case the universe, without being mapped as a whole in the fancy, will be enriched at one point, by the happy life enacted there, in one human focus of art and vision. The purer and more distinct the spirit which a philosopher can bring to light in his thoughts, the greater the intellectual achievement; and the greater the moral achievement also, if the policy so set forth is actually carried out in his whole life and conversation.

As for me, in stretching my canvas and taking up my palette and brush, I am not vexed that masters should have painted before me in styles which I have no power and no occasion to imitate; nor do I expect future genera- **Legitimate variety in speculation.** tions to be satisfied with always repainting my pictures. Agreement is sweet, being a form of friendship; it is also a stimulus to insight, and helpful, as contradiction is not; and I certainly hope to find agreement in some quarters. Yet I am not much concerned about the number of those who may be my friends in the spirit, nor do I care about their chronological distribution, being as much pleased to discover one intellectual kinsman in the past as to imagine two in the future. That in the world at large alien natures should prevail, innumerable and perhaps infinitely various, does not disturb me. On the contrary, I hope fate may manifest to them such objects as they need and can love; and although my sympathy with them cannot be so vivid as with men of my own mind, and in some cases may pass into antipathy, I do not conceive that they are wrong or inferior for being different from me, or from one another. If God and nature can put up with them, why should I raise an objection? But let them take care; for if they have sinned against the facts (as I suspect is often the case) and are kicking against the pricks of matter, they must expect to be brought to confusion on the day of doom, or earlier. Not only will their career be brief and troubled, which is the lot of all flesh, but their faith will be stultified by events, which is a needless and eternal ignominy for the spirit. But if somehow, in their chosen terms, they have balanced their accounts with nature, they are to be heartily congratulated on their moral diversity. It is pleasant to think that the fertility of spirit is inexhaustible, if matter only gives it a chance, and that the worst and most successful fanaticism cannot turn the moral world permanently into a desert.

The pity of it is only that contrary souls should often fight for the same bodies, natural or political, as if space and matter in the universe were inadequate (as on earth indeed they are) for every essence in its own time to see the sun. But existence is precipitate and blind; it cannot bide its time; and the seeds of form are often so wantonly and thickly scattered that they strangle one another, call one another weeds and tares, and can live only in the distracted effort to keep others from living. Seldom does any soul live through a single and lovely summer in its native garden, suffered and content to bloom. Philosophers and nations cannot be happy unless separate; then they may be single-minded at home and tolerant abroad. If they have a spirit in them which is worth cultivating (which is not always the case) they need to entrench it in some consecrated citadel, where it may come to perfect expression. Human beings allowed to run loose are vowed to perdition, since they are too individual to agree and too gregarious to stand alone. Hence the rareness of any polity founded on wisdom, like that of which ancient Greece affords some glimpses, and the equal rareness of a pure and complete philosophy, such as that of Dante or of Spinoza, conceived in some moment of wonderful unanimity or of fortunate isolation.

My own philosophy, I venture to think, is well-knit in the same sense, in spite of perhaps seeming eclectic and of leaving so many doors open both in physics and in morals. My eclecticism is not helplessness before sundry influences; it is detachment and firmness in taking each thing simply for what it is. Openness, too, is a form of architecture. The doctrine that all moralities equally are but expressions of animal life is a tremendous dogma, at once blessing and purging all mortal passions; and the conviction that

The temper of this system.

there can be no knowledge save animal faith positing external facts, and that this natural science is but a human symbol for those facts, also has an immense finality: the renunciation and the assurance in it are both radical and both invincible.

In confessing that I have merely touched the hem of nature's garment, I feel that virtue from her has passed into me, and made me whole. There is no more bewitching moment in childhood than when the boy, to whom someone is slyly propounding some absurdity, suddenly looks up and smiles. The brat has understood. A thin deception was being practised on him, in the hope that he might not be deceived, but by deriding it might prove he had attained to a man's stature and a man's wit. It was but banter prompted by love. So with this thin deception practised upon me by nature. The great Sphinx in posing her riddle and looking so threatening and mysterious is secretly hoping that I may laugh. She is not a riddle but a fact; the words she whispers are not oracles but prattle. Why take her residual silence, which is inevitable, for a challenge or a menace? She does not know how to speak more plainly. Her secret is as great a secret to herself as to me. If I perceive it, and laugh, instantly she draws in her claws. A tremor runs through her enigmatical body; and if she were not of stone she would embrace her boyish discoverer, and yield herself to him altogether. It is so simple to exist, to be what one is for no reason, to engulf all questions and answers in the rush of being that sustains them. Henceforth nature and spirit can play together like mother and child, each marvellously pleasant to the other, yet deeply unintelligible; for as she created him she knew not how, merely by smiling in her dreams, so in awaking and smiling back he somehow understands her; at least he is all the understanding she has of herself.

Various Approaches to Essence

The Realm of Essence: Book First of Realms of Being. New York: Charles Scribner's Sons; London: Constable and Co. Ltd., 1927, 1–17. Volume sixteen of the critical edition of *The Works of George Santayana.*

In this selection, Chapter I of The Realm of Essence, *Santayana considered how one might discover essence. Nothing in the being of essence requires that it be discovered, and there is no privileged way by which to approach it: Skepticism can reveal essence, but so can the dialectical activity of the logician, mathematician, or gamer. Even sense itself sometimes distinguishes essence from fact and beholds it in its ideal setting. This occurs when an accompanying sensation overcomes the practical interests of animal sensibility. Animal sensibility, being focussed on the eventual, takes no notice of what actually is presented to intuition, though this is "the entire reality for the spirit" (ES, 167). Essences are the natural objects of spirit and as such bear no moral value. Value and moral significance, resulting from the concerns of animal psyche, are extraneous to essence. Though psyche and its concerns determine which essences are presented to spirit in intuition, the concerns of psyche are not those of spirit. Spirit only intuits essences, and neither spirit nor essence play any role in the material realm of psyche.*

The modern or romantic man is an adventurer; he is less interested in what there may be to find than in the lure of the search and in his hopes, guesses, or experiences in searching. Essence is perfectly indifferent to being dis-

All approaches are adventitious.

covered and unaffected by the avenue through which any discoverer may approach it; and for that very reason the explorer ignores it, and asks what it can possibly be. Now the subjective attitude in philosophy is not only prevalent in these times, but always legitimate; because a mind capable of self-consciousness is always free to reduce all things to its own view of them. Before considering the realm of essence in itself, therefore, I will indicate some paths by which even the most rambling reflection may be led to it. Essence is indeed everywhere at hand; and a scrupulous scepticism, falling back on immediate appearance, is itself a chief means of discovering the pervasive presence of essences.

Approach through scepticism: Nothing indubitable save the character of some given essence.

In a volume on *Scepticism and Animal Faith*, to which the present work is a sequel, I have described in detail the approach to essence through scepticism. Knowledge such as animal life requires is something transitive, a form of belief in things absent or eventual or somehow more than the state of the animal knowing them. It needs to be information. Otherwise the animal mind would be the prisoner of its dreams, and no better informed than a stone about its environment, its past, or its destiny.

It follows that such transitive knowledge will always be open to doubt. It is a claim or presumption arising in a responsive organism; yet in spite of this biological status, it ventures upon assertions concerning facts elsewhere. This boldness exposes it to all sorts of errors; for opinion will vary with its organ and, on that irrelevant ground, will make varying assertions about its outlying objects. Nor is it to be presumed that initially the terms in which objects are conceived are their intrinsic qualities; the terms may be, in quality as in existence, generated in the organ of sense, as are words or optical perspectives. Knowledge of nature or of absent experience is accordingly no less questionable in its texture than in its scope. Its validity is only presumptive and its terms are merely symbols.

The sceptic once on this scent will soon trace essence to its lair. He will drop, as dubious and unwarranted, the belief in a past, an environment, or a destiny. He will dismiss all thought of any truth to be discovered or any mind engaged in that egregious chase; and he will honestly confine himself to noting the features of the passing apparition. At first he may still assume that he can survey the passage and transformation of his dreams; but soon, if he is truly sceptical and candid, he will confess that this alleged order of appearances and this extended experience are themselves only dreamt of, like the future or the remoter past or the material environment–those discarded idols of his dogmatic days. Nothing will remain but some appearance now; and that which appears, when all gratuitous implications of a world beyond or of a self here are discarded, will be an *essence*. Nor will his own spirit, or spirit absolute (which grammar may still seem to insert, under the form of the pronoun I, as a prior agent in this intuition of essence) be anything but another name for the absolute phantom, the unmeaning presence, into which knowledge will have collapsed.

This approach to essence through scepticism is by no means the only one possible, even for a critic of knowledge. Scepticism can impugn only such knowledge as is a form of faith, and posits a removed object; but the dialectician ignores this sort of knowledge as much as he can, and by his initial attitude plants himself in the realm of essence, and wishes to confine himself to it. What is dialectic? Precisely an analysis or construction of ideal forms which abstracts from such animal faith as might be stimulated by their presence, and traces instead the inherent patterns or logical relations of these forms as intuition reveals them. To the dialectician animal faith seems wanton and superfluous, and in his overt reasoning, if not in his secret assumptions, he neither posits any objects of natural knowledge nor seeks to describe them. Such preoccupation with dark external facts and hidden events seems to him but a grovelling instinct; and the persuasion that one's ideas describe natural objects, though inevitable perhaps in sniffing one's way through this nether world, he laughs at as a vain presumption, unworthy of the name of science. In practice, as a man amongst men, the dialectician may have mixed views. If he is an enthusiast or a naturalist in disguise, using dialectic for some ulterior purpose, he will probably embrace his conclusions not merely as implications of his premises, but as objects of hot animal faith; and he may even think he has discovered a metaphysical world, when in truth he has merely elaborated a system of essences, altogether imaginary, and in no way more deeply rooted in reality than any sys-

Approach through dialectic: every term intuited or defined is an essence.

tem of essences which a poet or a musician might compose. This eventual mystification, however, by which dialectic is represented as revealing facts, does not destroy its native competence to describe essences; in its purity it will be free from error, because free from any pretence to define ulterior existences. Now this very purity, this identity of the object envisaged with the definition given to it in thought, seems to the dialectician the perfection of science, because it is the last refuge of certitude. But certitude and dialectical cogency are far removed from animal faith, and unnecessary to it; and animal faith, when it describes in suitable symbols (of which a dialectical system may be one) the objects encountered in action, is what I call knowledge. The question of titles and preferences does not concern me here; in any case the dialectician, whether his art be called knowledge or not, has discovered the realm of essence (or some province in it) and has devoted himself to exploring it.

This acquaintance with essence I call intuition, whether it be passive, æsthetic, and mystical, or on the contrary analytical and selective, as in reasoned discourse; because at every point demonstration or inference depends for its force on intuition of the intrinsic relation between the given terms. So in planning a series of moves in chess, as in originally inventing that game, the mind *sees* the consequences implied at each stage by the rules of procedure: these rules are mere essences, but their implications are precise in any hypothetical position of the pieces. If chess were not a well-established game and if material chess-boards and chess-men had never existed, a day-dream in which particular imaginary matches were traced out, could hardly be called knowledge: but every possibility and every consequence involved at each juncture would be equally definite, and the science of chess—even if chess never had existed in the world—would be an exact science. Evidently an exact science is not without an object, ideal as this object may be: indeed, the ideal definition of that object, the absence of all ambiguity as to what it is, renders exact science of it possible. Such definable non-existent objects of exact science have being in an eminent degree; their nature and their eternal intrinsic relations to other comparable natures are perfectly determinate. They are what they are; and of all the meanings of the word *is*—existence, substance, equivalence, definition, etc., the most radical and proper is that in which I may say of anything that it is what it is. This asseveration does not commit me to any classification of the object or to any assertion of its existence. I merely note its idiosyncrasy, its qualitative identity, which enables me to distinguish it, study it, and hold it fast in my intent, so that I may eventually frame a definition of it, and perhaps assert or deny its existence. If any object had no such specific character, there would be no truth in saying that *it* was before me, or could ever again be the theme of memory or discourse. Essences, by being eternally what they are, enable existence to pass from one phase to another, and enable the mind to note and describe the change.

That what I see, I see, or what I am, I am, may seem a vain assertion: practical minds are not interested in anything except for the sake of something else. They are camp-followers or heralds of events, without self-possession. Yet if that which

Distinguishable essences, such as the terms of dialectic, are the most real of beings.

is actual and possessed at the moment never had a satisfying character, no satisfaction would ever be possible; the mind could never dip twice into the same subject or know its friends from its enemies, and life would be what a romantic philosophy would make it–an idle escape from one error into another. Radical flux is indeed characteristic of existence, where it is innocent, since there can be no mistake or regret where there is no purpose: but the mind, even if describing only the series of its own illusions, attempts to describe it with truth: and it could not so much as fail in this attempt unless that series of illusions and each of its terms had a precise inexpungible character. Then the question whether in some ulterior sense those phases were illusions or not, becomes a subsidiary question. In any case, internally, they were what they were; and to a simple and recollected spirit the obvious often is enough. Its identity may have a deep charm, like that of a jewel. I may long ruminate upon it and impress it upon myself by repetitions, which to a lover never seem vain. Even in the midst of distractions, if I say to myself "No, no", or "Business is business", the repetition serves to detach and to render indubitable the essence meant; it raises that material accident to the intellectual level, where my judgement henceforth may recognise it to the exclusion of circumstances, which do not alter essences, but only cases.

They are the only staunch possessions of the mind.

Sometimes sense itself, without any dialectical analysis, distinguishes essences from facts, and recognises them in their ideal sphere. This happens for a very simple reason. The stimulus that calls animal attention to some external fact, in provoking an act of the body, also presents some image to the mind. Moreover this labour of perception may be more or less welcome, pleasant, or life-enhancing, apart from its ulterior uses; and sometimes this incidental emotion is so strong that it overpowers the interest which I may have had originally in the external facts; and, I may suspend my action or continue it automatically, while my thought is absorbed in the image and arrested there. As I was jogging to market in my village cart, beauty has burst upon me and the reins have dropped from my hands. I am transported, in a certain measure, into a state of trance. I see with extraordinary clearness, yet what I see seems strange and wonderful, because I no longer look in order to understand, but only in order to see. I have lost my preoccupation with fact, and am contemplating an essence.

Approach through contemplation: Every intelligible pattern or harmony is an essence.

This experience, in modern times, is called æsthetic; but it has no exclusive connection with the arts or with the beautiful. It is really intellectual, and the high Platonic road. That the clearest and purest reality should be formal or ideal, and something on which no animal instinct could possibly be directed, may seem a paradox; it may be denied by cynics–often very dull people; it may be used by metaphysicians as an argument for the supernatural origin and destiny of the soul. It is important at once to discard any such inferences, not only because they are in themselves mistaken, thin, and superstitious, but particularly, at this point in my argument, because they encumber the notion of essence with a

Essences are beautiful when congruous with human faculty.

moral significance quite extraneous to it, and may distort and discredit it altogether. When a thing is beautiful, I stop to look at it; and in this way its beauty helps me to drink in the actual appearance, and to be satisfied with that ethereal draught. But if the thing were ugly or uninteresting, it would have an absolute appearance just as much, and would present an essence to intuition; only that in that case I should have no motive—no vital animal motive—for dwelling upon that essence, or noticing it at all. If the thing is beautiful, this is not because it manifests an essence, but because the essence which it manifests is one to which my nature is attuned, so that the intuition of it is a delightful exercise to my senses and to my soul. This pleasure and refreshment welling up in me, I courteously thank the object for, and call its intrinsic charm: but an intrinsic charm is a contradiction in terms, and all that the object possesses is affinity to my life, and power over it, without which it would be impossible for me to observe it or to think it beautiful.

The beautiful is itself an essence, an indefinable quality felt in many things which, however disparate they may be otherwise, receive this name by virtue of a special emotion, half wonder, half love, which is felt in their presence. The essence of the beautiful, when made an object of contemplation by itself, is rather misleading: like the good and like pure Being, it requires much dialectical and spiritual training to discern it in its purity and in its fullness. At first the impetuous philosopher, seeing the world in so many places flowering into beauty, may confuse his physics with a subjective or teleological reference to the beautiful, thereby turning this essence, which marks a spiritual consummation, into a material power: or, if he is not an enthusiast, he may dwell so much on the instinctive and pleasant bonds which attach men to what they call beautiful, that he may bury the essence of the beautiful altogether under heavy descriptions of the occasions on which perhaps it appears. I will not stop to discuss these complications: however apt to become entangled itself, the beautiful is a great liberator of other essences. The most material thing, in so far as it is felt to be beautiful, is instantly immaterialised, raised above external personal relations, concentrated and deepened in its proper being, in a word, sublimated into an essence: while on the other hand, many unnoticed Platonic ideas, relations, or unsubstantial aspects of things, when the thrill of beauty runs through them, are suddenly revealed, as in poetry the secret harmonies of feelings and of words. In this way innumerable natural themes of happiness, which no one could possibly mistake for things, become members of the human family, and in turn restore the prodigal mind, perhaps long wasted on facts, to its home circle of essence.

Beauty detaches them for contemplation from the flux of nature.

This native affinity of the mind to essence rather than to fact is mind itself, the very nature of spirit or intellectual light. The sort of intelligence which adapts one natural being to another, and may be found in the conduct of animals, or even in the structure of their bodies, does not consist in thinking; it is an adaptation of life to its conditions, a form of behaviour in matter, which must exist and flourish before thinking or even feeling can arise at all. Intuition would be impossible without an underlying animal life, a psyche; for how should the sheer light of intuition actualise itself, or choose the essence on which it should fall? A psyche, the hereditary organisation and movement of life in an animal, must first exist and sustain itself by its "intelligent" adaptations to the ambient world: but these adaptations are not conscious until, by virtue of their existence, intuition arises; and intuition arises when the inner life of the animal, or its contact with external things, is expressed in some actual appearance, in some essence given in feeling or thought. The psyche and the material circumstances, by their special character and movement, determine the choice and succession of themes on which intuition shall be employed in some particular person; in so far as spirit is kindled there at all, it will have raised those themes to the plane of essence; the whole movement of nature and of human affairs, which imposes those themes, becomes itself only another theme for contemplation, if present to the mind at all. This contemplation does not require a man to shut his eyes or to fix them exclusively on the stars; it does not require him to stop living or acting. Often the most contemplative minds are the most worldly-wise, and the most capable of directing business. But though they may survey or foresee action, they do not live in action, because they see it in its wholeness and in its results; as a spectator who sees the plot of a play understands the emotions of the characters; but does not succumb to them; or as a writer, very busy with his pen and conveying much ink from inkstand to paper, may be thinking of his subject; and the words will probably come most aptly when, as words, they come unconsciously, and when the truth which they express absorbs the whole mind. The same thing happens in a game of ball, or in the game of politics, when the player is good; the quick adjustment of his faculties and organs, being automatic, kindles in his mind a graphic image and a pure emotion, to be the signs of his achievement to his inner man.

There is concomitant contemplation in the midst of action whenever action is masterly.

The natural and the spiritual fruits of life are not opposed, but they are different. Its natural fruits are more life, persisting through readjustments and an incessant generation of new forms, so that youth may fill the place of age and attain an equal, though not identical, perfection. It is in these perfections, or in approaches which partly anticipate them, that the spiritual fruits are found. As we have seen, they may ripen early, and may be gathered at all seasons, when any phase of life is perfected in action; but the spiritual fruits are internal or tangential to this action, not consequent upon it, like the natural fruits: they may be omnipresent in existence, but only by everywhere transmuting existence into essence. Spirit is life looking out of the window; the work of the household must have been done first, and is best done by machinery. Moral triumphs are not æsthetic, because they have other occasions, but they are equally intellectual when realised in the spirit; they lie in the joy of having done *this:* they are a passage into essence. Finality, though it is not felt as beauty, marks the great moments of passion satisfied or purposes achieved. Into some scene, into some phrase, into some gesture in itself trivial, the whole burden of a long experience may then be cast, and happiness may be centred and realised in some simple event or in some silent moment.

Moral as well as æsthetic virtue is realised in the contemplation of essence.

I should need but to enlarge this canvass in order to paint the whole happiness possible to man. In what should it lie? In going on, and simply not stopping? In passing to some better experience? But in what would it be better? In being fuller or longer? I think the longer and the fuller a bad life is, the worse it is. How, then, should it be made better? Only surely, by bringing all its activities, as far as possible, to intrinsic perfection and mutual harmony, so that at each step, and in every high moment of synthesis and reflection, intuition may fall on an essence beyond which it need not look, finding in it peace, liberation, and a sufficient token that fate, so far as that expression of spirit is concerned, has lost its terrors. Without such vision realised at each of its stages, life would be a mere fatality, automatism at odds with itself, a procession of failures. Spirit would have been called into being by a false promise; its only hope would be that by sleep supervening, or by distraction so extreme as to destroy the organic harmonies on which intuition depends, that mistake should be corrected and forgotten.

This possible conflict between matter and spirit is a family quarrel; it is not a shock between independent forces brought together by accident, since spirit cannot exist except in matter, and matter cannot become interested in its formations and fortunes save by creating a spirit that may observe and celebrate them. How happily spirit and matter may lead their common life together appears in play at the beginning, and in contemplation at the end. It is only in the middle when animal faculties are inwardly perfect and keen enough to be conscious, but are outwardly ill-adjusted and ignorant, that trouble arises; because the mind sees and wants one thing, and circumstances impose something different, requiring a disposition and a form of imagination in the animal to which his play-life is not adapted. Spirit–the voice of the inner nature in so far as it is already formed and definite–accordingly suffers continual defeats, by the defeat of those animal impulses which it expresses; and if these impulses become confused or exhausted, it sinks with them into vice or discouragement. It would soon perish altogether, and annul the moral problem which its existence creates, unless in some way a harmony could be re-established between the individual and the world. This may be done in society at large by some firm political and moral regimen; or it may be done religiously by the discipline of the inner man, so that a part of him is weaned from the passions and interests which distract the world and is centred upon purely intellectual or spiritual aspiration. Religion is hard for external events to defeat, since ill-fortune stimulates it as much at least as good fortune. Thus within strict limits, and in a soberer garb, the play-life of childhood is restored to the soul.

In normal life, as in play, intuition is the innocent expression of action.

Hence that happy quarrel of philosophers–happy because both parties are right–as to whether wisdom is a meditation on life or on death. But in the midst of one we are in the other, not only in that existence is transition, but far more remarkably, in that life triumphant is life transmuted into something which is not life–into union with essence, with so much of the eternal as is then manifested in the transitory. This manifestation, with all the approaches to it, is life itself; and death is the fading of that vision, the passing of that essence back into its native heaven, depriving us by its obscuration of a part of ourselves, so that existence in us must lapse into some different phase, or into total darkness. Life, if by this word we understand the process of mutation, is itself death; to be fed is to kill, to advance is to reject and abandon. The truly creative movement is only upward, and life, in so far as it means light and accomplishment, is only some predestined intuition achieved, some wished-for essence made manifest. Existence itself is a momentary victory of essence: a victory over matter, in that matter, which might have taken any other form, takes this particular

> Life, death, and immortality all hang on the relation of existence to essence.

one and keeps circling about it, as if fascinated; not that there is really any magic here, but that matter, which has to have some form or other, is willing enough to be true to the one it has, and (so indifferent is it to form) to renounce for an indefinite time its native right to inconstancy: as a hardened traveller, not caring what inn he stays at, may remain good-naturedly at the one in which he happens to be lodged. Essence is victorious also over spirit, and no less amiably victorious; since it is in essence that spirit aspires to lose itself and to find its quietus, as it was from essence that matter managed to borrow some character and some beauty. What Spinoza meant by meditation on life was, I take it, the effort to wrest the truth of nature out of empirical confusion, so that all the vicissitudes of things might appear under the form of eternity; and what Socrates and Plato meant by meditation on death was almost the same thing. Only the Greeks, by distinguishing many gods and many divine ideas, could humanise and make friends with at least some of them; and in sympathy with those beautiful immortals they could survey and dismiss earthly existence with a touch of disdain; whereas the piety of thrifty and moralising nations, when enlightened, issues only in a scrupulous natural philosophy. Being overawed by the facts, and eager for existence and prosperity, they miss the liberal life; they prefer perpetual servitude, if well fed, to emancipation, such as interest in pure essences affords; and often (though not in Spinoza) they substitute a troubled hope in some fabulous resurrection for the present union with the eternal which is natural to spirit.

Thus scepticism, dialectic, contemplation, and spiritual discipline, all lead to the discrimination of essence; and anyone who has trodden any of these paths to the end will not need to be told what essence means, or that it is a most real and interesting realm of being. But it is not the whole of being: on the contrary, were there nothing but essence, not one of these approaches to it would be open: there would be no possible movement, no events, no life, and no preference. Considered in itself, essence is certainly the deepest, the only inevitable, form of reality; but I am here speaking of approaches to it, that is, of con-

> Essence, to which spirit is addressed, is not the source of spirit or of any existing fact.

siderations drawn from human experience that may enable us to discern that primary reality and to recognise it to be such in contrast to our own form of being. We stand, then, on another plane, the plane of scattered experience, brute fact, contingent existence; if we did not, the discernment of essence would have no novelty for us, it would reveal no night-firmament behind our day, it would not liberate us from ourselves or from the incubus of accidental things. If we were prompted, then, by our new insight to cry that our old life was all illusion, we might be turning this insight into a new folly. Enlightenment itself would be impossible if chance experiences had not preceded, perfectly real in their own way; indeed existence (something that has no foothold whatever in the realm of essence) is presupposed and contained in any assertion or denial, and in the intuition of essence itself. The existence and distribution of enlightenment, as of any other fact, places us to begin with in another realm, the realm of matter, which must be begged separately: without it there could be no manifestation of essence, whether in nature or in discourse.

The priority of the realm of essence is therefore not temporal or dynamic. It is an infinite field for selection; evidently it cannot select or emphasise any part of

Matter is the selective principle even among essences.

itself. When the selection takes place, we accordingly refer it to a different principle, which we may call chance, fact, or matter: but this principle would be a mere word, a term without indicative force, if it did not select some feature of the realm of essence to be its chosen form: in other words, if this brute accident were not some accident in particular, contrasted with the infinity of other forms which it has not chosen. To appeal to fact, to thump existence with empirical conviction, is accordingly but to emphasise some essence, like a virtuous bridegroom renouncing all others: the exclusion is opportune, but the bride after all is only one of a million, and the mind has simply wedded an essence. The principle of constancy, or perhaps of inconstancy—the selective principle—is matter; yet whatever way it may turn, it must embrace one essence or another.

The approaches to essence are therefore as various as those predispositions in matter which determine the poses of life. Or we may say that for the mind there

Through animal passions and interests, matter directs attention upon essence.

is a single avenue to essence, namely, attention. Awaken attention, intensify it, purify it into white flame, and the actual and unsubstantial object of intuition will stand before you in all its living immediacy and innocent nakedness. But notice: this attention, discovering nothing but essence, is itself an animal faculty: it is called forth by material stress, or by passion. The passions, in so far as they are impulses to action, entangle us materially in the flux of substance, being intent on seizing, transforming, or destroying something that exists: but at the same time, in so far as they quicken the mind, they are favourable to the discernment of essence; and it is only a passionate soul that can be truly contemplative. The reward of the lover, which also chastens him, is to discover that in thinking he loved anything of this world he was profoundly mistaken. Everybody strives for possession; that is the animal instinct on which everything hangs; but possession leaves the true lover unsatisfied: his joy is in the character of the thing loved, in the essence it reveals, whether it be here or there, now or then, his or another's. This essence, which for action was only a signal letting loose a generic animal impulse, to contemplation is the whole object of love, and the sole gain in loving. Naturally essences seem thin abstractions to those absorbed in action, whose heart is set on the eventual, and to whom the actual is never anything: the actual in experience is never more than an echo or supplement to deeper facts, a shimmer on the surface of the great sea labouring beneath; yet the actual in experience is never an abstraction from experience itself; it is the whole fruit of that hidden labour, the entire reality for the spirit. It is therefore not as a quality attributed to external things that essence is best distinguished; for the colour or the shape of an apple may be supposed to exist in it, and when drawn out and imagined existing alone they may seem ghostly; neither the roundness nor the redness of the apple would be edible. To a greedy child they would be miserable cheats; but not so to the painter or the geometer. The child might be better initiated into the nature of essence (which is not far from the innocent mind) if he chose as an instance the pleasure of eating the apple, or of snatching it from another boy's hand; essences which he would distinguish easily from their opposites, and which he would not be tempted to incorporate into apples. A little experience would convince him that these intangible pleasures gave importance to apples, and not apples to them; and he would join the painter of still life, and the geometer, in finding that things are mere instruments, and that only essences are essential. Interest, in marking the differences and precise characters of things, which are all that the mind can take from them, is the great revealer of essence. Herein appears the thoroughly intellectual or poetical virtue of spirit. The more intense and dominating it is, the less it dwells on the machinery which may control its existence, and the more exclusively it addresses itself to the true or the beautiful, that is, to the essences which experience would manifest if it were pure and perfect.

The Being Proper to Essences

The Realm of Essence: Book First of Realms of Being. New York: Charles Scribner's Sons; London: Constable and Co. Ltd., 1927, 18–25. Volume sixteen of the critical edition of *The Works of George Santayana.*

This selection, Chapter II of The Realm of Essence, *gives an account of essences and their realm. "The principle of essence," wrote Santayana, "is identity" (ES, 168). By this he means that the entire being of an essence lies in its character or in its being just what it is. This makes essence universal: it always is what it is irrespective of the time or place it might be exemplified in matter or intuition. It is what it is if it is never exemplified, and all essences are of equal worth whether exemplified or not. The multitude of essences infinitely exceeds what can be intuited by spirit and what nature can exhibit. The Realm of Essence is, according to Santayana, the basis of knowledge. An essence is the character of any existing thing such that the existing thing is what it is and no other. Hence, the existing object can be distinguished, noted, and known. Essences are inert; they are not the cause of any material objects. Rather they come to be exemplified through the contingent flux of matter taking one form and then another. Essence, being non-existent, is impervious to the contingency of matter and hence is eternal.*

The principle of essence, we have seen, is identity: the being of each essence is entirely exhausted by its definition; I do not mean its definition in words, but the character which distinguishes it from any other essence. Every **Each essence** essence is perfectly individual. There can be no question in the *is* **by being** realm of essence of mistaken identity, vagueness, shiftiness, or **identical and** self-contradiction. These doubts arise in respect to natural exis- **individual.** tences or the meanings or purposes of living minds: but in every doubt or equivocation both alternatives are genuine essences; and in groping and making up my mind I merely hesitate between essences, not knowing on which to arrest my attention. There is no possibility of flux or ambiguity within any of the alternatives which might be chosen at each step.

This inalienable individuality of each essence renders it a universal; for being perfectly self-contained and real only by virtue of its intrinsic character, it con- **Also** tains no reference to any setting in space or time, and stands in no **universal.** adventitious relations to anything. Therefore without forfeiting its absolute identity it may be repeated or reviewed any number of times. Such embodiments or views of it, like the copies of a book or the acts of reading of it, will be facts or events in nature (which is a net of external relations); but the copies would not be copies of the same book, nor the readings readings of it, unless (and in so far as) the same essence reappeared in them all. Physical obstacles to exact repetitions or reproductions do not affect the essential universality of every essence, even if by chance it occurs only once, or never occurs at all; because, in virtue of its perfect identity and individuality, it cannot fall out of the catalogue of essences, where it fills its particular place. If I try to delete it, I reinstate it, since in deleting *that* I have recognised and defined it anew, bearing witness to its possessing the whole being which it can claim as an essence. There accordingly it stands, waiting to be embodied or noticed, if nature or attention ever choose to halt at that point or to traverse it. Every essence in its own realm is just as central, just as normal, and just as complete as any other: it is therefore always just as open to exemplification or to thought, without the addition or subtraction of one iota of its being. Time and space may claim and repeat it as often or as seldom as they will: that is their own affair. The flux is free to have such plasticity as it has, and to miss all that it misses; and it is free to be as monotonous as it likes, if it finds it easier to fall again and again into the same form, rather than to run away into perpetual and unreturning novelties. The realm of essence is the scale of measurement, the continuum of variation, on which these repetitions or these novelties may be plotted and compared. Re-embodiments or re-surveys of an essence (if they occur) bind the parts of the flux together ideally, and render it amenable to description. The essential universality of these forms makes any fact, in so far as it exhibits them, distinct and knowable: the universal and the individual being so far from contrary that they are identical. I am not myself unless I re-enact now the essence of myself, which I may re-enact at all times and places.

Since essences are universals not needing to figure in any particular place or time, but fit to figure in any, it is not possible to investigate the realm of essence by empirical exploration. You cannot go in search of that which is nowhere. Some essences will appear or occur to you, since what- **Essences are infinite in number.** ever intuition life may awaken in you must light up some essence or other; but what further essences, if any, there may be is not discoverable by simply waiting for them to turn up. Nature is indeed very rich in forms, compared with the inertia and monotony of experience in home-keeping animals, revolving in their private circle of habits and ideas; but nature too is built on a single plan—all nuclei and planets, all life and death—and as much a slave of routine as any of her creatures. The unexemplified is not exemplified there, the unthought of is not thought of: not because in itself it resists being created or described, but because nature and thought happen not to bloom in any way but that in which they have taken to blooming. In part, indeed, this restriction may be due to local prejudice and ignorance in the observer, who draws the periphery of nature with his compass. Another man, a different animal, a spirit native to another world may even now be greeting the essences which it has not entered into my heart to conceive. Evidently my limitations cannot forbid them to rejoice in their different experience; nor can the limitations of any actual experience forbid the essences it leaves out to be just those which are absent. An essence is an inert theme, something which cannot bring itself forward, but must be chosen, if chosen, by some external agent; and evidently the choice made by this agent, contingent as it is and wholly arbitrary, cannot render unavailable the other inert themes which other agents, or itself in a different moment of its flux, might choose instead. The very contingency of existence, the very blindness of life, throw the doors wide open towards the infinity of being. Even if some philosopher or some god thought himself omniscient, surprises might be in store for him, and thoughts new to his thought; nay, even supposing that his whole experience and the entire history of his world lay synthesised before him under the form of eternity, and that he was not a victim of sheer egotism in asserting that nothing more could ever exist, still the wanton idiosyncrasy of that total fact, the enormity of that accident, could not be blustered away. Existence is irrational for a deeper and more intrinsic reason than because one part of it may not be deducible from another: any part, and all its parts together, are irrational in merely existing, and in being otherwise than as essences are, that is, identical with themselves and endowed with that formal being which it is impossible that anything, whatever it be, should not possess. Not that essence can resist or resent this irrational selection which existence makes of its riches: on the contrary, essence is a sort of invitation to the dance; it tempts nature with openings in every direction; and in so doing it manifests its own inexhaustible variety. Its very being is to set no limits to the forms of being. The multitude of essences is absolutely infinite.

This assertion has an audacious sound, and I should not venture upon it, had it not a counterpart or corollary which takes away all its venom, namely, that essences do not *exist*. If I were in pursuit of substance (as I shall be in the Second Book) I should distrust any description of it not purely tentative, empirical, and scrupulously modest: but the bold definition which Spinoza gives of what he calls substance that it is Being absolutely infinite, seems to me a perfect and self-justifying definition of the realm of essence: because in conceiving and defining such an object we prove it to possess the only being which we mean to ascribe to it. Denying it to be infinite, or denying that any supposed element in it existed, we should be designating these missing elements and that absent infinity: whereby we should be instituting them ideally, and recognising them to be essences. The realm of essence is comparable to an infinite Koran—or the Logos that was in the beginning—written in invisible but indelible ink, prophesying all that Being could ever be or contain: and the flux of existence is the magical reagent, travelling over it in a thin stream, like a reader's eye, and bringing here one snatch of it and there another to the light for a passing moment. Each reader may be satisfied with his own verse, and think it the whole of Scripture: but the mere assertion of this limit, or suspicion that other readers might find other texts, is enough to show that the non-existent cannot be limited, since the limits of the existent might always be changed. To deny the being of essence, because it may happen to be unrealised, is self-contradictory: for if it is not realised, it must have a quality, distinguishing it from realised forms. Unrealised forms may not interest a sluggish mind: an arithmetician who was happy in the thought of whole numbers, might deprecate all mention of vulgar fractions or repeating decimals, and might swear to die without them, lest his safe and honest arithmetic should be complicated with unrealities. But unrealities of that sort nevertheless envelop his realities on every side; and it is his arrest at his realities that, if you like, is unreal; there is no reason in it, and no permanence; whereas the unrealities are unchangeable, inevitable, and always standing behind the

But non-existent; they form an indelible background to all transitory facts.

door. Even if the whole realm of essence (as Spinoza assumed) were realised somewhere at some time in the life of nature, essence would remain a different and a non-existent realm: because the realisation of each part could be only local and temporary, and for all the rest of time and in all the worlds that excluded it, each fact would fade into the corresponding essence, and would remain certain and inevitable as an essence only, and as a fact merely presumptive.

Essence so understood much more truly *is* than any substance or any experience or any event: for a substance, event, or experience may change its form or may exist only by changing it, so that all sorts of things that are proper to it in one phase will be absent from it in another. It will not be a unit at all, save by external delimitation. Perhaps some abstract constancy in quantity, energy, or continuity may be discovered to run through it, but this constant element will never *Existence and truth borrow their individuality from essence.* be the actual experience, event, or substance in its living totality at any moment. Or perhaps all the phases of such an existence may be viewed together and synthesised into one historical picture; but this picture would again not be the existent substance, experience, or event unrolling itself in act. It would be only a description of that portion of the flux seen under the form of eternity; in other words, it would be an essence and not an existence. Essence is just that character which any existence wears in so far as it remains identical with itself and so long as it does so; the very character which it throws overboard by changing, and loses altogether when it becomes something else. To be able to become something else, to suffer change and yet endure, is the privilege of existence, be it in a substance, an event, or an experience; whereas essences can be exchanged, but not changed. Existence at every step casts off one essence and picks up another: we call it the same existence when we are able to trace its continuity in change, by virtue of its locus and proportions; but often we are constrained to give up the count, and to speak of a new event, a new thing, or a new experience. The essences or forms traversed in mutation render this mutation possible and describable: without their eternal distinctness no part of the flux could differ in any respect from any other part, and the whole would collapse into a lump without order or quality. So much more profound is the eternal being of the essences traversed in change, than that of the matter or attention or discourse which plays with those essences at touch and go.

Nothing, then, more truly *is* than character. Without this wedding garment no guest is admitted to the feast of existence: whereas the unbidden essences do not require that invitation (with which very low characters are sometimes honoured) in order to preserve their proud identity out in the cold. There those few privileged revellers will soon have to rejoin *Notion of the Realm of Essence.* them, not a whit fatter for their brief surfeit of being. After things lose their existence, as before they attain it, although it is true of them that they have existed or will exist, they have no internal being except their essences, quite as if they had never broached Existence at all: yet the identity of each essence with itself and difference from every other essence suffices to distinguish and define them all in eternity, where they form the Realm of Essence. True and false assertions may be made about any one of them, such, for instance, as that it does not exist; or that it includes or excludes some other essence, or is included or excluded by it.

Here is a further character inseparable from essence: all essences are eternal. No hyperbole or rhetorical afflatus is contained in this assertion, as if some prophet pronounced some law or some city to be everlasting. That any existing thing should be everlasting, though not impossible, is incongruous with the contingency of existence. God or matter, if they are everlasting, are so by a sort of iterated contingency and perpetual reproduction; for it is in the nature of existence to be here and perhaps not there, now and perhaps not then; it must be explored to discover how far it may stretch; it must wait and see how long it shall last. The assumption that it lasts or stretches for ever can be made only impetuously, by animal enthusiasm, when the feeling of readiness and omnipotence makes some living creature defy all threats of disaster. Yet so long as we live in time, the ghost of the murdered past will always fill the present with a profound uneasiness. If the eternity of essence were conceived after that fashion, it would indeed be a rash boast; no essence has an essential lien on existence anywhere, much less everywhere and always. Its eternity has nothing to do with such mortal hazards. It is merely the self-identity proper to each of the forms which existence may put on or off, illustrate somewhere or perhaps illustrate always, or very likely never illustrate at all.

Its eternity is the counterpart of its non-existence.

The Scope of Natural Philosophy

The Realm of Matter: Book Second of Realms of Being. New York: Charles Scribner's Sons; London: Constable and Co. Ltd., 1930, 1–9. Volume sixteen of the critical edition of *The Works of George Santayana*.

This selection appeared as Chapter I of The Realm of Matter, *the second volume of the four-volume* Realms of Being. *Santayana finished the manuscript of* The Realm of Matter *in August of 1929, and the book was published the following year. At the end of 1929 Santayana commented in letters that he was relieved to be finished with the book, and he wrote that it "was frightfully difficult to write, as I fear it may be to read" (LGS, 4:127). The chapter indicates the difference in aim when inquiring not into the Realm of Essence, where no belief is required, but rather into The Realm of Matter, in which belief is compulsory in the form of animal faith. The aim of Santayana's natural philosophy is to provide "a conception of nature by which the faith involved in action may be enlightened and guided" (ES, 174).*

The measure of confidence with which I have spoken of essence forsakes me when I approach existence. Logic, grammar, and poetry are free; no alien fact, no vociferation, can prevent intuition from beholding what it actually beholds. The public censor has indeed some rights over the persons in whom intuition arises, and may condemn their habit of mind if he thinks that it comports idleness or the disruption of happy national conventions; but, in this instance, fortune having relegated me, like the gods of Epicurus, to the interstices of the worlds, I may escape that censure or disregard it. Who knows? Perhaps some kindred spirit may tell me that I have chosen the better part. In any case, I deny nothing and prejudge nothing concerning the intuitions of others; if I cultivate my own with a certain ardour, it is only as any man cultivates his language and tastes, if his mind is at all liberal; and I am confident no god or man will be justly angry with me for browsing so innocently in my own pasture. But when the active impulse of curiosity and dogmatism asserts itself in its turn, as it must in the most contemplative mind, and I ask myself what dark objects or forces have created or are threatening my contemplation, then indeed I am at a loss: and as in positing such natural agencies at all I assume that they are objects obligatory to every other mind with which I can communicate, I bind myself to make my opinions conformable with their reports, and my reports agreeable to their experience. Of course the belief that I can communicate with other minds, and that the reports reaching me signify an experience of theirs over and above my own, is a part of this extraordinary compulsory assumption which I make in living; the assumption that I am surrounded by a natural world, peopled by creatures in whom intuition is as rife as in myself: and as all my concern in perception and action turns on what those external things may do, so half my interest in my own thoughts turns on what other people may be thinking.

Contrast between ideal and natural science.

It is not the task of natural philosophy to justify this assumption, which indeed can never be justified. Its task, after making that assumption, is to carry it out consistently and honestly, so as to arrive, if possible, at a con-

Assumption of an existing world.

ception of nature by which the faith involved in action may be enlightened and guided. Such a description of nature, if it were ever completed in outline, would come round full circle, and in its account of animals it would report how they came to have intuitions (among them this natural philosophy) and to use them in the description of the world which actually surrounded them. The whole field of action and of facts would then be embraced in a single view, summary and symbolic, but comprehensive.

The dream of the natural philosopher would be to describe the world from its beginning (if it had a beginning), tracing all its transformations; and he would like

Inevitable attempt to describe it.

to do this analytically, not pictorially—that is, not in the sensuous language of some local observer composing a private perspective, but in terms of the ultimate elements (if there are ultimate elements) concerned in the actual evolution of things. Out of those elements he would conceive each observer and his perspective arising, and of course varying from moment to moment. Even if the natural philosopher were an idealist, and admitted only observing spirits and their perspectives, he would endeavour to trace the evolution of these intuitions, which would be his atoms, in their universal order and march, by no means contenting himself with one intuition and one perspective; for, if he did so, his idealism (like that of some philosophies of history) would not be a system of physics or of logic, but a literary entertainment, the lyrical echo of many verbal reports in a romantic imagination. This echo might be interesting in itself: but it would remain only an incident in that natural world which indeed it presupposed, but which it deliberately ignored. So that when the idealist became a man again in the world of action, and began to live (as he must) by animal faith, his philosophy would entirely forsake him; yet it is in the service of this animal faith that philosophy exists, when it is science and wisdom. Indeed, a theoretical refusal to trust natural philosophy cannot absolve the most sceptical of us from framing one, and from living by it. I *must* conceive a surrounding world, even if in reflection I say to myself at every step: Illusion, Illusion. It then becomes almost as interesting to know what sort of illusions must accompany me through life, as it would be to imagine what sort of world I really live in. Indeed, if all spurious substitutes for natural philosophy were discarded (spurious because irrelevant to the animal faith which alone posits existence) those two positions might coincide, since the picture of the natural world framed by common sense and science, while framed with the greatest care, would be admittedly only a picture; and belief in the existence of that world, though assumed without wobbling, would be admittedly but an article of inevitable faith.

Non-scientific beliefs about existence, whether inspired by religious feeling, reasoning, or fancy, are alternatives to the current natural philosophy, or extensions of it. Nobody would believe in his ideas if he had not an initial propensity to believe in things, as if his ideas described them. Dogmatic religions are assertions about the nature of the universe; what is called supernatural is only ultra-mundane, an extension of this world on its own plane, and a recognition of forces ruling over it not reckoned with in vulgar commerce. The assertions made by such religious faith, if not superstitious errors, are ultimate truths of natural philosophy, which intu-ition or revelation has supplied in advance of experiment: but **Positive religions involve cosmologies.** if the assertions are true at all, experiment might one day confirm them. Thus Christian orthodoxy maintains that men will carry their memories and their bod-ies with them into hell or heaven. Theology is the natural philosophy of that larger world which religion posits as truly existing: it therefore has precise impli-cations in politics and science. The absence of such implications and commit-ments, far from showing that religion has become spiritual, proves it a sham; it is no longer a manly hypothesis, honestly made about the world confronted in action. No doubt there is an inner fountain of religious feeling which a person accepting his theology on hearsay might wholly lack; but it was religious instinct of some kind that originally prompted those hypotheses about the hidden nature of things, and if this instinct is lacking those hypotheses will soon be discarded. On the other hand, religious feeling may not always require ultra-mundane extensions of the natural world; it may find a sufficient object and sanction in the course of earthly history and domestic life, as was the case, at bottom, with Jewish and Protestant righteousness: the politics and science dictated by religious faith will then coincide with those recommended by worldly wisdom. Religious feel-ing may take still other forms; for instance, it may smile mystically at action and belief altogether, retreating into the invisible sanctuary of the spirit, or floating incredulously amid mere music and dreams. But mysticism, whether austere or voluptuous, since it regards the absolute, ceases to regard existence which, by definition, is relative, since it consists in having external relations. Positive and virile minds may find indulgence in such mysticism irreligious, because their earnestness is directed upon alleged facts, in this world or in another: facts essen-tially relevant to action and policy, and open to natural philosophy.

Much restraint, and some disillusion, may enable a man to entertain ideas without believing them to describe any matter of fact: such ideas will be avowedly mere terms of grammar, logic, or fancy, to be discarded, or at least discounted, on broaching a serious natural philosophy. They may still be indispensable as a medium, as some language is indispensable to science; but they will be optional and inter-**Idolatrous character of metaphysics.** changeable, as the scientific part of a book of science (which is never the whole of it) is perfectly translatable from one language into another. This is not to say that the medium of intuition, even in natural philosophy, is indifferent in itself; nothing is dearer to a man or a nation than congenial modes of expression; I would rather be silent than use some people's language; I would rather die than think as some people think. But it is the quality of life that is concerned here, not the truth of ideas. To attempt to impose such modes of intuition or expression, as if they were obligatory tenets, is metaphysics: a projection of the constraints or the creations of thought into the realm of matter. The authority of intuition would be entire if it kept to the definition of essences, and of their essential relations; but when zeal intervenes, and we profess to find our favourite dialectic in things, we are betrayed into disrespect for nature, and are inflating our egotism into cosmic proportions. At best the metaphysician has given a useful hint to the naturalist: he has supplied categories which may be convenient or even indispensable for expressing the ways of nature in human discourse. The palmary instance of this is mathematics, which, long after having ceased to be empirical and become dialectical, still continues to serve for construction and even for prophecy in the material sphere: yet the symbols employed grow more abstruse and tenuous as they grow more exact, so that people are little tempted to substitute the notation for the thing denoted; and they thus escape metaphysics.

When the experience interpreted is spiritual or passionate, the categories used are, as in religion and poetry, clearly mythological: yet they are not without a real, though indirect, object in the realm of matter. This object is the psyche, with all those profound currents in her life which create the passions, and create the spirit which expresses the passions, yet which in expressing them is so entangled that it often comes to regard them as its enemies. Those psychic currents, being dynamic, are material; but they are hidden from the eye of spirit, which alone is spiritual, by layer upon layer of vague sensation, rhetoric, and imagery.

Belief, in its very soul, is belief about nature; it is animal faith. To entangle belief in anything non-natural, or avowedly tangential to action, would be to cheat at the game. Honest speculative belief is always specula-

Nature is the nexus of all substances and forces. tive physics. But its terms are inevitably the essences present to intuition; and the very faith which, in the presence of these essences, posits existing things, drags something of the given apparition into the presumed substance of the thing revealed: the theophany humanises the god. In correcting this illusion, and in discarding one mythical or metaphysical image after another, science must still retain some symbol for the overpowering reality of the world. This reality is not that symbol itself, nor a collection of such symbols: if we cling to these we shall never quit the realm of essence. Nor am I sure that the most learned symbols are the least deceptive; if any human ideas must be idolized, I should almost prefer those of the senses and of the poets. Yet it would be ignominious for a philosopher voluntarily to succumb to illusion at all, when the artificiality and relativity of all human views, especially of learned and beautiful systems, is so patent to reflection. Yet views we must have, none the worse, surely, if they are beautiful and learned; so that the natural philosopher is driven to a deeper question, to which I mean to devote this book: How much, when cleared as far as possible of idolatry, can sense or science reveal concerning the dark engine of nature? In what measure do they truly enlighten animal faith?

In broaching this question I am not concerned with repeating, correcting, or forecasting the description which men of science may give of the world. I accept

How far is science knowledge? gladly any picture of nature honestly drawn by them, as I accept gladly any picture drawn by my own senses. Different circumstances or different faculties would certainly have produced different pictures. From Genesis to Thales, to Ptolemy, to Copernicus, to Newton, and to Einstein the landscape has pleasantly varied; and it may yet open other vistas. These variations and prospects show the plasticity of human thought, for it is not the facts that have much varied, nor the material station of man, nor his senses and destiny. The incubus of existence remains exactly the same. Is it merely imagination that has become more laboured but no less fantastic? Or has the path of destiny been really cleared and the forces that control destiny been better understood? Within what limits does any description of nature, picturesque or scientific, retain its relevance to animal faith and its validity as knowledge of fact, and at what point does it become pure speculation and metaphor? That is the only question which I shall endeavour to answer.

My survey of the realm of matter will accordingly be merely transcendental, and made from the point of view of a sceptic and a moralist criticising the claims of experience and science to be true knowledge.

By transcendental reflection I understand reversion, in the presence of any object or affirmation, to the immediate experience which discloses that object or prompts that affirmation. Transcendental reflection is a challenge to all dogmatism, a demand for radical evidence. It therefore tends to disallow substance and, when it is thorough, even to disallow existence. Nothing is ultimately left except the passing appearance or the appearance of something passing. How, then, if transcendental reflection disallows substance, can it lead me to distinguish the properties of substance?

The transcendental method applied to animal faith.

In *Scepticism and Animal Faith* I have considered the transcendental motives which oblige me to believe in substance. The belief must always remain an assumption, but one without which an active and intelligent creature cannot honestly act or think. Transcendentalism has two phases or movements—the sceptical one retreating to the immediate, and the assertive one by which objects of belief are defined and marshalled, of such a character and in such an order as intelligent action demands. The enterprise of life is precarious, and to the sceptic it must seem an adventure in the dark, without origins or environment or results. Yet this flying life, by its forward energy, breeds from within certain postulates of sanity, certain conceptions of the conditions which might surround it and lend it a meaning, so that its own continuance and fortunes may be conceived systematically and affirmed with confidence. Thus the faith that posits and describes a world is just as transcendental as the criticism which reduces that world to an appearance or a fiction. If so many transcendental philosophers stop at the negative pole, this arrest is not a sign of profundity in them, but of weakness. It is by boldly believing what transcendental necessity prompts any hunting animal to believe, that I separate myself from that arrested idealism, and proceed to inquire what existences, what substances, and what motions are involved in the chase.

In the chase, for those who follow it, the intensity of experience is not like the intensity (limitless if you will) of contemplating pure Being—immutable, equable, and complete. The hunter and the hunted believe in something ambushed and imminent:

Action posits a field existing substantially for science to describe.

present images are little to them but signs for coming events. Things are getting thick, agents are coming together, or disappearing: they are killing and dying. The assurance of this sort of being is assurance of existence, and the belief in this sort of agent is belief in substance. If this belief and assurance are not illusions (which the acting animal cannot admit them to be), several properties must belong to substances and to the world they compose. These properties I may distinguish in reflection and call by philosophical names, somewhat as follows.

Indispensable Properties of Substance

The Realm of Matter: Book Second of Realms of Being. New York: Charles Scribner's Sons; London: Constable and Co. Ltd., 1930, 10–25. Volume sixteen of the critical edition of *The Works of George Santayana.*

In this selection, Chapter II of The Realm of Matter, *Santayana distinguished five properties of substance. First, substance is external to the thought of it that is prompted by animal faith. This entails that transitions in nature are distinct from transitions in thought. Thought moves from one object to another by faith only. Second, since substance is posited in the actions of the animal, it must be external to the agent and in parts; else there could be no interaction. Third, substance changes perpetually and constitutes time, but this perpetual change does not exclude permanence. If change were total, there could be no transformation and no existence. Change and succession require a medium for external relations among the things changing and succeeding one another. Fourth, substance is unequally distributed, because it must be discriminated among various agents who interact and effect changes. It cannot be homogeneous and undivided. Fifth, substance lies in a common field of action. Substantial objects recognized by an agent must have an effect, direct or indirect, on the action of the agent; and these dynamic relations unify the field of action and make up a cosmos.*

1. Since substance is posited, and not given in intuition, as essences may be given, *substance is external to the thought which posits it.*

2. Since it is posited in action, or in readiness for action, the substance posited is external not merely to the positing thought (as a different thought would be) but is external to the physical agent which is the organ of that action, as well as of that thought. In other words, *Substance has parts and constitutes a physical space.* Conversely, the substantial agent in action and thought is external to the surrounding portions of substance with which it can interact. *All the parts of substance are external to one another.*

> A world in which action is to occur must be external, spatial, and temporal, possessing variety and unity.

3. Since substance is engaged in action, and action involves change, *substance is in flux and constitutes a physical time.* Changes are perpetually occurring in the relations of its parts, if not also in their intrinsic characters.

4. Since the agents in action and reaction are distinct in position and variable in character, and since they induce changes in one another, *substance is unequally distributed.* It diversifies the field of action, or physical time and space.

5. Since there is no occasion for positing any substance save as an agent in the field of action, all recognisable substance must lie in the same field in which the organism of the observer occupies a relative centre. Therefore, wherever it works and solicits recognition, *substance composes a relative cosmos.*

A mutual externality, or *Auseinandersein*—an alternation of centres such as moment and moment, thing and thing, place and place, person and person—is characteristic of existence. Each centre is equally actual and equally central, yet each is dependent on its neighbours for its position and on its predecessors for its genesis. The existential interval from one centre to another is bridged naturally by generation or motion—by a transition actually taking place from one moment, place, or character to another, in such a manner that the former moment, place, or character is abandoned and lost. The same interval may still be bridged cognitively by faith or intent, cognition being a substitute for a transition which cannot be executed materially, because the remote term of it is past or not next in the order of genesis or transformation. But this interval can never be bridged by synthesis in intuition. Synthesis in intuition destroys the existential status of the terms which it unites, since it excludes any alternation or derivation between them. It unites at best the essences of some natural things into an ideal picture. On the other hand the conjunction of existences in nature must always remain successive, external, and unsynthesised. Nature shows no absolute limits and no privileged partitions; whereas the richest intuition, the most divine omniscience, is imprisoned in the essence which it beholds. It cannot break through into existence unless it loses itself and submits to transition; and the foretaste or aftertaste of such transition, present in feeling, must posit something eventual, something absent from intuition, if even the sense or idea of existence is to arise at all. Then the mind engaged in action may begin to live by faith in the outlying conditions of life, and by an instinctive tension towards obscure events.

The first property, externality to thought belongs to all existence.

It might seem that memory eludes this necessity, and actually encloses some parts of the past in the present, and brings the movement of events bodily within the circle of intuition. But this is an illusion founded on the fact that memory contains both imagery and knowledge: the imagery is all present, but that of which it gives knowledge, when memory is true, is past and gone. Even if, by a rare favour, the original aspect of the past experience should be reproduced exactly, it will not be the past event, nor even the present one, that will be given in intuition, but the dateless essence common to both.

Memory, when cognitive, a relation between separate natural facts.

The cognitive value of this apparition will hang on the ulterior fact that such an apparition, or the event which it reports, occurred before, at a point of time which was its own centre, and not a marginal feature in the present perspective. Memory, then, in so far as it is, or even claims to be, knowledge, is faith in the absent, and bridges external relations by intent only, not by synthesis in intuition.

A mutual externality is also requisite among the instances of spirit, that is, among thoughts that are to be regarded as existences and events. This at first sight might seem contrary to the apparent self-existence and self-evidence of conscious being, and to the transcendental status of spirit, which, because it is a logical counterpart to any datum, might be alleged to be an omnipresent fact, existing absolutely. But this, although it may pass for criticism, is the sophistry of reflection, which can readily take its verbal terms

Existing thoughts are separate events lodged each in its place in nature.

for existences or substances, and ignore the natural springs of feeling and of reflection itself. An instance of spirit, a pure feeling or intuition, if it had no date or place in nature, would not be an event or existence at all, but only another name, and a mythical name, for the essence conceived to be present there. The life of thought, in its conscious intensity, lies in the syntheses which it is perpetually making among its changing materials. These acts of synthesis, these glances and insights, are historical facts; they arise and are distinguishable on the level of experience from their material conditions; but they are not substances. Their substance is their organ in its movement and in its changing tensions: it is the psyche. The case is like that of a collision between two vehicles, or checkmate in a game of chess. The collision is a new fact, on the plane of human affairs, as is the checkmate which ends the game; so, too, are the chagrin or the severe pain which these events may occasion. But the pain or the chagrin could no more arise, or come into existence, without the living persons who endure them—persons moving in the realm of matter—than the checkmate could occur without the match, or the collision without the vehicles. If a feeling or thought is to be actual, and not a metaphorical name for some eternal essence, it must therefore arise out of material events, and in the midst of them: it must stand in external relations.

Thus the first indispensable condition for the being of substance is indispensable also to any form of existence, mental or historical as well as physical. Existence, like substance, is essentially diffuse and many-centred. One fact can be reached cognitively from another fact only by faith, and materially only by transition; and the cognitive or the initial fact itself can exist only by virtue of its position or action in a natural system extending beyond it.

It follows that substance is in flux, virtual, if not actual. External relations are such as are due to the position, not to the inherent character, of the terms. They are, therefore, always variable, and existence, although it may endure by accident for any length of time, is inherently mortal and transitory, being adventitious to the essences which figure in it. When Hamlet says, *To be or not to be,* he is pondering the alternative between existence and non-existence, and feeling the contingency of both. The question is not whether he shall be or not be Hamlet: death might cause him to forget his essence, but could not abolish it or transform it into another essence. In the realm of essence all these essences are eternally present and no alternative arises: which is perhaps the ultimate truth conveyed by the doctrine of eternal salvation or punishment. But the accidents of death, or dreams, or oblivion continually confront this life, and existence is an optional form of being. Shall this beloved or detested essence presently lose it? And on what other essence shall it fall next? To this pressing question the realm of essence supplies no answer, and the contemplative mind is hopelessly puzzled by it. *Solvitur ambulando:* the event, the propulsive currents of substance merging and rushing into new forms, will precipitate a solution without ever considering alternatives; and it is perhaps because they never stop to think before they act, that they are able to act at all.

Something not essence, then, actualises and limits the manifestation of every

Existence being contingent is essentially unstable.

essence that figures in nature or appears before the mind. To this dark principle of existence we give the name of substance; so that substance, by definition, is the soil, the medium, and the creative force which secretly determines any option

The substance which determines events is itself in motion.

like that of Hamlet. Every such option is momentary and local; for although substance is external to essence and to thought, and its parts are external to one another, yet substance is internal to the things which it forms by occupying those contrasted places and assuming these various qualities. It is *their* substance, the principle of their existence, the ground of all the spontaneous changes which they undergo. It is indefinitely, perhaps infinitely, deep and inhuman; but whatever else its intrinsic essence may be, it is certainly complex, local, and temporal. Its secret flux involves at least as many contrasts and variations as the course of nature shows on the surface. Otherwise the ultimate core of existence would not exist, and the causes of variation would not vary. But how shall that which puts on this specious essence here and not there, be in the same inner condition in both places? Or how shall that which explodes now, have been equally active before? Substance, if it is to fulfil the function in virtue of which it is recognised and posited, must accordingly be for ever changing its own inner condition. It must be in flux.

Undoubtedly the word substance suggests permanence rather than change, because the substances best known to man (like the milk and the wet sand of the

Permanence need not be attributed to substance otherwise than as implied in flux.

young architect) evidently pass from place to place and from form to form while retaining their continuity and quantity. Such permanence is not contrary to flux, but a condition of flux. The degree of permanence which substance may have in any particular process, and the name which should be given to this permanent factor, are questions for scientific discussion. They may

not, and need not, receive any ultimate answer. But that *some* permanence, not the casual persistence of this or that image, is interwoven with the flux of things, follows from the reality of this flux itself. If change were total at any point, there transformation and existence would come to an end. The next, completely new, fact would not be next; it would be the centre, or the beginning, of a separate world. In other words, events, if they are to be successive or contiguous, must be pervaded by a common medium, in which they may assume relations external to their respective essences; for the internal or logical relations between these essences will never establish any succession or continuity among them, nor transport them at all into the sphere of existence. The critics of empiricism who have insisted that a series of sensations is not the sensation of a series, might well have added that the sensation of a series is no more than an isolated term on its own account, unless there is a background common to those terms and to this synthetic idea—a background in relation to which they may respectively take such places as shall render them contiguous or successive, although there is nothing within any of them to indicate such a position. This background, for human perception, is the field of vision symbolising the field of action; in this specious field the position of objects is distinguished before the objects are clearly specified or posited; but this unity of perspective, relative to the momentary station and thought of the observer, cannot embrace the existential flux itself, in which the events reported and the observer, with his thought, are incidental features. For the continuity and successiveness of this existing series, synthesis in apprehension is useless: it merely creates one more item—a living thought—to be ranged among its neighbours in the flux of existence. That which is requisite is the *natural derivation* of one phase in this flux from another, or a *natural tension* between them, determining their respective characters and positions. Such derivation and such tension, essential to action, involve a substance within or between events. There may be very much more in substance than that; but this is enough to disclose the existence of a substance, and to begin the human description of it by its functions.

Permanence, therefore, need not be set down separately among the radical properties attributed to substance: it is sufficiently expressed in the possibility of change, of continuity, of succession, and of the inclusion of actual events in a natural series, which shall not be a mere perspective in imagination.

Action and animal faith look in some specific direction; the butt of action, which is what I call substance, must be particular, local, and circumscribed. It must be capable of varying its position or its condition; for otherwise I could neither affect it by my action, nor await and observe its operation. In battle, in the chase, or in labour, attention is turned to a particular quarter, to something substantial there: it would defeat all action and art if all quarters were alike, and if I **Action presupposes a diversified field.** couldn't face a fact without turning my back on exactly the same fact in the rear; and the price of bread would be indifferent, if one substance being everywhere present I could find the same substance in the air. Action evidently would be objectless in an infinite vacuum or a homogeneous plenum; and even the notion or possibility of action would vanish if I, the agent, had not distinguishable parts, so that at least I might swim forward rather than backward in that dense vacuity.

A field of action must, then, be diversified substantially, not pictorially only; that which is at work in it here must not be equally at work in it there; the opportunities which it opens to me now must not be the same which it opened and will open always. Any conception of substance which represents it as undivided and homogeneous is accordingly not a conception of nature or of existence: and if such an object is ever called substance, it must be in a metaphysical sense which I do not attach to the word. One test of such eva- **The substance of things is physical: metaphysical substance is only a grammatical term.** sions into the realm of essence is ability, or ambition, to give a precise definition of what substance is. *Materia prima* may be defined—Plotinus has an admirable exposition of it, like the Athanasian creed—because it is avowedly something incapable of existence, and at best one of those ideal terms which serve to translate nature into the language of thought. *Materia prima* is a grammatical essence, comparable to the transcendental ego, the "I think", which according to Kant must accompany all experience. The discrimination of such essences distinguishes one logic from another, and leaves everything in nature, except human language, just as it was. The existing substance of things, on the contrary, is that which renders them dynamic; it is wherever dynamic things are, not where they are not; it determines their aspects and powers; and we may learn, since it exists in us also, to play with it and to let it play on us, in specific ways. But it would be frivolous to attempt to define it, as if a set of words, or of blinking ideas, could penetrate to the heart of existence and determine how, from all eternity, it must have been put together. What we may discover of it is not its essence but its place, its motion, its aspects, its effects. Were it an essence given in intuition, a visionary presence to sense or to language, it would forfeit those very functions which compel us to posit it, and which attest its formidable reality. Chief of these functions is a perpetual and determinate revolution in the heavens, and fertility and decay upon earth. In this flux there is a relative permanence and continuity; but substance is not for that reason less agitated than the familiar face of nature, or nearer to the impassibility of an eternal essence. Far otherwise. Investigation rather shows that this substance (which may be traced experimentally in many of its shifts) is in a continual silent ferment, by which gross visible objects are always being undermined and transformed: so much so that science often loses its way amid those subtle currents of the elements, and stops breathless at some too human image.

There are certain celebrated doctrines which, in their forms of expression, are excluded at once from natural philosophy by these considerations. I may not say, for instance, with Parmenides that Being is and Not-Being is not, if what I am seeking to describe is the substance of nature. If for dialectical reasons, which are not directly relevant to physics, I wished to regard pure Being as the essence of matter, I should be compelled to distribute this pure Being unequally in a void: a result which would contradict my premise that Not-Being is not, since this void would not only exist but would be the only true theatre of existence, because it would be the only seat of change. The pure Being or matter distributed in it, by hypothesis, is impassible and everywhere identical. Nature and life would therefore be due to the redistribution in the bosom of Not-Being of a pure Being in itself immutable. We should thus be led to the system of Democritus: a possible and even a model system of physics, although, in its expression, too Eleatic, and borrowing from that dialectical school a false air of necessity.

In physics Parmenides must give way to Democritus.

Similarly, at the threshold of natural philosophy, the Vedanta system must yield to the Samkhya: and this the Indians seem to have admitted by regarding the two systems as orthodox and compatible. It might be well if in the West we could take a hint from this comprehensiveness. The unity and simplicity of pure Being is not incompatible with the infinite variety of essences implied in it; and many things are true in the realm of essence which, if taken to describe existence, would be unmeaning or contrary to fact. It would suffice to distinguish the two spheres more carefully, for the legitimacy of systems, verbally most unlike, to become equal: although certainly those which were drawn from insight into essence

The Vedanta must give way to the Samkhya system.

would be more profound and unshakable than those drawn from observation of nature, since nature might as well have offered quite a different spectacle. On the other hand, it is the order and ground of this spectacle that interests the natural philosopher; and to him that more inward and more sublime intuition of essential Being is a waste of time, or a rhetorical danger.

One more illustration: the language of Spinoza about substance ought to yield, in physics, to that of Aristotle, in spite of the fact that a follower of Descartes could not help being more enlightened in mechanical matters than a follower of Socrates. Nevertheless it was Aristotle who **And Spinoza must give way to Aristotle.** gave the name of substance to compound natural things actually existing, and Spinoza who bestowed it on an ambiguous metaphysical object, now pure Being, now the universe in its infinity—in either case an ideal unity and an essence incapable of realisation all at once, if at all, in any natural locus. No discrimination of infinite Being into infinitely numerous attributes would ever generate existence, since all would remain eternal; and no enumeration of the possible modes of each attribute would turn them into particular things or into living minds, since each mode would imply all the others, and all would be equally rooted everywhere. In Aristotle, on the contrary, the name of substance is given where the office of substance is performed, and where one fact here asserts itself against another fact there; so that substance is the principle of individuation and exclusion, the condition of existence, succession, and rivalry amongst natural things. Even if these things, as conceived by Aristotle, have too much of an animate unity, and are mysteriously fixed in their genera and species, and redolent of moral suggestions, all this is but the initial dramatic rendering of their human uses, and the poetry of good prose. It does not prevent a more disinterested analysis, a microscopic and telescopic science, from disclosing in time the deeper mechanisms and analogies of nature, and its finer substance: just as the static zoology and the political psychology of Aristotle do not prevent us from peeping into the seething elementary passions beneath those classical masks. Things have not ceased to wear the sensuous and moral forms which interested the Greeks; but we may discover how those shells were generated, and what currents of universal substance have cast them up.

Finally, the practical intellect, in positing substance, imposes on it a certain relevance to the agent, who is to be in dynamic relations with it. The objects which art and sanity compel me to recognise as substantial, **The field of action must have a dynamic unity.** must affect me together, even if in very different ways. They must all impinge, directly or indirectly, on my action now; and it is by this test that I distinguish fact from fiction and true memory from fancy. Facts are dynamically connected with that which I now posit as substantial, and objects of fancy are not so connected. The field of animal faith spreads out from a living centre; observation cannot abandon its base, but from this vital station it may extend its perspectives over everything to which it can assign existence. Among these accredited things there may be other centres of observation, actual or eventual; but if the original organ and station, and these other stations and organs accredited by it, were not parts of one and the same substantial world, no means would remain of identifying the objects observed from one centre with those observed from another. I can acknowledge the existence of other moral centres in the world which I posit, but only if these centres are agencies, earthly or celestial, at work in my field of action, and dynamically connected with my own existence. All credible animation, of ascertainable character, must animate substances found in the same world with myself, and collateral with my own substance.

Perhaps this argument has some analogy to Spinoza's proof of the unity of substance. He tells us that substance is one, because if there were two or more

This system is relative and need not cover all reality.

substances they could bear no relation to one another. In other words, there can be but one universe, since anything outside, by being outside, would be related to it and collateral, and so after all would form a part of it. Yet if one universe, or one substance, can exist absolutely, and out of all relation to anything else, why should not any number of them exist, each centred in itself? The necessity of lying in external relations in order to exist, far from proving that only one system of facts is possible, proves that any closed circle of facts, in interplay with one another and with nothing else, will form a complete universe. Each part of this system will exist by virtue of its active position there, and may be discovered by any members of it who are sufficiently intelligent and adventurous; but from no part of that universe will anything beyond that universe be discoverable. Does this fact preclude the being of a different system, a separate universe, possessing the same sort of inward life and reality? I cannot think so. Transcendental necessities are relative to particular centres of experience; they have no jurisdiction beyond. Those other universes, to us, would be undiscoverable; but ours, too, would be undiscoverable to them; and yet we exist here without their leave. Might they not exist without ours?

What logic enables us to assert, therefore, is not that there is only one universe, but that each universe must be one, by virtue of a domestic economy

If there are many worlds their mutual relations are not physical, but are the eternal relations of their essences in the realm of truth.

determining the relative position and character of the events which compose it. Anything beyond this dynamic field is beyond the field of posited existence and possible knowledge. If there are other centres and active substances moving in other spheres, the relation of these disconnected spheres is not a physical relation: no journey and no transformation can bridge it: it lies in the realm of truth. Each of these worlds will exemplify its chosen essence; and the internal and unchangeable relations between these essences will be the only relations between those worlds. One will not exist before the other, nor will they be simultaneous; nor will either lie in any direction from the other, or at any distance. No force or influence will pass between them of any traceable physical or historical kind. If omniscience should see any harmony, contrast, or mutual fulfilment between their natures, that spiritual bond would be of the sort which links essences together by a logical necessity, and which a contemplative spirit may stop to disentangle and admire if it can and will.

Indeed, we may go further and say even of a single universe taken as a whole that its status is that of a truth rather than of an existence. Each part of it will exist, and if animate may truly feel its internal tension and life, and may truly assert the existence of the other parts also; yet the whole system—perhaps endless in its time and space—never exists at once or in any assignable quarter. Its existence is only posited from within its limits: externally its only status is that of a truth. Its essence was not condemned to be a closet-tragedy; living actors have been found to play it and a shifting stage to exhibit for a moment those convincing scenes. This essence has therefore the eternal dignity of a truth: it is the complete description of an event. Yet this event, taken as a whole, being unapproachable from outside, dateless, and nowhere, is in a sense a supernatural event. Those scenes are undiscoverable, save to those who play them, and that tumult is an ancient secret in the bosom of truth.

Indeed, good sense might suffice to convince anyone that no arguments or definitions can prevent things from being as numerous and as separate as they may chance to be. There is an infinite diversity of essences: what shall dissuade the fatality of existence, which must be groundless, from composing such changeful systems as it likes, on planes of being utterly incommensurable and incommunicable? The most a man can say for himself, or for any other *The first object of animal faith is nature as a whole.* element from which exploration may start, is that whatever is to enter his field of action must belong to the same dynamic system with himself. In experience and art, as in the nebular hypothesis, this dynamic oneness of the world is primitive. It is not put together by conjoining elements found existing separately, but is the locus in which they are found; for if they were not found there, they would be essences only and not facts. In mature human perception the essences given are doubtless distinct and the objects which they suggest are clearly discriminated: here is the dog, there the sun, the past nowhere, and the night coming. But beneath all this definition of images and attitudes of expectancy, there is always a voluminous feeble sensibility in the vegetative soul. Even this sensibility posits existence; the contemplation of pure Being might supervene only after all alarms, gropings, and beliefs had been suspended—something it takes all the discipline of Indian sages to begin to do. The vegetative soul enjoys an easier and more Christian blessedness: it sees not, yet it believes. But believes in what? In whatever it may be that envelopes it; in what we, in our human language, call space, earth, sunlight, and motion; in the throbbing possibility of putting forth something which we call leaves, for which that patient soul has no name and no image. The unknown total environment is what every intellect posits at birth; whatever may be attempted in action or discovered in nature will be a fresh feature in that field. Everything relevant to mortal anxiety lies within that immensity, be it an object of earthly fear or pursuit or of religious hope. Animal faith and material destiny move in a relative cosmos.

Teleology

The Realm of Matter: Book Second of Realms of Being. New York: Charles Scribner's Sons; London: Constable and Co. Ltd., 1930, 118–35. Volume sixteen of the critical edition of *The Works of George Santayana.*

In this selection, Chapter VII of The Realm of Matter, *Santayana rejected teleology understood as an explanation of material nature based on the excellence or ideal end of a natural existence. But he did not deny natural correspondences such as the adaptation of an organ and its function, the fit of a creature and its environment, or the fulfillment of an impulse in its resulting action; and he was happy to regard these correspondences as teleology, albeit a teleology distinct from explanatory principles such as efficacious ends or final causes (ES, 193). Final causes exist as wishes or ideas in human conduct, but they fail to account for the natural events in which they arise. Human art, as "an extension of natural teleology" (ES, 194), exhibits correspondences between wishes or ideas and products of labor; but these wishes and ideas have a physical basis and are consequences, not causes of material changes. The effects of humans on material nature are the outcome of animal forces deeper than ideas. Final causes are impositions of human values on natural events. One attends to final causes not because of their material efficacy but rather because of their value to spirit.*

We have already seen that explanation by habit or law is a reduction of events to their rhythms or repetitions; we gain no insight into why or how a thing happens by saying that it has often happened before. Did we really wish to understand, we should inquire into the inner elements of such a mutation in any one of its instances: because a thing must happen each time by a concourse of motions there, and not because the same thing happens also in other places; although naturally it will happen again if the conditions which produced it here are repeated. Now a different form of mock explanation appears in what is called teleology, when the ground of things is sought in their excellence, in their harmony with their surroundings, or in the adaptation of organs to their functions and of actions to their intentions.

Like explanation by law, explanation by purpose is verbal only.

Such correspondences exist: teleology, if it be only a name for them, is a patent and prevalent fact in nature. Indeed the adaptation of things to one another is involved in their co-existence: a thing can arise only by finding and taking its place where other things make room for it. Everything in the moving equilibrium of nature is necessarily co-operative. But the question becomes interesting (and unanswerable) when we ask why, at any point, this so singular thing should have found such a singular set of conditions as to permit or compel it to exist there. A wider view, exploring antecedents and consequents, and discovering analogies, may enlarge the prospect, and, as happens in the books of naturalists, may so pleas-

Nature a web of adaptations.

antly occupy the mind with pictures and stories, that we may stop asking for reasons. And to invoke adaptation itself, as if this were a cause of adaptation, would be to halt at a word, adding perhaps to it, as an element of power, the bated breath with which we pronounce it.

Yet this human scale and these human emotions, which we impose so fatuously on the universe, bear witness, on the plane of thought, to the existence of organisms and of life on the plane of matter; for we should have no emotions and no scale to impose on other things if our own being were not definite, animate, and self-assertive.

In human society teleology takes a special and conscious form: it becomes art. Not only do tropes—which here we call methods—everywhere dominate the scene, but very often the method is explicitly adopted or modified, and the action planned; foresight and intention occupy the first moment of it, and execution of that prevision occupies the second moment. Here the preformation of events and the pre-adaptation of instruments to their uses is a simple fact of history. Knowing how our passions and purposes watchfully realise their avowed ends, may we not reasonably assimilate obscure events to these deliberate actions, the causes of which seem clear to us and intimately confessed? As we do things when we wish, must not all nature, or God working through nature, wish everything when they do it? Must not some idea, seen under the form of the good, guide and attract every movement in nature?

Might art be the key to nature?

Yes: that is the normal way of speaking, the rhetorical or poetical way of describing nature in human terms from the human point of view. But moral sentiment, poetry, and theology are forms of literature, not of science; they are not wrong in their own sphere, and their rightness becomes intelligible, and takes its place in natural history, when we see its relativity to human experience, and its psychic seat. There, in literature, a sceptic should be the last to quarrel with the use of moral analogies in describing nature: poetry does not contradict science, because in daring to be poetry, it avows a complete ignorance and disdain of the prose of things. Poetry is poetry, and opens up a legitimate vista within its own world, but only to a poetic spirit; in its material existence it is a flood of verbiage incidental to human passions and their rhetorical automatisms. In its biological capacity poetry can be described only in prose; and all its insights reappear as incidents and as subjective creations bred in the realm of matter.

Yes, but only in the realm of art.

Before indicating, in the tentative way which alone is possible, the material basis of teleology, it may be well to examine the logic of it in the imagination; for the contrast between poetry and prose is by no means absolute, and any scrupulous study of moral philosophy compels us to restore that subject, and ourselves who pursue it, to our place in nature. The clearness of moral life after all is only a verbal clearness; a sort of facility and acceleration by which our acts and feelings come to a climax and fulfil their natural tropes. We are left in the dark concerning the manner of this fulfilment. We are even more in the dark as to the

Moral being has physical roots and works only through them.

ground of the ideas and wishes which, as we say, guide our conduct; when all goes well, we need not stop to question them, but presently when they clash with one another and fail of fulfilment, the easy miracle of their power begins to seem dubious, and subterranean bonds between them and the world of action become visible in a new, a biological, direction.

Consider first the existential presence of human wishes and ideas. Is it conceivably an original fact and unconditioned? Why should any wish or idea arise at all here and now? Is the mid-void peopled with them, as with little **All wishes** winged heads of cherubs, without bodies and without support? **and ideas** **have** Surely if anything ever had a cause and was evidently secondary, it **physical** is human will and fancy; to take them for absolute beings, or origi- **occasions,** nal powers, would be to allow theoretical sophistries to blind us to the plainest facts. If I want water, it is because my throat is parched; if I dream of love, it is because sex is ripening within me. Nature has fixed the character, and circumstances have fixed the occasion, for this ferment of desire and conception. Conscious will is a symptom, not a cause; its roots as well as its consequences are invisible to it, material, and often incongruous and astonishing.

But suppose that the mind, like some morose tyrant, determines to shut all doors and windows against the outer world, and to see only by the lamp of self-consciousness. What will be the stuff of its meditations? Nothing but **and** **physical** animal wishes and barn-yard ideas; demands for food, air, liberty of **objects.** motion; dreams of wild things to be chased, eaten, played with, or hidden; or perhaps of fame to be won, empires conquered, friend-ship and love and praise. How comes absolute free-will or a groundless moral energy to choose these singular objects? Could it not have employed its inviola-ble leisure and its infinite invention in conceiving something better than such a very humble, cruel, and nasty animal world? And could not its sentiment have been less sentimental, less unctuous and constrained, less tainted by terror and desperate delusion? Why are human love and religion so tormented, if they are masters of the world? If they command miraculously and matter obeys, is it not because matter had first created them and dictated the commands which they were to issue?

Evidence of this, if it were needed, might also be found in the loose character of ideas and wishes compared with their fulfilments, even when they are materi-ally fulfilled. These ideas and wishes are personal, confused, and **They are** incomplete. When a law-giver designs a constitution or an archi- **inadequate** **feelings** tect an edifice, a thousand contrary principles and suggestions **accompanying** assault his mind. Unless he is very precipitate, or an absolute **action.** slave of habit, the plan will take shape in his mind to his own surprise; it will be a sudden concretion of subtle currents and accidents within him, the harmony and relevance of which, if any, we call his genius or his ability. Even when these are greatest, and most seasoned by experience, their prophetic virtue will be only abstract and partial; the event will be a new surprise, as was the idea. For it is hardly possible that the edifice when complete, or the constitu-tion when in actual operation, should produce the same impression on the mind as the plan conceived there originally. The plan arose by a synthesis of acquired impulses within one body: the work arises by a concourse of actions which, even if still those of the same person only, and obedient to the same vital impulses as the idea (as happens in singing, speaking, or making a gesture) yet occur now in the outer world, in a comparatively foreign material, and with a greater admixture of accidental concomitants. Therefore a man's actions and works seem to him less a part of himself than his intentions, but to others seem more so: because to others he is a personage and to himself he is a mind.

Ideas and wishes, then, are mental echoes of movements proper to bodily life; were they not, they could have no application and no relevance to the world. The more accurately they prefigure events and seem to control them by prescribing their tropes, the better they prove their own fidelity to the ruling impulses of matter. Clear ideas are evidences of clean arts; a firm and victorious will bears witness to a strong and opportune economy in the organism. Indeed, for a scientific psychology behaviour is the only conceivable seat of mind, and intelligence simply a certain plasticity in organisms which enables them to execute tropes in subtle harmony with their material opportunities. True, mind and intelligence are something more in fact. This we perceive when, in reflection, we gather up sensuous images, memories, lyric effusions, and dramatic myths into a literary psychology, which may be remarkably convincing but remains purely literary; for it cannot follow the flux of its subject-matter by observation and measurement, but must recreate it in imagination, and leave it at that. Similarly, the history which interweaves intentions with events and ideas with motions may give a capital description of moral perspectives, but it is simply literature.

Scientific psychology itself is a study of behaviour, *i.e.* of matter.

Total events in nature are never wholly mental, and it is on their material side, through their substance and physical tensions, that they are derived from previous events and help to shape the events which follow. But this doctrine is based on far-reaching considerations which may often be ignored; and when only the mental side of an event is discovered, the material and substantial side of it may be denied, and states of mind, in their purity, may be regarded as total natural events. It will then seem plausible to regard them as links in the chain of natural causes, for are they not moments in experience, as memory or dramatic reconstruction may survey it? But this amphibious psycho-physics, even if we admitted it, would not be teleological. Each mental event would transmit existence and energy to its successor in proportion to its own intensity and quality, just as if it were a form of matter. It would not thereby exercise any magical moral control over its consequences. Thus intense thought might make the head ache, fear might cause paralysis, amusement laughter, or love a want of appetite and early death. The teleological virtue of wishes and ideas is accordingly something quite distinct from their alleged physical influence; indeed it is only when we disregard this incongruous mechanical efficacy attributed to them that we begin to understand what their teleological virtue would mean: it would mean a miraculous pre-established harmony between the commands or wishes of the spirit and events in the

Mental events, if causal, would not be teleological.

world. It would mean the exercise of divine power, which a well-advised human being could never attribute to himself, but only to the grace of God, perhaps passing through him.

Teleology then retreats into a theology, or into a cosmological idealism, fraught with curious alternatives: for a divine mind, if conscious and omniscient as high theology would make it, would not be an event; it would be a decree, **The will** a commandment, or an eternal glory relative to all events, but on a **invoked,** **if cosmic,** different plane from any of them. If, on the contrary, the divine will **would be** was immanent in the world and intermingled with all natural events, **mythical.** it would evidently not be separate or self-conscious; indeed, it would be only a poetic synonym for the actual fertility of matter, and for the tropes exhibited in its evolution. In either case, after making our bow to this divine will, out of deference to antiquity and to human rhetoric, we should be reduced to studying as far as possible the crawling processes of nature. These will be the seat of such teleology as surely exists, and as a critical philosophy may record without falling into rhetorical ambiguities. Organic life is a circular trope which at each repetition touches or approaches a point which we regard as its culmination, and call maturity. In man, maturity involves feelings, intentions, and spiritual light: but it is idle to regard the whole trope as governed by these top moments in it, which are more highly conditioned, volatile, and immaterial than are their organs, their occasions, or their fruits.

Nature is full of coiled springs and predestined rhythms; of mechanisms so wound up that, as soon as circumstances permit, they unroll themselves through a definite series of phases. A seed, if suitable sown and watered, will **There is an** grow into one particular sort of plant, and into no other. At the **untraced** **pregnancy** inception of such a trope the predestined movement is said to be **in organic** "potential"; there is a "predisposition" in matter at that point to **matter.** execute the whole movement. What is this predisposition? Examination of a seed would probably never disclose in it a perfect model of the future flower, any more than examination of a young man's passions, or of his body, would disclose there the poems which these passions might ultimately inspire. Potentiality seems to be an imputed burden, a nominal virtue attributed to the first term of a trope because of the character of the rest of it. Yet, sometimes, as in a seed, the imputed burden is genuine, and potentiality is pregnancy. A true beginning and sufficient cause of what ensues is really found there; but this initial reality need not at all resemble that which it will become. Its nature is internal, hidden, perhaps inexpressible in the terms of human observation at all; so far is it from being an image cast into that well from the outside, or a reflex name given to it in view of the future. The tropes which mark the obvious metres of nature tell nothing of the inspiration, the secret labour, or the mechanism which brings them forth.

Heredity is an obvious case of repetition; but its temporal scale is so large in respect to an observer of his own species that individualities may seem to him more striking and self-grounded than uniformities. Yet from a little distance, or in an alien species, heredity recedes into a monotonous succession of waves and a multitudinous repetition of objects. Both impressions are just, and nature, here seen at close quarters, reveals the complexity of her endless pulsations. There is a curious involution of the organism in the seed. The seed is not merely the first state of the organism in the offspring but was also a part of a similar organism in the parent. This notable trope is apt to blind us to the mechanism requisite for its repetition. We are solicited by the magic rhyme of it to rest content with explaining the beginning of life by the end, the part by the whole, the actual by the ideal, the existent by the non-existent. Abandoning physics altogether as incapable of solving the mystery, we may wonderingly record the reappearance, by the will of God, of new generations of every species, each after its kind. But as in the Christian sacraments, so here in natural reproduction, the grace of God does not operate without physical continuity in its channels; and it would be by tracing that continuity, and the accidents which often cause it to deviate from its course, that reproduction might be seen in its natural setting. The multitude of successes would not then blind us to the far greater number of failures. To arise in this world and to become something specific is in each instance a fresh and doubtful undertaking.

Heredity is a trope revealing the separate and perilous realisation of its instances.

Prodigious complexity is something to which nature is not averse, like a human artist, but on the contrary is positively prone; and in animals the attainment of such prodigious complexity is made possible by the fact that a special environment is at hand, in the body of the parent, enabling the young organism to run through its earlier and fundamental phases safely, surely, and quickly. So unerring is this development that the animal is often born complete; yet there is enough wavering, with false starts in directions once taken by the species and since abandoned, to show that the core of the seed need contain no prefigurement of the whole result, but that this result is reached tentatively in reproduction, as it was originally in evolution; only that the ovum is a far better locus for a perfect development of the psyche than was the bleak outer world.

Nevertheless the manner of this quick and spontaneous growth is little understood, and only the total trope remains to furnish our imagination. Seeing its dramatic unity, we feel that the first term must be pregnant with the ultimate issue, as the first act of a good play—assuming human nature and the ways of the world—is pregnant with the last. We forget that poetic genius itself must have natural sources and reason external guides; and we attribute the perpetual attainment of some natural perfection to the miraculous power of the trope realised in it, or to the divine will contemplating that trope and, as if fascinated by its magic beauty, commanding matter to reproduce it for ever and ever.

Final causes certainly exist in the conduct of human beings, yet they are always inadequate to describe the events in which they are manifested, since such events always presuppose a natural occasion and a mechanical impulse; and these cannot flow from the purpose or choice which they make possible and pertinent. The whole operation of final causes therefore requires, beneath and within it, a deeper flow of natural forces which we may darkly assign to fate or matter or chance or the unfathomable will of God. Yet, since without this irrational occasion or afflatus those purposes and choices could never have taken shape, it ought to suffice for our reasonable satisfaction if, in some measure, the natural perfections of things are manifested in them, and if there is some degree of harmony between the world and the spirit. Moral tropes have their proper status and dignity if they are actually found in the human aspect of events; they are not rendered false or nugatory merely because the material existence presupposed in them has a different method of progression. Medicine and psychology are now disclosing a truth which men of experience have perceived in all ages, that virtues and vices are equally phases of a controllable physical life: a fact which takes nothing away from their beauty or horror. They are the moral qualities of a natural being.

Final causes exist, but are moral perspectives superposed on natural causation.

Mechanical tropes in their turn are incompetent to describe or measure spiritual realities, such as excellence or happiness or spirit itself; nor is it reasonable to require them to do so. They will be amply authenticated if they can serve to trace the whole material backing and occasions of those moral harmonies or spiritual lights. These, in order to arise do not require a different mechanism of their own, or a different occasion; the material mechanism and the material occasion fully suffice to introduce and to justify them. The physical terror of murder has made murder criminal; the animal warmth and transport of love have made love tender and deep. Of course, a deepening of apprehension is required, founded itself on a changed habit, a finer involution of responses in the organism; so that the same things which were done and regarded brutally may be done and regarded with a far-reaching sense of all that they involve. This new sense sees light and glow in the fire, of which the blinder senses could feel only the heat. Hence if either the naturalist or the moralist is a man of a single sense he must be left to grope in his professional half-light. Nature in his children will probably redress the balance.

The fact that natural organisms are far more closely purposeful than works of art, may itself serve to reveal the true superposition of art upon nature. Art is a human, marginal, not indispensable extension of natural teleology. The essential organic tropes, passions, and powers of man must have been first firmly rooted in the race, before anyone could conceive a project, or be able to execute it as conceived. Even highly civilised humanity forms its plans only dreamfully, and is cheated by its own impotence, or by contrary currents, in the execution of them. Often the most fixed purposes and the most vehement efforts are wasted; indeed, they are always wasted in some measure, because no designer can foresee all the circumstances of his work, or its ulterior uses. Any work, when it exists, is a part of the realm of matter, and has its fortunes there, far from all control or intention. The saintly Henry the Sixth founded Eton and King's College for the salvation of souls; they have served admirably together with the playing-fields to form the pensive but quite earthly ethos of the modern Englishman. In the works of nature there is not this division, nor this irony; the uses are not forecast in any purpose, consciously prophetic; they are simply the uses which the thing finds or develops, as it changes under the control of the changing circumstances. Thus the precision

Art is a marginal imperfect form of natural organisation.

of adjustment between organs and functions, far from being a miracle, is in one sense a logical necessity or tautology; since nothing has any functions but those which it has come to have, when plasticity here with stimulus and opportunity there have conspired to establish them.

An organism is a concretion in matter which can feed, defend, and reproduce itself. Its initial form of expansion finds a natural limit, beyond which circumstances do not suffer it to go: then, unless it perishes altogether, it reproduces itself: that is, it breaks up into parts, some of which repeat the original form of expansion, while the others dissolve into their elements and die. Expansion thus becomes rhythmical, **Brief natural history of organisms.** repeating a constant trope; except that, if the force of concretion and accretion is powerful at that centre, and if the circumstances are favourable, that trope may become internally more complex: in other words, the organism may acquire fresh organs. These will reappear in each generation in their due place and season, if the environment continues to give them play; and in this way a race and a species will be established, individual and recognisable, yet subject to private variations and also to generic shifts, by the atrophy of some organs and the development of others.

If, then, we understood genesis we should understand heredity; for an organ cannot arise, either the first time or the last, except spontaneously, and as if it had never existed before. But how can it arise at all? By what genetic impulse does some nucleus of matter modify its parts, and complicate their sympathetic movements, without losing its unity of action in respect to external things? It is for the naturalists to reply, **Need final causes be operative to form them?** in so far as observation or experiment enables them to trace the actual genesis of bodies; for as to the verbal explanations which they may offer, they are not likely to be on the scale or in the terms proper to the flux or to the concretions of matter at a depth so far below that of human language. Let matter take shape as it will: all that concerns me here is the nature of the teleology present in the result. Organs must arise before they can exercise what we call their function, and this function must be one which the circumstances usually render possible and self-maintaining. Is the philosopher reduced to impressions on the human scale? Must he blankly confess that nature is mysteriously inspired, and that matter gathers itself into organisms as if it were magically guided by the love of that life and those achievements of which such organisms will be capable?

Not quite. Moralistic physics is wiser than natural science in not ignoring eventual spiritual issues; but these issues are no factors in generation. On the contrary, they are themselves uncertain, conditioned, and precarious; so that if we reach any depth or honesty in our reflection we cannot attribute the movement of nature to the antecedent influence of the future good which she might realise. Instead, we must attribute the **No: because purposes presuppose organisms.** pursuit of this good, and its eventual realisation, to her previous blind disposition, fortified by the fact that circumstances were favourable to that development: and this last fact is no accident, since (as we have just seen) the adaptation of the parts of nature to one another is necessary to their existence, and nature could not retain any disposition for which circumstances did not make room, at least for the moment. In a word, the teleology present in the world must be distinguished from final causes. The latter are mythical and created by a sort of literary illusion. The germination, definition, and prevalence of any good must be grounded in nature herself, not in human eloquence.

The conditions of existence, as I conceive it, involve change and involve adaptation: perhaps if we ponder these necessities we shall gain some insight into the origin of organisms and the secret of life. Each natural moment

Concretions arise inevitably in a flux of substance.

has a forward tension, it is a moment of transition. Its present quality was determined by the force of lateral tensions guiding the previous dynamic stress of its substance; and the issue, as this moment passes into the next, will be determined by the lateral tensions to which its inner or forward tension is now subject. Is it not then native and proper to existence in its primary elements to congregate and to roll itself together into shells fashioned by its seeds, and into seeds fostered by its climate? And will not this initial concretion at any point go on swallowing what it can, destroying what it must, and harmonising its own complexity, until some contrary wind or some inner exhaustion disperses its elements? May not this disruption itself become less frequent with the extension of any cosmos, and the better co-ordination of the motions within it? A natural moment may be prolonged or reiterated; it may be caught up in a trope itself indefinitely recurrent, so that associated moments, duly spaced and controlled by their mutual tensions, may for a long time reappear in a fixed order. Any trope will recur if within its substance, or near by, there is generated a fresh natural moment, like the original one, and under similar conditions. Nothing more is required for a swarming or a hereditary life to cover the face of nature.

Every natural moment, in which matter at any point holds some essence unchanged, is fit to be the seed of all creatures and the centre of all thought. Some

All matter is fit to be the matter of anything, if circumstances draw it into that form.

sequels might be reached only by a great and prosperous development from that moment outward; others might require the dissolution of this complex, and a fresh beginning, in some other direction, from one of its radical elements. But forwards or backwards, everything might be arranged round any nucleus, without the least violence or suppression of its original life, if only it were planted in the requisite soil. This profound naturalness of the greatest complications becomes clear to us in health, when we move spontaneously and think smoothly; it is only in disease that we tremble at our own incredible complexity, and that harmony becomes a problem. In fact harmony in itself is neither more difficult nor rarer than disorder: that which demands a rare concourse of circumstances is harmony *of this sort, here;* and yet, in the special circumstances in which anything arises, harmony with that thing is presupposed, otherwise that particular thing would not have arisen. When our own ready-made being and action are the facts in the foreground, we instinctively and justifiably take it for granted that surrounding nature is in harmony with them and will give them suitable play; they are not unconditioned or omnipotent, but they are co-operative with their world. It is only when a different harmony, not native to us, is suggested, that it seems to us impossibly difficult of attainment and, if actual, miraculous. Before we could adapt our presumptions and impulses to that alien order we should need to retrace our steps and follow that other path of development. Everything that is, except where it is, would be infinitely improbable.

Thus the very fluidity of the flux, in its moving equilibrium, causes every concretion that can arise to arise, and every organism to maintain itself which can maintain itself. Such is the feeble yet ineradicable sympathy in the poor heart of matter towards the whole realm of essence. With many a false start, with a momentum and an organic memory often disastrous, with an inertia always trustfully blind, existence passes inevitably and in many streams from what it is to what it can be; it changes in the very act of continuing, and undermines its condition in surrounding it with developments and supports. Then, when any of these concretions collapses, as they must all collapse in turn, it returns to the charge, perhaps in the same direction, like Sisyphus, or like Proteus, in quite another. In the first case we speak of reproduction, in the second of evolution: but these words do not stand for different forces or principles but only for different results. In reproduction the flux repeats the same trope, in evolution it changes that trope for one more complex or appropriate, imposed by a new balance of forces.

Repetition and variation flow indifferently from the same principle.

That collapse is inevitable follows from the fact that existence is essentially chaotic. Its parts, perhaps infinite in multitude, will be always readjusting their mutual tensions, so that, ultimately, the ground gives way under any edifice. And the catastrophe may ruin more than that confident system; it may radically transmute the elements which composed it, since every essence which matter may wear is arbitrary and, if occasion offers, may be exchanged for some other. Moreover, any trope has limits. The matter which executes or reproduces it, having done so, falls back into the relative chaos which remains the background of everything; so that death, in every instance, is the end of life; and in nature at large death can be only temporarily and imperfectly circumvented by fertility. I speak of fertility in a particular species and within one moral world: for of new creations there is presumably no end, and one perfection can neither remember nor desire another.

Enough for the day is the good thereof.

I confess that the life of the spider, or my own life, is not one which, if I look at it as a whole, seems to me worth realising; and to say that God's ways are not our ways, and that human tastes and scruples are impertinent, is simply to perceive that moral values cannot preside over nature, and that what arises is not the good, in any prior or absolute sense, but only the possible at that juncture: a natural growth which as it takes form becomes a good in its own eyes, or in the eyes of a sympathetic poet. Then this good realised endows with a relative and retrospective excellence all the conditions favourable to its being, as if with prophetic kindness and parental devotion they had conspired to produce it. The spider is a marvel of pertinacity, and I am not without affection for my own arts and ideas; we both of us heartily welcome the occasions for our natural activities; but when those occasions and activities have passed away, they will not be missed.

The Psyche

The Realm of Matter: Book Second of Realms of Being. New York: Charles Scribner's Sons; London: Constable and Co. Ltd., 1930, 136–62. Volume sixteen of the critical edition of *The Works of George Santayana.*

This selection, Chapter VIII of The Realm of Matter, *considers psyche and its relation to spirit. According to Santayana, psyche is the self that one immediately cares about and is more essentially the body than the body itself. While psyche is not material, it is the organization of matter in living creatures or the "habit in matter" reproduced in organisms after their kind (ES, 200). The life of psyche is observable and a topic for biological study, and its behavior and the events that influence it belong to the realm of matter. Spirit is different from psyche and lies outside of the realm of matter, yet it depends on psyche. Spirit–"the actual light of consciousness" (ES, 200)–is called forth by the sensitivity of psyche and is a culmination of psychic activity. Santayana wrote that consciousness "is a commentary on events, in the language of essence; and while its light is contemplative, its movement and intent strictly obey the life of the psyche in which it is kindled" (ES, 210). Spirit is impotent in the material realm even as it observes the changing shapes of the material flux. Spirit is an expression of that flux and cannot deny its material basis.*

Of all tropes the most interesting to the moralist is that which defines a life, and marks its course from birth to death in some human creature. But a life is also the

Life not an effect of spirit agitating matter.

most crucial of tropes for the natural philosopher; for here his congenial mathematical categories leave him in the lurch, and he must either recognise their inadequacy to express the intimate flux of substance, or else cut his world in two, appending a purely literary or moral psychology to his mathematical physics. If emotional life preoccupies him, and he cannot simply ignore it, he may even be tempted to revert to the most primitive of dualisms, and to conceive the flux of existence as the resultant of two opposite agents: one an inert matter only capable of sinking into a dead sea of indistinction: the other a supernatural spirit, intrinsically disembodied, but swooping down occasionally upon that torpid matter, like the angel into the pool of Bethesda, and stirring it for a while into life and shape.

Need I give reasons, after all that has preceded, for discarding this last conception? In the first place it would be a materialistic and superstitious view of spirit

Matter is, by definition, the principle of all motions.

to regard it as a wind, an effort, or any kind of physical force. On the other hand, in conceiving matter to be inert, merely heavy, and intrinsically blank, we should be forgetting our original reason for positing matter at all; and instead of that existing substance, filling the field of action, and necessarily fertile in everything to be

encountered there, we should be considering some casual symbol for matter, such as ignorant sensation or abstract science may have created. To say that matter, as it truly exists, is inert or incapable of spontaneous motion, organisation, life, or thought, would be flatly to contradict the facts: because the real matter, posited in action, and active in our bodies and in all other instruments of action, evidently possesses and involves all those vital properties.

Nevertheless, the venerable tradition which attributes the fashioning of the body to the soul might be retained, if only we could restore to the word "soul" all its primitive earthliness, potency, and mystery. Soul, as often in antiquity, would then signify an animating current widely diffused throughout the cosmos, a breath uncreated and immortal as a whole, but at each point entering some particular body and **A soul moulding the body would be itself material.** quitting it, in order to mingle again with the air, the light, the nether darkness, or the life of the god from which it came. Such a warm, fluid, transmissible agent would evidently be material. Industry requires hands: a traceable cause of specific motions must travel through space in particular channels. And indeed, that the soul was material, was once taken for granted both in India and in Greece. On the other hand, the Platonic and Christian tradition has come to identify the soul with a bodiless spirit, a sort of angel, at first neglecting and afterwards denying the biological functions which were the primitive essence of the soul; until in modern times the soul has been discarded altogether and its place taken by consciousness, something which in reality is the last and most highly conditioned of the works of a natural soul.

Thus a soul or an angel became, for the Christian imagination, a supernatural substance, a personal spirit without material organs, yet somehow still capable of seeing, loving, and thinking, and even of exercising physical force and making its presence felt in particular places. In man, and perhaps in other creatures, an evil fate had imprisoned some of these angelic souls in a natural body, and contaminated them with the **Christian notion of the soul.** vital principle—the old animal heathen soul—proper to such a body. Sometimes, under the influence of Aristotle and of the Apostolic doctrine of the resurrection of the flesh, theologians have endeavoured to bridge the chasm between these two souls, one generative and the other degenerate. Thus the orthodox Catholic doctrine declares that by a special act of creation a rational immortal soul, previously non-existent, is substituted during gestation for the animal soul of the embryo: the new supernatural soul taking on the functions of the previous natural soul in addition to its own, and by that union becoming subject to their influence; an influence which marks the fallen state of the supernatural soul and its participation in the sin of Adam. A forced conjunction of two incompatible beings is obvious here, yet this conjunction is not without its dramatic propriety in expressing theoretically the moral conflicts of the Christian life; and the same incongruities reappear in any doctrine which would make the soul immaterial and its functions physical. A soul essentially generative and directive must be capable of existing unconsciously and of exerting material energy. If it were ever clearly identified with consciousness it would evaporate into a passing feeling or thought, something unsubstantial, volatile, evanescent, non-measurable and non-traceable. Once recognised in its spiritual actuality, this thought would not only be obviously incapable of exercising the vegetative and propulsive functions of animal life, but would loudly call for such an animal life to support its own intuitions and lend them their place in nature and their moral significance.

Avoiding, then, this poetical word, the soul, laden with so many equivocations, I will beg the reader to distinguish sharply two levels of life in the human body, one of which I call *the spirit,* and the other *the psyche.* By spirit I understand the actual light of consciousness falling upon anything– the ultimate invisible emotional fruition of life in feeling and thought.

Definition of the psyche.

On the other hand, by the psyche I understand a system of tropes, inherited or acquired, displayed by living bodies in their growth and behaviour. This psyche is the specific form of physical life, present and potential, asserting itself in any plant or animal; it will bend to circumstances, but if bent too much it will suddenly snap. The animal or plant will die, and the matter hitherto controlled by that psyche will be scattered. Such a moving equilibrium is at once vital and material, these qualities not being opposed but coincident. Some parcels of matter, called seeds, are predetermined to grow into organisms of a specific habit, producing similar seeds in their turn. Such a habit in matter is a psyche.*

In literary psychology the psychic often means simply the mental; and the reader may be disconcerted by the suggestion that the truly psychic, the dynamic life of both body and mind, is on the contrary material. Let me remind him, in that case, of the following fundamental points:

1. The psyche is not another name for consciousness or mind. Everything truly conscious or mental–feeling, intuition, intent–belongs to the realm of spirit. We may say of spirit, but not of the psyche, that its essence is to think. The psyche is a natural fact, the fact that many organisms are alive, can nourish and reproduce themselves, and on occasion can feel and think. This is not merely a question of the use of words: it is *a deliberate refusal to admit the possibility of any mental machinery.* The machinery of growth, instinct, and action, like the machinery of speech, is all physical: but this sort of physical operation is called psychical, because it falls within the trope of a life, and belongs to the self-defence and self-expression of a living organism. How should any unsophisticated person doubt that the movements of matter have the nature of matter for their principle, and not the nature of spirit?

2. By the word matter I do not understand any human idea of matter popular or scientific, ancient or recent. Matter is properly a name for the actual substance of the natural world, whatever that substance may be. It would therefore be perfectly idle, and beside the point, to take some arbitrary idea of matter and to prove dialectically that from that idea none of the consequences follow with which the true substance of the world is evidently pregnant. What would be thereby proved would not be that matter cannot have the developments which it has, but that that particular idea of matter was wrong or at least inadequate.

3. In calling the psyche material I do not mean to identify her with any piece or kind of substance, an atom or monad or ether or energy. Perhaps all sorts of

---

* A further illustration of this definition of the psyche may be found in my *Soliloquies in England,* pp. 217–224.

substances may enter into her system; she is not herself a substance, except relatively to consciousness, of which her movements and harmonies are the organ and the immediate support. She is a *mode* of substance, a trope or habit established in matter; she is made of matter as a cathedral is made of stone, or the worship in it of sounds and motions; but only their respective forms and moral functions render the one a cathedral or a rite, and the other a psyche.

4. The whole life of the psyche, even if hidden by chance from human observation, is essentially observable: it is the object of biology. Such is the only scientific psychology, as conceived by the ancients, including Aristotle, and now renewed in behaviourism and psycho-analysis. This conception of the psyche also allows the adepts of psychical research to retain a congenial name for the very real region, far removed from everything that I call spiritual, in which occult processes, unusual powers, and subtle survivals may be actually discovered.

Biology aspires to be a part of physics, and this for the best of reasons, since in describing the spontaneous tropes that prevail in the flux of matter, physics is simply biology universalised. The problem is not where to place the frontier between two disparate regions, but only to discover how the tropes most obvious in each of them are superposed or grow out of one another. The inanimate world must needs concern **Continuity of physics and biology.** the zoologist, since it pervades and unites all living creatures; and the animate world must needs concern the physicist, since it is the crown of nature, the focus where matter concentrates its fires and best shows what it is capable of doing. Obviously, if we could understand the inmost machinery of motion we should understand life, which on the biological level is simply a system of motions.

In one sense, indeed, all matter is alive. Its deadest principles, like gravity and inertia, are principles of motion. The dry dust and the still waters which the wind sweeps into a vortex, if mingled, will breed. Even celestial matter, which might seem too tenuous and glowing to be alive after our fashion, is fertile in light, which may be, perhaps, the primary stimulus to life, or a first form of it. Yet this universal ethereal trepidation is too diffuse and elusive to seem life to our **Not all the energies of matter are properly vital or psychic.** human judgment, accustomed as we are to the crude contrast between a barking dog and a dead one. Even in animals and plants the life in which, so to speak, nature is interested, the life which is transmitted and preserved, is not their individual life, describable in a biography. Its vegetative continuity takes a course which, from our point of view, seems subterranean and unfriendly; for it does not pass from one complete animal or plant to the next (as the phases of each life succeed one another for the observant spirit), but the child buds at mid-branch, and the tree obdurately outlives its seeded flowers. In fact, individuality and tenacity never are more pronounced than in that old age which, as far as the life of nature is concerned, is so much dead wood and obstructive rubbish. Life at our level has adopted a vehicle which—like all natural vehicles—has a form and a story of its own, apart from the inherited movement which it serves to propagate. The individual has outgrown his character of a mere moment in a flux; his trope is not simply the general trope repeated and passed on. It has become a redundant trope, surrounding that other with epicycles and arabesques and prolongations useless to the march of transmissible life, yet enriching it at its several stations.

It is only metaphorically, therefore, that the general movement of nature can be called a life, or said to be animated by a cosmic psyche. Nor would the attribu-

There is no cosmic soul. tion of these tropes to the universe as a whole explain why they should arise again within it. On the contrary, it is more natural to find fish in the sea than within other fishes. We may rather say that matter, although perhaps everywhere organic or at least ready to be organised, becomes animate only when it forms hereditary organisms; and that a psyche exists only in bodies that can assimilate and redistribute the substances suitable for preserving and propagating their type. Thus the cosmos–not feeding or breeding–can have no psyche, but only psyches within it; and the spirit is no psyche, but always has some psyche beneath, which sustains it.

Embryology, the most obscure part of biology, is accordingly the fundamental part of it. In the present state of knowledge, the psychologist is condemned to

Profound obscurity of the psychic mechanism. taking summary and superficial views of his subject, for he sees gross results, gross variations, gross repetitions, and all the fine, individual, intricate labour of the psyche escapes him. Physiology and organic chemistry work only with ready-made materials, which already possess inexplicable specific virtues and habits; and psychoanalysis, in really opening a trap-door, as disease does, into the dim carpentry of the stage, is compelled to transcribe that intricacy into metaphors. Its reports come to it in hectic language, the latest, most wayward, most hypocritical ebullition of psychic life; while its own theories, for lack of physiological knowledge, must be couched in mythological terms. Thus the psyche remains a mystery in her intrinsic operations; and if something of that mystery seems to hang about the feminine name we are giving her, so much the better: we are warned that we do not, and probably cannot, understand.

What our knowledge of the psyche lacks in precision it makes up, after a fashion, in variety and extent. All that is called knowledge of the world, of human

The psyche, like other natural mechanisms, is known to us by her fruits. nature, of character, and of the passions is a sort of auscultation of the psyche; and the familiarity of our verbal and dramatic conventions often blinds us to their loose application, and to our profound ignorance of the true mechanism of life. Not knowing what we are, we at least can discourse abundantly about our books, our words, and our social actions; and these manifestations of the psyche, though peripheral, are faithful enough witnesses to her nature. She is that inner moving equilibrium from which these things radiate, and which they help to restore–the equilibrium by which we live, in the sense of not dying; and to keep us alive is her first and essential function. It follows naturally from this biological office that in each of us she is one, vigilant, and predetermined; that she is selfish and devoted, intrepid and vicious, intelligent and mad; for her quick potentialities are solicited and distracted by all sorts of accidents. She slept at first in a seed; there, and from there, as the seed softened, she distributed her organs and put forth her energies, always busier and busier in her growing body, almost losing control of her members, yet reacting from the centre, perhaps only slowly and partially, upon events at her frontiers. If too deeply thwarted her industry becomes distraction; and what we sometimes call her plan, which is only her propensity, may be developed and transformed, if she finds new openings, until it becomes quite a different plan. But against brutal obstacles she will struggle until death; that is, until her central control, her total equilibrium and power of recuperation, are exhausted. Her death may as easily occur by insurrection within her organism—each part of which is a potential centre on its own account—as by hostile action from outside.

I hardly venture to say more. To watch a plant grow, or draw in its leaves, to observe the animals in a zoological garden, is to gain some knowledge of the psyche; to study embryology or the nervous system or insanity or politics, is (or ought to be) to gain more: and every system of science or religion is rich in this sort of instruction for a critic who studies it in order to distinguish whatever may be arbitrary in it, based on human accidents, and without any but a psychic ground. All the errors ever made about other things, if we understand their cause, enlighten us about ourselves; for the psyche is at once the spring of curiosity and the ground of refraction, selection, and distortion in our ideas. Summary reaction, symbolisation, infection with relativity and subjective colouring begins in the senses and is continued in the passions; and if we succeed in removing, by criticism, this personal equation from our science of other things, the part withdrawn, which remains on our hands, is our indirect knowledge of the psyche.

Each man also has direct experience of the psyche within himself, not so much in his verbal thoughts and distinct images—which if they are knowledge at all are knowledge of other things—as in a certain sense of his personal momentum, a pervasive warmth and power in the inner man. As he thinks and acts, intent on external circumstances, he is not unaware of the knot of latent determinate impulses within him which respond to those circumstances. Our thoughts—which we may be said to know well, in that we know we have had them often before—are about anything and everything. We shuffle and iterate them, and live in them a verbal, heated, histrionic life. Yet we little know *why* we have them, or how they arise and change. Nothing could be more obscure, more physical, than the dynamics of our passions and dreams; yet, especially in moments of suspense or hesitation, nothing could be more intensely felt. There is the coursing of the blood, the waxing and waning of the affections, a thousand starts of smothered eloquence, the coming on of impatience, of invention, of conviction, of sleep. There are laughter and tears, ready to flow quite unbidden, and almost at random. There is our whole past, as it were, knocking at the door; there are our silent hopes; there are our future discourses and decisions working away, like actors rehearsing their parts, at their several fantastic arguments. All this is the psyche's work; and in that sense deeply our own; and our superficial mind is carried by it like a child, cooing or fretting, in his mother's arms. Much of it we feel going on unmistakably within our bodies, and the whole of it in fact goes on there. But the form which belongs to it in its truly physical and psychic character,

And also directly, though vaguely, by self-consciousness.

in its vital bodily tropes, is even less known to us than the mechanism of the heart, or that by which our nerves receive, transmit, and return their signals. The psyche is an object of experience to herself, since what she does at one moment or in one organ she can observe, perhaps, a moment later, or with another organ; yet of her life as a whole she is aware only as we are aware of the engines and the furnaces in a ship in which we travel, half-asleep, or chattering on deck; or as we are aware of a foreign language heard for the first time, perceived in its globular sound and gesticulation and even perhaps in its general issue—that all is probably a dispute about money—yet without distinguishing the words, or the reasons for those precise passionate outbursts. In this way we all endure, without understanding, the existence and the movement of our own psyche: for it is the body that speaks, and the spirit that listens.

The psyche is the self which a man is proud or ashamed of, or probably both at once: not his body in its accidental form, age, and diseases, from which he instinctively distinguishes those initial impulses and thwarted powers which are much more truly himself. And this is the self which, if he lives in a religious age, he may say that he wishes to save, and to find reviving in another world. Yet this self is far from being a stranger to the body; on the contrary, it is more deeply and persistently the essence of the body than is the body itself. It is human, male or female, proper to a particular social and geographical zone; it is still the fountain of youth in old age; it deprecates in a measure the actions and words which circumstances may have drawn from it, and which (it feels) do it enormous injustice; and yet the words and actions which it might have wished to produce instead are all words and actions of the same family, slightly more eloquent in the same human language, slightly more glorious in the same social sphere. The psyche is so much of us, and of our works, as is our own doing.

She is the internal source of the organism and of its action.

Conflicts between the flesh and the spirit, between habit and idea, between passion and reason, are real conflicts enough, but they are conflicts between one movement in the psyche and another movement there. Hers is a compound life, moulded by compromise, and compacted of tentative organs, with their several impulses, all initially blind and mechanical. Rarely will any particular psychic impulse or habit move in sympathy with all the rest, or be unquestionably dominant. It follows that what in religion or in moral reflection we call the spirit is a precarious harmony. It is threatened by subject powers always potentially rebellious, and it necessarily regards them as wicked and material in so far as they do not conspire to keep its own flame vivid and pure. And yet the spirit itself has no other fuel. Reason is not a force contrary to the passions, but a harmony possible among them. Except in their interests it could have no ardour, and, except in their world, it could have no point of application, nothing to beautify, nothing to dominate. It is therefore by a complete illusion, though an excusable one, that the spirit denies its material basis, and calls its body a prison or a tomb. The impediments are real, but mutual; and sometimes a second nucleus of passion or fleshliness rises against that nucleus which the spirit expresses, and takes the

All moral conflicts or dualisms are internal to her life.

name of spirit in its turn. Every virtue, and in particular knowledge and thought, have no other root in the world than the co-ordination of their organs with one another and with the material habitat. Certainly such a co-ordination could never arise except in a psyche: the psyche is another name for it: but neither could the psyche have any life to foster and defend, nor any instruments for doing so, if she were not a trope arising in a material flux, and enjoyed a visible dominance there more or less prolonged and extended.

Thus the first function of the psyche in the seed is to create the outer body. With every organ which she brings forth she acquires a new office and a new type of life. These changes and developments are not devised and suggested to the psyche by some disembodied spirit, whisper-ing in her ear. Were they not the natural continuation of her innate tensions she would be justified in regarding these prompt-ings as deceits and snares of the devil. For from the point of view of the psyche (whose innate impulse is the arbiter of mor-als) every change of purpose is a change for the worse: either a vain complication or a hideous surrender. It is only lateral tensions, circumstances, external pres-sure, that can compel her to recast her habits and become, to that extent, a new psyche. Surrenders are indeed inevitable when the action for which the soul is ready happens to be impossible, or organs once agile are atrophied by disuse; and new acquisitions of function are inevitable too, when new occasions induce a different mode of action, and preserve and solidify it. The burden of the psyche is in this way continually lightened in one quarter and accumulated in another. If crippled at first by some loss, she may ultimately heal the wound (healing being one of her primary functions) and may live on with her residual equipment all the more nimbly. On the other hand she often hardens herself to some novel exer-tion which at first was forced and distracting, until that exercise becomes instinc-tive and necessary to her health and peace, so that it is performed with alacrity and sureness whenever an occasion occurs. Habituation tames the spirit, or rather kills it in one form and recreates it in another. This forced attention to instrumen-talities, this awkwardness, which marks the acquisition of a new art, yields in time to love and mastery; and the spirit rises again from its troubles and threatened death to happiness and confidence.

Formation and variation of the psyche equally a resultant of material tensions.

At bottom, however, the whole psyche is a burden to herself, a terrible inner compulsion to care, to watch, to pursue, and to possess. Yet to evade this predes-tined career would be a worse fate; and the psyche is more terri-bly corroded and tormented for not doing, than she would be harassed in doing, or disappointed at having done. Original sin must be purged, the burden discharged, the message delivered. Happiness—for the surface of the psyche is normally happy—lies for her in jogging on without too much foresight or retrospect, along the middle way, exercising her central functions heartily, and reverting to them, as to hearth and home, from those gambler's losses or commitments into which she may be tempted. In this way she may healthfully deliver herself in a long life of her native burden, transmit the same in a healthful measure, and sleep in peace.

Her mission is to discharge an imposed burden.

Sleep is in a manner the normal condition of the psyche, from which in her vegetative and somatic labours she never awakes, unless it be to suffer; and we may fancy that a sort of sub-soul or potential life sleeps, and will always sleep, in the universe of matter, ready to shape it, when opportunity occurs, into the likeness of all essence. Yet as this labour must be in time, and in some one of many alternative courses, the greater part of that sleeping psyche remains unoccupied, and the occupied part anxious and full of the fear of death: from which indeed she cannot escape except by falling asleep again and forgetting, but never really removing, the peril of a new birth.

To be completely mastered by the psyche makes the health, agility, and beauty of the body. This sort of virtue is common among the brutes. It would seem to suffice that a very potent psyche—one to which its matter completely submits—should have entrenched herself in the seed and should surround it later with outworks so staunch and perfect that no ordinary hazard will pierce or bend them. Unquestioning fidelity to type is always a marvel, a victory of form over matter, which delights the contemplative spirit. In fragile organisms, such as children or flowers, this fidelity seems to us an appealing innocence; but in hard-shell organisms, which attempt to resist change by force of rigidity, it seems rather stupid. Brave and proud the conservative psyche may be: she will not suffer minor accidents to distract her from her first vows and native intentions; but against major accidents she has no resource save a total death; and on earth she must be extraordinarily prolific to survive at all.

Completely determinate psyches are beautiful but not safe.

The peculiarity of the human psyche, on the contrary, is her great relative plasticity. I will not call it intelligence, because that presupposes a fixed good to be attained, and invention only of new means of attaining it. A total plasticity, that for greater convenience consents to change its most radical direction, would hardly be life; its only assignable purpose would seem to be survival, and even this would be illusory, since the psyche that was to survive would have abdicated in doing so, and would have committed suicide. This the human soul is capable of doing, morally as well as physically, as we see in madness, in conversion, and in the wilder passions; but ordinarily her plasticity remains only a means to a native end, an incidental adjustment in the interests of the major radical passions, which remain supreme at the centre. Yet this alert human psyche, more intelligent than wise, often forgets the treasure locked in the citadel, and lives by preference in her own suburbs, in the outer organs of action and perception. She then becomes distracted, frivolous, loquacious; and we may doubt whether all this agitation and knowingness relieve her of her inner burden, or only add a dreadful fatigue to a profound dissatisfaction.

Nor is this all: friction at the periphery more or less recoils to the centre and modifies the organisation there. Changes of food, temperature, climate, and rhythm may extend to the very substance of the seed whence the next generation is to grow; so that the psyche transmitted is not always exactly similar to the psyche inherited. In the history of the earth, the evolution and transformation of psyches must have gone on from the beginning; and this reconstruction, which in some directions seems to have come to a temporary end and produced stable types of animals, in the human race still continues at an unusual rate. Not so much in the body—unless we regard clothes and weapons as equivalents to fur and claws—but in the singular equipment with instruments by which modern man has surrounded himself, and in the management of which he lives. The changes are so rapid **Some adaptations extend to the germ.** that we can observe and record them: something perhaps impossible and inconceivable to any psyche except the human.

All this may be studied and described behaviouristically, as a chapter in natural history; yet we know that the psyche so occupied has an inner invisible experience, which under these circumstances becomes very complex. The eloquence of language, the multitude of sights and sounds, the keen edge of silent emotion compose a perpetual waking dream—a view of the world which is not a part of the world and which even in sleep continues and shifts fantastically in many a muted development. **The feeling always involved in psychic life becomes in animals perception and in man thought.** This unsubstantial experience, which is alone immediate, is nothing new or paradoxical in kind. The psyche is probably never unconscious; she always feels, in some vague emotional form, the inherent stress of her innumerable operations. Her maturing instincts have their false dawn in her mind; she warms and awakes for a moment at their satisfaction, and simmers pleasantly when replete. But external perception is a keener, more inquisitive form of attention; it is less interested in what is given æsthetically, or even in what might be given, than in the action of things upon one another and on our bodies. At the same time, perception cannot fail to supply us with images—products of the inner psyche, like the feelings of blind animals—which serve to name and to clothe in our poetic consciousness those external objects of her concern. These images and those feelings, together with the constant flow of unspoken words which we call thinking, compose a mental or inner life. Its moments, though probably intent on external material events, are yet directly but symptoms of psychic movements; so that it requires only a shift in apperception to transform all this immediate experience from active consideration of dubious external objects into a certain and accurate index to an internal psychic life.

Not that these moments of spirit, these mental notes and mental vistas, *are* the psychic life in question. They form a thin flux of consciousness, chiefly verbal in most of us, which in reflective moods becomes self-consciousness, recollection, autobiography, and literature: all only the topmost synthesis, or play of shooting relations, on the surface of the unconscious. In this capacity, however, as a mental symptom or expression, self-consciousness gives infallible renderings **Secondary or expressive nature of consciousness.** of the agitation beneath. We may therefore use it, in so far as we can recollect it or reconstruct it, to describe the psyche and her passions, just as we use the essences given in perception to describe pictorially those parts of the material world on which the organs of perception react.

Hence a second approach to a science of the psyche, this time not biological or behaviouristic, but personal, through memory and repeatable mental discourse; and this imagination of imagination may fill our whole lives, composing

Possibility of literary psychology.

a dramatic, social, religious world in which we suppose ourselves to be living. Such a moral world, the world of humanism, need not mislead in practice the psyche that creates it. Sometimes she may become more interested in this play-world—in religion, landscape, fiction, and eloquence—than in her natural circumstances. Yet all her imaginative life is interfused with language and akin to language, so that it often becomes a convenient or indispensable transcript for the march of things on the human scale. It may be so disciplined and adjusted to facts as to compose history and literary psychology.

The two sorts of psychology, the scientific and the literary, are clearly distinguished by Aristotle where he says that anger is a name for two different things,

Its relation to the natural science of the psyche.

anger being physically a boiling of the humours and dialectically a desire for revenge. Boiling of the humours would be an exterior and gross effect of the total movement of the psyche, and the natural history of a passion is far more complicated and far-reaching than any such symptom; yet the boiling is on the same plane as the whole object of biology, on the plane of behaviour, and gives us a first glimpse of what anger is, substantially considered. On the other hand, "a desire for revenge" is a current verbal and dramatic expression for such a passion: this too is summary and might be elaborated in each case into an almost infinite network of motives, memories, likes and dislikes, and delicate juxtapositions of images and words; yet whatever figments we might substitute for the conventional terms "anger" or "desire" would be further literary figments, verbal or intuitive units formed and re-formed by the discoursing spirit, and non-existent in the realm of matter. For this reason the most adequate and confident knowledge of human nature, rendered in literary terms, as in novels and plays, or in the gossip of busybodies, covers only what might be called the reasoned element in life—although it is for the most part foolish at bottom. The same psychology remains helpless in the presence of all the radical passions and all the natural collocations of persons and events by which the life of mind is determined.

Literature and literary philosophy are nevertheless the most natural and eloquent witnesses to the life of the psyche. Literature is conserved speech, speech is significant song, and song is a pure overflow of the psyche in her moments of free play and vital leisure. And this overflow is itself double: biological and ontological. Biologically it resembles the exuberance of the psyche in all her well-fed and happy moments, in the gambols of young animals, the haughtiness of all accomplished strength, or the endless experimentation in colours, forms, and habits characteristic of the psyche in fashioning her strange menagerie of bodies. Yet the ontological overflow, the concomitant emergence of consciousness, alone seems to arrest the wonder, not to say the wrath, of philosophers; and they are so surprised at it, and so wrathful, that they are inclined to deny it, and to call it impossible. I have not myself such an intrinsic knowledge of matter as to be sure that it cannot do that which it does: nor do I see why the proudest man should be ashamed of the parents who after all have produced him. I am not tempted seriously to regard consciousness as the very essence of life or even of being. On the contrary, both my personal experience and the little I know of nature at large absolutely convince me that consciousness is the most highly conditioned of existences, an overtone of psychic strains, mutations, and harmonies; nor does its origin seem more mysterious to me than that of everything else.

Let us, in this important matter, go back to first principles. From the beginning it was in the very nature of existence to be involved in indirect commitments. Being transitive, anything existing is always in the act of becoming something which it was not, and yet which it was the sufficient cause for producing, according to those irresponsible impulses which animate its matter and predetermine its fate. The sequel is always spontaneous and, if we are not dulled by habit, seems miraculous; yet it is always natural, since no other development would have been more so, and some development was inevitable. Nature is not that realm of essence where all variety and all relations are perspicuous and intrinsically necessary. Necessity, in nature, is only an irrational propulsion which, as a matter of fact, is prevalent; existence could not have begun to be, it could not have taken the first step from one form of being to another, if it had not been radically mad. But this madness not only has method in it—a method in itself arbitrary and doubtless variable—it has also a certain glorious profusion, a rising, cumulative intensity and volume, coming to a climax and then dying down. The flux thus runs inevitably into dramatic episodes, even in its own plane of matter; episodes in our eyes far more interesting than its general movement, which is perhaps only itself an episode in some more radical genesis of existence.

Change, concretion, dissolution, and variation are intrinsic to a flux.

But the tacit commitments of such existence are not limited to the material plane. Every fact involves many a truth about it; it casts its shadow through infinite distances and makes relevant to it everything that it resembles and everything that it contradicts. By arising and by disappearing it introduces an unalterable event into history; it verifies or stultifies all prophecies concerning it and concerning the place which it fills in the context of nature, and which might have been filled otherwise; and it either justifies or renders false everything that anyone may say or think of it in future.

The eternal truth about it is also involved in it.

Here, then, is a whole infinite world, visible only to the intellect, but actually created and made precise by the blind flux of matter, whatsoever that flux may be. These are the indelible footprints which existence, thoughtlessly running on, neither knows nor cares that it is making, and which yet are its only memorial, its only redemption from death, the eternal truth about it.

Now, when the flux falls into the trope which we call a psyche, existence commits itself unawares to yet another complication; for now the reverberation of its movement in the realm of truth becomes, so to speak, vocal and audible to itself. Not indeed in its entirety—unless there be some divine sensorium to gather all its echoes together—but in snatches. At certain junctures animal life, properly a habit in matter, bursts as with a peal of bells into a new realm of being, into the realm of spirit. When does this happen, and how is this consciousness diversified and guided? We may presume that some slumbering sensibility exists in every living organism, as an echo or foretaste of its vital rhythms; and even when no assignable feeling comes to a head, if there is life at all, there is a sort of field of consciousness, or canvas spread for attention, ready to be occupied by eventual figures. Not by *any* figures, as if essences of their own initiative could come down and appear; but only by certain predetermined classes and intensities of sensation, possible to the particular organs whose suspended animation, or busy growth, spreads that canvas and rings that ground-tone of potential feeling. When ambient influences or inner ripening modify this vital rhythm, or cause the psyche actively to assimilate or to repel that stimulant, organic slumber may easily awake to some special feeling or image. Thus sensations and ideas always follow upon organic reactions and express their quality; and intuition merely supplies a mental term for the animal reaction already at work unconsciously. With each new strain or fresh adjustment, a new feeling darts through the organism; digestive sleep breaks into moral alertness and sharp perception; and, once initiated, these modes of sensibility may persist even in quiescent hours—for they leave neurograms or seeds of habit in the brain—and may be revived in thought and in dreams.

Where the flux is a psyche, some truths about it become occasions for feeling.

Consciousness, then, in its genesis and natural status, is one of the indirect but inevitable outpourings proper to an existence which is in flux and gathers itself into living bodies. In consciousness the psyche becomes festive, lyrical, rhetorical; she caps her life by considering it, and talking to herself about the absent parts of it. Consciousness is a spiritual synthesis of organic movements; and were it not this, no spirit and no consciousness would ever have any transcendent significance or any subject-matter other than the essences which it might weave together. Yet in fact, on account of its organic seat and material conditions, consciousness is significant. Its every datum is an index, and may become in its eyes a symbol, for its cause. In other words, consciousness is naturally cognitive. Its spiritual essence renders it an imponderable sublimation of organic life, and invisible there; yet it is attached historically, morally, and indicatively to its source, by being knowledge of it.

Being spiritual in essence, yet materially conditioned, consciousness can be knowledge of its source.

Thus, like truth, consciousness is necessarily faithful to its basis in the flux of nature; it is a commentary on events, in the language of essence; and while its light is contemplative, its movement and intent strictly obey the life of the psyche in which it is kindled. Hence the whole assertive or dogmatic force of intelligence, by which the spirit ventures to claim knowledge of outspread facts, and not merely to light up and inspect a given essence. This whole extraordinary pretension rests on a vital compulsion, native to the body, imposing animal faith on a spirit in itself contemplative. For in animals the organs are inevitably addressed to intercourse with relevant external things, as well as to internal growth and reproduction. Suspense outwards, towards an object not within her organism, is habitual

This knowledge is natural in its origin, validity, and scope.

to the psyche. Her tentacles and her actions hang and grope in mid-air, like a drawbridge confidently let down to meet its appropriate ulterior point of contact and support. Even her vegetative life is prophetic, conscious of maturation, and rich in preparations for coming crises, vaguely prefigured but unhesitatingly pursued. Under such circumstances and with such organs, consciousness could not be pure intuition: it must needs be intuition carried by intent. The intent is adventurous; its object or ulterior development is hidden and merely posited. Yet by thus torturing itself, and uprooting itself from its immediate datum, spirit becomes perception, and perception knowledge, in all its transitive and realistic force. And this perception and knowledge are, for the same reason, normally and virtually true: not true literally, as the fond spirit imagines when it takes some given picture, summary, synthetic, and poetical, for the essence of the world; but true as language may be true, symbolically, pragmatically, and for the range of human experience in that habitat and at that stage in its history.

So much for the claims of spirit to possess knowledge, and for the range of it. But whence the original qualities of feeling itself, the choice of essences that shall appear in intuition, the spectrum of each sense, the logic and grammar of each type of intelligence? How does the psyche arrive at any of these creations, rather than at any other? Certainly out of her own substance, and by the natural diversity and fertility of the tropes which she imposes on her own matter. The presumption of common sense, that these essences belong in the first place to objects and pass from them into the organs of sense, and somehow become evident to spirit in the dark caverns of the brain, is unfortunately untenable. We find it plausible—in spite of its incoherence and the many contrary facts—because we begin our reflection at the end, armed with our working conventions and dogmatic habits. We should readily understand the enormous illusion involved, and the false reduplication of our data, if we began at the beginning, where in the natural world the psyche begins. Surely pleasure and pain, hunger, lust, and fear, do not first reside in external objects and pass from them into the mind: and these are the primary, typical data of intuition. All the rest—colours, sounds, shapes, specious spaces and times and sensations of motion—is hatched in the same nest; it all has a similar psychic seat and dramatic occasion. If such essences seem to be found in external things, it is for the good and sufficient reason that outer things are perceived by us in these sensible terms, and could not be perceived were not the psyche sensitive, and fertile in such signals to the spirit. All things might stand facing one another for ever, clad in all the colours of the rainbow; and were there no poetic psyche in any of them, to turn those colours into feelings of colour and intuitions of the soul, never would anything perceive anything else.

The psyche is a poet, a creator of language; and there is no presumption that she will perceive material things, including her own substance and movement, at all in the terms or in the order and scale in which they exist materially. On the contrary, only the reactions of her organism are represented in her feelings; and these reactions, which are tropes subsisting only in the realm of truth, resemble

The spectrum of sense and the categories of thought are original creations of the psyche.

in nothing the imponderable feelings which are involved in executing them. The fountain of sense and of sensible qualities lies indeed in the forward and inner tensions of natural moments, with their conjunctions and flow in a psyche. Pain, novel in essence, signalises a special nervous affection, not another pain elsewhere; and this signal is suitable, in as much as just such a cry would be uttered by any psyche in such a predicament, and for all psyches

They express directly her own movements and only indirectly and relatively their external occasion.

signifies predicaments of that sort. The whole of life is a predicament, complex and prolonged; and the whole of mind is the cry, prolonged and variously modulated, which that predicament wrings from the psyche.

After the spirit is born, and in the midst of business has begun to take note silently of the actual aspectsand essences of things, the psyche may extend her action with more circumspection, in what we call the arts. That pause, as we may think it, for wonder and contemplation, was only, from her housewife's point of view, a pause for breath: in stopping to gaze, she gives herself time to readjust her impulses and increase her range. Having, among other organs, formed the human hand,

Psychic origin and control of the arts.

she may proceed through that instrument to transform matter outside her body; so that artificial instruments and works become, as it were, organs of the psyche too. With this extension of her instruments her spirit, which is the fruition of them in act, also extends its basis. From her centre, where the spirit lives, she may now control and watch a whole political, industrial, and learned world. Civilisation may accumulate for her benefit a great fund of traditions, which will foster the spirit systematically and direct it rationally. Just as in the growth of the embryo there was a marvellous precision and timeliness in the production of the various organs hereditary in the species, so in animal society there is a great, though much looser, predetermination of what the arts shall produce.

Art, as I use the word here, implies moral benefit: the impulsive modification of matter by man to his own confusion and injury I should not call art, but vice or folly. The tropes of art must be concentric with those of health in the psyche, otherwise they would not, on the whole, extend her dominion or subserve her need of discharging her powers. Nature is everywhere full of vices, partly apathetic, in that the impulse at work does not avail to transmute new matter into its instrument,

The psyche and all her works are subject to disease.

and partly aberrant, in that the impulse itself runs wild, and destroys, instead of buttressing, its original organ—for without an organ an impulse can neither exist nor operate. Thus the psyche continually creates diseases in her substance, or invents scourges and trammels to oppress her from without, as does a false civilisation, through the mad work of her own hands. These aberrations, if extreme, soon defeat themselves by the ruin which they cause; but often they interweave themselves permanently into the strong woof of life, rendering life wretched but not impossible.

In the very inertia of habit, however, as in inveterate vices, there may be a certain luxury or compensation. Impulse, having taken to that trope, may find a certain pleasure in repeating it, a sort of dogged allegiance and sense of rightness, more intimately native and satisfying than any overt proof of its folly. The virtuous human soul, so to speak, is then long dead and buried, and the omnivorous vice has become a soul in its stead. We are compacted of devils. Love and conscience, like the rest, are initially irrational; and the conservative inner man may strenuously cling to methods in art and to forms of sentiment which defeat his eventual rational nature. The fatal imperative of his daemon may lie deeper in him than any ulterior claim of beauty or happiness.

Thus the spiritual function of the psyche is added to her generative and practical functions, creating a fresh and unprecedented realm of being, the realm of spirit, with its original æsthetic spectrum and moral range and values incommensurable with anything but themselves. Yet this whole evocation is a concomitant function of the same psyche which presides over bodily growth and action. Were it not so, spirit would have no place in time or in nature, no relevance to existence, and indeed, no existence of its own; and even if by a flight of mythological fancy we imagined it existing disembodied, it would thereby have forfeited all its dramatic breathlessness, all its moral aspiration, all its piety and potential wisdom. It would be an abstract intellect without a spiritual life, a hypostasis of the realm of truth or of essence, and not a human virtue. So that the dependence of spirit on animal life is no brutal accident, no inexplicable degradation of a celestial being into the soul of a beast. All the themes and passions of spirit, however spiritual or immaterial in themselves, celebrate the vicissitudes of a natural psyche, like a pure poet celebrating the adventures of lovers and kings.

Meantime she has given birth to spirit and attached it to earthly interests.

There Are No Necessary Truths

The Realm of Truth: Book Third of Realms of Being. London: Constable and Co. Ltd.; Toronto: Macmillan Company, 1937; New York: Charles Scribner's Sons, 1938, 1–10. Volume sixteen of the critical edition of *The Works of George Santayana.*

This selection appeared as Chapter I in The Realm of Truth, *the third volume of the four-volume* Realms of Being. *He jokingly remarked that "there are some signs of senility in this volume; I can't avoid repetitions and ramblings, yet, as in the Curate's egg, <u>parts of it are excellent</u>" (LGS, 6:49). In this selection, Santayana disputed four claims often regarded as necessary truths. First, he disputed the statement 2 + 2 = 4, which he thought true of the realm of matter but not the realm of spirit. Second, he disputed the claim that space and time are infinitely divisible, which he thought true of space and time as they are intuited but false in natural spheres independent of intuition such as chemical interaction, animal life, or astronomy. Here space and time have no pre-existence that one may later analyze; material flux creates time through its rhythmic motion and space through its diversity. Third, he disputed the statement that everything has a cause, which lacks logical cogency. He further denied that the sum of all causes has a cause itself. Fourth, he disputed the claim that God necessarily exists, which he found to involve an equivocation of realms of being.*

Tradition is rich in maxims called necessary truths, such as that $2 + 2 = 4$, that space and time are infinitely divisible, that everything has a cause, and that God, or the most real of beings, necessarily exists. Many such propositions may be necessary, by virtue of the definitions given to their terms; many may be true, in that the facts of nature confirm them; and some may be both necessary logically and true materially, but even then the necessity will come from one quarter and the truth from another.

Logical necessity connects ideal terms.

This conclusion would be evident to anyone who had clearly conceived the nature of infinite Being or the realm of essence; a conception in itself easy and inevitable, when once attention has lighted upon it. So obvious and easy is this conception that it may be regarded as trivial and not worth dwelling on: yet here it finds a momentous echo, which dispels half the doubts and worries of speculation. For if essences, or possible terms of thought, are infinite in number and variety, it follows that every particular fact is contingent, arbitrary, and logically unnecessary, since infinite alternatives were open to existence, if existence had chosen to take a different form. Now it is precisely this unnecessary, arbitrary, contingent chance or fatality, making existence at each point such as it is, that determines what shall be true: that is, what elements of essence shall figure in that existence. So that, truth being descriptive of existence and existence being contingent, truth will be contingent also.

But truth, being a radiation of existence, is contingent.

Let me analyse, on these principles, the four maxims adduced above.

That $2 + 2 = 4$, like all the rest of mathematics, is an equation making explicit certain essential relations between certain terms. Essential relations are all necessary, being based on the definitions or intuitions which distinguish those related terms; though it is by no means necessary or even possible to explore and make explicit in human discourse all the essential relations of the terms selected.* Naturally in human mathematics there is a human element. Each intuitive mind darts in its own congenial direction, and sees what a differently intuitive mind might have overlooked: and the range of thought also is human, like its pace and direction. One mind crawls where another wears seven-league boots; yet by whatever leaps or on whatever scale the survey be made, if the essences first chosen are not dropped and confused with others, all explorations will help to fill in the same map, and the science of essence, in that region, will be enriched and consolidated.

Mathematical equations cogent formally.

So far truth has not been broached and mathematics is like music, freely exploring the possibilities of form. And yet, notoriously, mathematics holds true of things; hugs and permeates them far more closely than does confused and inconstant human perception; so that the dream of many exasperated critics of human error has been to assimilate all science to mathematics, so as to make knowledge safe by making it, as Locke wished, direct perception of the relations between ideas. Unfortunately, knowledge would then never touch those matters of fact on which Locke was intent. The only serious value of those logical explorations would lie in their possible relevance to the accidents of existence. It is only in that relation and in that measure that mathematical science would cease to be mere play with ideas and would become *true:* that is, in a serious sense, would become *knowledge.* Now the seriousness of mathematics comes precisely of its remarkable and exact relevance to material facts, both familiar and remote: so that mathematical equations, besides being essentially necessary in themselves, are often also true of the world we live in. And this in a surprising measure. For when once any essence falls within the sphere of truth, all its essential relations do so too: and the necessity of these relations will, on that hypothesis, form a necessary complement to a proposition that happens to be true. This same necessity, however, would have nothing to do with truth if the terms it connects were not exemplified in existence.

Their applicability a matter of fact.

In this way mathematical calculations far out-running experiment often turn out to be true of the physical world, as if, *per impossibile,* they could be true *à priori.* But in fact nature, that had to have some form or other, is organized and deployed on principles which, in human language, are called number, shape, and measurable time; categories which for that reason have taken root in human language

They are actually true of the material sphere, at least in the gross.

*The question does not arise whether mathematical judgments are analytic or synthetic. Psychologically all judgments and all intuitions of the complex are synthetic, because the terms given are distinguished and compared in thought. But if the judgments are necessary, they must be analytical logically, i.e. founded on the nature of the terms.

and science. Yet these categories would have no truth or applicability whatever, if existence were entirely mental and sentimental. They would then be ideal fictions or games of apperception, with their own sporting rules, like the game of chess, but with no cognitive function in respect to the dynamic world in which life would arise, and in which these games would be carried on.

Now as a matter of fact there is a psychological sphere to which logic and mathematics do not apply. There, the truth is dramatic. That $2 + 2 = 4$ is not true of ideas. One idea added to another, in actual intuition, makes still only one idea, or it makes three: for the combination, with the relations perceived, forms one complex essence, and yet the original essences remain distinct, as elements in this new whole.

But irrelevant to the realm of spirit.

This holds of all moral, æsthetic, and historical units: they are merged and reconstituted with every act of apperception. Each essence evoked reverts, when lost sight of, to its limbo of latent forms. It cannot contribute genetically or dynamically, being unsubstantial, to compose the next apparition. Although life in plants and animals may be capable of mathematical treatment at one pervasive material level, none of the vital unities or tropes are so capable. Moreover, this is not due altogether to the imagination superposing its views on the flux of existence: for the special organic unity which breeds imagination and will, and superposes them on events, cannot be itself imaginary, since it creates a specific fact—namely, this very will or imagination. There are therefore levels of reality, and these the most important to mankind, that elude all mathematical axioms.

In the second maxim adduced, that space and time are infinitely divisible, we pass to an axiom the truth of which is extremely doubtful, even in the physical world. Specious space and time (that is, extension and duration as given to intuition, and space and time as defined geometrically) are indeed infinitely divisible. Scale in them is elastic and utterly unsubstantial, so that there is room for the most elaborate ideal event or object within the smallest fraction of time or space. But this hardly seems to be true in the chemical or animal or astronomical spheres, where scale is not variable fantastically: and this for the best of reasons—namely, that in nature empty space and time do not pre-exist, so that existent beings of extensible and unascertainable dimensions may drop into them later; but on the contrary a physical flux, pulsing through natural moments and carrying a definite volume of events with it, creates a real time by its rhythms and a real space by its organic complexity. These native dimensions of the real may indeed be measured and graphically noted in our science, as living music may be measured and noted in a musical score: but the ideal qualities of the medium for such a transcription can no more be imposed on nature by our definitions than the flatness or infinite divisibility of the paper, or the lines of the clef, can impose their graphic qualities upon music.

Physical space and time not subject to dialectic.

For want of making this distinction, hopeless difficulties and fatuous assertions have been imported into philosophy. Sometimes nature has been abolished for not conforming to logic: and sometimes logic has corrected nature so as to secure an agreement. Yet the *true* agreement existed from the first, within its natural limits: a friendly concomitance between material events and the free symbolism proper to animal sense or imagination, excited as these must be by those material contacts and organic tensions. There is both precision and poetry in the intricacies of essence, if selectively explored: but the scientific imagination is idolatrous when it interpolates its creations in the dynamic structure of nature. They describe that structure from without, they are not contained within it: they are transcripts, not insights.

When we pass to the third maxim, that everything has a cause, the balance between necessity and truth is reversed. This maxim has no logical cogency, but the presumption it expresses is backed by a good deal of evidence. In search of necessity we might correct the statement and say that every *effect* has a cause; but this truism would leave us to consider whether every event is actually an effect. Certainly not, unless the series of events runs back to infinity: and even in that case—apart from the heavy strain imposed on human imagination and credulity—the question would arise whether every part of every event was caused by its antecedents, or only its initial phase or its approximate outline. The latter is the plausible view, adopted by Aristotle, and reasonable if we believe in the dominance of a conceptual pattern over the flux of existence. Events will fall into certain classes, animals and their passions will exemplify certain permanent types, but there will be a margin of incalculable variation due to accidental conjunctions or lapses in the execution of the dominant themes. And here again, there are alternative possibilities. These lapses or conjunctions may all have mechanical causes, according to deeper laws of matter, traceable beneath the moral morphology of events; or on the contrary, variations may be free and groundless, though kept within certain bounds by the magic of hereditary types; so that the old equilibrium of the cosmos will right itself after each casual oscillation. Or perhaps these oscillations are casual only in appearance, and from the point of view of their antecedents, while by a secret conspiracy they, or some of them, steadily make for one far-off divine event: and it may have been these successive variations, mechanically uncaused but prophetically inspired, that have created, as it were on the way, the stock genera and species of our transitory world. These would then be restive in their trammels and destined to be superseded. If all variations and free choices were so directed, they might all be said to have a cause, not in the past, but in the future: and the providential harmony of all the parts and of all the incidents would seem, in one sense, to render them necessary. Not that logically a different issue would not be conceivable, but that morally and emotionally it would be "unthinkable" that any absurd accident should ever come groundlessly to mar so perfect a plan.

> No actual sequence can be necessary and the sum of causes can have no cause.

Nevertheless, the necessity of each element for the perfection of a particular design confers no necessity upon that design as a whole, nor compels nature to adopt it. Whatever regularity or unity the existing world may exhibit, the existence of such unity or regularity remains a perfectly contingent matter of fact.

But have we not heard of an ontologically necessary Being, the essence of which involves existence? We have heard of it: and this typically metaphysical contention brings to a head, and exhibits boldly, the equivocation involved in the idea that any truth is necessarily true. The most real of beings, said St. Anselm, necessarily exists: for evidently if it did not exist, far from being most real, it would not be real at all. Is then reality, we may ask, the same as existence? And can existence have degrees? St. Anselm explains that by greater reality he means more than greater quantity of material being: he means also greater dignity, perfection, and moral greatness. Now, a non-existent essence would woefully lack moral greatness, perfection or dignity: it would be a contemptible host, a miserable nothing. Undoubtedly for a care-laden mind seeking salvation—unless it sought salvation from existence—power, which certainly involves existence, must be the first mark of reality and value: what is without power will be without importance. Granting this, the ontological proof is cogent: the most powerful of beings necessarily exists, because power is only another name for the difference which the existence of one thing makes in the existence of another. But a less religious or more practical investigator of power might well come to the conclusion that this greatest, most formidable, and most real of beings was matter, meaning by this not only the substance of interacting things but the principles of their interaction.

The ontological proof ambiguous.

At the other pole of reflection, on the contrary, as among the Indians or the Eleatics, the most real of things might seem to be pure Being, or the realm of essence, excluding change and existence altogether: because in change and existence there is essential privation. That from which we lapse or to which we aspire is no longer or not yet; and in being for the moment something in particular we renounce and reject Being in every other form. The truly ontological proof, for a pure ontologist, would therefore assert, not that the most real of beings necessarily exists, but that the most real of beings necessarily does not exist. In other words, reality would be identified with necessary Being, or essence, and this existing world of limitation, contrariety and care would be pronounced an illusion.

I do not mention this paradox in order to laugh at St. Anselm or at his many solemn disciples, but precisely to show that behind the sophistry of their words there is, or may be, a secret allegiance to pure and necessary Being. Their play on the word reality perhaps masked an instinctive revolt against worldliness, a desire to throw off somehow the incubus of alien facts and irrational compulsions and find a way back into safety and peace. They called pure Being most real because to their hearts it was most satisfying. Consequently their argument was fallacious and even ridiculous, if by "necessary existence" we understand a necessity attaching to events or to facts, that is, to contingencies. Yet the same argument breathes a fervent intuition and a final judgment of the spirit, if it intends rather to deny final validity to an existential order which, by definition, is arbitrary, treacherous, and self-destructive: a realm of being over which inessential relations are compulsory and essential relations are powerless.

The word reality, used eulogistically, may indicate essences rather than facts.

When we are asked to shift the meaning of terms so that, at least in God, essence may involve existence, we are left in doubt as to the direction in which the assimilation is to take place. Are we to idealize existence so that it may be nothing but essence, or to hypostatize essence so as to make it exist? When we speak of being or reality, are we intent on the miracle of existence, and do we pass from that mystery to the conviction that the divine essence is just this miracle, this absolute power, this abysmal fact? Or free from all trouble or wonder, and in placid intellectual clear-ness, do we first demonstrate to ourselves the necessity and infinity of possible being or essence; so that for us the miracle of existence becomes rather a scan-dal? For why should innocent and merely possible being be raised for a moment at this or that point into an insane prominence, impossible to sustain or to justify, whilst all the rest of essence is veiled by a passionate ignorance and proclaimed to be nothing? In the latter case, existence would involve privation, partiality, ignorance, instability, and grotesque pride, with a consequent perpetual misery. Instead of the word existence the ontological argument should then employ the word reality, meaning the fullness and indestructibility—*essential indestructibility*—of being. If we make this substitution, feeling the pregnancy of our terms, we may come to see how the maximum of reality might logically involve infinity, impas-siveness, and eternity: all of which are contrary to the limitation, flux, and crav-ing inherent in existence. No essence, not even this essence of existence, has any power to actualize itself in a fact; nor does such actualization bring to any essence an increment in its logical being; only an alien ambiguous status, no sooner acquired than lost.

Essence and existence contrasted afresh.

The existence of God is therefore not a necessary truth: for if the proposi-tion is necessary, its terms can be only essences; and the word God itself would then designate a definable idea, and would not be a proper name indicating an actual power. If, on the contrary, the word is such a proper name, and God is a psychological moral being energizing in space and time, then his existence can be proved only by the evidence of these natural manifestations, not by dialectical reasoning upon the meanings of terms.

Facts Arbitrary, Logic Ideal

The Realm of Truth: Book Third of Realms of Being. London: Constable and Co. Ltd.;
Toronto: Macmillan Company, 1937; New York: Charles Scribner's Sons, 1938,
11–19. Volume sixteen of the critical edition of *The Works of George Santayana.*

In this selection, Chapter II of The Realm of Truth, *Santayana denied that fact is necessary. The capacity of spirit to contemplate an infinity of essences is the capacity to go beyond
the apparent limitations of material facts in imagination. The infinite Realm of Essence
reveals that there is no limit to the forms matter may embody, and it is the contingency of
the flux of matter that determines which essences are in fact embodied. While there is logical
necessity, it is not truth in Santayana's view, truth being "the complete ideal description
of existence" (ES, 222). Logic traces a system of essences; it expresses truth when in fact
those essences are embodied in matter. It is a mistake to set up logic over the facts of nature:
"Logic is a child of fact, as spirit in general is a child of the psyche" (ES, 221). And just
as spirit enriches the life of the conscious creature so does logic. And like grammar, rhetoric,
and music it "humanizes the world" and can reveal the realm of essence (ES, 223).*

That one philosopher should profess to have proved some metaphysical tenet,
and that another philosopher should profess to have refuted it, might leave the
reader cold. It is not in those regions that he ordinarily feels sure

**Physical
necessity is
conditional
on an order
of nature
itself not
necessary.**
of the truth. Are there no truths obviously necessary to common
sense? If I have mislaid my keys, *mustn't* they be somewhere? If a
child is born, *mustn't* he have had a father? *Must* is a curious word,
pregnant for the satirist: it seems to redouble the certainty of a
fact, while really admitting that the fact is only conjectured. The
necessity asserted foolishly parades the helplessness of the mind
to imagine anything different. Yet this helplessness, on which dogmatism rests, is
shameful, and is secretly felt to be shameful. Spirit was born precisely to escape
such limitations, to see the contingency and finitude of every fact, and to imagine
as many alternatives and extensions as possible, some of which may be true, and
may put that casual fact in its true setting. Truth is groped after, not imposed, by
the presumptions of the intellect: and if these presumptions often are true, the
reason is that they are based upon and adjusted to the actual order of nature,
which is thoroughly unnecessary, and most miraculous when most regular. This
blessed regularity, logically unforeseeable, is indeed the basis of human safety,
wisdom, and science; it teaches us what *must* happen under particular circumstances; but accommodation to the truth in these regions leaves the mind, when
not mechanized, full of wonder at the truth.

The mechanized mind, that cannot wonder at the commonplace, is apt to
carry its mechanical presumptions over into logic, as if necessity there too were
simply truth to fact. A large part of the confidence felt in numerical and geometrical measurements is an emotional confidence. It comes from a sense of

what would surely happen to bodies having those numerical or geometrical properties. We seldom stop to consider narrowly the logical relations between defined essences, as pure mathematics would require us to do; but we rely on common knowledge of the world become in ourselves an irresistible mode of imagination; and this precipitation of ideas in ourselves we call necessity in the object. Anything else would be "impossible": that is to say, impossible for us to *believe*. Interest in fact, or confident judgment about fact, here overcomes or confuses interest in essence. Yet wonder at the commonplace—at the stars or a flower or a word—comes to almost everybody at certain moments: because these things are too improbable in themselves and too inexplicably juxtaposed for a spirit whose natural field is the perspicuous.

Practical certainty mistaken for logical necessity.

A rationalistic reader might still ask: "Is there no truth within your realm of essence? Are not unity and distinctness present in all essences, and is it not true to say so? And all that you yourself have written, here and elsewhere, about essence, is it not true?" No, I reply, it is not true, nor meant to be true. It is a grammatical or possibly a poetical construction having, like mathematics or theology, a certain internal vitality and interest; but in the direction of truth-finding, such constructions are merely instrumental like any language or any telescope. A man may fall into an error in grammar or in calculation. This is a fault in the practice of his art, at bottom a moral defect, a defect in attention, diligence, and capacity: and in my dialectic I have doubtless often clouded my terms with useless or disturbing allusions. But when consistently and conscientiously worked out and stripped to their fighting weight, my propositions will be logically necessary, being deducible from the definitions or intuitions of the chosen terms, and especially of this chosen term "essence" itself. But logic is only logic: and the systems of relation discoverable amongst essences do not constitute truths, but only other more comprehensive essences, within which the related essences figure as parts. The systems, like the logical elements, become a means of expressing truth only when truth can be otherwise discovered and brought face to face with our deductive reasonings. Truth will then domesticate our logic in the world: until perhaps the dialectical guest so hospitably received forgets his essential foreignness and undertakes to drive the poor native facts out of house and home. Our idealisms, in their moral autonomy, can hardly abstain from claiming a divine right to govern the world, to correct it, or at least to scold it for being so unaccountably wrong. And far from right the world indeed is, and must be, judged by human interests and even by human logic, because man and his moral aspirations are only incidents in the universe; but there is one ideal measure that the actual world cannot fall short of: it cannot be far from true.

Correctness or error within logic a question of art, not of truth.

This truth, if the world had been chaotic, might have excluded the existence of mind altogether, or kept mind down to the sensuous level; but there was a partial rationality or promise of rationality in things that encouraged the mind to clarify its ideas, and to develop logic. Logic is a child of fact, as spirit in general is a child of the psyche: a headstrong child quick to forget or deny the sweet milk that has nurtured it; yet the bond with earth remains notwithstanding. It remains not only in the past, fundamentally determining the choice of essences that logic shall play with, but it remains also contemporaneously, in that even the logician's thoughts are controlled at every turn by physical accidents and social pressure. It is important to distinguish this nether contact of logic with fact in the biological genetic direction, from the ideal contact established or rather claimed, when logic is used to express or to extend natural knowledge. Biological contact exists also between vital facts and music; it exists between vital facts and illusions, errors, or myths; but music luckily is not expected (until it is coined into language) to convey *knowledge* of facts. That is the secret of its magnificent development: the life of music is free from everything except its natural sources, from everything except the biological impulses and multiple harmonies internal to the organism. Sight and touch, on the contrary, though no less sensuous, animal and subjective than sound, are more readily and completely caught up by the cognitive impulse, and idolatrously treated as *true:* exactly how literally or consistently, it would be endless to trace.

Double contact of logic with fact.

By the truth, as the reader knows, I understand the complete ideal description of existence; and any part of this description will be a truth, that is, a part of the truth. The ideal complete description of an essence, on the contrary, or of the relations between essences, unless this description is rehearsed psychologically by some living mind, is simply that very essence and those very relations: it can be neither false nor true, but only articulate. And the realm of essence being infinite and omnimodal, any other description of any other essence, or relations between essences, would be equally articulate up to its own degree of elaboration; so that there would be nothing to choose, in the way of truth, between any two descriptions.

In respect to essences, all definitions are equally valid, since each selects the essence which it defines.

This insight removes a problem sometimes needlessly proposed about the choice of definitions, for instance in the case of number or numbers. Mathematicians are unanimous and clear on the point that $2 + 2 = 4$; but they are obscure and divided as to the nature of 2 and of 1, of + and of =. And we are allowed to infer that there is a *true* nature of = and +, of 1 and of 2. But that, in logic, is nonsense. Each of these essences is whatever it is by *any* definition: the rest is merely a question of names, perhaps pre-empted by custom to some one definition rather than to another. Essentially, all conceivable natures and definitions are on a par: the only question is historical and psychological, regarding the prevalence of particular notions in the human mind, or else physical, as to the applicability of these notions to the cosmos. In both directions, obscurity is inevitable, and differences of opinion, if modest, are legitimate. It may be expedient to limit the interpretation of mathematical signs to particular humanly chosen ideas: but other interpretations, perhaps less fertile or useful, would not be essentially less cogent. Truth, then, never enters the field of mathematics at all; and there is no *true* view about the nature of number or numbers, until the discussion veers from mathematics altogether, to physics, history or psychology.

From this it follows that we may intelligently adopt and apply the category of truth to current perceptions and opinions, inasmuch as they profess to be knowledge and are asserted of positive facts: but when, in reflection, we make some supposition deliberately contrary to fact, the relevance of truth to that supposition is exhausted before we begin to develop it. The supposition is admittedly false; and in considering it further we are exploring the relations it may have in the realm of essence only, where questions of truth do not arise. Romantic people think of what might have been: some danger narrowly escaped, some bet almost won: possibilities near enough to the truth to seem false, and perhaps bitter. In this moodiness we may say that the poets lie: but the poets did not lie, they were inspired. Their suppositions were contrary to fact only by accident, and quite apart from their innocent intention. No doubt common waking perception is truer than poetry, and the poets in their sane moments will not deny it: but inspiration liberates them from that interest. The crucial point is this: that not only are all particular truths and facts contingent, but the very categories of fact and truth, like all other essences, if they are exemplified at all, are exemplified unnecessarily and by a groundless chance.

Logic, when once its foothold in fact has been secured at any point, has a moral part to play, and this in two directions. It humanizes the world, since we now can think and reason about it with some relevance; and it vivifies speculation, by allying the furthest reaches of it with real life. Logic traces the radiation of truth: I mean that when one term of a logical system is known to describe a fact, the whole system **Contact with truth adds moral value to logic.** attachable to that term becomes, as it were, incandescent, and forms a part of the aura of truth. The terms of logic are themselves originally glimpses of facts: we deepen this apprehension humanly and morally when we develop ideally the qualities which a fact truly wears either in itself or in relation to human faculties and interests; as a poet deepens his sense of beauty, if one beauty in his mind recalls another, and he finds metaphors and musical words that may re-echo his passion. But we may also deepen our apprehension by buttressing it with apprehensions of kindred or neighbouring facts, which though interlopers in that argument, support it by analogy or qualify its value. Here is where allusions, logically redundant, may help to brighten the faint rays of truth still colouring high speculation. Between the branchings of our logic, that spread aloft forgetful of the truth in which, after all, they are remotely rooted, we may catch fresh glimpses of earth and sky, and so gain, as we go, circumstantial support or correction for our deductions.

Thus grammar, rhetoric, and logic enrich enormously the phenomenon of being alive. They embroider every image with a thousand latent analogies and concordant rhymes; and they enshrine this image in the ideal world to which, after all, every image belongs. Because the truth or applicability of ideas, as of words, though it may be the chief or only **And lends it a tragic force.** source of their importance, is irrelevant to their sensuous or intrinsic character: so that when an idea, weighted with the dignity of truth, is lifted out again from the alien context and accidental occasion which allied it with fact, that idea seems to be clarified and to sing hallelujah; for it finds itself free at last to be itself, and to trace its internal affinities in its native element. Nor is this merely a sensual or logical holiday for the mind: it is a holiday or holy day also in a religious sense; because weighted with truth as the idea now is, it drags, as it were, the whole workaday world with it into the light. The world which was but a too familiar fact suddenly becomes beautiful: and at the same time the idea, only a graphic pattern before, now touches the heart and becomes poetical.

Finally, turning the doctrine here defended against itself, we might ask whether it is not necessarily true that the truth is contingent and not necessary. Here again

My own logic, even if made cogent, not therefore true. I must repeat that what is necessary logically is not necessarily *true*. In this case, that truth is contingent is a necessary proposition, because facts, by definition, make the truth true and all facts, again by definition, are contingent. But there is no necessity in the choice or in the applicability of such categories as necessity, truth, or fact. These categories are not necessarily true. I find that, as a matter of fact, they are true, or at least true enough: they articulate human thought in a normal way which reality on the whole seems to sanction. They are the lungs and heart-valves of the mind. And while we use these categories, we shall be obliged on pain of talking nonsense to stick to their connotations, and to acknowledge, among other things, that there are no necessary truths. But the possession of such categories is after all a psychological or even a personal accident; and the fact that they are convenient, or even absolutely true in describing the existing world, is a cosmic accident.

The thesis of the first chapter, then, that there are no necessary truths, is itself made necessary only by virtue of certain assumed intuitions or definitions which

It is true only in so far as it is applicable. fix the meaning of terms necessity, contingency, existence, and truth. But no definition and no intuition can render true the term that it distinguishes. My thesis will therefore be a true thesis only in so far as in the realm of existence facts may justify my definitions and may hang together in the way that those definitions require. The case is the same in principle as in the homely equation, $2 + 2 = 4$; only that in arithmetic the terms are simpler and more familiar, so that the necessary relation between them is obvious to more people. It happens at the same time that the application of arithmetic, where it applies, is most constant and exact, so that its truth in those regions is beyond doubt; whereas any general logic applied to describing the universe, however ancient and well tried this logic may be, remains rather a form of human grammar. We are in a region of free intuition and construction, as in music, with no claims to propounding a revealed or a revealing truth.

Interplay between Truth and Logic

The Realm of Truth: Book Third of Realms of Being. London: Constable and Co. Ltd.; Toronto: Macmillan Company, 1937; New York: Charles Scribner's Sons, 1938, 20–30. Volume sixteen of the critical edition of *The Works of George Santayana.*

In this selection, Chapter III of The Realm of Truth, *Santayana explained how logic might be called true. He was concerned to defend both truth and logic against idealistic philosophy that would set up logic, a system of essences, in the place of truth, which Santayana regarded as the complete record of existence. Logic could be called true when it was the analysis of the implications of some truth. But because actual analysis often drifts from the truth, one must be on guard against idealism usurping the name of logical truth for this wandering dialectic. Santayana preferred to acknowledge the irrationality of existence and the limitation of human intuition. Logic and truth can be preserved and the critic avoids the fallacies of blaming discourse for human infidelity to ideas and of exporting human uncertainty and uneasiness to the material realm.*

Having laid down this distinction between logic and truth, and shown that truth, as I define it, is wholly contingent, I have no desire to quarrel with mankind for using words as they choose, and talking of truth also in cases where there is only consistency. There is much truth, even in my sense, possible in respect to ideas: not only psychological and historical truth, in describing the ideas that may have actually arisen in the human mind, but also formal truth in the description of an accepted idea in terms different from those in which it was couched at first; a change in expression which may serve to analyse that idea and bring out its essential affinities. Mathematics, logic, and a certain kind of psychology may thus create a phenomenological science; that is, a faithful description of some field of essence already selected and duly named; and we must allow that, at least according to the genius of the English language, whatever is faithful and trusty may be called true.

There is a kind of truth internal to discourse, depending on fidelity.

This idiomatic use of the word true is semi-moral. It turns on not belying one's professions and being constant to a plighted troth. Serious thought requires this sort of fidelity. We begin by noticing and liking some idea, and the very earnestness of our attention becomes a pledge in our own minds not to drop that idea, nor adulterously to slip another idea in its place. Truth—truth to it and to ourselves—now demands that we make it clearer and clearer, more and more unmistakable; and perhaps, by an illusion not unknown to lovers, we attribute to our first intuition a prophetic force, as if it had irresistibly predestined us to these later developments. But ideas, if by ideas we mean essences and not impressions, are as Berkeley termed them, inert. They do not compose a world but a vocabulary: and their logical relations, though immutable, have no aggressive force compelling us to notice them. We evoke ideas for a moment of our own motion; and they vanish like sounds and shadows, without leaving a trace. Thus if our intuition had been careless and not vitally rooted, the essence evoked in passing would never have been retained or recovered adequately in a second intuition. Its fleeting definiteness for sense would never have become an express definition for thought. In dismissing and forgetting that image we should then be committing no infidelity. Obviously we could never falsify our old ideas if we never thought of them again.

This drift of ideation, however, which would be innocent if it were purely sensuous, may invade dialectic and explicit recollection, becoming a perpetual fountain of sophistry. Each time we mention a word we may give it a different meaning, and the more we shift and vary, the deeper we may think we go. We lie, either idly or maliciously, when we allow invention to transform our memories; and we contradict ourselves if we allow invention or the flux of accidental thought to vitiate the sense of our original terms. Dialectic then becomes, as in Hegel, a romantic alternation of ideal or moral impulses. Infidelity to one's thoughts is here felt to be truth to one's deeper self and to one's destiny; and it may really be so when the thin pretence to logic covers a shrewd perception of the instability of life. For there are mental reservations and insincerities hiding in our explicit assertions, treasons latent in our promises, and unforeseen social currents destined to carry our thoughts suddenly in new directions. All this may make excellent dramatic history or phenomenology of morals; and if it seems to skirt dangerously a Mephistophelean abyss of mockery and biting scorn, it may be rendered unexpectedly edifying by the assurance that our dead selves are stepping-stones to higher things, that the sum of illusions is the only truth, and that a sufficient experience of folly produces wisdom, not by repentance, but by approximation. Yet even supposing that this romantic idealism truly represented the facts, in calling this description of the facts logic we should be turning the irony of logic upon logic itself; and dialectic, far from developing faithfully the implications of ideas, would glorify the infidelities of things to those ideas.

> **Infidelity to a first meaning is sometimes called dialectic, and may adjust ideas to facts.**

Whether glorious or feeble these infidelities are inevitable, since things are in flux and ideas, in the logical sense, are unchangeable. Moreover, there is necessarily some novel idea or pattern illustrated in the flux itself, and a special trope in each turn of affairs; so that the truth of history perpetually gives the lie to the maxims of men, and defeats their politics and ambition. Yet looked at from outside, with the wisdom that comes after the fact, people's actions may seem to the historian to have been directed upon the ends actually achieved; whereas in fact the result was unintended and probably unforeseen; though it is easier to foresee the future than to command it, and only those seem to command it who pre-figure it with enthusiasm. Infinitely deeper than the logic of our thoughts is the fertility of our destiny; and circumstances keep us alive by continually defeating us. In strictness no man ever succeeds: the only question is whether he shall be defeated by the action of others or by his own action.

> **History laughs at politics.**

The notion that history might be dialectical would hardly have seemed plausible to anybody, had not dialectic been conceived in a satirical sense; as when each speaker in a dialogue refutes the others, and the argument ends in the refutation of everybody. The author in such a case speaks for nature, and laughs at opinions. If he is candid he even laughs at his own opinion, and what he exhibits in his dialectic is not logic triumphant but logic losing itself in the sea of fact.

Nor is captious disputation requisite to this end. So long as logic is not thoroughly purified and abstracted, but is applied to things, a man's most honest ideas may issue in the same contrariety. Existence is once for all irrational and cannot be wholly elucidated in terms of essence. **Ontological divergence between logic and fact.** And since, at the same time, it is only in terms of essence that facts can be described, partiality and instability beset all description. If a thing is small, it is also large, compared with something smaller. If it is good, it is also bad; if true also false. Nor does this hold only of relatives. If a thing has being, or definite character, it also lacks being, because in being what it is it rejects and banishes all that it is not, so that all positive wealth is shadowed by privation.

This famous union of opposites, philosophers being naturally rapt in the excitement of assertion and not having time to be quite honest, gives rise to no less famous fallacies. A first fallacy is this: that the relativity and self-disruption found in the description of facts is transferred to the terms of the description, that is, to the essences confronting each other there. But these essences have no inherent ambiguity or tendency to pass into their opposites. **The union of contraries in things imports no contradiction into essences.** Large has no proclivity to mean small, good to mean bad, or true false, or wealth privation, or being not-being. If each of these essences could alienate its character, they could not remain terms in consistent assertions; they could not be so much as compared or opposed, and all discourse and perception would sink into black night. It is only in describing half-hidden, complex, substantial facts that ambiguities and contradictions appear; for here essences essentially different (since each is invincibly itself) are found alternately or simultaneously present. Were the essences not still different and absolutely fixed in character, there would be no problem in their co-presence, and no dialectic: only a flow of indistinguishables, if so much as a flow could be distinguished.

It may be noted in passing that essences are not intrinsically predicates or adjectives, but primordial and distinct forms of possible being. They become predicates or adjectives when an animal psyche apprehending them is vitally preoccupied with the pressure of matter, and with reacting upon that pressure; so that the given essences are taken for portions or qualities of the dynamic fact by which the psyche is **The nature of pure Being recalled.** confronted. Save for that material preoccupation, the spirit would regard the essences evoked before it in their intrinsic characters as the adequate furniture of life for the moment, like an eagle in repose observing the sun. Moreover, pure Being is not a substance in which individual essences inhere, so that the essences might be predicates of it. Pure Being is itself only an essence. Expressly, it is that which all essences have in common—namely, character or distinguishableness and self-identity; but pregnantly, pure Being covers the whole realm of essence or the sum of all essences, since all essences are needed to display fully all that is self-identical and distinguishable, and that has being or character.

A second fallacy incidental to the dialectic of opposites suggests a superstitious origin. Contradiction (which exists only in human language describing facts that in themselves cannot be contradictory) is transferred to the facts themselves, as if a moral uneasiness existed in them compelling them to shift their ground. Heraclitus seems to have hinted at something of the sort, in his oracular fashion: we learn that war is the parent of all things, and that justice or punishment condemns everything definite to destruction, as if it were a sin to be finite. In Hegel the same pantheistic sentiment was doubtless reinforced by intimate acquaintance with self-contradiction and self-dissolution in Protestant theology. Here sometimes there may really have been an uneasy conscience and a conflict of contrary feelings driving the mind to the next stage of enlightenment, and from that stage on. Yet the progress of dialectic even in this field, where there was a primary contradiction between tradition and enquiry, has suffered many reversals and has taken a long time. Not the logic of the beliefs, but the ripeness of society or of private sentiment for a change of view has determined the direction of reform and the halting-places of opinion. In general, it is fabulous to represent phenomenology, or the drama of ideas, as the motive force in history. Phenomena are inert results, æsthetic figments: while the derivation of event from event is a natural flow, with crises and cataclysms here and there, but for the most part lapsing with a serene monotony and a tireless self-repetition. This steady underlying vortex of nature keeps mankind alive and keeps it human: which does not prevent civilizations and empires from rising and falling, not always by mutual conflict or direct succession, but often by some local accretion of martial and social energy, vegetating spontaneously, as the Greeks and the Romans vegetated, and sucking their neighbours up into their more vigorous organism, not at all by dialectic. Nor is it dialectic, or any new idea, that commonly destroys the victor in his turn; ruin comes by the dissolution of his fighting organization and the changed habits that his very victory leads him to form. We may personify these habits in a miracle play, and show how virtues and vices rule the destinies of nations. Heraclitus had said so too: every man's character is his dæmon, presiding over his fate. And this interplay of the causes of life and death we may call, if we like, the dialectic of existence.

In Hegel's miracle play there are indeed many stretches of genuine logic, where he dissects the meanings of given ideas. Such analysis clarifies its own terms, and no cataclysms of nature or opinion can annul the validity of the deductions made from those terms logically. Whether the deduction is logical or empirical and arbitrary can be tested by this circumstance: that true analysis leaves the original idea whole and uncontaminated, in the centre of all the radiating ideas that may be brought to surround it: whereas in a psychological flux, as in a dream, additions transform

(marginal note:) Natural instability represented mythically as logical contradiction.

(marginal note:) Logic, sophistry and truth in Hegel's dialectic.

the original datum, identifications are fallacious, progress is made through oblivion, and the whole torrent is lost in sand. Yet as the sand itself is a quicksand, and moves, the romantic historian sees nothing tragic in the evaporation of his original stream: there will always be something on foot to undergo interesting transformations. Hegel's attention was accordingly not long arrested on pure analysis. Analysis served chiefly to loosen ideas, and open some breach for destructive criticism. The point was to produce a pregnant confusion in which the logician might drop the thread of his argument and pick up some contrary fact. The air of this dialectic is thick with the fumes of earth; this makes its strength and its charm; and such a picture of mutation, by its very homeliness and allegiance to truth, confirms my contention that truth and logical necessity are independent things.

Pleasant as well as tragic is the perpetual excitement of finding that which there was no reason to expect. If our prudence is discouraged, our vitality is stimulated; and existence, for the romantic soul, becomes a Gothic marvel, infinitely extensible in quality and quantity, unmapped and incalculable. If any eternal fitness seems nevertheless attributable to the course of things, this fitness will lie entirely in an occasional æsthetic or religious emotion arising during the process itself. **Romantic chaos.**

The taste for chaos, however, is hardly normal, because even in the act of demanding chaos the mind throws out a postulate that, by a secret necessity, this chaos shall never lapse into order. And what assurance can the empirical observer or pure experimenter possess that the indetermination he observes is not specious, and due to the superficial external cognizance which he takes of events? Might there not be a rationality in them hidden from his eyes? And, indeed, it is almost inevitable that, among events which interest him and remain in his memory, there should exist some mutual relevance. Every event, though unnecessary and spontaneous, will probably be pertinent to what went before, as each fresh episode in a serial story, unexpected as it may be to the reader, must somehow be grafted upon the previous characters and episodes. Even to break in and interrupt an experience, events must have a certain dramatic continuity, and fall into a temporal and moral order in the mind that records them. This psychological compulsion soon generates superstitions and prophecies about the secretly meaningful and fatal order of events; and the supposed paths of destiny are explored with as much intellectual ardour and foretaste of truth as were ever the laws of nature. **Any view of reality when taken to be true becomes imposing.**

Cognitive ambition, on the physical side, is inherent in hunting and fighting; and on the spiritual side and for reflection it involves something like a taste for truth. To be deceived is as hateful to the mind as it is dangerous to the body. Impatience and vanity, however, at once intervene; so that it is not facts so much that dominate human knowledge, in its sweep and intensity, as imagination that lends importance and felt reality to alleged facts. Impetuous thought is then led to claim a double truth: one sort of truth legitimately, truth to inspiration; and another sort of truth abusively, truth to fact. The vital and moral heat inseparable from thinking thus often ren- **Natural origin of dogmatism.**

ders logic dogmatic, and seduces it from its ideal cogency to posing as material truth. The mathematician has this justification, that his original data are simple and true. They have been tested and clarified in daily life from time immemorial; so that his speculative superstructure has a certain diminishing affinity or relevance to material truth, apart from its logical validity. Yet the glory of his science does not reside, for him, in that link with contingent fact, but rather in a certain almost humorous compulsiveness in its logical development: whence its reputation for certitude (not merited in the higher reaches of his speculation) which can make it, even for an empiricist like Locke, the ideal of knowledge.

Here, however, the pride of mathematics, like that of theology, comes before a fall. There is no end of science, no end of learning, in both pursuits; but mathematics, like theology, is not knowledge of anything but itself. *True* knowledge, *natural* knowledge, should be the cognizance that one existing thing takes of another; and this perforce is a form of faith, though justified in continual physical contacts between the knower and the known: whereas mathematics and theology trace ideal relations for their own sake and end in the air.

The bad repute into which logic fell at the Renaissance, for being tautological, might at any moment overtake mathematics, were it not for the utility of mathematics in the applied arts. For in themselves the higher mathematics, in spite of their exactitude, or because of it, have not the direct savour of truth. They are scholastic, they are almost occult; and the hearty shrewd lover of truth distrusts such acrobatic marvels. What he trusts is experiment, exploration, and the warm immediacy of action and passion in his own person; he would like to laugh at all abstract speculation as the most ridiculous of shams. And he would be right in laughing, if logic or mathematics pretended to truth: but that is a claim foisted on them by the dogmatism of common perception, contrary to their proper genius. It is like the claim to truth or utility foisted by pedagogues on the fine arts. Philosophy has too long been pedagogical, and the best schooldays are half-holidays. If liberty has opened a window for us towards the infinite realm of essence, it has not authorized us to regard the prospect visible to us there as the truth about nature. Much less are we authorized to set up our visions as moral standards to which things ought to conform. The order of subordination is the opposite one. Nature being what she is, and we being in consequence what we are, certain special reaches of essence are obvious to our senses and intellect. Sights and sounds, pains and pleasures assail us; and our leisure is free to develop in music and language, in mathematics and religion, the moral burden of our animal existence. Nor will this play of ideas be sheer truancy. Our toys may become instruments, our sensations signs; and a part of the truth about nature and about ourselves will be necessarily revealed to us, directly or indirectly, by the mere existence and sequence of those apparitions. Directly, in emotion, perception, and dramatic sympathy, we may learn to know the human world, the world of images, morals, and literature: and indirectly, in close connection with the flow of sensation, we may learn to posit permanent objects and to pick our way among them to good purpose, as a child finds his way home.

> **Logic, when turned into metaphysics, spoils both physics and logic.**

Dramatic Truth

The Realm of Truth: Book Third of Realms of Being. London: Constable and Co. Ltd.;
Toronto: Macmillan Company, 1937; New York: Charles Scribner's Sons, 1938,
59–66. Volume sixteen of the critical edition of *The Works of George Santayana.*

This selection, Chapter VII of The Realm of Truth, *makes a place for myth and drama
in the Realm of Truth. While the flux of matter is not itself dramatic, it can be read in
dramatic terms when intuition is directed by passion. Passion is a material force often running deeper than consciousness of it. Dramatic readings of existence may distort facts, but
they express something about the forces guiding human action and experience. Dramatic
enlightenment of this sort could be wearying with its partialities and bias, but without dramatic intuition thought would be paralyzed and lack direction. To eliminate the passions
that give rise to mythical or dramatic readings of nature would yield an echo or index, "a
part of the world" rather than "a part of the truth about the world" (ES, 234). In other
words, such a report would mirror existence but exclude mind or spirit. Mind is born out
of the the exemplification of essence in matter, that is, out of the being of truth; but truth is
discoverable only by mind. And some material passion must direct intuition toward truth.*

The dramatic moral climate in which our lives are passed is not other than the
climate of matter but only a passionate experience of the same. Society does not
present two separable worlds, one the world of men's bodies and
another less earthly one, that of men's minds. A world of mere
minds, a heaven with its legions of invisible and bodiless angels, if
conceived at all, exacts no belief from the sceptic. I am as far as
possible a sceptic, and a world of that sort does not figure in my
philosophy. On the other hand, a world of mindless automata, like
the *bêtes-machines* of Descartes, is a violently artificial object, con-

> **Moral
> dimensions
> found in the
> world are
> readings of
> matter in
> dramatic
> terms.**

ceived in purely mathematical and mechanical terms, although the terms in
which that object is actually perceived are primarily sensuous and dramatic. The
object is a body with the motions perceived or expected in that body; but these
bodies do more than amuse the eye. Some are noxious or wild beasts; some are
members of your own family. They suckle or hit you; and you know them apart
by their works before you distinguish them clearly by their aspect. Even the most
crudely physical forces wear a dramatic aspect when their action is violent, or for
any reason arouses violent emotion. Spirit in us then rises or falls; and the cause
is felt to be the action of spirits and gods: mythical beings not added fancifully to
physical beings clearly conceived to be physical, but moral energies recognized
as the very core and secret of the material facts. That souls exist and that they
move bodies is indeed the primary form in which any sensitive soul will conceive
the forces of nature.

A soul, a dramatic centre of action and passion, is utterly unlike what in modern philosophy we call consciousness. The soul causes the body to grow, to

assume its ancestral shape, to develop all its ancestral instincts, to wake and to sleep by turns. The soul determines what images shall arise in the mind and what emotions, and at the same time determines the responses that the living body shall make to the world. Consciousness is only an inner light kindled in the soul during these vicissitudes, a music, strident or sweet, made by the friction of existence. With this light and music, purified and enlarged, fancy has peopled heaven; but on earth the course of consciousness is helplessly distracted: a miscellany of conventional half-thoughts and evanescent images. A sympathetic intuition of such actual consciousness in another person often comes by imitation or by unison in action. When caught in a common predicament, we involuntarily understand one another. Each feels what everybody else is feeling; and the same thing happens, less voluminously, in ordinary conversation. Such mutual understanding is not in itself dramatic, though the occasion of it may be so; it is neighbourly, attentive, playful, as when we understand a child, a comrade, or an author. Spirit is essentially disinterested, even in tracing the fortunes of spirit. But when physical contagion ceases and this brotherly spell is broken, we remain as profoundly ignorant of the fountains of life in others as in ourselves. The volatile spirit which was ours for a moment is fled we know not where. Hence in consecutive politics or economics the experts are quite blind, lost in a labyrinth of facts not understood, and appalled at the insidious transformation of these avowed motives and ideas by which action was supposed to be guided.

The actual flux of events, either in nature or consciousness, is not dramatic.

Dramatic intuition, on the contrary, springs from the passions, that is to say, from the principles of action. A man may be conscious of his passion, in that he feels strangely agitated and is affected by everything in a strange way. But the passion itself is a force, a physical automatism let loose within him, and altogether other and deeper than his consciousness of it. If he attempts to put it into words, or to conceive its proper nature, he is driven to dramatic fictions in one sense more remote from actual passion than were his inarticulate feelings or hot words: he is driven to myth or to dialectic. In a fable, or in a logical trope, he imaginatively draws the outline and traces the movement of that mysterious influence which troubles him; and the truth facing his passion, as he is best able to conceive it, is a dramatic truth.

The dramatic sense depicts not consciousness elsewhere, but tropes affecting one's own passions.

Here all is expectation, partiality, superstition, hyperbole, rage, and enthusiasm. The accuracy possible in prosaic literary psychology is sacrificed to a summary eloquence. Yet not without compensation in the direction of truth. Dramatic genius can afford to be unfair to the surface facts, to foreshorten, crowd, and caricature everything. It is not interested in accompaniments, however real in themselves, which it finds irrelevant; it is not interested in justice; it is interested only in great issues, and in the secret tendencies that may be making for the ultimate triumph or defeat of one's own soul. If the facts are to be dramatized, they must not be reproduced. They must be recast selectively on a grand scale, and precipitated towards some climax in which the heart is concerned.

Yet if they are to be truly dramatic, these relations must not be invented. They must subsist in the realm of truth. Intuition simply comes to disengage them from what is morally irrelevant, and to trace the red vein of destiny running through the world.

Dramatic intuition, or apt myth, has many forms or stages, from animism to dialectic and wit, from superstition to natural law. These intellectual unities may be true of the world without being parts of it. Every trope discerned in nature, every self-repeating movement, assumes a vital unity in the mind. Whatever happens, when it elicits a living idea, seems to have happened with a purpose. This illusion is normal and even a sign of intellectual force, because the first phase of any trope, when that trope has once been noticed and *Mythical units may express important movements otherwise untraceable.* has taken root in the psyche, comes essentially as merely the beginning of what ought to follow, and a sure omen of the total movement to come. So the first part of a sentence, especially in an inflected language, can hardly appear without prophetic reference to the remainder. In nature, however, any trope may be cut short. It is not a power, as intellectual superstition may fancy, but only a customary rhythm established contingently and subject to interference from every quarter, until it finally becomes unrecognizable or vanishes altogether. Yet so long as it subsists, it describes as well as is humanly possible a whole obscure region of nature from the point of view of some soul. Dramatic fiction may thus reveal to us the gist of existence, as flat experience and prosaic observation could never do.

That which lifts dramatic perception above mere poetry or fiction is its moral origin and its practical sanction. Taken for cool descriptions of the facts, what would the myths of Freud be, or the dialectics of Hegel and Marx, except grotesque fancies? But there is method in this madness. Freud is an alienist, a healer of souls, Hegel fundamentally a theologian, Marx a revolutionary. Each studies a practical momentous problem, how to restore health and sanity, or justify a progressive worldly religion, or provoke and guide a social upheaval. They review the history of their moral problem in its own fantastic terms. They seek to understand and to govern passion by passion. In such treatment—for it is a treatment—the total cosmic truth must be denied or left in the shadow. Instead we have a sort of war-map in which nothing is set down but what touches the campaign of the season. Yet even so, the perspectives opened up may be infinite, since everything in the world touches everything else at a certain remove and at a certain angle; and we may be dramatically enlightened, in the service of our passions, whilst perhaps by these passions themselves we are being intellectually deceived.

The enormous infusion of error that sense, passion, and language bring with them into human knowledge is therefore less misleading than might be supposed. Knowledge is not truth, but a view or expression of the truth; a glimpse of it secured by some animal with special organs under special circumstances. A lover of paradox might say that to be *Error itself a true index to its causes.* partly wrong is a condition of being partly right; or more soberly, that to be partial is, for knowledge, a condition of existing at all. To be partial and also to be relative: so that all the sensuous colour and local perspective proper to human views, and all the moral bias pervading them, far from rendering knowledge impossible, supply instruments for exploration, divers sensitive centres and divers inks, whereby in divers ways the facts may be recorded.

A radical instance of dramatic truth appears in sentimental time. Time is not *in truth* sentimental: the past is not fading, the future is not empty or unreal; and when a man is moral and rational he recognizes the intrinsic reality and importance of both those regions, vitally so obscure and intangible. Yet if he could be absolutely rational and moral, if his mind could possess impartially all the past and all the future, he would be dead, he would be deified, he would have become motionless and eternal like the truth itself. The forward direction of his thought and the backward vista of his memory would be neutralized. He would be omnipresent; and this intimate identity of his mind with all possible knowledge would make experience, in any tentative progressive sense, impossible for him. And unless he somehow removed himself from the whole reality of himself and held it at arm's length, even the eternal and complete truth of it would elude him: because he would be that totality, and could not survey it. So the irrational finitude and bias of animal life, far from denying us the truth, summons us to pursue the truth, and gives us, in some measure, the means of attaining it.

Dramatic element inherent in knowledge.

I know how irritating constantly superstitious, rhetorical, moralistic views can be to the truth-lover; yet we must give the devil his due, and consider the consequences of refusing to think humanly when we are human. Thought itself would have to be abandoned in favour of mechanical notation of details. Such notation, in chronicles, statistics and pointer-readings, would not enter the realm of truth at all, if a certain selection and synthesis did not preside over the record: it would otherwise not be descriptive, as truth is, but merely a concomitant echo or mechanical index to certain features in the world; a part of the world, then, and not a part of the truth about the world. To this, indeed, a certain positivistic and ultra-empirical philosophy professes to reduce science, replacing science in act, which is a category of spirit, with the instrumentalities or procedure of science, which lie in the realm of matter. Here, out of respect for the truth, we have an attempt on the part of mind to suppress mind; but although the truth is ontologically no more mental than physical, it is a form, an essence, that intelligence may find in an object, or in a system of objects, and by no means of part or member of that existential reality. Truth is therefore something that only mind can detach, something, as it were, addressed essentially to mind; although in the order of genesis it is the being of truth, the fact that facts exemplify essences and have relations, that makes it possible and appropriate that animals should develop minds: that is, should become aware not only of their organic processes expressed in blind feeling, but should become aware also of the causes or the objects of those feelings, and discover some part of the truth about them.

Foolish effort to eliminate it.

Truth is therefore not discoverable at all without some vital moral impulse prompting to survey it, and some rhetorical or grammatical faculty, synthesizing that survey and holding it up to attention in the form of a recognizable essence. Dramatic myth, however poetical it may be or merely analogous to the facts, in that at least it responds to the facts reflectively, has entered the arena of truth; it is more cognitive, more intelligent, and more useful than a mechanical record of those facts without any moral synthesis. I think it very doubtful whether, if religion and poetry should dry up altogether, mankind would be nearer the truth; or whether science would gain anything by correcting its philosophical pretensions, for instance the pretension to truth, in order to become merely the technology of the mechanical arts. Certainly nothing would be gained intellectually: and if we condemned intelligence, as well as imagination, to ticking like a clock, if not to total silence, we might outrage human nature too deeply, and provoke a violent reaction. It is more prudent for the critic of illusion to consider the truth that myth may possess rather than to attempt to escape from myth altogether.

Affinity of mind to truth.

Sanity requires spirit to practise a certain duplicity, and continually to correct its necessary language by a no less necessary mental reservation. We live in this human scene as in a theatre, where an adult mind never loses itself so completely in the play as to forget that the play is a fiction; and he judges it, not for what it pretends to present, but for the stimulus and scope of the presentation. So in the whole verbal, sensuous, and moral medium through which we see the world we may learn not to see the world falsely but to see ourselves truly, and the world in its true relation to ourselves. With this proviso, all the humorous and picturesque aspects of experience may be restored to the world with dramatic truth. The near is truly near, when the station of the speaker is tacitly accepted as the point of reference. The good is truly good, the foreign truly foreign, if the absoluteness of the judgment is made relative to the judge. And this judge is no vagrant pure spirit. He is a man, an animal, a fragment of the material world; and he can no more annul or reverse his hereditary nature, in reference to which things are truly foreign or good, than he can annul the external forces playing upon his organism. Thus in reporting his passionate judgments, as if they were self-justified and obligatory, the dogmatist is unwittingly reporting a truth of natural history—namely, that at that juncture such judgments on his part are normal indexes to the state of the world, and not the least interesting element in it.

This dramatic medium is itself knowable and good.

Moral Truth

The Realm of Truth: Book Third of Realms of Being. London: Constable and Co. Ltd.;
Toronto: Macmillan Company, 1937; New York: Charles Scribner's Sons, 1938,
67–78. Volume sixteen of the critical edition of *The Works of George Santayana.*

In this selection, Chapter VIII of The Realm of Truth, *Santayana considered the specifically moral passions and how they might lead to the expression of truth. Moral passion, the
feeling or impulse that gives rise to preference, directs moral judgment. Such judgments are
true insofar as they answer to the vital impulses of the one making the judgments. Hence,
moral truth is the sincere expression of preferences and a reflection of perfect self-knowledge.
Santayana denied that true morality extended beyond the one making the moral judgments.
He believed in good and evil, but he also acknowledged the existence of genuine moral
conflict in which sincere parties may make true moral judgments about what is good and
yet not agree.*

Moral ideas are usually hybrid. On the one hand, they may contain truth about
matters of fact, such as that arsenic is poison, or that a man with more than the
desired courage will be called rash, and with less, a coward. On
the other hand, in recording these facts the moralist probably
adopts and asserts in his own person the preference implied in
those eulogistic or disparaging terms. He takes for granted that life
is a good, that the approved degree of courage is a virtue, and that
cowardice or rashness is a vice. He thus insinuates, as if self-evident, a moral
judgment into his historical or psychological observations; and the possible truth
of the latter may seem to him to support the truth of the former. But the nerve of
moral judgment is preference: and preference is a feeling or an impulse to action
which cannot be either false or true.

> **Confusion
> between
> ethical truth
> and moral
> preference.**

It might conduce to clearness in this subject if we limited the term *morality* to
actual allegiance in sentiment and action to this or that ideal of life; while the history of such allegiances, and of the circumstances and effects involved, would form
a descriptive science to be called ethics or the science of manners. Truth in ethics
would then be like truth in any other part of natural philosophy, and particularly
rich and discoverable: because it would not require us to investigate the mysteries of physics or biology, but would accept large material and historical facts on
the human scale, would treat them as units, and would be satisfied with presenting them to the human conscience, to be judged *morally.* In this *moral* judgment,
however, it is hard to see how there could be any truth. The only truth concerned
would be that such a judgment was passed, that it was more or less general and
lasting, and more or less passionate. But there would seem to be no conceivable
object or reality in reference to which any type of morality could be called *true.*

Yet how many moralists or political philosophers are content with the support
that physical facts and physical forces may lend to their maxims, and do not also

claim a moral rightness for these maxims themselves? Such moral rightness in moral sentiment is either a tautology, meaning that what you prize you prize, and what you want you want, or it is a tangle of confusion. Any first moral reaction, perhaps of anger, can harden into a fierce absolute command. Any feeling, nursed and kept close in the dark, may fester into a categorical imperative. The imperative of life, the **Fanatical abuse of the word true.** imperative of every unchecked impulse, is no doubt categorical; and a certain group of these impulses may easily become a code of duty or honour, traditional in some society, or in mankind at large. Utility or calculation or what Kant called heteronomy may have nothing to do with such maxims: they may be as spontaneous and free as laughter or love. But how should these automatisms be *true*? The word *true* in such a case is unmeaning, except perhaps as a vague term of praise, a mere reiteration of some automatic impulse, as if we cried Amen. Such repetition might seem harmless; yet verbal self-confirmation, coming to one's notions as it seems from nowhere or from above, tends to fanaticism. Language then becomes an accomplice and a sanction of the will: and from honest opposition to our enemies in battle, we pass to envenomed refutation of their feelings as false. Each party hugs its maxims not as its own and worth being true to, but as the *only true* maxims. We might dismiss this as excusable heat and vapour, or as a technical solecism; yet when passion usurps the name of truth, the very idea of truth is tarnished and defiled.

Nevertheless, as usage leads us to speak of truth within the spheres of logic and of convention, so it leads us to speak of truth in morals. And there are good reasons for acquiescing in this extension of the range within which judgment may be called true or false. In willing as in knowing there is a good deal of substitution and representation. Moral passions, carried by words and ideas in themselves automatic, may be deceptive, may be hollow; they may pass **A moral precept may be true or false in respect to moral interests in general.** like storm-clouds over the conscience, tragically misinterpreting the inmost and ultimate allegiance of the soul. Such passions, and the judgments they dictate, may be called false, since besides blinding us to many a matter of fact, they deceive us about our own fundamental needs and demands. Integrity, on the contrary, the clear allegiance of a transparent soul to its radical will, without being true to anything external, makes a man's choices true to himself. It banishes moral illusions. And the same true representation of latent interests may extend to political action; a government or a party may pursue true or false aims, in the sense of being or not being in line with the radical and permanent interests of the people. Thus truth and error may be possible in morals, in so far as they are truths or errors in self-knowledge.

Take, for example, the commandment: *Love thy neighbour as thyself.* Purely hortatory as this seems, it may be almost entirely translated into propositions that would be either true or false. In the sphere of action—which if we distinguish moral from spiritual life would also be the sphere of morals—an imperative is an order to a dependent, intended to be, by suggestion, a form of indirect or suspended compulsion. A commandment to love would then be in reality an order to act as if we loved, implying that if we did not do so, our neighbours and God would act as if they did not love us. This would be a true or a false prophecy, and

Ethical matters of fact are also involved. it might guide the will as might any other credible report about the field of action. But love, spiritually considered, is a feeling: and an imperative in the sphere of feeling becomes a little nebulous. How should love be commanded? It might perhaps be awakened by contagion, in return for love–*amor che a nullo amato amar perdona.* Or it might be extended from an object already loved to some kindred object. Then, in terms of pure feeling, the precept might run thus: Love thy neighbour, because God loves him; and thou lovest God, because God loves thee. Or less emotionally: Value others for their own sake, because they too are centres of life and of values. Consider them, as Kant counselled, always as ends and never merely as means. In fact and by nature they are ends to themselves as much as you are an end to yourself. Here, in respect to all living beings, and not merely to other men, we reach a necessary truth, since life means precisely the power in organisms to grow and to propagate, as if they loved their own being.

Yet this ethical truth is not, and cannot become, a moral commandment. The categorical nerve of every imperative is vital, it expresses an actual movement of

But ethical truths cannot inspire or annul natural moral preferences. the will. And evident as the truth may be that life in every form has its intrinsic values, and attributes radiating values to all felt events, it by no means follows that these values are unanimous or that life in one form can adopt, or morally ought to adopt, the interests of life in every other form. This would indeed be the death of all morality, not the perfection of it. The will of the storm, the will of Neptune or of Jupiter Tonans, cannot with self-knowledge be adopted by the struggling and trembling creature about to be destroyed. The will of the enemy cannot be incorporated into that of the soldier. The will of the tempter, the interests of a rival in love, the tastes of the vulgar, cannot be weighed in the balance against the constitutive will and radical virtue of one's own being. Reason may harmonize the impulses of a soul: it would not be reason but self-betrayal if it abdicated these impulses in a brotherly compromise with cobras, monkeys, idiots, sophists and villains. Against a threatening deity, there is always some protecting deity to be invoked, or some other side of the same deity; and licence may be freely allowed to beasts and barbarians to live in their own way in their own preserves, so long as they do not trespass upon ours. Moreover, there is a mystical insight proper to spirit within ourselves–spirit not being specifically human–that perceives the universal innocence of life in the midst of universal war: but this insight cannot impose on the psyche in which it arises ways contrary to her native ways: nor has impartial spirit any reason for wishing to do so. Life is a form of order, a great rhythmic self-responsive organization in parcels of matter: but it arises in a thousand places and takes a thousand forms. If reason or spirit or any mystic influence whatsoever attempted to impose on each living creature the contrary impulses of all the others, it would induce not universal harmony but universal death. It would solve the moral problem only by dissolving all goods, all arts, all species and all individuals.

Just because moral life is inwardly grounded, physical truths are the only guide that it will willingly accept. A contrary purpose merely arouses hostility, but a contrary fact may inspire caution. I remember in childhood the warning of my nurse against swallowing cherry-stones. If I swallowed them, she said, a cherry-tree would grow out of my mouth. This is the principle on which moralists usually recommend their system of morality. The preacher is honestly actuated by an unexplained intense sentiment which he wishes to propagate; and in order to do so he invents circumstances of a startling nature calculated to justify that sentiment. But the method is dangerous. The images evoked under such stress of feeling are likely to be grotesque, like the traditional picture of hell-torments, or the atrocities imputed to an enemy in war; and even if by chance the invention were true, or the fraud never discovered, the sentiments thereby aroused in a half-moralized public would wholly lack the intensity and purity of those that originally animated the preacher. Where he was all moral enthusiasm or sinister superstition, his flock will be lazy, prudential, or prim. For that which creates morality is not facts, nor the consequences of facts, but human terror or desire feeling its way amid those facts and those consequences.

Moral sentiment invents ethical fables.

Suppose that instead of laughing at my nurse I had been horrified at my thoughtless sin and terrible danger in having swallowed a cherry-stone: then moral experience in me would certainly have become vivid. Sundry *ethical truths* would incidentally become unpleasantly clear, such as that a tree growing out of my mouth would be embarrassing, not to say fatal; or that other little boys lacking that ornament would probably jeer at me. From these ethical truths my mind would be expected to jump automatically to the *moral judgment* that annoyance, derision and especially death are absolute evils, which ought to be avoided. Life indeed involves the moral judgment that life is a good, since, while life lasts, the organism tends to maintain or to restore the continuity and harmony of its functions, defending itself with a blind concentrated fury against mutilation, disease and death. Even when in some tragic moment reflection turns against instinct and prefers physical death to life, not everything in life is judged to be evil; for at least this high condemnation or renunciation of life is regarded as a glorious victory and liberation for the spirit; and what is spirit but the quintessence of life here purified into tragic knowledge, into clear loyalty to what is felt to be best? It is therefore an ethical truth that moral judgments of some sort are inevitable in man. He cannot help having some radical preference. However sublimated this preference may be, it will express his vital feeling, the last cry of his animal nature, morally groundless. This cry may be absolutely sincere and true to the heart; but there is no meaning in saying that the preference so uttered is a truth in itself.

Such sentiment is inevitable.

In strictness we might even say that every moral judgment is repugnant to the truth, and that if consciousness fundamentally gave voice to truth rather than to life, and to the animal partiality involved in life, moral sentiment would be impossible. The cry, *How beautiful!* or *How good!* may be sincere, and it may be applauded, but it is never true. If sincere such a cry is also never false, even if not re-echoed by the public conscience; because the public feeling that contradicts it can also never be true, but at best also sincere. Where sentiment is diffused and

But if turned into a predicate of things dictates a falsehood. unanimous, if one person utters those exclamations, all the rest may no doubt murmur, *How true!* And indeed, to that extent, the judgment will then be *true morally:* that is, it will express the bias of human nature. That mercy is good or the sunset beautiful may be true dramatically and conventionally, for the soul and in the speech of a particular moral society: a society that need not retract its judgments if by chance some harder head or colder heart contradicts them; rather it will judge those contrary judgments to be wicked and blind. And so they will be in respect to the standards of that society. There would be no further meaning, only a greater shrillness, in insisting that they are blind and wicked in themselves. If for the emotional words *beautiful* and *good* we now substitute the analytic words *admired* and *welcome,* all moral contradiction disappears, the fog lifts, and we restore our moral intuitions to their legitimate field, the field of self-knowledge.

This Socratic self-knowledge is not scientific but expressive, not ethical but moral; and here if anywhere, in the discovery of what one ultimately wants and ultimately loves, *moral truth* might be found. This is no easy discovery; and we must be prepared for surprises in morals, no less than in physics, as investigation and analysis proceed. As the blue vault vanishes under the telescope, so moral conventions might dissolve in an enlightened conscience, and we might be abashed to perceive how disconcerting, how revolutionary, how ascetic the inmost oracle of the heart would prove, if only we had ears to hear it. Perhaps a premonition of this ultimate moral disillusion rendered Socrates so endlessly patient, diffident and ironical, so impossible to corrupt and so impossible to deceive.

I think, however, that there was one ethical illusion unextirpated even from the mind of Socrates (as also from that of Emerson); an illusion that warped the

False assumption in dogmatic morals. moral impartiality of his precepts and rendered him partisan and dogmatic in spite of his intention to be absolutely courteous and fair. He assumed that human nature was single and immutable, and the soul qualitatively identical in all men. The good that glimmered like buried gold in his own heart must lie also in the hearts of others, and only ignorance or sophistry could keep them from seeing it. But the roots of the good are alive; they are far more tentative and curiously entangled than verbal debate might indicate at Athens amid a bevy of rationalizing demagogues and sophists. Even in the individual, in whom actual preference has its only possible seat, ultimate sincerity presupposes a definite psyche, with assignable aspirations; and indeed some degree of definiteness any psyche must possess, else that psyche could not be the hereditary principle of organization in the body or of direction in the will. Yet this vital definiteness is not absolute. At each moment there is a limit, inwards, below which the psyche is not sensitive to variations in her own substance; and there is a margin outwards toward the infinite, beyond which what happens does not affect her specific life. Moreover, the most radical demands of the psyche are not immutable. Unfelt variations in her substance transform and undermine her desires. She is mortal; presently she will make no demands at all; and in the interval, from germination to birth and from childhood to old age, she successively develops and outgrows functions which are essentially temporary. In her origin she was a new equilibrium that changing circumstances had rendered possible; and her organism remains always potentially plastic and internal to the flux of nature at large.

Hence the absence of a need or a passion in one phase of life cannot be taken for an argument that such a need or passion is false or wicked elsewhere. The contrary assumption is the root of much idle censoriousness and injustice in moralists, who are probably old men, and sapless even in youth, all their zeal being about phrases and maxims that run in their heads and desiccate the rest of their spirit. To reach moral truth, which like all truth is eternal, we should have to remember or foresee with absolute clearness the aspirations of all souls at all moments; and confronting these aspirations with their occasions, we should have to measure their relative vanity and physical compatibility. The question is not whether they happen to be identical or harmonious with our own sentiments. We are particular creatures at one point in space and time: and the most contrary goods are beyond mutual censure, if pursued at different times or by different spirits.

The problem for the moral imagination.

Moral dogmatism is an attempt to stretch moral unity beyond the range of natural organization. Spiritually it is a sinister thing, a sin against spirit elsewhere. Yet politically, and within the living organism, animal or social, moral dogmatism is morality itself; it is the effort of that organism to maintain its health and attain its perfection. Hatred or contempt for alien manners and ideas would be absurd in a philosopher sure of his own ground; he would be pleased by their zoological variety which like that of animals in cages would not seriously endanger his safety, freedom, or peace. But social morality—and all morality is deeply social—is necessarily divided at home and threatened from abroad. Invective and propaganda are instruments in this animal warfare; they are useful in maintaining discipline, in breaking the enemy's spirit, and in capturing as many loose ambient forces as possible to the support of your particular regimen. Liberals and Pacifists, who imagine they represent morality in general, are the first to announce the sure victory of their cause and the annihilation for ever of all their enemies, that is, of all moralities in particular. Yet morality in general, as we see in truly emancipated circles, is no morality at all. The root of morality is animal bias: and to renounce that bias would be to renounce life. Even the most general and tolerant of moral standards—harmony—is not a good in itself. There must be an actual will directed upon harmony in order to render harmony a good. Harmony demands many a sacrifice: in what direction, and at whose cost, shall those sacrifices be made? A strong and well-knit nature, brave with the perfect harmony within, will despise and detest harmony on a larger scale; it will refuse to sacrifice any part of its chosen good, and will declare eternal war on the devil, and on all his obsequious and insidious agents.

Yet conscience, being enlightened will, is indomitably positive.

Such, in whatever interest and on whatever scale, is the nerve of morality.

Reflected in the living soul, all the rays of nature instantly acquire a moral colour. Nothing can happen that will not be good or bad in a thousand directions. When all living souls are considered, the cross-lights and conflicts of these values spread an impenetrable tangle, through which it is impossible for mortal eye to see the ultimate balance of benefit and injury. But nature laughs at this perplexity. A man is a man, for all the apes and donkeys in the world. Instinct reasserts its primacy; the overwhelming immediacy of some great passion or hope breaks through the cobwebs of sentimental idleness, and sets a fresh clear work before us that will not brook delay.

This self-assertion is not always young and impulsive; it may survive all experience and disillusion, growing firmer in isolation, and cleaving to the chosen **Its ultimate** good even when this is known to be unrealizable. Such desperate **deliverance is** heroism is nevertheless contrary to all the lower unconsecrated **moral truth.** yielding parts of the psyche; and half the martyr's mind, together with the mind of posterity, will judge wholly unrealizable desires to have been unhealthy and undesirable. Moral truth, therefore, even at its purest, by no means bestows moral authority over alien lives. It signifies only complete, enlightened, ultimate sincerity.

Love and Hatred of Truth

The Realm of Truth: Book Third of Realms of Being. London: Constable and Co. Ltd.;
Toronto: Macmillan Company, 1937; New York: Charles Scribner's Sons, 1938,
102–18. Volume sixteen of the critical edition of *The Works of George Santayana*.

In this selection, Chapter XII of The Realm of Truth, *Santayana explained how ignorance of the nature of spirit and lack of self-knowledge lead to hatred of truth. Humans
judge nature in human terms, ignoring the vast difference in scale between human experience and nature. Hostility flares against the reality that would gainsay human passions
seeking to dictate objective truth rather than express sincere self-knowledge. Ignorance of
one's motives further confuses the relation to truth, as when the love of comfort or safety
are taken to be love of truth. Love of safety at least acknowledges that no peace comes with
delusion and may mark a tacit awareness of truth. But even when truth is the explicit aim
of the critic, Santayana found "love of ideas, novelties, adventure, controversy, and power"
to be more typical motives (ES, 246). Still, in positing truth, criticism honors truth. But
honor is not love. Love of truth entails understanding the natural love of spirit for truth.
The vocation of spirit is to contemplate essence, and the realm of truth is a subset of the
realm of essence and a natural home to spirit.*

The love of truth is often mentioned, the hatred of truth hardly ever, yet the latter
is the commoner. People say they love the truth when they pursue it, and they
pursue it when unknown: not therefore because of any felt affinity to
it in their souls, but probably because they need information for practical purposes, or to solve some conventional riddle. Where known,
on the contrary, truth is almost always dismissed or disguised, because
the aspect of it is hateful. And this apart from any devilish perversity
in the natural man, or accidental vices that may fear the light. On the
contrary, the cause is rather the natural man's innocence and courage in thinking
himself the measure of all things. Life imposes selfish interests and subjective
views on every inhabitant of earth: and in hugging these interests and these views
the man hugs what he initially assumes to be the truth and the right. So that aversion from the real truth, a sort of antecedent hatred of it as contrary to presumption, is interwoven into the very fabric of thought.

Truth naturally hated rather than loved.

Images and feelings do not arise without a certain vital enthusiasm in forming
or affirming them. To enjoy them is in some sense to hypostasize them and set
them up as models to which other images and feelings should conform. A child will protest and be inwardly wounded if a story once
told him is told differently the second time. His little soul has accepted
that world, and needs to build upon it undisturbed. Sensation, which
makes the foreground of what is called experience, is thus raised by innocent
faith to the level of truth. And false these images and feelings would not be, if
they provoked no assertions about further objects. They would compose the

Sense and fancy preempt belief.

ingredients of a true biography, although perhaps, when the circumstances are considered, the biography of a dupe.

Now love is a passion, and we might expect it not to be aroused at all by intellectual objects, such as truth, or theory purporting to be true: and yet the bitterest feuds, in families and nations, often turn on the love or hatred of particular beliefs, attacked or defended for the most fantastic reasons. Both sides may perhaps say that they are fighting for the truth; but evidently it is not any circumstantial evidence that supports the claims of the opposed ideas to be veridical; nor is there often much intrinsic beauty in those ideas. The theological notion of the Trinity was little affected by that iota for which nevertheless blood flowed in the streets of Byzantium; yet the metaphysical dignity of the Virgin Mary was involved, and nobody should be suffered to question the truth of a devout image so fondly lodged in the mind.

In such a case the passion concerned is not the love of truth, but a natural joy in thinking freely, and the self-assertion of each mind against all others. If meantime any attention is paid to the truth at all, it is only indirectly, in that the ideal authority of truth is recognized, whilst, by an absurd contradiction, its verdict is dictated to it by violence. The truth is needed, but not respected, not loved but raped; and that barbarous outrage to the truth in the concrete is still a sort of homage to truth as the coveted sanction of fancy.

Modern philosophers seem hardly aware of the extent to which they still reason on these principles. *Occam's Razor,* for instance, or economy as a criterion of truth, is the weapon of a monstrous self-mutilation with which

Parsimony in thinking shows indifference to truth.

British philosophy, if consistent, would soon have committed suicide. Only if all ideas were condemned to be blind and ugly, like a secret telegraphic code, would there be a human advantage in having the fewest and the baldest ideas possible: a gain, even then, only because thinking would be a loss, a waste of energy to be reduced to the practicable minimum. As to the truth of simple rather than elaborate ideas, what evidence does nature or history afford for such a presumption? Is nature sparing of atoms or seeds, of depths of organization and interrelation beyond the reach of human thought? Doubtless when applied to scholastic entities, conceived as dominant elements or powers (conceived, that is, as limiting the exuberance and waste in nature), Occam's Razor might serve to clear the ground for a richer crop of ideas. But for what ideas? I see no lilies of the field, I see only an expanse of coal-dust.

In fact, most scholastic distinctions were made in the effort to clarify the mind, and bring language nearer to the precise relations of things. This philosophy was not experimental physics; it did not trace the movements of matter on their own plane; it studied rather the functions that things might have in the life of reason, as classic rhetoric and morals had defined that life. Such humanism was itself a monument to self-complacency in the home mind and aversion from arctic and torrid truth; but at least in its own dimension it was diligent. So are modern mathematics and physics, to a degree that renders them more inventive and unintelligible than any philosophy; but though many of their terms, or all, may be figments of human method, they play respectfully round the profound complexity of things; and there is more modesty and love of truth in the better men of science than in the old scholastics, in that they admit that their conventions are largely arbitrary and symbolic.

A false truth is often attributed to human ideas, even when they are not taken for physical objects or powers. Æsthetic, moral or political sentiments, for instance, because they arouse a certain enthusiasm, are proclaimed as truths; individuals and parties entrench themselves within those maxims with all the ferocity of hatred and fear: hatred and fear of the besieging reality, that would prove that no such feelings can express any objective truth, but only the life of some biological or political organism. That every organism must have its own form of life and must love and defend it; goes without saying: but why poison the inevitable conflict of possible forms by insulting your rivals, and saying they have no right to attempt to live? Courage, that in a rational being would be courteous, then borrows the blindness and useless cruelty of instinct; and the legitimate will to live usurps the authority of destiny, which determines what forms of life, at any time and place, may actually prosper. Truly great men, nobly dominant wills, appeal, indeed, to that authority of destiny which they feel working within them: and common moralizing does the same thing when, without anger or false threats, it points to the vanity of some ambitions and the miserable consequences of some vices.

Pre-rational morality asserts its intuitions in defiance of moral truth.

Plato reports the humorous saying of Socrates that dogs are philosophical because they bark at strangers, thereby showing how much they prize knowledge. Intentionally or unintentionally there is a play here upon the word knowledge. This name is given at once, and sophistically, both to familiarity and to understanding; so that fondness for what we happen to know and hostility towards what we happen not to know are identified with the love of truth. Yet in fact they are the exact opposite. What we and the dogs love is our safety, our home-thoughts, our illusions and our undisputed confidence in habit. Undoubtedly, in controversial moments, we defend our ideas under the name of great and evident truths, as we defend our worldly possessions under the name of natural rights. In this we manifest our animal nature, like faithful dogs, and are biologically admirable and morally blameless. There is indeed something candid and honest in trusting appearance and in being loyal to convention; but to be dogged about these things with a clear conscience is hardly possible to an intelligent man. A dull child may tell the truth without understanding it, not in the least for the love of truth, but simply for lack of alternatives. Had he a less sluggish imagination he might have invented some aimless lie. Stupidity is positivistic, and sometimes, as in science, literal and uninterpreted reports are useful; they are trustworthy as far as they go, and allow us to do our own thinking. For the thinking spirit, however, literalness is simple slavery to appearance or to convention on the level of sense; a slavery that an intellectual coward may sometimes love. It saves him from discovering a truth secretly felt to be inhuman.

Attachment to familiar ideas shows love not of truth but of comfort.

Sensuous appearance and spontaneous language are nevertheless far from hostile to the truth: they are first steps in the pursuit of it. Nature takes good care

Fear of being deceived is again not a love of truth but of safety.
to discredit our young idolatries, and drives us from one image to another, from each thought to some alternative thought. Not, or not often, by the force of logic, which indeed would rather tighten its coils about us, and enclose us in an impenetrable cocoon of its own weaving. Conviction always abounds in its own sense, as in theology: but what breaks at last through such a charmed circle is wild nature, within and without. A thousand contrary facts, a thousand rebel emotions, drive us from our nest. We find that *there can be no peace in delusion:* and perhaps in this negative and moral guise the idea of truth first insinuates itself into the mind. No spiritual understanding, no generous interest in the truth on its own level and for its own sake: only discomfort in uncertainty, uneasiness about things hidden, and a prudent concern for the future. In positing the future and the hidden and also the past, we have already posited truth, but blindly, without distinguishing intellectually truth, which we might discover and possess, from facts extinct or unborn or incommunicable. We do not in the least care to discover or possess the truth; but we wish to be armed to face the obdurate facts; and our pride recoils from the confusion of finding ourselves mistaken. Better, then, examine everything suspiciously and form no idea, as we should buy no clothes, not likely to wear well. Hence a certain shrewdness and prudence in conceiving matters closely affecting us, each man in his own trade, each woman in her own circle; but this specialized sagacity is remote from the love of truth not only in motive but in scope. The foundation is laid in egotism, in partiality, in injustice; enormous tracts of relevant reality are wilfully ignored; and the result is some slander or some party tenet or some superstition, defended pugnaciously rather because it is preciously false than because it is presumably true. The more these self-indulgent minds fear and hate the truth, the more insistently they give the name of truth to the mask that hides it.

That fiction and convention should usurp in this manner the authority of truth—an authority which, however ideal it maybe, is logically absolute—naturally

Criticism is dogma on a different level.
arouses the ire of the critical; and it is not without reason that individual investigators, reformers, and heretics feel that they are champions of the truth. They are, in fact, rebels against imposture. Yet they ordinarily have many stronger and nearer motives for their zeal than love of truth for its own sake: love of ideas, novelties, adventure, controversy, and power. Take the case where bias and ulterior motives seem most radically absent: the case of the scientific empiricist, a compass in one hand and a balance in the other. He may say he is pursuing pure truth. Yet an exact record of his experiments would hardly disclose anything more enlightening than would the sights and gossip of the street. They would be glimpses and gossip about matter, not about human affairs: and this is far from implying that the glimpses or gossip would be truer. On the contrary, it is precisely about the social world that a man's surface impressions are apt to be adequate: the object is like the medium. And indeed the scientific man is not likely to be satisfied with the

bare record of his experiments, which would report the strict truth of his investigation. Instead, every experiment will suggest to him some new theory, or will seem to illustrate and confirm some old theory familiar to his mind. So fortified, he may be doubly ready to denounce the errors of his more conventional neighbours, whom he probably dislikes on other grounds, and wishes to supersede in public estimation. Nor is this always the merely inevitable admixture of different passions in a human being. The pure theory advanced is not likely in the end to be truer than the views it replaces. It is often truer in some particular; but when its tendency and oversights are considered, it very seldom increases the harmony between man and nature. Perhaps if critical and empirical motives governed science absolutely, science would disappear. Autobiography would replace it, with a perfect democracy of theories, as so many idle ideas, going with different moods; and when memory and solipsism had been criticized in their turn, the so-called zeal for truth would end by denying the notion of truth altogether.

That would be the second childhood of the mind. Instead of innocent joy in appearance and in language, as if nothing could be false, there would be a collapse into idiocy, as if nothing could be true. Vigorous critics and innovators are far from such apathy. They strip off one mask of truth only to substitute another, as the truer image: and they very likely join the elder dogmatists in maintaining that in the mask they propose the likeness to the original is perfect. Not all an honest man's zeal, be he a traditionalist or a reformer, is arrested at the specific doctrines which he identifies with the truth: the better part pierces *But all dogmas posit, and in that sense honour, the truth.* that symbol and rests in the truth itself, pure and absolute, which wears that mask for him for the moment. So that all is not hypocrisy in this partisan or fantastic zeal. Within the fanatical defence of vested illusions there may be a sacrificial respect for things beyond us, whatever those secret realities may be; and the martyr that on earth is ready to die for some false opinion may be judged in heaven to have died for the truth. The very absurdity of a tenet, or its groundlessness, at least proves that imagination is at work, and groping for an issue from animal darkness. At least the category of truth has been set up. Appearances, innocent and perfectly real in themselves, have begun to be questioned and discounted as deceptive; and this not merely against the blank background of a posited substance, known only as a force, but in contrast to a possible and more adequate description of that substance and of the manner in which it produces appearances. Intelligence has begun the pursuit of truth.

Does this pursuit ever really deserve the name of love? No doubt there must be a total and exact collocation of facts, and the universe must have a form which we call the truth of it; but why should anyone *love* that collocation, in its perhaps infinite and certainly inhuman minuteness and *Why should respect for truth turn into love?* extent? Why should anyone desire to know what that tiresome truth may be, except for human purposes in the region and on the scale of our gross experience? We may love our pleasures, our perceptions, our dogmas; we may love safety and dominion in action, and victory in argument; but if the truth is none of these things, why should we love it?

There is no *reason* why we should love the truth. There is no *reason* why we should love anything. There are only causes that, according to the routine of nature, bring about the love of various things on various occasions.

The forward strain for cosmic Eros in all existence becomes conscious in spirit.

As a matter of fact, nature breeds life, and life is everywhere aflame with love, and with its opposite; and there is also no reason why this spiritual passion—spiritual because it engages and colours the spirit— should stop short at bodily concerns or social affairs, and should not extend to all the relations radiating from bodily life into the realms of truth and of essence. This radiation, as I call it, is in itself passive and merely formal, yet physical organization must take account of it if life is to prosper; and this tension of life towards the eventual, the distant, the past and the future is what becomes conscious and bursts into actuality in spirit. Spirit is a child of truth. Matter in any one of its moments and in any one of its atoms offers no foothold for consciousness: but let certain tropes and cycles be established in the movement of matter, let certain kinds of matter cohere and pulse together in an organism, and behold, consciousness has arisen. Now tropes, cycles, organisms, and pulsations, with all the laws of nature, are units proper to the realm of truth; units that bridge the flux of existence and are suspended over it, as truth and spirit also are suspended. So that in conceiving and loving the truth spirit is not indulging in any caprice; it is surveying with pleasure the soil and the broad reaches of its native country.

Nor is love too warm a term for the sense of this radical affinity. There is cosmic justification for such a passion. Love is, biologically, an emotion proper to generation: and generation, in the cosmos at large, is the same thing as genesis or flux. Love, ever since Hesiod and Empedocles, has therefore been the poetic name for the instability and fecundity of transitive existence everywhere; life passing, and passing joyfully, from each phase to the next, and from one individual to another. Yet this joyful procreation of things is also tragic, because as Lucretius says, nothing is born save by the death of something else. In loving, in breeding, and in bringing up the young we make an unconscious sacrifice of ourselves to posterity. Such is the dominance of love in the realm of matter, where progression is, as it were, horizontal, and the thing generated continues and repeats the nature of its parents. But where the transmitted form is organic, and spirit inhabits it, life and love have also a vertical direction and a synthetic power, such that in precipitating the future, the present evokes some image of the past, and some notion of the outlying realities by which the present and the future are being controlled. In other words, life, in propagating itself, has also generated knowledge, and has become aware of the truth.

This by-product or hypostasis of organic life is also tragic, like physical reproduction, and accepts death; but instead of surrendering one life for another of the

And transcends the flux ideally by conceiving it.

same kind and on the same level, we now surmount or disregard physical life altogether, in order to define its form and consider its achievements. This consideration or definition of nature is itself a work of nature, occurring in time and requiring material organs. It therefore partakes of the joy proper to all vital functions in their perfection. The beauty of truth is loved as naturally as the beauty of women, and our ideas are cherished like our children. Enthusiasm and inspiration (which are other names of love addressed to the truth) have no less warmth and breed no less heroism than the love of home or of country.

Thus spirit is born and chooses its aims in sympathy with the movement of organic life, and is simply that movement become emotion and idea. For this radical reason spirit cannot be an independent power coming from nowhere to direct or accelerate animal action. We do not look about us because we love the truth, but we love the truth because we look about us. Were it merely a question of keeping alive or of controlling matter, business would actually be expedited if besides Occam's razor we used, so to speak, Occam's **This movement automatically assigns intrinsic value to truth.** glasses, and reduced our visions of things to pointer-readings, releasing appropriate reactions on our part without further rhetoric. Ignorance, when not materially dangerous, simplifies the fighting mind and is an economic advantage. It renders courage absolute and disturbs no comfortable or harmless illusions. Nature, however, being spontaneous and free, with no end of time before her, despises such thrift and is initially lavish and all-consenting. Her indefinite passive fertility is committed to no antecedent prejudices or desires. She adopts her laws and types unwittingly, as they avail to establish themselves; and they leave untouched her original potentialities. They may become, indeed, positive occasions for playful complications far out-turning those special terms and eluding their measure. Such a complication life seems to us to be in respect to mechanism, and consciousness in respect to life. In these cases the new fruit, while having an underivable character proper to itself, will draw all its existential sap from the tree on which it is grafted. Life requires food, warmth and air, yet is none of those things but an organization accruing to them; and spirit feeds on the life of the psyche, while establishing tangential and transcendent interests of its own. When feeling (a form of spirit evoked by organic processes in the body) becomes perception and begins to describe the objects that arouse feeling, spirit is already launched upon the pursuit of truth, an ideal reality altogether transcending the level of the psyche and of her world. When, moreover, the eye and the intellect have adequately surveyed the scene, or gathered the event observed into a dramatic unity, the organ of spirit is satisfied. It is satisfied in the very act by which a truth is discerned; so that by nature this discernment is a joy to the spirit, and the truth automatically conceived becomes an object of love for its own sake.

The vital and fundamentally physical quality of this love of truth appears clearly when it is thwarted. We see daily in young children and in impatient reformers how nothing is more hateful to a passionate being than obstruction, nothing more precious than liberty. The psyche will have her way in the first place, let the result be what it will. Indeed, the primitive horror of being stifled, of being held down and prevented from moving, is doubtless what lends its magic to the word **To stop short of the truth is a vital frustration.** liberty: any idea of what we might do with our liberty when we got it would have no such power. To be checked in our natural actions before we initiate them produces melancholy: to be checked in the middle of them produces rage. This intolerableness of suppression extends to the movement of our thoughts. It was in the act of spinning fine long threads of relationship that nature first evoked spirit: that web must not be torn, and nature demands that spirit should think the truth. We cannot endure to be cheated, to be deluded, even to suspect that we are deceiving ourselves. We may be incurious about remote truths, if our intellect is lazy; but at least we would not stultify what intellect we have by believing things positively false. Therefore when authority or public opinion would hold us down to some manifest error, however harmless and metaphysical, our impetuous souls resent the outrage. It is not the calm truth that calls for witnesses: martyrs usually die for some new error. It is the martyrs that cannot endure in themselves the arrest of the heart upon thoughts that the heart despises. No matter how tragic or arid the truth may be, the spirit follows and loves it, as the eye follows the light.

Automatic as the love of truth is, and internal as is the joy of discovering and holding the truth, this love has nothing narcissistic about it. It is as far as possible

Yet the standard of truth remains external and the love of truth is a form of worship. from being joy in the lustre or harmony of one's ideas. It is a clean, healthy, sacrificial love. In the form of childish curiosity it is turned from the beginning towards alien things, engaging the impulse to explore, to dissect, and to dare. The element of courage, united with submission and humility, belongs to the love of truth even in its ultimate reaches. Truth, in spite of what Platonists and poets may say, is not at all the same as beauty. Truth does not arrange or idealize its subject-facts. It can eliminate nothing. It can transfigure nothing, except by merely lifting it bodily from the plane of existence and exhibiting it, not as a present lure or as a disaster for some native ambition, but as a comedy or tragedy seen as a whole and liberating the spirit that understands it. In other words, truth is a moral, not an æsthetic good. The possession of it is not free intuition, but knowledge necessary to a man's moral integrity and intellectual peace.

That conventional truths, as exhibited to the senses, or in historical narrative or scientific exposition, may often be impressive æsthetically goes without saying: but it is not this æsthetic quality that makes their truth or satisfies the intellect. If truth at first entertains, as falsehood does also, it very soon sobers and rebukes. It is tragic even in comedy, since it looks to the end of every career and every achievement. The very movement of instinctive exploration that discloses truth, thereby discloses also the relativity, limits, and fugitiveness of this exploration. It shows life under the form of eternity, which is the form of death. Life thereby becomes an offering, a prayer, a sacrifice offered up to the eternal; and though there may be incense in that sacrifice, there is also blood.

Such affinity as there is between truth and beauty has various sources. When the word truth is coloured idealistically, to mean the types or potential perfec-

The true is akin to the beautiful when it means "true to type". tions of things, as when we speak of a true friend, evidently if this latent "truth" could only be brought out and raised to actual fact, it would also realize the beautiful. Love and charity are quick to perceive the latent perfections of the imperfect; and if we call this (perhaps imaginary) potentiality the truth, we indeed divine the principle of beauty also; of that beauty which the organic impulses of nature would bring to light if they had their way and did not interfere with one another.

Even this partial chaos and mutual destruction, when we see it to be the truth, for the very reason that we are interested in the beauties destroyed, has a cathartic effect. It is sublime; and if we call the sublime a part of the beautiful, the truth, even when distressing and ugly, will be horribly beautiful to us. Both naturalism and romanticism work this vein of merciless poetry. Religion often does the same thing indirectly, and aided by myths: the heart is taught to transmute **Also when the beautiful turns to the sublime or overwhelming.** its affections, so as to make them consonant with the will of God, that is, with the truth. But here we may see the danger of forced assimilations of the true to the good or to the beautiful. False views are often called true, in order to make the truth more consoling; and on the other hand moral and æsthetic values are often distorted by being torn from their roots in an animal soil and stretched on a rack of cosmic dimensions. The starry spaces bring us face to face with depths of reality hidden by the light of day: we find that spectacle beautiful, and sublime in its inhumanity; and the better part of our humanity then seems to be our capacity to rise above ourselves. But it is in fact one part of us that here eludes or rebukes another part. Nature is necessarily full of beauties, since our faculties of perception and sympathy would not subsist if they were not adapted to the facts of nature; and the truth is necessarily satisfying, for the same reason. Yet nature is also full of ugly, cruel and horrible things, and the truth in many ways is desolating: because our nature, though sufficiently harmonious with the universe to exist within it, is nevertheless finite and specific, with essential interests which nature and truth at large cannot but disregard. The truth, then, is often, in many ways, interesting, beautiful and sublime: but it is not identical with beauty either in quality or extension or status.

Undoubtedly, in their different ways, truth and beauty are both liberating; and when mystics identify them it may be because they are exalted by both above the travail of existence. In the case of beauty this deliverance is spontaneous and innocent: the spirit takes wing at birth, and **Also in freeing the spirit from private entanglements.** flutters from flower to flower, without suspecting that any other fate awaits it. But the deliverance that comes through the truth comes through sorrow: it is redemption by the cross. The more inhuman the truth turns out to be, the more dismal or cruel, so much greater is the self-conquest involved in facing it, in casting away false hopes, and entrenching ourselves impregnably in our insignificance. The very act of recognizing our insignificance, if sincere and not a mask for new claims, removes the sting of that insignificance. There is even something sadistic in the pleasure with which certain religious minds gloat on their own misery, as if they could never trample enough on their bleeding hearts or dance enough on their graves. But there is no occasion to exaggerate. To be finite is not a sin, to be ignorant is not a disgrace: the pleasures of illusion and those of disillusion are equally human. Pure insight into truth surmounts human bias in both directions impartially, without in the least hating or condemning the life that involves such bias; for to hate or condemn finitude is as finite as to cling to any particular form of finitude with an absolute fury. Intuition is liberating on every level, in each case defining the proper and adequate object of the faculty concerned. In sensation, intuition liberates some essence from the obscurity and tangle of fact; from passion it liberates eloquence, poetry and beauty; from the known world it liberates truth. The operation of each faculty, so perfected, turns into clear joy. To take the full measure of anything, especially of anything living, establishes (quite apart from practical advantages) a spiritual dominion over that thing. You have seen it, you have seen through it, you have seen round it. It no longer can hold you to any weak or unmerited regard. It no longer can torture you with a useless hatred. Moreover, in partly lifting your ignorance, the truth has liberated you from avidity for knowledge. Fortune can never unveil to you more than a part of the truth: such part as is important for you and as you can digest. This part, seen under the form of eternity, can then cease to be external to you; it can become a term and familiar rhythm in your own life. And this part of your life, being absorbed in pure intuition, will no longer seem consciously yours, nor concerned with your personal fortunes. It will be a light revealing the truth to you, and will be lost in the eternity of that which it knows.

Nevertheless, in the dead season of the mind, when every generous faculty is paralysed, it may become incredible that an immaterial reality, or material unreality, like the truth should ever be prized or even conceived. This doubt or denial is incidental to intellectual decay; but that fact does not count from the point of view of the decadence. We must therefore examine the position from within, in its subjective origin and logic.

Denials of Truth

The Realm of Truth: Book Third of Realms of Being. London: Constable and Co. Ltd.; Toronto: Macmillan Company, 1937; New York: Charles Scribner's Sons, 1938, 119–30. Volume sixteen of the critical edition of *The Works of George Santayana.*

In this selection, Chapter XIII of The Realm of Truth, *Santayana refuted denials of truth by distinguishing truth and the knowledge of truth. Despairing of transcending the limited and relative perspective of mortals, some have denied truth altogether. But this is the denial of knowledge of truth, not truth itself. The most honest and radical denial of truth would be the denial of any notion of or need for truth. While true of many animals, this claim among humans is "something late and artificial, a contorted, confused, and villainous effort to squirm away from one's intellectual conscience" (ES, 256). Santayana thought it indicated a society in which no particular perspective can entice allegiance: One might adopt whatever perspective is convenient and deny any notion of truth. This denial may entail psychologism: "the view that all we see, say, and think is false, but that the only truth is that we see, say and think it" (ES, 258). Santayana found this unconvincing as a denial of truth. He thought the truth in such circumstances would be that intelligence is irresolute and hesitant to pursue any particular dogma, but this would not exclude the being of truth.*

Pilate's question, *What is truth?* might be asked with varying intentions. It might be a sincere enquiry, assuming that the word truth stood for something assignable, and asking what that thing exactly was. A sincere answer might then be forthcoming, such for instance as is contained in this book. Very likely, however, the original demand would not have concerned so abstract a subject as the ontological nature of truth, considered as a logical category. The question would rather have touched what might be true in the concrete, in some such matter as religion or scientific theory; and then an adequate answer would be wellnigh endless, involving all conventional human knowledge.

> The nature of truth in the abstract and in the concrete is largely ascertainable.

Pilate, however, and those who have repeated his question were probably not desirous of learning anything. Their question was merely an exclamation of impatience, uttered in mockery or bravado, or perhaps in despair. If the sentiment were despair, it might be as honest as the innocent desire to know: in both cases we should be assuming the definite reality of the truth, in the one case by looking for it hopefully, and in the other

> Despair about it a passing mood.

case by thinking of it so grandly and placing it at so great a remove that the hope of ever possessing it would seem to us chimerical. Yet this honest kind of despair could only be momentary, and occasioned by some inordinate ambition to know all truth or to know the most comprehensive truths infallibly: something not consonant with the nature and station of man. Disappointment there, though sharp, would soon yield to contentment with such knowledge as is natural to us, and humanly interesting. Truth near home, in many a detail, is continually revealed to us; we cannot open a door or receive the answer to a letter without finding verified sundry assumptions made currently by instinct, and being assured that, in some sense, they were true. Amongst these familiar truths any educated man will place the elements of geography, biology, and history: and these, if his mind is open and unprejudiced, will suffice to show him the place of man in nature, the character of his organs of sense, and the images formed by these organs, together with the general history of human opinion. In view of these facts he would become aware that all human *knowledge* of truth, by virtue of its seat and function, must be relative and subjectively coloured. It expresses the sensations and expectations of a specific animal. It is therefore vastly different both in extent and in texture from the literal and complete truth about the universe.

This relativism no doubt shocks and humbles the spontaneously poetic mind. Spirit is initially addressed to omniscience, as it is to perfect freedom and happiness, and even to absolute power. These sweeping ambitions are **Primitive dogmatism must be renounced.** involved in the synthetic character of spirit, in its moral warmth and in its cognitive transcendence, in idea, over remote times and places; also in its inevitable isolation or egotism: and the same ambitions are encouraged by the real æsthetic and dialectical fertility of mind, when once an organism has flowered into consciousness, and begun to dream. To find itself harnessed to facts that it cannot control, to find itself helpless and mistaken, is therefore a hard lesson for the spirit. But this chastening is not fatal; on the contrary, it is positively enlightening and steadying. Not only does appropriate knowledge, in picturesque and infinite vistas, remain open, but spirit can now bring order into its own house, and consecrate itself to its essential vocation without being distracted by vain hopes.

Far, however, from denying or doubting the being of truth, such relativism as to knowledge doubly asserts it. On the one hand, it presupposes much true information about nature and human life; because criticism, even if we call it scepticism, is founded on knowledge. On the other hand, the reality of an unknown truth beyond the human sphere is thereby asserted emphatically and even pathetically: we should not need to beweep our ignorance if there were nothing to know. The post-religious agnosticism widespread in the nineteenth century was suffering from the vacuum left by a lost faith in revelation: in pottering about amongst appearances, and talking about science and progress, it felt secretly empty and bereaved. The truth, which had seemed to shine so warm and near upon a former age, had receded to an infinite distance and been eclipsed for ever. The agnostics often felt some tenderness for their lost illusions: and what they smiled at bitterly, and regarded as inexcusable, was rather the impudence of lay philosophers who ventured to proclaim the absolute truth of their toy systems. That was a double insult to the wise and the sorrowful: it ignored the depths of nature about us; it ignored also the depths of imagination and religion within us, by which the old faith had been inspired. As belief in the reality of material objects is never more acute than in the dark, when we are groping cautiously and intently amongst them, so the reality of overarching truth was never more painfully acknowledged than by these agnostics, conscious of not being able to define its form.

Luckily, honest agonies are brief. We become callous to ignorance, as we do to poverty, danger, or solitude: and presently a new healthy equilibrium is established in the mind. Custom and necessity carry us bodily along in conventional speech and action; we live with our images and metaphors without prying too closely into their credentials, as we live with our friends. And if in speculative moments misgivings overtake us, either we deliberately cover our heads with the hood of resignation, or perhaps we are visited by some sudden revelation and conspire with ourselves to trust it. In either case, whether by abstinence or divination, we join mankind in positing a comprehensive and inviolate truth hanging above us, and making our falsehoods false and our truths true.

In Pilate's question, however, we may detect a subtler and more insidious suggestion. He feels he has hold of nothing, and he mocks reality. Mockery is a means of restoring our self-respect by universalizing our own hollowness. As if he said: *Did I ever trouble about truth? No. Then why are these fools talking about it? The truth is that there is no truth.* **The real challenge to truth lies in blind impulse.**

Self-contradiction could not be franker. Evidently to deny the truth is to make an assertion, and thereby to allege that there is a truth. Yet a formal refutation of this sort remains rather puerile. It would ignore the depth of irritation and animal courage in that self-contradiction, the scorn of words, the reversion to primitive slumber. Even on the rational level, the verbal contradiction may be easily removed by a *distinguo* which is itself necessary and important. In saying, "The truth is that there is no truth", we use the word truth in two different senses. In the first clause "truth" means the truth; in the second **That which is denied and may be absent is not truth but knowledge of truth.** clause it means *knowledge* of the truth. Now the truth might well be that there were no true human opinions or criteria of certainty: and although a Cretan may not properly say that all Cretans are always liars, a laughing god might say so with perfect consistency. In fact the truth has a superhuman status: so that an absence of true opinions or criteria would not in the least abolish it. Moreover, spirit, which also is human only by accident and may forget its physical seat, can readily conceive an experience that should be inwardly irrelevant to truth altogether, so that within that experience there should be no problems, no alleged true opinions, and no category of truth or of error. It would suffice that such an experience should remain æsthetic and should never posit any removed object, even any removed part of itself. Music, for instance, is in this case: and if certain philosophies, like fine arts, aspire to the condition of music, they actually aspire not indeed to deny but to forget the truth. Of course the most irresponsible dance of feelings and images would be shadowed in all its convolutions by the truth about it, as any existence is inevitably shadowed; but it need not see its own shadow; it need never stop to consider the truth about itself. If the word truth fell somehow from outside into those buzzing ears, the retort might come from within with perfect sincerity: *There is no truth.*

Such, I think, would be the only radical and wholly honest denial of truth: an avowal that, in one's own mind, the notion of truth was absent and needless.

Background of opportunism in belief.
Great multitudes of animals would doubtless say so, if they could speak. But in human philosophy the denial of truth is something late and artificial, a contorted, confused, and villainous effort to squirm away from one's intellectual conscience. In a compact society, where all the world is of one opinion, the worldling will be cocksure of the truth; but when society is loose and decadent, why should he commit himself to any one of a thousand conflicting, exacting, and narrowing systems? To choose rationally he would need to dig down to first principles: but to what first principles? He is probably decayed himself at the core, and can find no first principles there. His obvious course is then to choose at each turn whatever views may be convenient, and to proclaim that there is no truth.

Civilizations are often partly rotten before they are ripe; so that chronologically there may be no great interval between the sophists who deny the being of truth and the philosophers who endeavour to piece the truth together or to defend it, as it may have inspired an earlier age. Thus in Greece the chief Sophists were hardly later than the chief naturalists and law-givers, and earlier than Socrates, Plato, and Aristotle.

In respect to truth the two famous sayings reported of Protagoras suffice to set the essential problem. "Man," he said, "is the measure of all things, of that which is, that it is, and that which is not, that it is not." And he also said,

The maxims of Protagoras.
"True is what appears to each man at each moment." I am not concerned with the historical question, vain and insoluble in itself, as to what may have been the exact connotation of these phrases in their author's mind. I take them as public property, to be turned to the best uses of which they are still capable. The first maxim will serve admirably for the first principle of humanism. Humanism begins in the moral sphere, with the perception that every man's nature is, for him, the arbiter of values. So far, this view merely universalizes the Gospel text that the Sabbath was made for man and not man for the Sabbath. From such moral enlightenment, however, we may easily slip into equivocations that will land us in moral chaos. In saying that a man's *nature* is, for him, the arbiter of values, we may understand that nothing is good or bad but *thinking* makes it so. We shall then have confused what a man is with what he thinks he is, and identified his interests with his wishes. Under cover of freedom to be ourselves we shall be denying that we have any true nature; and under cover of asserting our native rights we shall be denying that we have any ultimate interests. Humanism, so understood, will have disintegrated humanity, declared all passions equally good and proclaimed moral anarchy.

These equivocations may extend beyond the sphere of morals and may end in identifying all reality with consciousness. The first maxim of Protagoras, that *man* is the criterion, will have become equivalent to his second maxim, that the criterion is the present *moment*. Yet even in regard to the present moment there is a serious ambiguity. The word which I have translated by "appears," δοχεῖ, might rather mean "seems true", or "is thought to be true". If we took this second meaning seriously, far from denying the being of truth we should be regarding truth as omnipresent, and revealed by every thought or perception. In other words, we should be asserting that consciousness is never a passive feeling but always cognitive, capable of entertaining no appearance without regarding it as a description, and thinking it true. This may well be the case in action, when consciousness is on the wing and carried by animal faith to intend what is not given: but to make this self-transcendence universal would be the extreme of intellectualism, something impossible to attribute to Protagoras or to his modern emulators. Moreover, if all consciousness were cognitive, it could hardly be regarded as always veridical; and this claim to infallibility is only a playful or sarcastic way of saying that no opinion is true in a significant sense, because no moment of consciousness can have a removed object but must necessarily regard only the image or idea then present to the mind. For this reason I have rendered the term used by Protagoras by "appears" rather than by "seems true" or "is thought to be true"; because the ultimate position can hardly be other than this: that when that which appears is thought true the appearance becomes an illusion; and that this appearance is true only in the sense that it verily appears: in which sense all appearances are true equally.

Moral anarchy extended to the intellect.

The Greek Sophists were great men of the world addressing little men of the world: they could not be expected to push scepticism into the sphere of common sense; its use was merely to discredit speculation and authority. The Greeks in general were given to speech-making before the crowd. They might cast ridicule on all reported knowledge, and raise a laugh: they could hardly expect to carry their audience with them, if they denied the existence of that audience, or the intimate shrewd ratiocinations of each man in the crowd, hugging his own thoughts and his own interests. Therefore the unchallenged and unexpressed presuppositions of all criticism in this school must be the existence of conventional human society and the intelligent egoism of each of its members. All else in heaven and earth might be challenged with applause, if reduced to these comfortable and convincing terms.

This denial of truth assumes the truth of psychologism.

Was the being of truth, then, denied by the Sophists, or could they deny it? Yes, if we think only of the truth as proclaimed by particular opinions. All things *said* to be true might be false. Whatsoever depended on argument might be challenged by an opposed cleverer argument; whatsoever depended on usage, faith, or preference might be reversed by a contrary pose; so that every man remained free to think and do what he liked, and to deny all authority. This, though with a different moral tone and intention, was also the position of the Sceptics. They despised opinion, and collected contradictory arguments in order to liberate the mind from every pledge and the heart from every earthly bond. These indomitable doubters stood firm as rocks in their philosophy; and even the Sophists were sure of their wisdom and knowingness in playing their chosen parts in the world. For both schools, then, there was an *unspoken truth:* namely, that life was a treacherous predicament

Personal pride hid this from the ancients.

in which they found themselves without a reason, and that they were determined, whether nobly or nimbly, to make the best of it. Their moral philosophy left the cosmos problematical, while taking for granted abundant knowledge of human affairs and human character. If that age had had a turn for introspection and autobiography, it might have erected a doctrine of the march of experience. Trust in memory, in expectation, in the mutual communication of many minds might have issued in a system like modern psychologism: the view that all we see, say, and think is false, but that the only truth is that we see, say and think it. If nothing be real except experience, nothing can be true except biography. Society must then be conceived as carried on in a literary medium, with no regard to the natural basis of society. If the ancients never hit upon such a system of biographical metaphysics, the reason doubtless was that they were too intelligent. In filling out their fragmentary natural knowledge with myths, they had originally invented other and more beautiful natural beings to help carry on the world: but when the conflict of theories had made the natural world seem problematical, they preferred to abstain from voluntary follies, and not to credit anything so fantastic as that one sight or sound or pleasure or pain might generate another in a vacuum. It mattered little how events might be generated; the point was bravely to enjoy and endure and mock them as they came. Such spiritual courage, however, is physically barren. Heroic scepticism soon withered, and officious sophistry soon found nobody to listen to it. A new image of truth was rising in the east, evoked by inspiration, frankly miraculous, and destined to be sustained and rekindled for ages only by faith.

The dominance of this imposing speculative doctrine, long identified with the truth, has caused the denial of truth in modern times to assume a special character. It has seemed to go with enlightenment, with science, with the pursuit of truth. How, indeed, should anyone pursue the truth, if he were sure he possessed it? Trust in inspiration is something retrograde: it reinstates the primitive dogmatism of the senses, but reinstates it on the imaginative plane, where the object is some speculative idea or vision of the invisible, in regard to which a clear faith is harder to maintain. Protestants had freely criticized the doctrines of the Church, but only by appealing to the infallible text of the Bible, or to some new inspired image of the truth formed in their private meditations; and each had claimed for his shade of doctrine the authority of absolute truth. In view of so many wrangling "truths", the wiser and more humorous heads could not but distrust all conclusions. Free thought became romantic. Ever to decide what you thought would be to stop thinking, and the eternal search for the truth demanded that you should never find it. But for a humanist or an empiricist a truth never to be found differs little from a nonentity. How then avoid the conviction that fruitful science and adventurous philosophy imply a denial that there is any such thing as truth?

This conviction, suggested by that chaos of inspired opinions which was the weak side of Protestantism, was fortified by what gave Protestantism its strength—namely, subjective depth and sincerity. When sensuous dogmatism breaks down and we discover an optical illusion, *ipso facto* we discover a scientific truth; and we

Character of modern scepticism.

clarify the contrast, inherent in all investigation, between superficial appearance and material reality. When on the contrary some illusion of the intellect is detected, or we lose faith in a revealed "truth", no other compara- **Refuge in** ble conception is at hand to take the place of the discredited view. **romantic** Revelation and "truth" go by the board together, and we are driven **subjectivity.** back upon immediate experience and the inner fountain of ideas. These we must continue to accept, unless we should stop living; but we accept them now only as phenomena of life in ourselves, only as a kind of intellectual music which we cannot help making, because such is the fertility of our genius or the marvellous influence upon us of we know not what cosmic climate.

Some lurid romantic cloud land, in that case, truly envelops and contains us; and though the truth might then seem chaotic to us, because not amenable to our moral or grammatical categories, it would be nevertheless precisely the truth it was, and would display all our random visions and emotions precisely in their true places and true relativity. We should then be talking nonsense when we said we denied the being of truth, this truth being avowedly, in respect to us, that we were in a plastic and ill-determined phase of intelligence, and honourably unwilling to pin our faith on any hasty dogma.

Thus as among the ancients, so among the moderns, the denial of truth is due to palpable confusions between truth and knowledge of truth, between essence and existence, between the ideal and the actual. It might seem that **To deny** matters might easily be set right by recalling a few definitions. Yet **the truth** these verbal equivocations are not merely perverse: they are inci- **reported** dental to slow voluminous shifts in morals and culture. The truth **is to posit** posited by animal faith, in action or in curiosity, is posited as **the truth** unknown, as something to be investigated and discovered; and **unreported.** truth in this transcendent sense can never be denied by an active mind. But when animal faith has already expressed itself in conventional ideas, its own further action finds those ideas obstructive. Truth has now been rashly posited as known. An idea, an idol, has taken the place of the god originally and intrinsically invoked by the mind, and posited as unknown. But this is a scandal: how should the thoughts of the wisest human head coincide with the intrinsic essence of any object or event, not to speak of the universe in its totality? The "truth" that the critic or heretic then denies was itself a blasphemy, and in denying it he is secretly animated by the love of truth. What he denies is only the existence of any view in which truth is contained once for all and without qualification. Even if we admit prophecy and supernatural inspiration, the most rapt of prophets can only signalize, adumbrate, and clothe metaphorically the truth revealed through his lips, and not fathomed by his own rational mind: the most explicit of creeds is called a symbol of the faith. The relation which any such symbol may bear to the truth is evidently a historical accident; and the more clearly we perceive the inevitable, all-comprehensive, eternal being of truth, the more improbable or even impossible must seem the notion that any human conception should ever do it justice.

III

Rational Life in Art, Religion, and Spirituality

Santayana's early writings, such as *The Life of Reason,* are distinguished by their humanistic themes from his later ontological works, such as *The Realms of Being;* yet he maintained that his philosophy never changed. Writing seventeen years after the first publication of *The Life of Reason,* he claimed "there has been no change in my deliberate doctrine, only some changes of mental habit" ("Preface to the Second Edition," in *Reason in Common Sense,* 2nd edition [Charles Scribner's Sons, 1922], v). Elsewhere he acknowledged changes in perspective and emphasis, and in sentiment and the material he took up in his writing; but he claimed that his theory and vision of human life did not alter (*PGS,* 560; *PP,* 159, 167). His earlier perspective he thought more transcendental and egotistical, and he characterized his earlier approach as "sentimental self-consciousness" (*LGS,* 3:14). Later, human belief occupied him less and nature or the enveloping environment of such belief took on greater significance. But his work always looked to the free rational life or "the healthy life of the spirit" ("Preface to the Second Edition," in *Reason in Common Sense,* 2nd edition [Charles Scribner's Sons, 1922], xii), and this section attempts to show how this concern runs through his early works on poetry, religion, reason, and art and culminates in his later speculations on spirituality.

In "The Elements and Function of Poetry" Santayana observed that poetry can organize sounds in pleasing and elegant ways and challenge conventions through the expression of passion, but he thought the highest function of poetry to be organizing human passions through the creation of ideals true to the highest capacities of human nature. He thought poetry that performed this task perfectly would be identical to religion without illusion. "Religion," he wrote, "is poetry become the guide of life" (*ES,* 280).

The guide of life, according to Santayana, orients one toward excellence, which is the defining aim of reason. He characterized the Life of Reason as "the happy marriage of . . . impulse and ideation" (*ES,* 284). When impulse is enlightened by reflection and memory, reason appears. The Life of Reason is a life consciously realizing its ideal perfection, a harmony of impulses that is its natural happiness. "The Birth of Reason" relates the naturalistic basis of both excellence and reason. The living organism's efforts to preserve one set of conditions rather than another begin at a point assigned by fate, but this is the beginning of an instinctual discrimination among possibilities that shapes bias or interest. Reason, or the love and pursuit of the good, is a better form of interest because it is ultimately more assured, being concerned not with the shifting material flux but rather with ideals.

The ideals of excellence that distinguish the Life of Reason relate it to religion. Religion can be a means to the ultimate goods of the Life of Reason, such as happiness, harmony, and freedom. Both religion and reason establish standards of right and wrong, and both emancipate one from personal limitations. But where reason is simply a form or a principle and does not call out emotion, religion involves ideas, hopes, enthusiasms, and objects of worship, making the latter volatile and subject to illusion. Indeed, religion can go astray by asserting the literal truth of its poetic doctrines. But Santayana did not think religion to blame for hindering science and moral reflection. Obstacles to insight in these fields lie deeper than religion, and he found religion praiseworthy for promoting speculative insight.

In "The Justification of Art" Santayana considered the contribution of art to the Life of Reason. He thought that art, being concerned with the ideal, does not directly influence the material world; rather it renders the world of matter into ideas and is a rehearsal of a life not yet realized. The power of art lies in its rejuvenation of imagination and the life of ideas. But taste in art does not begin in the life of ideas; instead it has a material basis in one's natural affinities, making it dogmatic and inevitable. If one escapes the trap of believing one's own dogma to be absolute, then taste may be refined in reflection, made sympathetic with a wider range of experience, and articulated as the criterion of taste. Good taste is appreciation for those things that harmonize with the Life of Reason or that secure and promote richer satisfactions, such as pleasures that go beyond chance feelings and have the support of reason. Such pleasures include living artfully and enriching experience with keener intuition of essences.

Art is not an escape from reality; rather it is realization of the potentials of nature, including the potential for human happiness. Art absorbed into the Life of Reason endows all activities with beauty and makes all works into works of art. Art and happiness come together through intelligence, which consists in self-knowledge and an understanding of nature's laws. The harmonies made or discovered between humans and nature are the source of happiness and liberation from superstition and convention. The artist, no longer merely a tool or an observer of nature, becomes creative and so capable of honest expression and clearer articulation of human ideals.

In turning from the Life of Reason to the spiritual life, Santayana was not endorsing one form of life over another. He thought that rational living harmonized the life of spirit among other interests, and he remained concerned with disillusion and freedom as he took up spirit as his subject matter. In his earlier work, he had asked how religion embodies reason, a question about an ideal of actual human living. In "Ultimate Religion" Santayana asked, in the context of praising Spinoza, what a religion would be like that suited a free and disillusioned spirit.[1] This is not a survey of historical religions with an eye to the right one; rather it is speculation on the ultimate aims of spirit in its highest flights of

---

1. For an insightful discussion of the differences between Santayana's earlier and later views on this question, see James Gouinlock, "Ultimate Religion" (*Overheard in Seville: Bulletin of the Santayana Society*, 16 [1998]: 1–13), and the response by Henry Samuel Levinson, "Charity, Interpretation,

intuition. An ultimate religion acknowledges and respects the universal power of the realm of matter, honors the realm of truth, and loves all perfections arising as goals of life. The religious spirit loves the perfection and beauty inherent in every living thing.

In "The Nature of Spirit," Santayana provided a glossary of terms, including "body," "organism," "psyche," "animal," "soul," "self or person," and "spirit," and this last he characterized as "the *witness* of the cosmic dance" (*ES*, 350). It is "an immaterial invisible inward intensity of being" (*ES*, 351) without power in the physical world and distinct from the material body. But spirit is not disembodied; "[i]t is the moral fruition of physical life" (*ES*, 350). Santayana wrote that "[m]y whole description of the spiritual life is . . . an extension of my materialism and a consequence of it" (*PGS*, 504). Without a body spirit would lack consciousness or a particular moral destiny; it could not be a focus of knowledge engendered by the demands of the world on the animal organism. Spirit is infinitely open to all essences; but despite this lack of anxiety about what may be presented to it, it suffers because of its connection to psyche. Psyche must be concerned with threats to animal life and so distracts spirit from its proper activity.

Santayana considered spirit's distraction and deliverance in "Liberation." Distraction cannot be attributed to the flesh or the world, because spirit is a natural culmination of them. Liberation cannot be new life or elimination of life; the first would reinstate the same entanglements and the second would eliminate spirit altogether. Distraction of spirit is moral ignorance of the proper vocation of spirit. Santayana held that spirit is "by its own intellectual insight to introduce us into the spheres of truth or of essence, detaching us from each thing with humility and humour, and attaching us to all things with justice, charity and pure joy" (*ES*, 362). Distraction occurs when spirit concerns itself about itself rather than intuiting essences. It forgets its natural calling when assailed by the worries of the animal psyche. Liberation is not the rejection of animal psyche; rather it is the purification of the deliverances of psyche to spirit, "to view them as accidents, to enjoy them without claiming them, to transcend without despising them" (*ES*, 367).

Liberation prepares the way for spiritual "Union." But union with what and united in what sense? Spirit is to be united with the Good understood as "the end that life proposes to itself when conscious and rational" (*ES*, 405). This union is not a relation of interdependence or a material merger, and it does not require dissolution of spirit. In fact, spiritual integrity is a condition of union. In other words, union requires that spirit accept its animal origins even as it seeks its rational end. Santayana thought this possible through a kind of love understood as sympathy with vital origins, compassion for the perfection of any passion, and charity as a spiritualized sympathy allowing spirit to understand worldly passions without adopting them. This love would be "a pitying and forgiving insight into [the world's] loves" such as the world could never feel toward itself (*ES*, 382). Even though union with the Good must remain ideal, the commitment to union

Disintoxication: A Comment on Gouinlock's 'Ultimate Religion'" (*Overheard in Seville: Bulletin of the Santayana Society*, 16 [1998]: 13–18).

can become actual through "the life of prayer" (*ES*, 393) or "intellectual worship, in which spirit, forgetting itself, becomes pure vision and pure love" (*ES*, 407). Such an act is never final, just as spirit itself is "always a consummation, never a finality" (*ES*, 402).

The Elements and Function of Poetry

Interpretations of Poetry and Religion. Volume three of the critical edition of *The Works of George Santayana.* Edited by William G. Holzberger and Herman J. Saatkamp Jr., with an Introduction by Joel Porte. Cambridge, MA: The MIT Press, 1989, 151–72.

This selection appeared as Chapter X in Santayana's second philosophical book, an essay collection published in 1900 entitled Interpretations of Poetry and Religion. *Santayana wrote to his publisher "that this book will arouse more interest—doubtless more adverse criticism too—than did the other; but that, if it comes, will not do you or me any harm" (LGS, 1:203). William James reported that on reading the book he "literally squealed with delight at the imperturbable perfection with which the position is laid down on page after page" (*The Correspondence of William James, *volume 9, edited by Ignas K. Skrupskelis and Elizabeth M. Berkeley [Charlottesville and London: University Press of Virginia, 2001], 180). This selection describes three functions of poetry. On the lowest level poetry organizes sounds and displays virtuosity in language. On the intermediate level poetry undermines convention to release passions and communicate experiences previously ignored. On the highest level poetry is creative reason and aims not merely to tap emotion and experience but to use them "to build new structures, richer, finer, fitter to the primary tendencies of our nature, truer to the ultimate possibilities of the soul" (ES, 273). "The highest example of this kind of poetry is religion" (ES, 278).*

If a critic, in despair of giving a serious definition of poetry, should be satisfied with saying that poetry is metrical discourse, he would no doubt be giving an inadequate account of the matter, yet not one of which he need be ashamed or which he should regard as superficial. Although a poem be not made by counting of syllables upon the fingers, yet "numbers" is the most poetical synonym we have for verse, and "measure" the most significant equivalent for beauty, for goodness, and perhaps even for truth. Those early and profound philosophers, the followers of Pythagoras, saw the essence of all things in number, and it was by weight, measure, and number, as we read in the Bible, that the Creator first brought Nature out of the void. Every human architect must do likewise with his edifice; he must mould his bricks or hew his stones into symmetrical solids and lay them over one another in regular strata, like a poet's lines.

Measure is a condition of perfection, for perfection requires that order should be pervasive, that not only the whole before us should have a form, but that every part in turn should have a form of its own, and that those parts should be coördinated among themselves as the whole is coördinated with the other parts of some greater cosmos. Leibnitz lighted in his speculations upon a conception of organic nature which may be false as a fact, but which is excellent as an ideal; he tells us that the difference between living and dead matter, between animals and machines, is that the former are composed of parts that are themselves organic, every portion of the body being itself a machine, and every portion of that machine still a machine, and so *ad infinitum;* whereas, in artificial bodies the organisation is not in this manner infinitely deep. Fine Art, in this as in all things, imitates the method of Nature and makes its most beautiful works out of materials that are themselves beautiful. So that even if the difference between verse and prose consisted only in measure, that difference would already be analogous to that between jewels and clay.

The stuff of language is words, and the sensuous material of words is sound; if language therefore is to be made perfect, its materials must be made beautiful by being themselves subjected to a measure, and endowed with a form. It is true that language is a symbol for intelligence rather than a stimulus to sense, and accordingly the beauties of discourse which commonly attract attention are merely the beauties of the objects and ideas signified; yet the symbols have a sensible reality of their own, a euphony which appeals to our senses if we keep them open. The tongue will choose those forms of utterance which have a natural grace as mere sound and sensation; the memory will retain these catches, and they will pass and repass through the mind until they become types of instinctive speech and standards of pleasing expression.

The highest form of such euphony is song; the singing voice gives to the sounds it utters the thrill of tonality,–a thrill itself dependent, as we know, on the numerical proportions of the vibrations that it includes. But this kind of euphony and sensuous beauty, the deepest that sounds can have, we have almost wholly surrendered in our speech. Our intelligence has become complex, and language, to express our thoughts, must commonly be more rapid, copious, and abstract than is compatible with singing. Music at the same time has become complex also, and when united with words, at one time disfigures them in the elaboration of its melody, and at another overpowers them in the volume of its sound. So that the art of singing is now in the same plight as that of sculpture,–an abstract and conventional thing surviving by force of tradition and of an innate but now impotent impulse, which under simpler conditions would work itself out into the proper forms of those arts. The truest kind of euphony is thus denied to our poetry. If any verses are still set to music, they are commonly the worst only, chosen for the purpose by musicians of specialised sensibility and inferior intelligence, who seem to be attracted only by tawdry effects of rhetoric and sentiment.

When song is given up, there still remains in speech a certain sensuous quality, due to the nature and order of the vowels and consonants that compose the sounds. This kind of euphony is not neglected by the more dulcet poets, and is now so studied in some quarters that I have heard it maintained by a critic of relative authority that the beauty of poetry consists entirely in the frequent utterance of the sound of "j" and "sh," and the consequent copious flow of saliva in the mouth. But even if saliva is not the whole essence of poetry, there is an unmistakable and fundamental diversity of effect in the various vocalisation of different poets, which becomes all the more evident when we compare those who use different languages. One man's speech, or one nation's, is compact, crowded with consonants, rugged, broken with emphatic beats; another man's, or nation's, is open, tripping, rapid, and even. So Byron, mingling in his boyish fashion burlesque with exquisite sentiment, contrasts English with Italian speech:–

> *I love the language, that soft bastard Latin*
> *Which melts like kisses from a female mouth*
> *And sounds as if it should be writ on satin*
> *With syllables which breathe of the sweet South,*
> *And gentle liquids gliding all so pat in*
> *That not a single accent seems uncouth,*
> *Like our harsh Northern whistling, grunting guttural*
> *Which we're obliged to hiss and spit and sputter all.*

And yet these contrasts, strong when we compare extreme cases, fade from our consciousness in the actual use of a mother-tongue. The function makes us unconscious of the instrument, all the more as it is an indispensable and almost invariable one. The sense of euphony accordingly attaches itself rather to another and more variable quality; the tune, or measure, or rhythm of speech. The elementary sounds are prescribed by the language we use, and the selection we may make among those sounds is limited; but the arrangement of words is still undetermined, and by casting our speech into the moulds of metre and rhyme we can give it a heightened power, apart from its significance. A tolerable definition of poetry, on its formal side, might be found in this: that poetry is speech in which the instrument counts as well as the meaning–poetry is speech for its own sake and for its own sweetness. As common windows are intended only to admit the light, but painted windows also to dye it, and to be an object of attention in themselves as well as a cause of visibility in other things, so, while the purest prose is a mere vehicle of thought, verse, like stained glass, arrests attention in its own intricacies, confuses it in its own glories, and is even at times allowed to darken and puzzle in the hope of casting over us a supernatural spell.

Long passages in Shelley's *Revolt of Islam* and Keats' *Endymion* are poetical in this sense; the reader gathers, probably, no definite meaning, but is conscious of a poetic medium, of speech euphonious and measured, and redolent of a kind of objectless passion which is little more than the sensation of the movement and sensuous richness of the lines. Such poetry is not great; it has, in fact, a tedious vacuity, and is unworthy of a mature mind; but it is poetical, and could be produced only by a legitimate child of the Muse. It belongs to an apprenticeship, but in this case the apprenticeship of genius. It bears that relation to great poems which scales and aimless warblings bear to great singing–they test the essential endowment and fineness of the organ which is to be employed in the art. Without this sensuous background and ingrained predisposition to beauty, no art can reach the deepest and most exquisite effects; and even without an intelligible superstructure these sensuous qualities suffice to give that thrill of exaltation, that suggestion of an ideal world, which we feel in the presence of any true beauty.

The sensuous beauty of words and their utterance in measure suffice, therefore, for poetry of one sort–where these are there is something unmistakably poetical, although the whole of poetry, or the best of poetry, be not yet there.

Indeed, in such works as *The Revolt of Islam* or *Endymion* there is already more than mere metre and sound; there is the colour and choice of words, the fanciful, rich, or exquisite juxtaposition of phrases. The vocabulary and the texture of the style are precious; affected, perhaps, but at any rate refined.

This quality, which is that almost exclusively exploited by the Symbolist, we may call euphuism—the choice of coloured words and rare and elliptical phrases. If great poets are like architects and sculptors, the euphuists are like goldsmiths and jewellers; their work is filigree in precious metals, encrusted with glowing stones. Now euphuism contributes not a little to the poetic effect of the tirades of Keats and Shelley; if we wish to see the power of versification without euphuism we may turn to the tirades of Pope, where metre and euphony are displayed alone, and we have the outline or skeleton of poetry without the filling.

> *In spite of pride, in erring reason's spite,*
> *One truth is clear, Whatever is, is right.*

We should hesitate to say that such writing was truly poetical; so that some euphuism as well as metre would seem to be necessary to the formal essence of poetry.

An example of this sort, however, takes us out of the merely verbal into the imaginative region; the reason that Pope is hardly poetical to us is not that he is inharmonious,—not a defect of euphony,—but that he is too intellectual and has an excess of mentality. It is easier for words to be poetical without any thought, when they are felt merely as sensuous and musical, than for them to remain so when they convey an abstract notion,—especially if that notion be a tart and frigid sophism, like that of the couplet just quoted. The pyrotechnics of the intellect then take the place of the glow of sense, and the artifice of thought chills the pleasure we might have taken in the grace of expression.

If poetry in its higher reaches is more philosophical than history, because it presents the memorable types of men and things apart from unmeaning circumstances, so in its primary substance and texture poetry is more philosophical than prose because it is nearer to our immediate experience. Poetry breaks up the trite conceptions designated by current words into the sensuous qualities out of which those conceptions were originally put together. We name what we conceive and believe in, not what we see; things, not images; souls, not voices and silhouettes. This naming, with the whole education of the senses which it accompanies, subserves the uses of life; in order to thread our way through the labyrinth of objects which assault us, we must make a great selection in our sensuous experience; half of what we see and hear we must pass over as insignificant, while we piece out the other half with such an ideal complement as is necessary to turn it into a fixed and well-ordered conception of the world. This labour of perception and understanding, this spelling of the material meaning of experience is enshrined in our work-a-day language and ideas; ideas which are literally poetic in the sense that they are "made" (for every conception in an adult mind is a fiction), but which are at the same time prosaic because they are made economically, by abstraction, and for use.

When the child of poetic genius, who has learned this intellectual and utilitarian language in the cradle, goes afield and gathers for himself the aspects of Nature, he begins to encumber his mind with the many living impressions which the intellect rejected, and which the language of the intellect can hardly convey; he labours with his nameless burden of perception, and wastes himself in aimless impulses of emotion and revery, until finally the method of some art offers a vent to his inspiration, or to such part of it as can survive the test of time and the discipline of expression.

The poet retains by nature the innocence of the eye, or recovers it easily; he disintegrates the fictions of common perception into their sensuous elements, gathers these together again into chance groups as the accidents of his environment or the affinities of his temperament may conjoin them; and this wealth of sensation and this freedom of fancy, which make an extraordinary ferment in his ignorant heart, presently bubble over into some kind of utterance.

The fulness and sensuousness of such effusions bring them nearer to our actual perceptions than common discourse could come; yet they may easily seem remote, overloaded, and obscure to those accustomed to think entirely in symbols, and never to be interrupted in the algebraic rapidity of their thinking by a moment's pause and examination of heart, nor ever to plunge for a moment into that torrent of sensation and imagery over which the bridge of prosaic associations habitually carries us safe and dry to some conventional act. How slight that bridge commonly is, how much an affair of trestles and wire, we can hardly conceive until we have trained ourselves to an extreme sharpness of introspection. But psychologists have discovered, what laymen generally will confess, that we hurry by the procession of our mental images as we do by the traffic of the street, intent on business, gladly forgetting the noise and movement of the scene, and looking only for the corner we would turn or the door we would enter. Yet in our alertest moment the depths of the soul are still dreaming; the real world stands drawn in bare outline against a background of chaos and unrest. Our logical thoughts dominate experience only as the parallels and meridians make a checker-board of the sea. They guide our voyage without controlling the waves, which toss for ever in spite of our ability to ride over them to our chosen ends. Sanity is a madness put to good uses; waking life is a dream controlled.

Out of the neglected riches of this dream the poet fetches his wares. He dips into the chaos that underlies the rational shell of the world and brings up some superfluous image, some emotion dropped by the way, and reattaches it to the present object; he reinstates things unnecessary, he emphasises things ignored, he paints in again into the landscape the tints which the intellect has allowed to fade from it. If he seems sometimes to obscure a fact, it is only because he is restoring an experience. We may observe this process in the simplest cases. When Ossian, mentioning the sun, says it is round as the shield of his fathers, the expression is poetical. Why? Because he has added to the word sun, in itself sufficient and unequivocal, other words, unnecessary for practical clearness, but serving to restore the individuality of his perception and its associations in his mind. There is no square sun with which the sun he is speaking of could be confused; to stop and call it round is a luxury, a halting in the sensation for the love of its form. And to go on to tell us, what is wholly impertinent, that the shield of his fathers was round also, is to invite us to follow the chance wanderings of his fancy, to give us a little glimpse of the stuffing of his own brain, or, we might almost say, to turn over the pattern of his embroidery and show us the loose threads hanging out on the wrong side. Such an escapade disturbs and interrupts the true vision of the object, and a great poet, rising to a perfect conception of the sun and forgetting himself, would have disdained to make it; but it has a romantic and pathological interest, it restores an experience, and is in that measure poetical. We have been made to halt at the sensation, and to penetrate for a moment into its background of dream.

But it is not only thoughts or images that the poet draws in this way from the store of his experience, to clothe the bare form of conventional objects: he often adds to these objects a more subtle ornament, drawn from the same source. For the first element which the intellect rejects in forming its ideas of things is the emotion which accompanies the perception; and this emotion is the first thing the poet restores. He stops at the image, because he stops to enjoy. He wanders into the by-paths of association because the by-paths are delightful. The love of beauty which made him give measure and cadence to his words, the love of harmony which made him rhyme them, reappear in his imagination and make him select there also the material that is itself beautiful, or capable of assuming beautiful forms. The link that binds together the ideas, sometimes so wide apart, which his wit assimilates, is most often the link of emotion; they have in common some element of beauty or of horror.

The poet's art is to a great extent the art of intensifying emotions by assembling the scattered objects that naturally arouse them. He sees the affinities of things by seeing their common affinities with passion. As the guiding principle of practical thinking is some interest, so that only what is pertinent to that interest is selected by the attention; as the guiding principle of scientific thinking is some connection of things in time or space, or some identity of law; so in poetic thinking the guiding principle is often a mood or a quality of sentiment. By this union of disparate things having a common overtone of feeling, the feeling is itself evoked in all its strength; nay, it is often created for the first time, much as by a new mixture of old pigments Perugino could produce the unprecedented limpidity of his colour, or Titian the unprecedented glow of his. Poets can thus arouse sentiments finer than any which they have known, and in the act of composition become discoverers of new realms of delightfulness and grief. Expression is a misleading term which suggests that something previously known is rendered or imitated; whereas the expression is itself an original fact, the values of which are then referred to the thing expressed, much as the honours of a Chinese mandarin are attributed retroactively to his parents. So the charm which a poet, by his art of combining images and shades of emotion, casts over a scene or an action, is attached to the principal actor in it, who gets the benefit of the setting furnished him by a well-stocked mind.

The poet is himself subject to this illusion, and a great part of what is called poetry, although by no means the best part of it, consists in this sort of idealisation by proxy. We dye the world of our own colour; by a pathetic fallacy, by a false projection of sentiment, we soak Nature with our own feeling, and then celebrate her tender sympathy with our moral being. This aberration, as we see in the case of Wordsworth, is not inconsistent with a high development of both the faculties which it confuses,–I mean vision and feeling. On the contrary, vision and feeling, when most abundant and original, most easily present themselves in this undivided form. There would be need of a force of intellect which poets rarely possess to rationalise their inspiration without diminishing its volume: and if, as is commonly the case, the energy of the dream and the passion in them is greater than that of the reason, and they cannot attain true propriety and supreme beauty in their works, they can, nevertheless, fill them with lovely images and a fine moral spirit.

The pouring forth of both perceptive and emotional elements in their mixed and indiscriminate form gives to this kind of imagination the directness and truth which sensuous poetry possesses on a lower level. The outer world bathed in the hues of human feeling, the inner world expressed in the forms of things,–that is the primitive condition of both before intelligence and the prosaic classification of objects have abstracted them and assigned them to their respective spheres. Such identifications, on which a certain kind of metaphysics prides itself also, are not discoveries of profound genius; they are exactly like the observation of Ossian that the sun is round and that the shield of his fathers was round too; they are disintegrations of conventional objects, so that the original associates of our perceptions reappear; then the thing and the emotion which chanced to be simultaneous are said to be one, and we return, unless a better principle of organisation is substituted for the principle abandoned, to the chaos of a passive animal consciousness, where all is mixed together, projected together, and felt as an unutterable whole.

The pathetic fallacy is a return to that early habit of thought by which our ancestors peopled the world with benevolent and malevolent spirits; what they felt in the presence of objects they took to be a part of the objects themselves. In returning to this natural confusion, poetry does us a service in that she recalls and consecrates those phases of our experience which, as useless to the understanding of material reality, we are in danger of forgetting altogether. Therein is her vitality, for she pierces to the quick and shakes us out of our servile speech and imaginative poverty; she reminds us of all we have felt, she invites us even to dream a little, to nurse the wonderful spontaneous creations which at every waking moment we are snuffing out in our brain. And the indulgence is no mere momentary pleasure; much of its exuberance clings afterward to our ideas; we see the more and feel the more for that exercise; we are capable of finding greater entertainment in the common aspects of Nature and life. When the veil of convention is once removed from our eyes by the poet, we are better able to dominate any particular experience and, as it were, to change its scale, now losing ourselves in its infinitesimal texture, now in its infinite ramifications.

If the function of poetry, however, did not go beyond this recovery of sensuous and imaginative freedom, at the expense of disrupting our useful habits of thought, we might be grateful to it for occasionally relieving our numbness, but we should have to admit that it was nothing but a relaxation; that spiritual discipline was not to be gained from it in any degree, but must be sought wholly in that intellectual system that builds the science of Nature with the categories of prose. So conceived, poetry would deserve the judgment passed by Plato on all the arts of flattery and entertainment; it might be crowned as delightful, but must be either banished altogether as meretricious or at least confined to a few forms and occasions where it might do little harm. The judgment of Plato has been generally condemned by philosophers, although it is eminently rational, and justified by the simplest principles of morals. It has been adopted instead, although unwittingly, by the practical and secular part of mankind, who look upon artists and poets as inefficient and brainsick people under whose spell it would be a serious calamity to fall, although they may be called in on feast days as an ornament and luxury together with the cooks, hairdressers, and florists.

Several circumstances, however, might suggest to us the possibility that the greatest function of poetry may be still to find. Plato, while condemning Homer, was a kind of poet himself; his quarrel with the followers of the Muse was not a quarrel with the goddess; and the good people of Philistia, distrustful as they may be of profane art, pay undoubting honour to religion, which is a kind of poetry as much removed from their sphere as the midnight revels upon Mount Citheron, which, to be sure, were also religious in their inspiration. Why, we may ask, these apparent inconsistencies? Why do our practical men make room for religion in the background of their world? Why did Plato, after banishing the poets, poetise the universe in his prose? Because the abstraction by which the world of science and of practice is drawn out of our experience, is too violent to satisfy even the thoughtless and vulgar; the ideality of the machine we call Nature, the conventionality of the drama we call the world, are too glaring not to be somehow perceived by all. Each must sometimes fall back upon the soul; he must challenge this apparition with the thought of death; he must ask himself for the mainspring and value of his life. He will then remember his stifled loves; he will feel that only his illusions have ever given him a sense of reality, only his passions the hope and the vision of peace. He will read himself through and almost gather a meaning from his experience; at least he will half believe that all he has been dealing with was a dream and a symbol, and raise his eyes toward the truth beyond.

This plastic moment of the mind, when we become aware of the artificiality and inadequacy of what common sense conceives, is the true moment of poetic opportunity,–an opportunity, we may hasten to confess, which is generally missed. The strain of attention, the concentration and focussing of thought on the unfamiliar immediacy of things, usually brings about nothing but confusion. We are dazed, we are filled with a sense of unutterable things, luminous yet indistinguishable, many yet one. Instead of rising to imagination, we sink into mysticism.

To accomplish a mystical disintegration is not the function of any art; if any art seems to accomplish it, the effect is only incidental, being involved, perhaps, in the process of constructing the proper object of that art, as we might cut down trees and dig them up by the roots to lay the foundations of a temple. For every art looks to the building up of something. And just because the image of the world built up by common sense and natural science is an inadequate image (a skeleton which needs the filling of sensation before it can live), therefore the moment when we realise its inadequacy is the moment when the higher arts find their opportunity. When the world is shattered to bits they can come and "build it nearer to the heart's desire."

The great function of poetry is precisely this: to repair to the material of experience, seizing hold of the reality of sensation and fancy beneath the surface of conventional ideas, and then out of that living but indefinite material to build new structures, richer, finer, fitter to the primary tendencies of our nature, truer to the ultimate possibilities of the soul. Our descent into the elements of our being is then justified by our subsequent freer ascent toward its goal; we revert to sense only to find food for reason; we destroy conventions only to construct ideals.

Such analysis for the sake of creation is the essence of all great poetry. Science and common sense are themselves in their way poets of no mean order, since they take the material of experience and make out of it a clear, symmetrical, and beautiful world; the very propriety of this art, however, has made it common. Its figures have become mere rhetoric and its metaphors prose. Yet, even as it is, a scientific and mathematical vision has a higher beauty than the irrational poetry of sensation and impulse, which merely tickles the brain, like liquor, and plays upon our random, imaginative lusts. The imagination of a great poet, on the contrary, is as orderly as that of an astronomer, and as large; he has the naturalist's patience, the naturalist's love of detail and eye trained to see fine gradations and essential lines; he knows no hurry; he has no pose, no sense of originality; he finds his effects in his subject, and his subject in his inevitable world. Resembling the naturalist in all this, he differs from him in the balance of his interests; the poet has the concreter mind; his visible world wears all its colours and retains its indwelling passion and life. Instead of studying in experience its calculable elements, he studies its moral values, its beauty, the openings it offers to the soul: and the cosmos he constructs is accordingly an ideal theatre for the spirit in which its noblest potential drama is enacted and its destiny resolved.

This supreme function of poetry is only the consummation of the method by which words and imagery are transformed into verse. As verse breaks up the prosaic order of syllables and subjects them to a recognisable and pleasing measure, so poetry breaks up the whole prosaic picture of experience to introduce into it a rhythm more congenial and intelligible to the mind. And in both these cases the operation is essentially the same as that by which, in an intermediate sphere, the images rejected by practical thought, and the emotions ignored by it, are so marshalled as to fill the mind with a truer and intenser consciousness of its memorable experience. The poetry of fancy, of observation, and of passion moves on this intermediate level; the poetry of mere sound and virtuosity is confined to the lower sphere; and the highest is reserved for the poetry of the creative reason. But one principle is present throughout,–the principle of Beauty,–the art of assimilating phenomena, whether words, images, emotions, or systems of ideas, to the deeper innate cravings of the mind.

Let us now dwell a little on this higher function of poetry and try to distinguish some of its phases.

The creation of characters is what many of us might at first be tempted to regard as the supreme triumph of the imagination. If we abstract, however, from our personal tastes and look at the matter in its human and logical relations, we shall see, I think, that the construction of characters is not the ultimate task of poetic fiction. A character can never be exhaustive of our materials: for it exists by its idiosyncrasy, by its contrast with other natures, by its development of one side, and one side only, of our native capacities. It is, therefore, not by characterisation as such that the ultimate message can be rendered. The poet can put only a part of himself into any of his heroes, but he must put the whole into his noblest work. A character is accordingly only a fragmentary unity; fragmentary in respect to its origin,—since it is conceived by enlargement, so to speak, of a part of our own being to the exclusion of the rest,—and fragmentary in respect to the object it presents, since a character must live in an environment and be appreciated by contrast and by the sense of derivation. Not the character, but its effects and causes, is the truly interesting thing. Thus in master poets, like Homer and Dante, the characters, although well drawn, are subordinate to the total movement and meaning of the scene. There is indeed something pitiful, something comic, in any comprehended soul; souls, like other things, are only definable by their limitations. We feel instinctively that it would be insulting to speak of any man to his face as we should speak of him in his absence, even if what we say is in the way of praise: for absent he is a character understood, but present he is a force respected.

In the construction of ideal characters, then, the imagination is busy with material,—particular actions and thoughts,—which suggest their unification in persons; but the characters thus conceived can hardly be adequate to the profusion of our observations, nor exhaustive, when all personalities are taken together, of the interest of our lives. Characters are initially imbedded in life, as the gods themselves are originally imbedded in Nature. Poetry must, therefore, to render all reality, render also the background of its figures, and the events that condition their acts. We must place them in that indispensable environment which the landscape furnishes to the eye and the social medium to the emotions.

The visible landscape is not a proper object for poetry. Its elements, and especially the emotional stimulation which it gives, may be suggested or expressed in verse; but landscape is not thereby represented in its proper form; it appears only as an element and associate of moral unities. Painting, architecture, and gardening, with the art of stage setting, have the visible landscape for their object, and to those arts we may leave it. But there is a sort of landscape larger than the visible, which escapes the synthesis of the eye; it is present to that topographical sense by which we always live in the consciousness that there is a sea, that there are mountains, that the sky is above us, even when we do not see it, and that the tribes of men, with their different degrees of blamelessness, are scattered over the broad-backed earth. This cosmic landscape poetry alone can render, and it is no small part of the art to awaken the sense of it at the right moment, so that the object that occupies the centre of vision may be seen in its true lights, coloured by its wider associations, and dignified by its felt affinities to things permanent and great. As the Italian masters were wont not to paint their groups of saints about the Virgin without enlarging the canvas, so as to render a broad piece of sky, some mountains and rivers, and nearer, perhaps, some decorative pile; so the poet of larger mind envelops his characters in the atmosphere of Nature and history, and keeps us constantly aware of the world in which they move.

The distinction of a poet—the dignity and humanity of his thought—can be measured by nothing, perhaps, so well as by the diameter of the world in which he lives; if he is supreme, his vision, like Dante's, always stretches to the stars. And Virgil, a supreme poet sometimes unjustly belittled, shows us the same thing in another form; his landscape is the Roman universe, his theme the sacred springs of Roman greatness in piety, constancy, and law. He has not written a line in forgetfulness that he was a Roman; he loves country life and its labours because he sees in it the origin and bulwark of civic greatness; he honours tradition because it gives perspective and momentum to the history that ensues; he invokes the gods, because they are symbols of the physical and moral forces by which Rome struggled to dominion.

Almost every classic poet has the topographical sense; he swarms with proper names and allusions to history and fable; if an epithet is to be thrown in anywhere to fill up the measure of a line, he chooses instinctively an appellation of place or family; his wine is not red, but Samian; his gorges are not deep, but are the gorges of Hæmus; his songs are not sweet, but Pierian. We may deride their practice as conventional, but they could far more justly deride ours as insignificant. Conventions do not arise without some reason, and genius will know how to rise above them by a fresh appreciation of their rightness, and will feel no temptation to overturn them in favour of personal whimsies. The ancients found poetry not so much in sensible accidents as in essential forms and noble associations; and this fact marks very clearly their superior education. They dominated the world as we no longer dominate it, and lived, as we are too distracted to live, in the presence of the rational and the important.

A physical and historical background, however, is of little moment to the poet in comparison with that other environment of his characters,—the dramatic situations in which they are involved. The substance of poetry is, after all, emotion; and if the intellectual emotion of comprehension and the mimetic one of impersonation are massive, they are not so intense as the appetites and other transitive emotions of life; the passions are the chief basis of all interests, even the most ideal, and the passions are seldom brought into play except by the contact of man with man. The various forms of love and hate are only possible in society, and to imagine occasions in which these feelings may manifest all their inward vitality is the poet's function,—one in which he follows the fancy of every child, who puffs himself out in his day-dreams into an endless variety of heroes and lovers. The thrilling adventures which he craves demand an appropriate theatre; the glorious emotions with which he bubbles over must at all hazards find or feign their correlative objects.

But the passions are naturally blind, and the poverty of the imagination, when left alone, is absolute. The passions may ferment as they will, they never can breed an idea out of their own energy. This idea must be furnished by the senses, by outward experience, else the hunger of the soul will gnaw its own emptiness for ever. Where the seed of sensation has once fallen, however, the growth, variations, and exuberance of fancy may be unlimited. Only we still observe (as in the child, in dreams, and in the poetry of ignorant or mystical poets) that the intensity of inwardly generated visions does not involve any real increase in their scope or dignity. The inexperienced mind remains a thin mind, no matter how much its vapours may be heated and blown about by natural passion. It was a capital error in Fichte and Schopenhauer to assign essential fertility to the will in the creation of ideas. They mistook, as human nature will do, even when at times it professes pessimism, an ideal for a reality: and because they saw how much the will clings to its objects, how it selects and magnifies them, they imagined that it could breed them out of itself. A man who thinks clearly will see that such self-determination of a will is inconceivable, since what has no external relation and no diversity of structure cannot of itself acquire diversity of functions. Such inconceivability, of course, need not seem a great objection to a man of impassioned inspiration; he may even claim a certain consistency in positing, on the strength of his preference, the inconceivable to be a truth.

The alleged fertility of the will is, however, disproved by experience, from which metaphysics must in the end draw its analogies and plausibility. The passions discover, they do not create, their occasions; a fact which is patent when we observe how they seize upon what objects they find, and how reversible, contingent, and transferable the emotions are in respect to their objects. A doll will be loved instead of a child, a child instead of a lover, God instead of everything. The differentiation of the passions, as far as consciousness is concerned, depends on the variety of the objects of experience,–that is, on the differentiation of the senses and of the environment which stimulates them.

When the "infinite" spirit enters the human body, it is determined to certain limited forms of life by the organs which it wears; and its blank potentiality becomes actual in thought and deed, according to the fortunes and relations of its organism. The ripeness of the passions may thus precede the information of the mind and lead to groping in by-paths without issue; a phenomenon which appears not only in the obscure individual whose abnormalities the world ignores, but also in the starved, half-educated genius that pours the whole fire of his soul into trivial arts or grotesque superstitions. The hysterical forms of music and religion are the refuge of an idealism that has lost its way; the waste and failures of life flow largely in those channels. The carnal temptations of youth are incidents of the same maladaptation, when passions assert themselves before the conventional order of society can allow them physical satisfaction, and long before philosophy or religion can hope to transform them into fuel for its own sacrificial flames.

Hence flows the greatest opportunity of fiction. We have, in a sense, an infinite will; but we have a limited experience, an experience sadly inadequate to exercise that will either in its purity or its strength. To give form to our capacities nothing is required but the appropriate occasion; this the poet, studying the world, will construct for us out of the materials of his observations. He will involve us in scenes which lie beyond the narrow lane of our daily ploddings; he will place us in the presence of important events, that we may feel our spirit rise momentarily to the height of his great argument. The possibilities of love or glory, of intrigue and perplexity, will be opened up before us; if he gives us a good plot, we can readily furnish the characters, because each of them will be the realisation of some stunted potential self of our own. It is by the plot, then, that the characters will be vivified, because it is by the plot that our own character will be expanded into its latent possibilities.

The description of an alien character can serve this purpose only very imperfectly; but the presentation of the circumstances in which that character manifests itself will make description unnecessary, since our instinct will supply all that is requisite for the impersonation. Thus it seems that Aristotle was justified in making the plot the chief element in fiction: for it is by virtue of the plot that the characters live, or, rather, that we live in them, and by virtue of the plot accordingly that our soul rises to that imaginative activity by which we tend at once to escape from the personal life and to realise its ideal. This idealisation is, of course, partial and merely relative to the particular adventure in which we imagine ourselves engaged. But in some single direction our will finds self-expression, and understands itself; runs through the career which it ignorantly coveted, and gathers the fruits and the lesson of that enterprise.

This is the essence of tragedy: the sense of the finished life, of the will fulfilled and enlightened: that purging of the mind so much debated upon, which relieves us of pent-up energies, transfers our feelings to a greater object, and thus justifies and entertains our dumb passions, detaching them at the same time for a moment from their accidental occasions in our earthly life. An episode, however lurid, is not a tragedy in this nobler sense, because it does not work itself out to the end; it pleases without satisfying, or shocks without enlightening. This enlightenment, I need hardly say, is not a matter of theory or of moral maxims; the enlightenment by which tragedy is made sublime is a glimpse into the ultimate destinies of our will. This discovery need not be an ethical gain—Macbeth and Othello attain it as much as Brutus and Hamlet—it may serve to accentuate despair, or cruelty, or indifference, or merely to fill the imagination for a moment without much affecting the permanent tone of the mind. But without such a glimpse of the goal of a passion the passion has not been adequately read, and the fiction has served to amuse us without really enlarging the frontiers of our ideal experience. Memory and emotion have been played upon, but imagination has not brought anything new to the light.

The dramatic situation, however, gives us the environment of a single passion, of life in one of its particular phases; and although a passion, like Romeo's love, may seem to devour the whole soul, and its fortunes may seem to be identical with those of the man, yet much of the man, and the best part of him, goes by the board in such a simplification. If Leonardo da Vinci, for example, had met in his youth with Romeo's fate, his end would have been no more ideally tragic than if he had died at eighteen of a fever; we should be touched rather by the pathos of what he had missed, than by the sublimity of what he had experienced. A passion like Romeo's, compared with the ideal scope of human thought and emotion, is a thin dream, a pathological crisis.

Accordingly Aristophanes, remembering the original religious and political functions of tragedy, blushes to see upon the boards a woman in love. And we should readily agree with him, but for two reasons,–one, that we abstract too much, in our demands upon art, from nobility of mind, and from the thought of totality and proportion; the other, that we have learned to look for a symbolic meaning in detached episodes, and to accept the incidental emotions they cause, because of their violence and our absorption in them, as in some sense sacramental and representative of the whole. Thus the picture of an unmeaning passion, of a crime without an issue, does not appear to our romantic apprehension as the sorry farce it is, but rather as a true tragedy. Some have lost even the capacity to conceive of a true tragedy, because they have no idea of a cosmic order, of general laws of life, or of an impersonal religion. They measure the profundity of feeling by its intensity, not by its justifying relations; and in the radical disintegration of their spirit, the more they are devoured the more they fancy themselves fed. But the majority of us retain some sense of a meaning in our joys and sorrows, and even if we cannot pierce to their ultimate object, we feel that what absorbs us here and now has a merely borrowed or deputed power; that it is a symbol and foretaste of all reality speaking to the whole soul. At the same time our intelligence is too confused to give us any picture of that reality, and our will too feeble to marshal our disorganised loves into a religion consistent with itself and harmonious with the comprehended universe. A rational ideal eludes us, and we are the more inclined to plunge into mysticism.

Nevertheless, the function of poetry, like that of science, can only be fulfilled by the conception of harmonies that become clearer as they grow richer. As the chance note that comes to be supported by a melody becomes in that melody determinate and necessary, and as the melody, when woven into a harmony, is explicated in that harmony and fixed beyond recall; so the single emotion, the fortuitous dream, launched by the poet into the world of recognisable and immortal forms, looks in that world for its ideal supports and affinities. It must find them or else be blown back among the ghosts. The highest ideality is the comprehension of the real. Poetry is not at its best when it depicts a further possible experience, but when it initiates us, by feigning something which as an experience is impossible, into the meaning of the experience which we have actually had.

The highest example of this kind of poetry is religion; and although disfigured and misunderstood by the simplicity of men who believe in it without being capable of that imaginative interpretation of life in which its truth consists, yet this religion is even then often beneficent, because it colours life harmoniously with the ideal. Religion may falsely represent the ideal as a reality, but we must remember that the ideal, if not so represented, would be despised by the majority of men, who cannot understand that the value of things is moral, and who therefore attribute to what is moral a natural existence, thinking thus to vindicate its importance and value. But value lies in meaning, not in substance; in the ideal which things approach, not in the energy which they embody.

The highest poetry, then, is not that of the versifiers, but that of the prophets, or of such poets as interpret verbally the visions which the prophets have rendered in action and sentiment rather than in adequate words. That the intuitions of religion are poetical, and that in such intuitions poetry has its ultimate function, are truths of which both religion and poetry become more conscious the more they advance in refinement and profundity. A crude and superficial theology may confuse God with the thunder, the mountains, the heavenly bodies, or the whole universe; but when we pass from these easy identifications to a religion that has taken root in the hearts of men, we find its objects and its dogmas purely ideal, transparent expressions of moral experience and perfect counterparts of human needs. The evidence of history or of the senses is left far behind and never thought of; the evidence of the heart, the value of the idea, are alone regarded.

Take, for instance, the doctrine of transubstantiation. A metaphor here is the basis of a dogma, because the dogma rises to the same subtle region as the metaphor, and gathers its sap from the same soil of emotion. Religion has here rediscovered its affinity with poetry, and in insisting on the truth of its mystery it unconsciously vindicates the ideality of its truth. Under the accidents of bread and wine lies, says the dogma, the substance of Christ's body, blood, and divinity. What is that but to treat facts as an appearance, and their ideal import as a reality? And to do this is the very essence of poetry, for which everything visible is a sacrament—an outward sign of that inward grace for which the soul is thirsting.

In this same manner, when poetry rises from its elementary and detached expressions in rhythm, euphuism, characterisation, and story-telling, and comes to the consciousness of its highest function, that of portraying the ideals of experience and destiny, then the poet becomes aware that he is essentially a prophet, and either devotes himself, like Homer or Dante, to the loving expression of the religion that exists, or like Lucretius or Wordsworth, to the heralding of one which he believes to be possible. Such poets are aware of their highest mission; others, whatever the energy of their genius, have not conceived their ultimate function as poets. They have been willing to leave their world ugly as a whole, after stuffing it with a sufficient profusion of beauties. Their contemporaries, their fellow-countrymen for many generations, may not perceive this defect, because they are naturally even less able than the poet himself to understand the necessity of so large a harmony. If he is short-sighted, they are blind, and his poetic world may seem to them sublime in its significance, because it may suggest some partial lifting of their daily burdens and some partial idealisation of their incoherent thoughts.

Such insensibility to the highest poetry is no more extraordinary than the corresponding indifference to the highest religion; nobility and excellence, however, are not dependent on the suffrage of half-baked men, but on the original disposition of the clay and the potter; I mean on the conditions of the art and the ideal capacities of human nature. Just as a note is better than a noise because, its beats being regular, the ear and brain can react with pleasure on that regularity, so all the stages of harmony are better than the confusion out of which they come, because the soul that perceives that harmony welcomes it as the fulfilment of her natural ends. The Pythagoreans were therefore right when they made number the essence of the knowable world, and Plato was right when he said harmony was the first condition of the highest good. The good man is a poet whose syllables are deeds and make a harmony in Nature. The poet is a rebuilder of the imagination, to make a harmony in that. And he is not a complete poet if his whole imagination is not attuned and his whole experience composed into a single symphony.

For his complete equipment, then, it is necessary, in the first place, that he sing; that his voice be pure and well pitched, and that his numbers flow; then, at a higher stage, his images must fit with one another; he must be euphuistic, colouring his thoughts with many reflected lights of memory and suggestion, so that their harmony may be rich and profound; again, at a higher stage, he must be sensuous and free, that is, he must build up his world with the primary elements of experience, not with the conventions of common sense or intelligence; he must draw the whole soul into his harmonies, even if in doing so he disintegrates the partial systematisations of experience made by abstract science in the categories of prose. But finally, this disintegration must not leave the poet weltering in a chaos of sense and passion; it must be merely the ploughing of the ground before a new harvest, the kneading of the clay before the modelling of a more perfect form. The expression of emotion should be rationalised by derivation from character and by reference to the real objects that arouse it—to Nature, to history, and to the universe of truth; the experience imagined should be conceived as a destiny, governed by principles, and issuing in the discipline and enlightenment of the will. In this way alone can poetry become an interpretation of life and not merely an irrelevant excursion into the realm of fancy, multiplying our images without purpose, and distracting us from our business without spiritual gain.

If we may then define poetry, not in the formal sense of giving the minimum of what may be called by that name, but in the ideal sense of determining the goal which it approaches and the achievement in which all its principles would be fulfilled, we may say that poetry is metrical and euphuistic discourse, expressing thought which is both sensuous and ideal.

Such is poetry as a literary form; but if we drop the limitation to verbal expression, and think of poetry as that subtle fire and inward light which seems at times to shine through the world and to touch the images in our minds with ineffable beauty, then poetry is a momentary harmony in the soul amid stagnation or conflict,—a glimpse of the divine and an incitation to a religious life.

Religion is poetry become the guide of life, poetry substituted for science or supervening upon it as an approach to the highest reality. Poetry is religion allowed to drift, left without points of application in conduct and without an expression in worship and dogma; it is religion without practical efficacy and without metaphysical illusion. The ground of this abstractness of poetry, however, is usually only its narrow scope; a poet who plays with an idea for half an hour, or constructs a character to which he gives no profound moral significance, forgets his own thought, or remembers it only as a fiction of his leisure, because he has not dug his well deep enough to tap the subterranean springs of his own life. But when the poet enlarges his theatre and puts into his rhapsodies the true visions of his people and of his soul, his poetry is the consecration of his deepest convictions, and contains the whole truth of his religion. What the religion of the vulgar adds to the poet's is simply the inertia of their limited apprehension, which takes literally what he meant ideally, and degrades into a false extension of this world on its own level what in his mind was a true interpretation of it upon a moral plane.

This higher plane is the sphere of significant imagination, of relevant fiction, of idealism become the interpretation of the reality it leaves behind. Poetry raised to its highest power is then identical with religion grasped in its inmost truth; at their point of union both reach their utmost purity and beneficence, for then poetry loses its frivolity and ceases to demoralise, while religion surrenders its illusions and ceases to deceive.

Introduction *[The Life of Reason]*

Reason in Common Sense. Volume 1 of *The Life of Reason: or, the Phases of Human Progress.* New York: Charles Scribner's Sons; London: Constable and Co. Ltd., 1905, 1–32. Volume seven of the critical edition of *The Works of George Santayana.*

This introduction appeared in Reason in Common Sense, *volume 1 of the five-volume* The Life of Reason; or the Phases of Human Progress. *Santayana began working on* The Life of Reason *in 1896, was reading page-proofs in autumn 1904, and saw the first four volumes published in 1905 and the fifth in 1906. He characterized it as "a sort of retrospective politics, an estimate of events in reference to the moral ideal which they embodied or betrayed" (LR5, 58), Santayana's moral ideal being the harmonious relation of impulses or reason. The Life of Reason is "that part of experience which perceives and pursues ideals—all conduct so controlled and all sense so interpreted as to perfect natural happiness" (ES, 283). Reason is not instrumental or incidental to human progress: "it is the total and embodied progress itself, in which the pleasures of sense are included in so far as they can be intelligently enjoyed and pursued" (ES, 283). John Dewey called the five-volume work "the most adequate contribution America has yet made—always excepting Emerson—to moral philosophy" (John Dewey, The Middle Works, 1899–1924, volume 4, edited by Jo Ann Boydston [Carbondale and Edwardsville: Southern Illinois University Press, 1983], 241).*

THE SUBJECT OF THIS WORK, ITS METHOD AND ANTECEDENTS

Whatever forces may govern human life, if they are to be recognised by man, must betray themselves in human experience. Progress in science or religion, no less than in morals and art, is a dramatic episode in man's career, a welcome variation in his habit and state of mind; although this variation may often regard or propitiate things external, adjustment to which may be important for his welfare. The importance of these external things, as well as their existence, he can establish only by the function and utility which a recognition of them may have in his life. The entire history of progress is a moral drama, a tale man might unfold in a great autobiography, could his myriad heads and countless scintillas of consciousness conspire, like the seventy Alexandrian sages, in a single version of the truth committed to each for interpretation. What themes would prevail in such an examination of heart? In what order and with what emphasis would they be recounted? In which of its adventures would the human race, reviewing its whole

Progress is relative to an ideal which reflection creates.

experience, acknowledge a progress and a gain? To answer these questions, as they may be answered speculatively and provisionally by an individual, is the purpose of the following work.

A philosopher could hardly have a higher ambition than to make himself a mouth-piece for the memory and judgment of his race. Yet the most casual consideration of affairs already involves an attempt to do the same thing. Reflection is pregnant from the beginning with all the principles of **Efficacious** synthesis and valuation needed in the most comprehensive criticism. **reflection** **is reason.** So soon as man ceases to be wholly immersed in sense, he looks before and after, he regrets and desires; and the moments in which prospect or retrospect takes place constitute the reflective or representative part of his life, in contrast to the unmitigated flux of sensations in which nothing ulterior is regarded. Representation, however, can hardly remain idle and merely speculative. To the ideal function of envisaging the absent, memory and reflection will add (since they exist and constitute a new complication in being) the practical function of modifying the future. Vital impulse, however, when it is modified by reflection and veers in sympathy with judgments pronounced on the past, is properly called reason. Man's rational life consists in those moments in which reflection not only occurs but proves efficacious. What is absent then works in the present, and values are imputed where they cannot be felt. Such representation is so far from being merely speculative that its presence alone can raise bodily change to the dignity of action. Reflection gathers experiences together and perceives their relative worth; which is as much as to say that it expresses a new attitude of will in the presence of a world better understood and turned to some purpose. The limits of reflection mark those of concerted and rational action; they circumscribe the field of cumulative experience, or, what is the same thing, of profitable living.

Thus if we use the word life in a eulogistic sense to designate the happy maintenance against the world of some definite **The Life of** ideal interest, we may say with Aristotle that life is reason in **Reason a name** operation. The *Life of Reason* will then be a name for that part **for all practical** of experience which perceives and pursues ideals—all conduct **thought and all** so controlled and all sense so interpreted as to perfect natural **action justified** happiness. **by its fruits in** **consciousness.**

Without reason, as without memory, there might still be pleasures and pains in existence. To increase those pleasures and reduce those pains would be to introduce an improvement into the sentient world, as if a devil suddenly died in hell or in heaven a new angel were created. Since the beings, however, in which these values would reside, would, by hypothesis, know nothing of one another, and since the betterment would take place unprayed-for and unnoticed, it could hardly be called a progress; and certainly not a progress in man, since man, without the ideal continuity given by memory and reason, would have no moral being. In human progress, therefore, reason is not a casual instrument, having its sole value in its service to sense; such a betterment in sentience would not be progress unless it were a progress in reason, and the increasing pleasure revealed some object that could please; for without a picture of the situation from which a heightened vitality might flow, the improvement could be neither remembered nor measured nor desired. The Life of Reason is accordingly neither a mere means nor a mere incident in human progress; it is the total and embodied progress itself, in which the pleasures of sense are included in so far as they can be intelligently enjoyed and pursued. To recount man's rational moments would be to take an inventory of all his goods; for he is not himself (as we say with unconscious accuracy) in the others. If he ever appropriates them in recollection or prophecy, it is only on the ground of some physical relation which they may have to his being.

Reason is as old as man and as prevalent as human nature; for we should not recognise an animal to be human unless his instincts were to some degree conscious of their ends and rendered his ideas in that measure relevant to conduct. Many sensations, or even a whole world of dreams, do not amount to intelligence until the images in the mind begin to represent in some way, however symbolic, the forces and realities confronted in action. There may well be intense consciousness in the total absence of rationality. Such consciousness is suggested in dreams, in madness, and may be found, for all we know, in the depths of universal nature. Minds peopled only by desultory visions and lusts would not have the dignity of human souls even if they seemed to pursue certain objects unerringly; for that pursuit would not be illumined by any vision of its goal. Reason and humanity begin with the union of instinct and ideation, when instinct becomes enlightened, establishes values in its objects, and is turned from a process into an art, while at the same time consciousness becomes practical and cognitive, beginning to contain some symbol or record of the co-ordinate realities among which it arises.

Reason accordingly requires the fusion of two types of life, commonly led in the world in well-nigh total separation, one a life of impulse expressed in affairs and social passions, the other a life of reflection expressed in religion, science, and the imitative arts. In the Life of Reason, if it were brought to perfection, intelligence would be at once the universal method of practice and its continual reward. All reflection would then be applicable in action and all action fruitful in happiness. Though this be an ideal, yet everyone gives it from time to time a partial embodiment when he practises useful arts, when his passions happily lead him to enlightenment, or when his fancy breeds visions pertinent to his ultimate good. Everyone leads the Life of Reason in so far as he finds a steady light behind the world's glitter and a clear residuum of joy beneath pleasure or success. No experience not to be repented of falls without its sphere. Every solution to a doubt, in so far as it is not a new error, every practical achievement not neutralised by a second maladjustment consequent upon it, every consolation not the seed of another greater sorrow, may be gathered together and built into this edifice. The Life of Reason is the happy marriage of two elements—impulse and ideation—which if wholly divorced would reduce man to a brute or to a maniac. The rational animal is generated by the union of these two monsters. He is constituted by ideas which have ceased to be visionary and actions which have ceased to be vain.

Thus the Life of Reason is another name for what, in the widest sense of the

word, might be called Art. Operations become arts when their purpose is conscious and their method teachable. In perfect art the whole idea is
creative and exists only to be embodied, while every part of the product is rational and gives delightful expression to that idea. Like art,
again, the Life of Reason is not a power but a result, the spontaneous
expression of liberal genius in a favouring environment. Both art and reason

It is the sum of Art.

have natural sources and meet with natural checks; but when a process is turned
successfully into an art, so that its issues have value and the ideas that accompany
it become practical and cognitive, reflection, finding little that it cannot in some
way justify and understand, begins to boast that it directs and has created the
world in which it finds itself so much at home. Thus if art could extend its sphere
to include every activity in nature, reason, being everywhere exemplified, might
easily think itself omnipotent. This ideal, far as it is from actual realisation, has so
dazzled men, that in their religion and mythical philosophy they have often spoken as if it were already actual and efficient. This anticipation amounts, when
taken seriously, to a confusion of purposes with facts and of functions with causes,
a confusion which in the interests of wisdom and progress it is important to avoid;
but these speculative fables, when we take them for what they are—poetic expressions of the ideal—help us to see how deeply rooted this ideal is in man's mind,
and afford us a standard by which to measure his approaches to the rational perfection of which he dreams. For the Life of Reason, being the sphere of all human
art, is man's imitation of divinity.

To study such an ideal, dimly expressed though it be in human existence, is no
prophetic or visionary undertaking. Every genuine ideal has a natural basis; anyone may understand and safely interpret it who is attentive to the
life from which is springs. To decipher the Life of Reason nothing is
needed but an analytic spirit and a judicious love of man, a love
quick to distinguish success from failure in his great and confused
experiment of living. The historian of reason should not be a roman-

It has a natural basis which makes it definable.

tic poet, vibrating impotently to every impulse he finds afoot, without a criterion
of excellence or a vision of perfection. Ideals are free, but they are neither more
numerous nor more variable than the living natures that generate them. Ideals
are legitimate, and each initially envisages a genuine and innocent good; but they
are not realisable together, nor even singly when they have no deep roots in the
world. Neither is the philosopher compelled by his somewhat judicial office to be
a satirist or censor, without sympathy for those tentative and ingenuous passions
out of which, after all, his own standards must arise. He is the chronicler of human
progress, and to measure that progress he should be equally attentive to the
impulses that give it direction and to the circumstances amid which it stumbles
toward its natural goal.

There is unfortunately no school of modern philosophy to which a critique of
human progress can well be attached. Almost every school, indeed, can furnish
something useful to the critic, sometimes a physical theory, sometimes a piece of
logical analysis. We shall need to borrow from current science and speculation
the picture they draw of man's conditions and environment, his history and men-

tal habits. These may furnish a theatre and properties for our drama; but they
offer no hint of its plot and meaning. A great imaginative apathy has
fallen on the mind. One-half the learned world is amused in tinker-
ing obsolete armour, as Don Quixote did his helmet; deputing it,
after a series of catastrophes, to be at last sound and invulnerable.
The other half, the naturalists who have studied psychology and evolution, look
at life from the outside, and the processes of Nature make them forget her uses.

Modern philosophy not helpful.

Bacon indeed had prized science for adding to the comforts of life, a function
still commemorated by positivists in their eloquent moments. Habitually, however, when they utter the word progress it is, in their mouths, a
synonym for inevitable change, or at best for change in that direction which they conceive to be on the whole predominant. If they
combine with physical speculation some elements of morals, these
are usually purely formal, to the effect that happiness is to be pursued (probably,
alas! because to do so is a psychological law); but what happiness consists in we
gather only from casual observations or by putting together their national prejudices and party saws.

Positivism no positive ideal.

The truth is that even this radical school, emancipated as it thinks itself, is
suffering from the aftereffects of supernaturalism. Like children escaped from
school, they find their whole happiness in freedom. They are proud of what they
have rejected, as if a great wit were required to do so; but they do not know what
they want. If you astonish them by demanding what is their positive ideal, further
than that there should be a great many people and that they should be all alike,
they will say at first that what ought to be is obvious, and later they will submit
the matter to a majority vote. They have discarded the machinery in which their
ancestors embodied the ideal; they have not perceived that those symbols stood
for the Life of Reason and gave fantastic and embarrassed expression to what, in
itself, is pure humanity; and they have thus remained entangled in the colossal
error that ideals are something adventitious and unmeaning, not having a soil in
mortal life nor a possible fulfilment there.

The profound and pathetic ideas which inspired Christianity were attached in
the beginning to ancient myths and soon crystallised into many new ones. The
mythical manner pervades Christian philosophy; but myth succeeds in expressing ideal life only by misrepresenting its history
and conditions. This method was indeed not original with the
Fathers; they borrowed it from Plato, who appealed to parables
himself in an open and harmless fashion, yet with disastrous consequences to his school. Nor was he the first; for the instinct to
regard poetic fictions as revelations of supernatural facts is as old as the soul's
primitive incapacity to distinguish dreams from waking perceptions, sign from
thing signified, and inner emotions from external powers. Such confusions,
though in a way they obey moral forces, make a rational estimate of things impossible. To misrepresent the conditions and consequences of action is no merely
speculative error; it involves a false emphasis in character and an artificial balance and co-ordination among human pursuits. When ideals are hypostasised

Christian philosophy mythical: it misrepresents facts and conditions.

into powers alleged to provide for their own expression, the Life of Reason cannot be conceived; in theory its field of operation is pre-empted and its function gone, while in practice its inner impulses are turned awry by artificial stimulation and repression.

The Patristic systems, though weak in their foundations, were extraordinarily wise and comprehensive in their working out; and while they inverted life they preserved it. Dogma added to the universe fabulous perspectives; it interpolated also innumerable incidents and powers which gave a new dimension to experience. Yet the old world remained standing in its strange setting, like the Pantheon in modern Rome; and, what is more important, the natural springs of human action were still acknowledged, and if a supernatural discipline was imposed, it was only because experience and faith had disclosed a situation in which the pursuit of earthly happiness seemed hopeless. Nature was not destroyed by its novel appendages, nor did reason die in the cloister: it hibernated there, and could come back to its own in due season, only a little dazed and weakened by its long confinement. Such, at least, is the situation in Catholic regions, where the Patristic philosophy has not appreciably varied. Among Protestants Christian dogma has taken a new and ambiguous direction, which has at once minimised its disturbing effect in practice and isolated its primary illusion. The symptoms have been cured and the disease driven in.

The tenets of Protestant bodies are notoriously varied and on principle subject to change. There is hardly a combination of tradition and spontaneity which has not been tried in some quarter. If we think, however, of broad tendencies and ultimate issues, it appears that in Protestantism myth, without disappearing, has changed its relation to reality: instead of being an extension to the natural world myth has become its substratum. Religion no longer reveals divine personalities, future rewards, and tenderer Elysian consolations; nor does it seriously propose a heaven to be reached by a ladder nor a purgatory to be shortened by prescribed devotions. It merely gives the real world an ideal status and teaches men to accept a natural life on supernatural grounds. The consequence is that the most pious can give an unvarnished description of things. Even immortality and the idea of God are submitted, in liberal circles, to scientific treatment. On the other hand, it would be hard to conceive a more inveterate obsession than that which keeps the attitude of these same minds inappropriate to the objects they envisage. They have accepted natural conditions; they will not accept natural ideals. The Life of Reason has no existence for them, because, although its field is clear, they will not tolerate any human or finite standard of value, and will not suffer extant interests, which can alone guide them in action or judgment, to define the worth of life.

Liberal theology a superstitious attitude toward a natural world.

The after-effects of Hebraism are here contrary to its foundations; for the Jews loved the world so much that they brought themselves, in order to win and enjoy it, to an intense concentration of purpose; but this effort and discipline, which had of course been mythically sanctioned, not only failed of its object, but grew far too absolute and sublime to think its object could ever have been earthly; and the supernatural machinery which was to have secured prosperity, while that still enticed, now had to furnish some worthier object for the passion it had artificially fostered. Fanaticism consists in redoubling your effort when you have forgotten your aim.

An earnestness which is out of proportion to any knowledge or love of real things, which is therefore dark and inward and thinks itself deeper than the earth's foundations—such an earnestness, until culture turns it into intelligent interests, will naturally breed a new mythology. It will try to place some world of Afrites and shadowy giants behind the constellations, which it finds too distinct and constant to be its companions or supporters; and it will assign to itself vague and infinite tasks, for which it is doubtless better equipped than for those which the earth now sets before it. Even these, however, since they are parts of an infinite whole, the mystic may (histrionically, perhaps, yet zealously) undertake; but as his eye will be perpetually fixed on something invisible beyond, and nothing will be done for its own sake or enjoyed in its own fugitive presence, there will be little art and little joy in existence. All will be a tossing servitude and illiberal mist, where the parts will have no final values and the whole no pertinent direction.

The Greeks thought straight in both physics and morals.
In Greek philosophy the situation is far more auspicious. The ancients led a rational life and envisaged the various spheres of speculation as men might whose central interests were rational. In physics they leaped at once to the conception of a dynamic unity and general evolution, thus giving that background to human life which shrewd observation would always have descried, and which modern science has laboriously rediscovered. Two great systems offered, in two legitimate directions, what are doubtless the final and radical accounts of physical being. Heraclitus, describing the immediate, found it to be in constant and pervasive

Heraclitus and the immediate.
change: no substances, no forms, no identities could be arrested there, but as in the human soul, so in nature, all was instability, contradiction, reconstruction, and oblivion. This remains the empirical fact; and we need but to rescind the artificial division which Descartes has taught us to make between nature and life, to feel again the absolute aptness of Heraclitus's expressions. These were thought obscure only because they were so disconcertingly penetrating and direct. The immediate is what nobody sees, because convention and reflection turn existence, as soon as they can, into ideas; a man who discloses the immediate seems profound, yet his depth is nothing but innocence recovered and a sort of intellectual abstention. Mysticism, scepticism, and transcendentalism have all in their various ways tried to fall back on the immediate; but none of them has been ingenuous enough. Each has added some myth, or sophistry, or delusive artifice to its direct observation. Heraclitus remains the honest prophet of immediacy: a mystic without raptures or bad rhetoric, a sceptic who does not rely for his results on conventions unwittingly adopted, a transcendentalist without false pretensions or incongruous dogmas.

The immediate is not, however, a good subject for discourse, and the expounders of Heraclitus were not unnaturally blamed for monotony. All they could do was to iterate their master's maxim, and declare everything to be in flux. In suggesting laws of recurrence and a reason in which what is common to many might be expressed, Heraclitus had opened the door into another region: had he passed through, his philosophy would have been greatly modified, for permanent forms would have forced themselves on his attention no less than shifting materials. Such a Heraclitus would have anticipated Plato; but the time for such a synthesis had not yet arrived.

At the opposite pole from immediacy lies intelligibility. To reduce phenomena to constant elements, as similar and simple as possible, and to conceive their union and separation to obey constant laws, is what a natural philosopher will inevitably do so soon as his interest is not merely to utter experience but to understand it. Democritus brought this scientific ideal to its ultimate expression. By including psychic existence in his atomic system, he indicated a problem which natural **Democritus and the naturally intelligible.** science has since practically abandoned but which it may some day be compelled to take up. The atoms of Democritus seem to us gross, even for chemistry, and their quality would have to undergo great transformation if they were to support intelligibly psychic being as well; but that very grossness and false simplicity had its merits, and science must be for ever grateful to the man who at its inception could so clearly formulate its mechanical ideal. That the world is not so intelligible as we could wish is not to be wondered at. In other respects also it fails to respond to our ideals; yet our hope must be to find it more propitious to the intellect as well as to all the arts in proportion as we learn better how to live in it.

The atoms of what we call hydrogen or oxygen may well turn out to be worlds, as the stars are which make atoms for astronomy. Their inner organisation might be negligible on our rude plane of being; did it disclose itself, however, it would be intelligible in its turn only if constant parts and constant laws were discernible within each system. So that while atomism at a given level may not be a final or metaphysical truth, it will describe, on every level, the practical and efficacious structure of the world. We owe to Democritus this ideal of practical intelligibility; and he is accordingly an eternal spokesman of reason. His system, long buried with other glories of the world, has been partly revived; and although it cannot be verified in haste, for it represents an ultimate ideal, every advance in science reconstitutes it in some particular. Mechanism is not one principle of explanation among others. In natural philosophy, where to explain means to discover origins, transmutations, and laws, mechanism is explanation itself.

Heraclitus had the good fortune of having his physics absorbed by Plato. It is a pity that Democritus' physics was not absorbed by Aristotle. For with the flux observed, and mechanism conceived to explain it, the theory of existence is complete; and had a complete physical theory been incorporated into the Socratic philosophy, wisdom would have lacked none of its parts. Democritus, however, appeared too late, when ideal science had overrun the whole field and initiated a verbal and dialectical physics; so that Aristotle, for all his scientific temper and studies, built his natural philosophy on a lamentable misunderstanding, and condemned thought to confusion for two thousand years.

If the happy freedom of the Greeks from religious dogma made them the first natural philosophers, their happy political freedom made them the first moralists.

Socrates and the autonomy of mind. It was no accident that Socrates walked the Athenian agora; it was no petty patriotism that made him shrink from any other scene. His science had its roots there, in the personal independence, intellectual vivacity, and clever dialectic of his countrymen. Ideal science lives in discourse; it consists in the active exercise of reason, in signification, appreciation, intent, and self-expression. Its sum total is to know oneself, not as psychology or anthropology might describe a man, but to know, as the saying is, one's own mind. Nor is he who knows his own mind forbidden to change it; the dialectician has nothing to do with future possibilities or with the opinion of anyone but the man addressed. This kind of truth is but adequate veracity; its only object is its own intent. Having developed in the spirit the consciousness of its meanings and purposes, Socrates rescued logic and ethics for ever from authority. With his friends the Sophists, he made man the measure of all things, after bidding him measure himself, as they neglected to do, by his own ideal. That brave humanity which had first raised its head in Hellas and had endowed so many things in heaven and earth, where everything was hitherto monstrous, with proportion and use, so that man's works might justify themselves to his mind, now found in Socrates its precise definition; and it was naturally where the Life of Reason had been long cultivated that it came finally to be conceived.

Socrates had, however, a plebeian strain in his humanity, and his utilitarianism, at least in its expression, hardly did justice to what gives utility to life. His

Plato gave the ideal its full expression. condemnation for atheism—if we choose to take it symbolically— was not altogether unjust: the gods of Greece were not honoured explicitly enough in his philosophy. Human good appeared there in its principle; you would not set a pilot to mend shoes, because you knew your own purpose; but what purposes a civilised soul might harbour, and in what highest shapes the good might appear, was a problem that seems not to have attracted his genius. It was reserved to Plato to bring the Socratic ethics to its sublimest expression and to elicit from the depths of the Greek conscience those ancestral ideals which had inspired its legislators and been embodied in its sacred civic traditions. The owl of Minerva flew, as Hegel says, in the dusk of evening; and it was horror at the abandonment of all creative virtues that brought Plato to conceive them so sharply and to preach them in so sad a tone. It was after all but the love of beauty that made him censure the poets; for like a true Greek and a true lover he wished to see beauty flourish in the real world. It was love of freedom that made him harsh to his ideal citizens, that they might be strong enough to preserve the liberal life. And when he broke away from political preoccupations and turned to the inner life, his interpretations proved the absolute sufficiency of the Socratic method; and he left nothing pertinent unsaid on ideal love and ideal immortality.

Beyond this point no rendering of the Life of Reason has ever been carried. Aristotle improved the detail, and gave breadth and precision to many a part. If Plato possessed greater imaginative splendour and more enthusiasm in austerity,

Aristotle had perfect sobriety and adequacy, with greater fidelity to the common sentiments of his race. Plato, by virtue of his scope and plasticity, together with a certain prophetic zeal, outran at times the limits of the Hellenic and the rational; he saw human virtue so surrounded and oppressed by physical dangers that he wished to give it mythical sanctions, and his fondness for transmigration and nether punishments was somewhat more than playful. If as a work of imagination his philosophy holds the first place, Aristotle's has the decisive advantage of being the unalloyed expression of reason. In Aristotle the conception of human nature is perfectly sound; everything ideal has a natural basis and everything natural an ideal development. His ethics, when thoroughly digested and weighed, especially when the meagre outlines are filled in with Plato's more discursive expositions, will seem therefore entirely final. The Life of Reason finds there its classic explication.

Aristotle supplied its natural basis.

As it is improbable that there will soon be another people so free from preoccupations, so gifted, and so fortunate as the Greeks, or capable in consequence of so well exemplifying humanity, so also it is improbable that a philosopher will soon arise with Aristotle's scope, judgment, or authority, one knowing so well how to be both reasonable and exalted. It might seem vain, therefore, to try to do afresh what has been done before with unapproachable success; and instead of writing inferior things at great length about the Life of Reason, it might be simpler to read and to propagate what Aristotle wrote with such immortal justness and masterly brevity. But times change; and though the principles of reason remain the same the facts of human life and of human conscience alter. A new background, a new basis of application, appears for logic, and it may be useful to restate old truths in new words, the better to prove their eternal validity. Aristotle is, in his morals, Greek, concise, and elementary. As a Greek, he mixes with the ideal argument illustrations, appreciations, and conceptions which are not inseparable from its essence. In themselves, no doubt, these accessories are better than what in modern times would be substituted for them, being less sophisticated and of a nobler stamp; but to our eyes they disguise what is profound and universal in natural morality by embodying it in images which do not belong to our life. Our direst struggles and the last sanctions of our morality do not appear in them. The pagan world, because its maturity was simpler than our crudeness, seems childish to us. We do not find there our sins and holiness, our love, charity, and honour.

Philosophy thus complete, yet in need of restatement.

The Greek too would not find in our world the things he valued most, things to which he surrendered himself, perhaps, with a more constant self-sacrifice—piety, country, friendship, and beauty; and he might add that his ideals were rational and he could attain them, while ours are extravagant and have been missed. Yet even if we acknowledged his greater good fortune, it would be impossible for us to go back and become like him. To make the attempt would show no sense of reality and little sense of humour. We must dress in our own clothes, if we do not wish to substitute a masquerade for practical existence. What we can adopt from Greek morals is only the abstract principle of their development;

their foundation in all the extant forces of human nature and their effort toward establishing a perfect harmony among them. These forces themselves have perceptibly changed, at least in their relative power. Thus we are more conscious of wounds to stanch and wrongs to fight against, and less of goods to attain. The movement of conscience has veered; the centre of gravity lies in another part of the character.

Another circumstance that invites a restatement of rational ethics is the impressive illustration of their principle which subsequent history has afforded. Mankind has been making extraordinary experiments of which Aristotle could not dream; and their result is calculated to clarify even his philosophy. For in some respects it needed experiments and clarification. He had been led into a systematic fusion of dialectic with physics, and of this fusion all pretentious modern philosophy is the aggravated extension. Socrates' pupils could not abandon his ideal principles, yet they could not bear to abstain from physics altogether; they therefore made a mock physics in moral terms, out of which theology was afterward developed. Plato, standing nearer to Socrates and being no naturalist by disposition, never carried the fatal experiment beyond the mythical stage. He accordingly remained the purer moralist, much as Aristotle's judgment may be preferred in many particulars. Their relative position may be roughly indicated by saying that Plato had no physics and that Aristotle's physics was false; so that ideal science in the one suffered from want of environment and control, while in the other it suffered from misuse in a sphere where it had no application.

What had happened was briefly this: Plato, having studied many sorts of philosophy and being a bold and universal genius, was not satisfied to leave all physical questions pending, as his master had done. He adopted, accordingly, Heraclitus's doctrine of the immediate, which he now called the realm of phenomena; for what exists at any instant, if you arrest and name it, turns out to have been an embodiment of some logical essence, such as discourse might define; in every fact some idea makes its appearance, and such an apparition of the ideal is a phenomenon. Moreover, another philosophy had made a deep impression on Plato's mind and had helped to develop Socratic definitions: Parmenides had called the concept of pure Being the only reality; and to satisfy the strong dialectic by which this doctrine was supported and at the same time to bridge the infinite chasm between one formless substance and many appearances irrelevant to it, Plato substituted the many Socratic ideas, all of which were relevant to appearance, for the one concept of Parmenides. The ideas thus acquired what is called metaphysical subsistence; for they stood in the place of the Eleatic Absolute, and at the same time were the realities that phenomena manifested.

Plato's myths in lieu of physics.

The technique of this combination is much to be admired; but the feat is technical and adds nothing to the significance of what Plato has to say on any concrete subject. This barren triumph was, however, fruitful in misunderstandings. The characters and values a thing possessed were now conceived to subsist apart from it, and might even have preceded it and caused its existence; a mechanism composed of values and definitions could thus be placed behind phenomena to constitute a substantial physical world. Such a dream could not be taken seriously, until good sense was wholly lost and a bevy of magic spirits could be imagined peopling the infinite and yet carrying on the business of earth. Aristotle rejected the metaphysical subsistence of ideas, but thought they might still be essences operative in nature, if only they were identified with the life or form of particular things. The dream thus lost its frank wildness, but none of its inherent incongruity: for the sense in which characters and values make a thing what it is, is purely dialectical. They give it its status in the ideal world; but the appearance of these characters and values here and now is what needs explanation in physics, an explanation which can be furnished, of course, only by the physical concatenation and distribution of causes.

Aristotle himself did not fail to make this necessary distinction between efficient cause and formal essence; but as his science was only natural history, and mechanism had no plausibility in his eyes, the efficiency of the cause was always due, in his view, to its ideal quality; as in heredity the father's human character, not his physical structure, might seem to warrant the son's humanity. Every ideal, before it could be embodied, had to pre-exist in some other embodiment; but as when the ultimate purpose of the cosmos is considered it seems to lie beyond any given embodiment, the highest ideal must somehow exist disembodied. It must pre-exist, thought Aristotle, in order to supply, by way of magic attraction, a physical cause for perpetual movement in the world.

Aristotle's final causes. Modern science can avoid such expedients.

It must be confessed, in justice to this consummate philosopher, who is not less masterly in the use of knowledge than unhappy in divination, that the transformation of the highest good into a physical power is merely incidental with him, and due to a want of faith (at that time excusable) in mechanism and evolution. Aristotle's deity is always a moral ideal and every detail in its definition is based on discrimination between the better and the worse. No accommodation to the ways of nature is here allowed to cloud the kingdom of heaven; this deity is not condemned to do whatever happens nor to absorb whatever exists. It is mythical only in its physical application; in moral philosophy it remains a legitimate conception.

Truth certainly exists, if existence be not too mean an attribute for that eternal realm which is tenanted by ideals; but truth is repugnant to physical or psychical being. Moreover, truth may very well be identified with an impassible intellect, which should do nothing but possess all truth, with no point of view, no animal warmth, and no transitive process. Such an intellect and truth are expressions having a different metaphorical background and connotation, but, when thought out, an identical import. They both attempt to evoke that ideal standard which human thought proposes to itself. This function is their effective essence. It insures their eternal fixity, and this property surely endows them with a very genuine and sublime reality. What is fantastic is only the dynamic function attributed to them by Aristotle, which obliges them to inhabit some fabulous extension to the physical world. Even this physical efficacy, however, is spiritualised as much as possible, since deity is said to move the cosmos only as an object of love or an object of knowledge may move the mind. Such efficacy is imputed to a hypostasised end, but evidently resides in fact in the functioning and impulsive spirit that conceives and pursues an ideal, endowing it with whatever attraction it may seem to have. The absolute intellect described by Aristotle remains, therefore, as pertinent to the Life of Reason as Plato's idea of the good. Though less comprehensive (for it abstracts from all animal interests, from all passion and mortality), it is more adequate and distinct in the region it dominates. It expresses sublimely the goal of speculative thinking; which is none other than to live as much as may be in the eternal and to absorb and be absorbed in the truth.

The rest of ancient philosophy belongs to the decadence and rests in physics on eclecticism and in morals on despair. That creative breath which had stirred the founders and legislators of Greece no longer inspired their descendants. Helpless to control the course of events, they took refuge in abstention or in conformity, and their ethics became a matter of private economy and sentiment, no longer aspiring to mould the state or give any positive aim to existence. The time was approaching when both speculation and morals were to regard the other world; reason had abdicated the throne, and religion, after that brief interregnum, resumed it for long ages.

Such are the threads which tradition puts into the hands of an observer who at the present time might attempt to knit the Life of Reason ideally together. The problem is to unite a trustworthy conception of the conditions under which man lives with an adequate conception of his interests. Both conceptions, fortunately, lie before us. Heraclitus and Democritus, in systems easily seen to be complementary, gave long ago a picture of nature such as all later observation, down to our own day, has done nothing but fill out and confirm. Psychology and physics still repeat their ideas, often with richer detail, but never with a more radical or prophetic glance. Nor does the transcendental philosophy, in spite of its self-esteem, add anything essential. It was a thing taken for granted in ancient and scholastic philosophy that a being dwelling, like man, in the immediate, whose moments are in flux, needed constructive reason to interpret his experience and paint in his unstable consciousness some symbolic picture of the world. To have reverted to this constructive process and studied its stages is an interesting achievement; but the construction is already made by common-sense and science, and it was visionary insolence in the Germans to propose to make that construction otherwise. Retrospective self-consciousness is dearly bought if it inhibits the intellect and embarrasses the inferences which, in its spontaneous operation, it has known perfectly how to make. In the heat of scientific theorising or dialectical argument it is sometimes salutary to be reminded that we are men thinking; but, after all, it is no news. We know that life is a dream, and how should thinking be more? Yet the thinking must go on, and the only vital question is to what practical or poetic conceptions it is able to lead us.

Transcendentalism true but inconsequential.

Similarly the Socratic philosophy affords a noble and genuine account of what goods may be realised by living. Modern theory has not done so much to help us here, however, as it has in physics. It seldom occurs to modern moralists that theirs is the science of all good and the art of its attainment; they think only of some set of categorical precepts or some theory of moral senti- ments, abstracting altogether from the ideals reigning in society, in sci- ence, and in art. They deal with the secondary question What ought I to do? without having answered the primary question, What ought to be? They attach morals to religion rather than to politics, and this religion unhappily long ago ceased to be wisdom expressed in fancy in order to become superstition overlaid with reasoning. They divide man into compartments and the less they leave in the one labelled "morality" the more sublime they think their morality is; and sometimes pedantry and scholasticism are carried so far that nothing but an abstract sense of duty remains in the broad region which should contain all human goods.

Verbal ethics.

Such trivial sanctimony in morals is doubtless due to artificial views about the conditions of welfare; the basis is laid in authority rather than in human nature, and the goal in salvation rather than in happiness. One great modern philosopher, however, was free from these preconceptions, and might have reconstituted the Life of Reason had he had a sufficient interest in culture. Spinoza brought man back into nature, and made him the nucleus of all moral values, showing how he may recognise his environment and how he may master it. But Spinoza's sympathy with mankind fell short of imagi- nation; any noble political or poetical ideal eluded him. Everything impassioned seemed to him insane, everything human necessarily petty. Man was to be a pious tame animal, with the stars shining above his head. Instead of imagination Spinoza cultivated mysticism, which is indeed an alternative. A prophet in specu- lation, he remained a levite in sentiment. Little or nothing would need to be changed in his system if the Life of Reason, in its higher ranges, were to be grafted upon it; but such affiliation is not necessary, and it is rendered unnatural by the lack of sweep and generosity in Spinoza's practical ideals.

Spinoza and the Life of Reason.

For moral philosophy we are driven back, then, upon the ancients; but not, of course, for moral inspiration. Industrialism and democracy, the French Revolu- tion, the Renaissance, and even the Catholic system, which in the midst of ancient illusions enshrines so much tenderness and wis- dom, still live in the world, though forgotten by philosophers, and point unmistakably toward their several goals. Our task is not to construct but only to interpret ideals, confronting them with one another and with the conditions which, for the most part, they alike ignore. There is no need of refuting anything, for the will which is behind all ideals and behind most dog- mas cannot itself be refuted; but it may be enlightened and led to reconsider its intent, when its satisfaction is seen to be either naturally impossible or inconsis- tent with better things. The age of controversy is past; that of interpretation has succeeded.

Modern and classic sources of inspiration.

Here, then, is the programme of the following work: Starting with the imme- diate flux, in which all objects and impulses are given, to describe the Life of Reason; that is, to note what facts and purposes seem to be primary, to show how the conception of nature and life gathers around them, and to point to the ideals of thought and action which are approached by this gradual mastering of experience by reason. A great task, which it would be beyond the powers of a writer in this age either to execute or to conceive, had not the Greeks drawn for us the outlines of an ideal culture at a time when life was simpler than at present and individual intelligence more resolute and free.

The Birth of Reason

Reason in Common Sense. Volume 1 of *The Life of Reason: or, the Phases of Human Progress.* New York: Charles Scribner's Sons; London: Constable and Co. Ltd., 1905, 35–47. Volume seven of the critical edition of *The Works of George Santayana.*

This selection, Chapter I of Reason in Common Sense, *gives a naturalistic account of reason as growing out of irrational instinct. When considering the place of mind in the universe, other thinkers have looked for an originating principle of either chaos or order, but Santayana sought to reconcile the two views. He thought chaos undeniable, but he also observed order in natural arrangements. Such natural arrangements are inherently unstable and relative to some local tendency or aim, but out of these develop reason. Life is an example of an unstable attempt to preserve some arrangement. Reason is the extension of this pursuit but in terms of excellence or ideals. Excellent experiences are preserved as ideals and become organizing principles for other impulses. Santayana wrote, "[w]hen definite interests are recognized and the values of things are estimated by that standard, action at the same time veering in harmony with that estimation, then reason has been born and a moral world has arisen" (ES, 302).*

Whether Chaos or Order lay at the beginning of things is a question once much debated in the schools but afterward long in abeyance, not so much because it had been solved as because one party had been silenced by social pressure. The question is bound to recur in an age when observation and dialectic again freely confront each other. Naturalists look back to chaos since they observe everything growing from seeds and shifting its character in regeneration. The order now established in the world may be traced back to a situation in which it did not appear. Dialecticians, on the other hand, refute this presumption by urging that every collocation of things must have been preceded by another collocation in itself no less definite and precise; and further that some principle of transition or continuity must always have obtained, else successive states would stand in no relation to one another, notably not in the relation of cause and effect, expressed in a natural law, which is presupposed in this instance. Potentialities are dispositions, and a disposition involves an order, as does also the passage from any specific potentiality into act. Thus the world, we are told, must always have possessed a structure.

> Existence always has an Order, called Chaos when incompatible with a chosen good.

The two views may perhaps be reconciled if we take each with a qualification. Chaos doubtless has existed and will return—nay, it reigns now, very likely, in the remoter and inmost parts of the universe—if by chaos we understand a nature containing none of the objects we are wont to distinguish, a nature such that human life and human thought would be impossible in its bosom; but this nature must be presumed to have an order, an order directly importing, if the

tendency of its movement be taken into account, all the complexities and beauties, all the sense and reason which exist now. Order is accordingly continual; but
only when order means not a specific arrangement, favourable to a given form
of life, but any arrangement whatsoever. The process by which an arrangement
which is essentially unstable gradually shifts cannot be said to aim at every stage
which at any moment it involves. For the process passes beyond. It presently
abolishes all the forms which may have arrested attention and generated love; its
initial energy defeats every purpose which we may fondly attribute to it. Nor is it
here necessary to remind ourselves that to call results their own causes is always
preposterous; for in this case even the mythical sense which might be attached to
such language is inapplicable. Here the process, taken in the gross, does not, even
by mechanical necessity, support the value which is supposed to guide it. That
value is realised for a moment only; so that if we impute to Cronos any intent to
beget his children we must also impute to him an intent to devour them.

Of course the various states of the world, when we survey them retrospectively, constitute another and now static order called historic truth. To this absolute and impotent order every detail is essential. If we wished to

Absolute order, or truth, is static, impotent, indifferent. abuse language so much as to speak of will in an "Absolute" where change is excluded, so that nothing can be or be conceived beyond it, we might say that the Absolute willed everything that ever exists, and that the eternal order terminated in every fact indiscriminately;

but such language involves an after-image of motion and life, of
preparation, risk, and subsequent accomplishment, adventures all presupposing
refractory materials and excluded from eternal truth by its very essence. The
only function those traditional metaphors have is to shield confusion and sentimentality. Because Jehovah once fought for the Jews, we need not continue to say
that the truth is solicitous about us, when it is only we that are fighting to attain it.
The universe can wish particular things only in so far as particular beings wish
them; only in its relative capacity can it find things good, and only in its relative
capacity can it be good for anything.

The efficacious or physical order which exists at any moment in the world and
out of which the next moment's order is developed, may accordingly be termed
a relative chaos: a chaos, because the values suggested and supported by the
second moment could not have belonged to the first; but merely a relative chaos,
first because it probably carried values of its own which rendered it an order in a
moral and eulogistic sense, and secondly because it was potentially, by virtue of
its momentum, a basis for the second moment's values as well.

Human life, when it begins to possess intrinsic value, is an incipient order in
the midst of what seems a vast though, to some extent, a vanishing chaos. This

In experience order is relative to interests, which determine the moral status of all powers. reputed chaos can be deciphered and appreciated by man only in proportion as the order in himself is confirmed and extended. For man's consciousness is evidently practical; it clings to his fate, registers, so to speak, the higher and lower temperature of his fortunes, and, so far as it can, represents the agencies on which those fortunes depend. When this dramatic vocation of consciousness has not been fulfilled at all, consciousness is wholly confused; the world it envisages seems consequently a chaos. Later, if experience has fallen into shape, and there are settled categories and constant objects in human discourse, the inference is drawn that the original disposition of things was also orderly and indeed mechanically conducive to just those feats of instinct and intelligence which have been since accomplished. A theory of origins, of substance, and of natural laws may thus be framed and accepted, and may receive confirmation in the further march of events. It will be observed, however, that what is credibly asserted about the past is not a report which the past was itself able to make when it existed nor one it is now able, in some oracular fashion, to formulate and to impose upon us. The report is a rational construction based and seated in present experience; it has no cogency for the inattentive and no existence for the ignorant. Although the universe, then, may not have come from chaos, human experience certainly has begun in a private and dreamful chaos of its own, out of which it still only partially and momentarily emerges. The history of this awakening is of course not the same as that of the environing world ultimately discovered; it is the history, however, of that discovery itself, of the knowledge through which alone the world can be revealed. We may accordingly dispense ourselves from preliminary courtesies to the real universal order, nature, the absolute, and the gods. We shall make their acquaintance in due season and better appreciate their moral status, if we strive merely to recall our own experience, and to retrace the visions and reflections out of which those apparitions have grown.

To revert to primordial feeling is an exercise in mental disintegration, not a feat of science. We might, indeed, as in animal psychology, retrace the situations in which instinct and sense seem first to appear and write, as it were, a genealogy of reason based on circumstantial evidence. Reason was born, as it has since discovered, into a world already wonderfully organised, in which it found its precursor in what is called life, its seat in an animal body of unusual plasticity, and its function in rendering that body's volatile instincts and sensations harmonious with one another and with the outer world on which they depend. It did not arise until the will or conscious stress, by which any modification of living bodies' inertia seems to be accompanied, began to respond to represented objects, and to maintain that inertia not absolutely by resistance but only relatively and indirectly through labour. Reason has thus supervened at the last stage of an adaptation which had long been carried on by irrational and even unconscious processes. Nature preceded, with all that fixation of impulses and conditions which gives reason its tasks and its *point-d'appui*. Nevertheless, such a matrix or cradle for reason belongs only externally to its life. The description of conditions involves their previous discovery and a historian equipped with many data and many analogies of thought. Such scientific resources are absent in those first moments of rational living which we here wish to recall; the first chapter in reason's memoirs would no more entail the description of its real environment than the first chapter in human history would include true accounts of astronomy, psychology, and animal evolution.

The discovered conditions of reason not its beginning.

In order to begin at the beginning we must try to fall back on uninterpreted feeling, as the mystics aspire to do. We need not expect, however, to find peace there, for the immediate is in flux. Pure feeling rejoices in a logical nonentity very deceptive to dialectical minds. They often think, when they fall back on elements necessarily indescribable, that they have come upon true nothingness. If they are mystics, distrusting thought and craving the largeness of indistinction, they may embrace this alleged nothingness with joy, even if it seem positively painful, hoping to find rest there through self-abnegation. If on the contrary they are rationalists they may reject the immediate with scorn and deny that it exists at all, since in their books they cannot define it satisfactorily. Both mystics and rationalists, however, are deceived by their mental agility; the immediate exists, even if dialectic cannot explain it. What the rationalist calls nonentity is the substrate and locus of all ideas, having the obstinate reality of matter, the crushing irrationality of existence itself; and one who attempts to override it becomes to that extent an irrelevant rhapsodist, dealing with thin after-images of being. Nor has the mystic who sinks into the immediate much better appreciated the situation. This immediate is not God but chaos; its nothingness is pregnant, restless, and brutish; it is that from which all things emerge in so far as they have any permanence or value, so that to lapse into it again is a dull suicide and no salvation. Peace, which is after all what the mystic seeks, lies not in indistinction but in perfection. If he reaches it in a measure himself, it is by the traditional discipline he still practises, not by his heats or his languors.

The flux first.

The seed-bed of reason lies, then, in the immediate, but what reason draws thence is momentum and power to rise above its source. It is the perturbed immediate itself that finds or at least seeks its peace in reason, through which it comes in sight of some sort of ideal permanence. When the flux manages to form an eddy and to maintain by breathing and nutrition what we call a life, it affords some slight foothold and object for thought and becomes in a measure like the ark in the desert, a moving habitation for the eternal.

Life begins to have some value and continuity so soon as there is something definite that lives and something definite to live for. The primacy of will, as Fichte and Schopenhauer conceived it, is a mythical way of designating this situation. Of course a will can have no being in the absence of realities or ideas marking its direction and contrasting the eventualities it seeks with those it flies from; and tendency, no less than movement, needs an organised medium to make it possible, while aspiration and fear involve an ideal world. Yet a principle of choice is not deducible from mere ideas, and no interest is involved in the formal relations of things. All survey needs an arbitrary starting-point; all valuation rests on an irrational bias. The absolute flux cannot be physically arrested; but what arrests it ideally is the fixing of some point in it from which it can be measured and illumined. Otherwise it could show no form and maintain no preference; it would be impossible to approach or recede from a represented state, and to suffer or to exert will in view of events. The irrational fate that lodges the transcendental self in this or that body, inspires

Life the fixation of interests.

it with definite passions, and subjects it to particular buffets from the outer world—this is the prime condition of all observation and inference, of all failure or success.

Those sensations in which a transition is contained need only analysis to yield two ideal and related terms—two points in space or two characters in feeling. Hot and cold, here and there, good and bad, now and then, are dyads that spring into being when the flux accentuates some term and so makes possible a discrimination of parts and directions in its own movement. **Primary dualities.** An initial attitude sustains incipient interests. What we first discover in ourselves, before the influence we obey has given rise to any definite idea, is the working of instincts already in motion. Impulses to appropriate and to reject first teach us the points of the compass, and space itself, like charity, begins at home.

The guide in early sensuous education is the same that conducts the whole Life of Reason, namely, impulse checked by experiment, and experiment judged again by impulse. What teaches the child to distinguish the nurse's breast from sundry blank or disquieting presences? What induces him to arrest that image, to mark its associates, and to recognise them with alacrity? The discomfort of its absence and the comfort of its possession. To that image is attached the chief satisfaction he **First gropings. Instinct the nucleus of reason.** knows, and the force of that satisfaction disentangles it before all other images from the feeble and fluid continuum of his life. What first awakens in him a sense of reality is what first is able to appease his unrest.

Had the group of feelings, now welded together in fruition, found no instinct in him to awaken and become a signal for, the group would never have persisted; its loose elements would have been allowed to pass by unnoticed and would not have been recognised when they recurred. Experience would have remained absolute inexperience, as foolishly perpetual as the gurglings of rivers or the flickerings of sunlight in a grove. But an instinct was actually present, so formed as to be aroused by a determinate stimulus; and the image produced by that stimulus, when it came, could have in consequence a meaning and an individuality. It seemed by divine right to signify something interesting, something real, because by natural contiguity it flowed from something pertinent and important to life. Every accompanying sensation which shared that privilege, or in time was engrossed in that function, would ultimately become a part of that conceived reality, a quality of that thing.

The same primacy of impulses, irrational in themselves but expressive of bodily functions, is observable in the behaviour of animals, and in those dreams, obsessions, and primary passions which in the midst of sophisticated life sometimes lay bare the obscure groundwork of human nature. Reason's work is there undone. We can observe sporadic growths, disjointed fragments of rationality, springing up in a moral wilderness. In the passion of love, for instance, a cause unknown to the sufferer, but which is doubtless the spring-flood of hereditary instincts accidentally let loose, suddenly checks the young man's gayety, dispels his random curiosity, arrests perhaps his very breath; and when he looks for a cause to explain his suspended faculties, he can find it only in the presence or image of another being, of whose character, possibly, he knows nothing and whose beauty may not be remarkable; yet that image pursues him everywhere, and he is dominated by an unaccustomed tragic earnestness and a new capacity for suffering and joy. If the passion be strong there is no previous interest or duty that will be remembered before it; if it be lasting the whole life may be reorganised by it; it may impose new habits, other manners, and another religion. Yet what is the root of all this idealism? An irrational instinct, normally intermittent, such as all dumb creatures share, which has here managed to dominate a human soul and to enlist all the mental powers in its more or less permanent service, upsetting their usual equilibrium. This madness, however, inspires method; and for the first time, perhaps, in his life, the man has something to live for. The blind affinity that like a magnet draws all the faculties around it, in so uniting them, suffuses them with an unwonted spiritual light.

Here, on a small scale and on a precarious foundation, we may see clearly illustrated and foreshadowed that Life of Reason which is simply the unity given

Better and worse the fundamental categories.
to all existence by a mind in love with the good. In the higher reaches of human nature, as much as in the lower, rationality depends on distinguishing the excellent; and that distinction can be made, in the last analysis, only by an irrational impulse. As life is a better form given to force, by which the universal flux is subdued to create and serve a somewhat permanent interest, so reason is a better form given to interest itself, by which it is fortified and propagated, and ultimately, perhaps, assured of satisfaction. The substance to which this form is given remains irrational; so that rationality, like all excellence, is something secondary and relative, requiring a natural being to possess or to impute it. When definite interests are recognised and the values of things are estimated by that standard, action at the same time veering in harmony with that estimation, then reason has been born and a moral world has arisen.

How Religion May Be an Embodiment of Reason

Reason in Religion. Volume 3 of *The Life of Reason: or, the Phases of Human Progress.* New York: Charles Scribner's Sons; London: Constable and Co. Ltd., 1905, 3–14. Volume seven of the critical edition of *The Works of George Santayana.*

This selection appeared as Chapter I of Reason in Religion. *On rereading this book in 1948, Santayana remarked, "What a horrible tone!", and continued, "[i]t was life in America and the habit of lecturing that dominated one half of my celebral cortex, while England, Greece, the poets, and my friends dominated the other half, and they took turns in guiding my pen. How I wish I could erase all that cheap work!" (LGS, 8:100). How-ever, two years later he admitted that he and his secretary Daniel Cory, working together on a one-volume abridgment of* The Life of Reason, *had "found the text better than we expected . . . easy to read for the most part, and clear" (LGS, 8:396). This particular chapter shows how religion and the Life of Reason share a desire for values, meanings, and excellence. They both aim at ideals, though religion tends to turn them into material powers and falsely regard them as scientific evidence for another world. The emotion that religion bestows on ideals can advance reflection and insight and is not to be shunned. Santayana denied that the superstitious interpretation of nature is inherent in religion.*

Experience has repeatedly confirmed that well-known maxim of Bacon's, that "a little philosophy inclineth man's mind to atheism, but depth in philosophy bringeth men's minds about to religion." In every age the most com-prehensive thinkers have found in the religion of their time and country something they could accept, interpreting and illustrating that religion so as to give it depth and universal application. Even

Religion certainly significant.

the heretics and atheists, if they have had profundity, turn out after a while to be forerunners of some new orthodoxy. What they rebel against is a religion alien to their nature; they are atheists only by accident, and relatively to a convention which inwardly offends them, but they yearn mightily in their own souls after the religious acceptance of a world interpreted in their own fashion. So it appears in the end that their atheism and loud protestation were in fact the hastier part of their thought, since what emboldened them to deny the poor world's faith was that they were too impatient to understand it. Indeed, the enlightenment com-mon to young wits and worm-eaten old satirists, who plume themselves on detecting the scientific ineptitude of religion—something which the blindest half see—is not nearly enlightened enough: it points to notorious facts incompatible with religious tenets literally taken, but it leaves unexplored the habits of thought from which those tenets sprang, their original meaning, and their true function. Such studies would bring the sceptic face to face with the mystery and pathos of mortal existence. They would make him understand why religion is so profoundly moving and in a sense so profoundly just. There must needs be something humane and necessary in an influence that has become the most general sanction of virtue, the chief occasion for art and philosophy, and the source, perhaps, of the best human happiness. If nothing, as Hooker said, is "so malapert as a splenetic religion," a sour irreligion is almost as perverse.

At the same time, when Bacon penned the sage epigram we have quoted he forgot to add that the God to whom depth in philosophy brings back men's **But not** minds is far from being the same from whom a little philosophy **literally** estranges them. It would be pitiful indeed if mature reflection bred no **true.** better conceptions than those which have drifted down the muddy stream of time, where tradition and passion have jumbled everything together. Traditional conceptions, when they are felicitous, may be adopted by the poet, but they must be purified by the moralist and disintegrated by the philosopher. Each religion, so dear to those whose life it sanctifies, and fulfilling so necessary a function in the society that has adopted it, necessarily contradicts every other religion, and probably contradicts itself. What religion a man shall have is a historical accident, quite as much as what language he shall speak. In the rare circumstances where a choice is possible, he may, with some difficulty, make an exchange; but even then he is only adopting a new convention which may be more agreeable to his personal temper but which is essentially as arbitrary as the old.

The attempt to speak without speaking any particular language is not more hopeless than the attempt to have a religion that shall be no religion in particular. A courier's or a dragoman's speech may indeed be often unusual **All religion** and drawn from disparate sources, not without some mixture of **is positive** personal originality; but that private jargon will have a meaning **and** **particular.** only because of its analogy to one or more conventional languages and its obvious derivation from them. So travellers from one religion to another, people who have lost their spiritual nationality, may often retain a neutral and confused residuum of belief, which they may egregiously regard as the essence of all religion, so little may they remember the graciousness and naturalness of that ancestral accent which a perfect religion should have. Yet a moment's probing of the conceptions surviving in such minds will show them to be nothing but vestiges of old beliefs, creases which thought, even if emptied of all dogmatic tenets, has not been able to smooth away at its first unfolding. Later generations, if they have any religion at all, will be found either to revert to ancient authority, or to attach themselves spontaneously to something wholly novel and immensely positive, to some faith promulgated by a fresh genius and passionately embraced by a converted people. Thus every living and healthy religion has a marked idiosyncrasy. Its power consists in its special and surprising message and in the bias which that revelation gives to life. The vistas it opens and the mysteries it propounds are another world to live in; and another world to live in—whether we expect ever to pass wholly into it or no—is what we mean by having a religion.

What relation, then, does this great business of the soul, which we call religion, bear to the Life of Reason? That the relation between the two is close seems clear from several circumstances. The Life of Reason is the seat of all ultimate values. Now the history of mankind will show us that whenever spirits at once lofty and intense have seemed to attain the highest joys, they have envisaged and attained them in religion. Religion would therefore seem to be a vehicle or a factor in rational life, since the ends of rational life are attained by it. Moreover, the Life of Reason is an ideal to which everything in the world should be subordinated; it establishes lines of moral cleavage everywhere and makes right eternally different from wrong. Religion does the same thing. It makes absolute moral decisions. It sanctions, unifies, and transforms ethics. Religion thus exercises a function of the Life of Reason. And a further function which is common to both is that of emancipating man from his personal limitations. In different ways religions promise to transfer the soul to better conditions. A supernaturally favoured kingdom is to be established for posterity upon earth, or for all the faithful in heaven, or the soul is to be freed by repeated purgations from all taint and sorrow, or it is to be lost in the absolute, or it is to become an influence and an object of adoration in the places it once haunted or wherever the activities it once loved may be carried on by future generations of its kindred. Now reason in its way lays before us all these possibilities: it points to common objects, political and intellectual, in which an individual may lose what is mortal and accidental in himself and immortalise what is rational and human; it teaches us how sweet and fortunate death may be to those whose spirit can still live in their country and in their ideas; it reveals the radiating effects of action and the eternal objects of thought.

It aims at the Life of Reason.

Yet the difference in tone and language must strike us, so soon as it is philosophy that speaks. That change should remind us that even if the function of religion and that of reason coincide, this function is performed in the two cases by very different organs. Religions are many, reason one. Religion consists of conscious ideas, hopes, enthusiasms, and objects of worship; it operates by grace and flourishes by prayer. Reason, on the other hand, is a mere principle or potential order, on which, indeed, we may come to reflect, but which exists in us ideally only, without variation or stress of any kind. We conform or do not conform to it; it does not urge or chide us, nor call for any emotions on our part other than those naturally aroused by the various objects which it unfolds in their true nature and proportion. Religion brings some order into life by weighting it with new materials. Reason adds to the natural materials only the perfect order which it introduces into them. Rationality is nothing but a form, an ideal constitution which experience may more or less embody. Religion is a part of experience itself, a mass of sentiments and ideas. The one is an inviolate principle, the other a changing and struggling force. And yet this struggling and changing force of religion seems to direct man toward something eternal. It seems to make for an ultimate harmony within the soul and for an ultimate harmony between the soul and all the soul depends upon. So that religion, in its intent, is a more conscious and direct pursuit of the Life of Reason than is society, science, or art. For these approach and fill out the ideal life tentatively and piecemeal, hardly regarding the goal or caring for the ultimate justification of their instinctive aims. Religion also has an instinctive and blind side, and bubbles up in all manner of chance practices and intuitions; soon, however, it feels its way toward the heart of things, and, from whatever quarter it may come, veers in the direction of the ultimate.

Nevertheless, we must confess that this religious pursuit of the Life of Reason has been singularly abortive. Those within the pale of each religion may prevail

But largely fails to attain it.
upon themselves to express satisfaction with its results, thanks to a fond partiality in reading the past and generous draughts of hope for the future; but any one regarding the various religions at once and comparing their achievements with what reason requires, must feel how terrible is the disappointment which they have one and all prepared for mankind. Their chief anxiety has been to offer imaginary remedies for mortal ills, some of which are incurable essentially, while others might have been really cured by well-directed effort. The Greek oracles, for instance, pretended to heal our natural ignorance, which has its appropriate though difficult cure, while the Christian vision of heaven pretended to be an antidote to our natural death, the inevitable correlate of birth and of a changing and conditioned existence. By methods of this sort little can be done for the real betterment of life. To confuse intelligence and dislocate sentiment by gratuitous fictions is a short-sighted way of pursuing happiness. Nature is soon avenged. An unhealthy exaltation and a one-sided morality have to be followed by regrettable reactions. When these come, the real rewards of life may seem vain to a relaxed vitality, and the very name of virtue may irritate young spirits untrained in any natural excellence. Thus religion too often debauches the morality it comes to sanction, and impedes the science it ought to fulfil.

What is the secret of this ineptitude? Why does religion, so near to rationality in its purpose, fall so far short of it in its texture and in its results? The answer is

Its approach imaginative.
easy: Religion pursues rationality through the imagination. When it explains events or assigns causes, it is an imaginative substitute for science. When it gives precepts, insinuates ideals, or remoulds aspiration, it is an imaginative substitute for wisdom—I mean for the deliberate and impartial pursuit of all good. The conditions and the aims of life are both represented in religion poetically, but this poetry tends to arrogate to itself literal truth and moral authority, neither of which it possesses. Hence the depth and importance of religion become intelligible no less than its contradictions and practical disasters. Its object is the same as that of reason, but its method is to proceed by intuition and by unchecked poetical conceits. These are repeated and vulgarised in proportion to their original fineness and significance, till they pass for reports of objective truth and come to constitute a world of faith, superposed upon the world of experience and regarded as materially enveloping it, if not in space at least in time and in existence. The only truth of religion comes from its interpretation of life, from its symbolic rendering of that moral experience which it springs out of and which it seeks to elucidate. Its falsehood comes from the insidious misunderstanding which clings to it, to the effect that these poetic conceptions are not merely representations of experience as it is or should be, but are

rather information about experience or reality elsewhere–an experience and reality which, strangely enough, supply just the defects betrayed by reality and experience here.

Thus religion has the same original relation to life that poetry has; only poetry, which never pretends to literal validity, adds a pure value to existence, the value of a liberal imaginative exercise. The poetic value of religion would initially be greater than that of poetry itself, because religion deals with higher and more practical themes, with sides of life which are in greater need of some imaginative touch and ideal interpretation than are those pleasant or pompous things which ordinary poetry dwells upon. But this initial advantage is neutralised in part by the abuse to which religion is subject, whenever its symbolic rightness is taken for scientific truth. Like poetry, it improves the world only by imagining it improved, but not content with making this addition to the mind's furniture–an addition which might be useful and ennobling–it thinks to confer a more radical benefit by persuading mankind that, in spite of appearances, the world is really such as that rather arbitrary idealisation has painted it. This spurious satisfaction is naturally the prelude to many a disappointment, and the soul has infinite trouble to emerge again from the artificial problems and sentiments into which it is thus plunged. The value of religion becomes equivocal. Religion remains an imaginative achievement, a symbolic representation of moral reality which may have a most important function in vitalising the mind and in transmitting, by way of parables, the lessons of experience. But it becomes at the same time a continuous incidental deception; and this deception, in proportion as it is strenuously denied to be such, can work indefinite harm in the world and in the conscience.

When its poetic method is denied its value is jeopardised.

On the whole, however, religion should not be conceived as having taken the place of anything better, but rather as having come to relieve situations which, but for its presence, would have been infinitely worse. In the thick of active life, or in the monotony of practical slavery, there is more need to stimulate fancy than to control it. Natural instinct is not much disturbed in the human brain by what may happen in that thin superstratum of ideas which commonly overlays it. We must not blame religion for preventing the development of a moral and natural science which at any rate would seldom have appeared; we must rather thank it for the sensibility, the reverence, the speculative insight which it has introduced into the world.

It precedes science rather than hinders it.

We may therefore proceed to analyse the significance and the function which religion has had at its different stages, and, without disguising or in the least condoning its confusion with literal truth, we may allow ourselves to enter as sympathetically as possible into its various conceptions and emotions. They have made up the inner life of many sages, and of all those who without great genius or learning have lived steadfastly in the spirit. The feeling of reverence should itself be treated with reverence, although not at a sacrifice of truth, with which alone, in the end, reverence is compatible. Nor have we any reason to be intolerant of the

It is merely symbolic and thoroughly human.

partialities and contradictions which religions display. Were we dealing with a science, such contradictions would have to be instantly solved and removed; but when we are concerned with the poetic interpretation of experience, contradiction means only variety, and variety means spontaneity, wealth of resource, and a nearer approach to total adequacy.

If we hope to gain any understanding of these matters we must begin by taking them out of that heated and fanatical atmosphere in which the Hebrew tradition has enveloped them. The Jews had no philosophy, and when their national traditions came to be theoretically explicated and justified, they were made to issue in a puerile scholasticism and a rabid intolerance. The question of monotheism, for instance, was a terrible question to the Jews. Idolatry did not consist in worshipping a god who, not being ideal, might be unworthy of worship, but rather in recognising other gods than the one worshipped in Jerusalem. To the Greeks, on the contrary, whose philosophy was enlightened and ingenuous, monotheism and polytheism seemed perfectly innocent and compatible. To say God or the gods was only to use different expressions for the same influence, now viewed in its abstract unity and correlation with all existence, now viewed in its various manifestations in moral life, in nature, or in history. So that what in Plato, Aristotle, and the Stoics meets us at every step—the combination of monotheism with polytheism—is no contradiction, but merely an intelligent variation of phrase to indicate various aspects or functions in physical and moral things. When religion appears to us in this light its contradictions and controversies lose all their bitterness. Each doctrine will simply represent the moral plane on which they live who have devised or adopted it. Religions will thus be better or worse, never true or false. We shall be able to lend ourselves to each in turn, and seek to draw from it the secret of its inspiration.

Justification of Art

Reason in Art. Volume 4 of *The Life of Reason: or, the Phases of Human Progress.* New York: Charles Scribner's Sons; London: Constable and Co. Ltd., 1905, 166–90. Volume seven of the critical edition of *The Works of George Santayana.*

This selection appeared as Chapter IX of Reason in Art. *Art is concerned mainly with the ideal and not with material nature. It makes matter more congenial to spirit by harmonizing impulses with nature and rendering nature more ideal. Santayana conceived art as "a rehearsal of rational living" in that it recasts the world imaginatively. He held such imaginative rehearsal superior to "miserable experiments" in reality because it better revealed the wonderful possibilities of what could be (ES, 312). He thought that, "[w]hat nature does with existence, art does with appearance; and while the achievement leaves us, unhappily, much where we were before in all our efficacious relations, it entirely renews our vision and breeds a fresh world in fancy, where all form has the same inner justification that all life has in the real world" (ES, 312). Art perpetuates itself by reshaping nature such that it better disciplines and enriches imagination, and this increases appreciation for ideals.*

It is no longer the fashion among philosophers to decry art. Either its influence seems to them too slight to excite alarm, or their systems are too lax to subject anything to censure which has the least glamour or ideality about it. Tired, perhaps, of daily resolving the conflict between science and religion, they prefer to assume silently a harmony between morals and art. Moral harmonies, however, are not given; they have to be made. The curse of superstition is that it justifies and protracts their absence by proclaiming their invisible presence. Of course a rational religion could not conflict with a rational science; and similarly an art that was wholly admirable would necessarily play into the hands of progress. But as the real difficulty in the former case lies in saying what religion and what science would be truly rational, so here the problem is how far extant art is a benefit to mankind, and how far, perhaps, a vice or a burden.

> Art is subject to moral censorship.

That art is *prima facie* and in itself a good cannot be doubted. It is a spontaneous activity, and that settles the question. Yet the function of ethics is precisely to revise *prima facie* judgments of this kind and to fix the ultimate resultant of all given interests, in so far as they can be combined. In the actual disarray of human life and desire, wisdom consists in knowing what goods to sacrifice and what simples to pour into the supreme mixture. The extent to which æsthetic values are allowed to colour the resultant or highest good is a point of great theoretic importance, not only for art but for general philosophy. If art is excluded altogether or given only a trivial rôle, perhaps as a necessary relaxation, we feel at once that a philosophy so judging human arts is ascetic or post-rational. It pretends to guide life from above and from without; it has discredited human nature and mortal interests, and has

> Its initial or specific excellence is not enough.

thereby undermined itself, since it is at best but a partial expression of that humanity which it strives to transcend. If, on the contrary, art is prized as something supreme and irresponsible, if the poetic and mystic glow which it may bring seems its own complete justification, then philosophy is evidently still prerational or, rather, non-existent; for the beasts that listened to Orpheus belong to this school.

To be bewitched is not to be saved, though all the magicians and æsthetes in the world should pronounce it to be so. Intoxication is a sad business, at least for a philosopher; for you must either drown yourself altogether, or else when sober again you will feel somewhat fooled by yesterday's joys and somewhat lost in today's vacancy. The man who would emancipate art from discipline and reason is trying to elude rationality, not merely in art, but in all existence. He is vexed at conditions of excellence that make him conscious of his own incompetence and failure. Rather than consider his function, he proclaims his self-sufficiency. A way foolishness has of revenging itself is to excommunicate the world.

It is in the world, however, that art must find its level. It must vindicate its function in the human commonwealth. What direct acceptable contribution does it make to the highest good? What sacrifices, if any, does it impose? What indirect influence does it exert on other activities? Our answer to these questions will be our apology for art, our proof that art belongs to the Life of Reason.

When moralists deprecate passion and contrast it with reason, they do so, if they are themselves rational, only because passion is so often "guilty," because it works havoc so often in the surrounding world and leaves, among other ruins, "a heart high-sorrowful and cloyed." Were there no danger of such after-effects within and without the sufferer, no passion would be reprehensible. Nature is innocent, and so are all her impulses and moods when taken in isolation; it is only on meeting that they blush. If it be true that matter is sinful, the logic of this truth is far from being what the fanatics imagine who commonly propound it. Matter is sinful only because it is insufficient, or is wastefully distributed. There is not enough of it to go round among the legion of hungry ideas. To embody or enact an idea is the only way of making it actual; but its embodiment may mutilate it, if the material or the situation is not propitious. So an infant may be maimed at birth, when what injures him is not being brought forth, but being brought forth in the wrong manner. Matter has a double function in respect to existence; essentially it enables the spirit to be, yet chokes is incidentally. Men sadly misbegotten, or those who are thwarted at every step by the times' penury, may fall to thinking of matter only by its defect, ignoring the material ground of their own aspirations. All flesh will seem to them weak, except that forgotten piece of it which makes their own spiritual strength. Every impulse, however, had initially the same authority as this censorious one, by which the others are now judged and condemned.

All satisfactions, however hurtful, have an initial worth.

If a practice can point to its innocence, if it can absolve itself from concern for a world with which it does not interfere, it has justified itself to those who love it, though it may not yet have recommended itself to those who do not. Now art, more than any other considerable pursuit, more even than speculation, is abstract and inconsequential. Born of suspended attention, it ends in itself. It encourages sensuous abstraction, and nothing concerns it less than to influence the world. Nor does it really do so in a notable degree. Social changes do not reach artistic expression until after their momentum is acquired and their other collateral effects are fully predetermined. Scarcely is a school of art established, giving expression to prevailing sentiment, when the sentiment changes and makes that style seem empty and ridiculous. The expression has little or no power to maintain the movement it registers, as a waterfall has little or no power to bring more water down. Currents may indeed cut deep channels, but they cannot feed their own springs—at least not until the whole revolution of nature is taken into account.

But, on the whole, artistic activity is innocent.

In the individual, also, art registers passions without stimulating them; on the contrary, in stopping to depict them it steals away their life; and whatever interest and delight it transfers to their expression it subtracts from their vital energy. This appears unmistakably in erotic and in religious art. Though the artist's avowed purpose here be to arouse a practical impulse, he fails in so far as he is an artist in truth; for he then will seek to move the given passions only through beauty, but beauty is a rival object of passion in itself. Lascivious and pious works, when beauty has touched them, cease to give out what is wilful and disquieting in their subject and become altogether intellectual and sublime. There is a high breathlessness about beauty that cancels lust and superstition. The artist, in taking the latter for his theme, renders them innocent and interesting, because he looks at them from above, composes their attitudes and surroundings harmoniously, and makes them food for the mind. Accordingly it is only in a refined and secondary stage that active passions like to amuse themselves with their æsthetic expression. Unmitigated lustiness and raw fanaticism will snarl at pictures. Representations begin to interest when crude passions recede, and feel the need of conciliating liberal interests and adding some intellectual charm to their dumb attractions. Thus art, while by its subject it may betray the preoccupations among which it springs up, embodies a new and quite innocent interest.

This interest is more than innocent, it is liberal. Not being concerned with material reality so much as with the ideal, it knows neither ulterior motives nor quantitative limits; the more beauty there is the more there can be, and the higher one artist's imagination soars the better the whole flock flies. In æsthetic activity we have accordingly one side of rational life;

It is liberal,

sensuous experience is dominated there as mechanical or social realities ought to be dominated in science and politics. Such dominion comes of having faculties suited to their conditions and consequently finding an inherent satisfaction in their operation. The justification of life must be ultimately intrinsic; and wherever such self-justifying experience is attained, the ideal has been in so far embodied. To have realised it in a measure helps us to realise it further; for there is a cumulative fecundity in those goods which come not by increase of force or matter, but by a better organisation and form.

Art has met, on the whole, with more success than science or morals. Beauty gives men the best hint of ultimate good which their experience as yet can offer; and the most lauded geniuses have been poets, as if people felt that those seers, **and typical of perfect activity.** rather than men of action or thought, had lived ideally and known what was worth knowing. That such should be the case, if the fact be admitted, would indeed prove the rudimentary state of human civilisation. The truly comprehensive life should be the statesman's, for whom perception and theory might be expressed and rewarded in action. The ideal dignity of art is therefore merely symbolic and vicarious. As some people study character in novels, and travel by reading tales of adventure, because real life is not yet so interesting to them as fiction, or because they find it cheaper to make their experiments in their dreams, so art in general is a rehearsal of rational living, and recasts in idea a world which we have no present means of recasting in reality. Yet this rehearsal reveals the glories of a possible performance better than do the miserable experiments until now executed on the reality.

When we consider the present distracted state of government and religion, there is much relief in turning from them to almost any art, where what is good is altogether and finally good, and what is bad is at least not treacherous. When we consider further the senseless rivalries, the vanities, the ignominy that reign in the "practical" world, how doubly blessed it becomes to find a sphere where limitation is an excellence, where diversity is a beauty, and where every man's ambition is consistent with every other man's and even favourable to it! It is indeed so in art; for we must not import into its blameless labours the bickerings and jealousies of criticism. Critics quarrel with other critics, and that is a part of philosophy. With an artist no sane man quarrels, any more than with the colour of a child's eyes. As nature, being full of seeds, rises into all sorts of crystallisations, each having its own ideal and potential life, each a nucleus of order and a habitation for the absolute self, so art, though in a medium poorer than pregnant matter, and incapable of intrinsic life, generates a semblance of all conceivable beings. What nature does with existence, art does with appearance; and while the achievement leaves us, unhappily, much where we were before in all our efficacious relations, it entirely renews our vision and breeds a fresh world in fancy, where all form has the same inner justification that all life has in the real world. As no insect is without its rights and every cripple has his dream of happiness, so no artistic fact, no child of imagination, is without its small birthright of beauty. In this freer element, competition does not exist and everything is Olympian. Hungry generations do not tread down the ideal but only its spokesmen or embodiments, that have cast in their lot with other material things. Art supplies constantly to contemplation what nature seldom affords in concrete experience—the union of life and peace.

The ideal, however, would not come down from the empyrean and be conceived unless somebody's thought were absorbed in the conception. **The ideal, when incarnate, becomes subject to civil society.** Art actually segregates classes of men and masses of matter to serve its special interests. This involves expense; it impedes some possible activities and imposes others. On this ground, from the earliest times until our own, art has been occasionally attacked by moralists, who have felt that it fostered idolatry or luxury or irresponsible dreams. Of these attacks the most interesting is Plato's, because he was an artist by temperament, bred in the very focus of artistic life and discussion, and at the same time a consummate moral philosopher. His æsthetic sensibility was indeed so great that it led him, perhaps, into a relative error, in that he overestimated the influence which art can have on character and affairs. Homer's stories about the gods can hardly have demoralised the youths who recited them. No religion has ever given a picture of deity which men could have imitated without the grossest immorality. Yet these shocking representations have not had a bad effect on believers. The deity was opposed to their own vices; those it might itself be credited with offered no contagious example. In spite of the theologians, we know by instinct that in speaking of the gods we are dealing in myths and symbols. Some aspect of nature or some law of life, expressed in an attribute of deity, is what we really regard, and to regard such things, however sinister they may be, cannot but chasten and moralise us. The personal character that such a function would involve, if it were exercised willingly by a responsible being, is something that never enters our thoughts. No such painful image comes to perplex the plain sense of instinctive, poetic religion. To give moral importance to myths, as Plato tended to do, is to take them far too seriously and to belittle what they stand for. Left to themselves they float in an ineffectual stratum of the brain. They are understood and grow current precisely by not being pressed, like an idiom or a meta-phor. The same æsthetic sterility appears at the other end of the scale, where fancy is anything but sacred. A Frenchman once saw in "Punch and Judy" a shocking proof of British brutality, destined further to demoralise the nation; and yet the scandal may pass. That black tragedy reflects not very pretty manners, but puppets exercise no suasion over men.

Plato's strictures: he exaggerates the effect of myths.

To his supersensitive censure of myths Plato added strictures upon music and the drama: to excite passions idly was to enervate the soul. Only martial or religious strains should be heard in the ideal republic. Furthermore, art put before us a mere phantom of the good. True excellence was the function things had in use; the horseman knew the bridle's value and essence better than the artisan did who put it together; but a painted bridle would lack even this relation to utility. It would rein in no horse, and was an impertinent sensuous reduplication of what, even when it had material being, was only an instrument and a means.

His deeper moral objections.

This reasoning has been little understood, because Platonists so soon lost sight of their master's Socratic habit and moral intent. They turned the good into an existence, making it thereby unmeaning. Plato's dialectic, if we do not thus abolish the force of its terms, is perfectly cogent: representative art has indeed no utility, and, if the good has been identified with efficiency in a military state, it can have no justification. Plato's Republic was avowedly a fallen state, a church militant, coming sadly short of perfection; and the joy which Plato as much as any one could feel in sensuous art he postponed, as a man in mourning might, until life should be redeemed from baseness.

Never have art and beauty received a more glowing eulogy than is implied in Plato's censure. To him nothing was beautiful that was not beautiful to the core, **Their rightness.** and he would have thought to insult art–the remodelling of nature by reason–if he had given it a narrower field than all practice. As an architect who had fondly designed something impossible, or which might not please in execution, would at once erase it from the plan and abandon it for the love of perfect beauty and perfect art, so Plato wished to erase from pleasing appearance all that, when its operation was completed, would bring discord into the world. This was done in the ultimate interest of art and beauty, which in a cultivated mind are inseparable from the vitally good. It is mere barbarism to feel that a thing is æsthetically good but morally evil, or morally good but hateful to perception. Things partially evil or partially ugly may have to be chosen under stress of unfavourable circumstances, lest some worse thing come; but if a thing were ugly it would *thereby* not be wholly good, and if it were *altogether* good it would perforce be beautiful.

To criticise art on moral grounds is to pay it a high compliment by assuming that it aims to be adequate, and is addressed to a comprehensive mind. The only way in which art could disallow such criticism would be to protest its irresponsible infancy, and admit that it was a more or less amiable blatancy in individuals, and not *art* at all. Young animals often gambol in a delightful fashion, and men also may, though hardly when they intend to do so. Sportive self-expression can be prized because human nature contains a certain elasticity and margin for experiment, in which waste activity is inevitable and may be precious: for this license may lead, amid a thousand failures, to some real discovery and advance. Art, like life, should be free, since both are experimental. But it is one thing to make room for genius and to respect the sudden madness of poets through which, possibly, some god may speak, and it is quite another not to judge the result by rational standards. The earth's bowels are full of all sorts of rumblings; which of the oracles drawn thence is true can be judged only by the light of day. If an artist's inspiration has been happy, it has been so because his work can sweeten or ennoble the mind and because its total effect will be beneficent. Art being a part of life, the criticism of art is a part of morals.

Maladjustments in human society are still so scandalous, they touch matters so much more pressing than fine art, that maladjustments in the latter are passed **Importance of æsthetic alternatives.** over with a smile, as if art were at any rate an irresponsible miraculous parasite that the legislator had better not meddle with. The day may come, however, if the state is ever reduced to a tolerable order, when questions of art will be the most urgent questions of morals, when genius at last will feel responsible, and the twist given to imagination will seem the most crucial thing in life. Under a thin disguise, the momentous character of imaginative choices has already been fully recognised by mankind. Men have passionately loved their special religions, languages, and manners, and preferred death to a life flowering in any other fashion. In justifying this attachment forensically, with arguments on the low level of men's named and consecrated interests, people have indeed said, and perhaps come to believe, that their imaginative interests were material interests at bottom, thinking thus to give them more weight and legitimacy; whereas in truth material life itself would be nothing worth, were it not, in its essence and its issue, ideal.

It was stupidly asserted, however, that if a man omitted the prescribed ceremonies or had unauthorised dreams about the gods, he would lose his battles in this world and go to hell in the other. He who runs can see that these expectations are not founded on any evidence, on any observation of what actually occurs; they are obviously a *mirage* arising from a direct ideal passion, that tries to justify itself by indirection and by falsehoods, as it has no need to do. We all read facts in the way most congruous with our intellectual habit, and when this habit drives us to effulgent creations, absorbing and expressing the whole current of our being, it not merely biasses our reading of this world but carries us into another world altogether, which we posit instead of the real one, or beside it.

Grotesque as the blunder may seem by which we thus introduce our poetic tropes into the sequence of external events or existences, the blunder is intellectual only; morally, zeal for our special rhetoric may not be irrational. The lovely Phœbus is no fact for astronomy, nor does he stand behind the material sun, in some higher heaven, physically superintending its movements; but Phœbus is a fact in his own region, a token of man's joyful piety in the presence of the forces that really condition his welfare. In the region of symbols, in the world of poetry, Phœbus has his inalienable rights. Forms of poetry are forms of human life. Languages express national character and enshrine particular ways of seeing and valuing events. To make substitutions and extensions in expression is to give the soul, in her inmost substance, a somewhat new constitution. A method of apperception is a spontaneous variation in mind, perhaps the origin of a new moral species.

The value apperceptive methods have is of course largely representative, in that they serve more or less aptly to dominate the order of events and to guide action; but quite apart from this practical value, expressions possess a character of their own, a sort of vegetative life, as languages possess euphony. Two reports of the same fact may be equally trustworthy, equally useful as information, yet they may embody two types of mental rhetoric, and this diversity in genius may be of more intrinsic importance than the raw fact it works upon. The non-representative side of human perception may thus be the most momentous side of it, because it represents, or even constitutes, the man. After all, the chief interest we have in things lies in what we can make of them or what they can make of us. There is consequently nothing fitted to colour human happiness more pervasively than art does, nor to express more deeply the mind's internal habit. In educating the imagination art crowns all moral endeavour, which from the beginning is a species of art, and which becomes a fine art more completely as it works in a freer medium.

How great a portion of human energies should be spent on art and its appreciation is a question to be answered variously by various persons and nations. There is no ideal *á priori;* an ideal can but express, if it is genuine, the balance of impulses and potentialities in a given soul. A mind at once sensuous and mobile will find its appropriate perfection in studying and reconstructing objects of sense. Its rationality will appear chiefly on the plane of perception, to render the circle of visions which makes up its life as delightful as possible. For such a man art will be the most satisfying, the most significant activity, and to load him with material riches or speculative truths or profound social loyalties will be to impede and depress him. The irrational is what does not justify itself in the end; and the born artist, repelled by the soberer and bitterer passions of the world, may justly call them irrational. They would not justify themselves in his experience; they make grievous demands and yield nothing in the end which is intelligible to him. His picture of them, if he be a dramatist, will hardly fail to be satirical; fate, frailty, illusion will be his constant themes. If his temperament could find political expression, he would minimise the machinery of life and deprecate any calculated prudence. He would trust the heart, enjoy nature, and not frown too angrily on inclination. Such a Bohemia he would regard as an ideal world in which humanity might flourish congenially.

The importance of æsthetic goods varies with temperaments.

A puritan moralist, before condemning such an infantile paradise, should remember that a commonwealth of butterflies actually exists. It is not any inherent wrongness in such an ideal that makes it unacceptable, but only the fact that human butterflies are not wholly mercurial and that even imperfect geniuses are but an extreme type in a society whose guiding ideal is based upon a broader humanity than the artist represents. Men of science or business will accuse the poet of folly, on the very grounds on which he accuses them of the same. Each will seem to the other to be obeying a barren obsession. The statesman or philosopher who should aspire to adjust their quarrel could do so only by force of intelligent sympathy with both sides, and in view of the common conditions in which they find themselves. What ought to be done is that which, when done, will most nearly justify itself to all concerned. Practical problems of morals are judicial and political problems. Justice can never be pronounced without hearing the parties and weighing the interests at stake.

The æsthetic temperament requires tutelage.

A circumstance that complicates such a calculation is this: æsthetic and other interests are not separable units, to be compared externally; they are rather strands interwoven in the texture of everything. Æsthetic sensibility colours every thought, qualifies every allegiance, and modifies every product of human labour. Consequently the love of beauty has to justify itself not merely intrinsically, or as a constituent part of life more or less to be insisted upon; it has to justify itself also as an influence. A hostile influence is the most odious of things. The enemy himself, the alien creature, lies in his own camp, and in a speculative moment we may put ourselves in his place and learn to think of him charitably; but his spirit in our own souls is like a private tempter, a treasonable voice weakening our allegiance to our own duty. A zealot might allow his neighbours to be damned in peace, did not a certain heretical odour emitted by them infect the sanctuary and disturb his own dogmatic calm. In the same way practical people might leave the artist alone

Aesthetic values everywhere interfused.

in his oasis, and even grant him a pittance on which to live, as they feed the animals in a zoological garden, did he not intrude into their inmost conclave and vitiate the abstract cogency of their designs. It is not so much art in its own field that men of science look askance upon, as the love of glitter and rhetoric and false finality trespassing upon scientific ground; while men of affairs may well deprecate a rooted habit of sensuous absorption and of sudden transit to imaginary worlds, a habit which must work havoc in their own sphere. In other words, there is an element of poetry inherent in thought, in conduct, in affection; and we must ask ourselves how far this ingredient is an obstacle in their proper development.

The fabled dove who complained, in flying, of the resistance of the air, was as wise as the philosopher who should lament the presence and influence of sense. Sense is the native element and substance of experience; all its refinements are still parts of it existentially; and whatever excellence belongs specifically to sense is a preliminary excellence, a **They are primordial.** value antecedent to any which thought or action can achieve. Science and morals have but representative authority; they are principles of ideal synthesis and safe transition; they are bridges from moment to moment of sentience. Their function is indeed universal and their value overwhelming, yet their office remains derivative or secondary, and what they serve to put in order has previously its intrinsic worth. An æsthetic bias is native to sense, being indeed nothing but its form and potency; and the influence which æsthetic habits exercise on thought and action should not be regarded as an intrusion to be resented, but rather as an original interest to be built upon and developed. Sensibility contains the distinctions which reason afterward carries out and applies; it is sensibility that involves and supports primitive diversities, such as those between good and bad, here and there, fast and slow, light and darkness. There are complications and harmonies inherent in these oppositions, harmonies which æsthetic faculty proceeds to note; and from these we may then construct others, not immediately presentable, which we distinguish by attributing them to reason. Reason may well outflank and transform æsthetic judgments, but can never undermine them. Its own materials are the perceptions which if full and perfect are called beauties. Its function is to endow the parts of sentience with a consciousness of the system in which they lie, so that they may attain a mutual relevance and ideally support one another. But what could relevance or support be worth if the things to be buttressed were themselves worthless? It is not to organise pain, ugliness, and boredom that reason can be called into the world.

When a practical or scientific man boasts that he has laid aside æsthetic prejudices and is following truth and utility with a single eye, he can mean, if he is judicious, only that he has not yielded to æsthetic preference after his problem was fixed, nor in an arbitrary and vexatious fashion. **To superpose them** He has not consulted taste when it would have been in bad taste **adventitiously** to do so. If he meant that he had rendered himself altogether **is to destroy** insensible to æsthetic values, and that he had proceeded to organ- **them.** ise conduct or thought in complete indifference to the beautiful, he would be simply proclaiming his inhumanity and incompetence. A right observance of æsthetic demands does not obstruct utility nor logic; for utility and logic are themselves beautiful, while a sensuous beauty that ran counter to reason could never be, in the end, pleasing to an exquisite sense. Æsthetic vice is not favourable to æsthetic faculty: it is an impediment to the greatest æsthetic satisfactions. And so when by yielding to a blind passion for beauty we derange theory and practice, we cut ourselves off from those beauties which alone could have satisfied our passion. What we drag in so obstinately will bring but a cheap and unstable pleasure, while a double beauty will thereby be lost or obscured–first, the unlooked-for beauty which a genuine and stable system of things could not but betray, and secondly the coveted beauty itself, which, being imported here into the wrong context, will be rendered meretricious and offensive to good taste. If a jewel worn on the wrong finger sends a shiver through the flesh, how disgusting must not rhetoric be in diplomacy or unction in metaphysics!

The poetic element inherent in thought, affection, and conduct is prior to their prosaic development and altogether legitimate. Clear, well-digested perception
They flow naturally from perfect function. and rational choices follow upon those primary creative impulses, and carry out their purpose systematically. At every stage in this development new and appropriate materials are offered for æsthetic contemplation. Straightness, for instance, symmetry, and rhythm are at first sensuously defined; they are characters arrested by æsthetic instinct; but they are the materials of mathematics. And long after these initial forms have disowned their sensuous values, and suffered a wholly dialectical expansion or analysis, mathematical objects again fall under the æsthetic eye, and surprise the senses by their emotional power. A mechanical system, such as astronomy in one region has already unveiled, is an inexhaustible field for æsthetic wonder. Similarly, in another sphere, sensuous affinity leads to friendship and love, and makes us huddle up to our fellows and feel their heart-beats; but when human society has thereupon established a legal and moral edifice, this new spectacle yields new imaginative transports, tragic, lyric, and religious. Æsthetic values everywhere precede and accompany rational activity, and life is, in one aspect, always a fine art; not by introducing inaptly æsthetic vetoes or æsthetic flourishes, but by giving to everything a form which, implying a structure, implies also an ideal and a possible perfection. This perfection, being felt, is also a beauty, since any process, though it may have become intellectual or practical, remains for all that a vital and sentient operation, with its inherent sensuous values. Whatever is to be representative in import must first be immediate in existence; whatever is transitive in operation must be at the same time actual in being. So that an æsthetic sanction sweetens all successful living; animal efficiency cannot be without grace, nor moral achievement without a sensible glory.

These vital harmonies are natural; they are neither perfect nor preordained. We often come upon beauties that need to be sacrificed, as we come upon events and practical necessities without number that are truly regrettable. There are a myriad conflicts in practice and in thought, conflicts between rival possibilities, knocking inopportunely and in vain at the door of existence. Owing to the initial disorganisation of things, some demands continually prove to be incompatible with others arising no less naturally. Reason in such cases imposes real and irreparable sacrifices, but it brings a stable consolation if its discipline is accepted. Decay, for instance, is a moral and æsthetic evil; but being a natural necessity it can become the basis for pathetic and magnificent harmonies, when once imagination is adjusted to it. The hatred of change and death is ineradicable while life lasts, since it expresses that self-sustaining organisation in a creature which we call its soul; yet this hatred of change and death is not so deeply seated in the nature of things as are death and change themselves, for the flux is deeper than the ideal. Discipline may attune our higher and more adaptable part to the harsh conditions of being, and the resulting sentiment, being the only one which can be maintained successfully, will express the greatest satisfactions which can be reached, though not the greatest that might be conceived or desired. To be interested in the changing seasons is, in this middling zone, a happier state of mind than to be hopelessly in love with spring. Wisdom discovers these possible accommodations, as circumstances impose them; and education ought to prepare men to accept them.

Even inhibited functions, when they fall into a new rhythm, yield new beauties.

It is for want of education and discipline that a man so often insists petulantly on his random tastes, instead of cultivating those which might find some satisfaction in the world and might produce in him some pertinent culture. Untutored self-assertion may even lead him to deny some fact that should have been patent, and plunge him into needless calamity. His Utopias cheat him in the end, if indeed the barbarous taste he has indulged in clinging to them does not itself lapse before the dream is half formed. So men have feverishly conceived a heaven only to find it insipid, and a hell to find it ridiculous. Theodicies that were to demonstrate an absolute cosmic harmony have turned the universe into a tyrannous nightmare, from which we are glad to awake again in this unintentional and somewhat tractable world. Thus the fancies of effeminate poets in violating science are false to the highest art, and the products of sheer confusion, instigated by the love of beauty, turn out to be hideous. A rational severity in respect to art simply weeds the garden; it expresses a mature æsthetic choice and opens the way to supreme artistic achievements. To keep beauty in its place is to make all things beautiful.

He who loves beauty must chasten it.

The Criterion of Taste

Reason in Art. Volume 4 of *The Life of Reason: or, the Phases of Human Progress.* New York: Charles Scribner's Sons; London: Constable and Co. Ltd., 1905, 191–215. Volume seven of the critical edition of *The Works of George Santayana.*

This selection appeared as Chapter X of Reason in Art. *Just as artistic inspiration and creation are grounded in nature, so is taste. Santayana believed it was rooted in unreflective preference but thought this no reason to reject the authority of taste. In fact, one's taste gains authority as one gains experience and engages in reflection. "Reflection refines particular sentiments," wrote Santayana, "by bringing them into sympathy with all rational life" (ES, 321). He believed that taste varied among people in intensity, quality, and relevance, and that good taste harmonized with a wide range of interests. In other words, good taste has a social aspect and a sense of broader human satisfactions beyond the personal and subjective. He wrote that, "[e]ither aesthetic experience would have remained a chaos . . . or it must have tended to conciliate certain general human demands and ultimately all those interests which its operation in any way affects" (ES, 325). He thought good taste to be based on experience and that "it comes from having united in one's memory and character the fruit of many diverse undertakings" (ES, 327).*

Dogmatism in matters of taste has the same status as dogmatism in other spheres. It is initially justified by sincerity, being a systematic expression of a man's preferences; but it becomes absurd when its basis in a particular disposition is ignored and it pretends to have an absolute or metaphysical scope. Reason, with the order which in every region it imposes on life, is grounded on an animal nature and has no other function than to serve the same; and it fails to exercise its office quite as much when it oversteps its bounds and forgets whom it is serving as when it neglects some part of its legitimate province and serves its master imperfectly, without considering all his interests.

Dogmatism is inevitable but may be enlightened.

Dialectic, logic, and morals lose their authority and become inept if they trespass upon the realm of physics and try to disclose existences; while physics is a mere idea in the realm of poetic meditation. So the notorious diversities which human taste exhibits do not become conflicts, and raise no moral problem, until their basis or their function has been forgotten, and each has claimed a right to assert itself exclusively. This claim is altogether absurd, and we might fail to understand how so preposterous an attitude could be assumed by anybody did we not remember that every young animal thinks himself absolute, and that dogmatism in the thinker is only the speculative side of greed and courage in the brute. The brute cannot surrender his appetites nor abdicate his primary right to dominate his environment. What experience and reason may teach him is merely how to make his self-assertion well balanced and successful. In the same way taste is bound to maintain its preferences but free to rationalise them. After a man has compared his feelings with the no less legitimate feelings of other creatures, he can reassert his own with more complete authority, since now he is aware of their necessary ground in his nature, and of their affinities with whatever other interests his nature enables him to recognise in others and to co-ordinate with his own.

A criterion of taste is, therefore, nothing but taste itself in its more deliberate and circumspect form. Reflection refines particular sentiments by bringing them into sympathy with all rational life. There is consequently the greatest possible difference in authority between taste and taste, and while delight in drums and eagle's feathers is perfectly genuine and has no cause to blush for itself, it cannot be compared in scope or representative value with delight in a symphony or an epic. The very instinct that is satisfied by beauty prefers one beauty to another; and we have only to question and purge our æsthetic feelings in order to obtain our criterion of taste. This criterion will be natural, personal, autonomous; a circumstance that will give it authority over our own judgment—which is all moral science is concerned about—and will extend its authority over other minds also, in so far as their constitution is similar to ours. In that measure what is a genuine instance of reason in us, others will recognise for a genuine expression of reason in themselves also.

Taste gains in authority as it is more and more widely based.

Æsthetic feeling, in different people, may make up a different fraction of life and vary greatly in volume. The more nearly insensible a man is the more incompetent he becomes to proclaim the values which sensibility might have. To beauty men are habitually insensible, even while they are awake and rationally active. Tomes of æsthetic criticism hang on a few moments of real delight and intuition. It is in rare and scattered instants that beauty smiles even on her adorers, who are reduced for habitual comfort to remembering her past favours. An æsthetic glow may pervade experience, but that circumstance is seldom remarked; it figures only as an influence working subterraneously on thoughts and judgments which in themselves take a cognitive or practical direction. Only when the æsthetic ingredient becomes predominant do we exclaim, How beautiful! Ordinarily the pleasures which formal perception gives remain an undistinguished part of our comfort or curiosity.

Different æsthetic endowments may be compared in quantity or force.

Taste is formed in those moments when æsthetic emotion is massive and distinct; preferences then grown conscious, judgments then put into words, will reverberate through calmer hours; they will constitute prejudices, habits of apperception, secret standards for all other beauties. A period of life in which such intuitions have been frequent may amass tastes and ideals sufficient for the rest of our days. Youth in these matters governs maturity, and while men may develop their early impressions more systematically and find confirmations of them in various quarters, they will seldom look at the world afresh or use new categories in deciphering it. Half our standards come from our first masters, and the other half from our first loves. Never being so deeply stirred again, we remain persuaded that no objects save

Authority of vital over verbal judgments.

those we then discovered can have a true sublimity. These high-water marks of æsthetic life may easily be reached under tutelage. It may be some eloquent appreciations read in a book, or some preference expressed by a gifted friend, that may have revealed unsuspected beauties in art or nature; and then, since our own perception was vicarious and obviously inferior in volume to that which our mentor possessed, we shall take his judgments for our criterion, since they were the source and exemplar of all our own. Thus the volume and intensity of some appreciations, especially when nothing of the kind has preceded, makes them authoritative over our subsequent judgments. On those warm moments hang all our cold systematic opinions; and while the latter fill our days and shape our careers it is only the former that are crucial and alive.

A race which loves beauty holds the same place in history that a season of love or enthusiasm holds in an individual life. Such a race has a pre-eminent right to pronounce upon beauty and to bequeath its judgments to duller peoples. We may accordingly listen with reverence to a Greek judgment on that subject, expecting that what might seem to us wrong about it is the expression of knowledge and passion beyond our range; it will suffice that we learn to live in the world of beauty, instead of merely studying its relics, for us to understand, for instance, that imitation is a fundamental principle in art, and that any rational judgment on the beautiful must be a moral and political judgment, enveloping chance æsthetic feelings and determining their value. What most German philosophers, on the contrary, have written about art and beauty has a minimal importance: it treats artificial problems in a grammatical spirit, seldom giving any proof of experience or imagination. What painters say about painting and poets about poetry is better than lay opinion; it may reveal, of course, some petty jealousy or some partial incapacity, because a special gift often carries with it complementary defects in apprehension; yet what is positive in such judgments is founded on knowledge and avoids the romancing into which litterateurs and sentimentalists will gladly wander. The specific values of art are technical values, more permanent and definite than the adventitious analogies on which a stray observer usually bases his views. Only a technical education can raise judgments on musical compositions above impertinent autobiography. The Japanese know the beauty of flowers, and tailors and dressmakers have the best sense for the fashions. We ask them for suggestions, and if we do not always take their advice, it is not because the fine effects they love are not genuine, but because they may not be effects which we care to produce.

This touches a second consideration, besides the volume and vivacity of feeling, which enters into good taste. What is voluminous may be inwardly confused

Tastes differ also in purity or consistency. or outwardly confusing. Excitement, though on the whole and for the moment agreeable, may verge on pain and may be, when it subsides a little, a cause of bitterness. A thing's attractions may be partly at war with its ideal function. In such a case what, in our haste, we call a beauty becomes hateful on a second view, and according to the key of our dissatisfaction we pronounce that effect meretricious, harsh, or affected. These discords appear when elaborate things are attempted without enough art and refinement; they are essentially in bad taste. Rudimentary effects, on the contrary, are pure, and though we may think them trivial when we are expecting something richer, their defect is never intrinsic; they do not plunge us, as impure excitements do, into a corrupt artificial conflict. So wild-flowers, plain chant, or a scarlet uniform are beautiful enough; their simplicity is a positive merit, while their crudity is only relative. There is a touch of sophistication and disease in not being able to fall back on such things and enjoy them thoroughly, as if a man could no longer relish a glass of water. Your true epicure will study not to lose so genuine a pleasure. Better forego some artificial stimulus, though that, too, has its charm, than become insensible to natural joys. Indeed, ability to revert to elementary beauties is a test that judgment remains sound.

Vulgarity is quite another matter. An old woman in a blond wig, a dirty hand covered with jewels, ostentation without dignity, rhetoric without cogency, all offend by an inner contradiction. To like such things we should have to surrender our better intuitions and suffer a kind of dishonour. Yet the elements offensively combined may be excellent in isolation, so that an untrained or torpid mind will be at a loss to understand the critic's displeasure. Oftentimes barbaric art almost succeeds, by dint of splendour, in banishing the sense of confusion and absurdity; for everything, even reason, must bow to force. Yet the impression remains chaotic, and we must be either partly inattentive or partly distressed. Nothing could show better than this alternative how mechanical barbaric art is. Driven by blind impulse or tradition, the artist has worked in the dark. He has dismissed his work without having quite understood it or really justified it to his own mind. It is rather his excretion than his product. Astonished, very likely, at his own fertility, he has thought himself divinely inspired, little knowing that clear reason is the highest and truest of inspirations. Other men, observing his obscure work, have then honoured him for profundity; and so mere bulk or stress or complexity have produced a mystical wonder by which generation after generation may be enthralled. Barbaric art is half necromantic; its ascendancy rests in a certain measure on bewilderment and fraud.

To purge away these impurities nothing is needed but quickened intelligence, a keener spiritual flame. Where perception is adequate, expression is so too, and if a man will only grow sensitive to the various solicitations which anything monstrous combines, he will thereby perceive its monstrosity. Let him but enact his sensations, let him pause to make explicit the confused hints that threaten to stupefy him; he will find that he can follow out each of them only by rejecting and forgetting the others. To free his imagination in any direction he must disengage it from the contrary intent, and so he must either purify his object or leave it a mass of confused promptings. Promptings essentially demand to be carried out, and when once an idea has become articulate it is not enriched but destroyed if it is still identified with its contrary. Any complete expression of a barbarous theme will, therefore, disengage its incompatible elements and turn it into a number of rational beauties.

When good taste has in this way purified and digested some turgid medley, it still has a progress to make. Ideas, like men, live in society. Not only has each a will of its own and an inherent ideal, but each finds itself conditioned for its expression by a host of other beings, on whose co-operation it depends. Good taste, besides being inwardly clear, has to be outwardly fit. A monstrous ideal devours and dissolves itself, but even a rational one does not find an immortal embodiment simply for being inwardly possible and free from contradiction. It needs a material basis, a soil and situation propitious to its growth. This basis, as it varies, makes the ideal vary which is simply its expression; and therefore no ideal can be ultimately fixed in ignorance of the conditions that may modify it. It subsists, to be sure, as an eternal possibility, independently of all further earthly revolutions. Once expressed, it has revealed the inalienable values that attach to a certain form of being, whenever that form is actualised. But its expression may have been only momentary, and that eternal ideal may have no further relevance to the living world. A criterion of taste, however, looks to a social career; it hopes to educate and to judge. In order to be an applicable and a just law, it must represent the interests over which it would preside.

They differ, finally, in pertinence, and in width of appeal.

There are many undiscovered ideals. There are many beauties which nothing in this world can embody or suggest. There are also many once suggested or even embodied, which find later their basis gone and evaporate into their native heaven. The saddest tragedy in the world is the destruction of what has within it no inward ground of dissolution, death in youth, and the crushing out of perfection. Imagination has its bereavements of this kind. A complete mastery of existence achieved at one moment gives no warrant that it will be sustained or achieved again at the next. The achievement may have been perfect; nature will not on that account stop to admire it. She will move on, and the meaning which was read so triumphantly in her momentary attitude will not fit her new posture. Like Polonius's cloud, she will always suggest some new ideal, because she has none of her own.

In lieu of an ideal, however, nature has a constitution, and this, which is a necessary ground for ideals, is what it concerns the ideal to reckon with. A poet, spokesman of his full soul at a given juncture, cannot consider eventualities or think of anything but the message he is sent to deliver, whether the world can then hear it or not. God, he may feel sure, understands him, and in the eternal the beauty he sees and loves immortally justifies his enthusiasm. Nevertheless, critics must view his momentary ebullition from another side. They do not come to justify the poet in his own eyes; he amply relieves them of such a function. They come only to inquire how significant the poet's expressions are for humanity at large or for whatever public he addresses. They come to register the social or representative value of the poet's soul. His inspiration may have been an odd cerebral rumbling, a perfectly irrecoverable and wasted intuition; the exquisite quality it doubtless had to his own sense is now not to the purpose. A work of art is a public possession; it is addressed to the world. By taking on a material embodiment, a spirit solicits attention and claims some kinship with the prevalent gods. Has it, critics should ask, the affinities needed for such intercourse? Is it humane, is it rational, is it representative? To its inherent incommunicable charms it must add a kind of courtesy. If it wants other approval than its own, it cannot afford to regard no other aspiration.

This scope, this representative faculty or wide appeal, is necessary to good taste. All authority is representative; force and inner consistency are gifts on which I may well congratulate another, but they give him no right to speak for me. Either æsthetic experience would have remained a chaos—which it is not altogether—or it must have tended to conciliate certain general human demands and ultimately all those interests which its operation in any way affects. The more conspicuous and permanent a work of art is, the more is such an adjustment needed. A poet or philosopher may be erratic and assure us that he is inspired; if we cannot well gainsay it, we are at least not obliged to read his works. An architect or a sculptor, however, or a public performer of any sort, that thrusts before us a spectacle justified only in his inner consciousness, makes himself a nuisance. A social standard of taste must assert itself here, or else no efficacious and cumulative art can exist at all. Good taste in such matters cannot abstract from tradition, utility, and the temper of the world. It must make itself an interpreter of humanity and think esoteric dreams less beautiful than what the public eye might conceivably admire.

There are various affinities by which art may acquire a representative or classic quality. It may do so by giving form to objects which everybody knows, by rendering experiences that are universal and primary. The human figure, elementary passions, common types and crises of fate— these are facts which pass too constantly through apperception not to have a normal æsthetic value. The artist who can catch that effect in its fulness and simplicity accordingly does immortal work. This sort of art immediately becomes popular; it passes into language and convention so that its æsthetic charm is apparently worn down. The old images after a while hardly stimulate unless they be presented in some paradoxical way; but in that case attention will be diverted to the accidental extravagance, and the chief classic effect will be missed. It is the honourable fate or euthanasia of artistic successes that they pass from the field of professional art altogether and become a portion of human faculty. Every man learns to be to that extent an artist; approved figures and maxims pass current like the words and idioms of a mother-tongue, themselves once brilliant inventions. The lustre of such successes is not really dimmed, however, when it becomes a part of man's daily light; a retrogression from that habitual style or habitual insight would at once prove, by the shock it caused, how precious those ingrained apperceptions continued to be.

Art may grow classic by idealising the familiar,

Universality may also be achieved, in a more heroic fashion, by art that expresses ultimate truths, cosmic laws, great human ideals. Virgil and Dante are classic poets in this sense, and a similar quality belongs to Greek sculpture and architecture. They may not cause enthusiasm in everybody; but in the end experience and reflection renew their charm; and their greatness, like that of high mountains, grows more obvious with distance. Such eminence is the reward of having accepted discipline and made the mind a clear anagram of much experience. There is a great difference

or by reporting the ultimate.

between the depth of expression so gained and richness or realism in details. A supreme work presupposes minute study, sympathy with varied passions, many experiments in expression; but these preliminary things are submerged in it and are not displayed side by side with it, like the foot-notes to a learned work, so that the ignorant may know they have existed.

Some persons, themselves inattentive, imagine, for instance, that Greek sculpture is abstract, that it has left out all the detail and character which they cannot find on the surface, as they might in a modern work. In truth it contains those features, as it were, in solution and in the resultant which, when reduced to harmony, they would produce. It embodies a finished humanity which only varied exercises could have attained, for as the body is the existent ground for all possible actions, in which as actions they exist only potentially, so a perfect body, such as a sculptor might conceive, which ought to be ready for all excellent activities, cannot present them all in act but only the readiness for them. The features that might express them severally must be absorbed and mastered, hidden like a sword in its scabbard, and reduced to a general dignity or grace. Though such immersed eloquence be at first overlooked and seldom explicitly acknowledged, homage is nevertheless rendered to it in the most unmistakable ways. When lazy artists, backed by no great technical or moral discipline, think they, too, can produce masterpieces by summary treatment, their failure shows how pregnant and supreme a thing simplicity is. Every man, in proportion to his experience and moral distinction, returns to the simple but inexhaustible work of finished minds, and finds more and more of his own soul responsive to it.

Human nature, for all its margin of variability, has a substantial core which is invariable, as the human body has a structure which it cannot lose without perishing altogether; for as creatures grow more complex a greater number of their organs become vital and indispensable. Advanced forms will rather die than surrender a tittle of their character; a fact which is the physical basis for loyalty and martyrdom. Any deep interpretation of oneself, or indeed of anything, has for that reason a largely representative truth. Other men, if they look closely, will make the same discovery for themselves. Hence distinction and profundity, in spite of their rarity, are wont to be largely recognised. The best men in all ages keep classic traditions alive. These men have on their side the weight of superior intelligence, and, though they are few, they might even claim the weight of numbers, since the few of all ages, added together, may be more than the many who in any one age follow a temporary fashion. Classic work is nevertheless always national, or at least characteristic of its period, as the classic poetry of each people is that in which its language appears most pure and free. To translate it is impossible; but it is easy to find that the human nature so inimitably expressed in each masterpiece is the same that, under different circumstance, dictates a different performance. The deviations between races and men are not yet so great as is the ignorance of self, the blindness to the native ideal, which prevails in most of them. Hence a great man of a remote epoch is more intelligible than a common man of our own time.

Both elementary and ultimate judgments, then, contribute to a standard of taste; yet human life lies between these limits, and an art which is to be truly adjusted to life should speak also for the intermediate experience. Good taste is indeed nothing but a name for those appreciations which the swelling incidents of life recall and reinforce. Good taste is that taste which is a good possession, a friend to the whole man. It must not alienate him from anything except to ally him to something greater and more fertile in satisfactions. It will not suffer him to dote on things, however seductive, which rob him of some nobler companionship. To have a foretaste of such a loss, and to reject instinctively whatever will cause it, is the very essence of refinement. Good taste comes, therefore, from experience, in the best sense of that word; it comes from having united in one's memory and character the fruit of many diverse undertakings. Mere taste is apt to be bad taste, since it regards nothing but a chance feeling. Every man who pursues an art may be presumed to have some sensibility; the question is whether he has breeding, too, and whether what he stops at is not, in the end, vulgar and offensive. Chance feeling needs to fortify itself with reasons and to find its level in the great world. When it has added fitness to its sincerity, beneficence to its passion, it will have acquired a right to live. Violence and self-justification will not pass muster in a moral society, for vipers possess both, and must nevertheless be stamped out. Citizenship is conferred only on creatures with human and co-operative instincts. A civilised imagination has to understand and to serve the world.

Good taste demands that art should be rational, i.e., harmonious with all other interests.

The great obstacle which art finds in attempting to be rational is its functional isolation. Sense and each of the passions suffers from a similar independence. The disarray of human instincts lets every spontaneous motion run too far; life oscillates between constraint and unreason. Morality too often puts up with being a constraint and even imagines such a disgrace to be its essence. Art, on the contrary, as often hugs unreason for fear of losing its inspiration, and forgets that it is itself a rational principle of creation and order. Morality is thus reduced to a necessary evil and art to a vain good, all for want of harmony among human impulses. If the passions arose in season, if perception fed only on those things which action should be adjusted to, turning them, while action proceeded, into the substance of ideas—then all conduct would be voluntary and enlightened, all speculation would be practical, all perceptions beautiful, and all operations arts. The Life of Reason would then be universal.

To approach this ideal, so far as art is concerned, would involve diffusing its processes and no longer confining them to a set of dead and unproductive objects called works of art.

Why art, the most vital and generative of activities, should produce a set of abstract images, monuments to lost intuitions, is a curious mystery. Nature gives her products life, and they are at least equal to their sources in dignity. Why should mind, the actualisation of nature's powers, produce something so inferior to itself, reverting in its expression to material being, so that its witnesses seem so many fossils with which it strews its path? What we call museums—mausoleums, rather, in which a

A mere "work of art" a baseless artifice.

dead art heaps up its remains—are those the places where the Muses intended to dwell? We do not keep in show-cases the coins current in the world. A living art does not produce curiosities to be collected but spiritual necessaries to be diffused.

Artificial art, made to be exhibited, is something gratuitous and sophisticated, and the greater part of men's concern about it is affectation. There is a genuine pleasure in planning a work, in modelling and painting it; there is a pleasure in showing it to a sympathetic friend, who associates himself in this way with the artist's technical experiment and with his interpretation of some human episode; and there might be a satisfaction in seeing the work set up in some appropriate space for which it was designed, where its decorative quality might enrich the scene, and the curious passer-by might stop to decipher it. The pleasures proper to an ingenuous artist are spontaneous and human; but his works, once delivered to his patrons, are household furniture for the state. Set up to-day, they are outworn and replaced to-morrow, like trees in the parks or officers in the government. A community where art was native and flourishing would have an uninterrupted supply of such ornaments, furnished by its citizens in the same modest and cheerful spirit in which they furnish other commodities. Every craft has its dignity, and the decorative and monumental crafts certainly have their own; but such art is neither singular nor pre-eminent, and a statesman or reformer who should raise somewhat the level of thought or practice in the state would do an infinitely greater service.

The joys of creating are not confined, moreover, to those who create things without practical uses. The merely æsthetic, like rhyme and fireworks, is not the only subject that can engage a playful fancy or be planned with a premonition of beautiful effects. Architecture may be useful, sculpture commemorative, poetry reflective, even music, by its expression, religious or martial. In a word, practical exigencies, in calling forth the arts, give them moral functions which it is a pleasure to see them fulfil. Works may not be æsthetic in their purpose, and yet that fact may be a ground for their being doubly delightful in execution and doubly beautiful in effect. A richer plexus of emotions is concerned in producing or contemplating something humanly necessary than something idly conceived. What is very rightly called a *sense* for fitness is a vital experience, involving æsthetic satisfactions and æsthetic shocks. The more numerous the rational harmonies are which are present to the mind, the more sensible movements will be going on there to give immediate delight; for the perception or expectation of an ulterior good is a present good also. Accordingly nothing can so well call forth or sustain attention as what has a complex structure relating it to many complex interests. A work woven out of precious threads has a deep pertinence and glory; the artist who creates it does not need to surrender his practical and moral sense in order to indulge his imagination.

Human uses give to works of art their highest expression and charm.

The truth is that mere sensation or mere emotion is an indignity to a mature human being. When we eat, we demand a pleasant vista, flowers, or conversation, and failing these we take refuge in a newspaper. The monks, knowing that men should not feed silently like stalled oxen, appointed some one to read aloud in the refectory; and the Fathers, obeying the same civilised instinct, had contrived in their theology intelligible points of attachment for religious emotion. A refined mind finds as little happiness in love without friendship as in sensuality without love; it may succumb to both, but it accepts neither. What is true of mere sensibility is no less true of mere fancy. The Arabian Nights—futile enough in any case—would be absolutely intolerable if they contained no Oriental manners, no human passions, and no convinced epicureanism behind their miracles and their tattle. Any absolute work of art which serves no further purpose than to stimulate an emotion has about it a certain luxurious and visionary taint. We leave it with a blank mind, and a pang bubbles up from the very fountain of pleasures. Art, so long as it needs to be a dream, will never cease to prove a disappointment. Its facile cruelty, its narcotic abstraction, can never sweeten the evils we return to at home; it can liberate half the mind only by leaving the other half in abeyance. In the mere artist, too, there is always something that falls short of the gentleman and that defeats the man.

Surely it is not the artistic impulse in itself that involves such lack of equilibrium. To impress a meaning and a rational form on matter is one of the most masterful of actions. The trouble lies in the barren and superficial character of this imposed form: fine art is a play of appearance. **The sad** Appearance, for a critical philosophy, is distinguished from reality **values of** by its separation from the context of things, by its immediacy and **appearance.** insignificance. A play of appearance is accordingly some little closed circle in experience, some dream in which we lose ourselves by ignoring most of our interests, and from which we awake into a world in which that lost episode plays no further part and leaves no heirs. Art as mankind has hitherto practised it falls largely under this head and too much resembles an opiate or a stimulant. Life and history are not thereby rendered better in their principle, but a mere ideal is extracted out of them and presented for our delectation in some cheap material, like words or marble. The only precious materials are flesh and blood, for these alone can defend and propagate the ideal which has once informed them.

Artistic creation shows at this point a great inferiority to natural reproduction, since its product is dead. Fine art shapes inert matter and peoples the mind with impotent ghosts. What influence it has—for every event has consequences—is not pertinent to its inspiration. The art of the past is powerless even to create similar art in the present, unless similar conditions recur independently. The moments snatched for art have been generally interludes in life and its products parasites in nature, the body of them being materially functionless and the soul merely represented. To exalt fine art into a truly ideal activity we should have to knit it more closely with other rational functions, so that to beautify things might render them more useful and to represent them most imaginatively might be to see them in their truth. Something of the sort has been actually attained by the noblest arts in their noblest phases. A Sophocles or a Leonardo dominates his dreamful vehicle and works upon the real world by its means. These small centres, where interfunctional harmony is attained, ought to expand and cover the whole field.

Art, like religion, needs to be absorbed in the Life of Reason.

What might help to bring about this consummation would be, on the one side, more knowledge; on the other, better taste. When a mind is filled with important and true ideas and sees the actual relations of things, it cannot relish pictures of the world which wantonly misrepresent it. Myth and metaphor remain beautiful so long as they are the most adequate or graphic means available for expressing the facts, but so soon as they cease to be needful and sincere they become false finery. The same thing happens in the plastic arts. Unless they spring from love of their subject, and employ imagination only to penetrate into that subject and interpret it with a more inward sympathy and truth, they become conventional and overgrown with mere ornament. They then seem ridiculous to any man who can truly conceive what they represent. So in putting antique heroes on the stage we nowadays no longer tolerate a modern costume, because the externals of ancient life are too well known to us; but in the seventeenth century people demanded in such personages intelligence and nobleness, since these were virtues which the ancients were clothed with in their thought. A knowledge that should be at once full and appreciative would evidently demand fidelity in both matters. Knowledge, where it exists, undermines satisfaction in what does violence to truth, and it renders such representations grotesque. If knowledge were general and adequate the fine arts would accordingly be brought round to expressing reality.

They need to be made prophetic of practical goods,

At the same time, if the rendering of reality is to remain artistic, it must still study to satisfy the senses; but as this study would now accompany every activity, taste would grow vastly more subtle and exacting. Whatever any man said or did or made, he would be alive to its æsthetic quality, and beauty would be a pervasive ingredient in happiness. No work would be called, in a special sense, a work of art, for all works would be such intrinsically; and even instinctive mimicry and reproduction would themselves operate, not when mischief or idleness prompted, but when some human occasion and some general utility made the exercise of such skill entirely delightful. Thus there would need to be no division of mankind into mechanical blind workers and half-demented poets, and no separation of useful from fine art, such as people make who have understood neither the nature nor the ultimate reward of human action. All arts would be practised together and merged in the art of life, the only one wholly useful or fine among them.

which in turn would be suffused with beauty.

Art and Happiness

Reason in Art. Volume 4 of *The Life of Reason: or, the Phases of Human Progress*. New York: Charles Scribner's Sons; London: Constable and Co. Ltd., 1905, 216–30. Volume seven of the critical edition of *The Works of George Santayana*.

In this selection, Chapter XI of Reason in Art, *Santayana contended it was a weakness and a vice to forsake practical matters for art understood as "rhythms and declamations, . . . imaginary passions and histrionic woes" (ES, 331). Such "detached indulgences" leave one alienated and paralyzed (ES, 333). By contrast "the happy imagination is one initially in line with things, and brought always closer to them by experience" (ES, 333). Santayana remarked that an "effect of growing experience is to render what is unreal uninteresting" suggesting that irresponsible fantasy and escapism lose their appeal as wisdom increases (ES, 333). Indeed, Santayana thought practical as well as artistic success depended on reason and intelligence, or the ability to decipher both the law of one's own heart and the law of nature. "We fail in practical affairs when we ignore the conditions of action and we fail in works of imagination when we concoct what is fantastic and without roots in the world" (ES, 334). Perfect arts come only with a rational society, and before a great and native art could arise we would have to discard our illusions, superstition, and sectarianism and "discover instead our genuine needs, the forms of our possible happiness" (ES, 335).*

The greatest enemy harmony can have is a premature settlement in which some essential force is wholly disregarded. This excluded element will rankle in the flesh; it will bring about no end of disorders until it is finally recognised and admitted into a truly comprehensive regimen. The more numerous the interests which a premature settlement combines the greater inertia will it oppose to reform, and the more self-righteously will it condemn the innocent pariah that it leaves outside.

Æsthetic harmonies are parodies of real ones,

Art has had to suffer much Pharisaical opposition of this sort. Sometimes political systems, sometimes religious zeal, have excluded it from their programme, thereby making their programme unjust and inadequate. Yet of all premature settlements the most premature is that which the fine arts are wont to establish. A harmony in appearance only, one that touches the springs of nothing and has no power to propagate itself, is so partial and momentary a good that we may justly call it an illusion. To gloat on rhythms and declamations, to live lost in imaginary passions and histrionic woes, is an unmanly life, cut off from practical dominion and from rational happiness. A lovely dream is an excellent thing in itself, but it leaves the world no less a chaos and makes it by contrast seem even darker than it did. By dwelling in its mock heaven art may inflict on men the same kind of injury that any irresponsible passion or luxurious vice might inflict. For this reason it sometimes passes for a misfortune in a family if a son insists on being a poet or an actor. Such gifts suggest too much incompetence and such honours too much disrepute. A man does not avoid real evils by having visionary pleasures, but besides exposing himself to the real evils quite unprotected, he probably adds fancied evils to them in generous measure. He becomes supersensitive, envious, hysterical; the world, which was perhaps carried away at first by his ecstasies, at the next moment merely applauds his performance, then criticises it supercil-iously, and very likely ends by forgetting it altogether.

Thus the fine arts are seldom an original factor in human progress. If they express moral and political greatness, and serve to enhance it, they acquire a cer-tain dignity; but so soon as this expressive function is abandoned they grow mer-etricious. The artist becomes an abstracted trifler, and the public is divided into two camps: the dilettanti, who dote on the artist's affectations, and the rabble, who pay him to grow coarse. Both influences degrade him and he helps to foster both. An atmosphere of dependence and charlatanry gathers about the artistic attitude and spreads with its influence. Religion, philosophy, and manners may in turn be infected with this spirit, being reduced to a voluntary hallucination or petty flattery. Romanticism, ritualism, æstheticism, symbolism are names this disease has borne at different times as it appeared in different circles or touched a different object. Needless to say that the arts themselves are the first to suffer. That beauty which should have been an inevitable smile on the face of society, an overflow of genuine happiness and power, has to be imported, stimulated artificially, and applied from without; so that art becomes a sickly ornament for an ugly existence.

Nevertheless, æsthetic harmony, so incomplete in its basis as to be fleeting and deceptive, is most complete in its form. This so partial synthesis is a synthesis indeed, and just because settlements made in fancy are altogether premature, and ignore almost everything in the world, in type they **yet** can be the most perfect settlements. The artist, being a born lover of **prototypes** the good, a natural breeder of perfections, clings to his insight. If the **of true** world calls his accomplishments vain, he can, with better reason, **perfections.** call vain the world's cumbrous instrumentalities, by which nothing clearly good is attained. Appearances, he may justly urge, are alone actual. All forces, substances, realities, and principles are inferred and potential only and in the moral scale mere instruments to bring perfect appearances about. To have grasped such an appearance, to have embodied a form in matter, is to have justified for the first time whatever may underlie appearance and to have put reality to some use. It is to have begun to live. As the standard of perfection is internal and is measured by the satisfaction felt in realising it, every artist has tasted, in his activity, what activ-ity essentially is. He has moulded existence into the likeness of thought and lost himself in that ideal achievement which, so to speak, beckons all things into being. Even if a thousand misfortunes await him and a final disappointment, he has been happy once. He may be inclined to rest his case there and challenge practical people to justify in the same way the faith that is in them.

That a moment of the most perfect happiness should prove a source of unhap-piness is no paradox to any one who has observed the world. A hope, a passion, a crime, is a flash of vitality. It is inwardly congruous with the will that breeds it, yet the happiness it pictures is so partial that even while it is felt it may be over-shadowed by sinister forebodings. A certain unrest and insecurity may con-sciously harass it. With time, or by a slight widening in the field of interest, this submerged unhappiness may rise to the surface. If, as is probable, it is caused or increased by the indulgence which preceded, then the only moment in which a good was tasted, the only vista that had opened congenially before the mind, will prove a new and permanent curse. In this way love often misleads individuals, ambition cities, and religion whole races of men. That art, also, should often be an indulgence, a blind that hides reality from ill-balanced minds and ultimately increases their confusion, is by no means incompatible with art's ideal essence. On the contrary, such a result is inevitable when ideality is carried at all far upon a narrow basis. The more genuine and excellent the vision the greater havoc it makes if, being inadequate, it establishes itself authoritatively in the soul. Art, in the better sense, is a condition of happiness for a practical and labouring creature, since without art he remains a slave; but it is one more source of unhappiness for him so long as it is not squared with his necessary labours and merely interrupts them. It then alienates him from his world without being able to carry him effectually into a better one.

Pros and cons of detached indulgences.

The artist is in many ways like a child. He seems happy, because his life is spontaneous, yet he is not competent to secure his own good. To be truly happy he must be well bred, reared from the cradle, as it were, under propitious influences, so that he may have learned to love what conduces to his development. In that rare case his art will expand as his understanding ripens; he will not need to repent and begin again on a lower key. The ideal artist, like the ideal philosopher, has all time and all existence for his virtual theme. Fed by the world he can help to mould it, and his insight is a kind of wisdom, preparing him as science might for using the world well and making it more fruitful. He can then be happy, not merely in the sense of having now and then an ecstatic moment, but happy in having light and resource enough within him to cope steadily with real things and to leave upon them the vestige of his mind.

The happy imagination is one initially in line with things,

One effect of growing experience is to render what is unreal uninteresting. Momentous alternatives in life are so numerous and the possibilities they open up so varied that imagination finds enough employment of a his-toric and practical sort in trying to seize them. A child plans Tow-ers of Babel; a mature architect, in planning, would lose all interest if he were bidden to disregard gravity and economy. The condi-tions of existence, after they are known and accepted, become conditions for the only pertinent beauty. In each place, for each situation, the plastic mind finds an appropriate ideal. It need not go afield to import something exotic. It need make no sacrifices to whim and to personal memories. It rather breeds out of the given problem a new and singular solution, thereby exercising greater invention than would be requisite for framing an arbitrary ideal and imposing it at all costs on every occasion.

and brought always closer to them by experience.

In other words, a happy result can be secured in art, as in life, only by intelligence. Intelligence consists in having read the heart and deciphered the promptings latent there, and then in reading the world and deciphering
its law and constitution, to see how and where the heart's ideal
may be embodied. Our troubles come from the colossal blunders
made by our ancestors (who had worse ancestors of their own) in
both these interpretations, blunders which have come down to us
in our blood and in our institutions. The vices thus transmitted cloud our intelligence. We fail in practical affairs when we ignore the conditions of action and we
fail in works of imagination when we concoct what is fantastic and without roots
in the world.

**Reason is the
principle of
both art and
happiness.**

The value of art lies in making people happy, first in practising the art and
then in possessing its product. This observation might seem needless, and ought
to be so; but if we compare it with what is commonly said on these subjects, we
must confess that it may often be denied and more often, perhaps, may not be
understood. Happiness is something men ought to pursue, although they seldom
do so; they are drawn away from it at first by foolish impulses and afterwards by
perverse laws. To secure happiness conduct would have to remain spontaneous
while it learned not to be criminal; but the fanatical attachment of men, now to
a fierce liberty, now to a false regimen, keeps them barbarous and wretched.
A rational pursuit of happiness—which is one thing with progress or with the
Life of Reason—would embody that natural piety which leaves to the episodes
of life their inherent values, mourning death, celebrating love, sanctifying civic
traditions, enjoying and correcting nature's ways. To discriminate happiness is
therefore the very soul of art, which expresses experience without distorting it,
as those political or metaphysical tyrannies distort it which sanctify unhappiness.
A free mind, like a creative imagination, rejoices at the harmonies it can find or
make between man and nature; and, where it finds none, it solves the conflict so
far as it may and then notes and endures it with a shudder.

A morality organised about the human heart in an ingenuous and sincere
fashion would involve every fine art and would render the world pervasively
beautiful—beautiful in its artificial products and beautiful in its underlying natural
terrors. The closer we keep to elementary human needs and to the natural agencies that may satisfy them, the closer we are to beauty. Industry, sport, and science, with the perennial intercourse and passions of men, swarm with incentives
to expression, because they are everywhere creating new moulds of being and
compelling the eye to observe those forms and to recast them ideally. Art is simply an adequate industry; it arises when industry is carried out to the satisfaction
of all human demands, even of those incidental sensuous demands which we call
æsthetic and which a brutal industry, in its haste, may despise or ignore.

Arts responsive in this way to all human nature would be beautiful according to reason and might remain beautiful long. Poetic beauty touches the world
whenever it attains some unfeigned harmony either with sense or with reason;
and the more unfeignedly human happiness was made the test of all institutions
and pursuits, the more beautiful they would be, having more numerous points of

fusion with the mind, and fusing with it more profoundly. To distinguish and to create beauty would then be no art relegated to a few abstracted spirits, playing with casual fancies; it would be a habit inseparable from practical efficiency. All operations, all affairs, would then be viewed in the light of ultimate interests, and in their deep relation to human good. The arts would thus recover their Homeric glory; touching human fate as they clearly would, they would borrow something of its grandeur and pathos, and yet the interest that worked in them would be warm, because it would remain unmistakably animal and sincere.

The principle that all institutions should subserve happiness runs deeper than any cult for art and lays the foundation on which the latter might rest safely. If social structure were rational its free expression would be so too. Many observers, with no particular philosophy to adduce, feel that the arts among us are somehow impotent, and they look for a better inspiration, now to ancient models, now to the raw phenomena of life. A dilettante may, indeed, summon inspiration whence he will; and a virtuoso will never lack some material to keep him busy; but if what is hoped for is a genuine, native, inevitable art, a great revolution would first have to be worked in society. We should have to abandon our vested illusions, our irrational religions and patriotisms and schools of art, and to discover instead our genuine needs, the forms of our possible happiness. To call for such self-examination seems revolutionary only because we start from a sophisticated system, a system resting on traditional fashions and superstitions, by which the will of the living generation is misinterpreted and betrayed. To shake off that system would not subvert order but rather institute order for the first time; it would be an *Instauratio Magna,* a setting things again on their feet.

Only a rational society can have sure and perfect arts.

We in Christendom are so accustomed to artificial ideals and to artificial institutions, kept up to express them, that we hardly conceive how anomalous our situation is, sorely as we may suffer from it. We found academies and museums, as we found missions, to fan a flame that constantly threatens to die out for lack of natural fuel. Our overt ideals are parasites in the body politic, while the ideals native to the body politic, those involved in our natural structure and situation, are either stifled by that alien incubus, leaving civic life barbarous, or else force their way up, unremarked or not justly honoured as ideals. Industry and science and social amenities, with all the congruous comforts and appurtenances of contemporary life, march on their way, as if they had nothing to say to the spirit, which remains entangled in a cobweb of dead traditions. An idle pottering of the fancy over obsolete forms–theological, dramatic, or plastic–makes that by-play to the sober business of life which men call their art or their religion; and the more functionless and gratuitous this by-play is the more those who indulge in it think they are idealists. They feel they are champions of what is most precious in the world, as a sentimental lady might fancy herself a lover of flowers when she pressed them in a book instead of planting their seeds in the garden.

It is clear that gratuitous and functionless habits cannot bring happiness; they do not constitute an activity at once spontaneous and beneficent, such as noble art is an instance of. Those habits may indeed give pleasure; they may bring extreme excitement, as madness notably does, though it is in the highest degree functionless and gratuitous. Nor is such by-play without consequences, some of which might conceivably be fortunate. What is functionless is so called for being worthless from some ideal point of view, and not conducing to the particular life considered. But nothing real is dissociated from the universal flux; everything—madness and all unmeaning cross-currents in being—count in the general process and discharge somewhere, not without effect, the substance they have drawn for a moment into their little vortex. So our vain arts and unnecessary religions are not without real effects and not without a certain internal vitality. When life is profoundly disorganised it may well happen that only in detached episodes, only in moments snatched for dreaming in, can men see the blue or catch a glimpse of something like the ideal. In that case their esteem for their irrelevant visions may be well grounded, and their thin art and far-fetched religion may really constitute what is best in their experience. In a pathetic way these poor enthusiasms may be justified, but only because the very conception of a rational life lies entirely beyond the horizon.

Why art is now empty and unstable.

It is no marvel, when art is a brief truancy from rational practice, that the artist himself should be a vagrant, and at best, as it were, an infant prodigy. The wings of genius serve him only for an escapade, enabling him to skirt the perilous edge of madness and of mystical abysses. But such an erratic workman does not deserve the name of artist or master; he has burst convention only to break it, not to create a new convention more in harmony with nature. His originality, though it may astonish for a moment, will in the end be despised and will find no thoroughfare. He will meantime be wretched himself, torn from the roots of his being by that cruel, unmeaning inspiration; or, if too rapt to see his own plight, he will be all the more pitied by practical men, who cannot think it a real blessing to be lost in joys that do not strengthen the character and yield nothing for posterity.

Anomalous character of the irrational artist.

Art, in its nobler acceptation, is an achievement, not an indulgence. It prepares the world in some sense to receive the soul, and the soul to master the world; it disentangles those threads in each that can be woven into the other. That the artist should be eccentric, homeless, dreamful may almost seem a natural law, but it is none the less a scandal. An artist's business is not really to cut fantastical capers or be licensed to play the fool. His business is simply that of every keen soul to build well when it builds, and to speak well when it speaks, giving practice everywhere the greatest possible affinity to the situation, the most delicate adjustment to every faculty it affects. The wonder of an artist's performance grows with the range of his penetration, with the instinctive sympathy that makes him, in his mortal isolation, considerate of other men's fate and a great diviner of their secret, so that his work speaks to them kindly, with a deeper assurance than they could have spoken with to themselves. And the joy of his great sanity, the power of his adequate vision, is not the less intense because he can lend it to others and has borrowed it from a faithful study of the world.

If happiness is the ultimate sanction of art, art in turn is the best instrument of happiness. In art more directly than in other activities man's self-expression is cumulative and finds an immediate reward; for it alters the material conditions of sentience so that sentience becomes at once more delightful and more significant. In industry man is still servile, preparing the materials he is to use in action. In action itself, though he is free, he exerts his influence on a living and treacherous medium and sees the issue at each moment drift farther and farther from his intent. In science he is an observer, preparing himself for action in another way, by studying its results and conditions. But in art he is at once competent and free; he is creative. He is not troubled by his materials, because he has assimilated them and may take them for granted; nor is he concerned with the chance complexion of affairs in the actual world, because he is making the world over, not merely considering how it grew or how it will consent to grow in future. Nothing, accordingly, could be more delightful than genuine art, nor more free from remorse and the sting of vanity. Art springs so completely from the heart of man that it makes everything speak to him in his own language; it reaches, nevertheless, so truly to the heart of nature that it co-operates with her, becomes a parcel of her creative material energy, and builds by her instinctive hand. If the various formative impulses afoot in the world never opposed stress to stress and made no havoc with one another, nature might be called an unconscious artist. In fact, just where such a formative impulse finds support from the environment, a consciousness supervenes. If that consciousness is adequate enough to be prophetic, an art arises. Thus the emergence of arts out of instincts is the token and exact measure of nature's success and of mortal happiness.

True art measures and completes happiness.

Ultimate Religion

Obiter Scripta: Lectures, Essays and Reviews. Edited by Justus Buchler and Benjamin Schwartz. New York: Charles Scribner's Sons; London: Constable and Co. Ltd., 1936, 280–97.

Santayana read this essay in September 1932 at a conference in The Hague celebrating the tricentennial of Spinoza's birth. It appeared in the conference proceedings, Septimana Spinozana *(Hagae Comitis: Martinus Nijhoff [1933], 105–15), then in* Obiter Scripta, *and had been intended for* The Realm of Spirit. *In this piece Santayana asked, "[w]hat inmost allegiance, what ultimate religion, would be proper to a wholly free and disillusioned spirit?" (ES, 338). One, he thought, in which spirit acknowledges and submits to an incomprehensible power and cultivates contemplation. This renunciation of will and judgment leads to an intellectual charity toward each thing in its aspiration toward its perfection. But problems remain, because contemplation cannot grasp the entire universe, and intellect is not the whole of human nature or even of spirit. Spirit is grounded in animal life, and good or "whatsoever increases our perfection" (ES, 343) is fundamentally biological and so quite variable. Hence, pure spirit must be radically pluralistic in its love of perfection: "To love things spiritually, that is to say, intelligently and disinterestedly, means to love the love in them, to worship the good which they pursue, and to see them all prophetically in their possible beauty" (ES, 344).*

Before this chosen audience, in this consecrated place, I may venture to pass over all subsidiary matters and come at once to the last question of all: What inmost allegiance, what ultimate religion, would be proper to a wholly free and disillusioned spirit? The occasion invites us to consider this question, and to consider it with entire frankness. Great as you and I may feel our debt to be to Spinoza for his philosophy of nature, there is, I think, something for which we owe him an even greater debt; I mean, the magnificent example he offers us of philosophic liberty, the courage, firmness, and sincerity with which he reconciled his heart to the truth. Any clever man may sometimes see the truth in flashes; any scientific man may put some aspect of the truth into technical words; yet all this hardly deserves the name of philosophy so long as the heart remains unabashed, and we continue to live like animals lost in the stream of our impressions, not only in the public routine and necessary cares of life, but even in our silent thoughts and affections. Many a man before Spinoza and since has found the secret of peace: but the singularity of Spinoza, at least in the modern world, was that he facilitated this moral victory by no dubious postulates. He did not ask God to meet him half way: he did not whitewash the facts, as the facts appear to clear reason, or as they appeared to the science of his day. He solved the problem of the spiritual life after stating it in the hardest, sharpest, most cruel terms. Let us nerve ourselves today

Paper read in the *Domus Spinozana* at The Hague during the commemoration of the tercentenary of the birth of Spinoza.

to imitate his example, not by simply accepting his solution, which for some of us would be easy, but by exercising his courage in the face of a somewhat different world, in which it may be even more difficult for us than it was for him to find a sure foothold and a sublime companionship.

There is a brave and humorous saying of Luther's, which applies to Spinoza better, perhaps, than to Luther himself. When asked where, if driven out of the Church, he would stand, he replied: "Under the sky." The sky of Luther was terribly clouded: there was a vast deal of myth tumbling and thundering about in it: and even in the clear sky of Spinoza there was perhaps something specious, as there is in the blue vault itself. The sun, he tells us, seemed to be about two hundred feet away: and if his science at once corrected this optical illusion, it never undermined his conviction that all reality was within easy reach of his thought. Nature was dominated, he assumed, by unquestionable scientific and dialectical principles; so that while the forces of nature might often put our bodily existence in jeopardy, they always formed a decidedly friendly and faithful object for the mind. There was no essential mystery. The human soul from her humble station might salute the eternal and the infinite with complete composure and with a certain vicarious pride. Every man had a true and adequate idea of God: and this saying, technically justified as it may be by Spinoza's definitions of terms, cannot help surprising us: it reveals such a virgin sense of familiarity with the absolute. There could not but be joy in the sweep of an intelligence that seemed so completely victorious, and no misgivings could trouble a view of the world that explained everything.

Today, however, we can hardly feel such assurance: we should be taking shelter in a human edifice which the next earthquake might shake down. Nor is it a question really of times or temperaments: anyone anywhere, if he does not wish to construct a plausible system, but to challenge his own assumptions and come to spiritual self-knowledge, must begin by abstention from all easy faith, lest he should be madly filling the universe with images of his own reason and his own hopes. I will therefore ask you today, provisionally, for an hour, and without prejudice to your ulterior reasonable convictions, to imagine the truth to be as unfavourable as possible to your desires and as contrary as possible to your natural presumptions; so that the spirit in each of us may be drawn away from its accidental home and subjected to an utter denudation and supreme trial. Yes, although the dead cannot change their minds, I would respectfully beg the shade of Spinoza himself to suspend for a moment that strict rationalism, that jealous, hard-reasoning, confident piety which he shared with the Calvinists and Jansenists of his day, and to imagine–I do not say to admit–that nature may be but imperfectly formed in the bosom of chaos, and that reason in us may be imperfectly adapted to the understanding of nature. Then, having hazarded no favourite postulates and invoked no cosmic forces pledged to support our aspirations, we may all quietly observe what we find; and whatever harmonies may then appear to subsist between our spirits and the nature of things will be free gifts to us and, so far as they go, unchallengeable possessions. We shall at last be standing unpledged and naked, under the open sky.

In what I am about to say, therefore, I do not mean to prejudge any cosmological questions, such as that of free will or necessity, theism or pantheism. I am concerned only with the sincere confessions of a mind that has surrendered every doubtful claim and every questionable assurance. Of such assurances or claims there is one which is radical and comprehensive: I mean, the claim to existence and to directing the course of events. We say conventionally that the future is uncertain: but if we withdrew honestly into ourselves and examined our actual moral resources, we should feel that what is insecure is not merely the course of particular events but the vital presumption that there is a future coming at all, and a future pleasantly continuing our habitual experience. We rely in this, as we must, on the analogies of experience, or rather on the clockwork of instinct and presumption in our bodies; but existence is a miracle, and, morally considered, a free gift from moment to moment. That it will always be analogous to itself is the very question we are begging. Evidently all interconnections and sequences of events, and in particular any consequences which we may expect to flow from our actions, are really entirely beyond our spiritual control. When our will commands and seems, we know not how, to be obeyed by our bodies and by the world, we are like Joshua seeing the sun stand still at his bidding; when we command and nothing happens, we are like King Canute surprised that the rising tide should not obey him: and when we say we have executed a great work and re-directed the course of history, we are like Chanticleer attributing the sunrise to his crowing.

What is the result? That at once, by a mere act of self-examination and frankness, the spirit has come upon one of the most important and radical of religious perceptions. It has perceived that though it is living, it is powerless to live; that though it may die, it is powerless to die; and that altogether, at every instant and in every particular, it is in the hands of some alien and inscrutable power.

Of this felt power I profess to know nothing further. To me, as yet, it is merely the counterpart of my impotence. I should not venture, for instance, to call this power almighty, since I have no means of knowing how much it can do; but I should not hesitate, if I may coin a word, to call it *omnificent:* it is to me, by definition, the doer of everything that is done. I am not asserting the physical validity of this sense of agency or cause: I am merely feeling the force, the friendliness, the hostility, the unfathomableness of the world. I am expressing an impression; and it may be long before my sense of omnipresent power can be erected, with many qualifications, into a theological theory of the omnipotence of God. But the moral presence of power comes upon a man in the night, in the desert, when he finds himself, as the Arabs say, alone with Allah. It re-appears in every acute predicament, in extremities, in the birth of a child, or in the face of death. And as for the unity of this power, that is not involved in its sundry manifestations, but rather in my own solitude; in the unity of this suffering spirit overtaken by all those accidents. My destiny is single, tragically single, no matter how multifarious may be the causes of my destiny. As I stand amazed, I am not called upon to say whether, if I could penetrate into the inner workings of things, I should discover omnificent power to be simple or compound, continuous or spasmodic, intentional or blind. I stand before it simply receptive, somewhat as, in Rome, I might stand before the great fountain of Trevi. There I see jets and cascades flowing in separate streams and in divers directions. I am not sure that a single Pontifex Maximus designed it all, and led all those musical waters into just those channels. Some streams may have dried up or been diverted since the creation; some rills may have been added today by fresh rains from heaven; behind one of those artificial rocks some little demon, of his own free will, may even now be playing havoc with the conduits; and who knows how many details, in my image, may not have been misplaced or multiplied by optical tricks of my own? Yet here, for the spirit, is one total marvellous impression, one thunderous force, confronting me with this theatrical but admirable spectacle.

Yet this is not all. Power comes down upon me clothed in a thousand phenomena; and these manifestations of power open to me a new spiritual resource. In submitting to power, I learn its ways; from being passive my spirit becomes active; it begins to enjoy one of its essential prerogatives. For like a child the spirit is attracted to all facts by the mere assault of their irrational presence and variety. It watches all that happens or is done with a certain happy excitement, even at the most fearful calamities. Although the essence of spirit may be merely to think, yet some intensity and progression are essential to this thinking; thinking is a way of living, and the most vital way. Therefore all the operations of universal power, when they afford themes for perception, afford also occasions for intellectual delight. Here will and intellect, as Spinoza tells us, coincide: for omnificent power flows in part through our persons; the spirit itself is a spark of that fire, or rather the light of that flame: it cannot have an opposite principle of motion. With health a certain euphoria, a certain alacrity and sense of mastery are induced in the spirit; and a natural effect of perspective, the pathos of nearness, turns our little spark for us into a central sun. The world moves round us, and we move gladly with the world. What if the march of things be destined to overwhelm us? It cannot destroy the joy we had in its greatness and in its victory. There may even be some relief in passing from the troubled thought of ourselves to the thought of something more rich in life, yet in its own sphere and progression, untroubled: and it may be easier for me to understand the motion of the heavens and to rejoice in it than to understand or rejoice in my own motions. My own eclipse, my own vices, my own sorrows, may become a subject to me for exact calculation and a pleasing wonder. The philosophical eye may compose a cosmic harmony out of these necessary conflicts, and an infinite life out of these desirable deaths.

Does it not begin to appear that the solitude of a naked spirit may be rather well peopled? In proportion as we renounce our animal claims and commitments, do we not breathe a fresher and more salubrious air? May not the renunciation of everything disinfect everything and return everything to us in its impartial reality, at the same time disinfecting our wills also, and rendering us capable of charity? This charity will extend, of course, to the lives and desires of others, which we recognize to be no less inevitable than our own; and it will extend also to their ideas, and by a curious and blessed consequence, to the relativity and misery of our own minds. Yet this intellectual charity, since it is inspired by respect for the infinite, will by no means accept all views passively and romantically, as if they were equal and not subject to correction; but doing better justice to the holy aspiration which animates them in common, it will rise from them all, and with them all, to the conception of eternal truth.

Here we touch the crown of Spinoza's philosophy, that intellectual love of God in which the spirit was to be ultimately reconciled with universal power and universal truth. This love brings to consciousness a harmony intrinsic to existence: not an alleged harmony such as may be posited in religions or philosophies resting on faith, but a harmony which, as far as it goes, is actual and patent. In the realm of matter, this harmony is measured by the degree of adjustment, conformity, and co-operation which the part may have attained in the whole; in a word, it is measured by *health*. In the realm of truth, the same natural harmony extends as far as do capacity and pleasure in understanding the truth: so that besides health we may possess *knowledge*. And this is no passive union, no dead peace; the spirit rejoices in it; for the spirit, being, according to Spinoza, an essential concomitant of all existence, shares the movement, the *actuosa essentia* of the universe; so that we necessarily *love* health and knowledge, and *love* the things in which health and knowledge are found. In so far as omnificent power endows us with health, we necessarily love that power whose total movement makes for our own perfection; and in so far as we are able to understand the truth, we necessarily love the themes of an intense and unclouded vision, in which our imaginative faculty reaches its perfect function.

Of this religion of health and understanding Spinoza is a sublime prophet. By overcoming all human weaknesses, even when they seemed kindly or noble, and by honouring power and truth, even if they should slay him, he entered the sanctuary of an unruffled superhuman wisdom, and declared himself supremely happy, not because the world as he conceived it was flattering to his heart, but because the gravity of his heart disdained all flatteries, and with a sacrificial prophetic boldness uncovered and relished his destiny, however tragic his destiny might be. And presently peace descended; this keen scientific air seemed alone fit to breathe, and only this high tragedy worthy of a heroic and manly breast. Indeed the truth is a great cathartic and wonderfully relieves the vital distress of existence. We stand as on a mountain-top, and the spectacle, so out of scale with all our petty troubles, silences and overpowers the heart, expanding it for a moment into boundless sympathy with the universe.

Nevertheless, the moral problem is not solved. It is not solved for mankind at large, which remains no less distracted than it was before. Nor is it solved even for the single spirit. There is a radical and necessary recalcitrancy in the finite soul in the face of all this cosmic pomp and all this cosmic pressure: a recalcitrancy to which Spinoza was less sensitive than some other masters of the spiritual life, perhaps because he was more positivistic by temperament and less specifically religious. At any rate many a holy man has known more suffering than Spinoza found in the long work of salvation, more uncertainty, and also, in the end, a more lyrical and warmer happiness. For in the first place, as I said in the beginning, a really naked spirit cannot assume that the world is thoroughly intelligible. There may be surds, there may be hard facts, there may be dark abysses before which intelligence must be silent, for fear of going mad. And in the second place, even if to the intellect all things should prove perspicuous, the intellect is not the whole of human nature, nor even the whole of pure spirit in man. Reason may be the *differentia* of man; it is surely not his essence. His essence, at best, is animality qualified by reason. And from this animality the highest flights of reason are by no means separable. The very life of spirit springs from animal predicaments: it moves by imposing on events a perspective and a moral urgency proper to some particular creature or some particular interest.

Good, as Spinoza would tell us, is an epithet which we assign to whatsoever increases our perfection. Such a doctrine might seem egotistical, but is simply biological; and on its moral side, the maxim is a greater charter of liberty and justice than ever politician framed. For it follows that every good pursued is genuinely good, and the perfection of every creature equally perfection. Every good therefore is a good forever to a really clarified, just, and disinterested spirit; such a spirit cannot rest in the satisfaction of any special faculty, such as intelligence, nor of any special art, such as philosophy. That the intellect might be perfectly happy in contemplating the truth of the universe, does not render the universe good to every other faculty; good to the heart, good to the flesh, good to the eye, good to the conscience or the sense of justice. Of all systems an optimistic system is the most oppressive. Would it not be a bitter mockery if, in the words of Bradley, this were the best of possible worlds, and everything in it a necessary evil? The universal good by which the spirit, in its rapt moments, feels overwhelmed, if it is not to be a mystical illusion, cannot fall short of being the sum of all those perfections, infinitely various, to which all living things severally aspire. A glint or symbol of this universal good may be found in any moment of perfect happiness visiting any breast: but it is impossible unreservedly to love or worship anything, be it the universe or any part of it, unless we find in the end that this thing is completely good: I mean, unless it is perfect after its kind and a friend to itself, and unless at the same time it is beneficent universally, and a friend to everything else. Pure spirit would be lame, and evidently biassed by some biological accident, if it did not love every good loved anywhere by anybody. These varied perfections are rivals and enemies in the press of the world, where there seems not to be matter or time enough for everything: but to impartial spirit no good can render another good odious. Physically, one good may exclude another: nature and natural morality must choose between them, or be dissolved into chaos: but in eternity the most opposite goods are not enemies; rather little brothers and sisters, as all odd creatures were to St. Francis. And that all these various perfections are not actually attainable is a material accident, painful but not confusing to a free spirit. Their contrariety increases sorrow, but does not diminish love; the very pain is a fresh homage to the beauty missed, and a proof of loyalty; so that the more the spirit suffers the more clearly, when it unravels its suffering, it understands what it loves. Every perfection then shines, washed and clear, separate and uncontaminated: yet all compatible, each in its place, and harmonious. To love things spiritually, that is to say, intelligently and disinterestedly, means to love the love in them, to worship the good which they pursue, and to see them all prophetically in their possible beauty. To love things as they are would be a mockery of things: a true lover must love them as they would wish to be. For nothing is quite happy as it is, and the first act of true sympathy must be to move with the object of love towards its happiness.

Universal good, then, the whole of that to which all things aspire, is something merely potential; and if we wish to make a religion of love, after the manner of Socrates, we must take universal good, not universal power, for the object of our religion. This religion would need to be more imaginative, more poetical, than that of Spinoza, and the word God, if we still used it, would have to mean for us not the universe, but the good of the universe. There would not be a universe worshipped, but a universe praying; and the flame of the whole fire, the whole seminal and generative movement of nature, would be the love of God. This love would be erotic; it would be really love and not something wingless called by that name. It would bring celestial glimpses not to be retained, but culminating in moments of unspeakable rapture, in a union with all good, in which the soul would vanish as an object because, as an organ, it had found its perfect employment.

For there is a mystery here, the mystery of seeming to attain emotionally the logically unattainable. Universal good is something dispersed, various, contrary to itself in its opposite embodiments; nevertheless, to the mystic, it seems a single living object, the One Beloved, a good to be embraced all at once, finally and forever, leaving not the least shred of anything good outside. Yet I think this mystery may be easily solved. Spirit is essentially synthetic; and just as all the known and unknown forces of nature make, in relation to experience and destiny, one single omnificent power; and just as all facts and all the relations between facts compose for the historical and prophetic mind one unalterable realm of truth; so exactly, for the lover, all objects of love form a single ineffable good. He may say that he sees all beauties in a single face, that all beauties else are nothing to him; yet perhaps in this hyperbole he may be doing his secret heart an injustice. Beauty here may be silently teaching him to discern beauty everywhere, because in all instances of love only the sheer love counts in his eyes: and in the very absoluteness of his love he may feel an infinite promise. His ecstasy, which passes for a fulfilment, remains a sort of agony: and though itself visionary, it may, by its influence, free his heart from trivial or accidental attachments and lead it instead to a universal charity. Beggars in Catholic and Moslem countries used to beg an alms, sometimes, for the love of God. It was a potent appeal; because God, according to the Socratic tradition, was the good to which all creation moved; so that any one who loved deeply, and loved God, could not fail, by a necessary inclusion, to love the good which all creatures lived by pursuing, no matter how repulsive these creatures might be to natural human feeling.

Thus the absolute love of anything involves the love of universal good; and the love of universal good involves the love of every creature.

Such, in brief, seems to me the prospect open to a mind that examines its moral condition without any preconceptions. Perhaps an empirical critic, strictly reducing all objects to the functions which they have in experience, might see in my meagre inventory all the elements of religion. Mankind, he might say, in thinking of God or the gods have always meant the power in events: as when people say: *God willing.* Sometimes they have also meant the truth, as when people say: *God knows.* And perhaps a few mystics may have meant the good, or the supreme object of love, union with whom they felt would be perfect happiness. I should then have merely changed the language of traditional religion a little, translated its myths into their pragmatic equivalents, and reduced religion to its true essence. But no: I make no such professions: they would be plainly sophistical. The functions which objects have in experience no doubt open to us different avenues to those objects: but the objects themselves, if they exist, are not mere names for those functions. They are objects of faith: and the religion of mankind, like their science, has always been founded on faith. Now there is no faith invoked in the examination of conscience which I have made before you this evening: and therefore, properly speaking, what I come to is not religion. Nor is it exactly philosophy, since I offer no hypotheses about the nature of the universe or about the nature of knowledge. Yet to be quite sincere, I think that in this examination of conscience there is a sort of secret or private philosophy perhaps more philosophical than the other: and while I set up no gods, not even Spinoza's infinite *Deus sive Natura,* I do consider on what subjects and to what end we might consult those gods, if we found that they existed: and surely the aspiration that would prompt us, in that case, to worship the gods, would be our truest heart-bond and our ultimate religion.

If then any of us who are so minded should ever hear the summons of a liturgical religion calling to us: *Sursum corda, Lift up your hearts,* we might sincerely answer, *Habemus ad Dominum, Our hearts by nature are addressed to the Lord.* For we recognize universal power, and respect it, since on it we depend for our existence and fortunes. We look also with unfeigned and watchful allegiance towards universal truth, in which all the works of power are eternally defined and recorded; since in so far as we are able to discover it, the truth raises all things for us into the light, into the language of spirit. And finally, when power takes on the form of life, and begins to circle about and pursue some type of perfection, spirit in us necessarily loves these perfections, since spirit is aspiration become conscious, and they are the goals of life: and in so far as any of these goals of life can be defined or attained anywhere, even if only in prophetic fancy, they become glory, or become beauty, and spirit in us necessarily worships them: not the troubled glories and brief perfections of this world only, but rather that desired perfection, that eternal beauty, which lies sealed in the heart of each living thing.

The Nature of Spirit

The Realm of Spirit: Book Fourth of Realms of Being. London: Constable and Co. Ltd.; New York: Charles Scribner's Sons, 1940, 1–18. Volume sixteen of the critical edition of *The Works of George Santayana.*

This selection appeared as Chapter I of The Realm of Spirit. *Santayana found this to be "a most difficult book to put into proper shape" (LGS, 6:208) and characterized it as "a funeral oration, if not a tombstone, on my opinions" (LGS, 6:330) (though he went on to publish a three-volume autobiography, two new books, and two extensive revisions before his death). In this chapter Santayana sought to clarify his notion of spirit as natural, intellectual, and immaterial. He considered mistaken conceptions of spirit and provided an account of its emergence from animal life. He also distinguished seven entities in illuminating his notion of spirit. A* body *is a unit in the realm of matter; an* organism *is a body capable of nutrition and reproduction;* psyche *is the self-sustaining pattern of an organism; an* animal *is psyche able to seek what it needs to survive.* Soul *is psyche considered morally or through self-reflection;* self *or* person *is soul involved in social relations. "Other names for spirit," wrote Santayana, "are consciousness, attention, feeling, thought, or any word that marks the total inner difference between being awake or asleep, alive or dead" (ES, 355).*

Everything that exists is confined to a specific character at a particular place and time; if it escaped from those bonds it would cease to be itself. Such an escape

Spirit shares the contingency of existence but surveys it morally. occurs continually in the realm of matter, where everything gradually lapses into something different; and this continuous flux, with its various tempos, composes the great symphony of nature. In living substance, plasticity and fertility are a virtue: matter might say, with Shelley's cloud, *I change but I never die.* That which dies at every turn is only the negligible cloud-rack of the moment, easily replaced or even improved upon. To lament that individuals or even species should vanish would be natural only to some elegiac poet who clung to lost occasions and to remembered forms, not being ready for the next, and lagging sentimentally behind the glorious march of time, always buoyant with victory and strewn with wreckage.

The case is otherwise when we come to the realm of spirit, as we do in that melancholy poet. Not that spirit is less mobile or elastic than matter. In its ideal vocation, as we shall find, it is infinitely more so. Even in its existence it is as evanescent as any cloud. But the inevitable concentration of existence at each point into something specific rises in the moral world to a higher power. Individuation from being passive and imputed here becomes positive and self-assured. Spirit, in its briefest and feeblest flash, sets up a moral centre for the universe.

Contingence and partiality, in one direction, embitter spiritual life. Why should "I" (that is, spirit in me) be condemned to lodge in this particular body, with these parents and nationality and education and ridiculous fate? Why choose this gro-tesque centre from which to view the universe? You may say that other people exist in plenty, viewing the universe from their several positions, so that in giving this involuntary pre-eminence to myself I am perhaps not more grotesque than the average man, or even than the most intelligent. But that only makes matters worse, if isolation, partiality, error, and conceit are multiplied indefinitely, and inevitably attached to conscious existence.

In another direction, however, the imprisoned spirit escapes from its cage as no physical fact can escape. Without quitting its accidental station it can look about; it can *imagine* all sorts of things unlike itself; it can take long views over the times and spaces surrounding its temporary home, it can even view itself quizzically from the outside, as in a mirror, and laugh at the odd figure that it cuts. Intelligence is in a humorous position: confinement galls it, it rebels against contingency; yet it sees that without some accidental centre and some specific interests and specific organs, it could neither exist nor have the means of survey-ing anything. It had better be reconciled to incarnation, if it is at all attached to existence or even to knowledge.

This is the force of intelligence, marvellous if we try to conceive it on the anal-ogy of material being, but perfectly natural and obvious if we look at it congru-ously and from within. Spirit in each of its instances assumes a transcendental station, and looks out from there on all the world. Wherever it is, is here; whenever it is, is now. Yet *here* and *now,* for intelligence, are not what they are for physical being, or for external indication, a particular, accidental, dead position. For intelligence *here* and *now* are movable essences, to be found wherever spirit may wander; and they name no particular material point, but the centre found, at each point, for all distances and direc-tions. So that the bitterness of confinement is mitigated by a continual change of prisons, and the accident of place by the inevitable vastness of the prospect.

> It is intellectual.

A consequence of this intellectual nature of spirit marks it particularly, or even defines it in popular philosophy. Spirit is invisible, intangible, unapproachable from the outside. The materialist might like to deny its existence; but that is not the inclination of mankind at large. Only, being necessarily familiar with material things, and having shaped lan-guage and expectation in conformity with physical happenings, people find it impossible not to materialize the spirit of which they are vividly conscious; so that critical philosophy sometimes, in clearing up the notion of spirit, and remov-ing superstitious and physical analogies, seems to have nothing left. But that comes of being, like the primitive mind, pre-occupied with matter, and disin-clined to conceive spirit in spiritual terms. This disinclination is not confined to scoffers: religious philosophers also love to materialize spirit, in order to make it seem more solid and important, the pure air of a truly spiritual sphere being far too thin and cold for their lusty constitution.

> And immaterial.

Let me consider the various ways in which the notion of spirit is apt to be materialized. The sequel will then be less exposed to gross misunderstanding.

Spirits, in folklore, legend, and dreams, are often ghosts; that is, they are visi-

ble but intangible spectres of dead, absent, or supernatural persons. Such apparitions, for a critical psychologist, might not be physical facts, since the images
have their basis in the observer's brain, and are falsely incorporated

Spirit not a ghost.

into outer space: an error that the waking dreamer himself discovers
when he attempts to embrace a ghost and finds nothing but air. Genuine believers in the survival and return of the dead, like doubting Thomas and
modern Spiritualists, require their spirits to be tangible as well as visible, to come
and go and preserve a continuous physical existence, to eat and especially to talk.
Their bodies may be called "spiritual", but are conceived as extracts or magical
restitutions of the human body, ethereal, astral, but not immaterial. They move
about in another world or in the margins of this world, and are not pure intelli-
gences but complete natural individuals, having a body and a soul.

The native land of ghosts is memory, memory transforming sensations, or
drowsily confusing, recasting, or exaggerating old impressions into dreams.

But the landscape open to spirit is ghost-like in being purely ideal.

Imagination is fertile; and the old maxim that there is nothing in the
mind which was not first in the senses seems to me far from accurate.
There is never anything in the mind that *at that time* is not given in a
kind of sensation, that is, given directly: but these images are not old
images or fragments of old images surviving and recombined, as the
fragments of an ancient temple might be built into a modern wall.
Images, considered in themselves and objectively, are essences and
perfectly immaterial. That which is immaterial has no substance, no
persistence, and no effects: it offers no possibility of being stored, divided, redis-
tributed, or recombined. Ideas are not animals that may breed other animals.
They may recur, wholly or in part, but only when a living psyche inwardly reverts
to much the same movement as on some former occasion. The given essence will
then be the same or nearly the same as formerly. But it must be evoked afresh,
and unless evoked it has no existence whatever. It is truly a ghost, belief in it is
illusion, and its apparition or specious presence depends entirely on the dreaming psyche that weaves it together.

Dreams, and all the sensuous garments that fancy bestows on nature, are made
of stuff much more spiritual than any "spirits" supposed to be persisting and

Inspiration the voice of the psyche rebuking or idealizing external facts.

active persons, stealthily revisiting the earth, or sending messages
to it from some neighbouring region. The primitive idea that when
the body sleeps the spirit may travel to distant places, and receive
monitions concerning secret or future things, though poetical, is
true in this sense: that in dreams the contribution that the psyche
makes to experience predominates over the contribution ordinarily made by external things. This predominance of the psychic we
call *inspiration;* the existence and the rush of it are spirit itself. When this predominance is excessive and persists in waking hours, we go mad; any strong
passion, in its recklessness and self-assurance, has madness in it. Yet the same
inspiration permeates sensibility and desire, perception and thought, all experience being but a dream controlled, and all reason but fancy domesticated and
harnessed to human labours. In dreams, when the spirit seems to travel, it merely

smoulders like a fire no longer fanned by the wind: and in that withdrawal and concentration, together with much fragmentary nonsense, it may develop and fancifully express its absolute impulses, building the world nearer to the heart's desire. Hence dreams may be morally prophetic: or a more voluminous inspiration, from the same source, may combine with waking intelligence and art to produce some work of genius. The notion that spirit can escape from the psyche, or comes into us originally, as Aristotle says, from beyond the gates, merely inverts mythologically a natural truth: namely that the spirit is immaterial and transcendental. It issues from the psyche like the genie from Sinbad's bottle, and becomes, in understanding and in judgment, an authority over its source, and a transcendental centre for making a survey of everything.

That the wildest imaginations are, in their origin, native to matter appears clearly in this, that they are produced by drugs. Nor is this incompatible with their æsthetic or prophetic or intellectual value. The priestess at Delphi inhaled the vapours of her cave before uttering her oracles; other ritual practices have an intentionally hypnotic or narcotic influence; wine and music, martial or religious, notoriously rouse the spirit to boldness and to conviction. Nor is this a scandal, as if pure reason could move either the heart or the world. Pure reason is an ideal brought to light in the spirit by the organization of forces all originally irrational and wild: and this organization in turn is a product of long friction and forced adjustments. So much so, that in human life inspiration and reason come to seem holiday marvels, appearing when some suppressed strain or forbidden harmony is allowed to assert itself, in fancy only, during some lull in action. Prophecy is the swan-song of lost causes. The action that accompanies it has no tendency to fulfil it. If it survives like Hebrew prophecy in later Judaism and in Christianity, it becomes a purely spiritual discipline, mystic where it was martial, and ascetic where it was political. The communism of Plato's Republic could be realized only in the cloister.

Spirit is thus, in a certain sense, the native land of ghosts, of ideas, of phenomena; but it is not at all a visible ghost or phenomenon in its own being. Its own essence is an invisible stress; the vital, intellectual, and moral actuality of each moment.

Another way in which spirit may be materialized is by confusion with the psyche and with those cosmic currents by which the psyche is fed. Wind and breath have given their name to spirit, and most aptly. The air is invisible, yet the winds are a terrible reality, and though they may soon be stilled, the calm supervening is no longer deceptive. I have learned that what seemed vacancy was a reservoir of power, that air, ether, and **Spirit not a fluid.** energy filled that apparent void. I discover that innumerable atoms are floating there, ready to make fresh havoc in the world, or to be breathed in and renew life in my breast. What is this life in me but vital oxygen drawn into my lungs; what is this warm breath exhaled but my very spirit and will? Invisible as it is, does it not quicken my body and inspire all my action? Is it not one with the spirit of the winds howling in the storm or ruffling the sea or carrying seeds far and wide over the fertile earth? Is not the world, then, full of spirits? And is not spirit perhaps the one universal power astir in all things, as it stirs in me?

Such poetic confusions are spontaneous in a candid mind. They may be corrected by science and by logical analysis; but it would be a foolish philosophy that should ignore the continuities and analogies that run through the universe and that at once impress the attentive poet. The principle of life is not exactly wind or air. Life began in the sea and a great seclusion and darkness are requisite for seeds to germinate and for organic patterns to take shape undisturbed. Storms and struggles come afterwards on occasion; a normal order and distribution of elements, or self-defending organisms, must have arisen first. Yet the currents within and without such organisms or such elements remain continuous. A psyche, the organic order and potentiality in a living body, depends upon ambient forces and reacts upon them; and the sense of this dependence and of this reaction is the spirit.

This spirit is something ontologically altogether incongruous with air, ether, energy, motion, or substance. Spirit is the *witness* of the cosmic dance; in respect to that agitation it is transcendental and epiphenomenal; yet it crowns

It is the moral fruition of physical life.
some impulse, raises it to actual unity and totality, and being the fruition of it, could not arise until that organ had matured. An immense concretion of elements to make a habitat and of tropisms to make an animal must have preceded. Being fetched from such depths, spirit feels a profound kinship with its mothering elements. It suffers with the body and it speaks for the heart. Even if it dreams that it travels to distant spheres, it merely reports in a fable the scope of physical sensibility and the depths from which messages are received. In its station, in its interests, in its language, it always remains at home. To say that it travels, or witnesses the distant, is as if we said that the radio conveyed us to the concert which it conveys to us. The travelling, the waves, the transmissions are all physical. How should they be anything else? Instruments are material; even the composer, when he first conceived those accords, was listening to a spontaneous music bred in his psyche out of theoretically traceable impressions, tensions and outbursts of potential energy within him. The chain of these motions is materially uninterrupted, else the composer's imagined music would never have reached our ears; and spiritual union, both in perception and in passion, depends upon physical concordance. The number of spirits that may have lived through the measures of that melody helps me not at all to hear it now; the physical source must be tapped afresh in each case, and the physical receiver must be capable of vibrating afresh to the message.

Spiritualists and mystics are often more perceptive than rationalists; but they are not for that reason perceptive of spiritual things. They are, more probably, supersensitive materially. They feel influences vibrating through the universe to which the din of vulgar affairs has deafened most of us: and they dream of physical survivals and renewals, of physical Elysiums, with endless vistas of warm physical love or physical peace. They hover, they glide, they wallow; and they think themselves spirits. But there is nothing less spiritual than the shallows of indistinction and of torpid oneness. The universe is per-force one, and its parts easily break down and are lost in one another; but such collapse destroys the very possibility of spirit, which is not an ether or a fluid coursing through space, but a moral focus of recollection, discrimination and judgment.

Language in these subjects is particularly ambiguous and charged with emotion; it serves less to discriminate one thing from another than to attribute to one thing, miraculously, the powers and dignities of something else. So the power of nature is often attributed to spirit or identified with it: with a curious result. For if spirit be only the laws or tendencies discoverable in nature, it is only a form to be found in matter, and not an immaterial invisible inward intensity of being. And there is malice in this abuse of language: for we are expected to conceive that laws or tendencies are thoughts (essences being confused with the intuition of essences) and that nature being describable in those intelligible terms is secretly governed by intelligence: so that we may attribute power also to our own wishes and imaginations, and depute ourselves to be co-rulers of the universe. *Confusions about the seat of power.*

Now our *selves,* our organisms or persons, undoubtedly play a more or less efficacious part in physical events. It would be a miracle if our bodies, with so much stored and redistributable energy as they contain, did not redirect by their action all sorts of other motions in the environment. A man habitually identifies himself as much with his body as with his spirit: and since both are called "I", it is no wonder if what happens in each is felt to be also the work of the other. And the connection is radical and intimate in reality; the problem not being how the two happen to be united but in what respects we may justly distinguish them. The difference between myself as a transcendental centre or spirit and myself as a fact in the world is, in one sense, unbridgeable; but not because they are two facts incongruously or miraculously juxtaposed in the same field, but because they are realizations of the same fact in two incomparable realms of being. There is only one fact, more or less complex and extended, an incident in the flux of existence; and this fact lying in the realm of matter by virtue of its origin, place, time, and consequences, contains a transcendental apprehension of all things, in moral terms and in violent perspective, taken from itself as centre. Such sensibility is proper to the natural fact, when this fact is a living animal; but you can no more pass, at the same level, from sensation to matter, than you can pass from extension to duration, from colour to sound, from sound to meaning, or from logic to love. The organization of matter is something logically incomparable with its mere persistence or energy, yet can only exist with the latter; so spirit is logically incomparable with body, yet is a moral integration and dignity accruing to body when body develops a certain degree of organization and of responsiveness to distant things. Nor does spirit, in its new language, discourse about anything save that very world, with all its radiations, in which it has arisen.

Perhaps it is not logically impossible that spirit should exist without a body: but in that case how should spirit come upon any particular images, interests, or categories? If occupied with nothing, it would not be a conscious being; and if occupied with everything possible, that is, with the whole realm of essence at once, it would not be the consciousness of a living soul, having a particular moral destiny, but only a hypostasis of intelligence, abstracted from all particular occasions. *Treacherous notion of disembodied spirit.*

But can intelligence be abstracted from particular occasions and from problems set by contingent facts? Logic and mathematics would surely never have taken shape if nature had not compelled attention to dwell on certain forms of objects or of language, and rewarded in practice the elaboration of those forms in thought. Indeed Spirit, once abstracted from animal life and independent of all facts, would have forfeited that intensity, trepidation, and movement, that capacity for inquiry and description, which make spirit a focus of knowledge. It would have evaporated into identity with the realm of essence. Even divine spirits, as conceived in human poetry and religion, are thinking, loving, and planning minds, functions which all belong to animal life, and presuppose it.

In some speculative myths spirit is represented as a self-existent potentiality pregnant with the seeds of a particular development; so that spirit, as in a dream, gradually creates world upon world, and the experience of them, out of its magic bosom. There is sometimes poetic truth in such myths, but they describe, from some local point of view, a perspective in the realm of matter, not at all the history of spirit. Spirit is not a seed, it is not a potentiality, it is not a power. It is not even—though this touches more nearly its actual character—a grammar of thought or divine Logos, predetermining the structure of creation and its destiny. That, if found anywhere, would be found in the realm of truth; but we may doubt that any alleged Logos, or any psychological system of categories or forms of intuition, prescribes limits to the truth. It prescribes at best one type of logic, one set of senses, in which a particular existent world might be apprehended by its inhabitants.

And of "Spirit" in history.

Yet these myths, as often happens, have a real foothold in the nature of the facts. They catch some transcendental privilege or predicament proper to spirit and transfer it, together with the name of spirit, to the spheres of matter or truth. Spirit has an initial vagueness; it awakes, it looks, it waits, it oscillates between universal curiosity and primeval sleep. Certainly the feelings and images arising are specific; and spirit has no *a priori* notion of any different feelings or images to contrast with the given ones. Yet it is in no way predisposed or limited to these; it is not essentially, like the psyche, even a slave of habit, so as to think the given necessary and the not given impossible. Spirit is infinitely open. And this is no ontological marvel or mystic affinity of spirit to the absolute. It is merely the natural indistinction of primitive wakefulness, of innocent attention. Spirit is like a child with eyes wide open, heart simple, faith ready, intellect pure. It does not suspect the trouble the world is going to give it. It little knows the contortions, the struggles, the disasters which the world imposes on itself. There is a horrid confusion in attributing to spirit the dogged conservatism and catastrophic evolution of the natural world.

Spirit essentially open and blank.

To the primitive blankness of spirit corresponds its eventual hospitality to all sorts of things. But this hospitality is not connivance, not complicity. It is an intellectual hospitality open to all truth, even to all fiction and to all essence, as these things may present themselves. It is not an equal pleasure in them all. Spirit is a product of the psyche; the psyche makes for a specific order and direction of life; spirit congenitally shares in this vitality and this specific impulse. The psyche needs to prepare for all things that may chance in its life: it needs to be universally vigilant, universally retentive. In satisfying this need it forms the spirit, which therefore initially tends to look, to remember, to understand. But the psyche takes this step, so impartial and unprejudiced officially, for a perfectly selfish domestic reason, namely, to prepare the home defences and enlarge the home dominion. The spirit, therefore, is like Goethe's Watchman, who was born to gaze, and possessed all the world in idea, yet was set on that **It suffers when thwarted in its proper life of free sympathy and understanding.** watch-tower for an urgent purpose, with a specific duty to be vigilant. Hence the storms and forest-fires, the invasions or rebellions that he might observe, would not leave him cold, but would distress him in his fidelity, disturb his power of vision, and perhaps bring him and his tower to the ground. Not that spirit trembles for its own being. It is the most volatile of things, and the most evanescent, a flame blown or extinguished by any wind: but no extinction here can prevent it from blazing up there, and its resurrection is as perpetual as its death. What torments it is no selfish fear but a vicarious sympathy with its native psyche and her native world, which it cannot bear to feel dragged hither and thither in tragic confusion, but craves to see everywhere well-ordered and beautiful, *so that it may be better seen and understood.* This is the specific function of spirit, which it lives by fulfilling, and dies if it cannot somehow fulfil. But as it is unresisting yet indomitable in its existence, so it is resourceful in its art, and ultimately victorious; because the worst horrors and absurdities in the world, when they are past or distant, so that life here is not physically disturbed by them, can be raised in the spirit to the level of reflection, becoming mere pictures of hell and marvellous in that capacity. Thus a constant suggestion and echo of sorrow, which cannot but suffuse existence, adds strange dignity to the tragedy and renders the spirit freer from the world and surer in its own intrinsic possessions.

It is not in respect to large cosmic fatalities, such as war and death, that spirit is most perplexed. Love, self-sacrifice, and martyrdom are capable of turning those fatalities into occasions for lyrical joy and tragic liberation. The worst entanglements, from the spirit's point of view, arise within the psyche, in what in religious parlance is called sin. This strangles spirit at its source, because the psyche is primarily directed upon all sorts of ambitions irrelevant to spirit, producing stagnation, inflation, self-contradiction, and hatred of the truth. It is with difficulty that spirit can make itself heard in such a tumult. Spirit is no random blast, no irresponsible free demand, but speaks for a soul reduced to harmony and for the sane mind. This sanity implies not only integrity within, but also adjustment to the outer universe. So that whilst spirit is physically the voice of the soul crying in the wilderness, it becomes vicariously and morally the voice of the wilderness admonishing the soul.

Let me tabulate, as briefly as possible, the principal words and ideas that mark the differences, the bonds, and the confusions that exist between matter and spirit. Such a glossary may help the reader to criticize his favourite modes of expression and to be patient with those of other people.

BODY. Ancient usage identifies a man with his body, as Homer in the first lines of the Iliad:* and in English we still speak of *nobody* and *everybody*. This places man quite correctly in the realm of matter amongst other bodies, but it treats him and them summarily and externally as gross units and dead weights, ignoring their immaterial properties and their subtle physical substance and relations.

Glossary of terms.

ORGANISM. This word still designates the body, since the organization of an organism must exist somewhere and on a particular scale, if it is to exist at all. But a body is an organism only by virtue of its vital power of nutrition and reproduction. By these functions bodily life becomes continuous with the ambient forces on which it feeds and theoretically with the whole dynamic universe. Thus an organism is both a closed system of vital tropes and a nucleus in the general cosmic process.

PSYCHE. The forms of inorganic matter, though distinct from matter logically, are clearly passive: matter may fall into them innumerable times, yet if anywhere disturbed, they show no tendency to reinstate themselves. This tendency defines an organism: its actual form hides a power to maintain or restore that form. This power or potentiality, often concentrated in a seed, dwells in the matter of the organism, but is mysterious; so that for observation the form itself seems to be a power (when locked in that sort of substance or seed) and to work towards its own manifestation. The self-maintaining and reproducing pattern or structure of an organism, conceived as a power, is called a psyche. The psyche, in its moral unity, is a poetic or mythological notion, but needed to mark the hereditary vehement movement in organisms towards specific forms and functions.

ANIMAL. All natural organisms have psyches, and are at the same time in dynamic relations to the whole physical world. When the organism waits for favourable opportunities to unfold itself, the psyche is vegetative; when it goes to seek favourable opportunities, it is animal.

This is an important step in laying the ground for spirit. The unity of the organism subtends the moral unity of the spirit, which raises that unity to an actual and intense existence; the impulse of the psyche, making for a specific perfection of form and action, underlies the spiritual distinction between good and evil; and the power of locomotion gives the spirit occasion for perception and knowledge. Will is no doubt deeper than intelligence in the spirit, as it is in the animal; yet will without intelligence would not be spirit, since it would not distinguish what it willed or what it suffered. So that the passage from vegetation to action seems to produce the passage from a dark physical excitability to the *qui vive* of consciousness.

SOUL. The same thing that looked at from the outside or biologically is called the psyche, looked at morally from within is called the soul. This change of aspect so transforms the object that it might be mistaken for two separate things, one a kind of physical organization and the other a pure spirit. And spirit is in fact involved in feeling and knowing life from the inside: not that spirit is then *self-conscious*, or sees nothing save its own states, but that it is then the medium and

---

*The wrath of Achilles cast many souls of heroes to Hades and *themselves* to dogs and vultures.

focus for apprehension, and imposes on its objects categories and qualities of its own. A psyche, when spirit awakes in it, is turned into a soul. Not only can the career of that psyche now be reviewed in memory, or conceived in prophecy, but many a private impulse or thought never exhibited to the world can now be added to one's history; so that oneself is now not merely the body, its power, and its experience, but also an invisible guest, the soul, dwelling in that body and having motions and hopes of its own. This soul can be conceived to issue out of the body, to pass into a different body, or to remain thinking and talking to itself without a body at all. This, for the psyche, would have been inconceivable; for, as Aristotle shows, the psyche, or specific form of organization and movement, in an elephant, can no more pass into the body of a fly, than the faculty of cutting can pass from an axe into a lyre, or the faculty of making music from the lyre into the axe. The soul, however, having an apparently independent discoursing and desiring faculty, and a power to imagine all sorts of non-existent things, may easily be conceived to pass from one body to another, as by a change of domicile, and to have had forgotten incarnations, with an endless future.

SELF OR PERSON. If memory, dreams, and silent musings seem to detach the soul from bodily life, social relations and moral qualities may re-attach the soul to the world, not now biologically but politically. Politically a man cannot be separated from his body; but it is not by his bodily faculties that he chiefly holds his own in society, or conceives his individuality. He is a person, a self, a character; he has a judicial and economic status; he lives in his ambitions, affections, and repute. All this again, as in the notion of the soul, cannot come about without the secret intervention of spirit: yet these ideas, although spirit must be there to entertain them, are not spiritual ideas; the interests chiefly concerned are those of animal or social bodies. Even moral worth or immortal life are ideals borrowed from animal impulses and animal conditions. In a different biological setting, or in a realm of pure spirits, those social duties and services would be impossible: and the will to live forever is nothing but the animal will to go on living expressed reflectively and transferred, somewhat incongruously, to the social self or historical person.

SPIRIT. Psyches, we have said, take on the character of souls when spirit awakes in them. Spirit is an awareness natural to animals, revealing the world and themselves in it. Other names for spirit are consciousness, attention, feeling, thought, or any word that marks the total *inner* difference between being awake or asleep, alive or dead. This difference is morally absolute; but physically the birth of spirit caps a long growth during which excitability and potentiality of various kinds are concentrated in organisms and become transmissible. The *outer* difference between sleeping and waking, life and death, is not absolute; and we may trace certain divergences between the path of transmission for the psyche and the basis of distribution for the spirit. Life follows the seed, through long periods of unconsciousness and moral nonexistence; whereas spirit lives in the quick interplay of each sensitive individual and the world, and often is at its height when, after keen experience, the brain digests the event at leisure, and the body is sexually quiescent or reduced by old age to a mere husk. In the spirit, by definition, there is nothing persistent or potential. It is pure light and perpetual actuality. Yet the intensity and scope of this moral illumination, as well as the choice of characters lighted up, the order of the scenes and how long each shall last, all hang on the preparations nature may have made for this free entertainment.

Liberation

The Realm of Spirit: Book Fourth of Realms of Being. London: Constable and Co. Ltd.; New York: Charles Scribner's Sons, 1940, 182–213. Volume sixteen of the critical edition of *The Works of George Santayana.*

In this selection, Chapter VIII of The Realm of Spirit, *Santayana considered how spirit might avoid what distracts it from its essential calling. Traditional views of spiritual liberation attributed distraction to nature or life and looked for salvation in a new life or in the rejection of life altogether. Santayana attributed spiritual distraction to ignorance of the true nature and activity of spirit. Spirit is properly called to the spheres of truth and essence and away from animal attachments. When this is forgotten, spirit is hamstrung by the concerns of animal life. Such animal concerns include a desire for immortality, which can be only distraction for spirit. Liberation occurs not through rejecting or forgetting the realm of matter and animal life, but rather through transcending attachment to the objects of animal concern. Santayana considered three examples of liberated spirits in the persons of Socrates, Jesus Christ, and St. John of the Cross.*

From what does distraction distract the spirit? If the flesh, the world, and the devil impede the proper movement of life, they must impinge upon something deeper than themselves or degrade something better. But what is this deeper or better thing? Those who regard spirit as a separate substance, and spiritual life as essentially another life in another world, seem to solve the problem clearly; but I fear they would find it still on their hands if they actually passed into that other world. The moral adventure of existence would simply have been extended; and if that life were really life and that world really a world, the spirit would find itself there as much entangled and beset, if not as much tormented, as it ever was in the human body. So too if we suppose spirit to have first inhabited some celestial sphere, according to the Platonic myth. Evidently even in that sphere, if we take the myth literally, the spirit must have been subject to distraction. How else were its incarnations determined, or how else was it tempted to quit heaven at all? From the beginning those two ill-matched horses gave the charioteer no end of trouble. And if we choose a milder fable, and conceive a Garden of Eden where all was health, safety, and abundance, we invoke only an animal placidity, into which spiritual joy might break perhaps at rare intervals and (I should think) wistfully; because animal peace, to spirit, is half cloying, half pathetic, except as some fleeting posture or aspect of it may be caught up and turned into a lyric note or a charming picture.

No escape possible from nature.

And why are such pictures or notes momentarily satisfying to the spirit, when the life from which they are drawn, in its monotony and decay, seems so gross and melancholy? Because spirit is essentially a culmination, and perfect happiness a quality to be attained occasionally by natural life, not another nonnatural life existing beyond. To say that we are distracted here because we belong by nature to a different region is simply contrary to fact. Nothing could bloom more naturally or tremble and sing more congruously than spirit does on earth; and the myths about a paradise, past or future, are transparent parables, expressing the rare, transporting, ecstatic quality that distinguishes the culminating moments of natural life from its endless difficulties, hardships, and embroiled hopes. These moments are sometimes the gift of a happy change in circumstances, as when agony ends and lovers are reunited; but sometimes, more spiritually, the supreme moment liberates us from circumstances altogether, and we feel withdrawn into an inner citadel of insight and exaltation. Let us consider how this can be.

Apocalypses and Last Judgments and cosmological wonders interest our moral or political passions: they give us a foretaste—conceivably not false—of catastrophes and triumphs awaiting the human race. They need not be **Liberation does not turn on changes in the facts.** inspired by a narrow partisanship, but may contain spontaneous insights into the genesis and fate of life in a thousand non-human or superhuman forms: dreams of angels and Titans, of Gods and devils. Like inspiration of any kind, such revelations may bring to light and may fortify the rebellion of the psyche against oppression and hopeless routine. So far, the thunders of prophecy, political or cosmic, will give voice to the spirit, and may promise to emancipate it. They may awaken it when perhaps it was sleeping; but they are not needed and not satisfying. Not needed, because clear and varied notes enough of the spiritual gamut are struck spontaneously at every turn in daily life, even if drowned in the hubbub; and not satisfying, because those lurid transformations of the scene into hells and heavens, or into marches and counter-marches of reforming hosts, only redouble the pressure of circumstances upon the spirit, and browbeat it into being joyful or revengeful. All this may involve fevers and nightmares of singular violence, but short-lived: nothing can be more dead than dead prophecies. The shouts of triumph in one camp cannot render the spirit, which is universal, deaf to the groans of the other; and by the indefinite prospect of fresh revolutions and fresh catastrophes, far from being redeemed, the spirit is tied more excruciatingly than ever to the wheel of fortune.

The Indians, who gave themselves time to unravel this question without private prejudices, saw that salvation could come only by *not* being born again: not **Indian testimony regarding salvation.** because another life was not possible and might not be more splendid, but because, being life, it would be subject to accident, confusion, and responsibility. It would be essentially distracted. But not being born again is a negative solution, and personal. The very notion of being born again confuses the psyche with the spirit; for the spirit is inevitably born again so long as there is consciousness anywhere, whereas the psyche might perhaps be restored to life by the resurrection or re-creation of a corresponding body, but would lose its identity in proportion to the transformations suffered by this body and by its habitat. If the moral heritage or Will of any soul were extinguished by discipline and penance, so much of the transmissible energy or burden of existence would be destroyed and the universe would continue to live somewhat diminished in volume. I have not read any-where that the universe was at last to be totally extinguished by this process, the last man being a saint by whose salvation existence came to an end altogether; nor would such a prospect make any difference in the moral issue. Under the form of eternity that finished history would remain a fact, with all the beauties and horrors that it may have contained; and the spirit said to have quitted it would still be faced by that fact, and be condemned to digest it forever, if by poetic licence we conceive the spirit to survive disembodied. Salvation, then, must not be the beginning of a new life, which would make salvation again urgent; nor can it be existence without life, which except for dead matter would be a contradiction in terms.

When each sage reaches Nirvana or reverts to perfect identity with Brahma, who then is it that is saved? Certainly not the man, for he has abandoned and disallowed his personal being, even to the extreme of assuring us that *he* never existed at all, but that there was never anything but Brahma existing in him. Not the world; for this, even if with some diminution of potency or debt, continues to wag. And surely not Brahma, or the trance of Nirvana itself, for this has never been and never can be troubled. How then is spirit ever liberated, when in its proper nature it was always free, and in every phase of vital illusion it is still cap-tive?

I think the Indians themselves give us the key to this enigma when they tell us that, in reality, the departed or finite being never existed, but only the One or the Absolute existed in him. This assertion, taken historically or physically, is indeed self-contradictory and contrary to fact: for only the finite and transitory property *exists*. But two genuine insights are conveyed by that mystic formula. In the first place, there is one plane, that of matter, or physical energy, on which the universe forms a single dynamic system and is presumably of one substance; so that all other realities, not being possessed of any substance, force, or permanence of their own, are called unre-alities by the impulsive realist. On this analogy, mind in its turn may be reduced to an alleged spiritual substance. As the dissolution of bodies or worlds turns them all into water or ether or electricity or dust, so the dissolution of ideas and emotions is conceived to leave pure spirit, deep sleep, Brahma or Nirvana stand-ing. Thus as matter was, in a dynamic sense, the only "reality" in this variegated world, so pure and calm spirit may seem to have been the only lasting "reality" in our distracted consciousness.

It is an inward transformation.

Modern philosophy has enabled us to dismiss this notion of an underlying substantial spirit. There is something substantial underlying our feelings and thoughts, but it is the psyche, or the organic life of the body, the substance of which, in its turn, is the common matter of the whole universe. Spirit is as far as possible from being a substance: it is at the other end of the scale, the very flower of appearance, actuality, light and evanescence.

But in the second place the Indians, in telling us that Brahma was always the only reality in our lives, summon us to turn from that physical problem about the one substance in the cosmos to the moral problem of finding the quintessence of peace and joy in ourselves. Their philosophy here takes the same turn that Greek philosophy took in Socrates, and substitutes morals for physics. Now, morally considered, the only "reality" is the good. To say that Brahma is the only reality in our souls will then amount to saying that the only *good* in our thoughts and feelings, and in our whole existence, comes of pure spirit being alive in us. In fact spirit in our thoughts and feelings is terribly distracted; but it can be more or less so; and the nearer we come, at any moment, to spontaneous, disinterested, pure intuition, so much more nearly has spirit within us been freed from ourselves, and so much more completely have we become, in that act, identical with Brahma. There was something in us always, since consciousness awoke, that saw our persons as part of the world. From the beginning there was a moral ambiguity in our souls. We might identify ourselves with the self which we found existing and at work; we might adopt its passions and limits; we might almost forget that there might be other selves or other passions morally as real as our own. Yet such egotism is naturally unstable and perverse, because in seeing our persons as part of the world and at work there, spirit in us cannot help assimilating our action and fate to that of the other creatures visible in the same world; and sincerity then compels us either to admit the other wills as equally important and legitimate with our own (which would undermine our fighting morality) or else to detach our genuine allegiance from ourselves also, regard our passions as follies, our views as illusions, and identify ourselves not with ourselves, but with the spirit within us. This spirit will be qualitatively the same as exists, or may exist, in other creatures also: not in so far as each accepts and pursues his animal or political impulses, but only in so far as, like spirit in us, he detaches himself from those impulses, regards them as pathetic accidents, and equates them with our contrasting impulses, and those of all other creatures.

The light which lighteth every man that cometh into the world.

Physically, existentially, historically, nothing will be changed by this second insight; but morally the whole natural world, with our own persons in it, will be removed to a distance. It will have become foreign. It will touch us, and exist morally for us, only as the scene of our strange exile, and as being the darkness, the cravings, the confusion in which the spirit finds itself plunged, and from which, with infinite difficulty and uncertainty, it hopes to be delivered.

Thus when the Indians tell us that only ignorance makes us suppose that a world exists or that we have a natural self living in that world, I would understand them to speak of *moral* ignorance only; for they themselves heartily believe, for instance, in the transmigration of souls or (what is morally the same thing) in Karma. Spirit therefore has a long variegated experience of this ignorance, which is at the same time knowledge of the world, and of the path to salvation; and the created selves that obscure and distract spirit in this process are parts of the vast realm of genesis, with all its earths and heavens. It is not scientific or natural ignorance to discover and understand this too real machinery; but it is ignorance in the heart, ignorance of its spiritual vocation, to attach itself absolutely to anything relative. Those sufferings and triumphs weigh upon spirit only

Distraction is called ignorance in that it obscures the true good.

because they arouse spirit; otherwise they would be indifferent and morally null; and they are good rather than evil, true monitors rather than false, only in so far as they liberate spirit and pass into it, as oil shines only when consumed and turned into flame. Once lighted, this flame turns back upon all that it illuminates and upon its own fuel, as upon alien if not hostile facts. Being light, it thinks it shines of itself; but this is only the most inward and subtlest form of its distraction, when it torments itself about its own existence, perpetuity, and prerogatives, instead of simply shining upon all that there may be to shine upon, and consuming all its gross substance in that spiritual office. It is from the fumes of untoward matter obscuring the flame that liberation is needed, not from the fit occasion of this burning. The burning forms the flame that is to be saved; to be saved from its own impurities, from its obstructions and vacillations, so that it may neither suffer in shining nor fear not to shine.

That it should cease to shine here, upon these circumstances from this odd animal centre, follows from the natural instability of existence, and of the world in which spirit is kindled. To have lighted those things once is enough, if not too much. In any case they cannot lapse from the purview of spirit, which is addressed to all truth; they cannot lose their pertinence to that spiritual life which they once diversified; much less can their passing prevent other occasions and other objects from arousing spirit afresh. Frankly, this irrepressible vitality of that fire which by its very essence is continually consuming itself and ceasing to be, devours rather than sustains the animal soul; and those elegiac sentiments which gather round death, loss, old age, and mutation are not in the least modified by the assurance that truth is eternal and that life and beauty may be perpetually renewed in other shapes. On the contrary, both the eternity of truth and the vitality of nature merely perpetuate the reign of death and of sorrow; and far from promising an escape from destruction; they overwhelm the natural soul with a sense of how thorough that destruction is, how pervasive, minute, and hopeless. To be told that spirit maybe inwardly emancipated from fortune, and that in innumerable other creatures it may live through endless adventures, sounds like bitter mockery to the poor wight mourning the loss of all his treasures, and shuddering horribly before his open grave. The soul so much concerned about its immortality is not spirit, but is an animal psyche, a principle of natural impulsive life. As thunderbolts, floods, famines and wars, sickness and blindness fill this human soul with horror, and as social obloquy torments it morally, so when by a sudden ray of intuition it foresees its own end, it is appalled and sometimes the thought of resurrection in the flesh, sometimes that of immortality for the soul only, arises in reflection to mitigate that despair.

The dominance of spirit cannot redeem the whole soul.

Both these thoughts spring from the same intelligence that brought the knowledge of death. Life is a perpetual resurrection; and spirit too is continually being born again. In essence it is incapable of growing old or weary or embarrassed by past errors. Wherever there is existence there is youth; and death at every stroke by intercepting memory restores spontaneity. In another direction all that perishes in time is in truth

Ambiguous resurrection and immortality.

and for spirit raised to immortality. Life moves on, but the achievement of life remains undeniable, even if forgotten. Here are two honest counterparts to death, not adventitious hopes or hypotheses, but implications inherent in the fact of death from the first. Resurrection is involved naturally, though not logically, in death, because life is a self-repeating trope, a rhythm in which death is the cæsura; and ideal immortality is implied logically in the truth of any finished life, which death rounds and frames in its wholeness. The Phoenix that continually rises again, however, is no individual psyche, but mere spirit: not impersonal, since it can exist only in some person, yet not the past personality of any dead man; only the same rational light breaking out anew in some fresh creature. Such a resurrection of the spirit does not liberate it: on the contrary, in this new incarnation it must begin its redemption again, or at least continue it, if by a moral heredity the new psyche takes up the task where the old psyche left off. This is not only the Indian and Platonic doctrine but in principle also the Christian. The number of incarnations is reduced to two (or to three, if we admit Purgatory), but spirit awakes in the second life with that degree of moral virtue which it had achieved in the first. This rank it now retains in each soul for ever, either in hell or in heaven; or else, according to Origen and some modern Protestants, it continues its moral adventures in circumstances perhaps more favourable than those it lived in on earth. We are not told whether the test of progress in either case would be an approach to liberation from existence altogether, as the Indians and other mystics aver. Probably not: the picture is rather that of an endless process, monotonous or varied, but essentially quite empirical and naturalistic.

Resurrection is the good old Hebraic hope. Such a prophecy satisfies the moral or political enthusiasm of the prophets and promises relief and compensation to Job. It does not profess to disengage the spirit from accidental bonds. Suppose the prophecy came true and we began to live in the Millennium or in the New Jerusalem. As we walked those golden streets and gazed at those crowned and white-robed phantoms that discoursed music in eternal peace, the still solitary spirit within us might well ask whether all this was not a dream, whether the heart was not deceived and disappointed by it, and whether reality possessed no other dimensions. Spirit would still need to do what it does on earth, what it is the nature of spirit to do everywhere, namely by its own intellectual insight to introduce us into the spheres of truth or of essence, detaching us from each thing with humility and humour, and attaching us to all things with justice, charity and pure joy. Is this what, after all, we should understand by heaven? In that case the heavenly kingdom is already come, and exists potentially within us; and there would be no occasion for spiritual pride to turn its back on heaven, since heaven would open wherever spiritual humility happened to look.

No dramatic eschatology would be involved in such inward salvation. We should simply return to innocence as before nature in us was distracted; or we should achieve natural perfection in some particular faculty, for the moment predominant, say in poetic intuition or in universal sympathy. It is an error to identify spirit with cold intelligence, or to think even intelligence primarily cold; however impartial our inspection

Common life has moments of spiritual freedom.

of truth might become—and it never is wholly impartial—that very impartiality and scope, that very perception of contrary movements crossing or ignoring one another, and all issuing in the least expected or desired of destinies, would excite a tremendous and exhilarating emotion in the heart. Spirit has its lyric triumphs in childhood and in the simple life: wedding-days and moonlight nights and victories in war and soft music and pious trust. It breaks out momentarily in the shabbiest surroundings, in laughter, understanding, and small surrenders of folly to reason. Such moments are far from permanently lifting the soul they visit into a high spiritual sphere; often they come to ne'er-do-wells, poets, actors, or rakes. The spark dies in the burnt paper; yet it had the quality of a flame or a star. All the saint or the sage can add is constancy to that light, so that it colours all their thoughts and actions, turning the material circumstances into almost indifferent occasions. Yet the least disciplined or integrated of us sometimes feel something within us rising above ourselves, a culmination, a release, a transport beyond distraction. It was but summer lightning, and the sultriness continues unabated; yet that flash has given us a taste of liberty.

This is a spiritual gift, a gift of grace; it is not an earthly or even a moral benefit. Against circumstances and vices there are natural correctives; to apply them is the task of war, medicine, and labour; but easier circumstances or healthier passions will not liberate the spirit from oppression by things not spiritual. Prosperity might even deaden and misguide it more completely than ever misfortune could. For instance, that erotic passion which moralists think of when the flesh is mentioned is a conspicuous source of inspiration and spiritual courage; before it entangles us in sordid complications, it liberates us from the drab world, where everything suddenly seems foreign and worthless. The snares and slavery that love prepares for mankind are like venereal diseases; surprises for the young lover, shocks to his confident emotions, emotions in which nature and spirit seemed at last to have flowed together into an intense harmony.

It is then the flesh as a power that liberates us from the flesh as an obsession. That which is liberated is still love. It may ignore the flesh that breeds it; it may turn its rays away from their source upon the most remote or ethereal objects; it may even consume its substance and exhaust its organ. But that would be the end, not merely of all possible relapses into fleshliness, but of love itself and the blessing of its ultimate visions. Love presupposes a creature addressed to objects naturally harmonious with its deepest needs: otherwise love (if it could be imagined still to subsist) would be a blind unsatisfiable longing, incapable of fixing upon any true object, or even distinguishing the predestined beauty for which it longed.

We find, then, that it was not the flesh in its simple animal functions that imprisoned the spirit, but the world and the mind, complicating those impulses or compelling them to hide, that overwhelmed the young Eros with all manner of extraneous reproaches, jealousies, sorrows, and cares. We should liberate the spirit quite enough from the flesh if we could liberate the flesh from all that, as flesh, distorts, starves, and degrades it.

Spirit is freed by the perfection of the body, not by its absence.

Nor is it liberation for the spirit to be removed from the world. This, too, is physically impossible: but even in the sense in which a hermit or a lover of nature may flee from the world of men, liberation is problematical. It will not ensue if the hermit or poet still takes thought for what he shall eat or drink, what people will think of him, or how he may persuade them to reform their ways. As the flesh is the necessary organ of spirit, so the world is its inevitable environment, and its appointed theme when spirit is intelligent. Perhaps a purely sensuous, musical, or conceptual life might never discern a material or social world beyond the sphere of linked images; but when images are acted upon and understood, when objects, events, possibilities and certainties loom before the mind, then spirit, by becoming intelligent, becomes a conscious and absorbed inhabitant of nature. It lives by finding itself in the world, by seeing how the world wags, by tracing with emotion the tragedies of history. The greater the range or deeper the insight of spirit the more inextricably will it live the life of the world, though not as the world lives it. Ignorance is not liberation; and for that reason the world is such a slave to itself, not in the least understanding its own mechanism or foreseeing its destiny. But spirit, in the measure in which, by attentive study and sympathy, it may have understood the world, will be liberated from it, that is, from distraction by it.

By under-
standing
the world,
not by
quitting it.

And as for the devil—all that mesh of deceit, which language, imagination, reasoning and self-consciousness weave round the spirit out of its own creations— the devil needs indeed to be exorcised, but cannot be destroyed so long as spirit endures, because in their substance the two are one. We have seen how the distraction of the spirit by the devil reaches its height in insanity and suicide: on the way to which there are many stages and devious paths of sophistication, obsession, delusion, and fanatical pride. We need only follow the thread backward through that diabolical labyrinth to find the gate to freedom: not always, or perhaps often, a gate by which we entered or which we recognize as opening upon fields native to our souls; because we are born in original sin, hatched within the labyrinth, and accustomed from childhood to be little spit fires and little devils rather than inno- cent clear minds. Yet, though probably never experienced, perfect health and simple knowledge would have awakened and filled full within any animal a spirit free from distraction, and so attuned to its successive intuitions as to find the devil's whisperings inane and utterly repulsive. To this innocence, armed with the strength of unclouded spiritual wisdom, we may penitentially return; but only a long discipline can avail in most cases to smooth out all sophistry and banish all pride, so that undisturbed by the devil, spirit may deploy all its notes and all its tints in a new springtime of inspiration.

By natural
faith not
by pure
reason.

Health and knowledge: essentially nothing more is requisite for liberation from distraction by the flesh, the world, and the devil. Negatively we may observe this liberation in placid sleep. A sleeping child is not distracted, yet he is alive. Nature has given him health; fortune has not yet taxed his powers unduly; and while consciousness is in abeyance, the feelings and images ready to appear, and forming his latent store of knowledge, will serve perfectly to express his simple contacts with the world. But spirit in the sleeping child is in what Aristotle would call its first entelechy: it is ready, it is perfect, but not employed. It must awake before all that brimming potentiality can pass into action. And then, after a first phase of confidence and eager experiment, trouble will begin. Foreseeing this, must we say with the Indians that liberation can come only by reverting to that deep sleep in which all things are alike and nothing ever happens? It

Treacherous primitive paradise of indistinction and peace.

would be foolish to deny both the physical and the moral insight enveloped in this doctrine, but discrimination is needed. There is, let us allow, a universal substance to which we all return and which was always the real force and agent within us; and a worshipper of mere force, permanence, or existence may see in all that is evanescent (that is, in all that is in any honest sense *spiritual*) a vain delusion from which it is blessed to relapse into unconsciousness. This unconsciousness will not be death, because unconscious substance retains all its energy and potentiality, and will still breed, very likely, endless worlds out of itself. But in a spiritual sense is this liberation? Is it even liberation from life, if you are tired of thinking, loving, hating, and hoping, and wish for eternal rest? It would be death indeed to *you*, if that is what you long for: but the unconsciousness of universal substance is immensely alive (else we should not be here, with our troubled phenomenal world) and the end of spiritual troubles in you will not dry up the fountain of spirit or of endless distraction in the universe. The liberation, if you call death a liberation, will therefore be personal only, material and unspiritual. The spirit will not have learned how to live; and to speak of freedom where there is no life, of freedom in non-existence, would surely be an abuse of language.

No: liberation cannot be liberation from spirit itself; and therefore not from those natural circumstances which make spirit possible. On the other hand, these circumstances plunge the spirit, as we have seen, into all sorts of distraction, since the organ of spirit, not by chance but essentially, forms a particular and specific nucleus in the organization of nature. Were not the psyche a special nucleus, subject to external interference and needing external support, it could never have become the organ of spirit, that is, of an intellectual and moral

Problem of being emancipated without being starved or uprooted.

self-transcendence. Living suspended upon circumstances the psyche felt this suspense, reached and covered those circumstances by its concern, and thereby became spirit. Individual life must subsist, with a station from which to survey the world, a set of organs and interests to canalize that survey, to render it graphic, lyrical, tragic, and moral, if ever spirit is to arise or to endure or if in any positive sense it is to be liberated. Yet how shall it be liberated if it must continue, while it exists, to face a world of circumstances not only alien in themselves but often inimical? Between extinction on the one hand, and endless distraction on the other, it might seem that for spirit there were no salvation at all.

Perhaps a surer and more positive idea of liberation may be drawn from observing what spiritual men are than by discussing what they say. They are not all alike. Some are initially spiritual and free, not needing liberation, but birdlike and gay like children, or bovine and steady like peasants. Others who are more sophisticated represent all degrees of regeneration, from comfortable worldly wisdom to the extreme of asceticism. Even frankly mundane sages, like Goethe, while blandly smiling on the world, the flesh and the devil, seem to disinfect those influences by the breadth of their knowledge and sympathy, being too mature to run amok with any one folly. But such equilibrium seems rather the gift of a sound temperament than of a renovating philosophy. Nature at a certain distance and on a large scale looks sublimely calm, as if God lived there; but all is strain, torment, and disaster in the parts, if we take them on the scale of their inner effort and animation. So an Olympian naturalism lives at peace with all the vices, and is more selfish than sympathetic, thinking that inevitableness and beauty justify nature as they justify woman, no matter how much she may entangle or how much she may suffer.

Appeal to actual types of spirituality.

In such pantheistic allegiance and respect for nature as a whole, spirit may be philosophical, absorbed in curiosity and wonder, impressed by the size, force, complexity, and harmony of the universe; the eyes are open, but the mind is still in leading strings. So it should be in natural science; so it was in that happy childhood of philosophy represented by the Ionian cosmologers. Yet at two points the existence of spirit, with its transcendental rights, is bound to assert itself. The naturalist, being a man, must also be a moralist; and he must find himself dividing this seamless garment of nature, by a sort of optical iridescence, into the shifting colours of good and evil; and he will probably turn his reflection from pure science to giving counsel to his soul and to his country about the wiser way of life. At the same time, within his natural philosophy, he must ultimately notice the existence of sensation and emotion in animals, with his own moral philosophy crowning that immaterial and invisible experience; he must discover the witnessing and judging spirit. This is the adolescence of philosophy, and has its sentimental dangers. Only in the most home-keeping, industrious, unheroic souls will spirit be content, when self-conscious, to accept reality uncritically, and to run every errand of instinct or opportunity with the alacrity of a trained dog. Either overwhelmed by the disproportion between outer and inner forces, they will turn against themselves in the hope of suppressing all moral distinction or rebellion; or they will reserve the moral sphere as a private retreat, a humorous or sarcastic or poetical oasis for the spirit in the environing desert.

Worldly wisdom involves a judgment on the world and a choice among the natural virtues.

This last was, at heart, the path chosen by Socrates and his less metaphysical followers, who were not also followers of Plato. Cynics and Cyrenaics, like Confucians and sceptics elsewhere, summoned the spirit to live on its own resources, in studious or domestic peace, dominating the world only intellectually, describing it sometimes scientifically, sometimes satirically, and cultivating abstention from passion and war, and from excessive confidence in fortune or in human virtue. The spirit, as these men saw, was invulnerable in its idyllic modesty, and far more divine

Feeble glow of satire and abstention.

than the thundering gods; yet the authority of this spirit over the rest of the human soul remained precarious, and philosophy when honest had to be composed in a minor key. Minor, that is, in its philosophical pretensions, yet often merry and running into *scherzo;* for in fact this homely strain in Socratic wisdom has flowed ever since through all the pleasant fields of literature and worldly wisdom, while religion and science, not always more spiritually, frowned from the heights. For can it be regarded as a triumph of spirit to live, artificially exalted, on its own illusions? The zeal, the trembling anxiety, the fanaticism with which these illusions are sometimes defended betray their non-spiritual source. They represent psychic and political forces struggling to maintain a particular form of life, and dragging the spirit into their vortex, which is by no means identical with the free and natural organ of spirit.

No doubt the metaphysical side of Socratic philosophy, the hypostasis of language and morals into cosmic powers, expressed spiritual enthusiasm, and seemed to support it; yet in the end we find that it contaminated and betrayed the spirit. Earthly warfare against the world is an earthly and worldly business; it impoverishes its own side by condemning too large a part of nature and of human nature, which might also have served the spirit; and it constrains such spirit as it fosters into a false alliance with particular opinions and moralities. Spirit soon has to cry aloud to be saved from such salvation. Plato, who had the soul of a poet, knew perfectly how much he was sacrificing to the desperate enterprise of maintaining an impregnable and incorruptible city on earth; and the Church afterwards acknowledged that on earth it was but a Church militant; triumph, liberation, happiness could come only in heaven. Mankind were to remain an enlisted army, heavily armed, narrowly hedged, covered with blood and mire; spirit was to visit them only in the weariness of the twilight, and to rise heavenward in the smoke of their camp-fires.

A dogged allegiance to a particular temperament or country or religion, though it be an animal virtue, is heroic; it keys the whole man up to sacrifice and to integrity; so that persons devoted to such a specific allegiance attain a high degree of spirituality more often, perhaps, than sceptics **More** or original philosophers. Yet pantheism, or joyful allegiance to nature **substance** as a whole, also has its saints; it too, in one sense, is a special alle- **yields** giance, since it excludes every irreconcilable passion. Indeed what **more fire.** essential difference can it make to the liberation of spirit from what world or what passions it is liberated? To be liberated, let me repeat, is not to lose or destroy the positive possessions to which the spirit was attached. It is merely to disinfect them, to view them as accidents, to enjoy them without claiming them, to transcend without despising them. So we find the pantheists, when they are spiritual, retreating from this infinitely deployed universe into an inner silence and simplicity that holds infinity, as it were, in suspense; and we also find the disciples of particular religions interpreting their tenets as symbols or occasions for an inward revelation that renders those tenets indifferent.

When St. John of the Cross, for instance, who knew that the accepted facts of religion did not prevent the spirit from passing into the darkest night, tells us that the one guide out of that and darkness must be *faith,* what does he understand by this word? The dogmas of the Catholic Church? But those he never seems to have questioned or lost sight of. Any partial heresy seemed to him perverse, and he had no intellectual or historical lights to show him the whole system of Christianity from the outside, as one figment of imagination among many. Faith in that system, as a materially true account of the facts, had not prevented his spiritual desolation. How should it save him from it? The faith to invoke would seem to be rather faith in salvation itself, allegiance to the whole enterprise of the religious life, *Fides caritate formata,* trust that beyond that blank negation and inner death which utter self-surrender involved there would come in the end a positive liberty, a clear vision, a living flame of love. And it could come, it did come; although even the most exquisite poetic inspiration could not avail to express its nature in adequate images. The verses of St. John of the Cross have the lyric brevity, simplicity, and passion that anonymous popular ditties in Spain borrow, perhaps, from the East; there is something so entire, frank and ultimate about such effusions, that they are not unspiritual even when merely amorous or witty. The man who sings them, and perhaps improvises them, sees himself and his feelings from above, as did Catullus when he wrote: *Odi et amo.* Here is a torment that, in seeing how animal it is, has become spiritual. At least it has become awareness of a double life; you are perishing in the sea of fortune and passion, and you are making a philosophy or a poem out of your shipwreck. Or while the whole world is asleep you are slipping out invisibly into the night on the secret errands of your love.

Living flame and traditional fuel in St. John of the Cross.

It was a godsend to Christian mystics that the Song of Solomon was canonical. It countenanced allegories that otherwise might have seemed scandalous. The flesh as we have seen is naturally a breeder of spirit; even vulgar infatuation often touches ultimate insights, defiance of the world, self-surrender. And spontaneous sublimation here may well be used as types of sublimation for all the passions. Yet I find two defects in erotic symbolism, even in the delicate hands of St. John of the Cross, in which it was comparatively safe; because he seems to have had a less erotic temperament, or a more manly control over it, than many other mystics. One defect is that (as in the Song of Solomon itself) the images overpower the thought, if indeed the thought ever existed; and we are charmed by a lascivious picture or a poetic sigh, when we ought to be transported into a perfectly spiritual, entirely sacrificial bliss. The Indians, with their metaphysical intensity, are better guides here. The other defect is that lovers asleep in each other's arms on a bed of roses represent a pleasant death rather than a sublime life. Appeasement of a sensual instinct makes a bad symbol for attainment of intellectual light. The true spiritual sublimation of love is charity, not inebriation, or blind transports, or happy sleep. So that if in its imagery I find erotic mysticism less instructive than Indian concentration on pure spirit, in their issue I find both schools alike too negative, too drowsy, too unintellectual. Blank ecstasy is a form of intoxication, not of disintoxication. Instead of cleansing the lamp, it puts out the light.

False erotic symbols.

St. John of the Cross is now in great favour even among the merely curious in spiritual matters, because he is the most poetical and psychologically expert of mystics; but neither in speculation nor in heroism was his genius of the first order. What the essence of liberation is might be more readily gathered from St. Francis of Assisi, or from Buddha: one would teach us the cheeriness of utter renunciation, and the other its infinite peace. But I am not writing a history, and will jump at once to the supreme instance obvious to all natives of Christendom. Obvi- **Appeal to the person of Christ as conceived by the Church.** ous to believers, because where could spirit be freer or less tainted than in God made man? Obvious also to unbelievers, if they have any discernment; because at the moment when ancient civilization touched the summit of its greatness and of its misery the Hellenized Jews were exiles in the midst of that world; they learned from it without loving it, and were weaned from their own national ambition and bigotry, sublimating these into a purely religious zeal, still filled with prophetic grandeur and fire: and, to be the heart of this new religion, they composed the legend and maxims of Christ. Christ was supreme spirit incarnate in a human creature, suffering and dying guiltlessly in that creature, and immediately rising again and carrying with him into eternity his earthly body strangely transfigured, and thus opening the way of salvation for the spirit in all flesh.

What is this salvation, not as the Christian myth describes it (we have settled our accounts with myth) but as the adored person of Christ exhibits it, and as his followers would experience it if they shared his passion and his resurrection?

Christ in the Gospels continually tells us that he is subject to "the Father", who has "sent" him into this world. Liberation as a Christian should desire it, cannot be liberation from fortune or domination over it. Spirit is *sent* into this world: it does not command this world, much less create it. It may **He is the Son, accepting his being and mission from the Father.** work miracles here, when it feels the silent consent or monition of the Father prompting it to invoke them; but they are secondary, and the fuss the world makes about them is disheartening. "The Father" represents the realm of matter, where the sun shines on the just and the unjust, where to him that hath shall be given, where the lilies of the field flourish and the sparrows fall, where the house built on a rock will stand (for a season), where the poor are always with us, and where there shall be weeping and gnashing of teeth. Miracles belong to that natural sphere, and manifest the hidden sympathies and harmonies between its parts. The spirit notes them, but does not dwell upon them, or value them except as evidences of the unfathomable fatherly power on which spirit itself depends.

Jewish tradition unhesitatingly identified this universal power with Jehovah, conceived at once as a national patron and as the divine vindicator prophetically invoked by an aggressive conscience; but these strains are separable and not spiritual. "The Father" we hear of in the Gospels **Is universally detached and universally compassionate.** bears a more intimate and a more universal relation to the spirit. He generates and inspires it, and at the same time subjects it to the chances and cruelties of an impartial natural economy. To this economy the spirit submits painfully yet gladly; because the beauty and terror of that impartiality liberate the spirit itself from its accidental bonds. Family, race, religion, human conceit, human hypocrisy are transfixed by the clear spirit in Christ with a terrible detachment; but where love is refused, this is not because it does not exist; it exists overpoweringly for everything that the Father has created, that is simple, that is young, that suffers and is mangled in the hideous madhouse of this world.

Thus we see by the example of Christ that spirit, even when conceived to have been originally disembodied and voluntarily incarnate, is neither contaminated by its descent nor made proud by its intrinsic elevation. In Christ spirit did not need to be saved, it was free initially; yet it was inspired to love and willing to suffer; neither tempted, like the gods of Greece, to become an accomplice to human passions, nor like Lucifer to shut itself up in solitary pride. It was humble towards universal power, wisely respectful towards the realm of matter. Salvation could not consist in pretending to be independent, that is, in becoming mad. It could not consist in correcting the divine economy, and becoming creative, that is, in becoming guilty. Humility, piety, is a prerequisite to spirituality. It is much more than a prudential virtue, good for those who wish to prosper in the world. It enables spirit to recognize the truth and to be inwardly steady, clear, fearless, and without reproach.

Spirit is not the whole of life, only a child of the family. The others, the uninspired, cry out even more urgently and need to be helped first. The good Samaritan is more spiritual than the Pharisee. Learning and science and art scarcely deserve to be mentioned, or only ironically, in that they refute and stultify themselves. Spirit, being at once vital and disinterested, cannot but be merciful. Wounds, weakness, conflicts are the immediate evils; when these are healed, we may turn to higher things. Nor is this last possible or necessary to everybody; the parting word rather is: "Sin no more." Enough, to strike at the source of each grief, to staunch this wound, stop this pain, banish this care. Why force anybody to be greater than he naturally is? There is nothing enlightened in moral snobbery; and spirit feels more at home amid simple things, if they are perfect, than in ambitious minds. Its own perfection consists in charity, in the perception and love of possible perfections in all other things.

Proud towards the proud, and humble towards the humble.

Thus the innate humility of spirit is turned not only towards the realm of matter, the universal power on which spirit depends, but also towards the realm of spirit itself, towards all the lives, languages, and loves into which spirit can enter. To corporal works of mercy Christ adds spiritual charities: patience, forgiveness, understanding, defence of the heart against cant, hypocrisy, isolation, and the insanities of conscience. Spirit, that suffers distraction by the disorder of its instruments, rejoices in the salvation and perfectness of all creatures and all aspirations, as in so many preludes or approaches to its own happiness. It is not spirit that sins, but the terrible cross-pressure of a thousand motions in nature that stifle and confuse it, when they allow it to open its lips at all.

St. Paul tells us that Christ liberates us from the law, and therefore from sin, saving us by faith and an infusion of the spirit. This might be (and has been) interpreted so as to countenance moral licence; as the charity of Jesus in the Gospels has been interpreted by sentimental or romantic moderns as an invitation to indulge all their corrupt inclinations. But health and morality are not based on spirit, spirit is based on them; and no spiritual insight can abolish or weaken the difference between what nature allows and rewards and what she punishes and condemns to everlasting torments. The point is that spirit, caught in this vice, suffers guiltlessly for that natural disease and corruption; and to rescue that guiltlessness, to extricate spirit from inner madness as well as from outward oppression, is the double work of mercy proper to Christian charity. The moral economy of the universe is not destroyed or suspended: rewards and punishments, saving miraculous exemptions, take their natural course; but sins are forgiven because they *ought* to be forgiven, because the suffering they bring to the spirit, *the spirit* never deserved.

Sins rightly forgiven because it is always nature that sins and spirit suffers.

Is it too bold an interpretation of Christian dogma to say that this inevitable innocence of the spirit, in all it suffers, is symbolized by the passion and death of Christ, and by his resurrection? The possible liberation of the spirit is not a liberation from suffering or death, but through suffering and death. This suffering and death need not be bloody; often some silent spirit is overwhelmed like a modest brook grown brackish and lost in a tidal river. Suffering and death come from the contrariety of motions in nature and, among these, from the way in which life rises into spirit and sinks away from it. Yet this spirit, however cruelly circumstances may play with it, remains congenitally positive, self-justified, heroic; it has been sent into the world by the very power by which the world was created; and it aspires to live, and to find a good and beautiful world to live in. It loves, and although it suffers only because it loves, it wills to love and to suffer. Our sufferings will chasten and transfigure our attachment to the circumstances and passions that caused those sufferings. Death will soon annul the ignominy that confined spirit in us to our private views and private interests. Even now, by accepting that death in advance, we may identify ourselves dramatically with the spirit in us that endures and surmounts those accidents and laugh at that death, since apart from those accidents spirit in us is identical with spirit everywhere, a divine witness, a divine sufferer, immortal, and only temporarily and involuntarily incarnate in a myriad distracted lives.

Its continual passion and death.

So the Cross is a symbol for the true liberation, the ultimate dominion, possible to the spirit in man.* Salvation comes by shifting the centre of appreciation from the human psyche to the divine spirit. It is a shift within the psyche, otherwise it would not enter at all into our lives; but in each human soul some spark of divine spirit cohabits with the animal nature of the rest; and shifting the living centre from some other faculty to this spark, which is the focus of intellect, by no means abol-

The soul redeemed by grace remains human.

---

* "L'Esprit saura se priver de puissance, de toute espèce de puissance; tel est le plus haut règne. Or, le calvaire annonce cela même, de si éloquente et de si violente façon, que je n'ajouterai aucun commentaire." *Alain, Les Dieux* (the last words of the book).

ishes the remaining faculties; these merely become, for appreciation, peripheral. This means a change of heart, a conversion, momentarily real, but relapsing and becoming more or less nominal and merely intended as life goes on. For genetically and substantially those non-spiritual faculties were not peripheral but primary, and the nucleus from which intelligence and spirit were put forth. So that man is irremediably a human person assuming and adopting a divine nature, and not, like the Christ of theology, a divine person assuming a human nature added to and subordinate to his native divinity. This religious image is formed in worship, it expresses an unattainable limit of aspiration, it is hyperbolic. It represents as a descent from heaven that inward darkness which is in fact a presupposition to the idea of heaven. It would be heaven to shed all these backsliding inclinations and distracting cares, and to live only in the spirit; but spirit would have nothing to live with and nothing to live for, if it had begun and ended by being a spirit. For us to wish to become divine persons like Christ would be chimerical and, for the pious Christian, blasphemous; but Christ may come and dwell within us, transfusing our human nature with divine light, so that our natural functions, while continuing to be performed, and performed perhaps more healthily and beautifully than before, will now be performed with detachment and humility and an eye seeing what lies beyond.

The fact that spirit is grafted on the animal psyche and is a continual hypostasis of natural life prevents the sacrifices imposed by spirit from being unrewarded, and the spiritual life from being merely negative. Calvary is not the end: there is the Resurrection. And this post-mortal life has two stages, or two dimensions. One is a rebirth by expansion and re-incarnation in all those phases of spirit in which the spirit is free, and therefore self-forgetful. Selflessness can see no difference in value between what is enjoyed here and what is enjoyed there, by one man or by another. Envy is abolished; the very limits of sense and imagination seem virtually to break down; you feel all you have not felt, know all you have not known, live in everyone who has ever lived. Yet with a happy partiality; because the endless evils and sufferings which fill actual lives fill them precisely because the will in those creatures has not been liberated. There the spirit cares for what does not concern it, wills things contrary to itself and to one another, and in a word is subject to distraction. This we are now supposed to have overcome: and surely the passions and illusions that are dead in ourselves are not to be replaced in us by adopting the passions and illusions alive in others. Only the clear spirit in each can be identified with the clear spirit in all the rest. The distracted spirit in the world will be succoured with charity, and not hated even in its madness; but only the liberated spirit will be embraced with joy. For this reason hell does not poison heaven. The modern sentiment that heaven could not help being poisoned by the mere existence of such an eternal contradiction to its bliss, though generous, is not intelligent. As all truths fall together into the truth and are perfectly welcome to the intellect, all errors being understood and rejected, so all sane joys add themselves together uncontaminated in the heart, when the heart is pure; while the sorrows and hatreds, though per-

Spirit may be liberated, first historically, by resurrection or reincarnation.

ceived, cannot be shared. Pain is itself a kind of hatred, and however intense it may be elsewhere, it cannot find its way into a free spirit. But this very freedom lifts the spirit, in its outlook and virtual attainment, into the presence of all good, wherever this good may be realized; so that it now clings to the earth, and to its native soil, only by the hidden roots of which it is unconscious, while its head flowers out and drinks the light from every quarter of the heavens. Self, so turned into a mere pedestal, ceases to intercept intuition, yet continues to make intuition a possible temporal and local fact, and determines its point of view, language, and perspectives. Spirit continues to live, and to inhabit persons; but it feels no drag in this attachment, can carry away and transform its body as it will, and rise into any heaven to which it has a natural bent.

This I seem to see symbolized in the risen Christ appearing unannounced, unrecognized, in various disguises; a real body, yet not as it was; the same person, and yet escaped from his trammels, having finished his mission, transmitting his work, without regret or anxiety, into other hands. There remain a few relics of the man, but the spirit has passed untraceably into new mansions. If we come sorrowfully at dawn to the grave where we thought he was laid yesterday, we behold young men, strangers, sitting by the stone that has been rolled away, and saying: "He is not here, he is risen. Why seek ye the living among the dead? He goeth before you into Galilee. There shall ye see him."

Such is the escape or migration, or resurrection of spirit horizontally, in the direction of further instances and developments. But there is also, and simultaneously, a possible liberation ideally, in the vertical direction, when at any moment, or habitually, the spirit in a man recalls its universality, its merely momentary lodgment here, or preoccupation with this trouble, and expands intuitively into the equilibrium of all moments, and the convergence of all insights, under the intense firmament of truth. *In the second place mystically, by identification with pure spirit.* Here there is no longer any pang of loss, any dubiousness in re-union, any groping in the twilight of birth and death. Birth and death have become integral to life, like the outburst and the close of a phrase in music: there are no winding-sheets or sepulchres or embalmings; we have been initiated into the mystery of the divinity of Christ. In Adam, in the human psyche, the spirit is secondary, dependent, intermittent, only a point of view occasionally taken histrionically, by transcending animal egotism only the better to serve it; but in Christ, in the spirit that then enters into us, the opposite happens. There the centre is divine, and what is put on like a garment or a dramatic mask is human nature. And though this assumption of humanity be voluntary, the very fact that it is voluntary makes it incomplete. The humanity that can coexist with divinity in the same person must be a singularly chastened, subordinated humanity. Such in fact is the humanity depicted in Christ and admitted by Christians into their ideal of life.

A divine person coming down into the world to redeem it could not adopt its errors or its vices. He could not even adopt its passions, however legitimate or inevitable in the natural man. He could not marry and have a family claiming his special affection in contrast to mankind at large. He could not possess a home or

a country that should tether his heart and compel him to defend them. He could not become a national hero, like Joshua or Solomon or Ezra. He might speak
Liberated spirit accepts life ascetically. figuratively, and with great pity in his heart, of the kingdom to come: but it was not one in which his disciples should sit on thrones, like Cæsar, judging the nations. The first condition was that they should leave their nets by the seashore, take up their cross, and follow him. Nor was this a temporary repentance, because the end of the world was at hand, and it was not worth while making earthly provision. The end of the world is always at hand. The world is transitory, not only because our lives in it are short, but because it is unstable and contradictory and self-devouring essentially. In the true kingdom to come, in the soul transformed into spirit, there would be no anxiety about place or person, no marriage or giving in marriage, no pride of knowledge or power, no rebellion against suffering. These things are in the order of nature. The Father has ordained them. There can be no thought of abolishing them in their sphere. Christ himself came eating and drinking, living with the poor, and even feasting with the rich. Why not, when these things were profoundly indifferent in themselves, and the spirit could strengthen itself and pray in the midst of them whatever they might be?

Christianity was thus a fundamentally new religion, a religion of the spirit. It completely reversed the inspiration of the Jews in their frank original hopes, and
And also clarifies it emotionally. rather resembled Neo-Platonism and Buddhism. The Jews did well, from their point of view, to reject it, and the Protestants, from theirs, to reform it so as to revert to the cultus of marriage, thrift, science, and nationality. Nevertheless a religion or philosophy without repentance, without disillusion or asceticism, reckons without its host. The Jews themselves produced Christianity, and the Greeks helped them to do it. After all, it is the spirit that makes human nature human; and in the confused, tormented, corrupt life of Christendom, not only do we find many a bright focus of mercy, sanctity, poetry, speculation, and love, but even the tone and habit of the common mind seem shot through with more wit and insight, more merriment and kindness, than in ages and nations that have never asked to be saved. Salvation is demanded, and in one sense is possible, because by virtue of his intelligence man already has one foot in eternity. Each passion, each period of life, each political enterprise, after its heats are over (or even in the midst of them, when spirit shines through) enacts a tragedy which though vain materially need not be vain morally. Error and suffering, by the very change of heart that they provoke, may be offered up as a holocaust; affections lost as joys may be preserved as allegiances; and all experience may be accepted for the insights which it brings. Brings, that is to the spirit and for the spirit; because if after stumbling we merely plodded on, and if after dying we were merely made flesh again, the wheel of nature would go on grinding brutally for ever, no music would be heard in those spheres, and the soul would have sinned and suffered only to go on sinning and suffering unredeemed.

Union

The Realm of Spirit: Book Fourth of Realms of Being. London: Constable and Co. Ltd.; New York: Charles Scribner's Sons, 1940, 214–71. Volume sixteen of the critical edition of *The Works of George Santayana*.

In this selection, Chapter IX of The Realm of Spirit, *Santayana looked beyond the negative goal of liberation to the positive ideal of spiritual union. Adapting the classical understanding of spiritual union with the Good, he characterized the union of spirit as "a moral unanimity or fellowship with the life of all substances in so far as they support or enlarge its own life" (ES, 378–79). This entails a spiritual love of the world that Santayana thought possible through sympathy, pity, and charity. If love and sympathy lead to recognition of the Good, ideal union with the Good is possible through the activity of prayer—understood spiritually, not superstitiously. Santayana acknowledged the possibility of spontaneous spiritual union through laughter, and he distinguished unhappy, cruel laughter from pure laughter that releases one from unhealthy attachments. He discussed the social aspect and relation to friendship of spiritual union, but ultimately union occurs within spirit itself. And any spiritual union is never permanent: Spirit's "happiness must always remain volatile, and its union with the Good ideal. This union is achieved . . . by intellectual worship, in which spirit, forgetting itself, becomes pure vision and pure love" (ES, 407).*

Liberation is something negative, as freedom itself is; yet the soul feels confident of finding great things to do, if only the enemy would let it alone. This is an illusion, because the soul could not live for a moment without the support and suggestions of the environment; and even if, by an unnatural abstraction, we imagine the soul living on by itself, as in a dream, then, when once the vestiges of its old dependence on the flesh and the world were erased, it would be reduced to feeling itself lingering on in a void, watching the flow of sheer duration, and wishing it might go to sleep. The illusion of a fertile freedom comes of not distinguishing dependence from distraction. The sources of life and Will flow into us, and become ourselves; and so long as we move in harmony with the part of them that remains outside, we think we are our own masters, and even masters over all other things. It is only when there is conflict, and our spontaneity is not only fed and guided by circumstances, but also thwarted by them, that we protest against them, and wish to be free. Liberation, however, would bring no positive benefit, but at best the peace of death, unless it were a mere preliminary to Union.

Having freedom to what shall we devote it?

This, though not always understood by politicians, has always been understood by mystics. Union, even identification, is their constant watchword; and words fail them to describe the fullness and rapture of that consummation. I trust their sincerity, but I doubt their self-knowledge; and in any case we must ask ourselves, since they fail to tell us, *with what* they are united, and *in what sense* union with such a thing may be possible.

To union with what, and to what sort of union?

It would be useless to recite the names given to this supreme object: God, Brahma, the One, the Absolute. The question is what these words stand for; and as a begin-

Classic reply: To union with the Good.

ning I will take the name given to this ultimate object by Plato and his followers, who are comparatively articulate, and the origin of whose doctrines we are able partly to trace. This name is the Good: it is with the Good that a liberated soul should be united.

Socrates, in whose mouth Plato puts his views on this subject, was an austere moralist, what we should call a reactionary and a man of the Right, inveighing

The Socratic Good both utilitarian and spiritual.

against the sophistry and luxury of the age, and idealizing the principles of simpler, harsher, and more religious times. But like all reactionaries that found a new order he was a man of the peo- ple, with the tone and manners of that corrupt society which he condemned; and though occasionally he seems to have reached extremes of asceticism and mystic abstraction, which made him the precursor of the Cynics and the monks, he ordinarily passed his days eating and drinking, reasoning and joking, and pushing a plebeian utilitarianism to its most comical consequences. Thus he maintained that his own pop-eyes, upturned nostrils, and voluminous gross mouth were better and more beautiful than regular features, because they served and expressed better the uses of those organs. Such para- doxes, in raising a laugh, were meant to awaken the conscience. Away, they sug- gested, with all prejudices, all whims, all empty pleasures. There is a true, a perfect, a sublime Good within reach, to which it would be a joy and a deliver- ance to sacrifice everything else.

This Good, as we learn ultimately, is harmony, to be established by the perfect definition and mutual adjustment of all natural functions, both in the individual

The harmony of natural goods becomes a spiritual good called the beautiful.

and in the State. Nothing could be soberer, more hygienic, more politic. Here is the ancient Greek sage, chosen to legislate for his city in earlier times, but now condemned to legislate only for his own thoughts. Othello's occupation's gone; yet this enforced futility, if it favours exaggeration in the moralist, also favours free- dom of mind and tongue, and poetic aspiration. Playfully on a small scale, solemnly in prophetic moments, we find the homely Socrates harping on love. That harmony, that rational Good, which seemed so abstract a conception in argument and so cold and repressive a Utopia in political philosophy, appeals visibly to the heart in everything young and beautiful and positively transports the soul in moments of religious rapture. The Good, then, is not merely a harmony to be established or approached in the economy of nature; it is an influence to be felt, an inner transformation to be experienced, a beatific vision and union with God.

Are we then in the presence of two Goods, and will union with one of them mean something entirely different from union with the other? Not altogether: for dissimilar as the two Goods are in description, they are one in origin and may converge in attainment. Erotic feeling permeates all mysticism; but erotic feeling belongs to the machinery of reproduction, that is to say, to one of the most elabo- rate and therefore precarious harmonies established by nature in the institution of animal life. No doubt it is precisely when this animal harmony is suspended or deranged that the feeling belonging to it overflows or is sublimated into ideal enthusiasms; but we need not conclude that the ideal enthusiasms cling now to no other, perhaps wider, harmonies and are wholly hectic and diseased. The boys with whom Socrates pretended to be in love were for the most part nonentities and the notion of breeding philosophy out of them was preposterous: yet Plato was among them, and a legitimate Socratic philosophy was begotten in him, and propagated to our own minds. So too those beautiful institutions, which were to be the stepping stones to the highest Good, though never realized as conceived, were missed instances of social harmony that, in other forms, may be often realized; they may actually enlist vivid devotion, and may support materially the happiness found in maintaining them. Even that union with God, more often talked of than experienced, need not be an illusion; because the universe has, at each moment, and in its total career, a particular form, with which everything that exists must needs be in an actual harmony: and nothing forbids some sense of this harmony to resound occasionally in a particular soul, and to overcome it.

I say advisedly, to *overcome* it: because in a union, even if called a union with the Good, some sacrifice is involved. In embracing the greater good, the soul abandons some, or all, of its former affections; it therefore abandons some forms of the Good; and the notion that *all* good can be found in one moment or in one object is merely rhetorical. Often, and not only in an ultimate mystic trance, all other goods may be forgotten; they may cease to be desired; but this exclusiveness of itself suffices to prove that a psyche in a special phase is pronouncing that judgment, and that this judgment, if made dogmatic, is egotistical. The other goods remain good for the other phases of the psyche; and the determination and discipline that fix allegiance and love on a single good, are sacrificial. For that very reason they are healthy, noble, and if achieved deliberately, even sublime; since this willingness to surrender true goods, admitted and felt to be good, for the sake of one good only, offers to the beloved a supreme proof of love, and to the world a supreme example of wisdom and humility.

Any intense love involves exclusion and sacrifice.

Commonly the word union is understood eulogistically, as signifying a new strength and range for the elements united, so that the gain overbalances any losses involved. Yet in marriage and other social partnerships the living unit remains the individual person, and the union is likely to be partly a disunion and a latent war. Therefore union, in the eulogistic sense, must be carefully distinguished from interdependence. Interdependence, whether logical or physical, may be like the interdependence of the man hanged and the hangman. Now spirit has no occasion to aspire to interdependence with the universe with the truth or with the residual life of the psyche, because it is allied with these already, genetically, totally, and compulsorily. This biological bond is worth mentioning, in view of the confused pantheistic sentiment that professes to see a marvellous consummation in this necessary cosmic unity or equilibrium. Conformity with fate or with the will of God (which cannot be defeated) is a

Physical interdependence or identity of substance involves no moral union.

needful though partial factor in spiritual peace; yet brings peace only when the spirit conforms spontaneously, in that the order of nature seems to us magnificent as well as irresistible, and the intuition of that order becomes our happiest employ-ment. Such epic or stoic sentiments are included, as occasional events, in the same universal order that includes every actual crime, folly, and torment; yet this fact by no means involves logically that spirit should aspire to nothing in its own life except this helpless acknowledgment and deadly resignation. Spirit can aspire to union in a eulogistic sense, only with the object of its congenital love, in union with which its own life would be perfected. Virtual knowledge of the truth, in so far as relevant, and conformity with it, are indeed involved in such a union, because spirit is natively intelligent; but much else is involved also, because spirit is not, as Aristotle supposed, a disembodied act of thinking about thinking, or a hypostasis of general ideas, but is the passionate and delicate flowering of some animal soul, to whom much that exists in the world is inimical, and much would be lovely that does not exist.

Socrates and Plato were therefore true spokesmen and great liberators of the spirit when they made the Good, and not the universe or even the truth, the goal of life, attainment of which was happiness. They thereby placed the object of union in the moral sphere, which is that of spirit; because in material union with the universe, or fusion with the Absolute, no spirit is required or even permitted to survive. There can be no union where there are not at least two things to be united. If one is suppressed, the other may remain, but not the union between them; and if the two are merged in a single thought or feeling this feeling or thought is a new fact, a material resultant, perhaps, of the two previous existents, but not a union between them, since both now have ceased to exist. Union in prayer or in love requires the persistent physical separateness of the two beings united; and their union can be only spiritual, a union in intent, a perfect unanimity. If it were more than that, it would not be a moral union at all, but a material fusion in the dark, with a total extinction of spirit. Everybody achieves that substantial union by dying and being dissolved into cosmic energy and the flux of change. It is a con-summation, in some cases, devoutly to be wished; we may thereby turn into the potentiality of many a better thing than ever we were actually. Yet that better thing in its day, and spirit in any of its instances, can exist only by distinction; not only by distinguishing one essence from another in intuition but by distinguish-ing one object or eventuality from another in appetition, aspiration, and love. The truth and the universe will enter into this union only under the form of the good; that is to say, in so far as they contribute, by support and by denial, to define both the adored and the attainable good, both religion and politics. But it is with the Good only that union is good; and only with the Good that it is spiritu-ally possible. Union with anything less, or with anything more, kills the hope that was to be brought to perfection and damns the soul that was to be saved.

One point, a fundamental point, is thus settled in our inquiry: The union sought by a liberated spirit is no fusion of its substance with any other substance, but a moral unanimity or fellowship with the life of all substances in so far as they

Fusion with the universe is not union but death.

support or enlarge its own life.

This first conclusion also arms us with a thread of spiritual security in our wandering through the labyrinth of religions and philosophies. Are our steps turned towards discovering the real or articulating the possible, with no reference to the good? Then in our philosophic dream we may accompany great naturalists and subtle logicians through unending windings; the eye may range over prospects vastly discursive or intensely concentrated; we may summon spirits and work magic; but the Will in us will never swerve from its first animal direction, from blind craving or idle play. We shall be studying matter or essence, but not harmony. In these reaches we shall find the peripatetic Aristotle, the reasoning Parmenides, the Stoics, Spinoza, and Hegel: all naturalists and historians in their ultimate allegiance, and never more so than when they raise pure intelligibles or sheer substance or infinite existence into a supreme idol. They may call it God, but it is still fact or truth that they are worshipping, not excellence. Or, weary of that pursuit, we may turn down other paths, less stately and trodden, but more fragrant, where the poets walk. At the end, not far distant (since repentance follows close upon love) we may find some saint in his hermitage or some cynic in his den, or perhaps Epicurus in his little walled garden. Here every alley will be blind, with no thoroughfare. We must turn back into the maze, or stay with these solitaries for ever.

The Good also a saving thread through the labyrinth of philosophies.

But the thread in our hands may not be broken, and may encourage us to look further; and finally we shall not fail to reach the very centre of the labyrinth, where there is a great marvel: Nature replanned and twisted into a green temple for the mind. Here dignified priests officiate—Pythagoras, Plato, Plotinus—while in a rival sanctuary the Fathers of the Church vehemently preach and gesticulate. Apart, in wider spaces, the Indian teachers sit cross-legged and sleepy, each in his little shrine, and Buddha under his Bo-tree. But the thread we holdfast, the pledge of our safety and sanity, while it suffers us to approach all these arbours, grottoes, and artificial rockeries, will not allow us to enter any of them; if we attempt to step nearer, it pulls us back. Pure Good is not worshipped here. Actual good, which can only be a consummation, a smile suddenly breaking out on the face of nature, or some great gift of fortune to the heart, here is magically materialized into a fantastic monument, not a good realized but a new set of conditions imposed upon the spirit. The Good, falsely petrified, is inverted into a power, limiting the possibilities of the Good; a power here bribing us to accept something not perfect, there forbidding us to love and to praise the inalienably beautiful. But fortunately, we were only dreaming. This inverted universe is in fact undiscoverable and non-existent; those revealed histories were but fables, contrived for the sake of their moral. Inspiration no doubt invented them well, and they in turn may have inspired many a holy life; but, the spell once broken, those deceived passions become mere pantomime and those doctrines dead words. It remains for us to pluck the secret out of that dream, and to trace our guiding thread back to the living Ariadne who spun it.

Moralistic systems of nature.

This Ariadne is the human soul. It is only the psyche that can conceive a good or can love it, or can uphold or misguide the spirit in the pursuit of that good. An original theologian is but a poetizing moralist, and the mystic who thinks he is becoming one with the deity is simply purifying himself and learning to see all things from the point of view of the spirit. For that reason those pious philosophers do not altogether waste their time studying their fabulous universes: for they are but reversed images of the spiritual life, and the deeper the devotee penetrates into their magic economy, the better he learns to know his own heart. He becomes very much wiser, in spite of his fables, than the positivist who rails at them as invented physics, without understanding the moral secret of those inventions.

They are fables expressing human aspirations.

Yet truth conveyed by a fiction is an ambiguous good, and if it deepens our insight in one direction, it is in danger of misleading us in another. The bigoted positivist, who ignores the existence of his own spirit, is unwittingly doing the spirit a clearer service. He does not endeavour to be edifying; yet his views, in their externality and darkness, may serve staunchly for edification, by leading the spirit to a more complete disillusion, a simpler hope, and a greater liberty. The spirit does not need a universe composed of pure spirits. It needs a world that will suffer spirit to live in it.

Hard facts the better counsellors.

Now, with gods conceived as powers, or with the real powers that they personify, a spirit seeking the Good may make alliances and compromises; it may offer propitiation and undertake service with a hope of reward. These are the normal expedients of primitive religion: the calculation is prudential, the aim preliminary, and the alliance political. There is no moral union involved, and the powers addressed are respected as much for being dangerous as for being friendly. Therefore when loyalty is merely political it remains conditional and essentially unstable. It is an accidental method of securing our personal ends. Yet since the psyche is plastic, an imposed subjection to some constant calculable power may grow into an easy habit and a happy allegiance. The servants of a great king at once annex pride to their servitude and ambition to their loyalty. The power, the kingdom, and the glory of their master become indistinguishable in their minds from their own safety, profit, and eminence. Nature in this way sometimes overflows calculation and restores spontaneity where there was at first some ungenerous artifice. So polite language turns to wit, labour to art, superstition to religious devotion; and the ultimate goal is touched unexpectedly in the midst of a tedious journey. The journey continues, but now free from haste and from despair, since the goal is known to be always at hand, not before us, but within.

Facts, in closing one gate to the spirit, may open another.

In fine, a spiritual good does not cease to be spiritual because matter supplies it, or a humble occasion. We may eat and drink to the glory of God; but when, and in what sense? And when may the arts and sacrifices imposed on us by external forces become free arts and fresh vocations? I reply: when the psyche has undergone a radical readaptation to the facts, so that in living in harmony with them, it can live in harmony

Provided that the psyche achieves a new unity.

with itself. This is genuine conversion or *metanoia,* a true education and disci-pline, that in trimming away all excrescences and parasitic growths allows the plant to shoot up straight to its predestined flower. We see signs of this when asceticism is joyful, limitation avowed, labour interested in its function and excel-lence, with the heart detached from the issue and set on no particular event. And we see signs of the opposite when the will is merely cowed and suppressed pro-visionally, the original passions remaining alive under banked fires, and watch-ing for some partial or mock satisfaction. Overt life, social life, then becomes one vast hypocrisy, all duties forced, all virtues conscious, all work sullen and unwill-ing and bargained for in terms of some irrelevant reward. Something of this ugly lining is visible even in the pursuit of spiritual perfection, when that pursuit is systematic, since conversion is seldom so thorough as wholly to purify the unre-generate will; and some strictly virtuous people are so artificially good that it is only in their lighter and unguarded moments that they are at all tolerable or at all spiritual. The two meanings of the English word *light,* in this respect, seem not wholly divergent, because in order that spirit may be wholly *luminous* it must be also *imponderable.* The creaking of a motor must not be heard in its flight.

Union cannot be attained by sacrificing integrity. With inner integrity a spirit might live in moral harmony with chaos, as the romantic spirit thinks it can live; the only trouble being that chaos could never breed a firm spirit, or any spirit at all; so that your romantic hero draws all **Inner integrity the first** his strength from the natural order that he despises, and dreams **condition of** of a congenial chaos only because his own integrity is shaky and **unity with** diseased. But admitting, in a myth, that a perfect spirit could **everything else.** exist facing a chaotic world, that spirit would make no further claims on that world and would find no fault with it. It would positively love that disorderly order, no matter how many torments and mutual hatreds might be involved. And this tragic exultation, like that of the Stoics, Calvinists and Hegelians, would not become cruel or egotistical, unless, in view of his own Olympian peace, the philosopher denied that the world was a great evil to the world, and tolerable only to a spirit that had overcome and renounced it; a solution easy enough for the fabulous Olympians, but almost unattainable to actual spirit, incarnate in that very world.

Thus we see that it is easier for a free spirit to live in charity and peace with an evil society, than for a distracted spirit to tolerate the most perfect universe. Soli-tude is morally the most social of states, since it knows no ene-mies; and the concentration it allows equalizes distances, material **It makes range and** and moral, and places the spirit at its own source, from which flow **insight** all the radiating varieties of moral life, none of which then seem **possible in** unnatural or alien. Inwardness makes moral scope possible, the **thought.** experience obtainable externally being a mere annexation of casual views, with-out insight or moral understanding. Moving time and endless evolution cannot survey themselves; they straggle and grope along from moment to moment, ignorant of what they were or are going to be, and incapable at each point of conceiving the burden of any other. They can be surveyed only by virtue of a quickened sensibility lodged in particular places within that flux, where long-range organs play upon long-range instincts and unused potentialities in the psyche. Every affection of the organism may then become a perspective for the spirit.

There might seem to be a paradox in the love of truth, and in being spiritually exalted by the spectacle of an evil world. If spirit were a power, its first concern would indeed be to reform this world, and (lest it should falter in that endless task) to sharpen and stiffen its own demands, so that the existence of any evil in the world should never pass as a matter of course, and excusable; much less that evil should come to seem an entertaining and pleasant thing, or a necessary shadow and relief to the high-lights of virtue. The least blot should then fill the spirit, to all eternity, with an irreconcilable horror. But spirit is not responsible for the world; it is the world that is responsible for the spirit, and guilty of often tormenting it to no purpose. Yet this happens, so to speak, only by mistake, since consciousness, by its very existence, marks a vital if imperfect harmony already achieved in nature; and the imperfection of this harmony could not be perceived unless the potentiality and need of harmony were at work, impatient to make it perfect. Partial failure is inevitable, because the life of spirit is only a small part of the world's life, and not synchronous with those wider vibrations. Spirit cannot *be* the world; it can only *think* the world; and this function of thinking has conditions that are local and specific: there must be integrity and clear sensibility in some animal psyche. Such perfection of function brings an inner light and happiness. Truth, in the appropriate terms and relevant measure, has been discovered and defined: and this truth is a pure good for the spirit, no matter what disorder, conflict, or dangers in regard to spirit itself the discovery may reveal. Storms are not appalling to the spirit, nor even death; what is appalling is only inner contradiction, delusion, and madness hugging its own torments. Integrity banishes all that; and it renders the truth lifegiving and refreshing, like pure air and the solid earth.

This spiritual love of the truth is not love of what the world loves, and therefore not hatred of what the world hates; but is understanding of both those passions. It is therefore a kind of love for the world, a pitying and forgiving insight into its loves, such as the fratricidal world is incapable of feeling towards itself, but such as we might imagine that God would feel for it. He would not *adopt* the passions of his creatures; he would be like a perfectly wise and infinitely sensitive tragic poet, holding all those passions in suspense, as possible sentiments, and seeing their interplay and their moral issue: things to which they themselves, except in some ultimate moment, would remain blind.

Many an old philosopher and theologian has denied that God, if conceived to be pure spirit, could love the world or could have created it. It could only be some Demiurgos, himself a natural wild being full of fatal passions and limitations, that could have contrived so many ingenious ways of using or circumventing the forces of matter, and could have nursed a fatherly fondness for his work and a tendency to pull his too

Union with the truth not connivance with what the truth reveals.

How spirit may love the world.

hapless creatures out of the traps that he had covertly laid for them. That seems speculatively correct; yet the notion of God as pure spirit is religiously inadequate. The God of religion must be also a power, the fundamental power in the universe, controlling our destiny: and he must also be the truth or the Logos, that specific contingent pattern which this power imposes on existence. I will return to this point later; here, taking spirit as we find it in ourselves, we may readily see in what sense it cannot help loving the world: cannot help at once enjoying it, and pitying it, and wishing to save the spirits that inhabit it from the troubles they endure.

In the first place, is not spirit an emanation of animal life? How then should it not enjoy breathing and eating and fighting and loving? How should it not enjoy the sights and sounds that arouse it and stimulate it to fix the terms in which all its thinking will flow? Here then, inseparable from the **By vital sympathy.** movement of the world, we find the pleasures of emotion and of perception, pleasures intrinsically spiritual. The vital dependence of spirit on nature involves a responsive affection towards nature on the part of spirit. And this affection (as just now explained) will survive all the buffets of fortune, so long as the power to think, to observe, or even to protest, remains in the spirit, the very badness of the world being a fountain of eloquence in a free mind.

Yet, in the second place, love is an exacting passion, and we cannot willingly allow the object of it to be less than perfect. When imperfection, folly, or shame invade that object, love turns into suffering. Shall we deny the facts? Shall we excuse and adopt them, betraying our own honour **By compassion** and conscience rather than forsake our darlings? Yet what would **and** these darlings be without the charms that we found in them? Shall **concern.** we detach our love altogether from existing beings and platonically worship only universal Ideas of the Beautiful and the Good? This might be wisdom or spiritual insight, but is it love? And can such sublimation really be professed without hypocrisy? Could it be realized without a mortal chill benumbing the heart? If ever we have ceased to suffer, have we not ceased to love?

Whence it follows that a pure spirit that loved all Good would necessarily suffer with all sufferers, since they suffer only because they are deprived of something that has become for them a need and a good. Union with the Good might then seem impossible and self-contradictory, since it involves participation in all evil, and in all loss of the Good. And it is very true that union with the Good, with all Good freed from all evil, becomes possible only by the prior renunciation of all impossible or contradicted desires. We must first let the sorrow involved in love correct the love that is vowed to sorrow, not by denying the natural charm of those contradicted sweets, but by not pursuing them or demanding them wherever the natural Will does, or where, at a later moment, it would curse itself for having obtained them. This necessity establishes the double level of moral life, here natural, there spiritual; and it is only at the spiritual level that perfect union with the Good is possible, union with it at the natural level being precarious, blind, and almost always infected with suffering, remorse, and injustice. These two levels are not to be conceived as separated like heaven and earth, or lived in by different persons: they are moral levels within each life, often within one moment, when we partly tremble at our predicament or that of our friends and partly accept our fate and admire their virtues. Our love of the world is natural in so far as it rests on kinship and contagion; it becomes spiritual in so far as it grows disinterested, looks before and after, and discriminates the dead loss from the clear gain.

When sympathy with the world reaches the spiritual level it receives a Christian name and is called charity. This charity is seldom pure or universal, but touches home sentiments with more or less spiritual light. We see this in the slowness and hesitation with which the notion of charity was first distinguished. In later Judaism and early Christianity, there was a fervent spirituality of the heart, but the intellect had not discerned the nature of spirit and looked for a miraculous transformation of this world into a celestial society. It was the speedy coming of this mythical revolution that inspired the quite unworldly and ascetic practice of charity that we find praised in the First Epistle to the Corinthians. There was prudence, there was speculative joy, in renouncing this world when this world was dissolving, and in making ready for the next, where only the converted would be admitted. Being forgiven, it was easy to forgive, to be patient, to succour all, and to think evil of none. But such charity was unawares an inner initiation into that new spiritual order which was expected to burst so dramatically into public existence; it involved detachment from all that made the glory of earth, not only from the glories of the heathen or of the natural man, but even from those of the saints, when they were filled with gifts such as prophecy, working miracles, or speaking with tongues, which though called gifts of the spirit were grossly psychical or demonic faculties. These were worthless spiritually without charity, without the insight that renders love universal and the humility that accepts all homely cares, forgives all injuries and, without disclaiming eminence where there is eminence, knows that it is no private possession but a gift of grace. Spirit is not essentially seated more in one man than in another, and in all suffers semi-darkness and tribulation. In all it has an equal need of salvation and an equal capacity for it. Respect for persons and their gifts is worldly; so is enthusiasm for their ambitions. These are seductions for the spirit, blinding it to the simplicity of the Good and of the true love of it.

By transmuting both sympathy and pity into charity.

If thus charity is sympathy with universal Will, it is a sympathy doubly chastened, first by understanding and then by renunciation. The world is seen to be in one sense innocent; its great sin is original sin, the sin of being a spontaneous world, self-contradicting and ignorant of its destiny. And this predicament runs deep, to the very centre of the heart. There is no spark of Will anywhere that circumstances might not blow up into the greatest crimes, and the world falls into no error the roots of which might not be found in any soul: so that charity implies repentance, not for this or that slip, but radically for willing otherwise than as God wills. Therefore the true saint unaffectedly thinks himself the greatest of sinners, because he finds in himself, in so far as he is himself and not pure spirit, the potentiality of all sins. Yet this

Rationality of charity.

sinfulness calls for grace and deserves it, because there is still spirit in it, and hunger for the Good.

To blame nature uncharitably is not to understand the circumstantial origin of evil. Law and morality must needs punish and suppress natural Will whenever it transgresses the prevalent order of society; and they can trace this transgression no further back than to the voluntary acts or thoughts of particular persons who may be fined, imprisoned, executed, or at least banished from good company. But these are stopping-places **It sees victims in sinners.** conceived on a gross human scale. Responsibility and freedom no doubt lodge in persons as they do in every contingent unit arising in this contingent world; but for a speculative eye the obliquity of those initiatives is not inherent, nor the evil absolute and all on one side. The world is as evil for the natural Will as the natural Will is evil for the world. The true sin is cosmic and constitutional; it is the heritage of Chaos. This is the sin of which spirit is the innocent victim, which it expiates with undeserved sufferings, and from which it is redeemed if those sufferings and its own insight avail to detach it from the natural Will altogether, not by abolishing that Will (since then spirit would be abolished) but by understanding it and its self-contradictions.

To have passed in this way to the spiritual level is the first prerequisite of charity. Love here walks hand in hand with renunciation: not followed by renunciation after love has been disappointed but clarified by renunciation at its very dawn. Not having any stake in the **Its transcendental point of view.** contest, the Will expressed in spirit can rehearse all the other passions, which are not this *intelletto d'amore,* this understanding and this lesson of passion. Love, when so universalized and so disentangled, can forgive all injuries, endure all injustice, malice, or madness, and this not by an affected meekness, as if one begged to be trodden upon, but intelligently, justly, in the light of truth. The initial aspiration of life is everywhere innocent, the perfection of it would everywhere be beautiful; and everything is disfigured only by confusion, inopportuneness, and a hostile fate. That which is here and now impossible, impossible for ever for me, must be renounced; but it remains a good and cannot be detested without blindness. It may have its day in eternity. Charity is a love that outlives defeat and foresees it, that embraces death and is immortal; a love not demanding the impossible nor imagining the false, but knowing the intentions of the heart in each instance, disregarding the rest, and not despising the least spark of spirit in the cinders.

· Charity comes to assist or modify some work already afoot, or one that the natural Will might prompt or might welcome: but the motive is different. Animal passions are claims to possession, or extensions of self-love to wife, children, kindred, or party. The psyche expands and operates in a **Its spiritual quality.** wider field, but remains an animal psyche. Love remains a pursuit, a need, a demand, and is represented in the spirit, if at all, by desire or anxiety, that is, by some form of distraction. Only if at some moment that natural Will is fulfilled, is the spirit liberated and does love attain to union. But union for the spirit cannot lie in physical possession or in material expansion of its domain, things which impose more problems than they solve. Union for the spirit can be nothing but *presence;* nor need this presence be uninterrupted. Presence to it anywhere, full presence, is virtual presence to it everywhere else; its treasure is laid up in heaven, that is to say, in its own depths. Spiritual love is therefore not anxious and is entirely free from desire; it lives in the virtual presence of all the fulfilments and all the possibilities that the natural Will pursues.

The world appreciates charity, and finds it cooperative, when remedial action is requisite and the Will is trying to recuperate from its follies. Yet morally a spiritual temperament has its pros and cons, like any other temperament. Some monarchs who have been spiritual men—Marcus Aurelius, Saint Louis, Henry VI—have been unfortunate politically. Their heart was not in the conduct of affairs, yet they were not strong enough to recognize their true vocation. A greatly inspired prophet like Buddha would have at once renounced his throne and his family. Even this might not have sufficed. The professed and professional prophet is sometimes entangled in a worse net than a king. He may be led into self-assertion, into denunciations, into controversy; he may find himself working reputed miracles and inspiring fables that he must wink at; he will probably be utterly misunderstood; a sect betraying his thought if not his person will follow at his heels. Martyrdom, in such a case, would not be an escape; it would turn him into a myth, into an idol. His spirit would be dead, and more solitary in the other world than it had been in this; while here his bones would be encrusted in jewels. Books, laws, and traditional religions, supposed to embody the spirit, are parts of the world; their effect is compounded of a thousand influences alien to one another. Undoubtedly, even in their midst, as anywhere in the midst of nature spirit may be reborn; perhaps a docile intelligent spirit that can avail itself of all symbols without worshipping any fetich, but more probably a spirit soured and made wrathful by those very fossils of spirit. The world then takes sides in spiritual quarrels, or rather introduces quarrels of its own into that spiritual life which in itself would be free from all human partiality.

False esteem and contamination of charity in the world.

If charity be a universal spiritual sympathy with the world how does it seem so contrary to more than half the impulses that flourish there? Only because intelligent sympathy halts wherever one good conflicts with another: and this arrest is a consequence of universal sympathy, not a contradiction to it. As in a complex psyche or a complex world almost all passions are competitive and hostile to one another, charity is reduced to befriending them rather when they are down than when they are up; because when wounded and helpless and already suffering for its rashness, a creature ceases to be aggressive, and its enemies would be vindictive and fiendish if they still continued to assail it. They can afford to leave it alone to its involuntary penance; and charity can then step in with its double work of mercy, corporal in alleviating suffering, spiritual in rendering suffering a means of salvation.

Why charity is chiefly remedial.

This is the rationale of that check which a superstitious moralism would impose on all natural Will. To check any living being for the sake of checking it would be diabolical: the hypertrophy of egotism, when one movement of Will not only asserts itself absolutely against all others, but declares that all others are wicked and ought never to have existed. Moral passion shouts about right and wrong; applying to ends terms proper only to means: that is the feminine eloquence of the psyche, blind to everything but her home interests. To reason and to charity this prejudice is nonsense; it amounts to saying that some goods are good and other goods are bad. All are good, but not all are compatible in the same family.

Good-will on the contrary is the disinterested sympathy of one Will with another; a natural sympathy in kindred beings, where there is affinity in their Wills, but requiring spiritual insight before it can turn into sympathy with aliens and enemies. The infusion of this insight into natural good-will has observable stages. A mother will defend her young with ferocity; their bodies are extensions of her own; their psyches are colonies of her psyche; and she will passionately forget herself **Gradual clarification of good-will into charity.** in serving them, as the hand forgets itself in defending the eyes. But as the young grow older, they become less a part of the mother's life; she will scold, beat, and enslave them. She will grow jealous and sarcastic about their separate interests; if she were not human, and bound to them by economic and legal ties, she might even lose them in the crowd of young ruffians, and not know them for her children. Nor is it otherwise in friendship, where there seems to be no material bond. Friendship is a union in play, in adventure, in war. It is essentially exclusive, clannish, founded on sympathies that are common antipathies to all that is different, a comradeship prized for being segregation, cut off by special tastes and powers from the rest of the world. Manly friendship is based on physical affinity, as brotherhood is, only that instead of being passive, hereditary, and often annoying, it is freely chosen and tested in common action and adventure and in community of thought. It flourishes on sympathy (not confluence) in matters of love and honour. Personal reserve and idiosyncrasy are accepted tacitly and always respected; they make no difference in the common field, and are gladly felt to exist beyond it. A friend is not the keeper of his friends' souls; mutual liability is limited, but within the field of their common life and *virtù,* they feel sure of one another; and this confidence, when well tried, may be not untouched with admiration. And here a spiritual element may supervene. Friends may club together in cultivating music or philosophy as they might in mountain climbing: yet if the common ideal object predominates over the social occasions, with their incidental humours, the original personal atmosphere gradually becomes transparent, indifferent, and finally disturbing. Friendship is at an end, and each must tread the winepress alone. Even in the mountain climbing the supreme moments are solitary; the comradeship reigns in the projects, the dangers, and the irrelevant human incidents.

Exclusiveness and pugnacity appear also in all intellectual, political, and religious bodies—called bodies not without unconscious wit. They glow with local affections, with privilege, with scorn and hatred of the damnable outsider. If ever some ray of speculative spirit or universal charity pierces those enclosures, friendship is saddened, party is transcended, religion can be endured only as a human convention and nationality as a physical accident. Whatever measure of truth, beauty, or happiness there may have been in those associations is not denied or diminished; but the heart has travelled beyond; and it is only in an infinite landscape transfiguring their values that they continue to be prized. What was before lived is now understood, and this understanding is a second life in another sphere.

For this reason personal friendships and cliques are discouraged in the cloister. They are distracting and equivocal. Charity should extend equally to all the brethren, without favouritism or attachment. Not that affection is anything but natural and generous; but in the spiritual life it is acci- dental, as are also the particular doctrines and cults of any religion. They are to be accepted as we have to accept ourselves, not as goals but as points of departure. When we come to a spiritual com- munion of poets, philosophers, or saints, it is avowedly the divine grace, truth, or beauty flowing through those human channels, and not the human channels, that we profit by and embrace; so much so that all important spiritual figures necessarily become mythical, even when they were originally historical. If they resist this transformation, they become irrelevant to their spiritual mis- sion, as Shakespeare the man is irrelevant to the poetic world that we find in his plays. The creation of mythical heroes seems deceptive only to the pedant who insists on proving them historical or proving them unhistorical. To the spirit those *numina* are true, as the gods are; since the real source of influence in both cases is some diffuse cosmic power at work in the dark, and exciting these graphic images in the mind. We therefore conceive plastically and love as kindred beings and charitable powers the powers that actually liberate spirit in ourselves. They make for the Good; or, as we say, the Good works through them. This last, if pressed too literally, becomes not thinkable, since the Good is a result, a harmony in the workings of power; yet this power often serves the Good, which therefore may dramatically be called its master, commanding its own realization.

> **Union through all channels is interior and only with the Good.**

There is a school of theology that would clip the wings of love, so as to prevent it from ascending and make it always descend. Love of the Good, they say, is self-centred and erotic; by it we aspire greedily to something that we might enjoy, to the perfection of our own being, in the possession or presence of something that, for us, is the Good. Charity, on the con- trary, searches out the victims of evil, like divine grace poured out regardless of merit, and dedicates itself to their service. Forgetting self, it labours to relieve and instruct others. In a word, these moralists see charity in Martha, a hard-working Evangelical Christian; but in Mary they see only a corrupt enthusiast of the Greek decadence, absorbed in the passions of her own battered soul.

> **Charity *versus* Eros.**

In one sense unselfish love is not only possible but primitive. The Will is directed upon its objects by nature, without any calculation of satisfactions to accrue or torments to be avoided. But it is perfectly impossible that any love should exist not rooted in a psyche and not directed upon an object chosen and pursued by spontaneous Will. There is therefore no love not directed upon the Good, not directed upon something that makes for the fulfilment of the lover's nature. This good may be the good of others, but doing good to others will to that extent be a good for oneself. Or shall we say that a social life, involving friendliness and a sense of duty, is in itself nobler than self-help? If the monkeys agreed always to pick the vermin from one another's skins and never from their own, the operation would indeed have become social but the benefit would remain private. Amiable as the impulse may be to benefit others, this impulse would be cruelly stultified if no benefit could be really conferred; and it is only because Will is already directed upon life, health, food, and liberty that the ministrations of intelligent charity are a benefit and not a nuisance. If to pursue the Good be pronounced selfish the most unselfish charity would be openly serving the selfishness of our neighbours, and secretly serving our own.

Perhaps, however, the good that charity aims to bestow might be no other than charity itself. "The greatest thing in the world" being love, by diffusing love, without any other benefit, we should be saving the world. But should we? Flattered as everyone would be by the idea of being loved and full **Folly of** of ready love in return, yet if it were impossible to benefit anybody, **love for** the whole world would be tormented by a perpetual desire to do good **love's** and a hopeless inability to do it. But perhaps we may here be the vic-**sake.** tims of an ambiguity in the word love. Love may mean loving actions or it may mean the emotion of love. Now the *emotion* of love might be diffused universally, even if no positive natural goods could be secured for society. But then love, love, love would be a vapid sentiment; yet this is the happiness that the sentimental saviours of the world seem to be pursuing. Thinking themselves disciples of St. Paul, or even of Christ, they have removed all disillusion and asceticism from their notion of charity, all austerity from their love, and have become in reality disciples of Rousseau.

The position becomes even more precarious if we extend it to theology. That God is love is an orthodox saying; and even if God were essentially power rather than love, in one sense love would be involved in his being: for **Possible** power selects what it shall do and this selection marks a prefer-**meanings of** ence and a kind of love. When the Creator said, *Let there be light,* **"God is love."** he exerted power; yet the direction in which he exerted it betrayed an innate affection and proved that he loved light. The Book of Genesis represents God as an artist, loving the world in idea before he had brought it into existence. But a world, like a child, has a life of its own and may soon begin to wander from the parental intention. The parent may even be tempted to disown his offspring; yet the artist, even if disappointed in his work, remembers the Platonic Idea that first inspired him, and still feels its magic. He will be inclined to preserve the erring thing to be revised and corrected. So we learn that God has resumed his labours, this time not to create the world but to redeem it. The absolute artist has been softened into a forgiving father, a miraculous physician, a patient teacher, even a propitiatory victim. God's love of the world has become charity.

Arabian subtlety has known how to refine on these intuitions and to maintain that creation itself was a work of charity. Allah is continually called the Merciful and the Compassionate, even when his decrees are most severe; and there might seem to be a voluntary one-sidedness in these epithets, seeing that Moslem theology makes Allah absolutely omnificent. How should universal Will be moved by charity, when there can be nothing outside to succour or to love? The

Was it a mercy to be created? psyche is not moved by charity to fashion the body, or to react with a healing power on diseases and wounds. Nor is spontaneous unanimity between various psyches an instance of charity: it is not charity that leads a crew to pull together in a race or in a storm.

Nevertheless we are told that charity moved the Creator to make the world, because non-existence is the worst of metaphysical evils and the most necessitous. Allah therefore took pity on the unwedded essences of things and entirely without any claims or merits on their part married them to existence. The worst of monsters and of torments has this to be thankful for, that at least it exists. We may smile at such an ambiguous mercy; yet the principle that *giving* is blessing, whether the gift were needed or not, has a great vogue in religion and in society; and even when the gift is needed, the question remains whether the need itself was not an evil. The Prayer Book thanks God for our creation; yet in being created we received nothing but needs with no assurance that they would be satisfied; for what is our organic Will, our psyche, but a vast concourse of needs, some urgent, others latent but brewing and rendering us fundamentally unhappy? Common sense is blunted to such unremitting perceptions, and takes for granted our existence, our needs, and our desire to satisfy them; and on this basis we may unfeignedly thank Providence or Fortune or the charity of mankind for any aid in satisfying them, however inadequate.

Charity has more insight into nature than conscience or self-interest can have; it understands the innocence of contrary wills and the goodness of contrary

Charity is humane, with roots in nature. goods. For this reason charity seems unnatural or supernatural to the conventional mind. It rebukes in assisting. But if no will can be unreservedly abetted by charity, this happens only because natural wills are in conflict; for although some of them involve worse consequences than others, even the best involve consequences that are

unfortunate in some direction. Human wisdom cannot consider everything or really look to the end; and charity must begin at home and never lose its moorings there. Therefore it is always quick to relieve bodily distress. To relieve suffering in anyone's body is an immediate mercy to the spirit there, and can hardly bring an immediate injury to the spirit in anyone else. For the same reason charity gives alms, even when rational economy might hold back; because the benefit is clear, even if undeserved, and the detachment just, even if ill-timed. Thus charity is a second birth of love, aware of many wills and many troubles. It is not creative or constructive of anything positive, unless it be hospitals and almshouses. Institutions produce rival ambitions, rights, and contentions. About all plans and projects charity is disenchanted and sure only of the ever-present propriety of charity itself.

If in saying that God is love we understand that God is charity, we are led to certain consequences perhaps unwelcome to theology. For if the whole essence of deity were bounty, evidently the creator could not exist without the creation; and if the whole essence of deity were mercy, God would depend for his existence on the existence of suffering and sin. These implications are pantheistic; they are incompatible with Christianity, the religion of charity. But a more insidious consequence follows. If the impulse to give and to help were the very spirit of God (the occasion and demand for such charity being presupposed naturalistically) what would God be but goodness in ourselves, in so far as we are good? This insight may rather satisfy a moralistic and mystical piety, as the pantheistic insight satisfies dialectical wit: but if we say that God is nothing but the brotherly love that we feel for one another, it is clear that we are atheists.

To deify it involves atheism.

Neither the animal psyche nor the Good to which the psyche aspires can ever be banished from morals. The psyche introduces the element of preference, the distinction between good and evil, success and failure; and the Good is thus set in its ideal place, as the goal and perfection of a natural life. If we call this vital aspiration Eros, which is its ancient poetic name, we may say that charity is a form of Eros, and thoroughly erotic; for if it were not erotic it would not be a psychic force nor a passion of the spirit. What turns Eros into charity is reason, recollection, comparison, justice. The great tragedy of Eros is its blindness: remove the blindness produced by a too narrow and intense light, remove the bandage that turned vision into dreams, and Eros is charity itself: the pursuit of all Good, guided by all knowledge.

It is natural Eros enlightened.

Now sympathy with all good and attention to all knowledge are not possible to an animal psyche in its physical action; they enter the field only as ideals of the spirit, evoked by the psyche in the act of becoming sensitive to *some* sympathy and to *some* knowledge. Correcting a first impulse in consequence, the psyche creates the principle of a rational conscience or of universal justice. The universality of both sympathy and knowledge is posited initially but never attained in act; yet charity (as also science) lives in the light of that ideal. Truth far outruns actual knowledge, or any experience possible to any individual or any species of living beings; and charity far outruns any actual code of politics or morality. Charity extends to all animals and, as the Indians tell us, to all gods, whatever gods there may be; because existence of every type involves difficulty and imperfection, defeat, and essential impermanence, so that everywhere existence deserves compassion and demands transmutation into eternal terms. This the spirit performs instinctively, wherever it can, clearing the gold everywhere from the dross, and laying it up for an eternal treasure.

How is this possible? How shall we be united, even in spirit, with a good that is absent, how recognize a truth inexpressible in our language, or be at peace with a power that is perhaps destroying us? There is a way: it is prayer. Prayer seems sheer foolishness to the world, and rather a puzzle to the materially pious. Why pray, an indoctrinated child may ask, when God loves us, when he knows everything, and when he has already decided what he will do? And the only answer might seem to be the one given in my first Spanish catechism to any hard question: "The Church has doctors that will know how to explain it." We may smile; but in this

Union with all good is possible only in prayer.

case the explanation is really at hand if, whether doctors or not, we can distinguish the spirit from the psyche, or in Christian language, the other world from this world. In this world, or for the psyche, prayer is an instrumentality, and it could not be efficacious except magically if incantations, or the unspoken desires of the heart, could compel the powers of nature to obey our commands. This is what superstition expects and asserts, even in the most modern psychology. But for a spiritual religion the idea of compelling God or compelling matter, by magic words or by tears, to do as we wish, is sacrilegious. Magic does not begin to be prayer until it leaves the issue in God's hands, and reconciles itself beforehand to a denial of the need or the hope expressed. It is not expressed for the preposterous purpose of changing the will of God, or causing nature to revise the contingency of things, which seen from within is freedom and seen from above is fate. It flows out spontaneously from the fullness of the heart, in confession, in reflection, in prophetic vistas, in resigned and transmuting union with the truth and with a different infinite Good at first hidden from the eyes.

In his life-long prayer the reflective man need not be especially inclined to address petitions to heaven; rational prayer is not a means but an end. Petitions **Double interpretation of the divine will.** enter into prayer inevitably, because its language is a social language; and the spirit has a direction in which it wishes to move, so that it lives in a perpetual alternative between *I would* and *I would not*. It therefore can hardly conceive anything without gladness or aversion; and this vital bias comes to clearness, as all things come to clearness, in prayer. Yet in prayer all these wishes and sorrows are uttered in the felt presence of omnificent power and eternal truth; so that all preferences are, as it were; suspended and neutralized by the sense of dependence and by the virtual acceptance of the perhaps contrary fact. The very expression *Thy will be done* which breathes resignation also defines a hope. The will of God on the one hand means whatsoever happens; on the other hand it means that which ought to happen. In the latter sense it seems as yet not to be done on earth as it is in heaven; and the Kingdom of God seems not yet to have come. But this postponement too must be according to God's will in the first sense; and if it were not we should not implore him to shorten the interval and to deliver us from evil. If the will of God be not conceived as omnificent (that being too pantheistic for a political religion) and if events are determined in part by the free-will of other agents, the ultimate union to be attained in prayer would not be union with God, but with the entire moral society of the universe. With this totality we should have to settle our ultimate accounts, dynamic and ideal, since it would be this conjunction of free agencies, with our own included, that would determine the total destiny and truth of things. A moral theism, in denying that God is omnificent, would still have left omnificence the ultimate court of appeal; and this court would not be composed merely of the sundry free agents visible within it, but also and most importantly of the manner and time of their conjunction, and its effects. Now these conjunctions and effects of various free wills are contingent to any one of them and a primary fatality for them all; yet these unintended conjunctions and results are conceived in orthodox theology to have been foreseen and accepted by God at the creation of the world; so that his will seems to be double. As the designer and ultimate sanction of destiny, God wills whatsoever happens; but as lawgiver, merciful saviour, and moral judge, he wills us, for instance, to do not those things which we do but those which we ought to have done; so that his moral and redeeming will is only one strand in his total handiwork.

But the language of prayer should not be pressed as if, when we are living the life of spirit in its full freedom and transcendence, we were still bargaining and plotting in a social and diplomatic world. In expressing our needs and our sorrows we do not ask ourselves whether we are calling on the Almighty to will what he does not will, or whether we are calling on ourselves to contradict our moral aspirations and to think our evil good. We are probably doing neither. We are recollecting, digesting, purifying our conscience. Essentially, we are addressing nobody; the names and forms of the gods are as mutable as our necessities. Even when we are expressing a wish, we are doing so in the face of the truth, or of fate impersonally, considering how excellent it would be if fortune came to our assistance. We pray as spontaneously as we curse, and cry *Would to God!* without any theory of divine government. The same exclamation, *iojalá!* is even more familiar in Spain, meaning *May Allah will it!* If the Moslems, the most prayerful and most manly of men, sometimes abstained from petitions as irreverent, they could not abstain from desire; and their most unfeigned prayer was not to God, but concerning God. They could not suppress the feeling how beautiful the beautiful would be, if it came true. And among us now there are good people who pray that there may be a God to pray to.

The language of prayer is poetical.

Moreover, sincere prayer need not affect that hushed tone and demure attitude which we associate with religious devotion in modern times. The spirit may often be sorrowful, but when it thinks, when it dominates, it cannot be afraid. Prayer is essentially *oratio,* the eloquence of destiny; it contains the whole free comment, lament, and jubilation of the spirit, challenging its fate: a continual contrite reconsideration of all things, for which memory and hope supply the materials; so that prayer, as a sincere spirit may utter it, abounds in regrets, praises, aspirations, laughter, and curses, but all transposed from the plane of action to that of reflection and prophecy. Omnificent power and eternal truth mightily sustain this contemplation, rendering it, in so far as it conforms to them, victorious and full of light. Action is not excluded, as it is not in the drama. Prayer may easily glow with an assurance of the direction in which omnificent power, perhaps through our own agency, is carrying the world. We may be fighting with the big battalions, or even leading them; yet in the midst of action that which is proper to spirit is only observation, wonder, comparison, judgment. What has happened, what is happening, and what is bound to happen fall into a dramatic vista, which the prophet or psalmist develops eloquently in his prayer; and he judges nothing and promises himself nothing except as the agent and messenger of God.

Need not be timorous or cringing.

Thus, strange as it may sound to the rationalist who thinks prayer ridiculous, the only perfectly rational form of life for a spirit that has attained self-knowledge is the life of prayer.

To this we must come morally in the end, accepting all inevitable evils for the sake of the good still possible; but there is a partial union that the spirit may reach

Transition to laughter. vitally at any moment, as in laughter. Here there is no acceptance of ultimates, only merriment at present absurdities and deceptions. The Olympians did not pray to Fate, they did not *care* enough for that; but being free and happy, they laughed at existence.

There are moments in childhood when spirit breaks through in a clear triumph. Children laugh, they laugh easily, whole-heartedly, at all sorts of things.

The pure laughter of children and the impure. In laughter there is a release of tensions, as in play; but the tensions released in play are vital only, and inarticulate, while laughter is provoked by release from little obsessions about things already familiar. Things and persons are imposing objects to a child; they seem stolidly committed to be and to remain themselves; but they grow more engaging when they change, and still more when they make faces and pretend not to be what they are. Yet the circle of their tricks and of their stories is soon run, and they become prosaic. In things and persons this commitment to remain as they were may make their individuality and force, but for the spirit it is a restriction. In reality that solemnity and dullness in things and persons is a false pretence. Things are not the essences they put forward; they are configurations of a matter that has indefinite potentialities, just as the spirit has. Any day some unforeseen accident will disclose their inside, or their miscalculation of their powers. The gods have always been laughing at them, and now the spirit in us may laugh too. Even in the silliest fun, when a word meant in one sense is taken in another, there is some release from a false restriction, a little flight from one perch to another; but a pun disappoints if it merely drops us at another chance station. Had it been true wit, it would have kept us on the wing.

Laughter loses this innocence when children lose theirs and become rancorous. In their boasts and jeers we see the difference. These grimaces of egotism are forced, cruel, essentially unhappy. Pure laughter is not malicious, not scornful; it is not a triumph of one self over another, but of the spirit over all selves. It is a joyous form of union with our defeats, in which the spirit is victorious. The bubble once pricked, everybody stands on homelier and firmer ground. In passing, there is exultation at having rung the dirge of something unreal. This pleasure is dear to children, even if a little shrill. They, poor creatures, are being cheated so regularly by their elders, by one another, and by their own fancies, that it is sweet to turn the tables for once and to mock the solemn fools in return. But the enlightenment of children is apt to be a fresh delusion, destined to end not in laughter, but in tears; and tears are not enlightening. They water the roots of passion in the psyche and pile up the fruits of Karma for the world. It is laughter that liberates once for all from error, without taking a new pledge. It therefore unites us freely with whatsoever may truly deserve our troth. Laughter rings the recess-bell in school hours; and then perhaps some ugly little seeds of learning, sown in us against our will, spring up beautiful, free and unrecognized in the playground of the mind.

In after years laughter becomes bitter; we have laughed enough to no purpose and can no longer laugh merrily at the old comedy of things. One half of us has despaired and smiles sadly at the other half for not having been able to do so. Meantime, at all ages, laughter can sink into ribaldry and become the by-play of vice, when vice throws off the mask, or wins a trick against its demure enemies. But cynicism is not itself inwardly free; its professed wit (as in the Roman satirists) is not very witty, being tarnished sometimes by savage zeal and sometimes by a base relish for scandal. Nevertheless true merriment may anywhere break in unofficially at the shams of vice as at those of virtue, lifting us out of both to the happy level of understanding.

The seamy side of cynicism.

Sometimes, however, this music changes its stops, and grows solemn. Laughter, for all its innocent spontaneity, is too bodily an affection to be wholly satisfying. It lapses sadly into a blank; the next thing is irrelevant and mutes the impulse. When the elevation can be sustained on a wider view, we no longer laugh, but grow speculative, commemorative, even liturgical. The catharsis found in tragedy is only a solemn universalized form of the solution that unravels some comic knot, and leaves us, for a moment, contented with the world. Elegy also leaves us content, not with some gain but with all losses. The *bourgeois* endeavours to explain his love of scandal, of reported crimes, horrors, and ruin, by throwing pleasing considerations into the balance, such as his own safety, or the incidental merits of the report, diction, images, or moral lessons. But this is all beside the point. The nature of spirit and the divine allegiances of spirit have not been discerned. Why is the diction poetical or the imagery sublime or the moral edifying? Because in those intuitions the spirit triumphs over the triumphs of limitation, error, and death. It is not a question of sugaring the pill, but of drinking the fatal cup to the dregs, and being reborn into another life. We should be only lying to ourselves if we pretended that troubles had ceased or that death was not ultimate; but by being ultimate death frames all troubles in, completes the picture, removes it to the plane of historic accidents, and renders it an object fit for intuition to rest in. *Memento mori* may suggest only worms and ghastly corruption; but we might say just as well, *Memento vixisse,* remember that you will have lived. Such is the eternity intrinsically native to spirit and visible from each of its moments, be they few or many. The judgment then passed on the spectacle may be favourable or unfavourable; but it is always a sublime judgment, a true last judgment. David and the Sibyl sing for ever of the Day of Wrath and of the world sunk in ashes, and they are deeply happy.

The victory of mind.

Spirit could never *see* the truth or conceive it in an actual thought if spirit were not a function of life; and the intuition of eternity must always be a passing or repeated intuition. Now life is a trope in matter, proper to an organism that can restore and reproduce itself. Such life cannot help being precarious. It is inwardly continuous with material processes that outrun it, so that some of its developments will be disruptive and contrary to one another. Life may be killed by life, as it may be stifled by lifeless forces. Therefore the good that a liberated spirit may embrace cannot be the truth, but at best some conception of the truth. This will be more than the truth, in being living and emotional and having an internal movement from

Union not with unvarnished truth.

potentiality to act; and it will be immensely less than the truth in being always partial, intermittent, and subjectively directed. For it is life, raised to the scintillating light of spirit, that notices this rather than that, sets problems, and finds solutions, which are privately exciting scents followed to ends privately gratifying; whereas the truth displays the whole eternal labyrinth of real relations through which question and answer miss their way a thousand times, for once that they find it.

The triumph that inwardly raises spirit to its height is intuition, not knowledge; for when fact and truth have to be regarded, spirit has mortgaged its freedom, and is as often depressed as exalted. Therefore before the truth, or behind it, and intercepting knowledge in a thousand ways, arises a ghost of that which is not but might have been: something better than the truth, or worse than the truth, and evoked by fear of what the truth may be. And this play of heated imagination, which the truth if it could speak might call impertinent, flows from the sources of spirit more directly, and prophesies the Good more truly, than knowledge could ever do. The function of such free intuition is by no means superseded by eventual knowledge; it persists to enlighten the spirit morally about the truth that may have enlightened it intellectually. Truth is contingent; but spirit, being addressed to essence, can rest only in what is necessary: in the form that a form has, and in the inevitable relation of that form to all others. More deeply, therefore, than with the truth, spirit is concerned with conceiving, loving, or hating what might have been true. Spirit speaks not for the truth or for the intellect alone by which truth is discovered, but speaks for all life, in so far as life has been perfected and harmonized. Even the intellect is an exercise of this spontaneous or poetic faculty that rebels against the intellect; because the categories of the intellect are variable and vital, like those of language, and knowledge, like any other art, trembles between a good and an evil fate.

The value of knowledge is moral.

The fine arts and the traditional religions are vast instruments in the realm of matter, that seem to serve the spirit directly, apart from utility or truth; yet even they carry an immense load of impedimenta. All the technical, scientific, historical, social, local, and temporal side of art and religion, that absorbs so much blood and ink, has nothing to say to the spirit about the Good. At best, the ground may be thereby cleared for a free spiritual life, which will begin where those distractions end. I do not mean where they end historically, for they can never end while life in this world continues. I mean where they culminate morally and provisionally and yield their spiritual fruits. These fruits are gathered in moments of insight, recollection, and prayer. They are not probably novel fruits historically, but they are always fresh and spontaneous for the spirit that develops them. They are not discoveries of facts in another world, such as religious dogmas seem to a simple mind to report, or such as the arts of fiction add to common reality as it were in a dream. We are not divorced from the facts of this world in order to be subjected to the facts of another world, expected to be better: that is an illusion of the animal Will, unteachable and bent on trying its luck for the second time. We are divorced by

So is the value of imagination.

a revelation about the old and familiar facts, and remarried to them by a new charity that understand their hidden virtues and forgives their vices; a revelation about our own lives and affections transfiguring them in a superhuman light that robs us of ourselves and of our world, only to return our world and ourselves to us drenched in a truer Lethe, not of forgetfulness but of eternity.

Might not the union to which we aspire be a union with other spirits? Might there not be a supreme spirit, or perfect form of spiritual life, to which all spirits were inwardly directed? At bottom, this suggestion introduces nothing new: if any spirit inwardly aspired to a specific form of life, that form of life would be its good; and if all spirits aspired to the same form of life, that form of life would be the Good, absolute because universally relative. A supreme spirit that should actualize that ideal, as for instance by being omniscient, would possess the Good; and all lovers of the Good would be united with him morally, but not existentially, since the other spirits that aspired to omniscience without possessing it would *ipso facto* not be that supreme spirit itself, and could embrace that good only in prayer. If, on the other hand, we conceive the supreme spirit not as simply actualizing the good pursued by each spirit, but as a power with which all must reckon, union with the supreme spirit could never be wholly spiritual but would remain in some measure political, and such as pious souls without spiritual insight seek to establish in their religion. In seeking union with any other spirit we are therefore seeking either the Good, in that this other spirit realizes the perfection to which we are inwardly addressed; or else we are seeking such conformity with power and with truth as is necessary to the attainment of our proper good.

> **Union with other spirits only incidental.**

So the matter seems to end, if we take spirits existentially, and conceive union with them materially, as union in a tug-of-war. But a tug-of-war, and social union generally, does produce spiritual union; not because the spirits pull, as an absurd moral materialism supposes, but because when bodies pull well together, and psyches are akin, spirits for the time being become unanimous. Each has the very purpose, the very hope, that animates each of the others; and this actual spiritual unison is not unconscious. Spirit is divided into spirits by its organs, and into intuitions by its occasions; but we have seen that spiritually it is homogeneous and everywhere transcendental and potentially infinite. When, therefore, in two souls it thinks the same thought or sees the same fact, while the intuitions remain two, their object is identical: else we could never think twice of the same thing privately, or ever think of the same thing together. Yet we know that we do so, because we are deeply aware of our animal separateness and cohabitation. The presence of the friend or enemy resets the whole soul, and there is nothing of which we are more quickly conscious than of thinking alike or of thinking differently. This feeling often leads to rash alliances in the world, rash because real cooperation does not depend on spiritual union but on confluence of functions and interests, often more harmonious and cooperative for being diverse: and the *spes animi credula mutui*, in this world, is an *ignis fatuus*. Yet not so in the other world, in the realm of spirit; for there we are not looking for fidelity or active support or common

> **Spirits can be united only by thinking alike.**

ascendancy over opinion, but for the miraculous rhyming of mind with mind, when a thought, we know not whence or why, re-echoes our thought, confirms and clarifies it, setting it apart from the flux of irrevocable sensation. This spiritual bond is enough: the occasions when it is discovered may or may not recur; the happiness lies in the sense of an intuition once shared, a thought once anchored and become domiciled in history. Then the clearness of the light that had once shone upon us ceases to seem barren: as if a star, burning alone, had news of another star alive with the same fire.

Such unanimity would be a fact in the realm of truth prior to being discovered: and when the discovery brought a sense of spiritual fellowship, the comfort of this added intuition would not make union less spiritual. For we suppose material contact to be absent or impossible, as when our unknown friend is dead or not yet born or perhaps non-human; and what we gain is only fellowship in worship, reduplicating the light that falls, within each of us, upon the realm of ideas. The repetition of insights, though it may fortify an uncertain mind, is not spiritually important, and each angel, according to St. Thomas Aquinas, is the only individual of his species. In fact, the consideration of instances of spirit as events in nature is external to their spiritual import. Their occasions distribute them through physical space and time; but internally, though they are living acts, and in that sense events, they are distributed only by the relations of their subject-matter and individuated only by the ideas that they light up. Intellectually, two exactly similar intuitions make but one idea, being intuitions of the same essence. The multitude of witnesses, therefore, though it has animal weight, adds nothing to the truth or beauty of any revelation. It adds nothing to the happiness of pure life in the spirit.

That no spirit can absorb any other is evident, since spirit (as I use the word) is an act, not a transferable or transformable substance. Therefore any spiritual union actually experienced is necessarily specious and a pure datum of intuition. Not that a real union between spirits may not exist, in that separate minds may be unanimous; but this unanimity would be a fact external to their experience of it, a truth about them, which they might conceive and credit, but which could not in itself be a condition or ecstasy attained by either of them. Yet the union that mystics speak of seems to be emphatically a state into which they pass, internal, certain, and overwhelmingly actual. It has the surprising and all-solving character of a datum: and the character of a datum, by definition, is exactly the same whether it happens to be true or merely imaginary. Therefore the only spiritual union that can be certain, obvious, and intrinsically blissful, must be not a union between two spirits but the unity of a spirit within itself.

Actual union an experience of inner unity.

This conclusion is a corollary from the general critical principle that nothing given exists. That which certainly exists in such a case is only the intuition of that datum, not the datum in its own specious field, which is that of essence. So mystic union resides in intuition; it is not a union of objects or with objects, but a synthesis reached in life and expressed in a given quality of feeling. This is a feeling of union and bliss; but

It is an essence given, not a fact discovered.

the given union does not exist (it would abolish the universe if it did), only the feeling of union exists; and if the bliss exists for a moment (not without a certain deceptiveness as to its absolute volume and finality) this is only because, in the case of inarticulate feelings, we give the same name to the intuition and to the quality revealed to that intuition. The feeling of bliss exists; the bliss, if taken for a secret reality revealed or for the truth of the universe, certainly does not exist. For the world continues to be just as divided, just as obscure, and just as little blissful as it was before.

Spiritual union with the Good does not, then, alter the general facts or discover any general truth. It is a new dawn within: where the sky was clouded, it is clear, namely, in the mind. The currents that confused and abolished one another before join now in one harmonious deliverance with an all-solving force. And we must not infer that there must be ignorance of the world or a pious monotony involved in this spiritual symphony. On the contrary, the whole torrent and violence of things swells within it and exalts it. There is nothing too painful or too audacious to be included, only it cannot be included as it would exist outside in separation and wilful blindness. The union into which it now enters transmutes it, and is a fact in another realm of being, a creation of the witnessing and recording spirit. Experience cannot contain bodily any of its posited objects, or even its own past, in its past existence; it can contain only the thought of them. It obviously cannot make identical the contradictory beliefs and desires afloat in the universe; but it can compose, in thought, a single drama out of their conflict, where the spectacle of their folly turns into wisdom, and their ruin into salvation.

There might seem to be æsthetic cruelty and intellectual selfishness in such an enjoyment of evil at a speculative distance; and this would indeed be the case, if spirit were a power and either produced or did not wish to abolish the horrors of this world, in order to gloat on them from a private heaven. But spirit has no power; and the Will that supports and evokes spirit (and exerts power to that extent) is entirely secondary and sympathetic, being the Will to understand all Will, and to love all the goods that Will anywhere aspires to create. Spirit therefore would not be expressing its own Will if it condoned any evil or was dead to any good; but its nature forbids it to *repeat* within itself the efforts, sufferings, or pleasures that it understands; for it could not then understand or transcend them. Such repetition would be igno-minious, and would reduce spirit again to utter captivity, while its vocation is precisely dominion, spiritual dominion, without distraction, responsibility, or power. Not, however, without joy, such as the full exercise of Will necessarily brings when it is conscious.

Is spiritual happiness selfish?

Thus it is at once a sad, a comic and a glorious spectacle that existence pres-ents to spirit. Spirit would never have *commanded* this performance, like a Nero, if that had been within its power; it understands and feels the inwardness of the matter far too well for that. Yet it watches and records the whole with avidity, though not without tears. How far this liberation of spirit from all it finds afoot differs from selfishness appears in this: that the evils spirit transcends are its own sufferings, since no catastrophe in nature would involve any evil if nature had remained unconscious. Spirit captive has endured whatsoever spirit free may turn into glowing tragedies; and it would contradict its own Will if it did not rejoice in its final freedom. Yet even this tragic wisdom and tearful rapture are imposed on the spirit by a power above it. Had it the choice, perhaps it would renounce this victory also, and humbly prefer silence and peace; but choosing is not its office; it cannot exist before it exists and decide whether or not to bring itself into existence; and if it thinks it can kill itself, that is a psychic illusion, for it cannot prevent its rebirth. Nor is it asked to decide how much is worth enduring in order that something may be enjoyed.

Accepting that which is offered as, be it pious or rebellious, spirit cannot help doing, it may distinguish the direction in which its Good lies. It lies in the direction of harmony; harmony between the Will and its fortunes, and harmony within the subject-matter open to apprehension. A world without evil in it, that is, without contradiction in the Wills animating the various parts, would be better than a world in conflict. And if this seems to wash the field of experience somewhat too clean, and to diminish too much the risks and excitements of living, this feeling must be pronounced vicious, and a remnant of perfectly mad cruelty and masochism. There are creatures that might, for a moment, find nothing interesting to do, if evils ceased to torment them; yet if they had eyes and hands they might soon find work without torment and images without stain. The thunder of chaos receding would render audible "the music of the spheres": the life of a universe where the Good was not posited but realized.

Evil, though it may be transmuted in reflection, is not thereby rendered desirable.

If we imagine this harmony hypostasized into an actual intuition, we conceive the mind of God in its omniscience and glory. It is therefore perfectly legitimate to say that the union craved is union with God, and that when we have experience of such union we are merged in God indistinguishably and feel that we become God. Yet this can be true only of the essence that we have hypostasized into a divine person; and nothing proves that such a God exists or that we have been really united with him, or ceased to be our separate physical selves. On the contrary, if a true union of this kind is to take place between two existing spirits, it must be more than the experience of union, and God must be more than ourselves thinking we have become God. Our experience must be derived from its object and God must be a power infusing that experience into us by an act of grace, as is evidently the case in human love or mutual understanding. There would be no union and no society if our friends, were all personages in our own novels; instead of being united with others we should only be deploying ourselves. This inner dialogue is indeed what the life of spirit terminates in at any given point or in any given person: it is all that *experience* can contain. Yet intelligence, which is the cream of experience, transcends experience by revealing to it its own secondary nature, and the existence of its thousand causes and companions; and union with these ambient realities, harmony between these free and independent facts, makes the surprise and the joy of friendship.

If the Good were hypostasized the union with it could be only political.

Here lies the human advantage that popular positive religion has over mystical insight: it brings us into communion with the gods, and socializes our inner comforts and aspiration by ascribing them to friendly intercessions and divine favours. The myth is deeply true and salutary. We are not self-created spirits, but everything, includ- ing our best inspirations, comes to us from beyond ourselves, from the primeval fountains of matter. But the *dramatis personæ* of popular religion are fabulous and grow more and more novelesque as we make them more and more human. Intercourse with these invisible persons is not, even in fancy, an ideal union between spirits, but only social intercourse between psychic agents interacting under common conditions in a natural world. Even miracles, when they are admitted, obey the proprieties and conventions of some divine economy. Rather than the Good hypostasized, God now seems a particular monarch against whom we might rebel or to whom we might swear allegiance. His existence becomes a question of cosmology and political history, to be established by rational evidence.

> **Advantage and disadvantage of religious impersonations.**

The point would be important morally, inasmuch as, being a natural psyche with a Will shown in sporadic action, an existing deity might greatly influence the fortunes of other souls. He might be a great friend to some, but others would surely find him an enemy, because action in a particular world cannot possibly pursue or secure all particular goods, and the lovers of the goods sacrificed would cry to heaven against God for ven- geance. "Heaven" would there signify all Good, unrealizable at any point in an existing world but inviolate in its essential authority and goodness. "God", on the other hand, would signify the power domi- nant over us for the time being. Job felt the conflict between these two claims to allegiance, that of the Good and that of the Lord; and the Whirlwind enforced the claims of power with a deafening eloquence, utterly unconvincing to the spirit. Many a pagan god might be blameless and perfect, and might point with pride to his mighty works, or even, like Apollo and the Muses, to his inspir- ing or healing influence. He might, in a sense, be holy, in that he realized his chosen good absolutely, and remained steadfast, whatever monstrous growths chaos might vomit around him. But before a god of power could speak persua- sively to the spirit he would need in his own person to be spiritual and religious. He would need to be inspired by a perfect understanding and love of all goods. In his action, however powerful he might be, he could never bring all these goods at once into existence. Probably, as no power can assure itself against the intru- sion of some other power, he would be incapable of bringing even some goods into existence in perfect order and uncontaminated; so that his choice of the greatest possible good at each moment would really be a choice of the least of evils. To such a patient and merciful power spirit might well cry, *Though thou slay me, yet will I trust in thee;* and there would be a spiritual union possible with the antecedent Will of God, addressed to universal Good, as well as political submis- sion and piety towards his consequent Will, determining actual events.

> **In society the greatest good is only the least of evils.**

Essentially, however, it is not with the gods of popular religion that spiritual union is possible: they are not themselves at peace with mankind, with one another, or with the universe. Mystics are normally believers in the orthodoxy of their day, not being curious about facts nor thinking opinion very important; yet

Without denying the gods, spirit looks to union within itself.

they cannot help piercing the reigning myths, not critically but interpretatively, and reaching truths about the spiritual life at once more abstruse than traditional dogmas and more intimate. Why does the mystic keep his vigils and fasts, if not to escape from subjection to things external, and in the first place from the cravings and illusions of his individual self, the most accidental of seats for the spirit and, as he feels, the most unworthy? It would be a sorry failure to relapse in the end into the worship of earthly prosperity or disputatious learning, or into subjection to new accidental passions and hypnotic powers; and what else are the benefits proposed by popular religions? Paradises, as the Indians know, are fit rewards for active virtue, temporal rewards for occasional good conduct; but paradises are but stepping-stones for the spirit; and what does it matter whether the stepping-stone be a lump of gold or of granite, if only the foot neither slips nor sticks there, but leaps easily to safety and freedom? And this safety and freedom cannot be found in union with any existing being. If we say it is union with Brahma we must understand by Brahma pure spirit present in all its instances, not any one instance, however extraordinary; and if in order to avoid mythology we speak rather of Nirvana, we must understand by this no passive lapse from existence but a moral victory over it, occasionally possible, though never physically final. What is suspended is not existence but ignorance, and what is gained is not indifference but equilibrium.

That spirit should have its centre in itself, wherever and whenever it may exist, so that all its adventures must be ideal and all its symbols internal and specious,

Spirit always a consummation, never a finality.

follows from its transcendental nature. This nature was clearly if inadequately expressed by Aristotle when he called it *intellect in act;* an act being a spontaneous, transitional, momentary exercise of life, and intellect being such an act in an animal psyche that has become perfectly cognitive and conscious. But intellect is only the side of spirit that is addressed to knowledge and system; and life may be perfectly actualized also in feeling and in imagination. Everywhere, however, this actuality will be conscious light, the dawn of attention making something present: so that spirit can neither escape from itself nor be confined to any given object or sentiment. For these are present only in act, by being felt or conceived; and they have no hold on spirit, to prevent it from living on, and being differently active. That which can hold spirit down to steady objects and fixed categories is only the power of matter, which also elicits spirit itself; and the healthy limitations of the psyche give to each special spirit its special circle of sane thoughts. But an act is necessarily self-limited and self-delivered: what it does or thinks it can never undo or unthink; and spirit may shine again in another act, similar or dissimilar to the last, according to psychic and physical occasions.

The idea of final union with anything specific, even with omniscience or with pure Being, therefore contradicts the very nature of spirit. In one sense there is always union with so much as the spirit has clearly felt or conceived, since it is the same act that makes the actuality of spirit and the actuality of the feeling or thought. But in another sense, there is never union, never completion or finality, since an absorbed datum dies with the actual absorption in it; and no act, dying as it must in the process of living, can abolish or prevent a further act.

A sustained act would be perfectly possible if there were, as Aristotle supposed, perfectly sustained celestial motions. But everlasting sameness is something non-natural and a fabulous materialization of ideal eternity. Eternity belongs properly only to essences and truths, and may be extended by assimilation to intuitions in their deliverance, but never in their existence. In their existence intuitions are events: they arise **The *nunc stans* how possible.** and vanish; and in the interval they illustrate a *nunc stans,* since they fill a natural moment and actualize some essence or truth, in itself eternal. But the duration of such an actual *nunc stans* is not to be measured astronomically in fractions of a second or in light-years. It is a unit, however long sustained or however fugitive, in the realm of spirit, spiritually individuated by its quality and deliverance, not by its station (which it borrows from its organ) in physical time and space. For although each intuition has a date and a home in the physical world, if viewed from the outside or historically, when viewed from within each always stands in the middle of the temporal and spatial universe, introducing a moral centre into a flux where probably no centre exists physically.

These moral centres are as many as they happen to be; so that the realm of spirit is intrinsically a democracy (as the realm of truth is not), spirit being everywhere sovereign in its own right. This sovereignty, however, is only spiritual, as human equality, when not a sham, is only spiritual; and the **The galaxy of spirit.** sovereignty of each at home expressly invites and rejoices in the home sovereignty of all the others. For spirit exists; it is not a tyrannical idea, to be imposed on spirit; and existence is intrinsically dispersed, tireless, inexhaustible in its youth, ready to die and to be reborn, to discover and to rediscover, to sing sometimes an old song and sometimes a new one. The only totality or finality is ideal, it is the truth; but no view of the truth can be final in the life of spirit. Even omniscience, if it were possible, would not be final there; it would be a single instance of spirit, a supremely complex intuition. Simpler and partly ignorant intuitions would remain possible, and perhaps better. The truth that is requisite for the honour and peace of spirit is not omniscience but the absence of delusions; and this, where humility exists, does not demand infinite information. So it happens also when a man surveys his personal history. There is no contribution of experience that need be excluded from recollection, but the new total at each moment forms a new object, caught in a new intuition. The various perspectives have arisen in the same world; they contain errors and contradictions if turned into absolute dogmas and made to debate every point face to face, as if they stood or ought to stand in one another's shoes; but seen in their origin and causes, they are always complementary, explicable naturally, and unified objectively in the realm of truth. Yet actually, in the realm of spirit, every intuition is a flying spark, private, momentary, and saved from total death only by its ideal bonds and its inner vision of eternity. Each spark, by the radiation of its light, has revealed for a moment one region of heaven; and in that heaven it is united, with its friends by mutual confirmation, with its enemies by the common risks of existence and a common appeal to the jurisdiction of fact. Intent on the same reality, material or ideal, and spreading over different parts of it, all intuitions, the greatest with the least, form the galaxy of spirit.

This is an unwitting conspiracy of free natural beings, each springing from its own seed in its own country, and growing into whatsoever may flow from the potentialities of its substance and fortunes. The union is a fact in the realm of truth: the fact that many spirits or instances of spirit exist in the same universe, partly similar, partly dissimilar, sometimes unanimous, sometimes complementary in their insights. I say again, complementary rather than contradictory; because although judgments may be contradictory if expressed in words they become supplementary phases in the history of judgment, when this history is surveyed as a whole. They may be judgments about different objects; or in regard to the same object, they may express different fractions of the relations between that object and different souls. The Babel is but the totality of languages; and if each seems gibberish to the others, there is always some analogy in their logics, for they are languages, and some identity in their object, since they exist in the same world. So the galaxy of spirits has a natural orderliness in its moral confusion, and each spirit, in its solitude, a great kinship to all the others. Even if some or all, at the Last Judgment, should discover this spiritual society, which they had always composed without knowing it, no mind would become another mind, or like another; for even their common discovery of their relations would present these relations, in each case, in a different perspective; and an omniscient mind, in holding all perspectives at once in suspense, would differ enormously from all the other minds held by one perspective exclusively. Were not these personal histories and feelings eternally distinct, they could never orchestrate their celestial symphony.

Thoughts remain individual.

On the other hand, it is not persons in their personal limitations, that can enter into a spiritual union; for the limitations are transcended in being understood, one's own limitations as well as other people's. Persons become translucent, like the souls in Dante's *Paradise,* and what each sees in the others is only that part of the truth which they saw. It is in them that this part became visible, for the truth is not visible to itself; therefore this remains a union of spirits, of thoughts living and thinking each its special thought. But the rest of the man disappears; as in reading a book, the material book is forgotten, and the reader lives in rehearsing the author's thoughts without thinking of the author. At least this happens when the book is interesting and the author was himself lost in his subject; the realm of spirit is not to be entered by literary peacocks, or by bibliophiles that do not read, but hoard their books, pat them, and talk about them. So in communion between spirits, the man or the god is rendered invisible by the light he diffuses, and we are inwardly united only with so much of him as by his gifts or his grace can exist also beyond his person and can become a part of ourselves. For the spirit, therefore, the dead are still living, and the living are present *numina,* like the remembered dead.

Persons become transparent.

This is not to say that the real existence of persons, or that contact or friendship with them, has not a real function, and one prior to the function of ideas. Friends are important for the spirit, as a man's own identity and fortunes are important. Without such special occasions and attachments, spirit would have no foothold in nature and could not exist. Occasions, we have said, distribute spirit among psyches and divide each spirit into intuitions. Yet intuition itself is born out of a synthesis, and the field it opens up embraces, in conception, all that the flux of existence may have diversified and separated. The world was not made for the spirit, nor by the spirit, as the beautiful is; but for this very reason the world and the truth about the world have a tutelary function, and a guiding function, in the life of spirit. They are the gates through which the garden of the beautiful may be safely entered, the walls by which that garden is circumscribed and defended. The first step towards union with the Good is to have settled one's accounts with the world and with the truth. After that, truth and fiction may be entertained together, and the difference between them may be ignored. Yet this licence, which the world takes for incompetence or madness in spiritual men, would really be madness or incompetence if it were not founded on health, on adjustment to universal power, and on a deep ironical allegiance to the truth. When such moral health is presupposed the perspectives of truth and of fiction may be developed together, with no spiritual fear of either, since the agile spirit can digest both.

The nest and the wings.

If union must be unity within the spirit, might we not say finally that the Good is the existence of spirit itself? Not at all. Spirit is evidently a prerequisite to union within the spirit; but spirit is more often distracted than harmonious; and the attainment of harmony depends on many other causes than those that suffice to evoke spirit. The causes and conditions of the Good are not themselves good: else matter and universal Will would be good, and more radically good than spirit, since they are needed to generate it. The Good lies not behind all this movement but before it; it is the end that life proposes to itself when conscious and rational. Each endeavour furnishes spirit, which is by nature sympathetic, with an initial criterion of values; whatsoever helps each flower to grow seems good to the dramatizing spirit, and whatsoever blights it, seems evil. But how shall the relative value of these endeavours be judged? The most considered judgment could only express some other instance of initial Will, a preference as contingent and groundless as those it criticizes. Shall the spirit succumb to this universal egotism and judge that whatsoever in the universe conduces to the free exercise of spirit shall be pronounced good, and whatsoever hinders that exercise shall be pronounced evil?

Spirit not itself the Good.

Such a shamelessly egotistical judgment is in fact implicit in so much of unconscious Will as rushes blindly to create spirit. But the peculiarity of spirit, when once it exists, is not to be blind, and to be eternally ashamed of egotism. Its Will is not to will, but to understand all Will; and so without willing any of the ends that universal Will pursues (not even the Will to create spirit) it sees the beauty of all those ends, including the beauty of its own impartial but enamoured vision. Spirit

Understanding and love must make no claims for themselves.

too is only an incident in the life of nature; the Will to be spiritual can as little be pronounced to be absolutely good as can any other natural impulse; yet like any other natural impulse, when once launched into life, it inevitably becomes a criterion, by which all other things may be judged relatively.

Therefore the spirit, if free to criticize its enemies, is free also to judge its own aspirations tragically or satirically; and the higher flights of wisdom and self-knowledge have always done so. Never, however, when spirit is vigorous and free, can it judge any fate coldly or any aspiration unsympathetically; because to be sympathetic and warm towards all endeavours (though they may know nothing of themselves) is the very essence of spirit; and how then should it not be so towards its own endeavours? Yet this acceptance and pursuit of its specific aims will never be safe or pure until they are qualified by a prior complete renunciation of all illusions about them. The spirit can never be altogether spiritual, or morally other than a caprice of blind Will, until it has traversed the *Dark Night* described by Saint John of the Cross, and adopted his motto: *Nothing, Nothing, Nothing.* It is only on this understanding that all things may be understood without confusion, loved without disgrace, and touched without infection, or that a life of action, for the spirit, can be a life of prayer. Henceforth we are playing a part: we do not become kings because we may wear a crown upon this stage, nor fools because it is set down for us to talk nonsense. We may give commands, when they are in character, without arrogance, follow our fortunes without greed, and declare our affections without fear of disillusion. The disillusion has come already, and the affection flows out notwithstanding, without any claims. We know that the power that creates us and shapes our passions and prompts our acts is the Poet's, and not our own; that our knowledge is but faith moving in the dark, our joy a gift of grace, our immortality a subtle translation of time into eternity, where all that we have missed is ours, and where what we call ours is the least part of ourselves. We are not impatient of injustice. It is not the fate that overtakes us that makes our dignity but the detachment with which we suffer it. All belongs to the necessary passion and death of the spirit, that to-day rides upon an ass into its kingdom, to be crucified to-morrow between two thieves, and on the third day to rise again from the dead.

In the animal psyche the passions follow one another or battle for supremacy, and the distracted spirit runs helter-skelter among them, impressed by the sophistical arguments which each of them offers for itself; but if the psyche grows integrated and rational, its centre, which is the organ of spirit, becomes dominant, and all those eloquent passions begin to be compared and judged, and their probable issue to be foreknown and discounted. The waves will not be stilled, but they will now beat against a rock. And with inner security comes a great inner clearness. We may now become aware of the world to any depth, in any degree of complexity. We shall have reduced our psychic centre to its precise function as a centre; and from this centre, in duly shaded perspectives, the spirit may spread its silent light over all nature and all essence.

Margin notes:
The great witness is the great victim.

Spirit concentrated is clarified.

By so fortifying the spirit we shall not have saved the world; all its titular saviours have left the world much as it was. But we can reconcile ourselves with the world by doing it justice. It is a natural process: why should it have been other than it happens to be? We shall also have reconciled ourselves with our own destiny. Materially, we could not be more than poor animal experiments, lame yet wonderful, defeated yet breaking out in places into a jubilant sympathy with all creation. Spirit may live in its universal affinities, forgiving itself its ignorant errors and childish woes. It could not have suffered if it had not loved, and to love is to have eyes for the beautiful. This privilege is bought at a great price, but spirit speaks for a part of universal Will, for that part which becomes conscious. It is therefore essentially brave, as it is essentially enamoured; and the goal once seen, it cannot count the cost.

Intermittence is intrinsic to life, to feeling, to thought; so are partiality and finitude. Spirit cannot achieve unity or perfection physically; the living flame must dance. It suffices that its light should fall on things steadfast and true, worthy to be discerned and returned to and treasured; so that though spirit be everywhere halting in achievement it may be always perfect in allegiance. Its happiness must always remain volatile, and its union with the Good ideal. This union is achieved not by physical possession or identity, but by intellectual worship, in which spirit, forgetting itself, becomes pure vision and pure love. Then to the spirit that has renounced all things, all things are restored: and having renounced itself also, it cannot resist any inspiration or think evil of any good, but embraces them all in the eternal object of its worship, not as they may have existed in the world in passing and in conflict, but as they lie ideally reconciled in the bosom of the Good, at peace at last with themselves and with one another.

And is united with all things, thinking itself nothing.

IV

Ethics and Politics

Santayana's ethics and politics are grounded in his materialism. This section traces the natural and prerational grounds of moral judgments through ethical reasoning and the desire for universal harmony and then takes up questions of political organization.

Judgments of good and evil are rooted in the prerational preferences of animal life. Such preferences may be excellent in their setting, but they lack understanding and awareness of context. They are modified by chance and expressed in traditional maxims, religious commandments, and ethical intuitions. This prerational morality, even if narrow, is not arbitrary; it expresses a human will formed according to typical human experience. But what is typical for one group is not so for another, hence this prerational or intuitive morality remains partial and provides no means besides force for resolving conflicts between different moralities. Conceiving different moralities is beyond the capacity of prerational morality. To go beyond traditional values requires "appeal to the only real authority, to experience, reason, and human nature in the living man" (*ES*, 421). By drawing on experience and universal sympathy, conscience becomes reason.

Santayana thought that a rational morality, or an organization of impulses under a harmonizing ideal, presupposes perfect self-knowledge; and this he thought impossible to realize. Yet the ideal of a rational morality suggests a universal and practical method of valuing and judging impulses that Santayana characterized as "Rational Ethics." Rational ethics consists in taking any sincere human value judgment and determining the dialectical relations of the judgment. This reveals the underlying values of the person making the judgment and so reveals what really ought to guide the conduct of that person. The method does not impose a predetermined system of values, but rather it overcomes the narrowness of prerational morality by pursuing consistency and completeness in its survey of impulses. Avoiding the torment of contradictory urges, illusions, and fears, the method of reason aims at harmony and so brings happiness.

Post-rational morality arises out of the despair and pessimism of disintegrated societies and a desire for refuge, redemption, or eternal peace. Reason is left behind, not because of prejudice or incoherence as in prerational morality, but rather because of an overwhelming sense of the vanity of everything. Reason is regarded, rightly, as one impulse among many, but post-rational morality seeks a precept to which *all* impulses are subordinate; it seeks universal harmony. Some standard, natural in its origin, is inflated to universal applicability and acquires a supernatural character. In pursuit of universal harmony, reason is cut loose from any determinate goal and loses any practical harmonizing influence; it is no longer an ethical ideal. Santayana regarded prerational morality, rational ethics, and post-rational morality as continuous, but he did not believe them to be successive historical phases.

In the context of an essay on the philosophy of Bertrand Russell, Santayana criticized Russell's "Hypostatic Ethics" and clarified his own understanding of good and bad. Russell claimed that good and bad belong to objects independently of what anyone might think, making them absolute rather than relative qualities. Santayana believed that ethics rested on felt preferences wholly conditioned by the constitution of the valuing animal. To think otherwise, claimed Santayana, made moral reasoning impossible because it eliminated any point of reference for value judgments. Without a criterion of good and bad with actual relevance to life, nothing but force could settle differences among values; but acknowledging the relativity of values would eliminate contempt for opposing views and introduce greater justice into social relations.

When Santayana considered social relations in the political sphere, he concluded that public opinion and 'the public' are conceptual fictions, yet he contended that they indicate something real. The act of a social group, such as a vote or demonstration, might be justified after the fact with an idea called public opinion. This idea has no influence over the group or the individuals, and in fact each individual's idea of public opinion is something personal and private. It is animal sympathy rather than any conscious idea that gives the individual a sense of being caught up by a social movement. And this animal sympathy points to the material conditions of concerted social action.

"Government of the People" is an ambiguous phrase: the "of" may be in the objective genitive indicating that the government governs the people or the "of" may be possessive meaning that the government belongs to the people. The complexity of the government requires specialists, using their expert judgment, to carry out the will of the people. So the will of the people is expressed only in selecting whose judgment to trust. Santayana thought such choices are made as "[w]aves of contagious feeling sweep through the public," and political success then depends on riding those waves by means of eloquence and foresight (*ES,* 465).

Santayana contended that who the 'people' are is determined not according to geography or race, but rather by shared vital interests and common moral heritage. These determinants change through time and fuse with other traditions as a result of migration. But Santayana did not think that everyone needed to belong to one people, and he conceived of various peoples flourishing under a universal government. Such a government would not be like the United Nations but rather a particular government, and this led him to consider the United States as leader of the world. Santayana believed that rational authority depends on a government representing "the material conditions of free life and free action" (*ES,* 471) and would consist in prudent management of the material economy. He thought the American people well qualified to lead because they appeared to him to have an established and widespread character, to be innovative and successful in business and technology, and to be self-interested in the material success of other countries. However, the desire to secure material success through education and training could tempt America to change traditional ways of life and go beyond the dictates of rational control.

In his political speculations, Santayana intended to be neither prescriptive nor predictive, not because he had abandoned reason and moral judgment but rather because he recognized them to be relative to the natural impulses of a society or individual. Hence, his reflections could be only descriptive of the material conditions of government and of the implications in various moral judgments. To impose a form of government determined ahead of time to be absolutely rational and right is to ignore the material world, thought Santayana, because it would ignore the actual natural impulses that make the methods and judgments of reason relevant.

A government that is rational with respect to the natural impulses in society would not impose some idea of the good life, but rather it would clear the way for each society and each individual to discover its particular and proper good. The true good, thought Santayana, lies in imagination and is determined by the inherent organization of the individual. He wrote, "it is generally alien domination that makes anyone mistake his vocation" (ES, 477).

Prerational Morality

Reason in Science. Volume 5 of *The Life of Reason: or, the Phases of Human Progress.* New York: Charles Scribner's Sons; London: Constable and Co. Ltd., 1906, 210–32.

This selection appeared as Chapter VIII of Reason in Science. *Santayana wrote to his publisher that the final volume of* The Life of Reason *"is in many ways the most important" (LGS, 1:267) and later asked for more time to finish it, explaining that, "I am trying to make clearness doubly clear in volume 5" (LGS, 1:312). In this chapter Santayana examines the nature of morality. Moral judgment is based on the natural intent of the animal. The reason one judges some particular thing good rather than another is not itself moral. Rather it is the result of instinctive tendencies and the material push of nature. Morality is the vigorous, sincere, and non-reflective perception of goods minus any dialectic examination. Such moral judgments are shaped by experience, but they are the result of chance, not of reason or an attempt at harmonizing conflicting intents. Considering the prerational moralities of the Greeks and Hebrews, Santayana observed that Hebraic integrity and devotion would have served better than Greek naturalistic religion and patriotism to further the Greek ideals of reason and harmony. The result could have greatly advanced the Life of Reason.*

When a polyglot person is speaking, foreign words sometimes occur to him, which he at once translates into the language he happens to be using. Somewhat in the same way, when dialectic develops an idea, suggestions for this development may come from the empirical field; yet these suggestions soon shed their externality and their place is taken by some genuine development of the original notion. In constructing, for instance, the essence of a circle, I may have started from a hoop. I may have observed that as the hoop meanders down the path the roundness of it disappears to the eye, being gradually flattened into a straight line, such as the hoop presents when it is rolling directly away from me. I may now frame the idea of a mathematical circle, in which all diameters are precisely equal, in express contrast to the series of ellipses, with very unequal diameters, which the floundering hoop has illustrated in its career. When once, however, the definition of the circle is attained, no watching of hoops is any longer requisite. The ellipse can be generated ideally out of the definition, and would have been generated, like asymptotes and hyperbolas, even if never illustrated in nature at all. Lemmas from a foreign tongue have only served to disclose a great fecundity in the native one, and the legitimate word that the context required has supplanted the casual stranger that may first have ushered it into the mind.

When the idea which dialectic is to elaborate is a moral idea, a purpose touching something in the concrete world, lemmas from experience often play a very large part in the process. Their multitude, with the small shifts in aspiration and

Empirical alloy in dialectic.

esteem which they may suggest to the mind, often obscures the dialectical process altogether. In this case the foreign term is never translated into the native medium; we never make out what ideal connection our conclusion has with our premises, nor in what way the conduct we finally decide upon is to fulfil the purpose with which we began. Reflection merely beats about the bush, and when a sufficient number of prejudices and impulses have been driven from cover, we go home satisfied with our day's ranging, and feeling that we have left no duty unconsidered; and our last bird is our final resolution.

When morality is in this way non-dialectical, casual, impulsive, polyglot, it is what we may call prerational morality. There is indeed reason in it, since every deliberate precept expresses some reflection by which impulses have been compared and modified. But such chance reflection amounts to **Arrested rationality in morals.** moral perception, not to moral science. Reason has not begun to educate her children. This morality is like knowing chairs from tables and things near from distant things, which is hardly what we mean by natural science. On this stage, in the moral world, are the judgments of Mrs. Grundy, the aims of political parties and their maxims, the principles of war, the appreciation of art, the commandments of religious authorities, special revelations of duty to individuals, and all systems of intuitive ethics.

Prerational morality is vigorous because it is sincere. Actual interests, rooted habits, appreciations the opposite of which is inconceivable and contrary to the current use of language, are embodied in special precepts; or they **Its emotional and practical power.** flare up of themselves in impassioned judgments. It is hardly too much to say, indeed, that prerational morality is morality proper. Rational ethics, in comparison, seems a kind of politics or wisdom, while postrational systems are essentially religions. If we thus identify morality with prerational standards, we may agree also that morality is no science in itself, though it may become, with other matters, a subject for the science of anthropology; and Hume, who had never come to close quarters with any rational or postrational ideal, could say with perfect truth that morality was not founded on reason. Instinct is of course not founded on reason, but *vice versa;* and the maxims enforced by tradition or conscience are unmistakably founded on instinct. They might, it is true, become materials for reason, if they were intelligently accepted, compared, and controlled; but such a possibility reverses the partisan and spasmodic methods which Hume and most other professed moralists associate with ethics. Hume's own treatises on morals, it need hardly be said, are pure psychology. It would have seemed to him conceited, perhaps, to inquire what ought really to be done. He limited himself to asking what men tended to think about their doings.

The chief expression of rational ethics which a man in Hume's world would have come upon lay in the Platonic and Aristotelian writings; but these were not then particularly studied nor vitally understood. The chief illustration of postrational morality that could have fallen under his eyes, the Catholic religion, he would never have thought of as a philosophy of life, but merely as a combination of superstition and policy, well adapted to the lying and lascivious habits of

Mediterranean peoples. Under such circumstances ethics could not be thought of as a science; and whatever gradual definition of the ideal, whatever prescription of what ought to be and to be done, found a place in the thoughts of such philosophers formed a part of their politics or religion and not of their reasoned knowledge.

There is, however, a dialectic of the will; and that is the science which, for want of a better name, we must call ethics or moral philosophy. The interweaving of this logic of practice with various natural sciences that have man or society for their theme, leads to much confusion in terminology and in point of view. Is the good, we may ask, what anybody calls good at any moment, or what anybody calls good on reflection, or what all men agree to call good, or what God calls good, no matter what all mankind may think about it? Or is true good something that perhaps nobody calls good nor knows of, something with no other characteristic or relation except that it is simply good?

Moral science is an application of dialectic, not a part of anthropology.

Various questions are involved in such perplexing alternatives; some are physical questions and others dialectical. Why any one values anything at all, or anything in particular, is a question of physics; it asks for the causes of interest, judgment, and desire. To esteem a thing good is to express certain affinities between that thing and the speaker; and if this is done with self-knowledge and with knowledge of the thing, so that the felt affinity is a real one, the judgment is invulnerable and cannot be asked to rescind itself. Thus if a man said hemlock was good to drink, we might say he was mistaken; but if he explained that he meant good to drink in committing suicide, there would be nothing pertinent left to say: for to adduce that to commit suicide is not good would be impertinent. To establish that, we should have to go back and ask him if he valued anything—life, parents, country, knowledge, reputation; and if he said no, and was sincere, our mouths would be effectually stopped—that is, unless we took to declamation. But we might very well turn to the bystanders and explain what sort of blood and training this man possessed, and what had happened among the cells and fibres of his brain to make him reason after that fashion. The causes of morality, good or bad, are physical, seeing that they are causes.

The science of ethics, however, has nothing to do with causes, not in that it need deny or ignore them but in that it is their fruit and begins where they end. Incense rises from burning coals, but it is itself no conflagration, and will produce none. What ethics asks is not why a thing is called good, but whether it is good or not, whether it is right or not so to esteem it. Goodness, in this ideal sense, is not a matter of opinion, but of nature. For intent is at work, life is in active operation, and the question is whether the thing or the situation responds to that intent. So if I ask, Is four really twice two? the answer is not that most people say so, but that, in saying so, I am not misunderstanding myself. To judge whether things are *really* good, intent must be made to speak; and if this intent may itself be judged later, that happens by virtue of other intents comparing the first with their own direction.

Hence good, when once the moral or dialectical attitude has been assumed, means not what is called good but what is so; that is, what *ought* to be called good.

For intent, beneath which there is no moral judgment, sets up its own standard, and ideal science begins on that basis, and cannot go back of it to ask why the obvious good is good at all. Naturally, there is a reason, but not a moral one; for it lies in the physical habit and necessity of things. The reason is simply the propulsive essence of animals and of the universal flux, which renders forms possible but unstable, and either helpful or hurtful to one another. That nature should have this constitution, or intent this direction, is not a good in itself. It is esteemed good or bad as the intent that speaks finds in that situation a support or an obstacle to its ideal. As a matter of fact, nature and the very existence of life cannot be thought wholly evil, since no intent is wholly at war with these its conditions; nor can nature and life be sincerely regarded as wholly good, since no moral intent stops at the facts; nor does the universal flux, which infinitely overflows any actual synthesis, altogether support any intent it may generate.

Philosophers would do a great discourtesy to estimation if they sought to justify it. It is all other acts that need justification by this one. The good greets us initially in every experience and in every object. Remove from anything its share of excellence and you have made it utterly insignificant, irrelevant to human discourse, and unworthy of even theoretic consideration. Value is the principle of perspective in science, **Estimation the soul of philosophy.** no less than of rightness in life. The hierarchy of goods, the architecture of values, is the subject that concerns man most. Wisdom is the first philosophy, both in time and in authority; and to collect facts or to chop logic would be idle and would add no dignity to the mind, unless that mind possessed a clear humanity and could discern what facts and logic are good for and what not. The facts would remain facts and the truths truths; for of course values, accruing on account of animal souls and their affections, cannot possibly create the universe those animals inhabit. But both facts and truths would remain trivial, fit to awaken no pang, no interest, and no rapture. The first philosophers were accordingly sages. They were statesmen and poets who knew the world and cast a speculative glance at the heavens, the better to understand the conditions and limits of human happiness. Before their day, too, wisdom had spoken in proverbs. *It is better,* every adage began: *Better this than that.* Images or symbols, mythical or homely events, of course furnished subjects and provocations for these judgments; but the residuum of all observation was a settled estimation of things, a direction chosen in thought and life because it was better. Such was philosophy in the beginning and such is philosophy still.

To one brought up in a sophisticated society, or in particular under an ethical religion, morality seems at first an external command, a chilling and arbitrary set of requirements and prohibitions which the young heart, if it trusted itself, would not reckon at a penny's worth. Yet while **Moral discriminations are natural and inevitable.** this rebellion is brewing in the secret conclave of the passions, the passions themselves are prescribing a code. They are inventing gallantry and kindness and honour; they are discovering friendship and paternity. With maturity comes the recognition that the authorised precepts of morality were essentially not arbitrary; that they expressed the genuine aims and interests of a practised will; that their alleged alien and super-natural basis (which if real would have deprived them of all moral authority) was but a mythical cover for their forgotten natural springs. Virtue is then seen to be admirable essentially, and not merely by conventional imputation. If traditional morality has much in it that is out of proportion, much that is unintelligent and inert, nevertheless it represents on the whole the verdict of reason. It speaks for a typical human will chastened by a typical human experience.

Gnomic wisdom, however, is notoriously polychrome, and proverbs depend for their truth entirely on the occasion they are applied to. Almost every wise

A choice of proverbs.

saying has an opposite one, no less wise, to balance it; so that a man rich in such lore, like Sancho Panza, can always find a venerable maxim to fortify the view he happens to be taking. In respect to foresight, for instance, we are told, Make hay while the sun shines, A stitch in time saves nine, Honesty is the best policy, Murder will out, Woe unto you, ye hypocrites, Watch and pray, Seek salvation with fear and trembling, and *Respice finem.* But on the same authorities exactly we have opposite maxims, inspired by a feeling that mortal prudence is fallible, that life is shorter than policy, and that only the present is real; for we hear, A bird in the hand is worth two in the bush, *Carpe diem, Ars longa, vita brevis,* Be not righteous overmuch, Enough for the day is the evil thereof, Behold the lilies of the field, Judge not, that ye be not judged, Mind your own business, and It takes all sorts of men to make a world. So when some particularly shocking thing happens one man says, *Cherchez la femme,* and another says, Great is Allah.

That these maxims should be so various and partial is quite intelligible when we consider how they spring up. Every man, in moral reflection, is animated by his own intent; he has something in view which he prizes, he knows not why, and which wears to him the essential and unquestionable character of a good. With this standard before his eyes, he observes easily—for love and hope are extraordi-narily keen-sighted—what in action or in circumstances forwards his purpose and what thwarts it; and at once the maxim comes, very likely in the language of the particular instance before him. Now the interests that speak in a man are differ-ent at different times; and the outer facts or measures which in one case promote that interest may, where other less obvious conditions have changed, altogether defeat it. Hence all sorts of precepts looking to all sorts of results.

Prescriptions of this nature differ enormously in value; for they differ enor-mously in scope. By chance, or through the insensible operation of experience

Their various representative value.

leading up to some outburst of genius, intuitive maxims may be so central, so expressive of ultimate aims, so representative, I mean, of all aims in fusion, that they merely anticipate what moral science would have come to if it had existed. This happens much as in physics ultimate truths may be divined by poets long before they are discovered by investigators; the *vivida vis animi* taking the place of much recorded experience, because much unrecorded experience has secretly fed it. Such, for instance, is the central maxim of Christianity, Love thy neighbour as thyself. On the other hand, what is usual in intuitive codes is a mixture of some elementary precepts, necessary to any society, with others representing local traditions or ancient rites: so Thou shalt not kill, and Thou shalt keep holy the Sabbath day, figure side by side in the Decalogue. When Antigone, in her sublimest exaltation, defies human enactments and appeals to laws which are not of to-day nor yesterday, no man knowing whence they have arisen, she mixes various types of obligation in a most instructive fashion; for a superstitious horror at leaving a body unburied—something decidedly of yesterday—gives poignancy in her mind to natural affection for a brother—something indeed universal, yet having a well-known origin. The passionate assertion of right is here, in consequence, more dramatic than spiritual; and even its dramatic force has suffered somewhat by the change in ruling ideals.

The disarray of intuitive ethics is made painfully clear in the conflicts which it involves when it has fostered two incompatible growths in two centres which lie near enough to each other to come into physical collision. Such ethics has nothing to offer in the presence of discord except an appeal to force and to ultimate physical sanctions. It can instigate, but cannot resolve, the battle of nations and the battle of religions. Precisely the same zeal, the same patriotism, the same readiness for martyrdom fires adherents to rival societies, and fires them especially in view of the fact that the adversary is no less uncompromising and fierce. It might seem idle, if not cruel and malicious, to wish to substitute one historical allegiance for another, when both are equally arbitrary, and the existing one is the more congenial to those born under it; but to feel this aggression to be criminal demands some degree of imagination and justice, and sectaries would not be sectaries if they possessed it.

Conflict of partial moralities.

Truly religious minds, while eager perhaps to extirpate every religion but their own, often rise above national jealousies; for spirituality is universal, whatever churches may be. Similarly politicians often understand very well the religious situation; and of late it has become again the general practice among prudent governments to do as the Romans did in their conquests, and to leave people free to exercise what religion they have, without pestering them with a foreign one. On the other hand the same politicians are the avowed agents of a quite patent iniquity; for what is their ideal? To substitute their own language, commerce, soldiers, and tax-gatherers for the tax-gatherers, soldiers, commerce, and language of their neighbours; and no means is thought illegitimate, be it fraud in policy or bloodshed in war, to secure this absolutely nugatory end. Is not one country as much a country as another? Is it not as dear to its inhabitants? What then is gained by oppressing its genius or by seeking to destroy it altogether?

Here are two flagrant instances where prerational morality defeats the ends of morality. Viewed from within, each religious or national fanaticism stands for a good; but in its outward operation it produces and becomes an evil. It is possible, no doubt, that its agents are really so far apart in nature and ideals that, like men and mosquitoes, they can stand in physical relations only, and if they meet can meet only to poison or to crush one another. More probably, however, humanity in them is no merely nominal essence; it is definable ideally, as essences are defined, by a partially identical function and intent. In that case, by studying their own nature, they could rise above their mutual opposition, and feel that in their fanaticism they were taking too contracted a view of their own souls and were hardly doing justice to themselves when they did such great injustice to others.

How prerational morality may approach the goal, and miss it, is well illustrated in the history of Hellenism. Greek morals may be said to have been

The Greek ideal. inspired by two prerational sentiments, a naturalistic religion and a local patriotism. Could Plato have succeeded in making that religion moral, or Alexander in universalising that patriotism, perhaps Greece might have been saved and we might all be now at a very different level of civilisation. Both Plato and Alexander failed, in spite of the immense and lasting influence of their work; for in both cases the after-effects were spurious, and the new spirit was smothered in the dull substances it strove to vivify.

Greek myth was an exuberant assertion of the rights of life in the universe. Existence could not but be joyful and immortal, if it had once found, in land, sea, or air, a form congruous with that element. Such congruity would render a being stable, efficient, beautiful. He would achieve a perfection grounded in skilful practice and in a thorough rejection of whatever was irrelevant. These things the Greeks called virtue. The gods were perfect models of this kind of excellence; for of course the amours of Zeus and Hermes' trickery were, in their hearty fashion, splendid manifestations of energy. This natural divine virtue carried no sense of responsibility with it, but it could not fail to diffuse benefit because it radiated happiness and beauty. The worshipper, by invoking those braver inhabitants of the cosmos, felt he might more easily attain a corresponding beauty and happiness in his paternal city.

The source of myth had been a genial sympathy with nature. The observer, at ease himself, multiplied ideally the potentialities of his being; but he went farther

Imaginative exuberance and political discipline. in imagining what life might yield abroad, freed from every trammel an necessity, than in deepening his sense of what life was in himself, and of what it ought to be. This moral reflection, absent from mythology, was supplied by politics. The family and the state had a soberer antique religion of their own; this hereditary piety, together with the laws, prescribed education, customs, and duties. The city drew its walls close about the heart, and while it fostered friendship and reason within, without it looked to little but war. A splendid physical and moral discipline was established to serve a suicidal egoism. The city committed its crimes, and the individual indulged his vices of conduct and estimation, hardly rebuked by philosophy and quite unrebuked by religion. Nevertheless, religion and philosophy existed, together with an incomparable literature and art, and an unrivalled measure and simplicity in living. A liberal fancy and a strict civic regimen, starting with different partial motives and blind purposes, combined by good fortune into an almost rational life.

It was inevitable, however, when only an irrational tradition supported the state, and kept it so weak amid a world of enemies, that this state should succumb; not to speak of the mean animosities, the license in life, and the spirit of mockery that inwardly infested it. The myths, too, faded; they had expressed a fleeting moment of poetic insight, as patriotism had expressed a fleeting moment of unanimous effort; but what force could sustain such accidental harmonies? The patriotism soon lost its power to inspire sacrifice, and the myth its power to inspire wonder; so that the relics of that singular civilisation were scattered almost at once in the general flood of the world.

The Greek ideal has fascinated many men in all ages, who have sometimes been in a position to set a fashion, so that the world in general has pretended also to admire. But the truth is Hellas, in leaving so many heirlooms to mankind, has left no constitutional benefit; it has taught the conscience no lesson. We possess a great heritage from Greece, but it is no natural endowment. An artistic renaissance in the fifteenth century and a historical one in the nineteenth have only affected the trappings of society. The movement has come from above. It has not found any response in the people. While Greek morality, in its contents or in the type of life it prescribes, comes nearer than any other prerational experiment to what reason might propose, yet it has been less useful than many other influences in bringing the Life of Reason about. The Christian and the Moslem, in refining their more violent inspiration, have brought us nearer to genuine goodness than the Greek could by his idle example. Classic perfection is a seedless flower, imitable only by artifice, not reproducible by generation. It is capable of influencing character only through the intellect, the means by which character can be influenced least. It is a detached ideal, responding to no crying and actual demand in the world at large. It never passed, to win the right of addressing mankind, through a sufficient novitiate of sorrow. *Sterility of Greek example.*

The Hebrews, on the contrary, who in comparison with the Greeks had a barbarous idea of happiness, showed far greater moral cohesion under the pressure of adversity. They integrated their purposes into a fanaticism, but they integrated them; and the integrity that resulted became a mighty example. It constituted an ideal of character not the less awe-inspiring for being merely formal. We need not marvel that abstract commandments should have impressed the world more *Prerational morality among the Jews.* than concrete ideals. To appreciate an ideal, to love and serve it in the full light of science and reason, would require a high intelligence, and, what is rarer still, noble affinities and renunciations which are not to be looked for in an undisciplined people. But to feel the truth and authority of an abstract maxim (as, for instance, Do right and shame the devil), a maxim applicable to experience on any plane, nothing is needed but a sound wit and common honesty. Men know better what is right and wrong than what is ultimately good or evil; their conscience is more vividly present to them than the fruits which obedience to conscience might bear; so that the logical relation of means to ends, of methods to activities, eludes them altogether. What is a necessary connection between the given end, happiness, and the normal life naturally possessing it, appears to them as a miraculous connection between obedience to God's commands and enjoyment of his favour. The evidence of this miracle astonishes them and fills them with zeal. They are strengthened to persevere in righteousness under any stress of misfortune, in the assurance that they are being put to a temporary test and that the reward promised to virtue will eventually be theirs.

Thus a habit of faithfulness, a trust in general principles, is fostered and ingrained in generation after generation—a rare and precious heritage for a race so imperfectly rational as the human. Reason would of course justify the same constancy in well-doing, since a course of conduct would not be right, but wrong, if its ultimate issue were human misery. But as the happiness secured by virtue may be remote and may demand more virtue to make it appreciable, the mere rationality of a habit gives it no currency in the world and but little moral glow in the conscience. We should not, therefore, be too much offended at the illusions which play a part in moral integration. Imagination is often more efficacious in reaching the gist and meaning of experience than intelligence can be, just because imagination is less scrupulous and more instinctive. Even physical discoveries, when they come, are the fruit of divination, and Columbus had to believe he might sail westward to India before he could actually hit upon America. Reason cannot create itself, and nature, in producing reason, has to feel her way experimentally. Habits and chance systems of education have to arise first and exercise upon individuals an irrational suasion favourable to rational ends. Men long live in substantial harmony with reality before they recognise its nature. Organs long exist before they reach their perfect function. The fortunate instincts of a race destined to long life and rationality express themselves in significant poetry before they express themselves in science.

The development of conscience.

The service which Hebraism has rendered to mankind has been instrumental, as that rendered by Hellenism has been imaginative. Hebraism has put earnestness and urgency into morality, making it a matter of duty, at once private and universal, rather than what paganism had left it, a mass of local allegiances and legal practices. The Jewish system has, in consequence, a tendency to propaganda and intolerance; a tendency which would not have proved nefarious had this religion always remained true to its moral principle; for morality is coercive and no man, being autonomous, has a right to do wrong. Conscience, thus reinforced by religious passion, has been able to focus a general abhorrence on certain great scandals—slavery and sodomy could be practically suppressed among Christians, and drunkenness among Moslems. The Christian principle of charity also owed a part of its force to Hebraic tradition. For the law and the prophets were full of mercy and loving kindness toward the faithful. What Moses had taught his people Christ and his Hellenising disciples had the beautiful courage to preach to all mankind. Yet this virtue of charity, on its subtler and more metaphysical side, belongs to the spirit of redemption, to that ascetic and quasi-Buddhistic element in Christianity to which we shall presently revert. The pure Jews can have no part in such insight, because it contradicts the positivism of their religion and character and their ideal of worldly happiness.

As the human body is said to change all its substance every seven years, and yet is the same body, so the Hebraic conscience might change all its tenets in seven generations and be the same conscience still. Could this abstract moral habit, this transferable earnestness, be enlisted in rational causes, the Life of Reason would have gained a valuable instrument. Men would possess the "single eye," and the art, so difficult to an ape-like creature with loose moral feelings, of acting on principle. Could the vision of an adequate natural ideal fall into the Hebraising mind, already aching for action and nerved to practical enthusiasm, that ideal vision might become efficacious and be largely realised in practice. The abstract power of self-direction, if enlightened by a larger experience and a more fertile genius, might give the Life of Reason a public embodiment such as it has not had since the best days of classic antiquity. Thus the two prerational moralities out of which European civilisation has grown, could they be happily superposed, would make a rational polity.

Need of Hebraic devotion to Greek aims.

The objects of human desire, then, until reason has compared and experience has tested them, are a miscellaneous assortment of goods, unstable in themselves and incompatible with one another. It is a happy chance if a tolerable mixture of them recommends itself to a prophet or finds an adventitious acceptance among a group of men. Intuitive morality is adequate while it simply enforces those obvious and universal laws which are indispensable to any society, and which impose themselves everywhere on men under pain of quick extinction—a penalty which many an individual and many a nation continually prefers to pay.

Prerational morality marks an acquisition but offers no programme.

But when intuitive morality ventures upon speculative ground and tries to guide progress, its magic fails. Ideals are tentative and have to be critically viewed. A moralist who rests in his intuitions may be a good preacher, but hardly deserves the name of philosopher. He cannot find any authority for his maxims which opposite maxims may not equally invoke. To settle the relative merits of rival authorities and of hostile consciences it is necessary to appeal to the only real authority, to experience, reason, and human nature in the living man. No other test is conceivable and no other would be valid; for no good man would ever consent to regard an authority as divine or binding which essentially contradicted his own conscience. Yet a conscience which is irreflective and incorrigible is too hastily satisfied with itself, and not conscientious enough: it needs cultivation by dialectic. It neglects to extend to all human interests that principle of synthesis and justice by which conscience itself has arisen. And so soon as the conscience summons its own dicta for revision in the light of experience and of universal sympathy, it is no longer called conscience, but reason. So, too, when the spirit summons its traditional faiths, to subject them to a similar examination, that exercise is not called religion, but philosophy. It is true, in a sense, that philosophy is the purest religion and reason the ultimate conscience; but so to name them would be misleading. The things commonly called by those names have seldom consented to live at peace with sincere reflection. It has been felt vaguely that reason could not have produced them, and that they might suffer sad changes by submitting to it; as if reason could be the *ground* of anything, or as if everything might not find its consummation in becoming rational.

Rational Ethics

Reason in Science. Volume 5 of *The Life of Reason: or, the Phases of Human Progress.* New York: Charles Scribner's Sons; London: Constable and Co. Ltd., 1906, 233–61. Volume seven of the critical edition of *The Works of George Santayana.*

In this selection, Chapter IX of Reason in Science, *Santayana considered the application of reason to morality. He acknowledged that a rational morality was impossible, because morality is grounded in material conditions and reason could never eliminate material conflicts. However, it is possible that conflicting parties can share common ideal interests in the midst of their material conflicts, the chivalry of war being an example. Common ideals, while not making rational morality possible, may introduce rational ethics. As an example of rational ethics, Santayana looked to Socrates' conversational method, which "consists in accepting any estimation which any man may sincerely make, and in applying dialectic to it, so as to let the man see what he really esteems. What he really esteems is what ought to guide his conduct" (ES, 425). After reflecting on the nature of altruism and self-love, Santayana turned next to happiness, which is the culmination of the harmony at which reason aims. He examined some impediments to harmony and concluded that the individual's purpose is to clarify his or her own intent in the interest of finite and particular harmony.*

In moral reprobation there is often a fanatical element, I mean that hatred which an animal may sometimes feel for other animals on account of their strange

Moral passions represent private interests. aspect, or because their habits put him to serious inconvenience, or because these habits, if he himself adopted them, might be vicious in him. Such aversion, however, is not a rational sentiment. No fault can be justly found with a creature merely for not resembling another, or for flourishing in a different physical or moral environment. It has been an unfortunate consequence of mythical philosophies that moral emotions have been stretched to objects with which a man has only physical relations, so that the universe has been filled with monsters more or less horrible, according as the forces they represented were more or less formidable to human life. In the same spirit, every experiment in civilisation has passed for a crime among those engaged in some other experiment. The foreigner has seemed an insidious rascal, the heretic a pestilent sinner, and any material obstacle a literal devil; while to possess some unusual passion, however innocent, has brought obloquy on every one unfortunate enough not to be constituted like the average of his neighbours.

Ethics, if it is to be a science and not a piece of arbitrary legislation, cannot pronounce it sinful in a serpent to be a serpent; it cannot even accuse a barbarian of loving a wrong life, except in so far as the barbarian is supposed capable of accusing himself of barbarism. If he is a perfect barbarian he will be inwardly, and therefore morally, justified. The notion of a barbarian will then be accepted by him as that of a true man, and will form the basis of whatever rational judg-ments or policy he attains. It may still seem dreadful to him to be a serpent, as to be a barbarian might seem dreadful to a man imbued with liberal interests. But the degree to which moral science, or the dialectic of will, can condemn any type of life depends on the amount of disruptive contradiction which, at any reflec-tive moment, that life brings under the unity of apperception. The discordant impulse therein confronted will challenge and condemn one another; and the court of reason in which their quarrel is ventilated will have authority to pro-nounce between them.

The physical repulsion, however, which everybody feels to habits and inter-ests which he is incapable of sharing is no part of rational estimation, large as its share may be in the fierce prejudices and superstitions which prerational moral-ity abounds in. The strongest feelings assigned to the conscience are not moral feelings at all; they express merely physical antipathies.

Toward alien powers a man's true weapon is not invective, but skill and strength. An obstacle is an obstacle, not a devil; and even a moral life, when it actually exists in a being with hostile activities, is merely a hostile power. It is not hostile, however, in so far as it is moral, but only in so far as its morality represents a material organism, physically incompatible with what the thinker has at heart.

Material conflicts cannot be abolished by reason, because reason is powerful only where they have been removed. Yet where opposing forces are able mutu-ally to comprehend and respect one another, common ideal inter-ests at once supervene, and though the material conflict may remain irrepressible, it will be overlaid by an intellectual life, partly common and unanimous. In this lies the chivalry of war, that we acknowl-edge the right of others to pursue ends contrary to our own. **Common ideal interests may supervene.** Competitors who are able to feel this ideal comity, and who leading different lives in the flesh lead the same life in imagination, are incited by their mutual understanding to rise above that material ambition, perhaps gratuitous, that has made them enemies. They may ultimately wish to renounce that temporal good which deprives them of spiritual goods in truth infinitely greater and more appeal-ing to the soul—innocence, justice, and intelligence. They may prefer an enlarged mind to enlarged frontiers, and the comprehension of things foreign to the destruction of them. They may even aspire to detachment from those private interests which, as Plato said,* do not deserve to be taken too seriously; the fact that we must take them seriously being the ignoble part of our condition.

Of course such renunciations, to be rational, must not extend to the whole material basis of life, since some physical particularity and efficiency are requisite for bringing into being that very rationality which is to turn enemies into friends. The need of a material basis for spirit is what renders partial war with parts of the world the inevitable background of charity and justice. The frontiers at which this warfare is waged may, however, be pushed back indefinitely. Within the sphere

---

*Laws. VII. 803. B.

organised about a firm and generous life a Roman peace can be established. It is not what is assimilated that saps a creative will, but what remains outside that ultimately invades and disrupts it. In exact proportion to its vigour, it wins over former enemies, civilises the barbarian, and even tames the viper, when the eye is masterful and sympathetic enough to dispel hatred and fear. The more rational an institution is the less it suffers by making concessions to others; for these concessions, being just, propagate its essence. The ideal commonwealth can extend to the limit at which such concessions cease to be just and are thereby detrimental. Beyond or below that limit strife must continue for physical ascendancy, so that the power and the will to be reasonable may not be undermined. Reason is an operation in nature, and has its root there. Saints cannot arise where there have been no warriors, nor philosophers where a prying beast does not remain hidden in the depths.

Perhaps the art of politics, if it were practised scientifically, might obviate open war, religious enmities, industrial competition, and human slavery; but it would certainly not leave a free field for all animals nor for all monstrosities in men. Even while admitting the claims of monsters to be treated humanely, reason could not suffer them to absorb those material resources which might be needed to maintain rational society at its highest efficiency. We cannot, at this immense distance from a rational social order, judge what concessions individual genius would be called upon to make in a system of education and government in which all attainable goods should be pursued scientifically. Concessions would certainly be demanded, if not from well-trained wills, still from inevitable instincts, reacting on inevitable accidents. There is tragedy in perfection, because the universe in which perfection arises is itself imperfect. Accidents will always continue to harass the most consummate organism; they will flow in both from the outer world and from the interstices, so to speak, of its own machinery; for a rational life touches the irrational at its core as well as at its periphery. In both directions it meets physical force and can subsist only by exercising physical force in return. The range of rational ethics is limited to the intermediate political zone, in which existences have attained some degree of natural unanimity.

To this extent there is rational society.

It should be added, perhaps, that the frontiers between moral and physical action are purely notional. Real existences do not lie wholly on one or the other side of them. Every man, every material object, has moral affinities enveloping an indomitable vital nucleus or brute personal kernel; this moral essence is enveloped in turn by untraceable relations, radiating to infinity over the natural world. The stars enter society by the light and knowledge they afford, the time they keep, and the ornament they lavish; but they are mere dead weights in their substance and cosmological puzzles in their destiny. You and I posses manifold ideal bonds in the interests we share; but each of us has his poor body and his irremediable, incommunicable dreams. Beyond the little span of his foresight and love, each is merely a physical agency, preparing the way quite irresponsibly for undreamt-of revolutions and alien lives.

A truly rational morality, or social regimen, has never existed in the world and is hardly to be looked for. What guides men and nations in their practice is always some partial interest or some partial disillusion. A rational morality would imply perfect self-knowledge, so that no congenial good should be needlessly missed—least of all practical reason or justice itself; so that no good congenial to other creatures would be needlessly taken from them. The total value which everything had from the agent's point of view would need to be determined and felt efficaciously; and, among other things, the total value which this point of view, with the conduct it justified, would have for every foreign interest which it affected. Such knowledge, such definition of purpose, and such perfection of sympathy are **A rational morality not attainable,** clearly beyond man's reach. All that can be hoped for is that the advance of science and commerce, by fostering peace and a rational development of character, may bring some part of mankind nearer to that goal; but the goal lies, as every ultimate ideal should, at the limit of what is possible, and must serve rather to measure achievements than to prophesy them.

In lieu of a rational morality, however, we have rational ethics; and this mere idea of a rational morality is something valuable. While we wait for the sentiments, customs, and laws which should embody perfect humanity and perfect justice, we may observe the germinal principle of these ideal things; we may sketch the ground-plan of a true commonweatlth. This **but its principle clear.** sketch constitutes rational ethics, as founded by Socrates, glorified by Plato, and sobered and solidified by Aristotle. It sets forth the method of judgment and estimation which a rational morality would apply universally and express in practice. The method, being very simple, can be discovered and largely illustrated in advance, while the complete self-knowledge and sympathy are still wanting which might avail to embody that method in the concrete and to discover unequivocally where absolute duty and ultimate happiness may lie.

This method, the Socratic method, consists in accepting any estimation which any man may sincerely make, and in applying dialectic to it, so as to let the man see what he really esteems. What he really esteems is what ought to guide his conduct; for to suggest that a rational being ought to do what he feels to be wrong, or ought to pursue what he genuinely thinks is worthless, would be to impugn that man's rationality **It is the logic of an autonomous will.** and to discredit one's own. With what face could any man or god say to another: Your duty is to do what you cannot know you ought to do; your function is to suffer what you cannot recognise to be worth suffering? Such an attitude amounts to imposture and excludes society; it is the attitude of a detestable tyrant, and any one who mistakes it for moral authority has not yet felt the first heart-throb of philosophy.

More even than natural philosophy, moral philosophy is something Greek: it is the appanage of freemen. The Socratic method is the soul of liberal conversation; it is compacted in equal measure of sincerity and courtesy. Each man is autonomous and all are respected; and nothing is brought forward except to be submitted to reason and accepted or rejected by **Socrates' science.** the self-questioning heart. Indeed, when Socrates appeared in Athens mutual respect had passed into democracy and liberty into license; but the stalwart virtue of Socrates saved him from being a sophist, much as his method, when not honestly and sincerely used, might seem to countenance that moral anarchy which the sophists had expressed in their irresponsible doctrines. Their sophistry did not consist in the private *seat* which they assigned to judgment; for what judgment is there that is not somebody's judgment at some moment? The sophism consisted in ignoring the living moment's *intent,* and in suggesting that no judgment could refer to anything ulterior, and therefore that no judgment could be wrong: in other words that each man at each moment was the theme and standard, as well as the seat, of his judgment.

Socrates escaped this folly by force of honesty, which is what saves from folly in dialectic. He built his whole science precisely on that intent which the sophists ignored; he insisted that people should declare sincerely what they meant and what they wanted; and on the living rock he founded the persuasive and ideal sciences of logic and ethics, the necessity of which lies all in free insight and in actual will. This will and insight they render deliberate, profound, unshakable, and consistent. Socrates, by his genial midwifery, helped men to discover the truth and excellence to which they were naturally addressed. This circumstance rendered his doctrine at once moral and scientific; scientific because dialectical, moral because expressive of personal and living aspirations. His ethics was not like what has since passed under that name—a spurious physics, accompanied by commandments and threats. It was a pliant and liberal expression of ideals, inwardly grounded and spontaneously pursued. It was an exercise in self-knowledge.

Socrates' liberality was that of a free man ready to maintain his will and conscience, if need be, against the whole world. The sophists, on the contrary, were sycophants in their scepticism, and having inwardly abandoned the

Its opposition to sophistry and moral anarchy. ideals of their race and nation—which Socrates defended with his homely irony—they dealt out their miscellaneous knowledge, or their talent in exposition, at the beck and for the convenience of others. Their theory was that each man having a right to pursue his own aims, skilful thinkers might, for money, furnish any fellow-mortal with instruments fitted to his purpose. Socrates, on the contrary, conceived that each man, to achieve his aims must first learn to distinguish them clearly; he demanded that rationality, in the form of an examination and clarification of purposes, should precede any selection of external instruments. For how should a man recognise anything useful unless he first had established the end to be subserved and thereby recognised the good? True science, then, was that which enabled a man to disentangle and attain his natural good; and such a science is also the art of life and the whole of virtue.

The autonomous moralist differs from the sophist or ethical sceptic in this: that he retains his integrity. In vindicating his ideal he does not recant his human nature. In asserting the initial right of every impulse in others, he remains the spokesman of his own. Knowledge of the world, courtesy, and fairness do not neutralise his positive life. He is thoroughly sincere, as the sophist is not; for every man, while he lives, embodies and enacts some special interest; and this truth, which those who confound psychology with ethics may think destructive of all authority in morals, is in fact what alone renders moral judgment possible and respectable. If the sophist declares that what his nature attaches him to is not "really" a good, because it would not be a good, perhaps, for a different creature, he is a false interpreter of his own heart, and rather discreditably stulifies his honest feelings and actions by those theoretical valuations which, in guise of a mystical ethics, he gives out to the world. Socratic liberality, on the contrary, is consistent with itself, as Spinozistic naturalism is also; for it exercises that right of private judgment which it concedes to others, and avowedly builds up the idea of the good on that natural inner foundation on which everybody who has it at all must inevitably build it. This functional good is accordingly always relative and good for something; it is the ideal which a vital and energising soul carries with it as it moves. It is identical, as Socrates constantly taught, with the useful, the helpful, the beneficent. It is the complement needed to perfect every art and every activity after its own kind.

Rational ethics is an embodiment of volition, not a description of it. It is the expression of living interest, preference, and categorical choice. It leaves to psychology and history a free field for the description of moral phenomena. It has no interest in slipping far-fetched and incredible myths **Its vitality.** beneath the facts of nature, so as to lend a non-natural origin to human aspirations. It even recognises, as an emanation of its own force, that uncompromising truthfulness with which science assigns all forms of moral life to their place in the mechanical system of nature. But the rational moralist is not on that account reduced to a mere spectator, a physicist acknowledging no interest except the interest in facts and in the laws of change. His own spirit, small by the material forces which it may stand for and express, is great by its prerogative of surveying and judging the universe; surveying it, of course, from a mortal point of view, and judging it only by its kindliness or cruelty to some actual interest, yet, even so, determining unequivocally a part of its constitution and excellence. The rational moralist represents a force energising in the world, discovering its affinities there and clinging to them to the exclusion of their hateful opposites. He represents, over against the chance facts, an ideal embodying the particular demands, possibilities, and satisfactions of a specific being.

This dogmatic position of reason is not uncritically dogmatic; on the contrary, it is the sophistical position that it uncritically neutral. All criticism needs a dogmatic background, else it would lack objects and criteria for criticism. The sophist himself, without confessing it, enacts a special interest. He bubbles over with convictions about the pathological and fatal origin of human beliefs, as if that could prevent some of them from being more trustworthy and truer than others. He is doubtless right in his psychology; his own ideas have their natural causes and their chance of signifying something real. His scepticism may represent a wider experience than do the fanaticisms it opposes. But this sceptic also lives. Nature has sent her saps abundantly into him, and he cannot but nod dogmatically on that philosophical tree on which he is so pungent a berry. His imagination is unmistakably fascinated by the pictures it happens to put together. His judgment falls unabashed, and his discourse splashes on in its dialectical march, every stepping-stone on unquestioned idea, every stride a categorical assertion. Does he deny this? Then his very denial, in its promptness and heat, audibly contradicts him and makes him ridiculous. Honest criticism consists in being consciously dogmatic, and conscientiously so, like Descartes when he said, "I am." It is to sift and harmonise all assertions so as to make them a faithful expression of actual experience and inevitable thought.

Now will, no less than that reason which avails to render will consistent and far-reaching, animates natural bodies and expresses their functions. It has a radical bias, a foregone, determinate direction, else it could not be a will nor a principle of preference. The knowledge of what other people desire does not abolish a man's own aims. Sympathy and justice are simply an expansion of the soul's interests, arising when we consider other men's lives so intently that something in us imitates and re-enacts their experience, so that we move partly in unison with their movement, recognise that reality and initial legitimacy of their interests, and consequently regard their aims in our action, in so far as our own status and purposes have become identical with theirs. We are not less ourselves, nor less autonomous, for this assimilation, since we assimilate only what is in itself intelligible and congruous with our mind and obey only that authority which can impose itself on our reason.

Genuine altruism is natural self-expression.

The case is parallel to that of knowledge. To know all men's experience and to comprehend their beliefs would constitute the most cogent and settled of philosophies. Thought would then be reasonably adjusted to all the facts of history, and judgment would grow more authoritative and precise by virtue of that enlightenment. So, too, to understand all the goods that any man, nay, that any beast or angel, may ever have pursued, would leave man still necessitous of food, drink, sleep, and shelter; he would still love; the comic, the loathsome, the beautiful would still affect him with unmistakable direct emotions. His taste might no doubt gain in elasticity by those sympathetic excursions into the polyglot world; the plastic or dramatic quality which had enabled him to feel other creatures' joys would grow by exercise and new overtones would be added to his gamut. But the foundations of his nature would stand; and his possible happiness, though some new and precious threads might be woven into it, would not have a texture fundamentally different.

The radical impulses at work in any animal must continue to speak while he lives, for they are his essence. A true morality does not have to be adopted; the parts of it best practised are those which are never preached. To be "converted" would be to pass from one self-betrayal to another. It would be to found a new morality on a new artifice. The morality which has genuine authority exists inevitably and speaks autonomously in every common judgment, self-congratulation, ambition, or passion that fills the vulgar day. The pursuit of those goods which are the only possible or fitting crown of a man's life is predetermined by his nature; he cannot choose a law-giver, nor accept one, for none who spoke to the purpose could teach him anything but to know himself. Rational life is an art, not a slavery;

and terrible as may be the errors and the apathy that impede its successful exercise, the standard and goal of it are given intrinsically. Any task imposed externally on a man is imposed by force only, a force he has the right to defy so soon as he can do so without creating some greater impediment to his natural vocation.

Rational ethics, then, resembles prerational precepts and half-systems in being founded on impulse. It formulates a natural morality. It is a settled method of achieving ends to which man is drawn by virtue of his physical and rational constitution. By this circumstance rational ethics is removed **Reason expresses impulses,** from the bad company of all artificial, verbal, and unjust systems of morality, which in absolving themselves from relevance to man's endowment and experience merely show how completely irrelevant they are to life. Once, no doubt, each of these arbitrary systems expressed (like the observance of the Sabbath) some practical interest or some not unnatural rite; but so narrow a basis of course has to be disowned when the precepts so originating have been swollen into universal tyrannical laws. A rational ethics reduces them at once to their slender representative rôle; and it surrounds and buttresses them on every side with all other natural ideals.

Rational ethics thus differs from the prerational in being complete. There is one impulse which intuitive moralists ignore: the impulse to reflect. Human instincts are ignorant, multitudinous, and contradictory. To satisfy them as they come is often impossible, and often disastrous, in that **but impulses reduced to harmony.** such satisfaction prevents the satisfaction of other instincts inherently no less fecund and legitimate. When we apply reason to life we immediately demand that life be consistent, complete, and satisfactory when reflected upon and viewed as a whole. This view, as it presents each moment in its relations, extends to all moments affected by the action or maxim under discussion; it has no more ground for stopping at the limits of what is called a single life than at the limits of a single adventure. To stop at selfishness is not particularly rational. The same principle that creates the ideal of a self creates the ideal of a family or an institution.

The conflict between selfishness and altruism is like that between any two ideal passions that in some particular may chance to be opposed; but such a conflict has no obstinate existence for reason. For reason the person itself **Self-love artificial.** has no obstinate existence. The *character* which a man achieves at the best moment of his life is indeed something ideal and significant; it justifies and consecrates all his coherent actions and preferences. But *the man's life,* the circle drawn by biographers around the career of a particular body, from the womb to the charnel-house, and around the mental flux that accompanies that career, is no significant unity. All the substances and efficient processes that figure within it come from elsewhere and continue beyond; while all the rational objects and interests to which it refers have a transpersonal status. Self-love itself is concerned with public opinion; and if a man concentrates his view on private pleasures, these may qualify the fleeting moments of his life with an intrinsic value, but they leave the life itself shapeless and infinite, as if sparks should play over a piece of burnt paper.

The limits assigned to the mass of sentience attributed to each man are assigned conventionally; his prenatal feelings, his forgotten dreams, and his unappropriated sensations belong to his body and for that reason only are said to belong to him. Each impulse included within these limits may be as directly compared with the represented impulses of other people as with the represented impulses expected to arise later in the same body. Reason lives among these represented values, all of which have their cerebral seat and present efficacy over the passing thought; and reason teaches this passing thought to believe in and to respect them equally. Their right is not less clear, nor their influence less natural, because they may range over the whole universe and may await their realisation at the farthest boundaries of time. All that is physically requisite to their operation is that they should be vividly represented; while all that is requisite rationally, to justify them in qualifying actual life by their influence, is that the present act should have some tendency to bring the represented values about. In other words, a rational mind would consider, in its judgment and action, every interest which that judgment or action at all affected; and it would conspire with each represented good in proportion, not to that good's intrinsic importance, but to the power which the present act might have of helping to realise that good.

If pleasure, because it is commonly a result of satisfied instinct, may by a figure of speech be called the aim of impulse, happiness, by a like figure, may be called the aim of reason. The direct aim of reason is harmony; yet harmony, when made to rule in life, gives reason a noble satisfaction which we call happiness. Happiness is impossible and even inconceivable to a mind without scope and without pause, a mind driven by craving, pleasure, and fear. The moralists who speak disparagingly of happiness are less sublime than they think. In truth their philosophy is too lightly ballasted, too much fed on prejudice and quibbles, for happiness to fall within its range. Happiness implies resource and security; it can be achieved only by discipline. Your intuitive moralist rejects discipline, at least discipline of the conscience; and he is punished by having no lien on wisdom. He trusts to the clash of blind forces in collision, being one of them himself. He demands that virtue should be partisan and unjust; and he dreams of crushing the adversary in some physical cataclysm.

The sanction of reason in happiness.

Such groping enthusiasm is often innocent and romantic; it captivates us with its youthful spell. But it has no structure with which to resist the shocks of fortune, which it goes out so jauntily to meet. It turns only too often into vulgarity and worldliness. A snow-flake is soon a smudge, and there is a deeper purity in the diamond. Happiness is hidden from a free and casual will; it belongs rather to one chastened by a long education and unfolded in an atmosphere of sacred and perfected institutions. It is discipline that renders men rational and capable of happiness, by suppressing without hatred what needs to be suppressed to attain a beautiful naturalness. Discipline discredits the random pleasures of illusion, hope, and triumph, and substitutes those which are self-reproductive, perennial, and serene, because they express an equilibrium maintained with reality. So long as the result of endeavour is partly unforeseen and unintentional, so long as the will is partly blind, the Life of Reason is still swaddled in ignominy and the animal barks in the midst of human discourse. Wisdom and happiness consist in having recast natural energies in the furnace of experience. Nor is this experience merely a repressive force. It enshrines the successful expressions of spirit as well as the shocks and vetoes of circumstance; it enables a man to know himself in knowing the world and to discover his ideal by the very ring, true or false, of fortune's coin.

With this brief account we may leave the subject of rational ethics. Its development is impossible save in the concrete, when a legislator, starting from extant interests, considers what practices serve to render those interests vital and genuine, and what external alliances might lend them support and a more glorious expression. The difficulty in carrying rational policy very far comes partly from the refractory materials at hand, and partly from the narrow range within which moral science is usually confined. The materials are individual wills naturally far from unanimous, lost for the most part in frivolous pleasures, rivalries, and superstitions, and little inclined to listen to a law-giver that, like a new Lycurgus, should speak to them of unanimity, simplicity, disciplines, and perfection. Devotion and single-mindedness, perhaps possible in the cloister, are hard to establish in the world; yet a rational morality requires that all lay activities, all sweet temptations, should have their voice in the conclave. Morality becomes rational precisely by refusing either to accept human nature, as it sprouts, altogether without harmony, or to mutilate it in the haste to make it harmonious. The condition, therefore, of making a beginning in good politics is to find a set of men with well-knit character and cogent traditions, so that there may be a firm soil to cultivate and that labour may not be wasted in ploughing the quicksands.

Moral science impeded by its chaotic data,

When such a starting-point is given, moral values radiate from it to the very ends of the universe; and a failure to appreciate the range over which rational estimation spreads is a second obstacle to sound ethics. Because of this failure the earnest soul is too often intent on escaping to heaven, while the gross politician is suffered to declaim about the national honour, and to promise this client an office, this district a favour, and this class an iniquitous advantage. Politics is expected to be sophistical; and in the soberest parliaments hardly an argument is used or an ideal invoked which is not an insult to reason. Majorities work by a system of bribes offered to the more barren interests of men and to their more blatant prejudices. The higher direction of their lives is relegated to religion, which, unhappily, is apt to suffer from hereditary blindness to natural needs and to possible progress. The idea that religion, as well as art, industry, nationality, and science, should exist only for human life's sake and in order that men may live better in this world, is an idea not even mooted in politics and perhaps opposed by an official philosophy. The enterprise of individuals or of small aristocratic bodies has meantime sown the world which we call civilised with some seeds and nuclei of order. There are scattered about a variety of churches, industries, academies, and governments. But the universal order once dreamt of and nominally

and its unrecognised scope.

almost established, the empire of universal peace, all-permeating rational art, and philosophical worship, is mentioned no more. An unformulated conception, the prerational ethics of private privilege and national unity, fills the background of men's minds. It represents feudal traditions rather than the tendency really involved in contemporary industry, science, or philanthropy. Those dark ages, from which our political practice is derived, had a political theory which we should do well to study; for their theory about a universal empire and a catholic church was in turn the echo of a former age of reason, when a few men conscious of ruling the world had for a moment sought to survey it as a whole and to rule it justly.

Modern rational ethics, however, or what approaches most nearly to such a thing, has one advantage over the ancient and mediæval; it has profited by Christian discipline and by the greater gentleness of modern manners. It has recognised the rights of the dumb majority; it has revolted against cruelty and preventable suffering and has bent itself on diffusing well-being—the well-being that people want, and not the so-called virtues which a supercilious aristocracy may find it convenient to prescribe for them. It has based ethics on the foundation on which actual morality rests; on nature, on the necessities of social life, on the human instincts of sympathy and justice.

Fallacy in democratic hedonism.

It is all the more to be regretted that the only modern school of ethics which is humane and honestly interested in progress should have given a bad technical expression to its generous principles and should have substituted a dubious psychology for Socratic dialectic. The mere fact that somebody somewhere enjoys or dislikes a thing cannot give direction to a rational will. That fact indicates a moral situation but does not prescribe a definite action. A partial harmony or maladjustment is thereby proved to exist, but the method is not revealed by which the harmony should be sustained or the maladjustment removed. A given harmony can be sustained by leaving things as they are or by changing them together. A maladjustment can be removed by altering the environment or by altering the man. Pleasures may be attached to anything, and to pursue them in the abstract does not help to define any particular line of conduct. The particular ideal preexists in the observer; the mathematics of pleasure and pain cannot oblige him, for instance, to prefer a hundred units of mindless pleasure enjoyed in dreams to fifty units diffused over labour and discourse. He need not limit his efforts to spreading needless comforts and silly pleasures among the million; he need not accept for a goal a child's caprices multiplied by infinity. Even these caprices, pleasures, and comforts doubtless have their claims; but these claims have to be adjudicated by the agent's autonomous conscience, and he will give them the place they fill in his honest ideal of what it would be best to have in the world, not the place which they might pretend to usurp there by a sort of physical pressure. A conscience is a living function, expressing a particular nature; it is a not a passive medium where heterogeneous values can find their balance by virtue of their dead weight and number.

A moralist is called upon, first of all, to decide in what things pleasure ought to be found. Of course his decision, if he is rational, will not be arbitrary; it will conscientiously express his own nature—on which alone honest ideals can rest—without attempting to speak for the deafening and inconstant convocation of the whole sentient universe. Duty is a matter of self-knowledge, not of statistics. A living and particular will therein discovers its affinities, broadens its basis, acknowledges its obligations, and co-operates with everything that will co-operate with it; but it continues throughout to unfold a particular life, finding its supports and extensions in the state, the arts, and the universe. It cannot for a moment renounce its autonomy without renouncing reason and perhaps decreeing the extinction both of its own bodily basis and of its ideal method and policy.

Utilitarianism needs to be transferred to Socratic and dialectical ground, so that interest in absent interests may take its place in a concrete ideal. It is a noble thing to be sensitive to others' hardships, and happy in their happiness; but it is noble because it refines the natural will without enfeebling it, offering it rather a new and congenial development, one entirely predetermined by the fundamental structure of human nature. **Sympathy a conditional duty.** Were man not gregarious, were he not made to be child, friend, husband, and father by turns, his morality would not be social, but, like that of some silkworm or some seraph, wholly industrious or wholly contemplative. Parental and sexual instincts, social life and the gift of co-operation carry sympathy implicitly with them, as they carry the very faculty to recognise a fellow-being. To make this sympathy explicit and to find one's happiness in exercising it is to lay one's foundations deeper in nature and to expand the range of one's being. Its limits, however, would be broken down and moral dissolution would set in if, forgetting his humanity, a man should bid all living creatures lapse with him into a delicious torpor, or run into a cycle of pleasant dreams, so intense that death would be sure to precede any awakening out of them. Great as may be the advance in charity since the days of Socrates, therefore, the advance is within the lines of his method; to trespass beyond them would be to recede.

This situation is repeated on a broader stage. A statesman entrusted with power should regard nothing but his country's interests; to regard anything else would be treason. He cannot allow foreign sentiment or private hobbies to make him misapply the resources of his fellow-countrymen to their own injury. But he may well have an enlightened view of the interests which he serves; he might indeed be expected to take a more profound and enlightened view of them than his countrymen were commonly capable of, else he would have no right to his eminent station. He should be the first to feel that to inflict injury or foster hatred among other populations should not be a portion of a people's happiness. A nation, like a man, is something ideal. Indestructible mountains and valleys, crawled over by any sort of race, do not constitute its identity. Its essence is a certain spirit, and only what enters into this spirit can bind it morally, or preserve it.

If a drop of water contains a million worlds which I, in swallowing, may ruin or transform, that is Allah's business; mine is to clarify my own intent, to cling to what ideals may lie within the circle of my experience and practical imagination, so that I may have a natural ground for my loyalties, and may be constant in them. It would not be a rational ambition to wish to multiply the population of China by two, or that of America by twenty, after ascertaining that life there contained an overplus of pleasure. To weed a garden, however, would be ratio-

All life, and hence right life, finite and particular.
nal, though the weeds and their interests would have to be sacrificed in the process. Utilitarianism took up false ground when it made right conduct terminate in miscellaneous pleasures and pains, as if in their isolation they constituted all that morality had to consider, and as if respect offered to them, somehow in proportion to their quan-

tity, were the true conscience. The true conscience is rather an integrated natural will, chastened by clear knowledge of what it pursues and may attain. What morality has to consider is the form of life, not its quantity. In a world that is perhaps infinite, moral life can spring only from definite centres and is neither called upon nor able to estimate the whole, not to redress its balance. It is the free spirit of a part, finding its affinities and equilibrium in the material whole which it reacts on, and which it is in that measure enabled to understand.

Post-Rational Morality

Reason in Science. Volume 5 of *The Life of Reason: or, the Phases of Human Progress.*
New York: Charles Scribner's Sons; London: Constable and Co. Ltd., 1906, 262–
300. Volume seven of the critical edition of *The Works of George Santayana.*

In this selection, Chapter X of Reason in Science, *Santayana considered morality in a
fragmented society that has abandoned the Life of Reason as a vain pursuit. This rejection
comes not from prejudice or ignorance, as in prerational morality, but rather from despair
at the transience of existence and the conclusion that all is vanity. Thinkers then regard
the Life of Reason as merely one end among many and seek a substitute for happiness in
a natural ideal raised to supernatural significance: they seek a principle of universal harmony. Epicureanism took pleasure for the supreme standard of harmony, Stoicism took conformity to laws of nature (and Islam refined it in practice), and a post-rational pantheism
took mystical union with the infinite (and Christianity combined it with a Hebrew desire
for a promised land). Santayana thought that no post-rational system could entirely escape
naturalism. As long as a system involves some degree of living, complete nihilism is held at
bay and faith in the fundamental traits of a natural world retained. In consequence, the
values of a post-rational system will reflect a basic faith in the natural world.*

When Socrates and his two great disciples composed a system of rational ethics
they were hardly proposing practical legislation for mankind. One by his irony,
another by his frank idealism, and the third by his preponderat-
ing interest in history and analysis, showed clearly enough how
little they dared to hope. They were merely writing an eloquent

Socratic ethics retrospective.

epitaph on their country. They were publishing the principles of what had been
its life, gathering piously its broken ideals, and interpreting its momentary achievement. The spirit of liberty and co-operation was already dead. The private citizen,
debauched by the largesses and petty quarrels of his city, had become indolent
and mean-spirited. He had begun to question the utility of religion, of patriotism,
and of justice. Having allowed the organ for the ideal to atrophy in his soul, he
could dream of finding some sullen sort of happiness in unreason. He felt that the
austere glories of his country, as a Spartan regimen might have preserved them,
would not benefit that baser part of him which alone remained. Political virtue
seemed a useless tax on his material profit and freedom. The tedium and distrust
proper to a disintegrated society began to drive him to artificial excitements and
superstitions. Democracy had learned to regard as enemies the few in whom public interest was still represented, the few whose nobler temper and traditions still
coincided with the general good. These last patriots were gradually banished or
exterminated, and with them died the spirit that rational ethics had expressed.
Philosophers were no longer suffered to have illusions about the state. Human
activity on the public stage had shaken off all allegiance to art or reason.

The biographer of reason might well be tempted to ignore the subsequent attitudes into which moral life fell in the West, since they all embodied a more or less complete despair, and, having abandoned the effort to express the will honestly and dialectically, they could support no moral science. The point was merely to console or deceive the soul with some substitute for happiness.

Rise of disillusioned moralities. Life is older and more persistent than reason, and the failure of a first experiment in rationality does not deprive mankind of that mental and moral vegetation which they possessed for ages in a wild state before the advent of civilisation. They merely revert to their uncivil condition and espouse whatever imaginative ideal comes to hand, by which some semblance of meaning and beauty may be given to existence without the labour of building this meaning and beauty systematically out of its positive elements.

Not to study these imaginative ideals, partial and arbitrary as they are, would be to miss one of the most instructive points of view from which the Life of Reason may be surveyed: the point of view of its satirists. For moral ideals may follow upon philosophy, just as they may precede it. When they follow, at least so long as they are consciously embraced in view of reason's failure, they have a quite particular value. Aversion to rational ideals does not then come, as the intuitionist's aversion does, from moral incoherence or religious prejudice. It does not come from lack of speculative power. On the contrary, it may come from undue haste in speculation, from a too ready apprehension of the visible march of things. The obvious irrationality of nature as a whole, too painfully brought home to a musing mind, may make it forget or abdicate its own rationality. In a decadent age, the philosopher who surveys the world and sees that the end of it is even as the beginning, may not feel that the intervening episode, in which he and all he values after all figure, is worth consideration; and he may cry, in his contemplative spleen, that *all* is vanity.

If you should still confront him with a theory of the ideal, he would not be reduced, like the pre-rational moralists in a similar case, to mere inattention and bluster. If you told him that every art and every activity involves a congruous good, and that the endeavour to realise the ideal in every direction is an effort of which reason necessarily approves, since reason is nothing but the method of that endeavour, he would not need to deny your statements in order to justify himself. He might admit the naturalness, the spontaneity, the ideal sufficiency of your conceptions; but he might add, with the smile of the elder and the sadder man, that he had experience of their futility. "You Hellenisers," he might say, "are but children; you have not pondered the little history you know. If thought were conversant with reality, if virtue were stable and fruitful, if pains and policy were ultimately justified by a greater good arising out of them—then, indeed, a life according to reason might tempt a philosopher. But unfortunately not one of those fond assumptions is true. Human thought is a meaningless phantasmagoria. Virtue is a splendid and laborious folly, when it is not a pompous garment that only looks respectable in the dark, being in truth full of spots and ridiculous patches. Men's best laid plans become, in the casual cross-currents of being, the occasion of their bitterest calamities. How, then, live? How justify in our eyes, let us not say the ways of God, but our own ways?"

Such a position may be turned dialectically by invoking whatever positive hopes or convictions the critic may retain, who while he lives cannot be wholly without them. But the position is specious and does not collapse, like that of the intuitionist, at the first breath of criticism. Pessimism, and all the moralities founded on despair, are not pre-rational but post-rational. **The illusion subsisting in them.** They are the work of men who more or less explicitly have conceived the Life of Reason, tried it at least imaginatively, and found it wanting. These systems are a refuge from an intolerable situation: they are experiments in redemption. As a matter of fact, animal instincts and natural standards of excellence are never eluded in them, for no moral experience has other terms; but the part of the natural ideal which remains active appears in opposition to all the rest and, by an intelligible illusion, seems to be no part of that natural ideal because, compared with the commoner passions on which it reacts, it represents some simpler or more attenuated hope—the appeal to some very humble or very much chastened satisfaction, or to an utter change in the conditions of life.

Post-rational morality thus constitutes, in intention if not in fact, a criticism of all experience. It thinks it is not, like pre-rational morality, an arbitrary selection from among co-ordinate precepts. It is an effort to subordinate all precepts to one, that points to some single eventual good. For it occurs to the founders of these systems that by estranging oneself from the world, or resting in the moment's pleasure, or mortifying the passions, or enduring all sufferings in patience, or studying a perfect conformity with the course of affairs, one may gain admission to some sort of residual mystical paradise; and this thought, once conceived, is published as a revelation and accepted as a panacea. It becomes in consequence (for such is the force of nature) the foundation of elaborate institutions and elaborate philosophies, into which the contents of the worldly life are gradually reintroduced.

When human life is in an acute crisis, the sick dreams that visit the soul are the only evidence of her continued existence. Through them she still envisages a good; and when the delirium passes and the normal world gradually re-establishes itself in her regard, she attributes her regeneration to the ministry of those phantoms, a regeneration due, in truth, to the restored nutrition and circulation within her. In this way post-rational systems, though founded originally on despair, in a later age that has forgotten its disillusions may come to pose as the only possible basis of morality. The philosophers addicted to each sect, and brought up under its influence, may exhaust criticism and sophistry to show that all faith and effort would be vain unless their particular nostrum was accepted; and so a curious party philosophy arises in which, after discrediting nature and reason in general, the sectary puts forward some mythical echo of reason and nature as the one saving and necessary truth. The positive substance of such a doctrine is accordingly pre-rational and perhaps crudely superstitious; but it is introduced and nominally supported by a formidable indictment of physical and moral science, so that the wretched idol ultimately offered to our worship acquires a spurious halo and an imputed majesty by being raised on a pedestal of infinite despair.

Socrates was still living when a school of post-rational morality arose among
the Sophists, which after passing quickly through various phases, settled down
into Epicureanism and has remained the source of a certain consolation to man-

Epicurean refuge in pleasure.

kind, which if somewhat cheap, is none the less genuine. The pursuit
of pleasure may seem simple selfishness, with a tendency to debauch-
ery; and in this case the pre-rational and instinctive character of the
maxim retained would be very obvious. Pleasure, to be sure, is not
the direct object of an unspoiled will; but after some experience and discrimination, a man may actually guide himself by a foretaste of the pleasures he has
found in certain objects and situations. The criticism required to distinguish what
pays from what does not pay may not often be carried very far; but it may sometimes be carried to the length of suppressing every natural instinct and natural
hope, and of turning the philosopher, as it turned Hegesias the Cyrenaic, into a
eulogist of death.

The post-rational principle in the system then comes to the fore, and we see
clearly that to sit down and reflect upon human life, picking out its pleasant
moments and condemning all the rest, is to initiate a course of moral retrenchment. It is to judge what is worth doing, not by the innate ambition of the soul,
but by experience of incidental feelings, which to a mind without creative ideas
may seem the only objects worthy of pursuit. That life ought to be accompanied
by pleasure and exempt from pain is certain; for this means that what is agreeable to the whole process of nature would have become agreeable also to the various partial impulses involved–another way of describing organic harmony and
physical perfection. But such a desirable harmony cannot be defined or obtained
by picking out and isolating from the rest those occasions and functions in which
it may already have been reached. These partial harmonies may be actual arrests
or impediments in the whole which is to be made harmonious; and even when
they are innocent or helpful they cannot serve to determine the form which the
general harmony might take on. They merely illustrate its principle. The organism in which this principle of harmony might find pervasive expression is still
potential, and the ideal is something of which, in its concrete form, no man has
had experience. It involves a propitious material environment, perfect health,
perfect arts, perfect government, a mind enlarged to the knowledge and enjoyment of all its external conditions and internal functions. Such an ideal is lost
sight of when a man cultivates his garden-plot of private pleasures, leaving it to
chance and barbarian fury to govern the state and quicken the world's passions.

Even Aristippus, the first and most delightful of hedonists, who really enjoyed
the pleasures he advocated and was not afraid of the incidental pains–even Aristippus betrayed the post-rational character of his philosophy by abandoning politics, mocking science, making his peace with all abuses that fostered his comfort,
and venting his wit on all ambitions that exceeded his hopes. A great temperament can carry off a rough philosophy. Rebellion and license may distinguish
honourable souls in an age of polite corruption, and a grain of sincerity is better,
in moral philosophy, than a whole harvest of conventionalities. The violence and
shamelessness of Aristippus were corrected by Epicurus; and a balance was found

between utter despair and utter irresponsibility. Epicureanism retrenched much: it cut off politics, religion, enterprise, and passion. These things it convicted of vanity, without stopping to distinguish in them what might be inordinate from what might be rational. At the same time it retained friendship, freedom of soul, and intellectual light. It cultivated unworldliness without superstition and happiness without illusion. It was tender toward simple and honest things, scornful and bitter only against pretence and usurpation. It thus marked a first halting-place in the retreat of reason, a stage where the soul had thrown off only the higher and more entangling part of her burden and was willing to live, in somewhat reduced circumstances, on the remainder. Such a philosophy expresses well the genuine sentiment of persons, at once mild and emancipated, who find themselves floating on the ebb-tide of some civilisation, and enjoying its fruits, without any longer representing the forces that brought that civilisation about.

The same emancipation, without its mildness, appeared in the Cynics, whose secret it was to throw off all allegiance and all dependence on circumstance, and to live entirely on inner strength of mind, on pride and inflexible humour. The renunciation was far more sweeping than that of Epicurus, and indeed wellnigh complete; yet the Stoics, in underpinning the Cynical self-sufficiency with a system of physics, introduced

Stoic recourse to conformity.

into the life of the sect a contemplative element which very much enlarged and ennobled its sympathies. Nature became a sacred system, the laws of nature being eulogistically called rational laws, and the necessity of things, because it might be foretold in auguries, being called providence. There was some intellectual confusion in all this; but contemplation, even if somewhat idolatrous, has a purifying effect, and the sad and solemn review of the cosmos to which the Stoic daily invited his soul, to make it ready to face its destiny, doubtless liberated it from many an unworthy passion. The impressive spectacle of things was used to remind the soul of her special and appropriate function, which was to be rational. This rationality consisted partly in insight, to perceive the necessary order of things, and partly in conformity, to perceive that this order, whatever it might be, could serve the soul to exercise itself upon, and to face with equanimity.

Despair, in this system, flooded a much larger area of human life; everything, in fact, was surrendered except the will to endure whatever might come. The concentration was much more marked, since only a formal power of perception and defiance was retained and made a sphere of moral life; this rational power, at least in theory, was the one peak that remained visible above the deluge. But in practice much more was retained. Some distinction was drawn, however unwarrantably, between external calamities and human turpitude, so that absolute conformity and acceptance might not be demanded by the latter; although the chief occasion which a Stoic could find to practise fortitude and recognise the omnipresence of law was in noting the universal corruption of the state and divining its ruin. The obligation to conform to nature (which, strictly speaking, could not be disregarded in any case) was interpreted to signify that every one should perform the offices conventionally attached to his station. In this way a perfunctory citizenship and humanity were restored to the philosopher. But the restored life was merely histrionic: the Stoic was a recluse parading the market-place and a monk disguised in armour. His interest and faith were centred altogether on his private spiritual condition. He cultivated the society of those persons who, he thought, might teach him some virtue. He attended to the affairs of state so as to exercise his patience. He might even lead an army to battle, if he wished to test his endurance and make sure that philosophy had rendered him indifferent to the issue.

The strain and artifice of such a discipline, with merely formal goals and no hope of earth or in heaven, could not long maintain itself; and doubtless it existed,
Conformity the core of Islam, at a particular juncture, only in a few souls. Resignation to the will of God, says Bishop Butler, is *the whole of piety;* yet mere resignation would make a sorry religion and the negation of all morality, unless the will of God was understood to be quite different from his operation in nature. To turn Stoicism into a workable religion we need to qualify it with some pre-rational maxims. Islam, for instance, which boasts that in its essence it is nothing but the primitive and natural religion of mankind, consists in abandoning oneself to the will of God or, in other words, in accepting the inevitable. This will of God is learned for the most part by observing the course of nature and history, and remembering the fate meted out habitually to various sorts of men. Were this all, Islam would be a pure Stoicism, and the Hebraic religion, in its ultimate phase, would be simply the eloquence of physics. It would not, in that case, be a moral inspiration at all, except as contemplation and the sense of one's nothingness might occasionally silence the passions and for a moment bewilder the mind. On recovering from this impression, however, men would find themselves enriched with no self-knowledge, armed with no precepts, and stimulated by no ideal. They would be reduced to enacting their incidental impulses, as the animals are, quite as if they had never perceived that in doing so they were fulfilling a divine decree. Enlightened Moslems, accordingly, have often been more Epicurean than Stoical; and if they have felt themselves (not without some reason) superior to Christians in delicacy, in *savoir vivre,* in kinship with all natural powers, this sense of superiority has been quite rationalistic and purely human. Their religion contributed to it only because it was simpler, freer from superstition, nearer to a clean and pleasant regimen in life. Resignation to the will of God being granted, expression of the will of man might more freely begin.

What made Islam, however, a positive and contagious novelty was the assumption that God's will might be incidentally revealed to prophets before the event,
enveloped in arbitrary doctrines. so that past experience was not the only source from which its total operation might be gathered. In its opposition to grosser idolatries Islam might appeal to experience and challenge those who trusted in special deities to justify their worship in face of the facts. The most decisive facts against idolators, however, were not yet patent, but were destined to burst upon mankind at the last day—and most unpleasantly for the majority. Where Mohammed speaks in the name of the universal natural power he is abundantly scornful toward that fond paganism which consists in imagining distinct patrons for various regions of nature or for sundry human activities. In turning to such patrons the pagan regards something purely ideal or, as the Koran

shrewdly observes, worships his own passions. Allah, on the contrary, is over-whelmingly external and as far as possible from being ideal. He is indeed the giver of all good things, as of all evil, and while his mercies are celebrated on every page of the Koran, these mercies consist in the indulgence he is expected to show to his favourites, and the exceeding reward reserved for them after their earthly trials. Allah's mercy does not exclude all those senseless and unredeemed cruelties of which nature is daily guilty; nay, it shines all the more conspicuously by contrast with his essential irresponsibility and wanton wrath, a part of his express purpose being to keep hell full of men and demons.

The tendency toward enlightenment which Islam represents, and the limits of that enlightenment, may be illustrated by the precept about unclean animals. Allah, we were told, being merciful and gracious, made the world for man's use, with all the animals in it. We may therefore justly slaughter and devour them, in so far as comports with health; but, of course, we may not eat animals that have died a natural death, nor those offered in sacrifice to false gods, nor swine; for to do so would be an abomination.

Unfortunately religious reformers triumph not so much by their rational insight as by their halting, traditional maxims. Mohammed felt the unity of God like a philosopher; but people listened to him because he preached it like a sectary. God, as he often reminds us, did not make the world for a plaything; he made it in order to establish distinctions and separate by an immense interval the fate of those who conform to the truth from the fate of those who ignore it. Human life is indeed beset with enough imminent evils to justify this urgent tone in the Semitic moral-ist and to lend his precepts a stern practical ring, absent from merely Platonic idealisms. But this stringency, which is called positivism when the conditions of welfare are understood, becomes fanaticism when they are misrepresented. Had Mohammed spoken only of the dynamic unity in things, the omnipresence of destiny, and the actual conditions of success and failure in the world, he would not have been called a prophet or have had more than a dozen intelligent follow-ers, scattered over as many centuries; but the weakness of his intellect, and his ignorance of nature, made the success of his mission. It is easier to kindle righ-teous indignation against abuses when, by abating them, we further our personal interests; and Mohammed might have been less zealous in denouncing false gods had his own God been altogether the true one. But, in the heat of his militancy, he descends so far as to speak of *God's interests* which the faithful embrace, and of fighting in *God's cause*. By these notions, so crudely pre-rational, we are allowed to interpret and discount the pantheistic sublimities with which in most places we are regaled; and in order that a morality, too weak to be human, may not wither altogether in the fierce light of the Absolute, we are led to humanise the Absolute into a finite force, needing our support against independent enemies. So com-plete is the bankruptcy of that Stoic morality which thinks to live on the worship of That which Is.

As extremes are said to meet, so we may say that a radical position is often the point of departure for opposite systems. Pantheism, or religion and morality

The latter alone lend it practical force.

abdicating in favour of physics, may, in practice, be interpreted in contrary ways. To be in sympathy with the Whole may seem to require us to outgrow and discard every part; yet, on the other hand, there is no obvious reason why Being should love its essence in a fashion that involves hating every possible form of Being. The worshipper of Being accordingly assumes now one, now the other, of two opposite attitudes, according as the society in which he lives is in a pre-rational or a post-rational state of culture. Pantheism is interpreted pre-rationally, as by the early Mohammedans, or by the Hegelians, when people are not yet acquainted, or not yet disgusted, with worldliness; the Absolute then seems to lend a mystical sanction to whatever existences or tendencies happen to be afoot. Morality is reduced to sanctioning reigning conventions, or reigning passions, on the authority of the universe. Thus the Moslems, by way of serving Allah, could extend their conquests and cultivate the arts and pleasures congenial to a self-sufficing soul, at once indolent and fierce; while the transcendentalists of our times, by way of accepting their part in the divine business, have merely added a certain speculative loftiness to the maxims of some sect or the chauvinism of some nation.

Moral ambiguity in pantheism.

To accept everything, however, is not an easy nor a tolerable thing, unless you are naturally well pleased with what falls to your share. However the Absolute may feel, a moral creature has to hate some forms of being; and if the age has thrust these forms before a man's eyes, and imposed them upon him, not being suffered by his pantheism to blame the Absolute he will (by an inconsistency) take to blaming himself. It will be his finitude, his inordinate claims, his enormous effrontery in having any will or any preference in particular, that will seem to him the source of all evil and the single blot on the infinite lucidity of things. Pantheism, under these circumstances, will issue in a post-rational morality. It will practise asceticism and look for a mystical deliverance from finite existence.

Under stress, it becomes ascetic and requires a mythology.

Under these circumstances myth is inevitably reintroduced. Without it, no consolation could be found except in the prospect of death and, awaiting that, in incidental natural satisfactions; whereby absorption in the Absolute might come to look not only impossible but distinctly undesirable. To make retreat out of human nature seem a possible vocation, this nature itself must, in some myth, be represented as unnatural; the soul that this life stifles must be said to come from elsewhere and to be fitted to breathe some element far rarer and finer than this sublunary fog.

A curious foothold for such a myth was furnished by the Socratic philosophy. Plato, wafted by his poetic vision too far, perhaps, from the utilitarianism of his master, had eulogised concretions in discourse at the expense of existences and had even played with cosmological myths, meant to express the values of things, by speaking as if these values had brought things into being. The dialectical terms thus contrasted with natural objects, and pictured as natural powers, furnished the dogmas needed at this juncture by a post-rational religion. The spell which dialectic can exercise over an abstracted mind is itself great; and it may grow into

A supernatural world made by the Platonist out of dialectic.

a sacred influence and a positive revelation when it offers a sanctuary from a weary life in the world. Out of the play of notions carried on in a prayerful dream wonderful mysteries can be constructed, to be presently announced to the people and made the core of sacramental injunctions. When the tide of vulgar superstition is at the flood and every form of quackery is welcome, we need not wonder that a theosophy having so respectable a core—something, indeed, like a true logic misunderstood—should gain many adherents. Out of the names of things and of virtues a mystic ladder could be constructed by which to leave the things and the virtues themselves behind; but the sagacity and exigencies of the school would not fail to arrange the steps in this progress—the end of which was unattainable except, perhaps, in a momentary ecstasy—so that the obvious duties of men would continue, for the nonce, to be imposed upon them. The chief difference made in morals would be only this: that the positive occasions and sanctions of good conduct would no longer be mentioned with respect, but the imagination would be invited to dwell instead on mystical issues.

Neo-Platonic morality, through a thousand learned and vulgar channels, permeated Christianity and entirely transformed it. Original Christianity was, though in another sense, a religion of redemption. The Jews, without dreaming of original sin or of any inherent curse in being finite, had found themselves often in the sorest material straits. They hoped, like all primitive peoples, that relief might come by propitiating the deity. They knew that the sins of the fathers were visited upon the children even to the third and fourth generation. They had accepted this idea of joint responsibility and vicarious atonement, turning in their unphilosophical way this law of nature into a principle of justice. Meantime the failure of all their cherished ambitions had plunged them into a penitential mood. Though in fact pious and virtuous to a fault, they still looked for repentance—their own or the world's—to save them. This redemption was to be accomplished in the Hebrew spirit, through long-suffering and devotion to the Law, with the Hebrew solidarity, by vicarious attribution of merits and demerits within the household of the faith.

The Hebraic cry for redemption.

Such a way of conceiving redemption was far more dramatic, poignant, and individual than the Neo-Platonic; hence it was far more popular and better fitted to be a nucleus for religious devotion. However much, therefore, Christianity may have insisted on renouncing the world, the flesh, and the devil, it always kept in the background this perfectly Jewish and pre-rational craving for a delectable promised land. The journey might be long and through a desert, but milk and honey were to flow in the oasis beyond. Had renunciation been fundamental or revulsion from nature complete, there would have been no much-trumpeted last judgment and no material kingdom of heaven. The renunciation was only temporary and partial; the revulsion was only against incidental evils. Despair touched nothing but the present order of the world, though at first it took the extreme form of calling for its immediate destruction. This was the sort of despair and renunciation that lay at the bottom of Christian repentance; while hope in a new order of this world, or of one very like it, lay at the bottom of Christian joy. A temporary sacrifice, it was thought, and a partial mutilation would bring the spirit miraculously into a fresh paradise. The pleasures nature had grudged or punished, grace was to offer as a reward for faith and patience. The earthly life which was vain as an experience was to be profitable as a trial. Normal experience, appropriate exercise for the spirit, would thereafter begin.

Christianity is thus a system of postponed rationalism, a rationalism intercepted by a supernatural version of the conditions of happiness. Its moral principle is reason—the only moral principle there is; its motive power

The two factors meet in Christianity.

is the impulse and natural hope to be and to be happy. Christianity merely renews and reinstates these universal principles after a first disappointment and a first assault of despair, by opening up new vistas of accomplishment, new qualities and measures of success. The Christian field of action being a world of grace enveloping the world of nature, many transitory reversals of acknowledged values may take place in its code. Poverty, chastity, humility, obedience, self-sacrifice, ignorance, sickness, and dirt may all acquire a religious worth which reason, in its direct application, might scarcely have found in them; yet these reversed appreciations are merely incidental to a secret rationality, and are justified on the ground that human nature, as now found, is corrupt and needs to be purged and transformed before it can safely manifest its congenital instincts and become again an authoritative criterion of values. In the kingdom of God men would no longer need to do penance, for life there would be truly natural and there the soul would be at last in her native sphere.

This submerged optimism exists in Christianity, being a heritage from the Jews; and those Protestant communities that have rejected the pagan and Platonic elements that overlaid it have little difficulty in restoring it to prominence. Not, however, without abandoning the soul of the gospel; for the soul of the gospel, though expressed in the language of Messianic hopes, is really post-rational. It was not to marry and be given in marriage, or to sit on thrones, or to unravel metaphysical mysteries, or to enjoy any of the natural delights renounced in this life, that Christ summoned his disciples to abandon all they have and to follow him. There was surely a deeper peace in his self-surrender. It was not a new thing even among the Jews to use the worldly promises of their exoteric religion as symbols for inner spiritual revolutions; and the change of heart involved in genuine Christianity was not a fresh excitation of gaudy hopes, nor a new sort of utilitarian, temporary austerity. It was an emptying of the will, in respect to all human desires, so that a perfect charity and contemplative justice, falling like the Father's gifts ungrudgingly on the whole creation, might take the place of ambition, petty morality, and earthly desires. It was a renunciation which, at least in Christ himself and in his more spiritual disciples, did not spring from disappointed illusion or lead to other unregenerate illusions even more sure to be dispelled by events. It sprang rather from a native speculative depth, a natural affinity to the divine fecundity, serenity, and sadness of the world. It was the spirit of prayer, the kindliness and insight which a pure soul can fetch from contemplation.

This mystical detachment, supervening on the dogged old Jewish optimism, gave Christianity a double aspect, and had some curious consequence in later times. Those who were inwardly convinced—as most religious minds were under the Roman Empire—that all earthly things were vanity, and that they plunged the soul into an abyss of nothingness if not of torment, could, in view of brighter possibilities in another world, carry their asceticism and their cult of suffering farther than a purely negative system, like the Buddhistic, would have allowed. For a discipline that is looked upon as merely **Consequent electicism.** temporary can contradict nature more boldly than one intended to take nature's place. The hope of unimaginable benefits to ensue could drive religion to greater frenzies than it could have fallen into if its object had been merely to silence the will. Christianity persecuted, tortured, and burned. Like a hound it tracked the very scent of heresy. It kindled wars, and nursed furious hatreds and ambitions. It sanctified, quite like Mohammedanism, extermination and tyranny. All this would have been impossible if, like Buddhism, it had looked only to peace and the liberation of souls. It looked beyond; it dreamt of infinite blisses and crowns it should be crowned with before an electrified universe and an applauding God. These were rival baits to those which the world fishes with, and were snapped at, when seen, with no less avidity. Man, far from being freed from his natural passions, was plunged into artificial ones quite as violent and much more disappointing. Buddhism had tried to quiet a sick world with anæsthetics; Christianity sought to purge it with fire.

Another consequence of combining, in the Christian life, post-rational with pre-rational motives, a sense of exile and renunciation with hopes of a promised land, was that esoteric piety could choose between the two factors, even while it gave a verbal assent to the dogmas that included both. Mystics honoured the post-rational motive and despised the pre-rational; positivists clung to the second and hated the first. To the spiritually minded, whose religion was founded on actual insight and disillusion, the joys of heaven could never be more than a symbol for the intrinsic worth of sanctity. To the worldling those heavenly joys were nothing but a continuation of the pleasures and excitements of this life, serving to choke any reflections which, in spite of himself, might occasionally visit him about the vanity of human wishes. So that Christianity, even in its orthodox forms, covers various kinds of morality, and its philosophical incoherence betrays itself in disruptive movements, profound schisms, and total alienation on the part of one Christian from the inward faith of another. Trappist or Calvinist may be practising a heroic and metaphysical self-surrender while the busy-bodies of their respective creeds are fostering, in God's name, all their hot and miscellaneous passions.

This contradiction, present in the overt morality of Christendom, cannot be avoided, however, by taking refuge again in pure asceticism. Every post-rational system is necessarily self-contradictory. Its despair cannot be universal nor its nihilism complete so long as it remains a coherent method **The negation of naturalism never complete.** of action, with particular goals and a steady faith that their attainment is possible. The renunciation of the will must stop at the point where the will to be saved makes its appearance: and as this desire may be no less troublesome and insistent than any other, as it may even become a tormenting obsession, the mystic is far from the end of his illusions when he sets about to dispel them. There is one rational method to which, in post-rational systems, the world is still thought to be docile, one rational endeavour which nature is sure to crown with success. This is the method of deliverance from existence, the effort after salvation. There is, let us say, a law of Karma, by which merit and demerit accruing in one incarnation pass on to the next and enable the soul to rise continuously through a series of stages. Thus the world, though called illusory, is not wholly intractable. It provides systematically for an exit out of its illusions. On this rational ordinance of phenomena, which is left standing by an imperfect nihilism, Buddhist morality is built. Rational endeavour remains possible because experience is calculable and fruitful in this one respect, that it dissolves in the presence of goodness and knowledge.

Similarly in Christian ethics, the way of the cross has definite stations and a definite end. However negative this end may be thought to be, the assurance that it may be attained is a remnant of natural hope in the bosom of pessimism. A complete disillusion would have involved the neglect of such an assurance, the denial that it was possible or at least that it was to be realised under specific conditions. That conversion and good works lead to something worth attaining is a new sort of positivistic hope. A complete scepticism would involve a doubt, not only concerning the existence of such a method of salvation, but also (what is more significant) concerning the importance of applying it if it were found. For to assert that salvation is not only possible but urgently necessary, that every soul is now in an intolerable condition and should search for an ultimate solution to all its troubles, a restoration to a normal and somehow blessed state—what is this but to assert that the nature of things has a permanent constitution, by conformity with which man may secure his happiness? Moreover, we assert in such a faith that this natural constitution of things is discoverable in a sufficient measure to guide our action to a successful issue. Belief in Karma, in prayer, in sacraments, in salvation is a remnant of a natural belief in the possibility of living successfully. The remnant may be small and "expressed in fancy." Transmigration or an atonement may be chimerical ideas. Yet the mere fact of reliance upon something, the assumption that the world is steady and capable of rational exploitation, even if in a supernatural interest and by semi-magical means, amounts to an essential loyalty to postulates of practical reason, an essential adherence to natural morality.

The pretension to have reached a point of view from which *all* impulse may be criticised is accordingly an untenable pretension. It is abandoned in the very systems in which it was to be most thoroughly applied. The instrument of criticism must itself be one impulse surviving the wreck of all the others; the vision of salvation and of the way thither must be one dream among the rest. A single suggestion of experience is thus accepted while all others are denied; and although a certain purification and revision of morality may hence ensue, there is no real penetration to a deeper principle than spontaneous reason, no revelation of a higher end than the best possible happiness. One sporadic growth of human nature may be substituted for its whole luxuriant vegetation; one negative or formal element of happiness may be preferred to the full entelechy of life. We may see the Life of Reason reduced to straits, made to express itself in a niggardly and fantastic environment; but we have, in principle and essence, the Life of Reason still, empirical in its basis and rational in its method, its substance impulse and its end happiness.

So much for the umbilical cord that unites every living post-rational system to the matrix of human hopes. There remains a second point of contact between these systems and rational morality: the reinstated natural duties which all religions and philosophies, in order to subsist among civilised peoples, are at once obliged to sanction and somehow to deduce from their peculiar principles. The most plausible evidence which a supernatural doctrine can give of its truth is the beauty and rationality of its moral corollaries. It is instructive to observe that a gospel's congruity with natural reason and common humanity is regarded as the decisive mark of its supernatural origin. Indeed, were inspiration not the faithful echo of plain conscience and vulgar experience there would be no means of distinguishing it from madness. Whatever poetic idea a prophet starts with, in whatever intuition or analogy he finds a hint of salvation, it is altogether necessary that he should hasten to interpret his oracle in such a manner that it may sanction without disturbing the system of indispensable natural duties, although these natural duties, by being attached artificially to supernatural dogmas, may take on a different tone, justify themselves by a different rhetoric, and possibly suffer real transformation in some minor particulars. Systems of post-rational morality are not original works: they are versions of natural morality translated into different metaphysical languages, each of which adds its peculiar flavour, its own genius and poetry, to the plain sense of the common original.

Spontaneous values rehabilitated.

In the doctrine of Karma, for instance, experience of retribution is ideally extended and made precise. Acts, daily experience teaches us, form habits; habits constitute character, and each man's character, as Heraclitus said, is his guardian deity, the artisan of his fate. We need but raise this particular observation to a solitary eminence, after the manner of post-rational thinking; we need but imagine it to underlie and explain all other empirical observations, so that character may come to figure as an absolute cause, of which experience itself is an attendant result. Such arbitrary emphasis laid on some term of experience is the source of each metaphysical system in turn. In this case the surviving dogma will have yielded an explanation of our environment no less than of our state of heart by instituting a deeper spiritual law, a certain balance of merit and demerit in the soul, accruing to it through a series of previous incarnations. This fabulous starting-point was gained by an imaginary extension of the law of moral continuity and natural retribution; but when, accepting this starting-point, the believer went on to inquire what he should do to be saved and to cancel the heavy debts he inherited from his mythical past, he would merely enumerate the natural duties of man, giving them, however, a new sanction and conceiving them as if they emanated from his new-born metaphysical theory. This theory, apart from a natural conscience and traditional code,

A witness out of India.

would have been perfectly barren. The notion that every sin must be expiated does not carry with it any information about what acts are sins.

This indispensable information must still be furnished by common opinion. Those acts which bring suffering after them, those acts which arouse the enmity of our fellows and, by a premonition of that enmity, arouse our own shame—those are assumed and deputed to be sinful; and the current code of morality being thus borrowed without begging leave, the law of absolute retribution can be brought in to paint the picture of moral responsibility in more glaring colours and to extend the vista of rewards and punishments into a rhetorical infinite. Buddhistic morality was natural morality intensified by this forced sense of minute and boundless responsibility. It was coloured also by the negative, pessimistic justification which this dogma gives to moral endeavour. Every virtue was to be viewed as merely removing guilt and alleviating suffering, knowledge itself being precious only as a means to that end. The ultimate inspiration of right living was to be hope of perfect peace–a hope generously bestowed by nature on every spirit which, being linked to the flux of things, is conscious of change and susceptible of weariness, but a hope which the irresponsible Oriental imagination had disturbed with bad dreams. A pathetic feminine quality was thereby imparted to moral feeling; we were to be good for pity's sake, for the sake of a great distant deliverance from profound sorrows.

The pathetic idiosyncrasy of this religion has probably enabled it to touch many a heart and to lift into speculation many a life otherwise doomed to be quite instinctive and animal. It has kept morality pure–free from

Dignity of post-rational morality.

that admixture of worldly and partisan precepts with which less pessimistic systems are encumbered. Restraint can be rationally imposed on a given will only by virtue of evils which would be involved in its satisfaction, by virtue, in other words, of some actual demand whose disappointment would ensue upon inconsiderate action. To save, to cure, to nourish are duties far less conditional than would be supposed duty to acquire or to create. There is no harm in merely not being, and privation is an evil only when, after we exist, it deprives us of something naturally requisite, the absence of which would defeat interests already launched into the world. If there is something in a purely remedial system of morality which seems one-sided and extreme, we must call to mind the far less excusable one-sidedness of those moralities of prejudice to which we are accustomed in the Occident–the ethics of irrational acquisitiveness, irrational faith, and irrational honour. Buddhistic morality, so reasonable and beautifully persuasive, rising so willingly to the ideal of sanctity, merits in comparison the profoundest respect. It is lifted as far above the crudities of intuitionism as the whisperings of an angel are above a schoolboy's code.

A certain bias and deviation from strict reason seems, indeed, inseparable from any moral reform, from any doctrine that is to be practically and immediately influential. Socratic ethics was too perfect an expression to be much of a force. Philosophers whose hearts are set on justice and pure truth often hear reproaches addressed to them by the fanatic, who contrasts the conspicuous change in this or that direction accomplished by his preaching with the apparent impotence of reason and thought. Reason's resources are in fact so limited that it is usually reduced to guerilla warfare: a general plan of campaign is useless when only insignificant forces obey our commands. Moral progress is for that reason often greatest when some nobler passion or more fortunate prejudice takes the lead and subdues its meaner companions without needing to rely on the consciousness of ultimate benefits hence accruing to the whole life. So a pessimistic and merely remedial morality may accomplish reforms which reason, with its broader and milder suasion, might have failed in. If certain rare and precious virtues can thus be inaugurated, under the influence of a zeal exaggerating its own justification, there will be time later to insist on the complementary truths and to tack in the other direction after having been carried forward a certain distance by this oblique advance.

At the same time neglect of reason is never without its dangers and its waste. The Buddhistic system itself suffers from a fundamental contradiction, because its framers did not acknowledge the actual limits of retribution nor the empirical machinery by which benefits and injuries are really propagated. It is an onerous condition which religions must fulfil, if they would prevail in the world, that they must have their roots **Absurdities nevertheless involved.** in the past. Buddhism had its mission of salvation; but to express this mission to its proselytes it was obliged to borrow the language of the fantastic metaphysics which had preceded it in India. The machinery of transmigration had to serve as a scaffolding to raise the monument of mercy, purity, and spirituality. But this fabulous background given to life was really inconsistent with what was best in the new morality; just as in Christianity the post-rational evangelical ideals of redemption and regeneration, of the human will mystically reversed, were radically incompatible with the pre-rational myths about a creation and a political providence. The doctrine of Karma was a hypostasis of moral responsibility; but in making responsibility dynamic and all-explaining, the theory discountenanced in advance the charitable efforts of Buddhism—the desire to instruct and save every fellow-creature. For if all my fortunes depend upon my former conduct, I am the sole artificer of my destiny. The love, the pity, the science, or the prayers of others can have no real influence over my salvation. They cannot diminish by one tittle my necessary sufferings, nor accelerate by one instant the period which my own action appoints for my deliverance. Perhaps another's influence might, in the false world of time and space, change the order or accidental vesture of my moral experiences; but their quantity and value, being the exact counterpart of my free merits and demerits, could not be affected at all by those extraneous doings.

Therefore the empirical fact that we can help one another remains in Buddhism (as in any retributive scheme) only by a serious inconsistency; and since this fact is the sanction of whatever moral efficacy can be attributed to Buddhism, in sobering, teaching, and saving mankind, anything inconsistent with it is fundamentally repugnant to the whole system. Yet on that repugnant and destructive dogma of Karma Buddhism was condemned to base its instruction. This is the heavy price paid for mythical consolations, that they invalidate the moral values they are intended to emphasise. Nature has allowed the innocent to suffer for the guilty, and the guilty, perhaps, to die in some measure unpunished. To correct this imperfection we feign a closed circle of personal retributions, exactly proportionate to personal deserts. But thereby, without perceiving it, we have invalidated all political and social responsibility, and denied that any man can be benefited or injured by any other. Our moral ambition has overleaped itself and carried us into a non-natural world where morality is impotent and unmeaning.

Post-rational systems accordingly mark no real advance and offer no genuine solution to spiritual enigmas. The saving force each of them invokes is merely some remnant of that natural energy which animates the human ani-

The soul of positivism in all ideals. mal. Faith in the supernatural is a desperate wager made by man at the lowest ebb of his fortunes; it is as far as possible from being the source of that normal vitality which subsequently, if his fortunes mend, he may gradually recover. Under the same religion, with the same posthumous alternatives and mystic harmonies hanging about them, different races, or the same race at different periods, will manifest the most opposite moral characteristics. Belief in a thousand hells and heavens will not lift the apathetic out of apathy or hold back the passionate from passion; while a newly planted and ungalled community, in blessed forgetfulness of rewards or punishments, of cosmic needs or celestial sanctions, will know how to live cheerily and virtuously for life's own sake, putting to shame those thin vaticinations. To hope for a second life, to be had gratis, merely because this life has lost its savour, or to dream of a different world, because nature seems too intricate and unfriendly, is in the end merely to play with words; since the supernatural has no permanent aspect or charm except in so far as it expresses man's natural situation and points to the satisfaction of his earthly interests. What keeps supernatural morality, in its better forms, within the limits of sanity is the fact that it reinstates in practice, under novel associations and for motives ostensibly different, the very natural virtues and hopes which, when seen to be merely natural, it had thrown over with contempt. The new dispensation itself, if treated in the same spirit, would be no less contemptible; and what makes it genuinely esteemed is the restored authority of those human ideals which it expresses in a fable.

The extent of this moral restoration, the measure in which nature is suffered to bloom in the sanctuary, determines the value of post-rational moralities. They may preside over a good life, personal or communal, when their symbolism, though cumbrous, is not deceptive; when the supernatural machinery brings man back to nature through mystical circumlocutions, and becomes itself a poetic echo of experience and a dramatic impersonation of reason. The peculiar accent and emphasis which it will not cease to impose on the obvious lessons of life need not then repel the wisest intelligence. True sages and true civilisations can accordingly flourish under a dispensation nominally supernatural; for that supernaturalism may have become a mere form in which imagination clothes a rational and humane wisdom.

People who speak only one language have some difficulty in conceiving that things should be expressed just as well in some other; a prejudice which does not necessarily involve their mistaking words for things or being practically misled by their inflexible vocabulary. So it constantly happens that supernatural systems, when they have long prevailed, are defended by persons who have only natural interests at heart; because these persons lack that specula- **Moribund** tive freedom and dramatic imagination which would allow them to **dreams and** conceive other moulds for morality and happiness than those to **perennial** which a respectable tradition has accustomed them. Sceptical states- **realities.** men and academic scholars sometimes suffer from this kind of numbness; it is intelligible that they should mistake the forms of culture for its principle, especially when their genius is not original and their chosen function is to defend and propagate the local traditions in which their whole training has immersed them. Indeed, in the political field, such concern for decaying myths may have a pathetic justification; for however little the life of or dignity of man may be jeopardised by changes in language, languages themselves are not indifferent things. They may be closely bound up with the peculiar history and spirit of nations, and their disappearance, however necessary and on the whole propitious, may mark the end of some stirring chapter in the world's history. Those whose vocation is not philosophy and whose country is not the world may be pardoned for wishing to retard the migrations of spirit, and for looking forward with apprehension to a future in which their private enthusiasms will not be understood.

The value of post-rational morality, then, depends on a double conformity on its part with the Life of Reason. In the first place some natural impulse must be retained, some partial ideal must still be trusted and pursued by the prophet of redemption. In the second place the intuition thus gained and exclusively put forward must be made the starting-point for a restored natural morality. Otherwise the faith appealed to would be worthless in its operation, as well as fanciful in its basis, and it could never become a mould for thought or action in a civilised society.

Hypostatic Ethics

Winds of Doctrine: Studies in Contemporary Opinion. New York: Charles Scribner's Sons; London: J. M. Dent & Sons Ltd., 1913, 110–54. Volume nine of the critical edition of *The Works of George Santayana.*

*An early and slightly different version of this selection appeared as part III of "Russell's Philosophical Essays" (*Journal of Philosophy, Psychology, and Scientific Methods, *8, [1911]: 421–32). This selection appeared as part IV of "The Philosophy of Mr. Bertrand Russell," Chapter IV in* Winds of Doctrine. *In a letter thanking Russell for his book* Philosophical Essays *(London and New York: Longmans, Green, 1910), Santayana mentioned the review from which this selection originated and wrote, "[y]ou will not expect me to agree with you in everything, but, whatever you may think of my ideas, I always feel that yours, and Moore's too, make for the sort of reconstruction in philosophy which I should welcome. It is a great bond to dislike the same things, and dislike is perhaps a deeper indication of our real nature than explicit affections, since the latter may be effects of circumstances, while dislike is a reaction against them" (LGS, 2:28). Santayana's concern with individual natures over external circumstances reflects ideas in this selection. He thought moral judgments are grounded in individual preference, contrary to Russell's belief in independently existing moral qualities. Santayana thought moral pluralism more conducive to social harmony than absolutism.*

If Mr. Russell, in his essay on "The Elements of Ethics," had wished to propitiate the unregenerate naturalist, before trying to convert him, he could not have chosen a more skilful procedure; for he begins by telling us that "what is called good conduct is conduct which is a means to other things which are good on their own account; and hence ... the study of what is good or bad on its own account must be included in ethics." Two consequences are involved in this: first, that ethics is concerned with the economy of all values, and not with "moral" goods only, or with duty; and second, that values may and do inhere in a great variety of things and relations, all of which it is the part of wisdom to respect, and if possible to establish. In this matter, according to our author, the general philosopher is prone to one error and the professed moralist to another. "The philosopher, bent on the construction of a system, is inclined to simplify the facts unduly ... and to twist them into a form in which they can all be deduced from one or two general principles. The moralist, on the other hand, being primarily concerned with conduct, tends to become absorbed in means, to value the actions men ought to perform more than the ends which such actions serve.... Hence most of what they value in this world would have to be omitted by many moralists from any imagined heaven, because there such things as self-denial and effort and courage and pity could find no place.... Kant has the bad eminence of combining both errors in the highest possible degree, since he holds that there is nothing good except the virtuous will–a view which simplifies the good as much as any philosopher could wish, and mistakes means for ends as completely as any moralist could enjoin."

Those of us who are what Mr. Russell would call ethical sceptics will be delighted at this way of clearing the ground; it opens before us the prospect of a moral philosophy that should estimate the various values of things known and of things imaginable, showing what combinations of goods are possible in any one rational system, and (if fancy could stretch so far) what different rational systems would be possible in places and times remote enough from one another not to come into physical conflict. Such ethics, since it would express in reflection the dumb but actual interests of men, might have both influence and authority over them; two things which an alien and dogmatic ethics necessarily lacks. The joy of the ethical sceptic in Mr. Russell is destined, however, to be short-lived. Before proceeding to the expression of concrete ideals, he thinks it necessary to ask a preliminary and quite abstract question, to which his essay is chiefly devoted; namely, what is the right definition of the predicate "good," which we hope to apply in the sequel to such a variety of things? And he answers at once: The predicate "good" is indefinable. This answer he shows to be unavoidable, and so evidently unavoidable that we might perhaps have been absolved from asking the question; for, as he says, the so-called definitions of "good"–that it is pleasure, the desired, and so forth–are not definitions of the predicate "good," but designations of the things to which this predicate is applied by different persons. Pleasure, and its rivals, are not synonyms for the abstract quality "good," but names for classes of concrete facts that are supposed to possess that quality. From this correct, if somewhat trifling, observation, however, Mr. Russell, like Mr. Moore before him, evokes a portentous dogma. Not being able to define good, he hypostasises it. "Good and bad," he says, "are qualities which belong to objects independently of our opinions, just as much as round and square do; and when two people differ as to whether a thing is good, only one of them can be right, though it may be very hard to know which is right." "We cannot maintain that for me a thing ought to exist on its own account, while for you it ought not; that would merely mean that one of us is mistaken, since in fact everything either ought to exist, or ought not." Thus we are asked to believe that good attaches to things for no reason or cause, and according to no principles of distribution; that it must be found there by a sort of receptive exploration in each separate case; in other words, that it is an absolute, not a relative thing, a primary and not a secondary quality.

That the quality "good" is indefinable is one assertion, and obvious; but that the presence of this quality is unconditioned is another, and astonishing. My logic, I am well aware, is not very accurate or subtle; and I wish Mr. Russell had not left it to me to discover the connection between these two propositions. Green is an indefinable predicate, and the specific quality of it can be given only in intuition; but it is a quality that things acquire under certain conditions, so much so that the same bit of grass, at the same moment, may have it from one point of view and not from another. Right and left are indefinable; the difference could not be explained without being invoked in the explanation; yet everything that is to the right is not to the right on no condition, but obviously on the condition that some one is looking in a certain direction; and if some one else at the same time is looking in the opposite direction, what is truly to the right will be truly to the left also. If Mr. Russell thinks this is a contradiction, I understand why the universe does not please him. The contradiction would be real, undoubtedly, if we suggested that the *idea* of good was at any time or in any relation the *idea* of evil, or the *intuition* of right that of left, or the *quality* of green that of yellow; these disembodied essences are fixed by the intent that selects them, and in that ideal realm they can never have any relations except the dialectical ones implied in their nature, and these relations they must always retain. But the contradiction disappears when, instead of considering the qualities in themselves, we consider the things of which those qualities are aspects; for the qualities of things are not compacted by implication, but are conjoined irrationally by nature, as she will; and the same thing may be, and is, at once yellow and green, to the left and to the right, good and evil, many and one, large and small; and whatever verbal paradox there may be in this way of speaking (for from the point of view of nature it is natural enough) had been thoroughly explained and talked out by the time of Plato, who complained that people should still raise a difficulty so trite and exploded.* Indeed, while square is always square, and round round, a thing that is round may actually be square also, if we allow it to have a little body, and to be a cylinder.

But perhaps what suggests this hypostasis of good is rather the fact that what others find good, or what we ourselves have found good in moods with which we retain no sympathy, is sometimes pronounced by us to be bad; and far from inferring from this diversity of experience that the present good, like the others, corresponds to a particular attitude or interest of ours, and is dependent upon it, Mr. Russell and Mr. Moore infer instead that the presence of the good must be independent of all interests, attitudes, and opinions. They imagine that the truth of a proposition attributing a certain relative quality to an object contradicts the

---

*Plato, *Philebus*, 14, D. The dialectical element in this dialogue is evidently the basis of Mr. Russell's, as of Mr. Moore's, ethics; but they have not adopted the other elements in it, I mean the political and the theological. As to the political element, Plato everywhere conceives the good as the eligible in life, and refers it to human nature and to the pursuit of happiness—that happiness which Mr. Russell, in a rash moment, says is but a name which some people prefer to give to pleasure. Thus in the *Philebus* (11, D) the good looked for is declared to be "some state and disposition of the soul which has the property of making all men happy"; and later (66, D) the conclusion is that insight is better than pleasure "as an element in human life." As to the theological element, Plato, in hypostasising the good, does not hypostasise it as good, but as cause or power, which is, it seems to me, the sole category that justifies hypostasis, and logically involves it; for if things have a ground at all, that ground must exist before them and beyond them. Hence the whole Platonic and Christian scheme, in making the good independent of private will and opinion, by no means makes it independent of the direction of nature in general and of human nature in particular; for all things have been created with an innate predisposition towards the creative good, and are capable of finding happiness in nothing else. Obligation, in this system, remains internal and vital. Plato attributes a single vital direction and a single moral source to the cosmos. This is what determines and narrows the scope of the true good; for the true good is that relevant to nature. Plato would not have been a dogmatic moralist, had he not been a theist.

truth of another proposition, attributing to the same object an opposite relative quality. Thus if a man here and another man at the antipodes call opposite directions up, "only one of them can be right, though it may be very hard to know which is right."

To protect the belated innocence of this state of mind, Mr. Russell, so far as I can see, has only one argument, and one analogy. The argument is that "if this were not the case, we could not reason with a man as to what is right." "We do in fact hold that when one man approves of a certain act, while another disapproves, one of them is mistaken, which would not be the case with a mere emotion. If one man likes oysters and another dislikes them, we do not say that either of them is mistaken." In other words, we are to maintain our prejudices, however absurd, lest it should become unnecessary to quarrel about them! Truly the debating society has its idols, no less than the cave and the theatre. The analogy that comes to buttress somewhat this singular argument is the analogy between ethical propriety and physical or logical truth. An ethical proposition may be correct or incorrect, in a sense justifying argument, when it touches what is good as a means, that is, when it is not intrinsically ethical, but deals with causes and effects, or with matters of fact or necessity. But to speak of the truth of an ultimate good would be a false collocation of terms; an ultimate good is chosen, found, or aimed at; it is not opined. The ultimate intuitions on which ethics rests are not debatable, for they are not opinions we hazard but preferences we feel; and it can be neither correct nor incorrect to feel them. We may assert these preferences fiercely or with sweet reasonableness, and we may be more or less incapable of sympathising with the different preferences of others; about oysters we may be tolerant, like Mr. Russell, and about character intolerant; but that is already a great advance in enlightenment, since the majority of mankind have regarded as hateful in the highest degree any one who indulged in pork, or beans, or frogs' legs, or who had a weakness for anything called "unnatural"; for it is the things that offend their animal instincts that intense natures have always found to be, intrinsically and *par excellence,* abominations.

I am not sure whether Mr. Russell thinks he has disposed of this view where he discusses the proposition that the good is the desired and refutes it on the ground that "it is commonly admitted that there are bad desires; and when people speak of bad desires, they seem to mean desires for what is bad." Most people undoubtedly call desires bad when they are generically contrary to their own desires, and call objects that disgust them bad, even when other people covet them. This human weakness is not, however, a very high authority for a logician to appeal to, being too like the attitude of the German lady who said that Englishmen called a certain object *bread,* and Frenchmen called it *pain,* but that it really was *Brod* [sic]. Scholastic philosophy is inclined to this way of asserting itself; and Mr. Russell, though he candidly admits that there are ultimate differences of opinion about good and evil, would gladly minimise these differences, and thinks he triumphs when he feels that the prejudices of his readers will agree with his own; as if the constitutional unanimity of all human animals, supposing it existed, could tend to show that the good they agreed to recognise was independent of their constitution.

In a somewhat worthier sense, however, we may admit that there are desires for what is bad, since desire and will, in the proper psychological sense of these words, are incidental phases of consciousness, expressing but not constituting those natural relations that make one thing good for another. At the same time the words desire and will are often used, in a mythical or transcendental sense, for those material dispositions and instincts by which vital and moral units are constituted. It is in reference to such constitutional interests that things are "really" good or bad; interests which may not be fairly represented by any incidental conscious desire. No doubt any desire, however capricious, represents some momentary and partial interest, which lends to its objects a certain real and inalienable value; yet when we consider, as we do in human society, the interests of men, whom reflection and settled purposes have raised more or less to the ideal dignity of individuals, then passing fancies and passions may indeed have bad objects, and be bad themselves, in that they thwart the more comprehensive interests of the soul that entertains them. Food and poison are such only relatively, and in view of particular bodies, and the same material thing may be food and poison at once; the child, and even the doctor, may easily mistake one for the other. For the human system whiskey is truly more intoxicating than coffee, and the contrary opinion would be an error; but what a strange way of vindicating this real, though relative, distinction, to insist that whiskey is more intoxicating in itself, without reference to any animal; that it is pervaded, as it were, by an inherent intoxication, and stands dead drunk in its bottle! Yet just in this way Mr. Russell and Mr. Moore conceive things to be dead good and dead bad. It is such a view, rather than the naturalistic one, that renders reasoning and self-criticism impossible in morals; for wrong desires, and false opinions as to value, are conceivable only because a point of reference or criterion is available to prove them such. If no point of reference and no criterion were admitted to be relevant, nothing but physical stress could give to one assertion of value greater force than to another. The shouting moralist no doubt has his place, but not in philosophy.

That good is not an intrinsic or primary quality, but relative and adventitious, is clearly betrayed by Mr. Russell's own way of arguing, whenever he approaches some concrete ethical question. For instance, to show that the good is not pleasure, he can avowedly do nothing but appeal "to ethical judgments with which almost every one would agree." He repeats, in effect, Plato's argument about the life of the oyster, having pleasure with no knowledge. Imagine such mindless pleasure, as intense and prolonged as you please, and would you choose it? Is it your good? Here the British reader, like the blushing Greek youth, is expected to answer instinctively, No! It is an *argumentum ad hominem* (and there can be no other kind of argument in ethics); but the man who gives the required answer does so not because the answer is self-evident, which it is not, but because he is the required sort of man. He is shocked at the idea of resembling an oyster. Yet changeless pleasure, without memory or reflection, without the wearisome intermixture of arbitrary images, is just what the mystic, the voluptuary, and perhaps the oyster find to be good. Ideas, in their origin, are probably signals of alarm; and the distress which they marked in the beginning always clings to them in some measure, and causes many a soul, far more profound than that of the young Protarchus or of the British reader, to long for them to cease altogether. Such a radical hedonism is indeed inhuman; it undermines all conventional ambitions, and is not a possible foundation for political or artistic life. But that is all we can say against it. Our humanity cannot annul the incommensurable sorts of good that may be pursued in the world, though it cannot itself pursue them. The impossibility which people labour under of being satisfied with pure pleasure as a goal is due to their want of imagination, or rather to their being dominated by an imagination which is exclusively human.

The author's estrangement from reality reappears in his treatment of egoism, and most of all in his "Free Man's Religion." Egoism, he thinks, is untenable because "if I am right in thinking that my good is the only good, then every one else is mistaken unless he admits that my good, not his, is the only good." "Most people ... would admit that it is better two people's desires should be satisfied than only one person's.... Then what is good is not good *for me* or *for you,* but is simply good." "It is, indeed, so evident that it is better to secure a greater good for *A* than a lesser good for *B,* that it is hard to find any still more evident principle by which to prove this. And if *A* happens to be some one else, and *B* to be myself, that cannot affect the question, since it is irrelevant to the general question who *A* and *B* may be." To the question, as the logician states it after transforming men into letters, it is certainly irrelevant; but it is not irrelevant to the case as it arises in nature. If two goods are somehow rightly pronounced to be equally good, no circumstance can render one better than the other. And if the locus in which the good is to arise is somehow pronounced to be indifferent, it will certainly be indifferent whether that good arises in me or in you. But how shall these two pronouncements be made? In practice, values cannot be compared save as represented or enacted in the private imagination of somebody: for we could not conceive that an alien good *was* a good (as Mr. Russell cannot conceive that the life of an ecstatic oyster is a good) unless we could sympathise with it in some way in our own persons; and on the warmth which we felt in so representing the alien good would hang our conviction that it was truly valuable, and had worth in comparison with our own good. The voice of reason, bidding us prefer the greater good, no matter who is to enjoy it, is also nothing but the force of sympathy, bringing a remote existence before us vividly *sub specie boni.* Capacity for such sympathy measures the capacity to recognise duty and therefore, in a moral sense, to have it. Doubtless it is conceivable that all wills should become co-operative, and that nature should be ruled magically by an exact and universal sympathy; but this situation must be actually attained in part, before it can be conceived or judged to be an authoritative ideal. The tigers cannot regard it as such, for it would suppress the tragic good called ferocity, which makes, in their eyes, the chief glory of the universe. Therefore the inertia of nature, the ferocity of beasts, the optimism of mystics, and the selfishness of men and nations must all be accepted as conditions for the peculiar goods, essentially incommensurable, which they can generate severally. It is misplaced vehemence to call them intrinsically detestable, because they do not (as they cannot) generate or recognise the goods we prize.

In the real world, persons are not abstract egos, like *A* and *B,* so that to benefit one is clearly as good as to benefit another. Indeed, abstract egos could not be benefited, for they could not be modified at all, even if somehow they could be distinguished. It would be the qualities or objects distributed among them that would carry, wherever they went, each its inalienable cargo of value, like ships sailing from sea to sea. But it is quite vain and artificial to imagine different goods charged with such absolute and comparable weights; and actual egoism is not the thin and refutable thing that Mr. Russell makes of it. What it really holds is that a given man, oneself, and those akin to him, are qualitatively better than other beings; that the things they prize are intrinsically better than the things prized by others; and that therefore there is no injustice in treating these chosen interests as supreme. The injustice, it is felt, would lie rather in not treating things so unequal unequally. This feeling may, in many cases, amuse the impartial observer, or make him indignant; yet it may, in every case, according to Mr. Russell, be absolutely just. The refutation he gives of egoism would not dissuade any fanatic from exterminating all his enemies with a good conscience; it would merely encourage him to assert that what he was ruthlessly establishing was the absolute good. Doubtless such conscientious tyrants would be wretched themselves, and compelled to make sacrifices which would cost them dear; but that would only extend, as it were, the pernicious egoism of that part of their being which they had allowed to usurp a universal empire. The twang of intolerance and of self-mutilation is not absent from the ethics of Mr. Russell and Mr. Moore, even as it stands; and one trembles to think what it may become in the mouths of their disciples. Intolerance itself is a form of egoism, and to condemn egoism intolerantly is to share it.

I cannot help thinking that a consciousness of the relativity of values, if it became prevalent, would tend to render people more truly social than would a belief that things have intrinsic and unchangeable values, no matter what the attitude of any one to them may be. If we said that goods, including the right distribution of goods, are relative to specific natures, moral warfare would continue, but not with poisoned arrows. Our private sense of justice itself would be acknowledged to have but a relative authority, and while we could not have a higher duty than to follow it, we should seek to meet those whose aims were incompatible with it as we meet things physically inconvenient, without insulting them as if they were morally vile or logically contemptible. Real unselfishness consists in sharing the interests of others. Beyond the pale of actual unanimity the only possible unselfishness is chivalry–a recognition of the inward right and justification of our enemies fighting against us. This chivalry has long been practised in the battle-field without abolishing the causes of war; and it might conceivably be extended to all the conflicts of men with one another, and of the warring elements within each breast. Policy, hypnotisation, and even surgery may be practised without exorcisms or anathemas. When a man has decided on a course of action, it is a vain indulgence in expletives to declare that he is sure that course is absolutely right. His moral dogma expresses its natural origin all the more clearly the more hotly it is proclaimed; and ethical absolutism, being a mental grimace of passion, refutes what it says by what it is. Sweeter and more profound, to my sense, is the philosophy of Homer, whose every line seems to breathe the conviction that what is beautiful or precious has not thereby any right to existence; nothing has such a right; nor is it given us to condemn absolutely any force–god or man–that destroys what is beautiful or precious, for it has doubtless something beautiful or precious of its own to achieve.

The consequences of a hypostasis of the good are no less interesting than its causes. If the good were independent of nature, it might still be conceived as relevant to nature, by being its creator or mover; but Mr. Russell is not a theist after the manner of Socrates; his good is not a power. Nor would representing it to be such long help his case; for an ideal hypostasised into a cause achieves only a mythical independence. The least criticism discloses that it is natural laws, zoological species, and human ideals, that have been projected into the empyrean; and it is no marvel that the good should attract the world where the good, by definition, is whatever the world is aiming at. The hypostasis accomplished by Mr. Russell is more serious, and therefore more paradoxical. If I understand it, it may be expressed as follows: In the realm of eternal essences, before anything exists, there are certain essences that have this remarkable property, that they ought to exist, or at least that, if anything exists, it ought to conform to them. What exists, however, is deaf to this moral emphasis in the eternal; nature exists for no reason; and, indeed, why should she have subordinated her own arbitrariness to a good that is no less arbitrary? This good, however, is somehow good notwithstanding; so that there is an abysmal wrong in its not being obeyed. The world is, in principle, totally depraved; but as the good is not a power, there is no one to redeem the world. The saints are those who, imitating the impotent dogmatism on high, and despising their sinful natural propensities, keep asserting that certain things are in themselves good and others bad, and declaring to be detestable any other saint who dogmatises differently. In this system the Calvinistic God has lost his creative and punitive functions, but continues to decree groundlessly what is good and what evil, and to love the one and hate the other with an infinite love or hatred. Meanwhile the reprobate need not fear hell in the next world, but the elect are sure to find it here.

What shall we say of this strangely unreal and strangely personal religion? Is it a ghost of Calvinism, returned with none of its old force but with its old aspect of rigidity? Perhaps: but then, in losing its force, in abandoning its myths, and threats, and rhetoric, this religion has lost its deceptive sanctimony and hypocrisy; and in retaining its rigidity it has kept what made it noble and pathetic; for it is a clear dramatic expression of that human spirit–in this case a most pure and heroic spirit–which it strives so hard to dethrone. After all, the hypostasis of the good is only an unfortunate incident in a great accomplishment, which is the discernment of the good. I have dwelt chiefly on this incident, because in academic circles it is the abuses incidental to true philosophy that create controversy and form schools. Artificial systems, even when they prevail, after a while fatigue their adherents, without ever having convinced or refuted their opponents, and they fade out of existence not by being refuted in their turn, but simply by a tacit agreement to ignore their claims: so that the true insight they were based on is too often buried under them. The hypostasis of philosophical terms is an abuse incidental to the forthright, unchecked use of the intellect; it substitutes for things the limits and distinctions that divide them. So physics is corrupted by logic; but the logic that corrupts physics is perhaps correct, and when it is moral dialectic, it is more important than physics itself. Mr. Russell's ethics *is* ethics. When we mortals have once assumed the moral attitude, it is certain that an indefinable value accrues to some things as opposed to others, that these things are many, that combinations of them have values not belonging to their parts, and that these valuable things are far more specific than abstract pleasure, and far more diffused than one's personal life. What a pity if this pure morality, in detaching itself impetuously from the earth, whose bright satellite it might be, should fly into the abyss at a tangent, and leave us as much in the dark as before!

Public Opinion

Dominations and Powers: Reflections on Liberty, Society, and Government. New York: Charles Scribner's Sons; London: Constable and Co. Ltd., 1951, 341–44. Volume nineteen of the critical edition of *The Works of George Santayana.*

This selection appeared as Chapter 11 in Book Third of Dominations and Powers. *As early as 1918 Santayana mentioned his intention to write this book (LGS, 2:314–15), which he described as "a sort of psychology of politics and attempt to explain how it happens that governments and religions, with so little to recommend them, secure such a measure of popular allegiance" (LGS, 2:327). He thought the phenomenon well exemplified by athletics and on learning that his* alma mater *Harvard had beaten Yale at football he wrote in a letter, "I used to care immensely about this: and [*Dominations and Powers*] is largely based on that experience: it seems to me to explain all politics and wars" (LGS, 3:113). He put the work aside in 1937 as political instability increased and decided to wait until "a calm retrospective view is made possible" (LGS, 6:78, 138–39, 268). He began work on the book again in 1944, finished in 1950, and published it–his last book–the next year. This selection expresses Santayana's long-held belief that ideas exert no material influence but rather reflect material circumstances.*

A scrupulous logician might insist that the phrase "public opinion" makes nonsense, since the public is not a person, has no brain, no consecutive memory, and cannot opine. It can only assemble and shout, and many shouts make a public demonstration; but many ballots do not make a public idea. And yet a public act may ensue which a possible idea might justify; and if the act excited a public interest which did not exist before, the possible idea might well become actual in the persons who had acquired that interest. A crowd or an electorate may vote for war, and thereby create a thousand commercial and moral interests in portions of the public; parties who will tend to embrace ideas that justify the interests so suddenly thrust upon them. Then each variety of interest will favour a different type of opinion: first, for instance, a common enthusiasm for war and confidence in victory (though none of the persons concerned may have originally desired that war or dreamt of its possibility). Later, perhaps, a common desire for peace may follow in order that one man may escape taxes, another bombs, another military service, and another the ignorant tumult of public passions.

Public opinion is therefore a most real thing, and often a dominant power; many individuals habitually and all individuals occasionally embrace opinions together, under a common provocation and expressed in the same words. This public opinion is a distinct psychological event in each person, with a different intensity, duration, and field of suggestion; and this seems public opinion to each only in the measure in which its special character in himself is not distinguished. Nothing is heeded except some public action, sentiment, or words in the midst of which that personal opinion arose, with a powerful sense of being backed or borne forward by an irresistible persuasion, at least momentarily unanimous. The force of such public opinion in the private mind comes in no way through argument or evidence; for even if some eloquent phrase or the report of some crucial fact has occasioned it in each person, its *public* force lies entirely in the social blast that carried it, with magic conviction, into many minds at once. If the argument or evidence that rationally justifies this conviction is considered separately, coolly, and reflectively, the opinion so revised becomes a purely private opinion, independent of the character and number of the people that may happen to agree with it. Only if the prevalence of that opinion is expressly made the ground for accepting it, as in the maxim *quod semper, quod ubique, quod ab omnibus,* does public opinion still govern the private mind; and we shall probably find on examination that the society so clothed with authority is strictly limited and congenial to the man who adheres to it, and contrary to the prevalent opinion of mankind at large and in most ages. Under criticism, such a trust in unanimity becomes a private preference; the man respects a public authority because that particular public authority teaches what he likes to believe.

The spell of unanimity can therefore be exercised by a small assembly, with all the emotional magic of profound, blessed, invincible agreement. Indeed, two persons are enough, when they agree, to defy emotionally all the edicts of earth and of heaven. It is finding the *alter ego* who thinks as I do that is the satisfying, the reassuring support for the misgivings of solitude. These misgivings are animal, not logical; and the logician can overcome them by repeatedly agreeing with himself.

Public opinion and "the public" itself are conceptual fictions; yet nature is full of compound bodies that count as units in physics as well as in politics. A constellation in the sky may be a mythical entity; but a bear and a crab on earth are concrete and vital agents. Even a snowball is a dynamic unit when it flies, well aimed, and hits the passer-by. Each snowflake was light and fragile, and floated through the air without apparent aim or momentum; but when a mischievous urchin has compressed it, together with a thousand others, they have become as hard and as tight as ice. So the vague notions and animosities of an irresolute individual may become compact fury in a crowd; and the words that some demagogue selects to fix that notion or to whet that animosity may turn, for a moment, into a sudden passion in a thousand minds. Is this passion then a public passion? Yes, politically, for the moment, that concourse is dominated by it, and asserts and perhaps enacts it with an intense outflow of free will. Nevertheless not one, except the orator, might ever have found those words to represent or to transform his feelings nor, without those imposed words, might any one of them have ever felt that irresistible and glorious passion.

All feelings, then, in their living actuality, are private feelings, and all passions private passions; but by animal sympathy and contagion, the *sense* of each single feeling or passion sweeping through a crowd may possess each member of that crowd. And such an experience, even if no overt action comes to turn it into a commitment, warms the whole heart and leaves a durable nucleus in the psyche for all further enthusiasms and opinions. Public opinion, for a politician or a journalist, may ultimately become the whole furniture of the private mind; that which everybody thinks, or that which the majority are likely to think before long, becomes his standard of solidity; solidity rather than truth, because public opinion having become the test of private opinion, there is no truth to be considered except the political trustworthiness of such opinions as the public entertains and esteems.

The individual, however, has a memory as the public has not; and civilisation implies records and institutions which, for the reflective, enlarge private memory into some knowledge of other times, and of other forms of public opinion. Current public opinion may therefore sink, for the critic, into a passing phenomenon, necessarily partial and possibly pathological. Private judgment here has its innings again; not through ignorant egotism but on the contrary through respect for a wider view and a better understanding of the causes of public opinion. Public opinion is inevitably vaguer, more variable, more impulsive than the opinion of such members of the public as are particularly well informed; and it is morally less responsible, less prudent, more animal than are the actions of any sane individual. For the reversion to reason and conscience from the intoxication of tribal passions is not confined to learned or exceptional minds. The most helpless of the shouting mob in the circus is capable of it on the way home. Suppose as the crowd thins, that a man finds himself alone with his mate, who has shouted hurrah as loudly as himself and nudged him to express how great a man the leading speaker was. The two, after stopping to light their pipes, might begin to question this or that phrase of the orator's, saying that they were not sure that they liked that. Perhaps he hadn't quite got their own idea. In this way the unanimous enthusiasm of that public at its height might conceivably not represent the sober opinion of a single one of those present, except that of the orator himself. And I am perhaps not doing justice to his eloquence. For the more extraordinary his eloquence was, the more likely it is that what he said had never been his real and final opinion before, but came to him from the depths in the heat of improvisation; and though probably, in that case, he would adopt and repeat it perpetually henceforth in his propaganda, it is not inconceivable that, in his waking meditations in the silence of night, he might say to himself that it was nonsense.

If this ever happened, public opinion would not, in that instance, represent the private opinion or sober judgment of a single one of those who had contributed to form, to swell, or to diffuse that public opinion.

Government of the People

Dominations and Powers: Reflections on Liberty, Society, and Government. New York: Charles Scribner's Sons; London: Constable and Co. Ltd., 1951, 395–97. Volume nineteen of the critical edition of *The Works of George Santayana.*

This selection appeared as Chapter 26 of Book Third in Dominations and Powers. *In this book, which Santayana thought "closer to reality than any of [his] other books" (LGS, 8:265), he proposed "that there are three Orders of Society: the <u>Generative</u>, that grows up of itself: the <u>Militant</u>, which is imposed on mankind in all sorts of contradictory ways by bandits, conquerors, prophets, reformers, and idealists; and the third, the <u>Rational</u> order, which doesn't exist except in the imagination of philosophers. These Orders are treated in the three Books into which the whole work is divided. . . . Book III . . . contains a minute analysis of government of the people, by the people and for the People" (LGS, 8:189). This selection, which Santayana thought would "attract most attention in the U.S." (LGS, 8:87), considers the ambiguous phrase "government of the people."*

If we suppose various families together with stray individuals to be wrecked on a desert island, we can understand how, finding themselves in a common predicament, they will sometimes co-operate and sometimes quarrel; and then leaders will spontaneously appear who by the force of their words and actions will secure the obedience or acquiescence of their companions. A government will thus have arisen. Its function will not be to defend the territory, which is not being attacked, nor to build houses or occupy lands, since everyone will be quick to do so for himself in his own fashion. No one will have had prior possession of the soil, or will put forth ideal prerogatives as a prophet. The function of this government will be only to control such voluntary cooperation as there may spring up among the people and to settle their contentions by natural equity or common law. Individuals and families will look after themselves, and government will interfere with them only when they interfere with one another. It will have nothing to govern except the People.

It is not, however, in this purely social function that most governments are interested. Their concern is chiefly with the resources and political greatness of their dominions; and the constant stream of anonymous inhabitants that are born and die there preoccupy them only as tenants of the land, labourers in the mines, soldiers and sailors, taxpayers, and persons who otherwise the rulers wish to see flourishing in the State committed to their care.

Had Abraham Lincoln this broad contrast in mind when in his Gettysburg speech he defined the ideal character of American democracy? If he had he was giving to the first phrase in that definition "a government of the people" a more realistic historical and descriptive meaning than it carries to-day when it is perfunctorily repeated. I remember what violent emphasis, in the 1870's and 1880's, boys declaiming at the Boston Latin School, and other orators generally, would lay on the three prepositions in that formula, shouting almost angrily that a government *of* the people, *by* the people, and *for* the people should not perish from the earth. Nobody (except me) felt that the phrase "of the people" might have been originally a calm objective genitive implying, if anything, that the people required a government. And the language of the Gettysburg speech is so noble, so sober, and so carefully studied, that even now I doubt that Lincoln, in composing it, could have meant that first phrase to be a vaguer anticipation of what the second and third phrase announce explicitly. But in the popular mind, with frequent repetition, rhythm and enthusiasm have merged the whole into a ritual symbol; and that legal objective genitive has become decidedly possessive. It means that the government to be preserved shall be not only democratic in form and beneficent in operation, but precious and dear in itself, popular and homely: the People's Own Government. To be drawn from one's very vitals is indeed the radical sense of the genitive case; so that grammatically as well as emotionally this reading of the clause "a government of the people" is legitimate; but what does it signify politically?

This expression, "the people," though now often used to designate all the inhabitants of a region or of the globe, retains a rhetorical and political quality that limits it rather to one class of the total population. The official title of the Roman Republic, *Senatus Populusque Romanus,* explicitly distinguishes the people from the patricians or original landed families; and it ignores the slaves and aliens altogether who may sometimes have outnumbered the plebeian citizens. And there was another People to whom at least the Puritans in America felt themselves akin, the chosen People of Israel, even more sharply opposed to mankind in general or to the mixed population of great cities or recognised States. Even apart from that religious and moral idiosyncrasy felt by those who called themselves the people, there were in almost all American colonists bitter memories of proprietary monarchy and landlord tyranny; if a government was necessary at all, let it at least be composed of persons of their own class, knowing their needs and sharing their thoughts. No government, then, of aristocrats: no king, no priests, no landlords, no generals, no bureaucrats, and (they might have added prophetically) no professional politicians. Let all officials be plain men, drawn for a short time of service, by the general voice of their comrades, from the plough, the mine, the workshop, or the counting-house; and let them—since power corrupts—return soon to their old occupations, to drink in again the healthful atmosphere of labour and the rude but sound wisdom of unlettered men. Such is, as the people understand it, the true burden of the phrase "a government of the people."

It is obvious, however, and soon confirmed by experience, that as the business of government becomes complex—and it is complex beyond imagination—specialists may be employed to prepare its plans and to execute them. The common people must trust in most things the judgment of others; and how shall they decide whose judgment to trust? Waves of contagious feeling sweep through the public; and on these waves men of eloquence and tact rise in turn to power. How far can the government of the people, in these circumstances, remain the people's own government?

Who Are "The People"?

Dominations and Powers: Reflections on Liberty, Society, and Government. New York: Charles Scribner's Sons; London: Constable and Co. Ltd., 1951, 397–402. Volume nineteen of the critical edition of *The Works of George Santayana.*

This selection appeared as Chapter 27 of Book Third in Dominations and Powers. *In a letter, Santayana related the surprise at the title question of a guest who "had never thought of asking that before. I got the impression that he was not clear what it was all about, or whether it was acceptable or all wrong at bottom" (LGS, 8:245–46). This selection reflects Santayana's belief that "[s]ociety is not based on ideas, but on the material conditions of existence, such as agriculture and defence; virtue is moral health, and when genuine rests on the same foundations" (LGS, 6:30). The chapter explains that the relevant material conditions that determine who the people are, are not geography or race but rather the life activities and concrete values rooted in activities such as agriculture and defense of the community.*

When moral philosophy passes from an oracular phase into one that, at least in theory, is exclusively humanitarian, the object and criterion of good government will be said to be "the good of the people." This way of expressing it does not exclude from the functions of government all concern for country, glory, monuments, science, letters, or religion. The cultivation of these interests might well form a part of the good proper to the people, or to a part of them. Yet humanitarian morality excludes ideal aims except as they may be psychological demands in living persons; that they may have been occasionally the goods chiefly prized by mankind, or may be such in the future, would not make them the good of the people now. Leaving for consideration later what the good of the people may be, I will first consider more carefully the scope of this term "the People."

At first blush it may seem obvious that "the People" means all the inhabitants and that the people whose good a good government must serve comprise all the population subject to its jurisdiction. But these words are scarcely uttered when questions come trooping into the mind. Are resident foreigners, or tourists momentarily in the country, a part of "the People" that the government should serve? It certainly affects the strangers' comfort or welfare; should it provide for them gratis out of universal goodwill, or only in view of reciprocal favours to be expected by its own citizens when travelling or trading abroad? May not a good government conduct its foreign policy in such a way as to support kindred nations even at the cost of some sacrifice of material interests at home? And here subtler questions begin to appear. Are the purposes pursued by a nation in the past to be counted among its true interests apart from the degree of attention that the public may be giving them at the present moment? Should not a good government direct the people to a recognition of their *true* good? Should it not, for instance, leave them free, if their true good is liberty, even if they clamour for protection, prohibition, compulsory education of all grades, and guaranteed work, lodgings, pensions, and social services? Or, if the clamour is against these alleged benefits, should not a good government make itself the representative of the people's higher selves, show them what they would be missing without its guidance, and for their own good compel them to be healthy, educated, virtuous, and happy?

Whatever course the government takes it would seem to be condemned to secure the good as recognised by only *some* people. And this theoretical difficulty becomes a burning political problem in fixing the limits actually set to "The People" at various times and places.

Thus the ancient Jews frankly called themselves the *chosen* people, limited in race to the children of Abraham and in moral identity to faithful adherents to the Law of Moses and the spirit of the Hebrew Prophets. The same principle of selection for membership in the one rightly dominant people on earth and triumphant society in heaven appears in Islam and in the various forms of Christianity, modified by historical circumstances; and it reappears now, disguised in secular terms, in the two rival "ideologies," communist and liberal, ready to exterminate each other. The "People" in the one case include only the Communist Party, faithful to its providentially self-imposed leaders; and in the other it includes all men in so far as they agree to differ in thought, but in action always follow the majority. The People, for the communists, must be unanimous. For the liberals all parties are admitted, except the "criminals" who attempt to impose their special opinions by force or by guile. Even here, therefore, the police must impose respect for what one party esteems most, namely, for liberty.

These attempts to be rational are really militant; and we must look to the generative order of society to see what "the People" in fact may signify. In tribal societies it naturally means the tribe; and when agriculture has domesticated and rooted them it means the *local* population in contrast to strangers and the *common* people in contrast to their natural leaders. The classical case, from which the word "people" is derived, is that of the *Senatus Populusque Romanus.* Verbally, the contrast here is between patricians—the landowners with their children and dependents—and the artisan free population of the City. But there was another class (or classes) excluded from the People politically: namely resident foreigners, chiefly merchants, and slaves who served the patrician and plebeian landlords or householders. It was only the natives that formed the *Senatus Populusque;* and those together formed, not the population, but the government.

This articulation of the contrast between the government and the governed was transformed by the barbarian conquest, the feudal system, and the Christian types of peasant serfdom and domestic service. Peasants and servants then joined the artisans in the towns in composing "the People"; and distinct, though often derived, from them were the clergy and men-at-arms, commanded by a nobility composed of military chiefs turned into local proprietors and potentates. A complicated hierarchy of lieges and vassals of different ranks arose both in Church and State, with Popes, Emperors, and Kings, by divine right, occupying exalted places, often rather dignities than powers. Yet, especially in the commercial or industrial cities, vestiges of the *Populusque Romanus* re-appeared in picturesque Christian guise. The trades became institutions, with legal privileges and rights, such as the plebeians had extorted in Rome from the patricians. These towns-people could well resist the exactions of their feudal overlords. Merchants, artists, doctors, and clergy began to form a bourgeois class, distinct from artisans and shopkeepers, and began to feel that they were not essentially part of the People. They became the upper middle class. Yet it has been they, backed by militant eruptions from the working class beneath and the aristocracy above, that have constituted the liberal and democratic parties of recent times, invoking and professing to serve the People, without being a part of them.

In modern England social and political custom has never sharply distinguished the "People" from the nation or from the government; and it can hardly be said that universal suffrage, for instance, has brought the government nearer to the heart of the people than it was under Queen Elizabeth. Nevertheless the social hierarchy has nowhere been more clearly defined or respected than in England until the twentieth century. Snobbery, of which satirists accused the nation, was a peculiar sentiment of duty, deference, and sympathy in the humbler persons, at each stage, towards those above them; and emotionally the Court and the government felt themselves to be as much a part of the people as the shopkeepers, servants, or sailors.

The same continuity of political consciousness runs in the United States through all degrees of wealth and forms of labour; and the same good-natured pleasure at the greater wealth of others is seen in the common people as in England at their higher station, which is not long distinguishable from hereditary wealth.

Perhaps the most genuine line of cleavage in human society, in all ages and countries, is that between the rich and the poor. The poor we have always with us, and in some form the rich and the privileged also; but while wealth, at least great wealth, is not visible in a man or woman, but only in their houses or other belongings, poverty can be recognised at sight, and is distress made visible. It also has the property, proper to the generative order of things, of being in flux and removable, at least in its casual forms and distribution. In the East, where extreme poverty is often patent and widespread, it seems too human and exchangeable a condition to form a particular people, especially where traditional wisdom and refinement of feeling may often be present in the poor more than in the rich.

It is precisely in the East that the naturally distinctive properties of a people become obvious, crossing all boundaries of States and established jurisdictions. A people is properly speaking a civilised tribe, united by blood, language, and religion. In its origins a people may be as hybrid as you please, but in so far as it is morally and politically one people it will tend to become, by inbreeding, a pure race. If a mixed population in a given territory tends to segregate rather than to merge (as whites and blacks seem to tend in the United States) they will become two peoples: which would not necessarily prevent them from living side by side in the same country under the same government, if this government were not totalitarian, but respected the moral and civic individuality of each people.

Contemporary support for this analysis of the political essence of a people may be found in the language of communist governments. They demand that all political parties and influences be inspired by the people: but this "People" is not the whole population, nor the majority of it, nor the part that preserves and transmits ancient tradition. It means often a small minority of the inhabitants who have recently embraced (even in Russia) a foreign theory of government. Yet these few converts compose a people, and even the People, precisely because they are the proletariat, that is to say, the outcasts, without possessions or allegiance of any sort, and are therefore called to gather from all nations, like the early Christians, and form together a new universal People, unanimous in faith and obedient to a rule of life which the whole world ought to adopt and must adopt if it is to establish peace on earth and to enjoy it for ever.

Government is an art, serving economic and moral interests. The limits of the people who inspire and obey it are properly vital and moral limits, not geographical or racial except by accident. A people may migrate, and in proportion to the strength of its vital unity it will tend to fuse its blood and its moral heritage into a single race and language. Tribal bonds are usually local; the local cohabitation may be the occasion of vital fusion among peoples originally strangers and rivals. On the other hand a purely moral bond, like religion, may sometimes suffice to cement and distinguish a scattered people. The Jews are the palmary example of great and long-lived people closely united without a government or a territory; and Islam, while essentially militant and haughty, can unite many different regions and races into one people by attachment to a common way of life and sentiment. And it seems to me not impossible that in a similar way the Catholic Church, without anywhere retaining political domination, might subsist throughout the world as a distinct people, in larger or smaller groups of different races and speech, everywhere faithful to the same religious customs, philosophy, and arts.

Such a diversity of civilised peoples, each with its vital inspiration and traditional regimen, flourishing perhaps on the same universal basis of a rational economic order, would seem to me highly desirable. Mankind walks on one material planet under one material firmament; these conditions it is to their common advantage to respect. But, that toll once paid to necessity, why should not vital liberty in each heart devise the private or social or ideal order by which it would live?

The United States as Leader

Dominations and Powers: Reflections on Liberty, Society, and Government. New York: Charles Scribner's Sons; London: Constable and Co. Ltd., 1951, 456–61. Volume nineteen of the critical edition of *The Works of George Santayana.*

In this selection, which appeared as Chapter 45 of Book Third in Dominations and Powers, *Santayana considered how the United States might be best-suited to lead a universal government that directed material conditions and left the various peoples of the world to manage their own moral affairs. But despite his sanguine view of the United States as leader, he recognized inherent difficulties. In a letter he wrote, "my chief divergence from American views lies in that I am not a dogmatist in morals or politics and do not think that the same form of government can be good for everybody; except in those matters where everybody is subject to the same influence and has identical interests. . . . But where the interests of people are moral and imaginative they ought to be free to govern themselves. . . . the universal authority ought to manage only economic, hygienic, and maritime affairs. . . . Now the Americans' . . . way of talking is doctrinaire, as if they were out to save souls and not to rationalize commerce. And the respect for majorities instead of for wisdom is out of place in any matter of ultimate importance. . . . It cuts off all possibility of a liberal civilization"* (LGS, 8:294–95).

There is a point in political theory in which events have confirmed the position adopted above. A universal government would have to be a particular government, rooted in the generative order of history, and not an alliance of sovereign states or a universal parliament. The League of Nations was still-born; and when it had been buried, almost the same group of victorious powers that had blindly set it up set up the Organisation of United Nations on the same blind principles. They even introduced the old Polish system of an individual right of veto for each of the Great Powers, as if to make executive impotence not only constitutional but expressly intended and prized.

Yet this impotence had a vital nerve in it. A decision cannot be universally satisfying unless it is unanimous. And Russia had already established at home the ideal of unanimity and the practice of autocratic government to impose that unanimity by education and training or, failing that, by terror. Russia too had been the most brilliant of the victors in this second war; and Stalin at once adopted the policy of vetoing everything that did not conduce to the extension of communist domination.

Here, then, is one living and powerful government, strongly national in its central seat and in its leading members, but theoretically liberal in the treatment of other nationalities and languages. At the same time there is a militant thirst for the political assimilation of all peoples to the social regimen of Russia, which in that claim forfeits all rational authority. Rational authority, according to my analysis, can accrue to governments only in so far as they represent the inescapable *authority of things,* that is to say, of the material conditions of free life and free action. In the Marxist theory this almost seems to be involved in its materialistic character; yet in Russian practice it is not the authority of things but nominally the material class interests and militant Will of the proletariat and really the ambition of the self-appointed inner circle of the Communist party that not only rule absolutely but intend to keep the whole world unanimous by "liquidating" all dissentients. And half by the wonderful power of propaganda and mass-suggestion and half by systematic extermination of all other ways of thinking, this artificial unanimity has actually seemed to cover vast regions of Europe and Asia like a blanket of Siberian snow. The depth of it is unknown, but the silence is impressive.

It is not, then, by the authority of universal physical conditions of existence that the Russian government would exercise control over all nations in military and economic matters; it would be rather by a revolutionary conspiracy fomented everywhere that it would usurp a moral and intellectual domination over all human societies. Such baseless pretensions cancel the right which economic science might have to guide a universal material economy.

What fitness have the United States, which have now come forward as a rival, to become the secular arm of Reason in checking the unreason of the world?

I had not, in 1934, ventured to name the United States as one of the powers that might be entrusted with that universal political duty. The American people had refused to join the League of Nations, more by an instinct of general distrust than by an insight into the folly of expecting an assembly of sovereign powers to possess or to carry out a consistent policy. The prevalence of representative government and the habit of being docile to majorities, when no fundamental interests were at stake, made Americans slow to feel that danger. And it was under this domestic illusion that, in 1946, a replica of the rejected and extinct League of Nations, with the aggravating feature of right of veto for each of the great powers, was established under American leadership on American soil. Except for that veto, which at once paralysed all decisive action, it would have been natural for the United States to have begun to offer its own forces, then very strong and fit, to carry out the decrees of the universal authority. This authority, indeed, would have been little but a chorus to approve, or at most to retard by some accidental scruple, the special foreign policy of the United States.

At the same moment, by the unprecedented election of a President for a third and fourth term of office, and by an immense extension and elaborate organisation of all the departments of State, the American Government was becoming an automatic power, far more intelligent and determined than any floating and temporary majority in Congress; so that a traditional great government, comparable to the Roman, might have arisen in the United States and might have legally, and by general consent, have established its universal jurisdiction.

Would such an American hegemony have operated justly and deserved to endure?

There are several respects in which it would seem eminently capable of doing so. In the first place, the American people are good; their mentality is settled and pervasive; they are devoted and ingenious in improving the instruments and methods of material economy: and it is precisely in this sphere that they would have been called upon to act for the welfare of all mankind. They would have done so honestly, diligently, guided by experts in every department; and while a cumbrous official system, with much pedantry and delay and some false and premature theories, might have intervened, there need not have been, in their government, that open, perhaps unconscious, selfishness which many imperial governments have shown in the past. And this not because Americans are superhumanly unselfish, but because in questions of universal peace and universal trade their self-interest coincides with that of all other nations, or would at least do so if it were clearly understood and strictly confined to material economy.

But would an American management of international affairs be really confined to the economic sphere? It is no doubt the desire to keep American enterprise alive and progressive, by establishing everywhere rational commercial relations advantageous to both sides, that fundamentally inspires what the Russians call American imperialism; but quickness and sagacity in the economic arts are human virtues, and in the human psyche which is the agent in politics, they cannot stand alone. By the obvious well-being which they bring, they breed self-satisfaction and complacency; and the technically just belief that rational trade is profitable even to the less enterprising party excites a pleasing passion for doing good. And there are so many other goods, like education and training, that help to secure prosperity and in turn are favoured by it! The authority that controlled universal economy, if it were in American hands, would irresistibly tend to control education and training also. It might set up, as was done in the American zone in occupied Germany, a cultural department, with ideological and political propaganda. The philanthropic passion for service would prompt social, if not legal, intervention in the traditional life of all other nations, not only by selling there innumerable American products, but by recommending, if not imposing, American ways of living and thinking.

Now, this is, perhaps unintentionally, to transgress the limits of rational control and to exercise an influence that may be justly resented. If you wish to practice a mechanical art, the expert mechanic can rationally teach you how to do it; but if you wish to think or to practice a liberal art, another man, because he is self-satisfied, must not run up unasked and tell you to do it otherwise than as your vital liberty directs. The restraints that circumstances and the nature of things impose on your Will may be kindly pointed out to you before you commit yourself to a hopeless course; but the choice of your way must be left to you, if the authority that controls society is rational and friendly.

If, for instance, some community preferred not to trade at all, seeing that it could live suitably on native products, the universal government ought to limit its action in regard to that community to preventing their interference with the peace and liberty of their neighbours. It is a government, not a religion with a militant mission, that is demanded. It comes to serve and to keep order, not to dominate where it has no moral roots.

The British Empire, which was not founded or held exclusively for economic reasons, had a way of governing at once more reserved and more spectacular than the American system seems likely to be. There was military pomp and official grandeur about it; and the sportsmen of aristocratic breeding who chiefly carried it on meddled as little as possible with the natives. If the measures dictated to them from Whitehall were sometimes oppressive and designed to maintain British trade, even perhaps in opium, the thoughts of the military men and civil servants who actually governed were fixed rather on national prestige and on home and family affairs. It was as Englishmen that they fought and ruled, not as experts in an impartial and international economy. The very idea of a rational moral regimen for mankind was unknown to them, and they quite naturally associated prosperity rather with brave military enterprise than, as Americans naturally associate it, with a rising volume of irresistible trade. The fruits of monopolist adventure and of incessant mechanical invention have dangled in America before the eyes of ambitious youth and of capitalist old age; it was a world in progress and ulterior repercussions and settlements were not considered. The militancy of trade and of political reform seemed vital and almost normal, and undoubtedly it lent a speed and brilliancy to the growth of industry and of wealth in the nineteenth century which seemed to contemporaries an unmixed good, to be pursued and intensified for ever.

It is only now that the multiplication of mechanisms has become a nightmare, omnipresent advertisements a plague, the overgrown proletariat a quicksand beneath the feet of wealth, and the hierarchy of occupations a reversion to a sort of serfdom. In Europe this tragedy of commercialism is perceived; in America it seems to rumble still invisible below the horizon. And it may be a serious question whether a universal government in American hands would not attempt to revitalise the commercial optimism of the nineteenth century, by the aid of new inventions and better coordination of resources. Or would it face the inevitable limit to industrial expansion, and establish a stable economic order in a world where labour might again merge with self-rewarding arts, and imagination turn from devising machines to cultivating liberal arts and enlarging moral freedom?

Conclusion *[Dominations and Powers]*

Dominations and Powers: Reflections on Liberty, Society, and Government. New York: Charles Scribner's Sons; London: Constable and Co. Ltd., 1951, 461–66. Volume nineteen of the critical edition of *The Works of George Santayana.*

This conclusion appeared as Chapter 43 of Book Third in Dominations and Powers. *Book Third, explained Santayana, is "concerned with <u>rationality</u> in government rather than with moral rightness in precepts or ideals. Moral rightness has its credentials in nature. All life, if not all existence, has an intrinsic <u>direction</u>; it therefore evokes phantoms of good and evil according as things (or words) seem to support or impede its own <u>élan</u>. There can be no question, no possibility, of abolishing moral allegiance: only, when it breaks down in part, to get it together again <u>rationally</u>, in its own interests" (LGS, 8:384). The conclusion takes a native rationality to be the standard of good government. But Santayana recognized that his idea of good government was imaginative and would not be popular, and in the conclusion "there is a satirical fable, before the end about how people would hate it if ruled by a universal government in economics and by local or party governments in education and 'culture'" (LGS, 8:271). The point of the fable is not to choose sides, but rather it indicates how one might "distinguish wisdom from folly" by tracing interests and possible goods (ES, 477).*

The reflections gathered together in this book have not been prompted by an innocent desire to proclaim a political creed. Would it not have been a strange impertinence to assert that Julius Caesar should behave like Coriolanus or Hamlet like Henry the Fifth, either on the stage or in the world? Even less should I venture to prophesy the course of history in the future. What wiseacre in the nineteenth century could have considered possible the things we have seen in the twentieth?

This view by no means abandons the distinction between rational and irrational or between right and wrong. It rather insists that they cannot be arbitrary distinctions but must have some natural ground. In pronouncing anything to be rational or right we presuppose an underlying direction of vital energy or endeavour (here called primal Will) which some suggested step would serve to carry out. So a policy proposed at a Cabinet meeting can be judged to be right only by its fitness to further the aims of the government, these aims in turn can be judged only by the interests of the nation, and these interests only by the philosophy of the judge.

Rationality and rightness thus appear to be essentially relative; for it is their relativity that makes them relevant to events in the world. Were they absolute, and irrelevant to human nature and circumstances, they would be pathological fixations, making for militant madness.

In politics conscious rationality begins with the economic arts which would become wholly rational if they were organised exclusively in view of their utility and employed materials, time, and labour as economically as possible. In reality, as already pointed out, there is often a margin of spontaneous interest and initiative in doing things, which makes work partly liberal art; and besides, as men are not machines, they inevitably waste time and materials; both workmen and employers lounge a good deal and are more numerous than necessary, as are the clerks, salesmen, auxiliaries of every description, and hangers-on from senior partners to office boys; for they all think that the business exists to employ them and not they to carry on the business. In this way, while the machine threatens to mechanise mankind, old human nature does its best to humanise the machine.

The automatic equilibrium essential to health also helps in another sphere to soften the severity of reason. For sometimes reason tends to substitute pure method or simplicity or symmetry, with their empty magic, for the natural impulses of the artist; impulses that reason might have enlightened if they were misled by appearances or if they were themselves as yet inarticulate.

Many philosophers and politicians indeed tell us that they already possess *a priori* an adequate knowledge of what human needs and capacities are, and that they are really identical in everybody. The contrasts and conflicts in society, and in each man, they attribute to the absence or perversity of education. All men, they say, *must* find the same moral political and scientific regimen, communism, or constitutional democracy, or the One True Religion, perfectly satisfying. If they hesitate or condemn all such regimens, it *must* be because they are ignorant of the facts and of their own true good.

I think that these philosophers and politicians have good knowledge of themselves. They are born dogmatists and congenitally militant. But this disposition of theirs, at once intolerant and uneasy, blinds them to the actual radical diversity among men. This they cannot admit because, if admitted, it would prove them to be born tyrants. If this word "tyrant" is taken for a term of reproach, they can never be convicted of it in their own courts; but if taken to signify the superman, they will claim it with pride. They say we are all super-animals, either fallen from heaven or about to make a heaven for ourselves on earth.

It is often the boldest minds that, inspired by some political or religious dream, impose needless duties and taboos upon one another. A government that would be rational, on the contrary, would imitate the modesty of the physician that recommends only what can enable us to escape or to overcome the assaults that natural accidents may make upon us. Only that while government imposes instead of recommending its legal diet, it may also invite us to meet opportunities open to our powers. In both directions, however, it only forestalls and discovers for us the dumb beckonings of fortune. All else a rational government would leave to the special genius of each free society and each free individual. In suggesting such a division of moral labour, order where the conditions are known, liberty where imagination makes its own laws, I am far from expecting that such a division will actually be made; nor, if by chance the thousand forces at work ever fell into this arrangement, do I imagine that it would last long. Reason is itself a method of imaginative thought. It insinuates itself with difficulty even into economic arts, by virtue of the regularity of natural processes, to which action has to adapt itself;

but it lives happy and safe only in ideal constructions, mathematical or poetical.

Fondly, then, as I might regard a final peace between order and liberty, secured by the rational separation of their spheres, yet I can imagine far more clearly, and not without some merriment, the shouts of joy with which one or another passion or irrepressible faith would hasten to break that agreement.

I picture to myself, almost in the clouds, a many-pavilioned International Institute of Rational Economy, faultless in architecture and appointments, like an Oxford set upon the Rock of Gibraltar. All strength and all learning to keep the world in the right path: what could be more satisfying? But at the foot of this citadel there would have to be a commercial and industrial town, with its own self-government and factions. There might be riots and revolutions there, too insignificant and local to demand international control. And in the spiral roads, or steep stairs, or funiculars that led to the citadel there might sometimes be scuffles between town and gown, or academic arguments, even more dangerous to moral peace. Nor would that be the greatest danger. Little knots of critical spirits would be formed in that high nursery of wisdom itself and would whisper their heresies in corners, or run down to join the demonstrations in the town square; for even supposing justice enforced in international relations, who could prevent local tyranny and deadly stagnation in free cities or free Churches? Moreover, economic order could not be maintained in the great world at long range by the International Institute without expeditionary forces of soldiers, sailors, airmen, and police, and all the holders of scholarships, experts, and young professors at that central nursery of peace would have begun by seeing military and inquisitorial service at the outposts of the Institute all over the world; they would all have seen something of the unregenerate edges of civilisation, and of political conspiracy at the heart of it. Imagination in some of these future guardians of universal peace would have been impressed by the lawless spirit they had come to root out. It may have seemed more human than the rational economy they were going to enforce. The excitement of lawlessness may have visited them in dreams. Why not try it in real life? Why not decamp to the mountains or run away to sea? Good luck might cast them on the smallest of islands in the widest of oceans where they might run about naked under the mangoes or paddle out boldly in double canoes beyond the horizon to capture and bring home each his innocent and loving bride. How much prouder they would be at having been ravished at sight by a young stranger than our spectacled sister-students who, after being wall-flowers on show for years, marry some elderly cousin!

But not all those emancipated minds would have been so selfishly pleasure-loving and, alas! so short-sighted! In rushing down from their Peace-Force Barracks, some of them would not have forgotten to fling open the cages of all the animals in the Zoological Gardens which, as an aid to understanding mankind, studded the flanks of that mountain. What new life they would bring to those unhappy brothers of theirs! Soon the old jungle and the old forests would teem with every sort of free creature, feeding, breeding, and fighting without respite! And the feasts would not be conventional like a dinner after a foxhunt, but truly royal, truly primitive, with the stag or boar or suckling-pigs on the table; and they themselves would sit like Nimrods enthroned and magnificently draped in the skins of their leopards and their lions, or like trappers or archers in a mountain camp, sporting the feathers of their quarry.

Other young pupils of Rational Economy might not have had time to shake off the dulcet diction of their former pedagogues; and they might attempt modestly to change the subject. "But how sad," they might murmur, "how sad to think that for so long we should have done that cruel wrong to our fellow-creatures by condemning them to undeserved captivity in dismal bare cells—so like our own, alas! in that prison!—with no outlook except on an artificial garden, with asphalt walks and arc-lights, when they were meant to range freely over wild and boundless spaces! Yes, and what's worse, we have condemned them to be fed on scanty, horrible, monotonous rations, thrown at them (think of the ignominy of this!) at precisely stated hours, while a crowd of grinning cockneys stare at them and poke them with umbrellas! As if our common Mother Nature had not commanded them to gorge their fill whenever and wherever they found what they wanted; and as for finding it, to have faith and to trust in *Her!*"

It would be to misread the moral of this fable simply to approve one party, the constitutional and rational, or the other party, the militant and romantic; or to propose a third regimen, no less absolute and universal in intention. The study of human behaviour and opinion would then have taught us nothing, except perhaps that we must put up with them, whatever they choose to be. If we wish to draw some moral from experience we must assume that we are living in a world where our behaviour has causes and consequences that recede in all directions until they become irrelevant to our interests; but at closer quarters they can be traced in terms of the sensations and ideas that events excite in us. In these terms we can observe or learn from history and general report what sort of conduct will further our interests and what sort will ruin them; so that the question at once becomes not what we like best, but whether any part, and how much, of what we think we should like we can possibly secure. In a word, we shall be able to distinguish wisdom from folly.

Knowledge of the world and of what is possible in it, though it may discourage some vices, will not solve for us the question of what is our true good. For what the world can offer, when tried, may seem to us vanity. There is therefore another sphere, that of potential goods, which each man may evoke according to the warmth and richness of his imagination; and if he has any integrity or moral strength he will easily discern where his chosen treasure lies. Whether it is attainable in the world or not will not shake his allegiance: it is based on a native bent in his soul without which he would cease to be himself.

It follows from the evolution of the psyche through plants and animals that its treasure is at each stage different; and in man I think it is generally alien domination that makes anyone mistake his vocation. Strictly there is a complete impossibility, even between brothers, to conceive each other's inner man. The catalogue of possible virtues is limited only by the capacity of the cataloguer. But existence imposes limitation and idiosyncrasy even on the imagination and the Will (which Descartes said is infinite); and how should any of us, with his inevitable bias, pronounce which moral vocation is "the best"? Comparison can only be made with reference to a chosen good, chosen by chance; and wisdom lies not in pronouncing what sort of good is best but in understanding each good within the lives that enjoy it as it actually is in its physical complexion and in its moral essence.

V

Literature, Culture, and Criticism

Santayana's literary and critical endeavors did not take second place to his philosophical works. In fact, his first published book was *Sonnets and Other Verses* (1894). *Interpretations of Poetry and Religion,* his third book (after his well-known *The Sense of Beauty*), was as much literary criticism as philosophy. The essays of philosophical criticism included in this section–focusing on Emerson, Nietzsche, James, Royce, and Dewey–each offer assessments of a figure in light of his cultural context.

The section begins with examples of Santayana's literary work: "Sonnet III," a famous and oft-anthologized poem; a series of poems for Warwick Potter, a student and close friend who died young; and short sections from the novel *The Last Puritan.*

The novel tells the tragic story of Oliver Alden, the intelligent, wealthy, and conscientious descendant of well-established New England families. He is doomed because his integrity and virtue simultaneously incapacitate him and urge him to reject his crippling excellences. In the "Prologue" to the novel Santayana imagined a conversation in Paris with a fictional former student, Mario Van de Weyer, a friend and cousin of Oliver. Mario proposes that Santayana write the life story of Oliver and explains the significance of the title with the claim that "in Oliver puritanism worked itself out to its logical end. He convinced himself, on puritan grounds, that it was wrong to be a puritan" (*ES,* 489). The character of Santayana remarks that the secret of Oliver was "the tragedy of the spirit when it's not content to understand but wishes to govern" (*ES,* 491).

In the "Epilogue" the character of Santayana points out that Mario represents a relationship to tradition that is healthier than Oliver's. Santayana says to Mario: "Your modernness sucks in all the sap of the past . . .; and any future worth having will spring from men like you, not from weedy intellectuals or self-inhibited puritans. Fortune will never smile on those who disown the living forces of nature" (*ES,* 494).

In his novel Santayana dramatized his philosophy, his observations of modern American culture, and his ideas about literary art. In his critical essays he often considered specific literary figures. In one such essay Santayana observed that contemporary artists lacked a total vision and a capacity for idealization. This left the culture without its own standards of beauty or perfection. In place of ideals, barbarous art celebrates subjective, undisciplined passions as the highest values. As examples of such artistic practice, "The Poetry of Barbarism" considers Walt Whitman and Robert Browning. Both had powerful imaginations, but each was limited: Whitman to collecting sensations, Browning to subjective thought and feeling. Neither could rise to the level of reason by which chaotic sensation and subjective feeling could be fashioned into an ideal.

In "Emerson," Santayana identified the hallowed American essayist's single theme as imagination. It allowed Emerson to escape convention and avoid formulating a doctrine. Idealization rather than any particular ideal was his aim. But this resulted in disorganized thought and mystical tendencies. These tendencies were supported not only by his freedom of imagination but also the "moral intensity and metaphysical abstraction" of his ancestral Calvinism freed from any literal doctrine (*ES,* 525). He was, claimed Santayana, "a Puritan mystic" (*ES,* 524).

Lingering Calvinism appears again in "The Genteel Tradition in American Philosophy," an essay diagnosing American intellectual life as detached from the active Will of the nation. American Will was seen in the skyscraper; but American intellect remained in the colonial mansion: "The one is all aggressive enterprise; the other is all genteel tradition" (*ES,* 527). The genteel tradition drew on an irrelevant Calvinism and an imported idealism, and these left American philosophy unable to express a meaningful vision of American life and unaware of its culture. Santayana observed that Walt Whitman and William James contributed in different ways to breaking the spell of the genteel tradition, but neither succeeded in overthrowing it.

In "English Liberty in America" Santayana examined the fate of another European import in America. He contrasted English Liberty with Absolute Liberty. The first is characterized by the cooperation of free individuals and requires unanimity in society and plasticity in individuals. The second is characterized by the single-minded pursuit of some clear and unchanging ideal. It forces cooperation in its pursuit thereby eliminating individual liberty. English Liberty is a method of organizing society, whereas Absolute Liberty is radically individual and exhibited by fanatics, poets, and martyrs. The advantage of the first is its acknowledgment of the natural plurality of aims; and the second, though impracticable, is in its purity of aim more perfect and more beautiful. But, Santayana observed, the curse of existence is to reject some things that are beautiful.

Santayana revisited the Genteel Tradition twenty years after his first diagnosis. He found that even though it seemed to have disappeared, really it had assumed a new form: namely the New Humanism of Irving Babbitt and Paul Elmer More, who championed classical principles. Santayana thought that the three "R"s of modern history—the Renaissance, the Reformation, and the modern political Revolutions—along with Romanticism, had left modern culture without unity or discipline. This result of the old Humanism disturbed the New Humanists who sought to reestablish a belief in a supernatural human soul by means of a Christian Platonism. Santayana preferred a naturalistic morality, which he defended in this essay.

Looking abroad, Santayana saw Nietzsche as the last in a series of German romantic egotists that began with Kant and ran through Hegel. While Santayana thought Nietzsche immature and disparaged his philosophical originality, he also thought Nietzsche's expressions significant as an indicator of a great shift in deep instincts: "What he said may be nothing, but the fact that he said it is all-important" (*ES*, 583). The doctrines may be foolish, but they may provide the materials for future philosophies after the old have been swept away.

Santayana's portraits of his American teachers, colleagues, and contemporaries show how their thought departed from his own naturalism. He observed in them subjectivism, romanticism, moralism, and metaphysics; and each of these distorts the reality of material nature by privileging some particular perspective or falsely attributing powers to immaterial things.

Santayana thought that William James' openness to experience led him to degrade the idea of truth and exchange substantive fact for theory and perception. James at his worst claimed that a belief in oneself could bring about successful execution of some action and thereby justify itself. This self-assurance Santayana thought worthless if it was mere self-delusion, and he held that a true belief in one's abilities was a symptom of really being able to accomplish something. This view followed James at his best as the psychologist who observed that the emotion of fear was the result of the shaking and trembling body in response to certain conditions.

Santayana found Josiah Royce's philosophy confused, moralistic, and rooted in sadness and trouble. Royce claimed that good is the struggle with and triumph over evil, hence good is possible because of evil. But then virtue becomes dependent on vice and pleasure exists only as contrast with or relief from suffering; there is no pure pleasure of understanding. Santayana saw in Royce "the aboriginal principle of all superstition: reverence for what hurts" (*ES*, 601).

John Dewey's emphasis on experience, according to Santayana, resulted in a philosophy marked by "*the dominance of the foreground*," that is, by the elevation of local interests or perspectives over nature, in which there is no absolute perspective, no foreground or background (*ES*, 613). To emphasize experience is to read the social world onto the entire universe. Because the social conditions in America happened to emphasize material activity, Dewey came by his naturalism accidentally, prompting Santayana's indictment that Dewey's "naturalism is half-hearted and short-winded" (*ES*, 614). On Santayana's view, Dewey believed immediate experience to influence the future; this would be a species of metaphysics and a departure from naturalism.

Sonnet III

The Complete Poems of George Santayana: A Critical Edition. Edited by William G. Holzberger. Lewisburg, PA: Bucknell University Press; London: Associated University Presses, 1979, 92.

This poem first appeared in the Harvard Monthly *in 1886. It was reprinted with some changes in* Sonnets and Other Verses *and thereafter often anthologized. Santayana wrote the sonnet while studying Greek tragedies as a sophomore at Harvard in 1884. It was inspired by a line from Euripides' play* The Bacchae, *"τὸ σοφὸν οὐ σοφία," which Santayana translated as "It is not wisdom to be only wise." He built the sonnet around this line and took the original as his personal motto, often including it with his autograph (LGS, 8:437). In his autobiography he claimed it was his first sonnet and that numbers I and II were "composed afterwards on purpose to frame in the earlier one and bring the argument to a head" (PP, 231), but the evidence of his notebooks suggests otherwise (See CP, fn. 16, 28–9). Santayana remarked that this poem, often entitled "Faith" by editors of anthologies, "passes into the religious calendars and anthologies as vindicating Christian faith, or some faith very nearly Christian" despite the Greek inspiration being "as sceptical as it is possible to be, since it fell back on Bacchic instinct, or animal faith" (LGS, 6:190–91).*

O world, thou choosest not the better part!
It is not wisdom to be only wise,
And on the inward vision close the eyes,
But it is wisdom to believe the heart.
Columbus found a world, and had no chart,
Save one that faith deciphered in the skies;
To trust the soul's invincible surmise
Was all his science and his only art.
Our knowledge is a torch of smoky pine
That lights the pathway but one step ahead
Across a void of mystery and dread.
Bid, then, the tender light of faith to shine
By which alone the mortal heart is led
Unto the thinking of the thought divine.

From *Sonnets and Other Verses* by George Santayana (Cambridge and Chicago: Stone and Kimball, 1894).

To W. P.

The Complete Poems of George Santayana: A Critical Edition. Edited by William G. Holzberger. Lewisburg, PA: Bucknell University Press; London: Associated University Presses, 1979, 125–27.

These four sonnets first appeared in Sonnets and Other Verses *(1894). Santayana wrote them in 1893 after the death of his former student and close friend Warwick Potter. Santayana and Potter had been "constant companions" in the two years before Potter's graduation from Harvard in 1893. Santayana, then teaching philosophy at Harvard, was nine years Potter's senior and wrote that, he "insensibly came to think of [Potter] as a younger brother and as a part of myself" (PP, 350). In summer 1893 Potter and his brother Robert joined a friend for an ocean cruise aboard his yacht. Weakened by severe seasickness, Potter contracted cholera and died in October in the harbor of Brest, France (PP, 350; LGS, 1:189). Santayana was shaken by this loss, but he wrote, "[t]he cause of my emotion was in myself. I was brimming over with the sense of parting, of being divided by fortune where at heart there was no division. . . . It was not good simple Warwick alone that inspired my verses about him. It was the thought of everything that was escaping me: the Good in all the modes of it that I might have caught a glimpse of and lost" (PP, 423).*

I

Calm was the sea to which your course you kept,
Oh, how much calmer than all southern seas!
Many your nameless mates, whom the keen breeze
Wafted from mothers that of old have wept.
All souls of children taken as they slept
Are your companions, partners of your ease,
And the green souls of all these autumn trees
Are with you through the silent spaces swept.
Your virgin body gave its gentle breath
Untainted to the gods. Why should we grieve,
But that we merit not your holy death?
We shall not loiter long, your friends and I;
Living you made it goodlier to live,
Dead you will make it easier to die.

II

With you a part of me hath passed away;
For in the peopled forest of my mind
A tree made leafless by this wintry wind
Shall never don again its green array.
Chapel and fireside, country road and bay,
Have something of their friendliness resigned;
Another, if I would, I could not find,
And I am grown much older in a day.
But yet I treasure in my memory
Your gift of charity, and young heart's ease,
And the dear honour of your amity;
For these once mine, my life is rich with these.
And I scarce know which part may greater be,—
What I keep of you, or you rob from me.

III

Your ship lies anchored in the peaceful bight
Until a kinder wind unfurl her sail;
Your docile spirit, wingèd by this gale,
Hath at the dawning fled into the light.
And I half know why heaven deemed it right
Your youth, and this my joy in youth, should fail;
God hath them still, for ever they avail,
Eternity hath borrowed that delight.
For long ago I taught my thoughts to run
Where all the great things live that lived of yore,
And in eternal quiet float and soar;

There all my loves are gathered into one,
Where change is not, nor parting any more,
Nor revolution of the moon and sun.

IV

In my deep heart these chimes would still have rung
To toll your passing, had you not been dead;
For time a sadder mask than death may spread
Over the face that ever should be young.
The bough that falls with all its trophies hung
Falls not too soon, but lays its flower-crowned head
Most royal in the dust, with no leaf shed
Unhallowed or unchiselled or unsung.
And though the after world will never hear
The happy name of one so gently true,
Nor chronicles write large this fatal year,
Yet we who loved you, though we be but few,
Keep you in whatsoe'er things are good, and rear
In our weak virtues monuments to you.

Prologue *[The Last Puritan]*

The Last Puritan: A Memoir in the Form of a Novel. Volume four of the critical edition of *The Works of George Santayana.* Edited by William G. Holzberger and Herman J. Saatkamp Jr., with an Introduction by Irving Singer. Cambridge, MA: The MIT Press, 1994, 11–17.

This prologue appeared in Santayana's only novel, The Last Puritan *(1935). The story was born in 1889 as sketches about college life composed when Santayana was a 25-year-old philosophy instructor and completed 45 years later. Santayana wrote that "the theme is the sentimental education, or disillusionment, of a superior young American: which involves a criticism of modern conventions, as well as a counter-criticism of any high-strung individual morality: the tragedy of which makes this Puritan the last puritan" (LGS, 5:194–95). In a letter Santayana explained that the character to whom the title refers "had reached the ultimate phase of puritanism, when it condemns itself. That doesn't kill it, but it kills the man who has it. . . . he "peters" out because his austerity rejects the ordinary religious and moral shams that satisfy most idealistic souls, while at the same time he can't identify himself with the life of the world. He is like the rich young man in the Gospel who turns away sadly: not in this case because he wasn't ready to sell all he had and give to the poor, but because he found no Christ to follow" (LGS, 5:308).*

In the first years after the war Mario Van de Weyer was almost my neighbour in Paris, for he lived just where the Left Bank ceases to be the Latin Quarter and I where it is not yet the Faubourg Saint Germain. This trifling interval, with the much greater one between our ages, was easily bridged by his bubbling good nature; and sometimes when in the evening twilight I was putting away my papers and preparing to sally forth to a solitary dinner, the bell would ring with a certain unmistakable decision and confidence, and almost before I had opened the door I was already saying, "Ah, Vanny" (for so his English friends called him), "how nice this is! It seems an age since we dined together." And for the rest of the evening our talk would run for the tenth time over the reminiscences which my old friendship with his family, long antedating his birth, furnished in abundance. Ours was hardly conversation; it was musing aloud; and repetitions troubled us as little in our talk as they did in our memories. Often we would recall the summer day at Windsor on which I had first spied him, still in jackets, gorging strawberry-mess in the garden of my inimitable friend and quasi-cousin, Howard Sturgis, host and hostess in one, who held court in a soft nest of cushions, of wit, and of tenderness, surrounded by a menagerie of outcast dogs, a swarm of friends and relations, and all the luxuries of life. Nor did I forget the reply which the youthful Vanny had made on that occasion to our compliments on the particularly nice curves of his hat. "Prettiest and cheapest topper in Eton; Busby's in the Arlington Mews, *'Whips, 'Ats, & Liveries';* eighteen pence off the price if cockade not required. Groom's hat, that's all."

Then Mario would pick up his thread in our recollections.

"Old Busby looked like Mr. Pickwick; had the breast of a pigeon, and would cock his head behind it to catch the effect of a new hat on the customer. 'Parfect fit, sir; you couldn't do better, sir; thenk you, sir.' We were fast friends from the first day I got a hat there. He was showing me to the door, when I stopped him short. 'I say, Mr. Busby: suppose my people are ruined and I have to look for a job. Do you think I'd do for a small footman?' 'Footman, sir? You, sir? 'Ope not, indeed—I mean, of course you would, sir; the prettiest young groom as you would make; none smarter in London, to jump off the box monkeylike—I beg pardon, sir, I mean, nimbly—and hold the door open for her ladyship.' 'Yes, Mr. Busby, but will you recommend me? She must be a countess at least,' I added with a wink, 'and young.' And I suddenly grew rigid and blank-faced, touched my hat with one wooden finger, and left him muttering. 'I'm blowed if a spry young gentleman like you wouldn't pretty well find a situation without a character.' But that's all a thing of the past. Old Busby's gone. Nobody wants whips, 'ats, or grooms any more; and where there's still a footman, he wears an absurd little motoring cap with a vizor. And even the Arlington Mews has disappeared."

"Never mind," I would answer, "perhaps when the common people set the fashions, men's clothes may recover their old rakishness. Grooms used to be more pleasantly dressed than gentlemen, because good form for gentlemen nowadays is simply to be scrupulously clean, correct, and inconspicuous. Even your military men hate anything that savours of swagger or aggressive virility, are uncomfortable in scarlet and gold braid, and take refuge whenever possible in the blessed obscurity of mufti. Not that the uniform of industrialism absolves the rest of us drab creatures from self-consciousness or from taking pains. We mustn't fall short of the right standard or overdo anything; but we compose our social figures sadly, with fear and trembling, and more in the dread of damnation than in the hope of glory."

"Not in my case," Mario said, smiling broadly and straightening his shoulders. "I rather fancy dressing up and giving people something to stare at."

"I know; but you're a rare exception, a professional lady-killer, a popinjay amid the millions of crows. You have the courage of your full human nature, as your father had the courage of his delicate tastes. To have been emancipated otherwise, in his day, would have seemed vicious and unkind; and he remained innocence itself in his person and affections, although his mental enthusiasms were boundless. That is why we all called him 'dear Harold'. You lost him when you were too young to appreciate his gifts or his weaknesses. How old were you exactly?"

"About seven."

"When to you he was simply papa, who drew amusing pictures and read Stevenson's stories aloud, to improve your English. There were many such Americans *de luxe* in my generation who prolonged their youth at the *École des Beaux-Arts* or at Julian's, confident of personally restoring the age of Pericles. Even in our Harvard days, I remember how he would burst into the Lampoon sanctum, flushed with the project of some comic illustration that had just occurred to him;

but the joke could never be brought to have a point, and the drawing, twice begun, would end in the wastepaper-basket. Later, whenever he despaired of becoming a great painter—as he did every other year—he would remember his enthusiasm for the science of genealogy, and would rush to Holland in quest of his ancestors. In that very garden at Windsor where we admired your hat, he had once discovered that in that neighbourhood there lived a well-known family of English Van de Weyers; and nothing would do but he must be taken at once to call on the old Colonel, and be informed about his family tree. But no researches availed to unearth the least connection between that family and the Van de Weyers of New York. Baffled in private genealogy, he would rebound to heraldry in general and to the monumental work which he was always about to compose on heraldic ornament in architecture. His great ambition, he used to say, was to devote his whole life to a very small subject, and heraldry held in a nutshell the secret of all the arts, which were nothing but self-exhibition upon the shield of self-defence. But once having laid down this brilliant first principle, he had nothing more to say on the subject; and the stream of his enthusiasm, rebuffed by that stone wall, gurgled back to the happiness of collecting bookplates."

"No harm," Mario would say, a cloud of gravity passing over his face, "no harm in amusing himself as he chose; only he was a brute to marry my mother and keep her from being the greatest *prima donna* of the age."

"But if your father hadn't married your mother, where would you be? Dear Harold would have loved nothing better than to see his beautiful wife a glorious *diva*, treading the boards with all the authority of genius, and borne along from ovation to ovation on an ocean of floral offerings. But she herself and her sensible Italian relations wouldn't hear of such a thing, once her respectable future was assured. In their view the rich young American, proposing just in time, had saved the situation."

So our talk would ramble on amongst memories that seemed pleasantest when they were most remote; yet sooner or later recent events would intrude, and Mario would tell me of one or another of his friends who had fallen in the war or who were blankly surviving, at a loss what to do with themselves. One evening— when the party of New York ladies at the other table had risen in a flurry fearing to miss the new curtain-raiser at *Le Vieux Colombier;* when Mario had seen them to their taxi and had promised to show them Montmartre on the following night after the Opera; and when quiet was restored in the little room at Lapérouse where we remained alone—our talk reverted, as it often did, to the young Oliver Alden, who of all the victims of the war was nearest to us both. He had been Mario's cousin and bosom friend and the most gifted of my pupils in my last days at Harvard.

"You know what I've been thinking," Mario said after a pause. "You ought to write Oliver's Life. Nobody else could do it."

"Oliver's Life? Had he a life to be written with a big L? And why should I, of all people, abandon philosophy in my old age and take to composing history, even supposing that in Oliver's history there were any actions to record?"

"No actions, but something you might take a wicked pleasure in describing:

Puritanism Self-condemned. Oliver was THE LAST PURITAN.*"*

"I am afraid," I answered with a melancholy which was only half feigned, "I am afraid there will always be puritans in this mad world. Puritanism is a natural reaction against nature."

"I don't mean that puritanism has died out everywhere. There may always be fresh people to take the thing up. But in Oliver puritanism worked itself out to its logical end. He convinced himself, on puritan grounds, that it was wrong to be a puritan."

"And he remained a puritan notwithstanding?"

"Exactly. That was the tragedy of it. Thought it his clear duty to give puritanism up, but couldn't."

"Then the case," I said laughing, "is like that of Miss Pickleworth of Boston who declared she envied me for not having a conscience, which I thought rather insolent of her, until she went on to explain, gasping with earnestness, that she was *sure* people were *far too* conscientious and self-critical; that it was so *wrong* and *cruel* to stunt oneself; so *cowardly* to avoid the greatest possible wealth of experience; and that every night before she went to bed she *made a point* of thinking over all she had said and done during the day, for fear she might have been *too particular.*"

"Good Lord! That's not like Oliver at all. He wasn't one of those romantic cads who want to experience everything. He kept himself for what was best. That's why he was a true puritan after all."

"Quite so. His puritanism had never been mere timidity or fanaticism or calculated hardness: it was a deep and speculative thing: hatred of all shams, scorn of all mummeries, a bitter merciless pleasure in the hard facts. And that passion for reality was beautiful in him, because there was so much in his gifts and in his surroundings to allure him and muffle up his mind in worldly conventions. He was a millionaire, and yet scrupulously simple and silently heroic. For that reason you and I loved him so much. You and I are not puritans; and by contrast with our natural looseness, we can't help admiring people purer than ourselves, more willing to pluck out the eye that offends them, even if it be the eye for beauty, and to enter halt and lame into the kingdom of singlemindedness. I don't prefer austerity for myself as against abundance, against intelligence, against the irony of ultimate truth. But I see that in itself, as a statuesque object, austerity is more beautiful, and I like it in others."

"I always knew that you thought more of Oliver than of me." Mario had been his mother's darling, and was so accustomed to having women make love to him that he sometimes turned his extreme manliness into coquetry. He liked flattery, he liked presents, and he liked the best cigarettes.

"Certainly I thought more of him as an experiment in virtue. But I prefer your conversation."

"At Oxford, when he had his nursing home, you used to talk with him for ever."

"Yes: but those were philosophical discussions, which are never very satisfying. Have you ever talked with monks and nuns? You may admit that some of these good souls may be saints, but their conversation, even on spiritual subjects, very soon becomes arid and stereotyped, always revolving round a few dulcet incorrigible maxims. Well, Oliver would have been a monk, if he had been a Catholic."

"Yes, and I think he would surely have become a Catholic if he had lived long enough."

"Do you really think so? He, so Nordic, leave the monorail of sheer will for the old Roman road of tradition? I grant you this road is just as straight on the map, or much straighter: but it dips down and soars up so unconcernedly with the lay of the land, like a small boat over great seas; and while the middle way is regularly paved for the militant faithful, there are such broad grassy alleys on either side for the sheep and the goats, and so many an attractive halting-place, and habitable terminus. You might forget you were on a mission, and think life a free tour, or even a picnic.–How Oliver hated picnics, with the messy food and waste paper and empty bottles and loud merriment and tussling and amorous episodes improvised on the grass! Yet, when necessary, he put up with it all gallantly and silently. There was his duty to democracy. No: not a Catholic. His imagination wasn't lordly and firm enough to set up a second world over against this one, and positively believe in it. He distrusted doubleness, but he couldn't admit chaos: and in order to escape chaos, without imposing any fictions or any false hopes upon mankind, he would have been capable of imposing no matter what regimen on us by force. Yes, free, rare and delicate soul as he was, he would have accepted for himself this red communist tyranny that puts a grimy revolver to our noses and growls: 'Be like me, or die.'"

"He wouldn't have found much puritanism among the Bolshies," said Mario, thinking of free love.

"It's a popular error to suppose that puritanism has anything to do with purity. The old Puritans were legally strict, they were righteous, but they were not particularly chaste. They had the virtues and vices of old age. An old man may be lecherous: but that vice in him, like avarice, gluttony, despotism, or the love of strong drink, soon becomes monotonous and sordid, and is easy to cover up hypocritically under his daily routine. The Bolshies have the one element of puritanism which was the most important, at least for Oliver: integrity of purpose and scorn of all compromises, practical or theoretical."

"I don't believe Oliver was ever really in love," Mario interposed, not having listened to my last speech, and evidently reviewing in his mind various incidents which he preferred to pass over in silence. "Women were rather a difficulty to him. He thought he liked them and they thought they liked him; but there was always something wanting. He regarded all women as ladies, more or less beautiful, kind, privileged, and troublesome. He never discovered that all ladies are women."

"Yes, and that is the side of them you see; but you forget that many of the ladies whom Oliver knew suffered from the same impediment as himself: it comes from being over-protected in one region and over-developed in another. Sex for them becomes simply a nuisance, and they can't connect it pleasantly with their feeling for the people they love. Therefore sensuality for them remains disgusting, and tenderness incomplete."

"Poor things!" Mario cried, full of genuine commiseration. "I suppose that's what I never could make out about Oliver, and then his philosophy. Certainly it's you that ought to write his Life. You understood him thoroughly, knew his people and his background, and can toy with all those German philosophers that he was always quoting."

"I'm not so sure of that. You and I have an immense advantage in belonging to the Catholic tradition. We were born clear, and don't have to achieve clearness. But the light of common day to which we are accustomed may blind us to what is going on in the dark, and the roots of everything are underground. We may be easily dupes of the blue sky and but foolish daylight astronomers."

"Well then, here's your chance of focussing your telescope upon the depths of poor Oliver, until you're used to the darkness and find that there's nothing there. Or rather, you'll find something perfectly commonplace. There's nothing less marvellous than what most mysterious people, especially women, think their secret: only they keep it shut up in a painted casket with seven keys, so that nobody may see what it is."

"To be frank," I replied, "I think I know what Oliver's secret was–common enough, if you like, and even universal, since it was simply the tragedy of the spirit when it's not content to understand but wishes to govern. The old Calvinists cut the Gordian knot by asserting that since the Fall, the spirit had ceased to rule over the world and over their own passions, but that nevertheless it was secretly omnipotent, and would burn up the world and their passions at the last day. Oliver suffered from no such delusion. The holocaust was real enough: it was the endless fire of irrational life always devouring itself: yet somehow the spirit rose from that flame, and surveyed the spectacle with some tears, certainly, but with no little curiosity and satisfaction. Oliver hardly got so far as to feel at home in this absurd world: I could never convince him that reason and goodness are necessarily secondary and incidental. His absolutist conscience remained a pretender, asserting in exile its divine right to the crown. I confess it would interest me to trace in Oliver this purification of puritanism, and this obstinacy in it. But where are the materials? I should have to invent half the story, and I'm no novelist."

"Oliver always kept a diary, and there are a lot of letters. He left me all his father's papers, as well as his own, which I can pass over to you, and we can ask his old German governess for her records, which are surely voluminous and more sentimental than any decent novel would dare to be nowadays. Of course, his mother might help, only she won't. We can't look for anything in that quarter."

"Nor is it necessary. I can easily imagine what *she* would say. Yet with all the documents in the world, I should have to fill many a gap and compose all the dialogues. I could never do that properly. And how, my dear Vanny, how am I to manage the love scenes?"

"Bah, there are love stories enough in the bookstalls for those who like them. But what is love in a book! This is to be a tale of sad life."

"Think, I shall have to draw the portrait of a lot of living people, and first and foremost of yourself."

"I trust you."

"It will be a delicate task, and perhaps impossible, to find words for tenderer feelings and more varied thoughts than my own. But I will make the attempt. They say we all have a fund of predispositions which circumstances have never developed, but which may be tapped under hypnotic influence. When my intuition gives out, I will summon you to renew the spell, and perhaps I may be able to recover as much of Oliver's thoughts, and of those of all of you, as the world might overhear without indiscretion."

Epilogue *[The Last Puritan]*

The Last Puritan: A Memoir in the Form of a Novel. Volume four of the critical edition of *The Works of George Santayana.* Edited by William G. Holzberger and Herman J. Saatkamp Jr., with an Introduction by Irving Singer. Cambridge, MA: The MIT Press, 1994, 569–72.

This epilogue appeared in Santayana's novel, The Last Puritan *(1935). Santayana wrote that "the book is really what I call it, 'a Memoir in the Form of a Novel' and, although not an autobiography, it is rooted throughout in my personal recollections" (LGS, 5:224). Santayana related to a friend that "the hardest thing for an author . . . is to conceive how [his characters] will seem to other people, when conveyed to them only by <u>words</u>. I have pictures, quite as distinct as memories; and my characters <u>speak to me</u>. . . . This doesn't contradict the fact which . . . I point to in the <u>Epilogue</u>, that these characters speak my language, and are in some sense masks for my own spirit. On the contrary, that makes, or ought to make, them more living, since they are fetched from an actual life, and only dressed, as an actor on the stage, for their social parts" (LGS, 5:296).*

Fifteen years and more had elapsed since Mario Van de Weyer had first urged me to write this biography. We were still almost neighbours, but no longer in Paris. Different motives had prompted each of us to shift his centre to Rome, he more than ever in the current of the world and I more than ever out of it. We seldom met. Our acquaintance had passed into that serene crepuscular phase in which nothing more is demanded, and every past episode is affectionately folded in the cedar-chest of memory, to be shaken out on occasion together with the fragrance of time long past. At length I was able to send him a rough draft of these pages, composed at odd moments in the intervals of other work. He knew that, like the Pope, I accepted no invitations and paid no visits; but I asked him, after he had had time to dip into my manuscript, to come some fine day to lunch with me at the Pincio and tell me his impressions.

Accordingly we sat one early afternoon, basking in the oblique warmth of the wintry sun, yet sheltered overhead by evergreen oak and ilex from the naked glare of the sky.

In respect to this novel, as I called it, I explained how insecure I had felt all these years, like an old schoolmaster for the first time in the saddle, at one moment innocently elated, and at the next in total distress. This wasn't my métier. However, I had got back alive to the stable, and safely dismounted. I stood again with both feet on my own ground; and I could laugh with him at my foolish excursion, if he pronounced it ridiculous.

My friend smiled amiably, looked about as if in doubt which of various observations to make first, and then said nothing.

Naturally he couldn't tell me outright to put the whole thing in the fire; but I was curious to know the grounds of his judgment.

"For instance," I said, "what of the characters, and in the first place of your own? Are you satisfied with your portrait?"

"It's no portrait; or so flattered that nobody would recognise it. You exaggerate enormously my favour with the fair sex. I wasn't different from any other young spark."

"You were more of a Don Juan than you now choose to remember. But you needn't disown your past. You are all of a piece, and your evolution has been natural. Don't you remember saying to Oliver that you wished to be a Knight of Malta? He thought the notion whimsical, but you have done even better. Gallantry in a gentleman passes easily into chivalry, and chivalry into religion."

"With my father-in-law's position at the Vatican," he replied colouring a little, "the thing came of itself."

"No, no. It wasn't mere nepotism; rather the outward sign of an inward grace. Your modernness sucks in all the sap of the past, like the modernness of the new Italy; and any future worth having will spring from men like you, not from weedy intellectuals or self-inhibited puritans. Fortune will never smile on those who disown the living forces of nature. You can well afford to let an old philosopher here and there anticipate death and live as much as possible in eternity. The truth cannot help triumphing at the last judgment. Perhaps it cannot triumph before. Perhaps, while life lasts, in order to reconcile mankind with reality, fiction in some directions may be more needful than truth. You are at home in the grand tradition. With the beautiful Donna Laura and your charming children, you will hand on the torch of true civilisation; or rather, in this classic Italy, you have little need of tradition or torches. You have blood within and sunlight above, and are true enough to the past in being true to yourselves."

"Yes. We are frankly animal—But to return to your book. Besides over-glorifying my peccadilloes, you almost turn me into a clever chap, which I never was. You put into my mouth a lot of good things of your own, or of Howard Sturgis's, or of other friends of yours. Moreover, in general, you make us all talk in your own philosophical style, and not in the least as we actually jabber. Your women are too intelligent, and your men also. There is clairvoyance in every quarter; whereas in the real world we are all unjust to one another and deceived about ourselves."

"Granted, granted," said I delighted that at last the ball was rolling merrily. "I hardly see anybody, and I don't know how people talk. But that doesn't matter for my purpose. If I had been absolutely true to life, half my possible readers wouldn't have understood me. I wasn't composing a philological document in which future antiquarians might study the dialects and slang of the early twentieth century. I have made you all speak the lingo natural to myself, as Homer made all his heroes talk in Ionian hexameters. Fiction is poetry, poetry is inspiration, and every word should come from the poet's heart, not out of the mouths of other people. If here and there I have hinted at a characteristic idiom, it's not for the sake of the idiom but for the sake of the character or the mood. Even in the simplest of us passion and temperament have a rich potential rhetoric that never finds utterance; and all the resources of a poet's language are requisite to convey not what his personages would have been likely to say, but what they were really feeling. So with the characters themselves, I am not photographing real people and changing their names. On the contrary, wherever discretion permits, I keep the real names and the real places, just as Homer does. Real names have a wonderful atmosphere. But I recast, I re-live, I entirely transform the characters. They are creatures of imagination. Imagination! We are of imagination all compact. You know how energetically I reject the old axiom that sights and sounds exist in the material world, and somehow cause us to perceive them. Sights and sounds are products of the organism; they are forms of imagination; and all the treasures of experience are nothing but spontaneous fictions provoked by the impacts of material things. How foolish, then, should I have been in my own eyes to reject the images which you and my other friends have excited within me, when I have no other pigments at my disposal with which to paint mankind! Yet though an image must be only an image, it may be more or less suitable and proper. And if we were not all clairvoyant at bottom, how should we ever recognise clairvoyance in others? How much poetic truth, for instance, is there in my picture of Oliver himself?"

"More than in your picture of me. You knew him well. But you idealise him, and make him too complex. You introduce something Freudian into him which I never saw a sign of: fixations, transferences, inhibitions, or whatever else you call them. To my mind, he was perfectly normal, only a little vague and undeveloped. He required a lot of time to mobilise his forces."

"Yes," I interrupted, "because his forces were very great and drawn from a vast territory."

"Perhaps: but then why do you make him so much more intelligent than he seemed? You endow him with altogether too much insight. In reality he was simply bewildered. There was a fundamental darkness within him, a long arctic night, as in all Nordics."

"But isn't the arctic night very brilliant? And after the *aurora borealis* isn't there an arctic day, no less prolonged? I think there is no great truth that sensitive Nordics don't sometimes discover: only they don't stick to their best insights. They don't recognise the difference between a great truth and a speculative whim, and they wander off again into the mist, empty-handed and puzzle-headed. As to moral complications in Oliver, you must allow me my diagnosis. He was the child of an elderly and weary man, and of a thin-spun race; from his mother he got only his bigness and athleticism, which notoriously don't wear well. A moral nature burdened and over-strung, and a critical faculty fearless but helplessly subjective—isn't that the true tragedy of your ultimate Puritan? However, suppose I am wrong about the facts. Shall I tear the book up, or will it do as a fable?"

"As a fable you may publish it. It's all your invention; but perhaps there's a better philosophy in it than in your other books."

"How so?"

"Because now you're not arguing or proving or criticising anything, but painting a picture. The trouble with you philosophers is that you misunderstand your vocation. You ought to be poets, but you insist on laying down the law for the universe, physical and moral, and are vexed with one another because your inspirations are not identical."

"Are you accusing me of dogmatism? Do I demand that everybody should agree with me?"

"Less loudly, I admit, than most philosophers. Yet when you profess to be describing a fact, you can't help antagonising those who take a different view of it, or are blind altogether to that sort of object. In this novel, on the contrary, the argument is dramatised, the views become human persuasions, and the presentation is all the truer for not professing to be true. You have said it somewhere yourself, though I may misquote the words: *After life is over and the world has gone up in smoke, what realities might the spirit in us still call its own without illusion save the form of those very illusions which have made up our story?*"

THE END

The Poetry of Barbarism

Interpretations of Poetry and Religion. Volume three of the critical edition of *The Works of George Santayana*. Edited by William G. Holzberger and Herman J. Saatkamp Jr., with an Introduction by Joel Porte. Cambridge, MA: The MIT Press, 1989, 103–30.

In this essay, which appeared as Chapter VII in Interpretations of Poetry and Religion (1900), *Santayana diagnosed the limitations of contemporary poetry. He found it lacking in wisdom and vision. The poets of the time had "no grasp of the whole reality, and consequently no capacity for a sane and steady idealisation" (ES, 498). Poetry at that time, thought Santayana, neglected articulation of the ideal and was dominated by subjectivism. The specific figures in this essay are the American poet Walt Whitman and the English poet Robert Browning. Santayana acknowledged their great gifts in escaping convention and honest expression, but neither progressed beyond these basic functions of poetry. Whitman, whom Santayana admired for his "fresh, manly, large, and healthy" imagination (LGS, 3:311), approached the world without standards and imposed no order on the sensations that came to him. Browning expressed emotions masterfully, but he had no sense for the perfection of things. He was, according to Santayana, "a lover of experience; the ideal did not exist for him" (ES, 511), and he had "a mind full of chaotic sensations, objectless passions, and undigested ideas" (ES, 511).*

I

It is an observation at first sight melancholy but in the end, perhaps, enlightening, that the earliest poets are the most ideal, and that primitive ages furnish the most heroic characters and have the clearest vision of a perfect life. The Homeric times must have been full of ignorance and suffering. In those little barbaric towns, in those camps and farms, in those shipyards, there must have been much insecurity and superstition. That age was singularly poor in all that concerns the convenience of life and the entertainment of the mind with arts and sciences. Yet it had a sense for civilisation. That machinery of life which men were beginning to devise appealed to them as poetical; they knew its ultimate justification and studied its incipient processes with delight. The poetry of that simple and ignorant age was, accordingly, the sweetest and sanest that the world has known; the most faultless in taste, and the most even and lofty in inspiration. Without lacking variety and homeliness, it bathed all things human in the golden light of morning; it clothed sorrow in a kind of majesty, instinct with both self-control and heroic frankness. Nowhere else can we find so noble a rendering of human nature, so spontaneous a delight in life, so uncompromising a dedication to beauty, and such a gift of seeing beauty in everything. Homer, the first of poets, was also the best and the most poetical.

From this beginning, if we look down the history of Occidental literature, we see the power of idealisation steadily decline. For while it finds here and there, as in Dante, a more spiritual theme and a subtler and riper intellect, it pays for that advantage by a more than equivalent loss in breadth, sanity, and happy vigour. And if ever imagination bursts out with a greater potency, as in Shakespeare (who excels the patriarch of poetry in depth of passion and vividness of characterisation, and in those exquisite bubblings of poetry and humour in which English genius is at its best), yet Shakespeare also pays the price by a notable loss in taste, in sustained inspiration, in consecration, and in rationality. There is more or less rubbish in his greatest works. When we come down to our own day we find poets of hardly less natural endowment (for in endowment all ages are perhaps alike) and with vastly richer sources of inspiration; for they have many arts and literatures behind them, with the spectacle of a varied and agitated society, a world which is the living microcosm of its own history and presents in one picture many races, arts, and religions. Our poets have more wonderful tragedies of the imagination to depict than had Homer, whose world was innocent of any essential defeat, or Dante, who believed in the world's definitive redemption. Or, if perhaps their inspiration is comic, they have the pageant of mediæval manners, with its picturesque artifices and passionate fancies, and the long comedy of modern social revolutions, so illusory in their aims and so productive in their aimlessness. They have, moreover, the new and marvellous conception which natural science has given us of the world and of the conditions of human progress.

With all these lessons of experience behind them, however, we find our contemporary poets incapable of any high wisdom, incapable of any imaginative rendering of human life and its meaning. Our poets are things of shreds and patches; they give us episodes and studies, a sketch of this curiosity, a glimpse of that romance; they have no total vision, no grasp of the whole reality, and consequently no capacity for a sane and steady idealisation. The comparatively barbarous ages had a poetry of the ideal; they had visions of beauty, order, and perfection. This age of material elaboration has no sense for those things. Its fancy is retrospective, whimsical, and flickering; its ideals, when it has any, are negative and partial; its moral strength is a blind and miscellaneous vehemence. Its poetry, in a word, is the poetry of barbarism.

This poetry should be viewed in relation to the general moral crisis and imaginative disintegration of which it gives a verbal echo; then we shall avoid the injustice of passing it over as insignificant, no less than the imbecility of hailing it as essentially glorious and successful. We must remember that the imagination of our race has been subject to a double discipline. It has been formed partly in the school of classic literature and polity, and partly in the school of Christian piety. This duality of inspiration, this contradiction between the two accepted methods of rationalising the world, has been a chief source of that incoherence, that romantic indistinctness and imperfection, which largely characterise the products of the modern arts. A man cannot serve two masters; yet the conditions have not been such as to allow him wholly to despise the one or wholly to obey the other. To be wholly Pagan is impossible after the dissolution of that civilisation which had seemed universal, and that empire which had believed itself eternal. To be wholly Christian is impossible for a similar reason, now that the illusion and cohesion of Christian ages is lost, and for the further reason that Christianity was itself fundamentally eclectic. Before it could succeed and dominate men even for a time, it was obliged to adjust itself to reality, to incorporate many elements of Pagan wisdom, and to accommodate itself to many habits and passions at variance with its own ideal.

In these latter times, with the prodigious growth of material life in elaboration and of mental life in diffusion, there has supervened upon this old dualism a new faith in man's absolute power, a kind of return to the inexperience and self-assurance of youth. This new inspiration has made many minds indifferent to the two traditional disciplines; neither is seriously accepted by them, for the reason, excellent from their own point of view, that no discipline whatever is needed. The memory of ancient disillusions has faded with time. Ignorance of the past has bred contempt for the lessons which the past might teach. Men prefer to repeat the old experiment without knowing that they repeat it.

I say advisedly ignorance of the past, in spite of the unprecedented historical erudition of our time; for life is an art not to be learned by observation, and the most minute and comprehensive studies do not teach us what the spirit of man should have learned by its long living. We study the past as a dead object, as a ruin, not as an authority and as an experiment. One reason why history was less interesting to former ages was that they were less conscious of separation from the past. The perspective of time was less clear because the synthesis of experience was more complete. The mind does not easily discriminate the successive phases of an action in which it is still engaged; it does not arrange in a temporal series the elements of a single perception, but posits them all together as constituting a permanent and real object. Human nature and the life of the world were real and stable objects to the apprehension of our forefathers; the actors changed, but not the characters or the play. Men were then less studious of derivations because they were more conscious of identities. They thought of all reality as in a sense contemporary, and in considering the maxims of a philosopher or the style of a poet, they were not primarily concerned with settling his date and describing his environment. The standard by which they judged was eternal; the environment in which man found himself did not seem to them subject of any essential change.

To us the picturesque element in history is more striking because we feel ourselves the children of our own age only, an age which being itself singular and revolutionary, tends to read its own character into the past, and to regard all other periods as no less fragmentary and effervescent than itself. The changing and the permanent elements are, indeed, everywhere present, and the bias of the observer may emphasise the one or the other as it will: the only question is whether we find the significance of things in their variations or in their similarities.

Now the habit of regarding the past as effete and as merely a stepping-stone to something present or future, is unfavourable to any true apprehension of that element in the past which was vital and which remains eternal. It is a habit of thought that destroys the sense of the moral identity of all ages, by virtue of its very insistence on the mechanical derivation of one age from another. Existences that cause one another exclude one another; each is alien to the rest inasmuch as it is the product of new and different conditions. Ideas that cause nothing unite all things by giving them a common point of reference and a single standard of value.

The classic and the Christian systems were both systems of ideas, attempts to seize the eternal morphology of reality and describe its unchanging constitution. The imagination was summoned thereby to contemplate the highest objects, and the essence of things being thus described, their insignificant variations could retain little importance and the study of these variations might well seem superficial. Mechanical science, the science of causes, was accordingly neglected, while the science of values, with the arts that express these values, was exclusively pursued. The reverse has now occurred and the spirit of life, innocent of any rationalising discipline and deprived of an authoritative and adequate method of expression, has relapsed into miscellaneous and shallow exuberance. Religion and art have become short-winded. They have forgotten the old maxim that we should copy in order to be copied and remember in order to be remembered. It is true that the multiplicity of these incompetent efforts seems to many a compensation for their ill success, or even a ground for asserting their absolute superiority. Incompetence, when it flatters the passions, can always find a greater incompetence to approve of it. Indeed, some people would have regarded the Tower of Babel as the best academy of eloquence on account of the variety of oratorical methods prevailing there.

It is thus that the imagination of our time has relapsed into barbarism. But discipline of the heart and fancy is always so rare a thing that the neglect of it need not be supposed to involve any very terrible or obvious loss. The triumphs of reason have been few and partial at any time, and perfect works of art are almost unknown. The failure of art and reason, because their principle is ignored, is therefore hardly more conspicuous than it was when their principle, although perhaps acknowledged, was misunderstood or disobeyed. Indeed, to one who fixes his eye on the ideal goal, the greatest art often seems the greatest failure, because it alone reminds him of what it should have been. Trivial stimulations coming from vulgar objects, on the contrary, by making us forget altogether the possibility of a deep satisfaction, often succeed in interesting and in winning applause. The pleasure they give us is so brief and superficial that the wave of essential disappointment which would ultimately drown it has not time to rise from the heart.

The poetry of barbarism is not without its charm. It can play with sense and passion the more readily and freely in that it does not aspire to subordinate them to a clear thought or a tenable attitude of the will. It can impart the transitive emotions which it expresses; it can find many partial harmonies of mood and fancy; it can, by virtue of its red-hot irrationality, utter wilder cries, surrender itself and us to more absolute passion, and heap up a more indiscriminate wealth of images than belong to poets of seasoned experience or of heavenly inspiration. Irrational stimulation may tire us in the end, but it excites us in the beginning; and how many conventional poets, tender and prolix, have there not been, who tire us now without ever having excited anybody? The power to stimulate is the beginning of greatness, and when the barbarous poet has genius, as he well may have, he stimulates all the more powerfully on account of the crudity of his methods and the recklessness of his emotions. The defects of such art–lack of distinction, absence of beauty, confusion of ideas, incapacity permanently to please–will hardly be felt by the contemporary public, if once its attention is arrested; for no poet is so undisciplined that he will not find many readers, if he finds readers at all, less disciplined than himself.

These considerations may perhaps be best enforced by applying them to two writers of great influence over the present generation who seem to illustrate them on different planes–Robert Browning and Walt Whitman. They are both analytic poets–poets who seek to reveal and express the elemental as opposed to the conventional; but the dissolution has progressed much farther in Whitman than in Browning, doubtless because Whitman began at a much lower stage of moral and intellectual organisation; for the good will to be radical was present in both. The elements to which Browning reduces experience are still passions, characters, persons; Whitman carries the disintegration further and knows nothing but moods and particular images. The world of Browning is a world of history with civilisation for its setting and with the conventional passions for its motive forces. The world of Whitman is innocent of these things and contains only far simpler and more chaotic elements. In him the barbarism is much more pronounced; it is, indeed, avowed, and the "barbaric yawp" is sent "over the roofs of the world" in full consciousness of its inarticulate character; but in Browning the barbarism is no less real though disguised by a literary and scientific language, since the passions of civilised life with which he deals are treated as so many "barbaric yawps," complex indeed in their conditions, puffings of an intricate engine, but aimless in their vehemence and mere ebullitions of lustiness in adventurous and profoundly ungoverned souls.

Irrationality on this level is viewed by Browning with the same satisfaction with which, on a lower level, it is viewed by Whitman; and the admirers of each hail it as the secret of a new poetry which pierces to the quick and awakens the imagination to a new and genuine vitality. It is in the rebellion against discipline, in the abandonment of the ideals of classic and Christian tradition, that this rejuvenation is found. Both poets represent, therefore, and are admired for representing, what may be called the poetry of barbarism in the most accurate and descriptive sense of this word. For the barbarian is the man who regards his passions as their own excuse for being; who does not domesticate them either by understanding their cause or by conceiving their ideal goal. He is the man who does not know his derivations nor perceive his tendencies, but who merely feels and acts, valuing in his life its force and its filling, but being careless of its purpose and its form. His delight is in abundance and vehemence; his art, like his life, shows an exclusive respect for quantity and splendour of materials. His scorn for what is poorer and weaker than himself is only surpassed by his ignorance of what is higher.

II

WALT WHITMAN

The works of Walt Whitman offer an extreme illustration of this phase of genius, both by their form and by their substance. It was the singularity of his literary form–the challenge it threw to the conventions of verse and of language–that first gave Whitman notoriety: but this notoriety has become fame, because those incapacities and solecisms which glare at us from his pages are only the obverse of a profound inspiration and of a genuine courage. Even the idiosyncrasies of his style have a side which is not mere perversity or affectation; the order of his words, the procession of his images, reproduce the method of a rich, spontaneous, absolutely lazy fancy. In most poets such a natural order is modified by various governing motives–the thought, the metrical form, the echo of other poems in the memory. By Walt Whitman these conventional influences are resolutely banished. We find the swarms of men and objects rendered as they might strike the retina in a sort of waking dream. It is the most sincere possible confession of the lowest–I mean the most primitive–type of perception. All ancient poets are sophisticated in comparison and give proof of longer intellectual and moral training. Walt Whitman has gone back to the innocent style of Adam, when the animals filed before him one by one and he called each of them by its name.

In fact, the influences to which Walt Whitman was subject were as favourable as possible to the imaginary experiment of beginning the world over again. Liberalism and transcendentalism both harboured some illusions on that score; and they were in the air which our poet breathed. Moreover he breathed this air in America, where the newness of the material environment made it easier to ignore the fatal antiquity of human nature. When he afterward became aware that there was or had been a world with a history, he studied that world with curiosity and spoke of it not without a certain shrewdness. But he still regarded it as a foreign world and imagined, as not a few Americans have done, that his own world was a fresh creation, not amenable to the same laws as the old. The difference in the conditions blinded him, in his merely sensuous apprehension, to the identity of the principles.

His parents were farmers in central Long Island and his early years were spent in that district. The family seems to have been not too prosperous and somewhat nomadic; Whitman himself drifted through boyhood without much guidance. We find him now at school, now helping the labourers at the farms, now wandering along the beaches of Long Island, finally at Brooklyn working in an apparently desultory way as a printer and sometimes as a writer for a local newspaper. He must have read or heard something, at this early period, of the English classics; his style often betrays the deep effect made upon him by the grandiloquence of the Bible, of Shakespeare, and of Milton. But his chief interest, if we may trust his account, was already in his own sensations. The aspects of Nature, the forms and habits of animals, the sights of cities, the movement and talk of common people, were his constant delight. His mind was flooded with these images, keenly felt and afterward to be vividly rendered with bold strokes of realism and imagination.

Many poets have had this faculty to seize the elementary aspects of things, but none has had it so exclusively; with Whitman the surface is absolutely all and the underlying structure is without interest and almost without existence. He had had no education and his natural delight in imbibing sensations had not been trained to the uses of practical or theoretical intelligence. He basked in the sunshine of perception and wallowed in the stream of his own sensibility, as later at Camden in the shallows of his favourite brook. Even during the civil war, when he heard the drum-taps so clearly, he could only gaze at the picturesque and terrible aspects of the struggle, and linger among the wounded day after day with a canine devotion; he could not be aroused either to clear thought or to positive action. So also in his poems; a multiplicity of images pass before him and he yields himself to each in turn with absolute passivity. The world has no inside; it is a phantasmagoria of continuous visions, vivid, impressive, but monotonous and hard to distinguish in memory, like the waves of the sea or the decorations of some barbarous temple, sublime only by the infinite aggregation of parts.

This abundance of detail without organisation, this wealth of perception without intelligence and of imagination without taste, makes the singularity of Whitman's genius. Full of sympathy and receptivity, with a wonderful gift of graphic characterisation and an occasional rare grandeur of diction, he fills us with a sense of the individuality and the universality of what he describes–it is a drop in itself yet a drop in the ocean. The absence of any principle of selection or of a sustained style enables him to render aspects of things and of emotion which would have eluded a trained writer. He is, therefore, interesting even where he is grotesque or perverse. He has accomplished, by the sacrifice of almost every other good quality, something never so well done before. He has approached common life without bringing in his mind any higher standard by which to criticise it; he has seen it, not in contrast with an ideal, but as the expression of forces more indeterminate and elementary than itself; and the vulgar, in this cosmic setting, has appeared to him sublime.

There is clearly some analogy between a mass of images without structure and the notion of an absolute democracy. Whitman, inclined by his genius and habits to see life without relief or organisation, believed that his inclination in this respect corresponded with the spirit of his age and country, and that Nature and society, at least in the United States, were constituted after the fashion of his own mind. Being the poet of the average man, he wished all men to be specimens of that average, and being the poet of a fluid Nature, he believed that Nature was or should be a formless flux. This personal bias of Whitman's was further encouraged by the actual absence of distinction in his immediate environment. Surrounded by ugly things and common people, he felt himself happy, ecstatic, overflowing with a kind of patriarchal love. He accordingly came to think that there was a spirit of the New World which he embodied, and which was in complete opposition to that of the Old, and that a literature upon novel principles was needed to express and strengthen this American spirit.

Democracy was not to be merely a constitutional device for the better government of given nations, not merely a movement for the material improvement of the lot of the poorer classes. It was to be a social and a moral democracy and to involve an actual equality among all men. Whatever kept them apart and made it impossible for them to be messmates together was to be discarded. The literature of democracy was to ignore all extraordinary gifts of genius or virtue, all distinction drawn even from great passions or romantic adventures. In Whitman's works, in which this new literature is foreshadowed, there is accordingly not a single character nor a single story. His only hero is Myself, the "single separate person," endowed with the primary impulses, with health, and with sensitiveness to the elementary aspects of Nature. The perfect man of the future, the prolific begetter of other perfect men, is to work with his hands, chanting the poems of some future Walt, some ideally democratic bard. Women are to have as nearly as possible the same character as men: the emphasis is to pass from family life and local ties to the friendship of comrades and the general brotherhood of man. Men are to be vigorous, comfortable, sentimental, and irresponsible.

This dream is, of course, unrealised and unrealisable, in America as elsewhere. Undeniably there are in America many suggestions of such a society and such a national character. But the growing complexity and fixity of institutions necessarily tends to obscure these traits of a primitive and crude democracy. What Whitman seized upon as the promise of the future was in reality the survival of the past. He sings the song of pioneers, but it is in the nature of the pioneer that the greater his success the quicker must be his transformation into something different. When Whitman made the initial and amorphous phase of society his ideal, he became the prophet of a lost cause. That cause was lost, not merely when wealth and intelligence began to take shape in the American Commonwealth, but it was lost at the very foundation of the world, when those laws of evolution were established which Whitman, like Rousseau, failed to understand. If we may trust Mr. Herbert Spencer, these laws involve a passage from the homogeneous to the heterogeneous, and a constant progress at once in differentiation and in organisation–all, in a word, that Whitman systematically deprecated or ignored. He is surely not the spokesman of the tendencies of his country, although he describes some aspects of its past and present condition: nor does he appeal to those whom he describes, but rather to the *dilettanti* he despises. He is regarded as representative chiefly by foreigners, who look for some grotesque expression of the genius of so young and prodigious a people.

Whitman, it is true, loved and comprehended men; but this love and comprehension had the same limits as his love and comprehension of Nature. He observed truly and responded to his observation with genuine and pervasive emotion. A great gregariousness, an innocent tolerance of moral weakness, a genuine admiration for bodily health and strength, made him bubble over with affection for the generic human creature. Incapable of an ideal passion, he was full of the milk of human kindness. Yet, for all his acquaintance with the ways and thoughts of the common man of his choice, he did not truly understand him. For to understand people is to go much deeper than they go themselves; to penetrate to their characters and disentangle their inmost ideals. Whitman's insight into men did not go beyond a sensuous sympathy; it consisted in a vicarious satisfaction in their pleasures, and an instinctive love of their persons. It never approached a scientific or imaginative knowledge of their hearts.

Therefore Whitman failed radically in his dearest ambition: he can never be a poet of the people. For the people, like the early races whose poetry was ideal, are natural believers in perfection. They have no doubts about the absolute desirability of wealth and learning and power, none about the worth of pure goodness and pure love. Their chosen poets, if they have any, will be always those who have known how to paint these ideals in lively even if in gaudy colours. Nothing is farther from the common people than the corrupt desire to be primitive. They instinctively look toward a more exalted life, which they imagine to be full of distinction and pleasure, and the idea of that brighter existence fills them with hope or with envy or with humble admiration.

If the people are ever won over to hostility to such ideals, it is only because they are cheated by demagogues who tell them that if all the flowers of civilisation were destroyed its fruits would become more abundant. A greater share of happiness, people think, would fall to their lot could they destroy everything beyond their own possible possessions. But they are made thus envious and ignoble only by a deception: what they really desire is an ideal good for themselves which they are told they may secure by depriving others of their preëminence. Their hope is always to enjoy perfect satisfaction themselves; and therefore a poet who loves the picturesque aspects of labour and vagrancy will hardly be the poet of the poor. He may have described their figure and occupation, in neither of which they are much interested; he will not have read their souls. They will prefer to him any sentimental story-teller, any sensational dramatist, any moralising poet; for they are hero-worshippers by temperament, and are too wise or too unfortunate to be much enamoured of themselves or of the conditions of their existence.

Fortunately, the political theory that makes Whitman's principle of literary prophecy and criticism does not always inspire his chants, nor is it presented, even in his prose works, quite bare and unadorned. In *Democratic Vistas* we find it clothed with something of the same poetic passion and lighted up with the same flashes of intuition which we admire in the poems. Even there the temperament is finer than the ideas and the poet wiser than the thinker. His ultimate appeal is really to something more primitive and general than any social aspirations, to something more elementary than an ideal of any kind. He speaks to those minds and to those moods in which sensuality is touched with mysticism. When the intellect is in abeyance, when we would "turn and live with the animals, they are so placid and self-contained," when we are weary of conscience and of ambition, and would yield ourselves for a while to the dream of sense, Walt Whitman is a welcome companion. The images he arouses in us, fresh, full of light and health and of a kind of frankness and beauty, are prized all the more at such a time because they are not choice, but drawn perhaps from a hideous and sordid environment. For this circumstance makes them a better means of escape from convention and from that fatigue and despair which lurk not far beneath the surface of conventional life. In casting off with self-assurance and a sense of fresh vitality the distinctions of tradition and reason a man may feel, as he sinks back comfortably to a lower level of sense and instinct, that he is returning to Nature or escaping into the infinite. Mysticism makes us proud and happy to renounce the work of intelligence, both in thought and in life, and persuades us that we become divine by remaining imperfectly human. Walt Whitman gives a new expression to this ancient and multiform tendency. He feels his own cosmic justification and he would lend the sanction of his inspiration to all loafers and holiday-makers. He would be the congenial patron of farmers and factory hands in their crude pleasures and pieties, as Pan was the patron of the shepherds of Arcadia: for he is sure that in spite of his hairiness and animality, the gods will acknowledge him as one of themselves and smile upon him from the serenity of Olympus.

III

ROBERT BROWNING

If we would do justice to Browning's work as a human document, and at the same time perceive its relation to the rational ideals of the imagination and to that poetry which passes into religion, we must keep, as in the case of Whitman, two things in mind. One is the genuineness of the achievement, the sterling quality of the vision and inspiration; these are their own justification when we approach them from below and regard them as manifesting a more direct or impassioned grasp of experience than is given to mildly blatant, convention-ridden minds. The other thing to remember is the short distance to which this comprehension is carried, its failure to approach any finality, or to achieve a recognition even of the traditional ideals of poetry and religion.

In the case of Walt Whitman such a failure will be generally felt; it is obvious that both his music and his philosophy are those of a barbarian, nay, almost of a savage. Accordingly there is need of dwelling rather on the veracity and simple dignity of his thought and art, on their expression of an order of ideas latent in all better experience. But in the case of Browning it is the success that is obvious to most people. Apart from a certain superficial grotesqueness to which we are soon accustomed, he easily arouses and engages the reader by the pithiness of his phrase, the volume of his passion, the vigour of his moral judgment, the liveliness of his historical fancy. It is obvious that we are in the presence of a great writer, of a great imaginative force, of a master in the expression of emotion. What is perhaps not so obvious, but no less true, is that we are in the presence of a barbaric genius, of a truncated imagination, of a thought and an art inchoate and ill-digested, of a volcanic eruption that tosses itself quite blindly and ineffectually into the sky.

The points of comparison by which this becomes clear are perhaps not in every one's mind, although they are merely the elements of traditional culture, æsthetic and moral. Yet even without reference to ultimate ideals, one may notice in Browning many superficial signs of that deepest of all failures, the failure in rationality and the indifference to perfection. Such a sign is the turgid style, weighty without nobility, pointed without naturalness or precision. Another sign is the "realism" of the personages, who, quite like men and women in actual life, are always displaying traits of character and never attaining character as a whole. Other hints might be found in the structure of the poems, where the dramatic substance does not achieve a dramatic form; in the metaphysical discussion, with its confused prolixity and absence of result; in the moral ideal, where all energies figure without their ultimate purposes; in the religion, which breaks off the expression of this life in the middle, and finds in that suspense an argument for immortality. In all this, and much more that might be recalled, a person coming to Browning with the habits of a cultivated mind might see evidence of some profound incapacity in the poet; but more careful reflection is necessary to understand the nature of this incapacity, its cause, and the peculiar accent which its presence gives to those ideas and impulses which Browning stimulates in us.

There is the more reason for developing this criticism (which might seem needlessly hostile and which time and posterity will doubtless make in their own quiet and decisive fashion) in that Browning did not keep within the sphere of drama and analysis, where he was strong, but allowed his own temperament and opinions to vitiate his representation of life, so that he sometimes turned the expression of a violent passion into the last word of what he thought a religion. He had a didactic vein, a habit of judging the spectacle he evoked and of loading the passions he depicted with his visible sympathy or scorn.

Now a chief support of Browning's popularity is that he is, for many, an initiator into the deeper mysteries of passion, a means of escaping from the moral poverty of their own lives and of feeling the rhythm and compulsion of the general striving. He figures, therefore, distinctly as a prophet, as a bearer of glad tidings, and it is easy for those who hail him as such to imagine that, knowing the labour of life so well, he must know something also of its fruits, and that in giving us the feeling of existence, he is also giving us its meaning. There is serious danger that a mind gathering from his pages the raw materials of truth, the unthreshed harvest of reality, may take him for a philosopher, for a rationaliser of what he describes. Awakening may be mistaken for enlightenment, and the galvanising of torpid sensations and impulses for wisdom.

Against such fatuity reason should raise her voice. The vital and historic forces that produce illusions of this sort in large groups of men are indeed beyond the control of criticism. The ideas of passion are more vivid than those of memory, until they become memories in turn. They must be allowed to fight out their desperate battle against the laws of Nature and reason. But it is worth while in the meantime, for the sake of the truth and of a just philosophy, to meet the varying though perpetual charlatanism of the world with a steady protest. As soon as Browning is proposed to us as a leader, as soon as we are asked to be not the occasional patrons of his art, but the pupils of his philosophy, we have a right to express the radical dissatisfaction which we must feel, if we are rational, with his whole attitude and temper of mind.

The great dramatists have seldom dealt with perfectly virtuous characters. The great poets have seldom represented mythologies that would bear scientific criticism. But by an instinct which constituted their greatness they have cast these mixed materials furnished by life into forms congenial to the specific principles of their art, and by this transformation they have made acceptable in the æsthetic sphere things that in the sphere of reality were evil or imperfect: in a word, their works have been beautiful as works of art. Or, if their genius exceeded that of the technical poet and rose to prophetic intuition, they have known how to create ideal characters, not possessed, perhaps, of every virtue accidentally needed in this world, but possessed of what is ideally better, of internal greatness and perfection. They have also known how to select and reconstruct their mythology so as to make it a true interpretation of moral life. When we read the maxims of Iago, Falstaff, or Hamlet, we are delighted if the thought strikes us as true, but we are not less delighted if it strikes us as false. These characters are not presented to us in order to enlarge our capacities of passion nor in order to justify themselves as processes of redemption; they are there, clothed in poetry and imbedded in plot, to entertain us with their imaginable feelings and their interesting errors. Shakespeare, without being especially a philosopher, stands by virtue of his superlative genius on the plane of universal reason, far above the passionate experience which he overlooks and on which he reflects; and he raises us for the moment to his own level, to send us back again, if not better endowed for practical life, at least not unacquainted with speculation.

With Browning the case is essentially different. When his heroes are blinded by passion and warped by circumstance, as they almost always are, he does not describe the fact from the vantage-ground of the intellect and invite us to look at it from that point of view. On the contrary, his art is all self-expression or satire. For the most part his hero, like Whitman's, is himself; not appearing, as in the case of the American bard, *in puris naturalibus,* but masked in all sorts of historical and romantic finery. Sometimes, however, the personage, like Guido in *The Ring and the Book* or the "frustrate ghosts" of other poems, is merely a Marsyas, shown flayed and quivering to the greater glory of the poet's ideal Apollo. The impulsive utterances and the crudities of most of the speakers are passionately adopted by the poet as his own. He thus perverts what might have been a triumph of imagination into a failure of reason.

This circumstance has much to do with the fact that Browning, in spite of his extraordinary gift for expressing emotion, has hardly produced works purely and unconditionally delightful. They not only portray passion, which is interesting, but they betray it, which is odious. His art was still in the service of the will. He had not attained, in studying the beauty of things, that detachment of the phenomenon, that love of the form for its own sake, which is the secret of contemplative satisfaction. Therefore, the lamentable accidents of his personality and opinions, in themselves no worse than those of other mortals, passed into his art. He did not seek to elude them: he had no free speculative faculty to dominate them by. Or, to put the same thing differently, he was too much in earnest in his fictions, he threw himself too unreservedly into his creations. His imagination, like the imagination we have in dreams, was merely a vent for personal preoccupations. His art was inspired by purposes less simple and universal than the ends of imagination itself. His play of mind consequently could not be free or pure. The creative impulse could not reach its goal or manifest in any notable degree its own ingenuous ideal.

We may illustrate these assertions by considering Browning's treatment of the passion of love, a passion to which he gives great prominence and in which he finds the highest significance.

Love is depicted by Browning with truth, with vehemence, and with the constant conviction that it is the supreme thing in life. The great variety of occasions in which it appears in his pages and the different degrees of elaboration it receives, leave it always of the same quality—the quality of passion. It never sinks into sensuality; in spite of its frequent extreme crudeness, it is always, in Browning's hands, a passion of the imagination, it is always love. On the other hand it never rises into contemplation: mingled as it may be with friendship, with religion, or with various forms of natural tenderness, it always remains a passion; it always remains a personal impulse, a hypnotisation, with another person for its object or its cause. Kept within these limits it is represented, in a series of powerful sketches, which are for most readers the gems of the Browning gallery, as the last word of experience, the highest phase of human life.

> *The woman yonder, there's no use in life*
> *But just to obtain her! Heap earth's woes in one*
> *And bear them—make a pile of all earth's joys*
> *And spurn them, as they help or help not this;*
> *Only, obtain her!*
>
> *When I do come, she will speak not, she will stand,*
> *Either hand*
> *On my shoulder, give her eyes the first embrace*
> *Of my face,*
> *Ere we rush, ere we extinguish sight and speech*
> *Each on each....*
> *O heart, O blood that freezes, blood that burns!*
> *Earth's returns*
> *For whole centuries of folly, noise, and sin—*

> *Shut them in—*
> *With their triumphs and their follies and the rest.*
> *Love is best.*

In the piece called "In a Gondola" the lady says to her lover:—

> *Heart to heart*
> *And lips to lips! Yet once more, ere we part,*
> *Clasp me and make me thine, as mine thou art.*

And he, after being surprised and stabbed in her arms, replies:—

> *It was ordained to be so, sweet!—and best*
> *Comes now, beneath thine eyes, upon thy breast:*
> *Still kiss me! Care not for the cowards; care*
> *Only to put aside thy beauteous hair*
> *My blood will hurt! The Three I do not scorn*
> *To death, because they never lived, but I*
> *Have lived indeed, and so—(yet one more kiss)—can die.*

We are not allowed to regard these expressions as the cries of souls blinded by the agony of passion and lust. Browning unmistakably adopts them as expressing his own highest intuitions. He so much admires the strength of this weakness that he does not admit that it is a weakness at all. It is with the strut of self-satisfaction, with the sensation, almost, of muscular Christianity, that he boasts of it through the mouth of one of his heroes, who is explaining to his mistress the motive of his faithful services as a minister of the queen:—

> *She thinks there was more cause*
> *In love of power, high fame, pure loyalty?*
> *Perhaps she fancies men wear out their lives*
> *Chasing such shades....*
> *I worked because I want you with my soul.*

Readers of the fifth chapter of this volume need not be reminded here of the contrast which this method of understanding love offers to that adopted by the real masters of passion and imagination. They began with that crude emotion with which Browning ends; they lived it down, they exalted it by thought, they extracted the pure gold of it in a long purgation of discipline and suffering. The fierce paroxysm which for him is heaven, was for them the proof that heaven cannot be found on earth, that the value of experience is not in experience itself but in the ideals which it reveals. The intense, voluminous emotion, the sudden, overwhelming self-surrender in which he rests was for them the starting-point of a life of rational worship, of an austere and impersonal religion, by which the fire of love, kindled for a moment by the sight of some creature, was put, as it were, into a censer, to burn incense before every image of the Highest Good. Thus love ceased to be a passion and became the energy of contemplation: it diffused over the universe, natural and ideal, that light of tenderness and that faculty of worship which the passion of love often is first to quicken in a man's breast.

Of this art, recommended by Plato and practised in the Christian Church by all adepts of the spiritual life, Browning knew absolutely nothing. About the object of love he had no misgivings. What could the object be except somebody or other? The important thing was to love intensely and to love often. He remained in the phenomenal sphere: he was a lover of experience; the ideal did not exist for him. No conception could be farther from his thought than the essential conception of any rational philosophy, namely, that feeling is to be treated as raw material for thought, and that the destiny of emotion is to pass into objects which shall contain all its value while losing all its formlessness. This transformation of sense and emotion into objects agreeable to the intellect, into clear ideas and beautiful things, is the natural work of reason; when it has been accomplished very imperfectly, or not at all, we have a barbarous mind, a mind full of chaotic sensations, objectless passions, and undigested ideas. Such a mind Browning's was, to a degree remarkable in one with so rich a heritage of civilisation.

The nineteenth century, as we have already said, has nourished the hope of abolishing the past as a force while it studies it as an object; and Browning, with his fondness for a historical stage setting and for the gossip of history, rebelled equally against the Pagan and the Christian discipline. The "Soul" which he trusted in was the barbarous soul, the "Spontaneous Me" of his half-brother Whitman. It was a restless personal impulse, conscious of obscure depths within itself which it fancied to be infinite, and of a certain vague sympathy with wind and cloud and with the universal mutation. It was the soul that might have animated Attila and Alaric when they came down into Italy, a soul not incurious of the tawdriness and corruption of the strange civilisation it beheld, but incapable of understanding its original spirit; a soul maintaining in the presence of that noble, unappreciated ruin all its own lordliness and energy, and all its native vulgarity.

Browning, who had not had the education traditional in his own country, used to say that Italy had been his university. But it was a school for which he was ill prepared, and he did not sit under its best teachers. For the superficial ferment, the worldly passions, and the crimes of the Italian Renaissance he had a keen interest and intelligence. But Italy has been always a civilised country, and beneath the trappings and suits of civilisation which at that particular time it flaunted so gayly, it preserved a civilised heart to which Browning's insight could never penetrate. There subsisted in the best minds a trained imagination and a cogent ideal of virtue. Italy had a religion, and that religion permeated all its life, and was the background without which even its secular art and secular passions would not be truly intelligible. The most commanding and representative, the deepest and most appealing of Italian natures are permeated with this religious inspiration. A Saint Francis, a Dante, a Michael Angelo, breathe hardly anything else. Yet for Browning these men and what they represented may be said not to have existed. He saw, he studied, and he painted a decapitated Italy. His vision could not mount so high as her head.

One of the elements of that higher tradition which Browning was not prepared to imbibe was the idealisation of love. The passion he represents is lava hot from the crater, in no way moulded, smelted, or refined. He had no thought of subjugating impulses into the harmony of reason. He did not master life, but was mastered by it. Accordingly the love he describes has no wings; it issues in nothing. His lovers "extinguish sight and speech, each on each"; sense, as he says elsewhere, drowning soul. The man in the gondola may well boast that he can die; it is the only thing he can properly do. Death is the only solution of a love that is tied to its individual object and inseparable from the alloy of passion and illusion within itself. Browning's hero, because he has loved intensely, says that he has lived; he would be right, if the significance of life were to be measured by the intensity of the feeling it contained, and if intelligence were not the highest form of vitality. But had that hero known how to love better and had he had enough spirit to dominate his love, he might perhaps have been able to carry away the better part of it and to say that he could not die; for one half of himself and of his love would have been dead already and the other half would have been eternal, having fed

> *On death, that feeds on men;*
> *And death once dead, there's no more dying then.*

The irrationality of the passions which Browning glorifies, making them the crown of life, is so gross that at times he cannot help perceiving it.

> *How perplexed*
> *Grows belief! Well, this cold clay clod*
> *Was man's heart:*
> *Crumble it, and what comes next? Is it God?*

Yes, he will tell us. These passions and follies, however desperate in themselves and however vain for the individual, are excellent as parts of the dispensation of Providence:–

> *Be hate that fruit or love that fruit,*
> *It forwards the general deed of man,*
> *And each of the many helps to recruit*
> *The life of the race by a general plan,*
> *Each living his own to boot.*

If we doubt, then, the value of our own experience, even perhaps of our experience of love, we may appeal to the interdependence of goods and evils in the world to assure ourselves that, in view of its consequences elsewhere, this experience was great and important after all. We need not stop to consider this supposed solution, which bristles with contradictions; it would not satisfy Browning himself, if he did not back it up with something more to his purpose, something nearer to warm and transitive feeling. The compensation for our defeats, the answer to our doubts, is not to be found merely in a proof of the essential necessity and perfection of the universe; that would be cold comfort, especially to so uncontemplative a mind. No: that answer, and compensation are to come very soon and very vividly to every private bosom. There is another life, a series of other lives, for this to happen in. Death will come, and

I shall thereupon
Take rest, ere I be gone
Once more on my adventure brave and new,
Fearless and unperplexed,
When I wage battle next,
What weapons to select, what armour to endue.

For sudden the worst turns the best to the brave,
The black minute's at end,
And the elements' rage, the fiend-voices that rave
Shall dwindle, shall blend,
Shall change, shall become first a peace out of pain,
Then a light, then thy breast,
O thou soul of my soul! I shall clasp thee again
And with God be the rest!

Into this conception of continued life Browning has put all the items furnished by fancy or tradition which at the moment satisfied his imagination—new adventures, reunion with friends, and even, after a severe strain and for a short while, a little peace and quiet. The gist of the matter is that we are to live indefinitely, that all our faults can be turned to good, all our unfinished business settled, and that therefore there is time for anything we like in this world and for all we need in the other. It is in spirit the direct opposite of the philosophic maxim of regarding the end, of taking care to leave a finished life and a perfect character behind us. It is the opposite, also, of the religious *memento mori,* of the warning that the time is short before we go to our account. According to Browning, there is no account: we have an infinite credit. With an unconscious and characteristic mixture of heathen instinct with Christian doctrine, he thinks of the other world as heaven, but of the life to be led there as of the life of Nature.

Aristotle observes that we do not think the business of life worthy of the gods, to whom we can only attribute contemplation; if Browning had had the idea of perfecting and rationalising this life rather than of continuing it indefinitely, he would have followed Aristotle and the Church in this matter. But he had no idea of anything eternal; and so he gave, as he would probably have said, a filling to the empty Christian immortality by making every man busy in it about many things. And to the irrational man, to the boy, it is no unpleasant idea to have an infinite number of days to live through, an infinite number of dinners to eat, with an infinity of fresh fights and new love-affairs, and no end of last rides together.

But it is a mere euphemism to call this perpetual vagrancy a development of the soul. A development means the unfolding of a definite nature, the gradual manifestation of a known idea. A series of phases, like the successive leaps of a water-fall, is no development. And Browning has no idea of an intelligible good which the phases of life might approach and with reference to which they might constitute a progress. His notion is simply that the game of life, the exhilaration of action, is inexhaustible. You may set up your tenpins again after you have bowled them over, and you may keep up the sport for ever. The point is to bring them down as often as possible with a master-stroke and a big bang. That will tend to invigorate in you that self-confidence which in this system passes for faith. But it is unmeaning to call such an exercise heaven, or to talk of being "with God" in such a life, in any sense in which we are not with God already and under all circumstances. Our destiny would rather be, as Browning himself expresses it in a phrase which Attila or Alaric might have composed, "bound dizzily to the wheel of change to slake the thirst of God."

Such an optimism and such a doctrine of immortality can give no justification to experience which it does not already have in its detached parts. Indeed, those dogmas are not the basis of Browning's attitude, not conditions of his satisfaction in living, but rather overflowings of that satisfaction. The present life is presumably a fair average of the whole series of "adventures brave and new" which fall to each man's share; were it not found delightful in itself, there would be no motive for imagining and asserting that it is reproduced *in infinitum.* So too if we did not think that the evil in experience is actually utilised and visibly swallowed up in its good effects, we should hardly venture to think that God could have regarded as a good something which has evil for its condition and which is for that reason profoundly sad and equivocal. But Browning's philosophy of life and habit of imagination do not require the support of any metaphysical theory. His temperament is perfectly self-sufficient and primary; what doctrines he has are suggested by it and are too loose to give it more than a hesitant expression; they are quite powerless to give it any justification which it might lack on its face.

It is the temperament, then, that speaks; we may brush aside as unsubstantial, and even as distorting, the web of arguments and theories which it has spun out of itself. And what does the temperament say? That life is an adventure, not a discipline; that the exercise of energy is the absolute good, irrespective of motives or of consequences. These are the maxims of a frank barbarism; nothing could express better the lust of life, the dogged unwillingness to learn from experience, the contempt for rationality, the carelessness about perfection, the admiration for mere force, in which barbarism always betrays itself. The vague religion which seeks to justify this attitude is really only another outburst of the same irrational impulse.

In Browning this religion takes the name of Christianity, and identifies itself with one or two Christian ideas arbitrarily selected; but at heart it has far more affinity to the worship of Thor or of Odin than to the religion of the Cross. The zest of life becomes a cosmic emotion; we lump the whole together and cry, "Hurrah for the Universe!" A faith which is thus a pure matter of lustiness and inebriation rises and falls, attracts or repels, with the ebb and flow of the mood from which it springs. It is invincible because unseizable; it is as safe from refutation as it is rebellious to embodiment. But it cannot enlighten or correct the passions on which it feeds. Like a servile priest, it flatters them in the name of Heaven. It cloaks irrationality in sanctimony; and its admiration for every bluff folly, being thus justified by a theory, becomes a positive fanaticism, eager to defend any wayward impulse.

Such barbarism of temper and thought could hardly, in a man of Browning's independence and spontaneity, be without its counterpart in his art. When a man's personal religion is passive, as Shakespeare's seems to have been, and is adopted without question or particular interest from the society around him, we may not observe any analogy between it and the free creations of that man's mind. Not so when the religion is created afresh by the private imagination; it is then merely one among many personal works of art, and will naturally bear a family likeness to the others. The same individual temperament, with its limitations and its bias, will appear in the art which has appeared in the religion. And such is the case with Browning. His limitations as a poet are the counterpart of his limitations as a moralist and theologian; only in the poet they are not so regrettable. Philosophy and religion are nothing if not ultimate; it is their business to deal with general principles and final aims. Now it is in the conception of things fundamental and ultimate that Browning is weak; he is strong in the conception of things immediate. The pulse of the emotion, the bobbing up of the thought, the streaming of the reverie–these he can note down with picturesque force or imagine with admirable fecundity.

Yet the limits of such excellence are narrow, for no man can safely go far without the guidance of reason. His long poems have no structure–for that name cannot be given to the singular mechanical division of *The Ring and the Book.* Even his short poems have no completeness, no limpidity. They are little torsos made broken so as to stimulate the reader to the restoration of their missing legs and arms. What is admirable in them is pregnancy of phrase, vividness of passion and sentiment, heaped-up scraps of observation, occasional flashes of light, occasional beauties of versification,–all like

> *the quick sharp scratch*
> *And blue spurt of a lighted match.*

There is never anything largely composed in the spirit of pure beauty, nothing devotedly finished, nothing simple and truly just. The poet's mind cannot reach equilibrium; at best he oscillates between opposed extravagances; his final word is still a *boutade,* still an explosion. He has no sustained nobility of style. He affects with the reader a confidential and vulgar manner, so as to be more sincere and to feel more at home. Even in the poems where the effort at impersonality is most successful, the dramatic disguise is usually thrown off in a preface, epilogue or parenthesis. The author likes to remind us of himself by some confidential wink or genial poke in the ribs, by some little interlarded sneer. We get in these tricks of manner a taste of that essential vulgarity, that indifference to purity and distinction, which is latent but pervasive in all the products of this mind. The same disdain of perfection which appears in his ethics appears here in his verse, and impairs its beauty by allowing it to remain too often obscure, affected, and grotesque.

Such a correspondence is natural: for the same powers of conception and expression are needed in fiction, which, if turned to reflection, would produce a good philosophy. Reason is necessary to the perception of high beauty. Discipline is indispensable to art. Work from which these qualities are absent must be barbaric; it can have no ideal form and must appeal to us only through the sensuousness and profusion of its materials. We are invited by it to lapse into a miscellaneous appreciativeness, into a subservience to every detached impression. And yet, if we would only reflect even on these disordered beauties, we should see that the principle by which they delight us is a principle by which an ideal, an image of perfection, is inevitably evoked. We can have no pleasure or pain, nor any preference whatsoever, without implicitly setting up a standard of excellence, an ideal of what would satisfy us there. To make these implicit ideals explicit, to catch their hint, to work out their theme, and express clearly to ourselves and to the world what they are demanding in the place of the actual— that is the labour of reason and the task of genius. The two cannot be divided. Clarification of ideas and disentanglement of values are as essential to æsthetic activity as to intelligence. A failure of reason is a failure of art and taste.

The limits of Browning's art, like the limits of Whitman's, can therefore be understood by considering his mental habit. Both poets had powerful imaginations, but the type of their imaginations was low. In Whitman imagination was limited to marshalling sensations in single file; the embroideries he made around that central line were simple and insignificant. His energy was concentrated on that somewhat animal form of contemplation, of which, for the rest, he was a great, perhaps an unequalled master. Browning rose above that level; with him sensation is usually in the background; he is not particularly a poet of the senses or of ocular vision. His favourite subject-matter is rather the stream of thought and feeling in the mind; he is the poet of soliloquy. Nature and life as they really are, rather than as they may appear to the ignorant and passionate participant in them, lie beyond his range. Even in his best dramas, like *A Blot in the 'Scutcheon* or *Colombe's Birthday,* the interest remains in the experience of the several persons as they explain it to us. The same is the case in *The Ring and the Book,* the conception of which, in twelve monstrous soliloquies, is a striking evidence of the poet's predilection for this form.

The method is, to penetrate by sympathy rather than to portray by intelligence. The most authoritative insight is not the poet's or the spectator's, aroused and enlightened by the spectacle, but the various heroes' own, in their moment of intensest passion. We therefore miss the tragic relief and exaltation, and come away instead with the uncomfortable feeling that an obstinate folly is apparently the most glorious and choiceworthy thing in the world. This is evidently the poet's own illusion, and those who do not happen to share it must feel that if life were really as irrational as he thinks it, it would be not only profoundly discouraging, which it often is, but profoundly disgusting, which it surely is not; for at least it reveals the ideal which it fails to attain.

This ideal Browning never disentangles. For him the crude experience is the only end, the endless struggle the only ideal, and the perturbed "Soul" the only organon of truth. The arrest of his intelligence at this point, before it has envisaged any rational object, explains the arrest of his dramatic art at soliloquy. His immersion in the forms of self-consciousness prevents him from dramatising the real relations of men and their thinkings to one another, to Nature, and to destiny.

For in order to do so he would have had to view his characters from above (as Cervantes did, for instance), and to see them not merely as they appeared to themselves, but as they appear to reason. This higher attitude, however, was not only beyond Browning's scope, it was positively contrary to his inspiration. Had he reached it, he would no longer have seen the universe through the "Soul," but through the intellect, and he would not have been able to cry, "How the world is made for each one of us!" On the contrary, the "Soul" would have figured only in its true conditions, in all its ignorance and dependence, and also in its essential teachableness, a point against which Browning's barbaric wilfulness particularly rebelled. Rooted in his persuasion that the soul is essentially omnipotent and that to live hard can never be to live wrong, he remained fascinated by the march and method of self-consciousness, and never allowed himself to be weaned from that romantic fatuity by the energy of rational imagination, which prompts us not to regard our ideas as mere filling of a dream, but rather to build on them the conception of permanent objects and overruling principles, such as Nature, society, and the other ideals of reason. A full-grown imagination deals with these things, which do not obey the laws of psychological progression, and cannot be described by the methods of soliloquy.

We thus see that Browning's sphere, though more subtle and complex than Whitman's, was still elementary. It lay far below the spheres of social and historical reality in which Shakespeare moved; far below the comprehensive and cosmic sphere of every great epic poet. Browning did not even reach the intellectual plane of such contemporary poets as Tennyson and Matthew Arnold, who, whatever may be thought of their powers, did not study consciousness for itself, but for the sake of its meaning and of the objects which it revealed. The best things that come into a man's consciousness are the things that take him out of it—the rational things that are independent of his personal perception and of his personal existence. These he approaches with his reason, and they, in the same measure, endow him with their immortality. But precisely these things—the objects of science and of the constructive imagination—Browning always saw askance, in the outskirts of his field of vision, for his eye was fixed and riveted on the soliloquising Soul. And this Soul being, to his apprehension, irrational, did not give itself over to those permanent objects which might otherwise have occupied it, but ruminated on its own accidental emotions, on its love-affairs, and on its hopes of going on so ruminating for ever.

The pathology of the human mind—for the normal, too, is pathological when it is not referred to the ideal—the pathology of the human mind is a very interesting subject, demanding great gifts and great ingenuity in its treatment. Browning ministers to this interest, and possesses this ingenuity and these gifts. More than any other poet he keeps a kind of speculation alive in the now large body of sentimental, eager-minded people, who no longer can find in a definite religion a form and language for their imaginative life. That this service is greatly appreciated speaks well for the ineradicable tendency in man to study himself and his destiny. We do not deny the achievement when we point out its nature and limitations. It does not cease to be something because it is taken to be more than it is.

In every imaginative sphere the nineteenth century has been an era of chaos, as it has been an era of order and growing organisation in the spheres of science and of industry. An ancient doctrine of the philosophers asserts that to chaos the world must ultimately return. And what is perhaps true of the cycles of cosmic change is certainly true of the revolutions of culture. Nothing lasts for ever: languages, arts, and religions disintegrate with time. Yet the perfecting of such forms is the only criterion of progress; the destruction of them the chief evidence of decay. Perhaps fate intends that we should have, in our imaginative decadence, the consolation of fancying that we are still progressing, and that the disintegration of religion and the arts is bringing us nearer to the protoplasm of sensation and passion. If energy and actuality are all that we care for, chaos is as good as order, and barbarism as good as discipline—better, perhaps, since impulse is not then restrained within any bounds of reason or beauty. But if the powers of the human mind are at any time adequate to the task of digesting experience, clearness and order inevitably supervene. The moulds of thought are imposed upon Nature, and the conviction of a definite truth arises together with the vision of a supreme perfection. It is only at such periods that the human animal vindicates his title of rational. If such an epoch should return, people will no doubt retrace our present gropings with interest and see in them gradual approaches to their own achievement. Whitman and Browning might well figure then as representatives of our time. For the merit of being representative cannot be denied them. The mind of our age, like theirs, is choked with materials, emotional, and inconclusive. They merely aggravate our characteristics, and their success with us is due partly to their own absolute strength and partly to our common weakness. If once, however, this imaginative weakness could be overcome, and a form found for the crude matter of experience, men might look back from the height of a new religion and a new poetry upon the present troubles of the spirit; and perhaps even these things might then be pleasant to remember.

Emerson

Interpretations of Poetry and Religion. Volume three of the critical edition of *The Works of George Santayana.* Edited by William G. Holzberger and Herman J. Saatkamp Jr., with an Introduction by Joel Porte. Cambridge, MA: The MIT Press, 1989, 131–40.

This essay appeared as Chapter VIII in Interpretations of Poetry and Religion (1900). *Its beginnings can be traced to an unpublished essay, "The Optimism of Ralph Waldo Emerson," that Santayana submitted in 1886 as a senior at Harvard for the Bowdoin Prize (which he did not win). In the essay, Santayana observed Emerson's love of idealization over any particular idea. Emerson's devotion to imagination tempted him to mysticism, which was fostered by a religious inheritance from his Calvinist ancestors. Santayana appreciated the effort Emerson made to escape the dead Puritan tradition, but he also noted Emerson's inability to replace it with any particular living ideal. This explains why Santayana would claim that Emerson "was in no sense a prophet for his age or country" (ES, 525).*

Those who knew Emerson, or who stood so near to his time and to his circle that they caught some echo of his personal influence, did not judge him merely as a poet or philosopher, nor identify his efficacy with that of his writings. His friends and neighbours, the congregations he preached to in his younger days, the audiences that afterward listened to his lectures, all agreed in a veneration for his person which had nothing to do with their understanding or acceptance of his opinions. They flocked to him and listened to his word, not so much for the sake of its absolute meaning as for the atmosphere of candour, purity, and serenity that hung about it, as about a sort of sacred music. They felt themselves in the presence of a rare and beautiful spirit, who was in communion with a higher world. More than the truth his teaching might express, they valued the sense it gave them of a truth that was inexpressible. They became aware, if we may say so, of the ultra-violet rays of his spectrum, of the inaudible highest notes of his gamut, too pure and thin for common ears.

This effect was by no means due to the possession on the part of Emerson of the secret of the universe, or even of a definite conception of ultimate truth. He was not a prophet who had once for all climbed his Sinai or his Tabor, and having there beheld the transfigured reality, descended again to make authoritative report of it to the world. Far from it. At bottom he had no doctrine at all. The deeper he went and the more he tried to grapple with fundamental conceptions, the vaguer and more elusive they became in his hands. Did he know what he meant by Spirit or the "Over-Soul"? Could he say what he understood by the terms, so constantly on his lips, Nature, Law, God, Benefit, or Beauty? He could not, and the consciousness of that incapacity was so lively within him that he never attempted to give articulation to his philosophy. His finer instinct kept him from doing that violence to his inspiration.

The source of his power lay not in his doctrine, but in his temperament, and the rare quality of his wisdom was due less to his reason than to his imagination. Reality eluded him; he had neither diligence nor constancy enough to master and possess it; but his mind was open to all philosophic influences, from whatever quarter they might blow; the lessons of science and the hints of poetry worked themselves out in him to a free and personal religion. He differed from the plodding many, not in knowing things better, but in having more ways of knowing them. His grasp was not particularly firm, he was far from being, like a Plato or an Aristotle, past master in the art and the science of life. But his mind was endowed with unusual plasticity, with unusual spontaneity and liberty of movement—it was a fairyland of thoughts and fancies. He was like a young god making experiments in creation: he blotched the work, and always began again on a new and better plan. Every day he said, "Let there be light," and every day the light was new. His sun, like that of Heraclitus, was different every morning.

What seemed, then, to the more earnest and less critical of his hearers a revelation from above was in truth rather an insurrection from beneath, a shaking loose from convention, a disintegration of the normal categories of reason in favour of various imaginative principles, on which the world might have been built, if it had been built differently. This gift of revolutionary thinking allowed new aspects, hints of wider laws, premonitions of unthought-of fundamental unities to spring constantly into view. But such visions were necessarily fleeting, because the human mind had long before settled its grammar, and discovered, after much groping and many defeats, the general forms in which experience will allow itself to be stated. These general forms are the principles of common sense and positive science, no less imaginative in their origin than those notions which we now call transcendental, but grown prosaic, like the metaphors of common speech, by dint of repetition.

Yet authority, even of this rational kind, sat lightly upon Emerson. To reject tradition and think as one might have thought if no man had ever existed before was indeed the aspiration of the Transcendentalists, and although Emerson hardly regarded himself as a member of that school, he largely shared its tendency and passed for its spokesman. Without protesting against tradition, he smilingly eluded it in his thoughts, untamable in their quiet irresponsibility. He fled to his woods or to his "pleachèd garden," to be the creator of his own worlds in solitude and freedom. No wonder that he brought thence to the tightly conventional minds of his contemporaries a breath as if from paradise. His simplicity in novelty, his profundity, his ingenuous ardour must have seemed to them something heavenly, and they may be excused if they thought they detected inspiration even in his occasional thin paradoxes and guileless whims. They were stifled with conscience and he brought them a breath of Nature; they were surfeited with shallow controversies and he gave them poetic truth.

Imagination, indeed, is his single theme. As a preacher might under every text enforce the same lessons of the gospel, so Emerson traces in every sphere the same spiritual laws of experience—compensation, continuity, the self-expression of the Soul in the forms of Nature and of society, until she finally recognises herself in her own work and sees its beneficence and beauty. His constant refrain is the omnipotence of imaginative thought; its power first to make the world, then to understand it, and finally to rise above it. All Nature is an embodiment of our native fancy, all history a drama in which the innate possibilities of the spirit are enacted and realised. While the conflict of life and the shocks of experience seem to bring us face to face with an alien and overwhelming power, reflection can humanise and rationalise that power by conceiving its laws; and with this recognition of the rationality of all things comes the sense of their beauty and order. The destruction which Nature seems to prepare for our special hopes is thus seen to be the victory of our impersonal interests. To awaken in us this spiritual insight, an elevation of mind which is at once an act of comprehension and of worship, to substitute it for lower passions and more servile forms of intelligence–that is Emerson's constant effort. All his resources of illustration, observation, and rhetoric are used to deepen and clarify this sort of wisdom.

Such thought is essentially the same that is found in the German romantic or idealistic philosophers, with whom Emerson's affinity is remarkable, all the more as he seems to have borrowed little or nothing from their works. The critics of human nature, in the eighteenth century, had shown how much men's ideas depend on their predispositions, on the character of their senses and the habits of their intelligence. Seizing upon this thought and exaggerating it, the romantic philosophers attributed to the spirit of man the omnipotence which had belonged to God, and felt that in this way they were reasserting the supremacy of mind over matter and establishing it upon a safe and rational basis.

The Germans were great system-makers, and Emerson cannot rival them in the sustained effort of thought by which they sought to reinterpret every sphere of being according to their chosen principles. But he surpassed them in an instinctive sense of what he was doing. He never represented his poetry as science, nor countenanced the formation of a new sect that should nurse the sense of a private and mysterious illumination, and relight the fagots of passion and prejudice. He never tried to seek out and defend the universal implications of his ideas, and never wrote the book he had once planned on the law of compensation, foreseeing, we may well believe, the sophistries in which he would have been directly involved. He fortunately preferred a fresh statement on a fresh subject. A suggestion once given, the spirit once aroused to speculation, a glimpse once gained of some ideal harmony, he chose to descend again to common sense and to touch the earth for a moment before another flight. The faculty of idealisation was itself what he valued. Philosophy for him was rather a moral energy flowering into sprightliness of thought than a body of serious and defensible doctrines. In practising transcendental speculation only in this poetic and sporadic fashion, Emerson retained its true value and avoided its greatest danger. He secured the freedom and fertility of his thought and did not allow one conception of law or one hint of harmony to sterilise the mind and prevent the subsequent birth within it of other ideas, no less just and imposing than their predecessors. For we are not dealing at all in such a philosophy with matters of fact or with such verifiable truths as exclude their opposites. We are dealing only with imagination, with the art of conception, and with the various forms in which reflection, like a poet, may compose and recompose human experience.

A certain disquiet mingled, however, in the minds of Emerson's contemporaries with the admiration they felt for his purity and genius. They saw that he had forsaken the doctrines of the Church; and they were not sure whether he held quite unequivocally any doctrine whatever. We may not all of us share the concern for orthodoxy which usually caused this puzzled alarm: we may understand that it was not Emerson's vocation to be definite and dogmatic in religion any more than in philosophy. Yet that disquiet will not, even for us, wholly disappear. It is produced by a defect which naturally accompanies imagination in all but the greatest minds. I mean disorganisation. Emerson not only conceived things in new ways, but he seemed to think the new ways might cancel and supersede the old. His imagination was to invalidate the understanding. That inspiration which should come to fulfil seemed too often to come to destroy. If he was able so constantly to stimulate us to fresh thoughts, was it not because he demolished the labour of long ages of reflection? Was not the startling effect of much of his writing due to its contradiction to tradition and to common sense?

So long as he is a poet and in the enjoyment of his poetic license, we can blame this play of mind only by a misunderstanding. It is possible to think otherwise than as common sense thinks; there are other categories beside those of science. When we employ them we enlarge our lives. We add to the world of fact any number of worlds of the imagination in which human nature and the eternal relations of ideas may be nobly expressed. So far our imaginative fertility is only a benefit: it surrounds us with the congenial and necessary radiation of art and religion. It manifests our moral vitality in the bosom of Nature.

But sometimes imagination invades the sphere of understanding and seems to discredit its indispensable work. Common sense, we are allowed to infer, is a shallow affair: true insight changes all that. When so applied, poetic activity is not an unmixed good. It loosens our hold on fact and confuses our intelligence, so that we forget that intelligence has itself every prerogative of imagination, and has besides the sanction of practical validity. We are made to believe that since the understanding is something human and conditioned, something which might have been different, as the senses might have been different, and which we may yet, so to speak, get behind—therefore the understanding ought to be abandoned. We long for higher faculties, neglecting those we have, we yearn for intuition, closing our eyes upon experience. We become mystical.

Mysticism, as we have said, is the surrender of a category of thought because we divine its relativity. As every new category, however, must share this reproach, the mystic is obliged in the end to give them all up, the poetic and moral categories no less than the physical, so that the end of his purification is the atrophy of his whole nature, the emptying of his whole heart and mind to make room, as he thinks, for God. By attacking the authority of the understanding as the organon of knowledge, by substituting itself for it as the herald of a deeper truth, the imagination thus prepares its own destruction. For if the understanding is rejected because it cannot grasp the absolute, the imagination and all its works—art, dogma, worship—must presently be rejected for the same reason. Common sense and poetry must both go by the board, and conscience must follow after: for all these are human and relative. Mysticism will be satisfied only with the absolute, and as the absolute, by its very definition, is not representable by any specific faculty, it must be approached through the abandonment of all. The lights of life must be extinguished that the light of the absolute may shine, and the possession of every-thing in general must be secured by the surrender of everything in particular.

The same diffidence, however, the same constant renewal of sincerity which kept Emerson's flights of imagination near to experience, kept his mysticism also within bounds. A certain mystical tendency is pervasive with him, but there are only one or two subjects on which he dwells with enough constancy and energy of attention to make his mystical treatment of them pronounced. One of these is the question of the unity of all minds in the single soul of the universe, which is the same in all creatures; another is the question of evil and of its evaporation in the universal harmony of things. Both these ideas suggest themselves at certain turns in every man's experience, and might receive a rational formulation. But they are intricate subjects, obscured by many emotional prejudices, so that the labour, impartiality, and precision which would be needed to elucidate them are to be looked for in scholastic rather than in inspired thinkers, and in Emerson least of all. Before these problems he is alternately ingenuous and rhapsodical, and in both moods equally helpless. Individuals no doubt exist, he says to him-self. But, ah! Napoleon is in every schoolboy. In every squatter in the western prairies we shall find an owner—

> *Of Caesar's hand and Plato's brain,*
> *Of Lord Christ's heart, and Shakespeare's strain.*

But how? we may ask. Potentially? Is it because any mind, were it given the right body and the right experience, were it made over, in a word, into another mind, would resemble that other mind to the point of identity? Or is it that our souls are already so largely similar that we are subject to many kindred promptings and share many ideals unrealisable in our particular circumstances? But then we should simply be saying that if what makes men different were removed, men would be indistinguishable, or that, in so far as they are now alike, they can understand one another by summoning up their respective experiences in the fancy. There would be no mysticism in that, but at the same time, alas, no eloquence, no paradox, and, if we must say the word, no nonsense.

On the question of evil, Emerson's position is of the same kind. There is evil, of course, he tells us. Experience is sad. There is a crack in everything that God has made. But, ah! the laws of the universe are sacred and beneficent. Without them nothing good could arise. All things, then, are in their right places and the universe is perfect above our querulous tears. Perfect? we may ask. But perfect from what point of view, in reference to what ideal? To its own? To that of a man who renouncing himself and all naturally dear to him, ignoring the injustice, suffering, and impotence in the world, allows his will and his conscience to be hypnotised by the spectacle of a necessary evolution, and lulled into cruelty by the pomp and music of a tragic show? In that case the evil is not explained, it is forgotten; it is not cured, but condoned. We have surrendered the category of the better and the worse, the deepest foundation of life and reason; we have become mystics on the one subject on which, above all others, we ought to be men.

Two forces may be said to have carried Emerson in this mystical direction; one, that freedom of his imagination which we have already noted, and which kept him from the fear of self-contradiction; the other the habit of worship inherited from his clerical ancestors and enforced by his religious education. The spirit of conformity, the unction, the loyalty even unto death inspired by the religion of Jehovah, were dispositions acquired by too long a discipline and rooted in too many forms of speech, of thought, and of worship for a man like Emerson, who had felt their full force, ever to be able to lose them. The evolutions of his abstract opinions left that habit unchanged. Unless we keep this circumstance in mind, we shall not be able to understand the kind of elation and sacred joy, so characteristic of his eloquence, with which he propounds laws of Nature and aspects of experience which, viewed in themselves, afford but an equivocal support to moral enthusiasm. An optimism so persistent and unclouded as his will seem at variance with the description he himself gives of human life, a description coloured by a poetic idealism, but hardly by an optimistic bias.

We must remember, therefore, that this optimism is a pious tradition, originally justified by the belief in a personal God and in a providential government of affairs for the ultimate and positive good of the elect, and that the habit of worship survived in Emerson as an instinct after those positive beliefs had faded into a recognition of "spiritual laws." We must remember that Calvinism had known how to combine an awestruck devotion to the Supreme Being with no very roseate picture of the destinies of mankind, and for more than two hundred years had been breeding in the stock from which Emerson came a willingness to be, as the phrase is, "damned for the glory of God."

What wonder, then, that when, for the former inexorable dispensation of Providence, Emerson substituted his general spiritual and natural laws, he should not have felt the spirit of worship fail within him? On the contrary, his thought moved in the presence of moral harmonies which seemed to him truer, more beautiful, and more beneficent than those of the old theology. An independent philosopher would not have seen in those harmonies an object of worship or a sufficient basis for optimism. But he was not an independent philosopher, in spite of his belief in independence. He inherited the problems and the preoccupations of the theology from which he started, being in this respect like the German idealists, who, with all their pretense of absolute metaphysics, were in reality only giving elusive and abstract forms to traditional theology. Emerson, too, was not primarily a philosopher, but a Puritan mystic with a poetic fancy and a gift for observation and epigram, and he saw in the laws of Nature, idealised by his imagination, only a more intelligible form of the divinity he had always recognised and adored. His was not a philosophy passing into a religion, but a religion expressing itself as a philosophy and veiled, as at its setting it descended the heavens, in various tints of poetry and science.

If we ask ourselves what was Emerson's relation to the scientific and religious movements of his time, and what place he may claim in the history of opinion, we must answer that he belonged very little to the past, very little to the present, and almost wholly to that abstract sphere into which mystical or philosophic aspiration has carried a few men in all ages. The religious tradition in which he was reared was that of Puritanism, but of a Puritanism which, retaining its moral intensity and metaphysical abstraction, had minimised its doctrinal expression and become Unitarian. Emerson was indeed the Psyche of Puritanism, "the latest-born and fairest vision far" of all that "faded hierarchy." A Puritan whose religion was all poetry, a poet whose only pleasure was thought, he showed in his life and personality the meagreness, the constraint, the frigid and conscious consecration which belonged to his clerical ancestors, while his inmost impersonal spirit ranged abroad over the fields of history and Nature, gathering what ideas it might, and singing its little snatches of inspired song.

The traditional element was thus rather an external and inessential contribution to Emerson's mind; he had the professional tinge, the decorum, the distinction of an old-fashioned divine; he had also the habit of writing sermons, and he had the national pride and hope of a religious people that felt itself providentially chosen to establish a free and godly commonwealth in a new world. For the rest, he separated himself from the ancient creed of the community with a sense rather of relief than of regret. A literal belief in Christian doctrines repelled him as unspiritual, as manifesting no understanding of the meaning which, as allegories, those doctrines might have to a philosophic and poetical spirit. Although, being a clergyman, he was at first in the habit of referring to the Bible and its lessons as to a supreme authority, he had no instinctive sympathy with the inspiration of either the Old or the New Testament; in Hafiz or Plutarch, in Plato or Shakespeare, he found more congenial stuff.

While he thus preferred to withdraw, without rancour and without contempt, from the ancient fellowship of the church, he assumed an attitude hardly less cool and deprecatory toward the enthusiasms of the new era. The national ideal of democracy and freedom had his entire sympathy; he allowed himself to be drawn into the movement against slavery; he took a curious and smiling interest in the discoveries of natural science and in the material progress of the age. But he could go no farther. His contemplative nature, his religious training, his dispersed reading, made him stand aside from the life of the world, even while he studied it with benevolent attention. His heart was fixed on eternal things, and he was in no sense a prophet for his age or country. He belonged by nature to that mystical company of devout souls that recognise no particular home and are dispersed throughout history, although not without intercommunication. He felt his affinity to the Hindoos and the Persians, to the Platonists and the Stoics. Like them he remains "a friend and aider of those who would live in the spirit." If not a star of the first magnitude, he is certainly a fixed star in the firmament of philosophy. Alone as yet among Americans, he may be said to have won a place there, if not by the originality of his thought, at least by the originality and beauty of the expression he gave to thoughts that are old and imperishable.

The Genteel Tradition in American Philosophy

Winds of Doctrine: Studies in Contemporary Opinion. New York: Charles Scribner's Sons; London: J. M. Dent & Sons Ltd., 1913, 186–215. Volume nine of the critical edition of *The Works of George Santayana.*

This essay was first delivered as an address to the Philosophical Union of the University of California on 25 August 1911. It appeared in the University of California Chronicle *(13 [1911]: 357–380), and then two years later as Chapter VI in* Winds of Doctrine. *On 23 January 1912, Santayana departed the United States for Europe. Later in the year he submitted his resignation to Harvard and never returned to the United States in his long life. This essay was, in effect, Santayana's farewell address to America. In it he claimed that America's intellectual life was cut off from American will. The former, symbolized by the colonial mansion, was dominated by the genteel tradition; while the latter, symbolized by the skyscraper, was enterprising and energetic. The genteel tradition was an intellectual conformity that traded in an enfeebled Calvinism and a foreign idealism—both philosophies that expressed nothing vital in contemporary American life. Twenty-six years later Santayana explained, "I never meant to find fault with America or to prescribe what people should become. I simply described what I saw, what I felt, and the relations, up to a certain point, of these things with particular philosophies" (LGS, 6:59).*

Ladies and gentlemen,–The privilege of addressing you to-day is very welcome to me, not merely for the honour of it, which is great, nor for the pleasures of travel, which are many, when it is California that one is visiting for the first time, but also because there is something I have long wanted to say which this occasion seems particularly favourable for saying. America is still a young country, and this part of it is especially so; and it would have been nothing extraordinary if, in this young country, material preoccupations had altogether absorbed people's minds, and they had been too much engrossed in living to reflect upon life, or to have any philosophy. The opposite, however, is the case. Not only have you already found time to philosophise in California, as your society proves, but the eastern colonists from the very beginning were a sophisticated race. As much as in clearing the land and fighting the Indians they were occupied, as they expressed it, in wrestling with the Lord. The country was new, but the race was tried, chastened, and full of solemn memories. It was an old wine in new bottles; and America did not have to wait for its present universities, with their departments of academic philosophy, in order to possess a living philosophy–to have a distinct vision of the universe and definite convictions about human destiny.

Now this situation is a singular and remarkable one, and has many consequences, not all of which are equally fortunate. America is a young country with

Address delivered before the Philosophical Union of the University of California, August 25, 1911.

an old mentality: it has enjoyed the advantages of a child carefully brought up and thoroughly indoctrinated; it has been a wise child. But a wise child, an old head on young shoulders, always has a comic and an unpromising side. The wisdom is a little thin and verbal, not aware of its full meaning and grounds; and physical and emotional growth may be stunted by it, or even deranged. Or when the child is too vigorous for that, he will develop a fresh mentality of his own, out of his observations and actual instincts; and this fresh mentality will interfere with the traditional mentality, and tend to reduce it to something perfunctory, conventional, and perhaps secretly despised. A philosophy is not genuine unless it inspires and expresses the life of those who cherish it. I do not think the hereditary philosophy of America has done much to atrophy the natural activities of the in habitants; the wise child has not missed the joys of youth or of manhood; but what has happened is that the hereditary philosophy has grown stale, and that the academic philosophy afterwards developed has caught the stale odour from it. America is not simply, as I said a moment ago, a young country with an old mentality: it is a country with two mentalities, one a survival of the beliefs and standards of the fathers, the other an expression of the instincts, practice, and discoveries of the younger generations. In all the higher things of the mind—in religion, in literature, in the moral emotions—it is the hereditary spirit that still prevails, so much so that Mr. Bernard Shaw finds that America is a hundred years behind the times. The truth is that one-half of the American mind, that not occupied intensely in practical affairs, has remained, I will not say high-and-dry, but slightly becalmed; it has floated gently in the back-water, while, alongside, in invention and industry and social organisation, the other half of the mind was leaping down a sort of Niagara Rapids. This division may be found symbolised in American architecture: a neat reproduction of the colonial mansion—with some modern comforts introduced surreptitiously—stands beside the sky-scraper. The American Will inhabits the sky-scraper; the American Intellect inhabits the colonial mansion. The one is the sphere of the American man; the other, at least predominantly, of the American woman. The one is all aggressive enterprise; the other is all genteel tradition.

Now, with your permission, I should like to analyse more fully how this interesting situation has arisen, how it is qualified, and whither it tends. And in the first place we should remember what, precisely, that philosophy was which the first settlers brought with them into the country. In strictness there was more than one; but we may confine our attention to what I will call Calvinism, since it is on this that the current academic philosophy has been grafted. I do not mean exactly the Calvinism of Calvin, or even of Jonathan Edwards; for in their systems there was much that was not pure philosophy, but rather faith in the externals and history of revelation. Jewish and Christian revelation was interpreted by these men, however, in the spirit of a particular philosophy, which might have arisen under any sky, and been associated with any other religion as well as with Protestant Christianity. In fact, the philosophical principle of Calvinism appears also in the Koran, in Spinoza, and in Cardinal Newman; and persons with no very distinctive Christian belief, like Carlyle or like Professor Royce, may be nevertheless, philosophically, perfect Calvinists. Calvinism, taken in this sense, is an expression of the agonised conscience. It is a view of the world which an agonised conscience readily embraces, if it takes itself seriously, as, being agonised, of course it must. Calvinism, essentially, asserts three things: that sin exists, that sin is punished, and that it is beautiful that sin should exist to be punished. The heart of the Calvinist is therefore divided between tragic concern at his own miserable condition, and tragic exultation about the universe at large. He oscillates between a profound abasement and a paradoxical elation of the spirit. To be a Calvinist philosophically is to feel a fierce pleasure in the existence of misery, especially of one's own, in that this misery seems to manifest the fact that the Absolute is irresponsible or infinite or holy. Human nature, it feels, is totally depraved: to have the instincts and motives that we necessarily have is a great scandal, and we must suffer for it; but that scandal is requisite, since otherwise the serious importance of being as we ought to be would not have been vindicated.

To those of us who have not an agonised conscience this system may seem fantastic and even unintelligible; yet it is logically and intently thought out from its emotional premises. It can take permanent possession of a deep mind here and there, and under certain conditions it can become epidemic. Imagine, for instance, a small nation with an intense vitality, but on the verge of ruin, ecstatic and distressful, having a strict and minute code of laws, that paints life in sharp and violent chiaroscuro, all pure righteousness and black abominations, and exaggerating the consequences of both perhaps to infinity. Such a people were the Jews after the exile, and again the early Protestants. If such a people is philosophical at all, it will not improbably be Calvinistic. Even in the early American communities many of these conditions were fulfilled. The nation was small and isolated; it lived under pressure and constant trial; it was acquainted with but a small range of goods and evils. Vigilance over conduct and an absolute demand for personal integrity were not merely traditional things, but things that practical sages, like Franklin and Washington, recommended to their countrymen, because they were virtues that justified themselves visibly by their fruits. But soon these happy results themselves helped to relax the pressure of external circumstances, and indirectly the pressure of the agonised conscience within. The nation became numerous; it ceased to be either ecstatic or distressful; the high social morality which on the whole it preserved took another colour; people remained honest and helpful out of good sense and good will rather than out of scrupulous adherence to any fixed principles. They retained their instinct for order, and often created order with surprising quickness; but the sanctity of law, to be obeyed for its own sake, began to escape them; it seemed too unpractical a notion, and not quite serious. In fact, the second and native-born American mentality began to take shape. The sense of sin totally evaporated. Nature, in the words of Emerson, was all beauty and commodity; and while operating on it laboriously, and drawing quick returns, the American began to drink in inspiration from it æsthetically. At the same time, in so broad a continent, he had elbow-room. His neighbours helped more than they hindered him; he wished their number to increase. Good will became the great American virtue; and a passion arose for counting heads, and square miles, and cubic feet, and minutes saved—as if there had been anything to save them for. How strange to the American now that saying of Jonathan Edwards, that men are naturally God's enemies! Yet that is an axiom to any intelligent Calvinist, though the words he uses may be different. If you told the modern American that he is totally depraved, he would think you were joking, as he himself usually is. He is convinced that he always has been, and always will be, victorious and blameless.

Calvinism thus lost its basis in American life. Some emotional natures, indeed, reverted in their religious revivals or private searchings of heart to the sources of the tradition; for any of the radical points of view in philosophy may cease to be prevalent, but none can cease to be possible. Other natures, more sensitive to the moral and literary influences of the world, preferred to abandon parts of their philosophy, hoping thus to reduce the distance which should separate the remainder from real life.

Meantime, if anybody arose with a special sensibility or a technical genius, he was in great straits; not being fed sufficiently by the world, he was driven in upon his own resources. The three American writers whose personal endowment was perhaps the finest—Poe, Hawthorne, and Emerson—had all a certain starved and abstract quality. They could not retail the genteel tradition; they were too keen, too perceptive, and too independent for that. But life offered them little digestible material, nor were they naturally voracious. They were fastidious, and under the circumstances they were starved. Emerson, to be sure, fed on books. There was a great catholicity in his reading; and he showed a fine tact in his comments, and in his way of appropriating what he read. But he read transcendentally, not historically, to learn what he himself felt, not what others might have felt before him. And to feed on books, for a philosopher or a poet, is still to starve. Books can help him to acquire form, or to avoid pitfalls; they cannot supply him with substance, if he is to have any. Therefore the genius of Poe and Hawthorne, and even of Emerson, was employed on a sort of inner play, or digestion of vacancy. It was a refined labour, but it was in danger of being morbid, or tinkling, or self-indulgent. It was a play of intra-mental rhymes. Their mind was like an old music-box, full of tender echoes and quaint fancies. These fancies expressed their personal genius sincerely, as dreams may; but they were arbitrary fancies in comparison with what a real observer would have said in the premises. Their manner, in a word, was subjective. In their own persons they escaped the mediocrity of the genteel tradition, but they supplied nothing to supplant it in other minds.

The churches, likewise, although they modified their spirit, had no philosophy to offer save a new emphasis on parts of what Calvinism contained. The theology of Calvin, we must remember, had much in it besides philosophical Calvinism. A Christian tenderness, and a hope of grace for the individual, came to mitigate its sardonic optimism; and it was these evangelical elements that the Calvinistic churches now emphasised, seldom and with blushes referring to hell-fire or infant damnation. Yet philosophic Calvinism, with a theory of life that would perfectly justify hell-fire and infant damnation if they happened to exist, still dominates the traditional metaphysics. It is an ingredient, and the decisive ingredient, in what calls itself idealism. But in order to see just what part Calvinism plays in current idealism, it will be necessary to distinguish the other chief element in that complex system, namely, transcendentalism.

Transcendentalism is the philosophy which the romantic era produced in Germany, and independently, I believe, in America also. Transcendentalism proper, like romanticism, is not any particular set of dogmas about what things exist; it is not a system of the universe regarded as a fact, or as a collection of facts. It is a method, a point of view, from which any world, no matter what it might contain, could be approached by a self-conscious observer. Transcendentalism is systematic subjectivism. It studies the perspectives of knowledge as they radiate from the self; it is a plan of those avenues of inference by which our ideas of things must be reached, if they are to afford any systematic or distant vistas. In other words, transcendentalism is the critical logic of science. Knowledge, it says, has a station, as in a watch-tower; it is always seated here and now, in the self of the moment. The past and the future, things inferred and things conceived, lie around it, painted as upon a panorama. They cannot be lighted up save by some centrifugal ray of attention and present interest, by some active operation of the mind.

This is hardly the occasion for developing or explaining this delicate insight; suffice it to say, lest you should think later that I disparage transcendentalism, that as a method I regard it as correct and, when once suggested, unforgettable. I regard it as the chief contribution made in modern times to speculation. But it is a method only, an attitude we may always assume if we like and that will always be legitimate. It is no answer, and involves no particular answer, to the question: What exists; in what order is what exists produced; what is to exist in the future? This question must be answered by observing the object, and tracing humbly the movement of the object. It cannot be answered at all by harping on the fact that this object, if discovered, must be discovered by somebody, and by somebody who has an interest in discovering it. Yet the Germans who first gained the full transcendental insight were romantic people; they were more or less frankly poets; they were colossal egotists, and wished to make not only their own knowledge but the whole universe centre about themselves. And full as they were of their romantic isolation and romantic liberty, it occurred to them to imagine that all reality might be a transcendental self and a romantic dreamer like themselves; nay, that it might be just their own transcendental self and their own romantic dreams extended indefinitely. Transcendental logic, the method of discovery for the mind, was to become also the method of evolution in nature and history. Transcendental method, so abused, produced transcendental myth. A conscientious critique of knowledge was turned into a sham system of nature. We must therefore distinguish sharply the transcendental grammar of the intellect, which is significant and potentially correct, from the various transcendental systems of the universe, which are chimeras.

In both its parts, however, transcendentalism had much to recommend it to American philosophers, for the transcendental method appealed to the individualistic and revolutionary temper of their youth, while transcendental myths enabled them to find a new status for their inherited theology, and to give what parts of it they cared to preserve some semblance of philosophical backing. This last was the use to which the transcendental method was put by Kant himself, who first brought it into vogue, before the terrible weapon had got out of hand, and become the instrument of pure romanticism. Kant came, he himself said, to remove knowledge in order to make room for faith, which in his case meant faith in Calvinism. In other words, he applied the transcendental method to matters of fact, reducing them thereby to human ideas, in order to give to the Calvinistic postulates of conscience a metaphysical validity. For Kant had a genteel tradition of his own, which he wished to remove to a place of safety, feeling that the empirical world had become too hot for it; and this place of safety was the region of transcendental myth. I need hardly say how perfectly this expedient suited the needs of philosophers in America, and it is no accident if the influence of Kant soon became dominant here. To embrace this philosophy was regarded as a sign of profound metaphysical insight, although the most mediocre minds found no difficulty in embracing it. In truth it was a sign of having been brought up in the genteel tradition, of feeling it weak, and of wishing to save it.

But the transcendental method, in its way, was also sympathetic to the American mind. It embodied, in a radical form, the spirit of Protestantism as distinguished from its inherited doctrines; it was autonomous, undismayed, calmly revolutionary; it felt that Will was deeper than Intellect; it focussed everything here and now, and asked all things to show their credentials at the bar of the young self, and to prove their value for this latest born moment. These things are truly American; they would be characteristic of any young society with a keen and discursive intelligence, and they are strikingly exemplified in the thought and in the person of Emerson. They constitute what he called self-trust. Self-trust, like other transcendental attitudes, may be expressed in metaphysical fables. The romantic spirit may imagine itself to be an absolute force, evoking and moulding the plastic world to express its varying moods. But for a pioneer who is actually a world-builder this metaphysical illusion has a partial warrant in historical fact; far more warrant than it could boast of in the fixed and articulated society of Europe, among the moonstruck rebels and sulking poets of the romantic era. Emerson was a shrewd Yankee, by instinct on the winning side; he was a cheery, child-like soul, impervious to the evidence of evil, as of everything that it did not suit his transcendental individuality to appreciate or to notice. More, perhaps, than anybody that has ever lived, he practised the transcendental method in all its purity. He had no system. He opened his eyes on the world every morning with a fresh sincerity, marking how things seemed to him then, or what they suggested to his spontaneous fancy. This fancy, for being spontaneous, was not always novel; it was guided by the habits and training of his mind, which were those of a preacher. Yet he never insisted on his notions so as to turn them into settled dogmas; he felt in his bones that they were myths. Sometimes, indeed, the bad example of other transcendentalists, less true than he to their method, or the pressing questions of unintelligent people, or the instinct we all have to think our ideas final, led him to the very verge of system-making; but he stopped short. Had he made a system out of his notion of compensation, or the over-soul, or spiritual laws, the result would have been as thin and forced as it is in other transcendental systems. But he coveted truth; and he returned to experience, to history, to poetry, to the natural science of his day, for new starting-points and hints toward fresh transcendental musings.

To covet truth is a very distinguished passion. Every philosopher says he is pursuing the truth, but this is seldom the case. As Mr. Bertrand Russell has observed, one reason why philosophers often fail to reach the truth is that often they do not desire to reach it. Those who are genuinely concerned in discovering what happens to be true are rather the men of science, the naturalists, the historians; and ordinarily they discover it, according to their lights. The truths they find are never complete, and are not always important; but they are integral parts of the truth, facts and circumstances that help to fill in the picture, and that no later interpretation can invalidate or afford to contradict. But professional philosophers are usually only apologists: that is, they are absorbed in defending some vested illusion or some eloquent idea. Like lawyers or detectives, they study the case for which they are retained, to see how much evidence or semblance of evidence they can gather for the defence, and how much prejudice they can raise against the witnesses for the prosecution; for they know they are defending prisoners suspected by the world, and perhaps by their own good sense, of falsification. They do not covet truth, but victory and the dispelling of their own doubts. What they defend is some system, that is, some view about the totality of things, of which men are actually ignorant. No system would have ever been framed if people had been simply interested in knowing what is true, whatever it may be. What produces systems is the interest in maintaining against all comers that some favourite or inherited idea of ours is sufficient and right. A system may contain an account of many things which, in detail, are true enough; but as a system, covering infinite possibilities that neither our experience nor our logic can prejudge, it must be a work of imagination and a piece of human soliloquy. It may be expressive of human experience, it may be poetical; but how should any one who really coveted truth suppose that it was true?

Emerson had no system; and his coveting truth had another exceptional consequence: he was detached, unworldly, contemplative. When he came out of the conventicle or the reform meeting, or out of the rapturous close atmosphere of the lecture-room, he heard Nature whispering to him: "Why so hot, little sir?" No doubt the spirit or energy of the world is what is acting in us, as the sea is what rises in every little wave; but it passes through us, and cry out as we may, it will move on. Our privilege is to have perceived it as it moves. Our dignity is not in what we do, but in what we understand. The whole world is doing things. We are turning in that vortex; yet within us is silent observation, the speculative eye before which all passes, which bridges the distances and compares the combatants. On this side of his genius Emerson broke away from all conditions of age or country and represented nothing except intelligence itself.

There was another element in Emerson, curiously combined with transcendentalism, namely, his love and respect for Nature. Nature, for the transcendentalist, is precious because it is his own work, a mirror in which he looks at himself and says (like a poet relishing his own verses), "What a genius I am! Who would have thought there was such stuff in me?" And the philosophical egotist finds in his doctrine a ready explanation of whatever beauty and commodity nature actually has. No wonder, he says to himself, that nature is sympathetic, since I made it. And such a view, one-sided and even fatuous as it may be, undoubtedly sharpens the vision of a poet and a moralist to all that is inspiriting and symbolic in the natural world. Emerson was particularly ingenious and clear-sighted in feeling the spiritual uses of fellowship with the elements. This is something in which all Teutonic poetry is rich and which forms, I think, the most genuine and spontaneous part of modern taste, and especially of American taste. Just as some people are naturally enthralled and refreshed by music, so others are by landscape. Music and landscape make up the spiritual resources of those who cannot or dare not express their unfulfilled ideals in words. Serious poetry, profound religion (Calvinism, for instance), are the joys of an unhappiness that confesses itself; but when a genteel tradition forbids people to confess that they are unhappy, serious poetry and profound religion are closed to them by that; and since human life, in its depths, cannot then express itself openly, imagination is driven for comfort into abstract arts, where human circumstances are lost sight of, and human problems dissolve in a purer medium. The pressure of care is thus relieved, without its quietus being found in intelligence. To understand oneself is the classic form of consolation; to elude oneself is the romantic. In the presence of music or landscape human experience eludes itself; and thus romanticism is the bond between transcendental and naturalistic sentiment. The winds and clouds come to minister to the solitary ego.

Have there been, we may ask, any successful efforts to escape from the genteel tradition, and to express something worth expressing behind its back? This might well not have occurred as yet; but America is so precocious, it has been trained by the genteel tradition to be so wise for its years, that some indications of a truly native philosophy and poetry are already to be found. I might mention the humorists, of whom you here in California have had your share. The humorists, however, only half escape the genteel tradition; their humour would lose its savour if they had wholly escaped it. They point to what contradicts it in the facts; but not in order to abandon the genteel tradition, for they have nothing solid to put in its place. When they point out how ill many facts fit into it, they do not clearly conceive that this militates against the standard, but think it a funny perversity in the facts. Of course, did they earnestly respect the genteel tradition, such an incongruity would seem to them sad, rather than ludicrous. Perhaps the prevalence of humour in America, in and out of season, may be taken as one more evidence that the genteel tradition is present pervasively, but everywhere weak. Similarly in Italy, during the Renaissance, the Catholic tradition could not be banished from the intellect, since there was nothing articulate to take its place; yet its hold on the heart was singularly relaxed. The consequence was that humorists could regale themselves with the foibles of monks and of cardinals, with the credulity of fools, and the bogus miracles of the saints; not intending to deny the theory of the church, but caring for it so little at heart that they could find it infinitely amusing that it should be contradicted in men's lives and that no harm should come of it. So when Mark Twain says, "I was born of poor but dishonest parents," the humour depends on the parody of the genteel Anglo-Saxon convention that it is disreputable to be poor; but to hint at the hollowness of it would not be amusing if it did not remain at bottom one's habitual conviction.

The one American writer who has left the genteel tradition entirely behind is perhaps Walt Whitman. For this reason educated Americans find him rather an unpalatable person, who they sincerely protest ought not to be taken for a representative of their culture; and he certainly should not, because their culture is so genteel and traditional. But the foreigner may sometimes think otherwise, since he is looking for what may have arisen in America to express, not the polite and conventional American mind, but the spirit and the inarticulate principles that animate the community, on which its own genteel mentality seems to sit rather lightly. When the foreigner opens the pages of Walt Whitman, he thinks that he has come at last upon something representative and original. In Walt Whitman democracy is carried into psychology and morals. The various sights, moods, and emotions are given each one vote; they are declared to be all free and equal, and the innumerable common-place moments of life are suffered to speak like the others. Those moments formerly reputed great are not excluded, but they are made to march in the ranks with their companions–plain foot-soldiers and servants of the hour. Nor does the refusal to discriminate stop there; we must carry our principle further down, to the animals, to inanimate nature, to the cosmos as a whole. Whitman became a pantheist; but his pantheism, unlike that of the Stoics and of Spinoza, was unintellectual, lazy, and self-indulgent; for he simply felt jovially that everything real was good enough, and that he was good enough himself. In him Bohemia rebelled against the genteel tradition; but the reconstruction that alone can justify revolution did not ensue. His attitude, in principle, was utterly disintegrating; his poetic genius fell back to the lowest level, perhaps, to which it is possible for poetic genius to fall. He reduced his imagination to a passive sensorium for the registering of impressions. No element of construction remained in it, and therefore no element of penetration. But his scope was wide; and his lazy, desultory apprehension was poetical. His work, for the very reason that it is so rudimentary, contains a beginning, or rather many beginnings, that might possibly grow into a noble moral imagination, a worthy filling for the human mind. An American in the nineteenth century who completely disregarded the genteel tradition could hardly have done more.

But there is another distinguished man, lately lost to this country, who has given some rude shocks to this tradition and who, as much as Whitman, may be regarded as representing the genuine, the long silent American mind–I mean William James. He and his brother Henry were as tightly swaddled in the genteel tradition as any infant geniuses could be, for they were born before 1850, and in a Swedenborgian household. Yet they burst those bands almost entirely. The ways in which the two brothers freed themselves, however, are interestingly different. Mr. Henry James has done it by adopting the point of view of the outer world, and by turning the genteel American tradition, as he turns everything else, into a subject-matter for analysis. For him it is a curious habit of mind, intimately comprehended, to be compared with other habits of mind, also well known to him. Thus he has overcome the genteel tradition in the classic way, by understanding it. With William James too this infusion of worldly insight and European sympathies was a potent influence, especially in his earlier days; but the chief source of his liberty was another. It was his personal spontaneity, similar to that of Emerson, and his personal vitality, similar to that of nobody else. Convictions and ideas came to him, so to speak, from the subsoil. He had a prophetic sympathy with the dawning sentiments of the age, with the moods of the dumb majority. His scattered words caught fire in many parts of the world. His way of thinking and feeling represented the true America, and represented in a measure the whole ultra-modern, radical world. Thus he eluded the genteel tradition in the romantic way, by continuing it into its opposite. The romantic mind, glorified in Hegel's dialectic (which is not dialectic at all, but a sort of tragi-comic history of experience), is always rendering its thoughts unrecognisable through the infusion of new insights, and through the insensible transformation of the moral feeling that accompanies them, till at last it has completely reversed its old judgments under cover of expanding them. Thus the genteel tradition was led a merry dance when it fell again into the hands of a genuine and vigorous romanticist like William James. He restored their revolutionary force to its neutralised elements, by picking them out afresh, and emphasising them separately, according to his personal predilections.

For one thing, William James kept his mind and heart wide open to all that might seem, to polite minds, odd, personal, or visionary in religion and philosophy. He gave a sincerely respectful hearing to sentimentalists, mystics, spiritualists, wizards, cranks, quacks, and impostors—for it is hard to draw the line, and James was not willing to draw it prematurely. He thought, with his usual modesty, that any of these might have something to teach him. The lame, the halt, the blind, and those speaking with tongues could come to him with the certainty of finding sympathy; and if they were not healed, at least they were comforted, that a famous professor should take them so seriously; and they began to feel that after all to have only one leg, or one hand, or one eye, or to have three, might be in itself no less beauteous than to have just two, like the stolid majority. Thus William James became the friend and helper of those groping, nervous, half-educated, spiritually disinherited, passionately hungry individuals of which America is full. He became, at the same time, their spokesman and representative before the learned world; and he made it a chief part of his vocation to recast what the learned world has to offer, so that as far as possible it might serve the needs and interest of these people.

Yet the normal practical masculine American, too, had a friend in William James. There is a feeling abroad now, to which biology and Darwinism lend some colour, that theory is simply an instrument for practice, and intelligence merely a help toward material survival. Bears, it is said, have fur and claws, but poor naked man is condemned to be intelligent, or he will perish. This feeling

William James embodied in that theory of thought and of truth which he called pragmatism. Intelligence, he thought, is no miraculous, idle faculty, by which we mirror passively any or everything that happens to be true, reduplicating the real world to no purpose. Intelligence has its roots and its issue in the context of events; it is one kind of practical adjustment, an experimental act, a form of vital tension. It does not essentially serve to picture other parts of reality, but to connect them. This view was not worked out by William James in its psychological and historical details; unfortunately he developed it chiefly in controversy against its opposite, which he called intellectualism, and which he hated with all the hatred of which his kind heart was capable. Intellectualism, as he conceived it, was pure pedantry; it impoverished and verbalised everything, and tied up nature in red tape. Ideas and rules that may have been occasionally useful it put in the place of the full-blooded irrational movement of life which had called them into being; and these abstractions, so soon obsolete, it strove to fix and to worship for ever. Thus all creeds and theories and all formal precepts sink in the estimation of the pragmatist to a local and temporary grammar of action; a grammar that must be changed slowly by time, and may be changed quickly by genius. To know things as a whole, or as they are eternally, if there is anything eternal in them, is not only beyond our powers, but would prove worthless, and perhaps even fatal to our lives. Ideas are not mirrors, they are weapons; their function is to prepare us to meet events, as future experience may unroll them. Those ideas that disappoint us are false ideas; those to which events are true are true themselves.

This may seem a very utilitarian view of the mind; and I confess I think it a partial one, since the logical force of beliefs and ideas, their truth or falsehood as assertions, has been overlooked altogether, or confused with the vital force of the material processes which these ideas express. It is an external view only, which marks the place and conditions of the mind in nature, but neglects its specific essence; as if a jewel were defined as a round hole in a ring. Nevertheless, the more materialistic the pragmatist's theory of the mind is, the more vitalistic his theory of nature will have to become. If the intellect is a device produced in organic bodies to expedite their processes, these organic bodies must have interests and a chosen direction in their life; otherwise their life could not be expedited, nor could anything be useful to it. In other words—and this is a third point at which the philosophy of William James has played havoc with the genteel tradition, while ostensibly defending it—nature must be conceived anthropomorphically and in psychological terms. Its purposes are not to be static harmonies, self-unfolding destinies, the logic of spirit, the spirit of logic, or any other formal method and abstract law; its purposes are to be concrete endeavours, finite efforts of souls living in an environment which they transform and by which they, too, are affected. A spirit, the divine spirit as much as the human, as this new animism conceives it, is a romantic adventurer. Its future is undetermined. Its scope, its duration, and the quality of its life are all contingent. This spirit grows; it buds and sends forth feelers, sounding the depths around for such other centres of force or life as may exist there. It has a vital momentum, but no predetermined goal. It uses its past as a stepping-stone, or rather as a diving-board, but has an absolutely fresh will at each moment to plunge this way or that into the unknown. The universe is an experiment; it is unfinished. It has no ultimate or total nature, because it has no end. It embodies no formula or statable law; any formula is at best a poor abstraction, describing what, in some region and for some time, may be the most striking characteristic of existence; the law is a description *a posteriori* of the habit things have chosen to acquire, and which they may possibly throw off altogether. What a day may bring forth is uncertain; uncertain even to God. Omniscience is impossible; time is real; what had been omniscience hitherto might discover something more to-day. "There shall be news," William James was fond of saying with rapture, quoting from the unpublished poem of an obscure friend, "there shall be news in heaven!" There is almost certainly, he thought, a God now; there may be several gods, who might exist together, or one after the other. We might, by our conspiring sympathies, help to make a new one. Much in us is doubtless immortal; we survive death for some time in a recognisable form; but what our career and transformations may be in the sequel we cannot tell, although we may help to determine them by our daily choices. Observation must be continual if our ideas are to remain true. Eternal vigilance is the price of knowledge; perpetual hazard, perpetual experiment keep quick the edge of life.

This is, so far as I know, a new philosophical vista; it is a conception never before presented, although implied, perhaps, in various quarters, as in Norse and even Greek mythology. It is a vision radically empirical and radically romantic; and as William James himself used to say, the visions and not the arguments of a philosopher are the interesting and influential things about him. William James, rather too generously, attributed this vision to M. Bergson, and regarded him in consequence as a philosopher of the first rank, whose thought was to be one of the turning-points in history. M. Bergson had killed intellectualism. It was his book on creative evolution, said James with humorous emphasis, that had come at last to "*écraser l'infâme.*" We may suspect, notwithstanding, that intellectualism, infamous and crushed, will survive the blow; and if the author of the Book of Ecclesiastes were now alive, and heard that there shall be news in heaven, he would doubtless say that there may possibly be news there, but that under the sun there is nothing new—not even radical empiricism or radical romanticism, which from the beginning of the world has been the philosophy of those who as yet had had little experience; for to the blinking little child it is not merely something in the world that is new daily, but everything is new all day.

I am not concerned with the rights and wrongs of that controversy; my point is only that William James, in this genial evolutionary view of the world, has given a rude shock to the genteel tradition. What! The world a gradual improvisation? Creation unpremeditated? God a sort of young poet or struggling artist? William James is an advocate of theism; pragmatism adds one to the evidences of religion; that is excellent. But is not the cool abstract piety of the genteel getting more than it asks for? This empirical naturalistic God is too crude and positive a force; he will work miracles, he will answer prayers, he may inhabit distinct places, and have distinct conditions under which alone he can operate; he is a neighbouring being, whom we can act upon, and rely upon for specific aids, as upon a personal friend, or a physician, or an insurance company. How disconcerting! Is not this new theology a little like superstition? And yet how interesting, how exciting, if it should happen to be true! I am far from wishing to suggest that such a view seems to me more probable than conventional idealism or than Christian orthodoxy. All three are in the region of dramatic system-making and myth to which probabilities are irrelevant. If one man says the moon is sister to the sun, and another that she is his daughter, the question is not which notion is more probable, but whether either of them is at all expressive. The so-called evidences are devised afterwards, when faith and imagination have prejudged the issue. The force of William James's new theology, or romantic cosmology, lies only in this: that it has broken the spell of the genteel tradition, and enticed faith in a new direction, which on second thoughts may prove no less alluring than the old. The important fact is not that the new fancy might possibly be true–who shall know that?–but that it has entered the heart of a leading American to conceive and to cherish it. The genteel tradition cannot be dislodged by these insurrections; there are circles to which it is still congenial, and where it will be preserved. But it has been challenged and (what is perhaps more insidious) it has been discovered. No one need be brow-beaten any longer into accepting it. No one need be afraid, for instance, that his fate is sealed because some young prig may call him a dualist; the pint would call the quart a dualist, if you tried to pour the quart into him. We need not be afraid of being less profound, for being direct and sincere. The intellectual world may be traversed in many directions; the whole has not been surveyed; there is a great career in it open to talent. That is a sort of knell, that tolls the passing of the genteel tradition. Something else is now in the field; something else can appeal to the imagination, and be a thousand times more idealistic than academic idealism, which is often simply a way of white-washing and adoring things as they are. The illegitimate monopoly which the genteel tradition had established over what ought to be assumed and what ought to be hoped for has been broken down by the first-born of the family, by the genius of the race. Henceforth there can hardly be the same peace and the same pleasure in hugging the old proprieties. Hegel will be to the next generation what Sir William Hamilton was to the last. Nothing will have been disproved, but everything will have been abandoned. An honest man has spoken, and the cant of the genteel tradition has become harder for young lips to repeat.

With this I have finished such a sketch as I am here able to offer you of the genteel tradition in American philosophy. The subject is complex, and calls for many an excursus and qualifying footnote; yet I think the main outlines are clear enough. The chief fountains of this tradition were Calvinism and transcendentalism. Both were living fountains; but to keep them alive they required, one an agonised conscience, and the other a radical subjective criticism of knowledge. When these rare metaphysical preoccupations disappeared–and the American atmosphere is not favourable to either of them–the two systems ceased to be inwardly understood; they subsisted as sacred mysteries only; and the combination of the two in some transcendental system of the universe (a contradiction in principle) was doubly artificial. Besides, it could hardly be held with a single mind. Natural science, history, the beliefs implied in labour and invention, could not be disregarded altogether; so that the transcendental philosopher was condemned to a double allegiance, and to not letting his left hand know the bluff that his right hand was making. Nevertheless, the difficulty in bringing practical inarticulate convictions to expression is very great, and the genteel tradition has subsisted in the academic mind for want of anything equally academic to take its place.

　The academic mind, however, has had its flanks turned. On the one side came the revolt of the Bohemian temperament, with its poetry of crude naturalism; on the other side came an impassioned empiricism, welcoming popular religious witnesses to the unseen, reducing science to an instrument of success in action, and declaring the universe to be wild and young, and not to be harnessed by the logic of any school.

　This revolution, I should think, might well find an echo among you, who live in a thriving society, and in the presence of a virgin and prodigious world. When you transform nature to your uses, when you experiment with her forces, and reduce them to industrial agents, you cannot feel that nature was made by you or for you, for then these adjustments would have been pre-established. Much less can you feel it when she destroys your labour of years in a momentary spasm. You must feel, rather, that you are an offshoot of her life; one brave little force among her immense forces. When you escape, as you love to do, to your forests and your sierras, I am sure again that you do not feel you made them, or that they were made for you. They have grown, as you have grown, only more massively and more slowly. In their non-human beauty and peace they stir the sub-human depths and the superhuman possibilities of your own spirit. It is no transcendental logic that they teach; and they give no sign of any deliberate morality seated in the world. It is rather the vanity and superficiality of all logic, the needlessness of argument, the relativity of morals, the strength of time, the fertility of matter, the variety, the unspeakable variety, of possible life. Everything is measurable and conditioned, indefinitely repeated, yet, in repetition, twisted somewhat from its old form. Everywhere is beauty and nowhere permanence, everywhere an incipient harmony, nowhere an intention, nor a responsibility, nor a plan. It is the irresistible suasion of this daily spectacle, it is the daily discipline of contact with things, so different from the verbal discipline of the schools, that will, I trust, inspire the philosophy of your children. A Californian whom I had recently the pleasure of meeting observed that, if the philosophers had lived among your mountains their systems would have been different from what they are. Certainly, I should say, very different from what those systems are which the European genteel tradition has handed down since Socrates; for these systems are egotistical; directly or indirectly they are anthropocentric, and inspired by the conceited notion that man, or human reason, or the human distinction between good and evil, is the centre and pivot of the universe. That is what the mountains and the woods should make you at last ashamed to assert. From what, indeed, does the society of nature liberate you, that you find it so sweet? It is hardly (is it?) that you wish to forget your past, or your friends, or that you have any secret contempt for your present ambitions. You respect these, you respect them perhaps too much; you are not suffered by the genteel tradition to criticise or to reform them at all radically. No; it is the yoke of this genteel tradition itself that these primeval solitudes lift from your shoulders. They suspend your forced sense of your own importance not merely as individuals, but even as men. They allow you, in one happy moment, at once to play and to worship, to take yourselves simply, humbly, for what you are, and to salute the wild, indifferent, non-censorious infinity of nature. You are admonished that what you can do avails little materially, and in the end nothing. At the same time, through wonder and pleasure, you are taught speculation. You learn what you are really fitted to do, and where lie your natural dignity and joy, namely, in representing many things, without being them, and in letting your imagination, through sympathy, celebrate and echo their life. Because the peculiarity of man is that his machinery for reaction on external things has involved an imaginative transcript of these things, which is preserved and suspended in his fancy; and the interest and beauty of this inward landscape, rather than any fortunes that may await his body in the outer world, constitute his proper happiness. By their mind, its scope, quality, and temper, we estimate men, for by the mind only do we exist as men, and are more than so many storage-batteries for material energy. Let us therefore be frankly human. Let us be content to live in the mind.

English Liberty in America

Character and Opinion in the United States: With Reminiscences of William James and Josiah Royce and Academic Life in America. New York: Charles Scribner's Sons; London: Constable and Co. Ltd.; Toronto: McLeod, 1920, 192–233. Volume eleven of the critical edition of *The Works of George Santayana.*

This essay appeared as Chapter VII in Character and Opinion in the United States, *which developed out of lectures delivered in England. In this chapter Santayana considered the English trait of free cooperation as manifested in America. It is a method of social organization that assumes unanimity and adaptability among the population, and Santayana thought it had been a great success in America. The result was individual freedom predicated on social conformity: "Even what is best in American life is compulsory—the idealism, the zeal, the beautiful happy unison of its great moments. You must wave, you must cheer, you must push with the irresistible crowd; otherwise you will feel like a traitor" (ES, 547). The freedom comes from being pretty much the same as your neighbor and wanting to be part of the public. By contrast absolute liberty is radically individual and primitive. It is fanatical commitment to a fixed ideal. It does not cooperate, but rather it subjugates others to its one ideal aim. "Certainly absolute freedom would be more beautiful if we were birds or poets" (ES, 554), but English liberty is more in harmony with the variety and variation of nature.*

The straits of Dover, which one may sometimes see across, have sufficed so to isolate England that it has never moved quite in step with the rest of Europe in politics, morals, or art. No wonder that the Atlantic Ocean, although it has favoured a mixed emigration and cheap intercourse, should have cut off America so effectually that all the people there, even those of Latin origin, have become curiously different from any kind of European. In vain are they reputed to have the same religions or to speak the same languages as their cousins in the old world; everything has changed its accent, spirit, and value. Flora and fauna have been intoxicated by that untouched soil and fresh tonic air, and by those vast spaces; in spite of their hereditary differences of species they have all acquired the same crude savour and defiant aspect. In comparison with their European prototypes they seem tough, meagre, bold, and ugly. In the United States, apart from the fact that most of the early colonists belonged to an exceptional type of Englishman, the scale and speed of life have made everything strangely un-English. There is cheeriness instead of doggedness, confidence instead of circumspection; there is a desire to quizz [*sic*] and to dazzle rather than a fear of being mistaken or of being shocked; there is a pervasive cordiality, exaggeration, and farcical humour; and in the presence of the Englishman, when by chance he turns up or is thought of, there is an invincible impatience and irritation that his point of view should be so fixed, his mind so literal, and the freight he carries so excessive (when you are sailing in ballast yourself), and that he should seem to take so little notice of changes in the wind to which you are nervously sensitive.

Nevertheless there is one gift or habit, native to England, that has not only been preserved in America unchanged, but has found there a more favourable atmosphere in which to manifest its true nature—I mean the spirit of free co-operation. The root of it is free individuality, which is deeply seated in the English inner man; there is an indomitable instinct or mind in him which he perpetually consults and reveres, slow and embarrassed as his expression of it may be. But this free individuality in the Englishman is crossed and biased by a large residue of social servitude. The church and the aristocracy, entanglement in custom and privilege, mistrust and bitterness about particular grievances, warp the inner man and enlist him against his interests in alien causes; the straits of Dover were too narrow, the shadow of a hostile continent was too oppressive, the English sod was soaked with too many dews and cut by too many hedges, for each individual, being quite master of himself, to confront every other individual without fear or prejudice, and to unite with him in the free pursuit of whatever aims they might find that they had in common. Yet this slow co-operation of free men, this liberty in democracy—the only sort that America possesses or believes in—is wholly English in its personal basis, its reserve, its tenacity, its empiricism, its public spirit, and its assurance of its own rightness; and it deserves to be called English always, to whatever countries it may spread.

The omnipresence in America of this spirit of co-operation, responsibility, and growth is very remarkable. Far from being neutralised by American dash and bravura, or lost in the opposite instincts of so many alien races, it seems to be adopted at once in the most mixed circles and in the most novel predicaments. In America social servitude is reduced to a minimum; in fact we may almost say that it is reduced to subjecting children to their mothers and to a common public education, agencies that are absolutely indispensable to produce the individual and enable him to exercise his personal initiative effectually; for after all, whatever metaphysical egotism may say, one cannot vote to be created. But once created, weaned, and taught to read and write, the young American can easily shoulder his knapsack and choose his own way in the world. He is as yet very little trammelled by want of opportunity, and he has no roots to speak of in place, class, or religion. Where individuality is so free, co-operation, when it is justified, can be all the more quick and hearty. Everywhere co-operation is taken for granted, as something that no one would be so mean or so short-sighted as to refuse. Together with the will to work and to prosper, it is of the essence of Americanism, and is accepted as such by all the unkempt polyglot peoples that turn to the new world with the pathetic but manly purpose of beginning life on a new principle. Every political body, every public meeting, every club, or college, or athletic team, is full of it. Out it comes whenever there is an accident in the street or a division in a church, or a great unexpected emergency like the late war. The general instinct is to run and help, to assume direction, to pull through somehow by mutual adaptation, and by seizing on the readiest practical measures and working compromises. Each man joins in and gives a helping hand, without a preconceived plan or a prior motive. Even the leader, when he is a natural leader and not a professional, has nothing up his sleeve to force on the rest, in their obvious good-will and mental blankness. All meet in a genuine spirit of consultation, eager to persuade but ready to be persuaded, with a cheery confidence in their average ability, when a point comes up and is clearly put before them, to decide it for the time being, and to move on. It is implicitly agreed, in every case, that disputed questions shall be put to a vote, and that the minority will loyally acquiesce in the decision of the majority and build henceforth upon it, without a thought of ever retracting it.

Such a way of proceeding seems in America a matter of course, because it is bred in the bone, or imposed by that permeating social contagion which is so irresistible in a natural democracy. But if we consider human nature at large and the practice of most nations, we shall see that it is a very rare, wonderful, and unstable convention. It implies a rather unimaginative optimistic assumption that at bottom all men's interests are similar and compatible, and a rather heroic public spirit—such that no special interest, in so far as it has to be overruled, shall rebel and try to maintain itself absolutely. In America hitherto these conditions happen to have been actually fulfilled in an unusual measure. Interests have been very similar—to exploit business opportunities and organise public services useful to all; and these similar interests have been also compatible and harmonious. A neighbour, even a competitor, where the field is so large and so little pre-empted, has more often proved a resource than a danger. The rich have helped the public more than they have fleeced it, and they have been emulated more than hated or served by the enterprising poor. To abolish millionaires would have been to dash one's own hopes. The most opposite systems of religion and education could look smilingly upon one another's prosperity, because the country could afford these superficial luxuries, having a constitutional religion and education of its own, which everybody drank in unconsciously and which assured the moral cohesion of the people. Impulses of reason and kindness, which are potential in all men, under such circumstances can become effective; people can help one another with no great sacrifice to themselves, and minorities can dismiss their special plans without sorrow, and cheerfully follow the crowd down another road. It was because life in America was naturally more co-operative and more plastic than in England that the spirit of English liberty, which demands co-operation and plasticity, could appear there more boldly and universally than it ever did at home.

English liberty is a method, not a goal. It is related to the value of human life very much as the police are related to public morals or commerce to wealth; and it is no accident that the Anglo-Saxon race excels in commerce and in the commercial as distinguished from the artistic side of industry, and that having policed itself successfully it is beginning to police the world at large. It is all an eminence in temper, good-will, reliability, accommodation. Probably some other races, such as the Jews and Arabs, make individually better merchants, more shrewd, patient, and loving of their art. Englishmen and Americans often seem to miss or force opportunities, to play for quick returns, or to settle down into ponderous corporations; for successful men they are not particularly observant, constant, or economical. But the superiority of the Oriental is confined to his private craft; he has not the spirit of partnership. In English civilisation the individual is neutralised; it does not matter so much even in high places if he is rather stupid or rather cheap; public spirit sustains him, and he becomes its instrument all the more readily, perhaps, for not being very distinguished or clear-headed in himself. The community prospers; comfort and science, good manners and generous feelings are diffused among the people, without the aid of that foresight and cunning direction which sometimes give a temporary advantage to a rival system like the German. In the end, adaptation to the world at large, where so much is hidden and unintelligible, is only possible piecemeal, by groping with a genuine indetermination in one's aims. Its very looseness gives the English method its lien on the future. To dominate the world co-operation is better than policy, and empiricism safer than inspiration. Anglo-Saxon imperialism is unintended; military conquests are incidental to it and often not maintained; it subsists by a mechanical equilibrium of habits and interests, in which every colony, province, or protectorate has a different status. It has a commercial and missionary quality, and is essentially an invitation to pull together—an invitation which many nations may be incapable of accepting or even of understanding, or which they may deeply scorn, because it involves a surrender of absolute liberty on their part; but whether accepted or rejected, it is an offer of co-operation, a project for a limited partnership, not a complete plan of life to be imposed on anybody.

It is a wise instinct, in dealing with foreigners or with material things (which are foreigners to the mind), to limit oneself in this way to establishing external relations, partial mutual adjustments, with a great residuum of independence and reserve; if you attempt more you will achieve less; your interpretations will become chimerical and your regimen odious. So deep-seated is this prudent instinct in the English nature that it appears even at home; most of the concrete things which English genius has produced are expedients. Its spiritual treasures are hardly possessions, except as character is a possession; they are rather a standard of life, a promise, an insurance. English poetry and fiction form an exception; the very incoherence and artlessness which they share with so much else that is English lend them an absolute value as an expression. They are the mirror and prattle of the inner man—a boyish spirit astray in the green earth it loves, rich in wonder, perplexity, valour, and faith, given to opinionated little prejudices, but withal sensitive and candid, and often laden, as in *Hamlet,* with exquisite music, tender humour, and tragic self-knowledge. But apart from the literature that simply utters the inner man, no one considering the English language, the English church, or English philosophy, or considering the common law and parliamentary government, would take them for perfect realisations of art or truth or an ideal polity. Institutions so jumbled and limping could never have been planned; they can never be transferred to another setting, or adopted bodily; but special circumstances and contrary currents have given them birth, and they are accepted and prized, where they are native, for keeping the door open to a great volume and variety of goods, at a moderate cost of danger and absurdity.

Of course no product of mind is *merely* an expedient; all are concomitantly expressions of temperament; there is something in their manner of being practical which is poetical and catches the rhythm of the heart. In this way anything foreign—and almost all the elements of civilisation in England and America are foreign—when it is adopted and acclimatised, takes on a native accent, especially on English lips; like the Latin words in the language, it becomes thoroughly English in texture. The English Bible, again, with its archaic homeliness and majesty, sets the mind brooding, not less than the old ballad most redolent of the native past and the native imagination; it fills the memory with solemn and pungent phrases; and this incidental spirit of poetry in which it comes to be clothed is a self-revelation perhaps more pertinent and welcome to the people than the alien revelations it professes to transmit. English law and parliaments, too, would be very unjustly judged if judged as practical contrivances only; they satisfy at the same time the moral interest people have in uttering and enforcing their feelings. These institutions are ceremonious, almost sacramental; they are instinct with a dramatic spirit deeper and more vital than their utility. Englishmen and Americans love debate; they love sitting round a table as if in consultation, even when the chairman has pulled the wires and settled everything beforehand, and when each of the participants listens only to his own remarks and votes according to his party. They love committees and commissions; they love public dinners with after-dinner speeches, those stammering compounds of facetiousness, platitude, and business. How distressing such speeches usually are, and how helplessly prolonged, does not escape anybody; yet every one demands them notwithstanding, because in pumping them up or sitting through them he feels he is leading the political life. A public man must show himself in public, even if not to advantage. The moral expressiveness of such institutions also helps to redeem their clumsy procedure; they would not be useful, nor work at all as they should, if people did not smack their lips over them and feel a profound pleasure in carrying them out. Without the English spirit, without the faculty of making themselves believe in public what they never feel in private, without the habit of clubbing together and facing facts, and feeling duty in a cautious, consultative, experimental way, English liberties forfeit their practical value; as we see when they are extended to a volatile histrionic people like the Irish, or when a jury in France, instead of pronouncing simply on matters of fact and the credibility of witnesses, rushes in the heat of its patriotism to carry out, by its verdict, some political policy.

The practice of English liberty presupposes two things: that all concerned are fundamentally unanimous, and that each has a plastic nature, which he is willing to modify. If fundamental unanimity is lacking and all are not making in the same general direction, there can be no honest co-operation, no satisfying compromise. Every concession, under such circumstances, would be a temporary one, to be retracted at the first favourable moment; it would amount to a mutilation of one's essential nature, a partial surrender of life, liberty, and happiness, tolerable for a time, perhaps, as the lesser of two evils, but involving a perpetual sullen opposition and hatred. To put things to a vote, and to accept unreservedly the decision of the majority, are points essential to the English system; but they would be absurd if fundamental agreement were not presupposed. Every decision that the majority could conceivably arrive at must leave it still possible for the minority to live and prosper, even if not exactly in the way they wished. Were this not the case, a decision by vote would be as alien a fatality to any minority as the decree of a foreign tyrant, and at every election the right of rebellion would come into play. In a hearty and sound democracy all questions at issue must be minor matters; fundamentals must have been silently agreed upon and taken for granted when the democracy arose. To leave a decision to the majority is like leaving it to chance—a fatal procedure unless one is willing to have it either way. You must be able to risk losing the toss; and if you do you will acquiesce all the more readily in the result, because, unless the winners cheated at the game, they had no more influence on it than yourself—namely none, or very little. You acquiesce in democracy on the same conditions and for the same reasons, and perhaps a little more cheerfully, because there is an infinitesimally better chance of winning on the average; but even then the enormity of the risk involved would be intolerable if anything of vital importance was at stake. It is therefore actually required that juries, whose decisions may really be of moment, should be unanimous; and parliaments and elections are never more satisfactory than when a wave of national feeling runs through them and there is no longer any minority nor any need of voting.

Free government works well in proportion as government is superfluous. That most parliamentary measures should be trivial or technical, and really devised and debated only in government offices, and that government in America should so long have been carried on in the shade, by persons of no name or dignity, is no anomaly. On the contrary, like the good fortune of those who never hear of the police, it is all a sign that co-operative liberty is working well and rendering overt government unnecessary. Sometimes kinship and opportunity carry a whole nation before the wind; but this happy unison belongs rather to the dawn of national life, when similar tasks absorb all individual energies. If it is to be maintained after lines of moral cleavage appear, and is to be compatible with variety and distinction of character, all further developments must be democratically controlled and must remain, as it were, in a state of fusion. Variety and distinction must not become arbitrary and irresponsible. They must take directions that will not mar the general harmony, and no interest must be carried so far as to lose sight of the rest. Science and art, in such a vital democracy, should remain popular, helpful, bracing; religion should be broadly national and in the spirit of the times. The variety and distinction allowed must be only variety and distinction of service. If they ever became a real distinction and variety of life, if they arrogated to themselves an absolute liberty, they would shatter the unity of the democratic spirit and destroy its moral authority.

The levelling tendency of English liberty (inevitable if plastic natures are to co-operate and to make permanent concessions to one another's instincts) comes out more clearly in America than in England itself. In England there are still castles and rural retreats, there are still social islands within the Island, where special classes may nurse particular allegiances. America is all one prairie, swept by a universal tornado. Although it has always thought itself in an eminent sense the land of freedom, even when it was covered with slaves, there is no country in which people live under more overpowering compulsions. The prohibitions, although important and growing, are not yet, perhaps, so many or so blatant as in some other countries; but prohibitions are less galling than compulsions. What can be forbidden specifically–bigamy, for instance, or heresy–may be avoided by a prudent man without renouncing the whole movement of life and mind which, if carried beyond a certain point, would end in those trespasses against convention. He can indulge in hypothesis or gallantry without falling foul of the positive law, which indeed may even stimulate his interest and ingenuity by suggesting some indirect means of satisfaction. On the other hand, what is exacted cuts deeper; it creates habits which overlay nature, and every faculty is atrophied that does not conform with them. If, for instance, I am compelled to be in an office (and up to business, too) from early morning to late afternoon, with long journeys in thundering and sweltering trains before and after and a flying shot at a quick lunch between, I am caught and held both in soul and body; and except for the freedom to work and to rise by that work–which may be very interesting in itself–I am not suffered to exist morally at all. My evenings will be drowsy, my Sundays tedious, and after a few days' holiday I shall be wishing to get back to business. Here is as narrow a path left open to freedom as is left open in a monastic establishment, where bell and book keep your attention fixed at all hours upon the hard work of salvation–an infinite vista, certainly, if your soul was not made to look another way. Those, too, who may escape this crushing routine– the invalids, the ladies, the fops–are none the less prevented by it from doing anything else with success or with a good conscience; the bubbles also must swim with the stream. Even what is best in American life is compulsory–the idealism, the zeal, the beautiful happy unison of its great moments. You must wave, you must cheer, you must push with the irresistible crowd; otherwise you will feel like a traitor, a soulless outcast, a deserted ship high and dry on the shore. In America there is but one way of being saved, though it is not peculiar to any of the official religions, which themselves must silently conform to the national orthodoxy, or else become impotent and merely ornamental. This national faith and morality are vague in idea, but inexorable in spirit; they are the gospel of work and the belief in progress. By them, in a country where all men are free, every man finds that what most matters has been settled for him beforehand.

Nevertheless, American life *is* free as a whole, because it is mobile, because every atom that swims in it has a momentum of its own which is felt and respected throughout the mass, like the weight of an atom in the solar system, even if the deflection it may cause is infinitesimal. In temper America is docile and not at all tyrannical; it has not predetermined its career, and its merciless momentum is a passive resultant. Like some Mississippi or Niagara, it rolls its myriad drops gently onward, being but the suction and pressure which they exercise on one another. Any tremulous thought or playful experiment anywhere may be a first symptom of great changes, and may seem to precipitate the cataract in a new direction. Any snowflake in a boy's sky may become the center for his *boule de neige,* his prodigious fortune; but the monster will melt as easily as it grew, and leaves nobody poorer for having existed. In America there is duty everywhere, but everywhere also there is light. I do not mean superior understanding or even moderately wide knowledge, but openness to light, an evident joy in seeing things clearly and doing them briskly, which would amount to a veritable triumph of art and reason if the affairs in which it came into play were central and important. The American may give an exorbitant value to subsidiary things, but his error comes of haste in praising what he possesses, and trusting the first praises he hears. He can detect sharp practices, because he is capable of them, but vanity or wickedness in the ultimate aims of a man, including himself, he cannot detect, because he is ingenuous in that sphere. He thinks life splendid and blameless, without stopping to consider how far folly and malice may be inherent in it. He feels that he himself has nothing to dread, nothing to hide or apologise for; and if he is arrogant in his ignorance, there is often a twinkle in his eye when he is most boastful. Perhaps he suspects that he is making a fool of himself, and he challenges the world to prove it; and his innocence is quickly gone when he is once convinced that it exists. Accordingly the American orthodoxy, though imperious, is not unyielding. It has a keener sense for destiny than for policy. It is confident of a happy and triumphant future, which it would be shameful in any man to refuse to work for and to share; but it cannot prefigure what that bright future is to be. While it works feverishly in outward matters, inwardly it only watches and waits; and it feels tenderly towards the unexpressed impulses in its bosom, like a mother towards her unborn young.

There is a mystical conviction, expressed in Anglo-Saxon life and philosophy, that our labours, even when they end in failure, contribute to some ulterior achievement in which it is well they should be submerged. This Anglo-Saxon piety, in the form of trust and adaptability, reaches somewhat the same insight that more speculative religions have reached through asceticism, the insight that we must renounce our wills and deny ourselves. But to have a will remains essential to animals, and having a will we must kick against the pricks, even if philosophy thinks it foolish of us. The spirit in which parties and nations beyond the pale of English liberty confront one another is not motherly nor brotherly nor Christian. Their valorousness and morality consist in their indomitable egotism. The liberty they want is absolute liberty, a desire which is quite primitive. It may be identified with the love of life which animates all creation, or with the pursuit of happiness which all men would be engaged in if they were rational. Indeed, it might even be identified with the first law of motion, that all bodies, if left free, persevere in that state of rest, or of motion in a straight line, in which they happen to find themselves. The enemies of this primitive freedom are all such external forces as make it deviate from the course it is in the habit of taking or is inclined to take; and when people begin to reflect upon their condition, they protest against this alien tyranny, and contrast in fancy what they would do if they were free with what under duress they are actually doing. All human struggles are inspired by what, in this sense, is the love of freedom. Even craving for power and possessions may be regarded as the love of a free life on a larger scale, for which more instruments and resources are needed. The apologists of absolute will are not slow, for instance, to tell us that Germany in her laborious ambitions has been pursuing the highest form of freedom, which can be attained only by organising all the resources of the world, and the souls of all subsidiary nations, around one luminous centre of direction and self-consciousness, such as the Prussian government was eminently fitted to furnish. Freedom to exercise absolute will methodically seems to them much better than English liberty, because it knows what it wants, pursues it intelligently, and does not rely for success on some measure of goodness in mankind at large. English liberty is so trustful! It moves by a series of checks, mutual concessions, and limited satisfactions; it counts on chivalry, sportsmanship, brotherly love, and on that rarest and least lucrative of virtues, fair-mindedness: it is a broad-based, stupid, blind adventure, groping towards an unknown goal. Who but an Englishman would think of such a thing! A fanatic, a poet, a doctrinaire, a dilettante—any one who has a fixed aim and clear passions—will not relish English liberty. It will seem bitter irony to him to give the name of liberty to something so muffled, exacting, and oppressive. In fact English liberty is a positive infringement and surrender of the freedom most fought for and most praised in the past. It makes impossible the sort of liberty for which the Spartans died at Thermopylæ, or the Christian martyrs in the arena, or the Protestant reformers at the stake; for these people all died because they would not co-operate, because they were not plastic and would never consent to lead the life dear or at least customary to other men. They insisted on being utterly different and independent and inflexible in their chosen systems, and aspired either to destroy the society round them or at least to insulate themselves in the midst of it, and live a jealous, private, unstained life of their own within their city walls or mystical conclaves. Any one who passionately loves his particular country or passionately believes in his particular religion cannot be content with less liberty or more democracy than that; he must be free to live absolutely according to his ideal, and no hostile votes, no alien interests, must call on him to deviate from it by one iota. Such was the claim to religious liberty which has played so large a part in the revolutions and divisions of the western world. Every new heresy professed to be orthodoxy itself, purified and restored; and woe to all backsliders from the reformed faith! Even the popes, without thinking to be ironical, have often raised a wail for liberty. Such too was the aspiration of those mediæval cities and barons who fought for their liberties and rights. Such was the aspiration even of the American declaration of independence and the American constitution: cast-iron documents, if only the spirit of co-operative English liberty had not been there to expand, embosom, soften, or transform them. So the French revolution and the Russian one of to-day have aimed at establishing society once for all on some eternally just principle, and at abolishing all traditions, interests, faiths, and even words that did not belong to their system. Liberty, for all these pensive or rabid apostles of liberty, meant liberty for themselves to be just so, and to remain just so for ever, together with the most vehement defiance of anybody who might ask them, for the sake of harmony, to be a little different. They summoned every man to become free in exactly their own fashion, or have his head cut off.

Of course, to many an individual, life even in any such free city or free church, fiercely jealous of its political independence and moral purity, would prove to be a grievous servitude; and there has always been a sprinkling of rebels and martyrs and scornful philosophers protesting and fuming against their ultra-independent and nothing-if-not-protesting sects. To co-operate with anybody seems to these *esprits forts* contamination, so sensitive are they to any deviation from the true north which their compass might suffer through the neighbourhood of any human magnet. If it is a weakness to be subject to influence, it is an imprudence to expose oneself to it; and to be subject to influence seems ignominious to any one whose inward monitor is perfectly articulate and determined. A certain vagueness of soul, together with a great gregariousness and tendency to be moulded by example and by prevalent opinion, is requisite for feeling free under English liberty. You must find the majority right enough to live with; you must give up lost causes; you must be willing to put your favourite notions to sleep in the family cradle of convention. Enthusiasts for democracy, peace, and a league of nations should not deceive themselves; they are not everybody's friends; they are the enemies of what is deepest and most primitive in everybody. They inspire undying hatred in every untamable people and every absolute soul.

It is in the nature of wild animal life to be ferocious or patient, and in either case heroic and uncompromising. It is inevitable, in the beginning, that each person or faction should come into the lists to serve some express interest, which in itself may be perfectly noble and generous. But these interests are posited alone and in all their ultimate consequences. The parties meet, however diplomatic their procedure, as buyers and sellers bargain in primitive markets. Each has a fixed programme or, as he perhaps calls it, an ideal; and when he has got as much as he can get to-day, he will return to the charge to-morrow, with absolutely unchanged purpose. All opposed parties he regards as sheer enemies to be beaten down, driven off, and ultimately converted or destroyed. Meantime he practises political craft, of which the climax is war; a craft not confined to priests, though they are good at it, but common to every missionary, agitator, and philosophical politician who operates in view of some vested interest or inflexible plan, in the very un-English spirit of intrigue, cajolery, eloquence, and dissimulation. His art is to worm his way forward, using people's passions to further his own ends, carrying them off their feet in a wave of enthusiasm, when that is feasible, and when it is not, recommending his cause by insidious half-measures, flattery of private interests, confidence-tricks, and amiable suggestions, until he has put his entangled victims in his pocket; or when he feels strong enough, brow-beating and intimidating them into silence. Such is the inevitable practice of every prophet who heralds an absolute system, political or religious, and who pursues the unqualified domination of principles which he thinks right in themselves and of a will which is self-justified and irresponsible.

Why, we may ask, are people so ready to set up absolute claims, when their resources are obviously so limited that permanent success is impossible, and their will itself, in reality, is so fragile that it abandons each of its dreams even before it learns that it cannot be realised? The reason is that the feebler, more ignorant, and more childlike an impulse is, the less it can restrain itself or surrender a part of its desire in order the better to attain the rest. In most nations and most philosophies the intellect is rushed; it is swept forward and enamoured by the first glimpses it gets of anything good. The dogmas thus precipitated seem to relieve the will of all risks and to guarantee its enterprises; whereas in fact they are rendering every peril tragic by blinding us to it, and every vain hope incorrigible. A happy shyness in the English mind, a certain torpor and lateness in its utterance, have largely saved it from this calamity, and just because it is not brilliant it is safe. Being reticent, it remains fertile; being vague in its destination, it can turn at each corner down the most inviting road. In this race the intellect has chosen the part of prudence, leaving courage to the will, where courage is indispensable. How much more becoming and fortunate is this balance of faculties for an earthly being than an intellect that scales the heavens, refuting and proving everything, while the will dares to attempt and to reform nothing, but fritters itself away in sloth, petty malice, and irony! In the English character modesty and boldness appear in the right places and in a just measure. Manliness ventures to act without pretending to be sure of the issue; it does not cry that all is sure, in order to cover up the mortal perils of finitude; and manliness has its reward in the joys of exploration and comradeship.

It is this massive malleable character, this vigorous moral youth, that renders co-operation possible and progressive. When interests are fully articulate and fixed, co-operation is a sort of mathematical problem; up to a certain precise limit, people can obviously help one another by summing their efforts, like sailors pulling at a rope, or by a division of labour; they can obviously help one another when thereby they are helping themselves. But beyond that, there can be nothing but mutual indifference or eternal hostility. This is the old way of the world. Most of the lower animals, although they run through surprising transformations during their growth, seem to reach maturity by a predetermined method and in a predetermined form. Nature does everything for them and experience nothing, and they live or die, as the case may be, true to their innate character. Mankind, on the contrary, and especially the English races, seem to reach physical maturity still morally immature; they need to be finished by education, experience, external influences. What so often spoils other creatures improves them. If left to themselves and untrained, they remain all their lives stupid and coarse, with no natural joy but drunkenness; but nurseries and schools and churches and social conventions can turn them into the most refined and exquisite of men, and admirably intelligent too, in a cautious and special fashion. They may never become, for all their pains, so agile, graceful, and sure as many an animal or *a priori* man is without trouble, but they acquire more representative minds and a greater range of material knowledge. Such completion, in the open air, of characters only half-formed in the womb may go on in some chance direction, or it may go on in the direction of a greater social harmony, that is, in whatever direction is suggested to each man by the suasion of his neighbours. Society is a second mother to these souls; and the instincts of many animals would remain inchoate if the great instinct of imitation did not intervene and enable them to learn by example. Development in this case involves assimilation; characters are moulded by contagion and educated by democracy. The sphere of unanimity tends to grow larger, and to reduce the margin of diversity to insignificance. The result is an ever-increasing moral unison, which is the simplest form of moral harmony and emotionally the most coercive.

Democracy is often mentioned in the same breath with liberty, as if they meant the same thing; and both are sometimes identified with the sort of elective government that prevails in Great Britain and the United States. But just as English liberty seems servitude to some people because it requires them to co-operate, to submit to the majority, and to grow like them, so English democracy seems tyranny to the wayward masses, because it is constitutional, historical, and sacred, narrowing down the power of any group of people at any time to voting for one of two or three candidates for office, or to saying yes or no to some specific proposal—both the proposals and the candidates being set before them by an invisible agency; and fate was never more inexorable or blinder than is the grinding of this ponderous political mill, where routine, nepotism, pique, and swagger, with love of office and money, turn all the wheels. And the worst of it is that the revolutionary parties that oppose this historical machine repeat all its abuses, or even aggravate them. It would be well if people in England and America woke up to the fact that it is in the name of natural liberty and direct democracy that enemies both within and without are already rising up against their democracy and their liberty. Just as the Papacy once threatened English liberties, because it would maintain one inflexible international religion over all men, so now an international democracy of the disinherited many, led by the disinherited few, threatens English liberties again, since it would abolish those private interests which are the factors in any co-operation, and would reduce everybody to forced membership and forced service in one universal flock, without property, family, country, or religion. That life under such a system might have its comforts, its arts, and its atomic liberties, is certain, just as under the Catholic system it had its virtues and consolations; but both systems presuppose the universality of a type of human nature which is not English, and perhaps not human.

The great advantage of English liberty is that it is in harmony with the nature of things; and when living beings have managed to adapt their habits to the nature of things, they have entered the path of health and wisdom. No doubt the living will is essentially absolute, both at the top and at the bottom, in the ferocious animal and in the rapt spirit; but it is absolute even then only in its deliverance, in what it asserts or demands; nothing can be less absolute or more precarious than the living will in its existence. A living will is the flexible voice of a thousand submerged impulses, of which now one and now another comes to the surface; it is responsive, without knowing it, to a complex forgotten past and a changing, unexplored environment. The will is a mass of passions; when it sets up absolute claims it is both tragic and ridiculous. It may be ready to be a martyr, but it will have to be one. Martyrs are heroic; but unless they have the nature of things on their side and their cause can be victorious, their heroism is like that of criminals and madmen, interesting dramatically but morally detestable. Madmen and criminals, like other martyrs, appeal to the popular imagination, because in each of us there is a little absolute will, or a colony of little absolute wills, aching to be criminal, mad, and heroic. Yet the equilibrium by which we exist if we are sane, and which we call reason, keeps these rebellious dreams under; if they run wild, we are lost. Reason is a harmony; and it has been reputed by egotistical philosophers to rule the world (in which unreason of every sort is fundamental and rampant), because when harmony between men and nature supervenes at any place or in any measure, the world becomes intelligible and safe, and philosophers are able to live in it. The passions, even in a rational society, remain the elements of life, but under mutual control, and the life of reason, like English liberty, is a perpetual compromise. Absolute liberty, on the contrary, is impracticable; it is a foolish challenge thrown by a new-born insect buzzing against the universe; it is incompatible with more than one pulse of life. All the declarations of independence in the world will not render anybody really independent. You may disregard your environment, you cannot escape it; and your disregard of it will bring you moral empoverishment and some day unpleasant surprises. Even Robinson Crusoe—whom offended America once tried to imitate—lived on what he had saved from the wreck, on footprints and distant hopes. Liberty to be left alone, not interfered with and not helped, is not English liberty. It is the primeval desire of every wild animal or barbarous tribe or jealous city or religion, claiming to live and to tramp through the world in its own sweet way. These combative organisms, however, have only such strength as the opposite principle of co-operation lends them inwardly; and the more liberty they assume in foreign affairs the less liberty their members can enjoy at home. At home they must then have organisation at all costs, like ancient Sparta and modern Germany; and even if the restraints so imposed are not irksome and there is spontaneous unison and enthusiasm in the people, the basis of such a local harmony will soon prove too narrow. Nations and religions will run up against one another, against change, against science, against all the realities they had never reckoned with; and more or less painfully they will dissolve. And it will not be a normal and fruitful dissolution, like that of a man who leaves children and heirs. It will be the end of that evolution, the choking of that ideal in the sand.

This collapse of fierce liberty is no ordinary mutation, such as time brings sooner or later to everything that exists, when the circumstances that sustained it in being no longer prevail. It is a deep tragedy, because the narrower passions and swifter harmonies are more beautiful and perfect than the chaos or the dull broad equilibrium that may take their place. Co-operative life is reasonable and long-winded; but it always remains imperfect itself, while it somewhat smothers the impulses that enter into it. Absolute liberty created these elements; inspiration, free intelligence, uncompromising conviction, a particular home and breeding-ground, were requisite to give them birth. Nothing good could arise for co-operation to diffuse or to qualify unless first there had been complete liberty for the artist and an uncontaminated perfection in his work. Reason and the principle of English liberty have no creative afflatus; they presuppose spontaneity and yet they half stifle it; and they can rest in no form of perfection, because they must remain plastic and continually invite amendments, in order to continue broadly adjusted to an infinite moving world. Their work is accordingly like those cathedrals at which many successive ages have laboured, each in its own style. We may regret, sometimes, that some one design could not have been carried out in its purity, and yet all these secular accretions have a wonderful eloquence; a common piety and love of beauty have inspired them; age has fused them and softened their incongruities; and an inexpressible magic seems to hang about the composite pile, as if God and man breathed deeply within it. It is a harmony woven out of accidents, like every work of time and nature, and all the more profound and fertile because no mind could ever have designed it. Some such natural structure, formed and reformed by circumstances, is the requisite matrix and home for every moral being.

Accordingly there seems to have been sober sense and even severe thought behind the rant of Webster when he cried, "Liberty *and* Union, now and for ever, one and inseparable!" because if for the sake of liberty you abandon union and resist a mutual adaptation of purposes which might cripple each of them, your liberty loses its massiveness, its plasticity, its power to survive change; it ceases to be tentative and human in order to become animal and absolute. Nature must always produce little irresponsible passions that will try to rule her, but she can never crown any one of them with more than a theatrical success; the wrecks of absolute empires, communisms, and religions are there to prove it. But English liberty, because it is co-operative, because it calls only for a partial and shifting unanimity among living men, may last indefinitely, and can enlist every reasonable man and nation in its service. This is the best heritage of America, richer than its virgin continents, which it draws from the temperate and manly spirit of England. Certainly absolute freedom would be more beautiful if we were birds or poets; but co-operation and a loving sacrifice of a part of ourselves—or even of the whole, save the love in us—are beautiful too, if we are men living together. Absolute liberty and English liberty are incompatible, and mankind must make a painful and a brave choice between them. The necessity of rejecting and destroying some things that are beautiful is the deepest curse of existence.

The Genteel Tradition at Bay

The Genteel Tradition at Bay. New York: Charles Scribner's Sons; London: "The Adelphi," 1931. Volume seventeen of the critical edition of *The Works of George Santayana.*

The three parts of this selection were first published in three issues of The Saturday Review of Literature *in January 1931 and then appeared together as a small book. It was commissioned by the editor of* The Saturday Review, *who had sent Santayana recent books on humanism in America by Irving Babbit (1863–1933) and others. In a letter Santayana wrote, "I am a Naturalist in general philosophy, whereas Babbit & [Paul Elmer] More begin with moralism. I admit their point of view only as an optional attitude, as if they were Roman patriots or Buddhist monks, but I feel no obligation to accept or enforce any special code or any special civilization" (LGS, 5:107). In Part I, "Analysis of Modernity," Santayana showed how the Renaissance, the Reformation and modern political revolutions along with the Romantic tradition have undone Christianity as a unifying cultural ideal. In Part II, "The Appeal to the Supernatural," he showed how the moralism of the New Humanists requires support from a Platonic-Christian theology. In Part III, "Moral Adequacy of Naturalism," he provided a detailed summary of his naturalism in morals.*

I

ANALYSIS OF MODERNITY

Twenty years ago the genteel tradition in America seemed ready to melt gracefully into the active mind of the country. There were few misgivings about the perfect health and the all-embracing genius of the nation: only go full speed ahead and everything worth doing would ultimately get done. The churches and universities might have some pre-American stock-in-trade, but there was nothing stubborn or recalcitrant about them; they were happy to bask in the golden sunshine of plutocracy; and there was a feeling abroad—which I think reasonable—that wherever the organisation of a living thing is materially perfected, there an appropriate moral and intellectual life will arise spontaneously. But the gestation of a native culture is necessarily long, and the new birth may seem ugly to an eye accustomed to some other form of excellence. Will the new life ever be as beautiful as the old? Certain too tender or too learned minds may refuse to credit it. Old Harvard men will remember the sweet sadness of Professor Norton. He would tell his classes, shaking his head with a slight sigh, that the Greeks did not play football. In America there had been no French cathedrals, no Venetian school of painting, no Shakespeare, and even no gentlemen, but only gentle-menly citizens. The classes laughed, because that recital of home truths seemed to miss the humour of them. It was jolly to have changed all that; and the heartiness of the contrary current of life in everybody rendered those murmurs useless and a little ridiculous. In them the genteel tradition seemed to be breathing its last. Now, however, the worm has turned. We see it raising its head more admonishingly than ever, darting murderous glances at its enemies, and protesting that it is not genteel or antiquated at all, but orthodox and immortal. Its principles, it declares, are classical, and its true name is Humanism.

The humanists of the Renaissance were lovers of Greek and of good Latin, scornful of all that was crabbed, technical, or fanatical: they were pleasantly learned men, free from any kind of austerity, who, without quarrelling with Christian dogma, treated it humanly, and partly by tolerance and partly by ridicule hoped to neutralise all its metaphysical and moral rigor. Even when orthodoxy was re-affirmed in the seventeenth century and established all our genteel traditions, some humanistic leaven was mixed in: among Protestants there remained a learned unrest and the rationalistic criticism of tradition: among Catholics a classical eloquence draping everything in large and seemly folds, so that nothing trivial, barbaric, or ugly should offend the cultivated eye. But apart from such influences cast upon orthodoxy, the humanists continued their own labours. Their sympathy with mankind was not really universal, since it stopped short at enthusiasm, at sacrifice, at all high passion or belief; but they loved the more physical and comic aspects of life everywhere and all curious knowledge, especially when it could be turned against prevalent prejudices or abuses. They believed in the sufficient natural goodness of mankind, a goodness humanised by frank sensuality and a wink at all amiable vices; their truly ardent morality was all negative, and flashed out in their hatred of cruelty and oppression and in their scorn of imposture. This is still the temper of revolutionaries everywhere, and of philosophers of the extreme Left. These, I should say, are more truly heirs to the humanists then the merely academic people who still read, or pretend to read, the classics, and who would like to go on thrashing little boys into writing Latin verses. Greek and Roman studies were called the humanities because they abstracted from Christian divinity; and it was for this paganising or humanising value that they were loved; much as Platonism is espoused by some theologians, because it enables them to preserve a metaphysical moralism independent of that historic religious faith of which they are secretly ashamed. The humanist would not deserve his name if he were not in sympathy with the suppressed sides of human nature (sometimes, as to-day perhaps, the highest sides of it); and he must change his aversions as the ruling convention changes its idols. Thus hatred of exact logic, of asceticism, and of Gothic earnestness, with praise of the misjudged pleasures of a young body and a free mind, could supply the humanist with a sufficient inspiration so long as Christian orthodoxy remained dominant; but when the strongholds of superstition and morose tyranny (as he called them) were in ruins, and tenanted only by a few owls or a bevy of cooing pigeons, his angry occupation was gone. The great courts and the great court preachers were humanistic enough. Nothing therefore remained for him but to turn wit, or savant, or polite poet, and to spread his philanthropic sympathies thinner and thinner over all human things. Eastern civilisations claimed a place in his affections side by side with the ancients: he must make room even for savage arts and savage virtues–they were so human– nor could he exclude for ever that wonderful mediæval art and philosophy which, in the flush of the Renaissance, he had derided and deposed. Thus humanism ended at last in a pensive agnosticism and a charmed culture, as in the person of Matthew Arnold.

It is against this natural consequence of the old humanism that the new American humanists, in a great measure, seem to be protesting. They feel the lameness of that conclusion: and indeed a universal culture always tolerant, always fluid, smiling on everything exotic and on everything new, sins against the principle of life itself. We exist by distinction, by integration round a specific nucleus according to a particular pattern. Life demands a great insensibility, as well as a great sensibility. If the humanist could really live up to his ancient maxim, *humani nil a me alienum puto,* he would sink into moral anarchy and artistic impotence–the very things from which our liberal, romantic world is so greatly suffering. The three R's of modern history, the Renaissance, the Reformation, and the Revolution, have left the public mind without any vestige of discipline. The old humanism itself is impotent and scattered; no man of the world any longer remembers his Latin. Indeed, those three R's were inwardly at war with one another. The Renaissance, if it had had full swing, would never have become, even locally or by mistake, either Protestant or revolutionary: what can a pure poet or humanist have in common with religious faction, or with a sentimental faith in liberty and democracy? Such a free mind might really have understood the ancients, and might have passed grandly with them into a complete naturalism, universal and impartial on its intellectual side (since the intellect is by right all-seeing) but in politics and morals fiercely determinate, with an animal and patriotic intensity of will, like Carthage and Sparta, and like the Soviets and the Fascists of to-day. Such political naturalism was clearly conceived by Bacon and Machiavelli, and by many princes and nobles who took the Protestant side, not in the least for religious reasons, but because they were supermen wishing to be free from all trammels, with a clergy to serve them, and all wealth and initiative in their own hands. Those princes and nobles had their day, but the same motives work to this hour in the nations or classes that have taken their place.

I think that in each of the three R's we may distinguish an efficacious hidden current of change in the unconscious world from the veneer of words and sentiments that may have served to justify that change, or to mask it in the popular mind, and often in the mind of the leaders. The Renaissance really tended to emancipate the passions and to exploit nature for fanciful and for practical human uses: it simply continued all that was vivacious and ornate in the Middle Ages. It called those ages barbarous, partly for writing dog Latin and partly for being hard, penitential, warlike, and migratory; one might almost say, for being religious. The mind of the Renaissance was not a pilgrim mind, but a sedentary city mind, like that of the ancients: in this respect and in its general positivism, the Renaissance was truly a revival of antiquity. If merchants and princelings travelled or fought, it was in order to enrich themselves at home, and not because of an inward unrest or an unreturning mission, such as life itself is for a pure soul. If here or there some explorer by vocation or some great philosopher had still existed (and I know of none) he would have been a continuator of the crusaders or the scholastics. A genius typical of the Renaissance, such as Leonardo or Shakespeare, could not be of that consecrated kind. In his omnivorous intelligence and zest, in his multiform contacts and observations, in so many lights kindled inconclusively, such a genius, except for the intensity of his apprehension, would not have been a master or a poet at all. He would have been, like Bacon and Machiavelli, a prophet of Big Business. There might still be passion and richness in the accents, but the tidings were mean. The Renaissance, for all its poetry, scholarship, and splendour, was a great surrender of the spirit to the flesh, of the essence for the miscellany of human power.

The Reformation in like manner had a mental façade which completely hid the forces that really moved it, and the direction in which its permanent achievements would lie. It gave out that it was a religious reform and revival, and it easily enlisted in its cause all the shocked consciences, restless intellects, and fanatical hearts of the day; but in its very sincerity it substituted religious experience for religious tradition, and that, if the goal had been really religious, would have been suicide: for in religious experience, taken as its own criterion, there is nothing to distinguish religion from moral sentiment or from sheer madness. Kant and other German philosophers have actually reduced religion to false postulates or dramatic metaphors necessary to the heroic practice of morality. But why practice folly heroically and call it duty? Because conscience bids. And why does conscience bid that? *Because society and empire require it.* Meantime, in popular quarters, we see religion, or the last shreds of it, identified with occult science or sympathetic medicine. The fact is, I think, that the Reformation from the beginning lived on impatience of religion and appealed to lay interests: to the love of independence, national and personal; to free thought; to local pride; to the lure of plunder and enterprise; to the sanctity of thrift. Many a writer (Macaulay, for instance) demonstrates the superiority of Protestantism by pointing to its social fruits: better roads, neater villages, less begging and cheating, more schools, more commerce, greater scientific advance and philosophic originality. Admirable things, except perhaps the last: and we learn that religion is to be regarded as an instrument for producing a liberal well-being. But when this is secured, and we have creature comforts, a respectable exterior, and complete intellectual liberty, what in turn are the spiritual fruits? None: for the spirit, in this system, is only an instrument, and its function is fulfilled if those earthly advantages are realised. It was so, at bottom, with the ancient Jews: and the intensity of religious emotions in the prophet or the revivalist must not blind us to the tragic materialism at his heart. I think we might say of Protestantism something like what Goethe said of Hamlet. Nature had carelessly dropped an acorn into the ancient vase of religion, and the young oak, growing within, shattered the precious vessel.

In the Revolution (which is not yet finished) the same doubleness is perhaps less patent: liberty, fraternity, and equality have been actually achieved in some measure, even if they lack that Arcadian purity and nobleness which the revolutionary prophets expected. Their cry had been for limpid virtue, antique heroism, and the radical destruction of unreason: the event has brought industrialism, populousness, comfort, and the dominance of the average man, if not of the average woman.

The whole matter is complicated by the presence of yet another R, Romance, which lies in an entirely different category from the Renaissance, the Reformation, and the Revolution. Romance is not, like these, inspired by any modern sense of outrage or by any moral or political theory. It is neither hortatory nor contemptuous; not a rebellion against anything. I don't know whether its springs should be called Celtic or Norse or simply primitive and human, or whether any subtle currents from Alexandria or Arabia, or from beyond, swelled the flood in the dark ages. Suffice it that Romance is something very old, and supplies that large element which is neither classical nor Christian in mediæval and modern feeling. It lies deeper, I think, in most of us than any conventional belief or allegiance. It involves a certain sense of homelessness in a chaotic world, and at the same time a sense of meaning and beauty there. To Romance we owe the spirit of adventure; the code of honour, both masculine and feminine; chivalry and heraldry; feudal loyalty; hereditary nobility; courtesy, politeness, and pity; the love of nature; rhyme and perhaps lyric melody; imaginative love and fidelity; sentimentality; humour. Romance was a great luminous mist blowing from the country into the ancient town; in the wide land of Romance everything was vaguely placed and man migratory; the knight, the troubadour, or the palmer carried all his permanent possessions on his back, or in his bosom. So did the wandering student and the court fool. There was much play with the picturesque and the miraculous; perhaps the cockiness of changing fashions has the same source. Fancy has freer play when men are not deeply respectful to custom or reason, but feel the magic of strangeness and distance, and the profound absurdity of things. Even the intellect in the romantic world became subject to moods: attention was arrested at the subjective. "Experience"–the story-teller's substance–began to seem more interesting and sure than the causes of experience or the objects of knowledge. The pensive mind learned to trace the Gothic intricacies of music and mathematics, and to sympathise too much with madness any longer to laugh at it. The abnormal might be heroic; and there could be nothing more sure and real than the intense and the immediate. In this direction, Romance developed into British and German philosophy, in which some psychological phantasm, sensuous or logical, interposes itself in front of the physical world, covers and absorbs it. Mixed with revolutionary passions, Romance also produced the philosophy of Rousseau; and mixed with learning and archæology, the classical revival of Goethe and his time; finally, by a sort of reduplication or reversion of romantic interest upon Romance itself, there followed the literary and architectural romanticism of the nineteenth century.

Romance is evidently a potent ingredient in the ethos of the modern world;

and I confess that I can hardly imagine in the near future any poetry, morality, or religion not deeply romantic. Something wistful, a consciousness of imperfection, the thought of all the other beauties destroyed or renounced in achieving anything, seems inseparable from breadth in sympathy and knowledge; and such breadth is the essence of modern enlightenment. But is not this intelligent humility itself a good? Is it not a prerequisite to a sane happiness? The accident of birth, with all its consequences, offers us the first and palmary occasion for renunciation, measure, and reason. Why not frankly rejoice in the benefits, so new and extraordinary, which our state of society affords? We may not possess those admirable things which Professor Norton pined for, but at least (besides football) haven't we Einstein and Freud, Proust and Paul Valéry, Lenin and Mussolini? For my part, though a lover of antiquity, I should certainly congratulate myself on living among the moderns, if the moderns were only modern enough, and dared to face nature with an unprejudiced mind and a clear purpose. Never before was the mental landscape so vast. What if the prospect, when the spirit explores it, seems rather a quagmire, as it were the Marshes of Glynn, rich only in weak reeds and rank grasses? Has not the spirit always loved the wilderness? Does not the wide morass open out here and there into a quiet pool, with water-lilies, and is not the sky, with all its wonders, often reflected there? Do not the screeching wild-fowl cleave this air with avidity? I think that the simple lover of the beautiful may well be content to take his turn and have his day almost anywhere in the pageant of human history. Wherever he might be born, or wherever banished, he could never be separated from his inner mind of from a fundamental kinship with his fellow-creatures. Even if his feet were without foothold in the dreary bog, his spirit need not be starved or impatient. Amid weeds and rushes, if he would only watch them, and breathing deep the very freedom of emptiness, he might forget the oaks and roses of terra firma, even for five hundred or a thousand years.

So far, then, the gist of modern history would seem to be this: a many-sided insurrection of the unregenerate natural man, with all his physical powers and affinities, against the regimen of Christendom. He has convinced himself that his physical life is not as his ghostly mentors asserted, a life of sin; and why should it be a life of misery? Society has gradually become a rather glorious, if troubled, organisation of matter, and of man for material achievements. Even our greatest troubles, such as the late war, seem only to accelerate the scientific bridling of matter: troubles do not cease, but surgery and aviation make remarkable progress. Big Business itself is not without its grave worries: wasted production, turbulent labour, rival bosses, and an inherited form of government, by organised parties and elections, which was based on revolutionary maxims, and has become irrelevant to the true work of the modern world if not disastrous for it. Spiritual distress, too, cannot be banished by spiritual anarchy; in obscure privacy and in the sordid tragedies of doubt and of love, it is perhaps more desperate than ever. We live in an age of suicides. Yet this spiritual distress may be disregarded, like bad dreams, so long as it remains isolated and does not organise any industrial revolt or any fresh total discouragement and mystic withdrawal, such as ushered in the triumph of Christianity. For the present, Big Business continues to generate the sort of intelligence and loyalty which it requires: it favours the most startling triumphs of mind in abstract science and mechanical art, without any philosophic commitments regarding their ultimate truth or value. Indeed, mechanical art and abstract science are other forms of Big Business, and congruous parts of it. They, too, are instinctive undertakings, in which ambition, co-operation, and rivalry keep the snowball rolling and getting bigger and bigger. Some day attention will be attracted elsewhere, and the whole vain thing will melt away unheeded. But while the game lasts and absorbs all a man's faculties, its rules become the guides of his life. In the long run, obedience to them is incompatible with anarchy, even in the single mind. Either the private anarchy will ruin public order, or the public order will cure private anarchy.

The latter, on the whole, has happened in the United States, and may be expected to become more and more characteristic of the nation. There, according to one of the new humanists, "The accepted vision of a good life is to make a lot of money by fair means; to spend it generously; to be friendly; to move fast; to die with one's boots on." This sturdy ideal has come to prevail naturally, despite the preachers and professors of sundry finer moralities; it includes virtue and it includes happiness, at least in the ancient and virile sense of these words. We are invited to share an industrious, cordial, sporting existence, self-imposed and self-rewarding. There is plenty of room, in the margin and in the pauses of such a life, for the intellectual tastes which anyone may choose to cultivate; people may associate in doing so; there will be clubs, churches, and colleges by the thousand; and the adaptable spirit of Protestantism may be relied upon to lend a pious and philosophical sanction to any instinct that may deeply move the national mind. Why should anyone be dissatisfied? Is it not enough that millionaires splendidly endow libraries and museums, that the democracy loves them, and that even the Bolsheviks prize the relics of Christian civilisation when laid out in that funereal documentary form? Is it not enough that the field lies open for any young professor in love with his subject to pursue it hopefully and ecstatically, until perhaps it begins to grow stale, the face of it all cracked and wrinkled with little acrid controversies and perverse problems? And when not pressed so far, is it not enough that the same studies should supply a pleasant postscript to business, a congenial hobby or night-cap for ripe rich elderly people? May not the ardent humanist still cry (and not in the wilderness): Let us be well-balanced, let us be cultivated, let us be high-minded; let us control ourselves, as if we were wild; let us chasten ourselves, as if we had passions; let us learn the names and dates of all famous persons; let us travel and see all the pictures that are starred in Baedeker; let us establish still more complete museums at home, and sometimes visit them in order to show them to strangers; let us build still more immense libraries, containing all known books, good, bad, and indifferent, and let us occasionally write reviews of some of them, so that the public, at least by hearsay, may learn which are which.

Why be dissatisfied? I am sure that the true heirs to the three R's would not ask for more. Even Romance gets its due; what could be more romantic than the modern world, like a many-decked towering liner, a triumph of mechanism, a hive of varied activities, sailing for sailing's sake? Big Business is an amiable monster, far kindlier and more innocent than anything Machiavelli could have anticipated, and no less lavish in its patronage of experiment, invention, and finery than Bacon could have desired. The discontent of the American humanists would be unintelligible if they were really humanists in the old sense; if they represented in some measure the soul of that young oak, bursting the limits of Christendom. Can it be that they represent rather the shattered urn, or some one of its fragments? The leaders, indeed, though hardly their followers, might pass for rather censorious minds, designed by nature to be the pillars of some priestly orthodoxy; and their effort, not as yet very successful, seems to be to place their judgments upon a philosophical basis. After all, we may actually be witnessing the demise of the genteel tradition, though by a death more noble and glorious than some of us had looked for. Instead of expiring of fatigue, or evaporating into a faint odour of learning and sentiment hanging about Big Business, this tradition, in dying, may be mounting again to its divine source. In its origin it was a severe and explicit philosophy, Calvinism; not essentially humanistic at all, but theocratic. Theocracy is what all the enemies of the three R's, and more, the enemies of Romance, must endeavour to restore, if they understand their own position. Wealth, learning, sport, and beneficence, even on a grand scale, must leave them cold, or positively alarm them, if these fine things are not tightly controlled and meted out according to some revealed absolute standard. Culture won't do, they must say, unless it be the one right culture: learning won't do, unless it fills out the one true philosophy. No more sentimentality, then, or intellectual snobbery; away with the sunset glow and the organ peals overheard in a churchyard. Let us have honest bold dogmas supported by definite arguments: let us re-establish our moral sentiments on foundations more solid than tradition or gentility. Boundless liberal opportunity, such as Big Business offers, is a futile romantic lure. Even the most favourable turn of the fashion in education, criticism, and literature would not last for ever. The opposite schools would continue to advertise their wares; and only the unpredictable shifts of human moods and customs could here or there decide the issue. The best fruits of time, in any case, are unexpected. If our edifice is to be safe, we must lay the foundations in eternity.

Is this really the meaning of the American humanists, which they have hardly ventured to propose, even to themselves? If so, the summons is bold and the programme radical: nothing less than to brush away the four R's from the education and the sentiment of the modern world, and to reinstate a settled belief in a supernatural human soul and in a precise divine revelation. These, as they say in Spain, are major words, and we shall have to proceed with caution.

II

THE APPEAL TO THE SUPERNATURAL

Almost all nations and religions, and especially the liberal party in them, think themselves the salt of the earth. They believe that only their special institutions are normal or just, and hope to see them everywhere adopted. They declare that only the scriptures handed down by their own clergy are divinely inspired; that only their native language is clear, convenient, deeply beautiful, and ultimately destined to become universal; that only the logic of their home philosophers is essentially cogent; and that the universal rule of morals, if not contained in tablets preserved in their temple, is concentrated in an insoluble pellet of moral prejudice, like the categorical imperative of Kant, lodged in their breast. Not being content, or not being able, to cultivate their local virtues in peace at home, they fiercely desire to sweep everything foreign from the face of the earth. Is this madness? No: I should say it was only haste, transposing a vital necessity into absurd metaphysical terms. Moral absolutism is the shadow of moral integrity.

Now moral integrity and its shadow, moral absolutism, were always a chief part of the genteel tradition in America. They were perhaps its essence; and we need not wonder that the heirs to this tradition, in order to reaffirm the integrity of soul which they feel to be slipping away from them, clutch at its shadow, ethical absolutism, which perhaps they think is its principle. But such principles are verbal; they are not sources; and absolutism, even if reinstated philosophically, would never actually reestablish integrity in a dissolute mind or in a chaotic society. The natural order of derivation and growth is the opposite, and nature must first produce a somewhat integrated soul before that soul can discover or pursue the ideal of integrity.

Nevertheless, merely to reinstate absolutism philosophically would be a great feat, and would prove the hopeless perversity of relaxing integrity in any degree whatever. If, for instance, the human soul were supernatural and had its proper life and perfection in another world, then indeed all the variety of human tastes, temperaments, and customs would be variety only in self-ignorance and error. There would be an eternal criterion, apart from all places, persons, and times, by which everything should be judged, namely: Does this conduce to the salvation of the soul? Salvation would mean self-recovery, emergence from distraction, life beginning anew, not romantically, in some arbitrary fresh adventure in an exotic landscape, but inwardly, by the pure exercise of those functions which are truly native and sufficient to the spirit. The supernatural constitution and affinities of the soul would supply a criterion for all human affairs; not one absurdly imposed by one earthly creature upon another, as I was just now protesting, but one imposed by the visiting spirit upon the whole natural world. For however admirable and innocent the whole life of nature might be in itself, it would probably be in some directions sympathetic and in others poisonous and horrible to the native of a different sphere.

What, then, would a supernatural world be if it existed? I don't mean to ask what such a world would contain: it might evidently contain anything. I am only asking what relation any occult world must bear to nature, as we know nature, if that other world is to deserve the titles of existent and of supernatural. If it is to be existent, and not like the realms of poetry or mathematics merely conceived, it must, I think, be in dynamic relations with ourselves and with our world. Miracles, reports, incarnations, and ascensions, or at least migrations of the soul, must connect the two worlds, and make them, in reality, parts of one and the same universe. The supramundane and the mundane taken together would compose the total reality with which human knowledge, morality, and sentiment must reckon if they would not be ultimately stultified by the facts.

Supernaturalism, in its own eyes, is accordingly simply a completed naturalism, a naturalism into which certain ulterior facts and forces, hidden from our near-sighted and imperfect science, have been duly admitted. The morality inspired by supernaturalism will also be a naturalistic morality in principle: only that the soul will then be confronted by other opportunities and other dangers than her earthly life contains. Reason will have to take longer views, and the passions will be arrested, excited, or transformed by a larger prospect.

On the other hand, if this possible other world is to be called supernatural in any significant sense, it must not be confused with the chaotic, the groundlessly miraculous, the *infra*-natural. I am far from wishing to deny that the infra-natural exists; that below the superficial order which our senses and science find in the world, or impose upon it, there may not be an intractable region of incalculable accidents, chance novelties, or inexplicable collapses. Perhaps what we call the order of nature may be only a cuticle imperfectly formed round a liquid chaos. This speculative possibility is worth entertaining in the interests of scientific modesty and spiritual detachment; and it positively fascinates some ultra-romantic minds, that detest to be caged even in an infinite world, if there is any order in it. Indetermination seems to them liberty; they feel that idiocy and accident are far more deeply rooted than method in their own being, and they think it must be so also in the world at large: and perhaps they are right. All this underlying chaos, however, if it exists, has nothing to do with that supernatural sphere–a sphere and not a medley–to which morality and religion may be tempted to appeal. As the Indian, Platonic, and Christian imagination has conceived it, the supernatural has an eternal nature and a sublime order of its own. It forms an elder cosmos surrounding our nether world and destined to survive it. In that cosmos a hierarchy of spirits continually descends and ascends all the steps of moral decline and exaltation; and there the inexplicable burdens and tantalising glories of this life find their origin and their fulfilment.

There is nothing impossible, therefore, in the existence of the supernatural: its existence seems to me decidedly probable; there is infinite room for it on every side. But, then, this almost tangible supernatural world is only the rest of nature, nature in her true depths and in her true infinity, which is presumably a rich and unmapped infinity of actual being, not the cheap ideal infinity of the geometers. The question is only what evidences we may have of the existence of this hidden reality, and of its character; whether, for instance, it is likely that the outlying parts of the universe should be more sympathetic to our moral nature than this particular part to which we are native, and which our science describes because this is the part which we have to reckon with in action.

Now to this question the Platonic and Christian tradition replies, among other things, that the soul herself is a sufficient witness to her own supernatural origin, faculties, and destiny, in-as-much as she knows herself to be a pure spirit, synthetic and intelligent, endowed with free will, and immortal. We are not really native to this world, except in respect to our bodies; our souls are native to a spiritual world, from which we fetch our standards of truth and beauty, and in which alone we can be happy. Such is the thesis: and we must never let this ancient citadel of absolutism fall into the enemy's hands if we expect safely to hold the outworks and to claim for ourselves a universal jurisdiction in taste, politics, and morals. Moreover, this citadel encloses a sanctuary: our philosophical supernaturalism would be uselessly vague without a positive revelation.

If we were not especially informed concerning the nature and destiny of all human souls, how could we legislate for them universally? How could we assert that all types of virtue, except our one official type, are either rudimentary or corrupt, and that although biologically various types radiate from a centre and diverge more and more the nearer they come to perfection, morally this is not so, but all human souls, in spite of what they may think, can be saved only by marching compulsorily in single file, after the same kind of happiness? We must possess a divine revelation to this effect, since without such a revelation our moral dogmatism would be avowedly only an expression of our particular temperament or local customs; and any romantic anarchist or dissolute epicurean might flout us, saying that his temperament and his customs were as good as our own or, to his feeling, better; and that he was innocent and happy in his way of life, and at peace with God—as indeed that loose, low creature, Walt Whitman, actually declared.

And the case would be particularly hopeless if the heretics, like us, were supernaturalists about the soul; because if they were mere naturalists we might rebuke them on medical grounds, as we warn a child munching too many sweets of the stomach-ache and the tooth-ache, lest he should be cloyed too late; or we might simply turn the cold shoulder of indifference and disgust upon the odious being, to signify his ostracism from our desirable society. But if he too was an immortal visitor from another world, he might well despise our earthly prudence and stupid persecutions, and he might assert against us his own unassailable vocation merely to will, or merely to laugh, or merely to understand. How, unless divinely illuminated, could we then pretend that we knew what was good for him better than he knew it himself? Nothing would be left for us except to thrash him: which at present we should be wisely disinclined to attempt; because in the arena of democratic jealousies and journalistic eloquence he would probably thrash us. No; we must boldly threaten him with hell fire; he shall be thrashed in the other world, in the world of spirit to which he appeals; and though the more picturesque forms of this threat may be out of date, and may raise a smile, there are other forms of it terrible enough in themselves and near to our daily experience. We have but to open the newspaper to read the last confidences of some suicide, and to learn how the torments and the darkness of hell descend on the desperate rebel and the forlorn pleasure seeker. We must rely on the horror which the facts of earthly life, when faced, inspire in the innocent conscience. We must appeal to the profound doubt, the profound unhappiness, the profound courage in the human soul, so that she may accept our revelation as the key to the mystery of her profound ignorance.

The alleged happiness of the epicurean or the romantic we must assert to be a lie. In them, too, we must believe, a supernatural Christian soul is leading a pain-ful and disgusted life; for nothing can be more unnatural to her than naturalism. Evil souls and ugly bodies are degenerate, not primitive; we are all wretchedly fallen from an estate to which we secretly aspire to return, although we may not clearly perceive our plight or understand the nature of that good which alone would render us happy. We need to have the way of salvation preached to us, whether it be salvation in this world or in another; and this preaching we must receive on authority, if not on that of a special religion, at least that of the high philosophic tradition, Indian, Neoplatonic, and Catholic, which represents the spiritual wisdom of all ages. If we reject this authority and neglect to seek the supernatural happiness which it prescribes, we shall be systematically sinning against ourselves, and literally losing our souls.

The same doctrine of a supernatural soul is indispensable if we would jus-tify another conviction dear to the absolute moralist; I mean, the consciousness of free will. A supernatural soul would have a life and direction of her own: she would be an efficacious member of an invisible cosmos, in which—since the whole is the work of God—every being would have its appropriate gifts, functions, and destiny. The soul cannot create herself: she cannot determine the point of space and time at which she will begin to show her colours: she cannot tell how long her influence may be allowed to count in this world. But while her union with the body endures, there will be a tug-of-war; and the issue will never be determined by either side taken alone. A man will therefore be no helpless slave of his body; his acts will not be predetermined physically without his soul's leave; they will be determined by the interplay of the physical with the spiritual forces in him: and on the spiritual side there will be two principal factors: his soul, with her native powers, affinities, and will, and the will and the grace of God, putting that soul in contact with particular circumstances and allowing her in that trial some measure of victory.

The soul, being an independent centre of force, would have come, on this hypothesis, into the body from without, and would continue to act upon it from within, until perhaps she escaped to pursue elsewhere her separate fortunes. This independent initiative of hers would be her free will: free in respect to material laws of solicitations, but of course conformable to her own instinct and native direction, as well as subject to the original dispositions and dynamic balance of the total universe, natural and supernatural. We must not confuse the dualism of origin in human acts, asserted by this theory of a supernatural soul, with any supposed absolute indetermination of either soul or body, or of their natural effects upon one another. Indeterminism, if it exists, belongs to the unintelligible foundations of things, to chaos, and to the sub-human: it is so far from vindicating the power of spirit over matter, that in this contest, as everywhere else, a real indeterminism would dislocate the normal relations of things and render them, to that extent, fortuitous.

The notion that absolute freedom might save many a critical situation, and that in general the intervention of groundless movements would tend towards a happy issue rests on a complete confusion. It is the gambler's fallacy. Empty possibility seems to him full of promise; but in fact sheer chance, throwing dice, would seldom throw sixes. The only force that really tends towards happy results is the innate force of the soul herself: for the soul, whether natural or supernatural, is an organising principle working, as in seeds, for a particular form of life which, if realised, would make her good and her perfection. If in this labour any groundless events occurred in her or in the circumstances, she would to that extent be the victim of chance. Energies dropped into her and not exerted by herself would evidently do no work of hers; they would not manifest her freedom, but only her helplessness; they would be irruptions into her life of that primitive contingency which is identical with fate. The result would, to that extent, not be after her own mind, and she would not be responsible for it. Sheer indeterminism like the danger of earthquakes, if the healthy mind did not disregard it, would put all human labour in jeopardy: it would dislocate all definite hopes and calculations; in a sane life it would be the worst and the most alien of agencies. Such a possibility is like the other face of the moon, for ever turned away from human interests.

The kind of free will which concerns the moralist asserts rather the autonomy of the soul, her power of manifesting herself, often surprisingly, in the realm of matter in ways which, since they express her innate impulses, may have been already vaguely prefigured and desired by her conscious mind. This freedom, or internal initiative, will be proper to the soul whether she be natural or supernatural: in either case she will have a chosen good to pursue, and a certain limited power of achieving it; but if she is natural, her dispositions may change with the evolution of animal life, and one of her forms will have no authority over another; whereas, if she is supernatural, these material shifts will change only the theatre of her activity or its instruments; her nature and her perfection will remain unchangeable.

If, then, the American humanists hope to maintain an absolute criterion of taste and morals, I think they should hasten to embrace supernaturalism, in case they have not done so already. The word supernatural has long been out of favour, partly because it denied to science an omniscience which, in theory, science never claimed, and partly because it pointed to possible realities far beyond that subjective sphere which is the only reality admitted by romantic idealism: but neither reason seems to have any serious force. Supernaturalism, being an extension of naturalism, is far sounder philosophically than subjectivism, and morally at once humbler and more sublime. And that form of supernaturalism which lies nearest at hand, Christian Platonism, has the further advantage, in this case, of being remarkably humanistic. It deifies human morality and human intelligence.

Socrates and Plato, and some of the Fathers of the Church, were excellent humanists. They had not, of course, that great rhetorical joy in all the passions which we find in the humanists of the Renaissance and, somewhat chastened, in Shakespeare. Platonism and Christianity, in their beginnings, were reactions against decadence, and necessarily somewhat disillusioned and ascetic. These philosophers were absorbed in preaching: I mean, in denouncing one-half of life and glorifying the other half; they were absolute moralists; and this dominance of ethical interests was confirmed by the Jewish and the Roman influences which permeated that age. Moreover a learned humanism was involved in the possession of Scriptures, demanding studies and eloquent expositions, which could not remain exclusively theological or legendary. In the Old Testament and even in the New, there were humanistic maxims, such as that the Sabbath was made for man, and not man for the Sabbath. Epicurus had crept into Ecclesiastes, and Plato into the Gospel of Saint John; and by a bolder stroke of humanism than anyone had yet thought of, God himself had been made man. Man consequently might be superlatively important in his own eyes, without offence to the higher powers. He might proclaim his natural preferences even more vehemently and tenaciously than the heathen since round his conscience and his intellect he believed that the universe revolved, and had indeed been created expressly for his dubious and tragic glory.

This marked, and even absolute, humanism in Platonism and Christianity seems to some of us, who have no prejudice against supernaturalism in general, an argument against supernaturalism of that kind. There is a sort of acoustic illusion in it: the voice that reverberates from the heavens is too clearly a human voice. Is it not obvious that the reports contained in this revelation are not bits of sober information, not genuine reminiscences of a previous life, not messages literally conveyed from other worlds by translated prophets or visiting angels? Are they not clearly human postulates, made by ignorant mortals in sheer desperation or in poetic self-indulgence? Are they not ways of imagining a material vindication of lost causes, by a miraculous reversal, in the last instance, of every judgment of fate? Don Quixote, after twice mending and testing his ancestral helmet, and finding it fall apart at the first blow, mended it for the third time with a green riband—green being the colour of hope—and, without testing it this time, deputed it to be henceforth a trusty and a perfect helmet. So when native zeal and integrity, either in nations or in persons, has given way to fatigue or contagion, a supernatural assurance needing no test may take possession of the mind. Plato wrote his "Republic" after Athens had succumbed, and his "Laws" after Syracuse had disappointed him; Neo-Platonism and Christianity became persuasive when ancient civic life had lost its savour. A wealth of wisdom survived, but little manly courage; a dreamful courage of another sort, supernatural faith, transposed that wisdom into meekness; and sanctity sprouted like the early crocus in the loam under the leafless giants of antiquity.

Far be it from me to suggest that anybody ought to exchange his native religion or morality for a foreign one: he would be merely blighting in himself the

only life that was really possible. But the travelling thoughts of the pure philosopher may compare the minds and manners of various men; and considering
the supernatural world of Platonism and Christianity, he may marvel to observe
how very mundane that supernatural world is, how moralistic and romantic, how
royal, ecclesiastical, legal, and dramatic an apotheosis of national or pious ambitions. At best, as in Plotinus, it lifts to cosmic dimensions the story of spiritual
experience. But how shall any detached philosopher believe that the whole universe, which may be infinite, is nothing but an enlarged edition, or an expurgated
edition, of human life? This is only a daylight religion; the heavens in its view are
near, and pleasantly habitable by the Olympians; the spheres fit the earth like a
glove; the sky is a tent spread protectingly or shaken punitively over the human
nest.

In the East, the philosopher will remember, there are, as it were, night religions, simpler perhaps than ours but more metaphysical, inspired by the stars or
the full moon. Taken as information, their account of the other world is no better
than ours, but their imagination is more disinterested and their ontology bolder.
They are less afraid that the truth might be disconcerting. Is the colour which
those inhuman religions lend to morality less suitable to mankind? I am sure that
a Hindu, a Moslem, or a Buddhist is amply sustained in his home virtues by his
traditional precepts and rites; he does not need to transpose these virtues out of
their human sphere; the universe can sanction in man the virtues proper to man
without needing to imitate them on its own immeasurable scale.

That was a confused and insolent ambition in Milton to justify the ways of
God to man. Impartial reflection upon ultimate things tends to purify, without
condemning, all the natural passions, because being natural, they are inevitable
and inherently innocent, while being *only* natural, they are all relative and, in a
sense, vain. Platonism and Christianity, on the contrary, except in a few natural
mystics and speculative saints, seem to sacrifice ruthlessly one set of passions
merely in order to intensify another set. Ultimate insights cannot change human
nature; but they may remove that obfuscation which accompanies any passion,
and a virtuous passion especially, when its relativity is not understood. Human
nature includes intelligence, and cannot therefore be perfected without such an
illumination, and the equipoise which it brings: and this would seem to be a better fruit of meditation upon the supernatural than any particular regimen to be
forced upon mankind in the name of heaven. Not that the particular regimen
sanctified by Platonic and Christian moralists is at all inacceptable; but they did
not require any supernatural assistance to draw it up. They simply received back
from revelation the humanism which they had put into it.

III

MORAL ADEQUACY OF NATURALISM

Suppose we discount as fabulous every projection of human morality into the supernatural: need we thereby relapse into moral anarchy? In one sense, and from the point of view of the absolute or monocular moralist, we must; because the whole moral sphere then relapses into the bosom of nature, and nature, though not anarchical, is not governed by morality. But for a philosopher with two eyes, the natural status of morality in the animal world does not exclude the greatest vigour in those moral judgments and moral passions which belong to his nature. On the contrary, I think that it is only when he can see the natural origin and limits of the moral sphere that a moralist can be morally sane and just. Blindness to the biological truth about morality is not favourable to purity of moral feeling: it removes all sense of proportion and relativity; it kills charity, humility, and humour; and it shuts the door against that ultimate light which comes to the spirit from the spheres above morality.

The Greeks—if I may speak like Professor Norton—the early Greeks, who as yet had little experience of philosophers, sometimes invited their philosophers to legislate for them. Their problem was not so unlike that which confronts us to-day: in the midst of increasing bustle and numbers, the preponderance of towns, the conflict of classes, close and dangerous foreign relations, freer manners, new ideas in science and art. How did those early sages set to work? In one way, they didn't mince matters: the rule of life which each of them proposed for his city covered the whole life of the citizen, military, political, intellectual, ceremonial, and athletic: but on the other hand, for each city the rule proposed was different: severe and unchangeable at Sparta, liberal and variable at Athens; while the idealistic brotherhood of the Pythagoreans prescribed astronomy and sweet numbers for Magna Græcia. It was in quite other circumstances that Socrates and Plato, Moses and President Wilson came forward to legislate unasked, and for the universe.

I am afraid that even some of those earlier sages were not perfect naturalists. They did not merely consider the extant organism for which they were asked to prescribe, or endeavour to disentangle, in its own interests, the diseases or dangers which might beset it. A legislating naturalist would be like a physician or horticulturalist or breeder of animals: he would remove obstructions and cut out barren deformities; he would have a keen eye for those variations which are spontaneous and fertile, gladly giving them free play; and he would know by experience those other variations into which nature may be coaxed by grafting and watering. In all his measures he would be guided by the avowed needs and budding potentialities of his client. Perhaps some of those Greek law-givers, the Pythagoreans, for instance, had something of the missionary about them, and while full of adoration for the harmonies of nature as they conceived them, conceived these harmonies idealistically, and felt called upon to correct nature by the authority of a private oracle. In this their philosophy, apart from some cosmological errors, may have proved its depth, and may have been prophetic of the revolution that was destined to undermine ancient society.

The only natural unit in morals is the individual man, because no other natural unit is synthesised by nature herself into a living spirit. The state is only a necessary cradle for the body of the individual, and nursery for his mind; and he can never really renounce his prescriptive right to shatter the state or to reform it, according to his physical and spiritual necessities. Even when his spontaneous fidelity causes him to forget or to deny this right, the force of fidelity is at that very moment exercising that right within him. Yet it was an intermediate and somewhat artificial unit, the ancient city, that was asking those early philosophers for counsel; and that counsel could not be good, or honestly given, unless it considered the life of the individual within the walls, and the life of the world outside, only as they might contribute to the perfection of the city.

Morality—by which I mean the principle of all choices in taste, faith, and allegiance—has a simple natural ground. The living organism is not infinitely elastic; if you stretch it too much, it will snap; and it justifiably cries out against you somewhat before the limit is reached. This animal obstinacy is the backbone of all virtue, though intelligence, convention, and sympathy may very much extend and soften its expression. As the brute unconditionally wills to live, so the man, especially the strong masterful man, unconditionally wills to live after a certain fashion. To be pliant, to be indefinite, seems to him ignominious.

Very likely, in his horror of dissipating his strength or deviating from his purpose, he will give opprobrious names to every opposite quality. His hot mind may not be able to conceive as virtues in others any traits which would not be virtues in himself. Yet this moral egotism, though common or even usual, is not universal in virtuous people. On the contrary, precisely those who are most perfect escape it: they do not need the support of the majority, or of the universal voice, in order to fortify them in some shaky allegiance. They know what they want and what they love: the evident beauty of the beautiful is not enhanced or removed by agreement. In its victorious actuality a man's work must be local and temporary; it satisfies his impulse in his day, and he is not forbidden to feel that in some secret sense the glory of it is eternal.

In this way aristocratic people, who are sure of their own taste and manners, are indifferent, except for a general curiosity, to the disputes of critics and pedants, and perhaps to the maxims of preachers; such things are imposing only to those who are inwardly wondering what they ought to do, and how they ought to feel. A truly enlightened mind is all the simpler for being enlightened and thinks, not without a modest sort of irony, that art and life exist to be enjoyed and not to be estimated. Why should different estimations annoy anyone who is not a snob, when, if they are sincere, they express different enjoyments?

Even in politics, the masters who are most determined and intelligent, like those diverse Greek lawgivers, or like the Fascists of our day, do not dream of imposing their chosen polity on all nations. They are proud, with a local and school-boy pride, of their special customs. Or perhaps the perfect aristocrat gets beyond that; he is too amiable, too well-informed, to feel the glow of a real pre-eminence, but smiles at his own ways as he might at the ways of the native anywhere. He seems to himself only an odd native of an odd world; but perhaps the chief advantage which his good breeding bestows upon him is that he can afford to regard the other odd natives without hatred or envy.

Accordingly, a reasonable physician of the soul would leave his patients to prescribe for themselves, though not before subjecting them to a Socratic or even Freudian inquisition, or searching of heart, in order to awaken in them a radical self-knowledge, such as amid conventions and verbal illusions they probably do not possess. Evidently a regimen determined in this way has no validity for any other being, save in the measure in which, as a matter of fact, that other being partakes in the same nature and would find his sincere happiness in the same things. This is seldom or never exactly the case. Nothing is more multiform than perfection. No interest, no harmony, shuts out the legitimacy or the beauty of any other. It only shuts out from itself those qualities which are incompatible with perfection of that kind, there: as the perfect diamond shuts out the ruby, and the perfect ruby rejects the lovely colour of the emerald. But from nature, in her indefinite plasticity, nothing is shut out *a priori;* and no sort of virtue need be excluded by a rational moralist from the place where that virtue is native, and may be perfect.

Perfection is the most natural form of existence, simply carrying out the organic impulse by which any living creature arises at all; nor can that impulse ever find its quietus and satisfaction short of perfection; and nevertheless perfection is rare and seems wonderful, because division or weakness within the organism, or contrariety without, usually nips perfection in the bud. These biological troubles have their echo in the conscience. The alternation between pride and cowardice, between lust and shame, becomes a horrible torment to the spirit; and the issue in any case is unhappy, because a divided soul cannot be perfected. This distress, grown permanent, probably infects the imagination. Mysterious half-external forces–demons and duties–are seen looming behind these contrary natural promptings; and fantastic sanctions, heaven and hell, are invented for the future, enormously exaggerating the terrors of the choice. Thus while on the whole the morality which men impose on themselves is rational, the reasons which they give for it are apt to be insane.

What is reason? There is a certain plasticity in some organisms which enables them to profit by experience. Instead of pushing for ever against a stone wall, they learn to go round it or over it. This plasticity, even when not under pressure, may take to play and experiment; toys are made which may become instruments; and the use of sounds as signals may enable the talking animal to recall absent things and to anticipate the future. Moreover, many animals mimic what they see; they transpose themselves dramatically into the objects surrounding them, especially into other animals of the same species. This transposition gives a moral reality, in their own spirit, to all their instinctive coaxing, deceiving, or threatening of one another. Their mind begins to conceive and to compare mere possibilities; it turns to story-telling and games; life becomes a tangle of eager plans and ambitions;

and in quiet moments the order of merely imaginary things grows interesting for its own sake. There is a pleasure in embracing several ideas in a single act of intuition so as to see how far they are identical or akin or irrevelant.

Such a power of intellectual synthesis is evidently the mental counterpart of the power of acting with reference to changing or eventual circumstances: whether in practice or in speculation, it is the faculty of putting two and two together, and this faculty is what we call reason. It is what the idiot lacks, the fool neglects, and the madman contradicts. But in no case is reason a code, an oracle, or an external censor condemning the perceptions of sense or suppressing animal impulses. On the contrary, in the moral life, reason is a harmony of the passions, a harmony which perceptions and impulses may compose in so far as they grow sensitive to one another, and begin to move with mutual deference and a total grace.

Such at least was the life of reason which the humanists of the Renaissance thought they discovered, as it were embalmed, in Greek philosophy, poetry, and sculpture. Socrates had expressed this principle paradoxically when he taught that virtue is knowledge—self-knowledge taken to heart and applied prudently in action. Not that spontaneous preferences, character, and will could be dispensed with: these were presupposed; but it was reason that alone could mould those animal components of human nature into a noble and modest happiness.

But is there anything compulsory in reason? Is there not still liberty for fools? Can reason reasonably forbid them to exist? Certainly not, if they like to be fools: I should be sorry to see reason so uselessly kicking against the pricks. But a naturally synthetic mind (and all mind is naturally synthetic) hates waste and confusion; it hates action and speech at cross purposes; and these instinctive aversions implicitly pledge all mind to the ideal of a perfect rationality. Nobody is forbidden to be mindless; but in the mindful person the passions have spontaneously acquired a sense of responsibility to one another; or if they still allow themselves to make merry separately—because liveliness in the parts is a good without which the whole would be lifeless—yet the whole possesses, or aspires to possess, a unity of direction, in which all the parts may conspire, even if unwittingly.

So far, reason might be said to be prescriptive, and to impose a method on all moral life. Yet even where this method is exemplified in action, and life has become to that extent rational, nothing is prescribed concerning the elements which shall enter into that harmony. The materials for the synthesis are such at each point as nature and accident have made them; even in the same man or in the same nation they will be shifting perpetually, so that equally rational beings may have utterly disconnected interests, or interests hopelessly opposed. This diversity will be acceptable, so long as the parties are isolated, like China before the age of discoverers and missionaries; but where there is physical contact and contagion, the appeal must be to war, or to some other form of continued material pressure, such as industrial development or compulsory education: and in such a conflict both sides are apt to lose their original virtues, while the unthought-of virtues of the compound arise in their place.

In another direction the criterion of reason leaves the texture of life undetermined: the degree of unison requisite for harmony may differ in different rational systems. It is perhaps a classical prejudice that all happiness should be architectural. It might be simple and, like disillusioned Christian charity, alms for the moment. The finality of the incidental is more certain, and may be no less perfect, than the finality of great totals, like a life or a civilisation. A good verse is much more unmistakably good than a good epic. Organisation is everywhere presupposed, otherwise there could be no bodily life and no moral intuition: but where the level of intuition is reached, which is the supreme or spiritual level, the dead mass of the pyramid beneath that apex becomes indifferent. Reason cannot prescribe the girth of a man, or his stature; it can only reveal to his imperfect self his possible perfection. On this account I am not sure that the romantic temperament or art can be condemned off-hand for not being organic enough. Why be so pervasively organic? A flood of details and an alteration of humours may possibly bring the human heart as near as it can come to the heart of things, which I suspect is very fluid; and perhaps the human spirit is not at its best in the spider-like task of construction. Contemplation is freer and may be contemplation of anything.

Why is naturalism supposed to be favourable to the lower sides of human nature? Are not the higher sides just as natural? If anything, the naturalist, being a philosopher, might be expected to move most congenially and habitually on the higher levels. Perhaps the prejudice comes from the accident that when one element of human nature is reinforced by a supernatural sanction, and falsely assigned to a specially divine influence, the unsanctioned remainder alone retains the name of the natural. So Zola can come to be regarded as more naturalistic than Shakespeare, because more sordid in his naturalism, and less adequate; and Shakespeare can be regarded as more naturalistic than Virgil, although Virgil's feeling for things rural as well as for the cosmos at large was more naturalistic than Shakespeare's. Virgil is less romantic, playful, and vague: for the ancients poetised the actual surroundings and destiny of man, rather than the travesty of these facts in human fancy, and the consequent dramas within the spirit.

I think that pure reason in the naturalist may attain, without subterfuge, all the spiritual insights which supernaturalism goes so far out of the way to inspire. Spirituality is only a sort of return to innocence, birdlike and childlike. Experience of the world may have complicated the picture without clouding the vision. In looking before and after, and learning to take another man's point of view, ordinary intelligence has already transcended a brutal animality; it has learned to conceive things as they are, disinterestedly, contemplatively. Although intellect arises quite naturally, in the animal act of dominating events in the interests of survival, yet essentially intellect disengages itself from that servile office (which is that of its organ only) and from the beginning is speculative and impartial in its own outlook, and thinks it not robbery to take the point of view of God, of the truth, and of eternity.

In this congenital spiritual life of his, man regards himself as one creature among a thousand others deserving to be subordinated and kept in its place in his own estimation: a spiritual life not at all at war with animal interests, which it presupposes, but detached from them in allegiance, withdrawn into the absolute, and reverting to them only with a charitable and qualified sympathy, such as the sane man can have for the madman, or the soul in general for inanimate things: and of course, it is not only others that the spiritual man regards in this way, but primarily himself. Yet this gift of transcending humanity in sympathy with the truth is a part, and the most distinctive part, of human nature. Reason vindicates insights and judgments which, though overruling those of the world, overrule them within the human heart, with its full consent and to its profound peace and satisfaction. The disillusioned philosopher is (at least in his own opinion) happier than the fool: the saint is at least as human as the man in the street, and far more steadfast and unrepining in his type of humanity.

That the fruition of happiness is intellectual (or as perhaps we should now call it, esthetic) follows from the comprehensive scope of that intuition in which happiness is realised, a scope which distinguishes happiness from carnal pleasures; for although happiness, like everything else, can be experienced only in particular moments, it is found in conceiving the total issue and ultimate fruits of life; and no passing sensation or emotion could be enjoyed with a free mind, unless the blessing of reason and of a sustained happiness were felt to hang over it. All experience can of course never be synthesised in act, because life is a passage and has many centres; yet such a synthesis is adumbrated everywhere; and when it is partially attained, in some reflective or far-seeing moment, it raises the mind to a contemplation which is very far from cold, being in fact ecstatic; yet this ecstasy remains intellectual in that it holds together the burden of many successive and disparate things, which in blind experience would exclude one another: somewhat as a retentive ear, in a silence following upon music, may gather up the mounting strains of it in a quiet rapture. In raising truth to intuition of truth, in surveying the forms and places of many things at once and conceiving their movement, the intellect performs the most vital of possible acts, locks flying existence, as it were, in its arms, and stands, all eyes and breathless, at the top of life.

Reason may thus lend itself to sublimation into a sort of virtual omniscience or divine ecstasy: yet even then reason remains a harmony of material functions spiritually realised, as in Aristotle the life of God realises spiritually the harmonious revolutions of the heavens. So it is with reason in morals. It is essential to the validity of a moral maxim that it should be framed in the interest of natural impulses: otherwise that maxim would be a whim or an impertinence. The human impulses to be harmonised should not be without a certain persistence and strength; they should be honest, self-renewing, and self-rewarding, so as not to prove treacherous factors in the method of life to be adopted; and this method in its turn, becoming a custom and an institution, should be a gracious thing, beautiful and naturally glorious, as are love, patriotism, and religion; else the passion for living in political and religious union, beyond the limits of utility, would be sheer folly. But there are fusions, transmutations, and self-surrenders in which a naturally social animal finds an ultimate joy. True reason restrains only to liberate; it checks only in order that all currents, mingling in that moment's pause, may take a united course.

As to conscience and the sense of imposed duty, we may suppose them to be the voice of reason conveyed by tradition, in words that have grown mysterious and archaic, and at the same time solemn and loud. In so far as conscience is not this, but really a personal and groundless sentiment, it may be left to cancel its own oracles. Those who have lived in Boston—and who else should know?—are aware how earnestly the reformed New England conscience now disapproves of its disapprovals. Positive blushes and an awkward silence fall on a worthy family of my acquaintance at the least mention of one of their ancestors, who once wrote a terrifying poem about the Day of Doom. Conscience is an index to integrity of character, and under varying circumstances may retain an iron rigidity, like the staff and arrow of a weather-vane; but if directed by sentiment only, and not by a solid science of human nature, conscience will always be pointing in a different direction.

And in what direction exactly, we may ask, does conscience point so impressively in the American humanists, that they feel constrained to invoke a supernatural sanction for their maxims and to go forth and preach them to the whole world? I am at a loss to reply; because I can find little in their recommendations except a cautious allegiance to the genteel tradition. But can the way of Matthew Arnold and of Professor Norton be the way of life for all men for ever? If there be really a single supernatural vocation latent in all souls, I can imagine it revealed to some supreme sage in a tremendous vision, like that which came to Buddha under the Bo-Tree, or to Socrates when he heard, or dreamt that he heard, the Sibyl of Mantinæa discoursing on mortal and immortal love. There is much in any man's experience, if he reflects, to persuade him that the circumstances of this life are a strange accident to him, and that he belongs by nature to a different world. If all the American humanists had become Catholics like Newman, or even like Mr. T. S. Eliot, I should understand the reason.

But can it be that all Latins and Slavs, all Arabs, Chinamen, and Indians, if they were not benighted in mind and degenerate in body, would be model Anglo-Americans? That is what British and American politicians and missionaries seem to believe: all nations are expected gladly to exchange their religion and their customs for the protestant genteel tradition. I am myself an ardent admirer of the Anglo-American character. I almost share that "extraordinary faith in the moral efficacy of cold baths and dumb-bells" which Mr. Bertrand Russell attributes to the Y.M.C.A. Sport, companionship, reading-rooms, with an occasional whiff of religious sentiment to stop foul mouths and turn aside hard questions—all this composes a saving tonic for the simple masculine soul habitually in the service of Big Business; while for the more fastidious, or the more fashionable, I can see the value of the English public school and the Anglican Church, which Mr. Russell thinks mere instruments of oppression. To me—seeing them, I confess, at a more romantic distance—they seem instruments rather of a beautiful integration: none of those fierce darts of intellectual sincerity which Mr. Russell would like, but something voluminous, comfortable, and sane, on a political, conventional, and sporting level.

The senses, which we use successfully in action, distort the objects on which we act, yet do so harmlessly and poetically, because our bodies are quick to understand those perceptions before our minds have had time to consider them narrowly. In the same way understanding relieves a truly intelligent man from fussiness about social institutions and conventions: they are absurd, yet absurdity is not incompatible with their natural function, which may be indispensable. But in philosophy, when ultimately the spirit comes face to face with the truth, convention and absurdity are out of place; so is humanism and so is the genteel tradition; so is morality itself.

The commandment *Thou shalt not kill,* for instance, is given out on divine authority, and infinite sanctions are supposed to confirm it in the other world. Yet the basis of this commandment is not cosmic or supernatural, but narrowly human. It expresses the natural affection of kindred for one another, an affection surviving and woefully rebuking any rash murder; and it expresses also the social and political need of living, within a certain territory, in safety and mutual trust. In its human atmosphere, the thunder of that precept is therefore not hollow; the sharp bolts of remorse and ruin follow closely upon it. But in the cosmos at large, is killing forbidden? If so, the fabric of creation must be monstrous and sinful indeed. The moving equilibrium of things, so blind and inexorable, yet often so magnificent, becomes a riddle to be deciphered, a labyrinth of punishments and favours, the work of some devil, or at least a work of God so contaminated with evil as to be a caricature of the divine intentions. And not in human life only: the ferocity and agony of the jungle and the strange gropings of life in the depths of the sea, become perverse and scandalous; existence seems a disease, and the world a garden of poisons, through which a man must pick his way with fear and trembling, girded high, and dreading to touch the earth with his bare foot, or a fellow-creature with his hand. Had it been the Creator who said *Thou shalt not kill,* and said it to the universe, existence would have been arrested.

When therefore a tender conscience extends its maxims beyond their natural basis, it not only ceases to be rational in its deliverances, and becomes fanatical, but it casts the livid colours of its own insanity upon nature at large. A strained holiness, never without its seamy side, ousts honourable virtue, and the fear of so many enemies becomes the greatest enemy of the soul. No true appreciation of anything is possible without a sense of its *naturalness,* of the innocent necessity by which it has assumed its special and perhaps extraordinary form. In a word, the principle of morality is naturalistic. Call it humanism or not, only a morality frankly relative to man's nature is worthy of man, being at once vital and rational, martial and generous; whereas absolutism smells of fustiness as well as of faggots.

The Ethics of Nietzsche

Egotism in German Philosophy. New York: Charles Scribner's Sons, 1915; London and Toronto: J. M. Dent & Sons Ltd., 1916. Volume ten of the critical edition of *The Works of George Santayana,* 123–35.

This selection appeared as Chapter XII in Egotism in German Philosophy. *Critics frequently regarded the book as a piece of war propaganda, but the subject of "egotism in German philosophy" had been current at Harvard for over fifty years prior to the publication of Santayana's book (H. S. Levinson,* Santayana, Pragmatism, and the Spiritual Life *[Chapel Hill and London: The University of North Carolina Press, 1992], 315). Santayana expressed his thoughts on the critical response in a letter to a friend: "[t]he ill-grace with which the professors of philosophy have received my little exposition (or exposure) shows how much it was needed" (LGS, 2:300). The ethics of Friedrich Nietzsche (1844–1900), thought Santayana, are an example of romantic egotism. He criticized Nietzsche's confusion of nature and ego, reverence for prejudice, and romantic demand for violent contrasts.*

Nietzsche occasionally spoke disparagingly of morality, as if the word and the thing had got a little on his nerves; and some of his best-known phrases might give the impression that he wished to drop the distinction between good and evil and transcend ethics altogether. Such a thought would not have been absurd in itself or even unphilosophical. Many serious thinkers, Spinoza for instance, have believed that everything that happens is equally necessary and equally expressive of the will of God, be it favourable or unfavourable to our special interests and, therefore, called by us good or bad. A too reverent immersion in nature and history convinces them that to think any part of reality better or worse than the rest is impertinent or even impious. It is true that in the end these philosophers usually stultify themselves and declare enthusiastically that whatever is is right. This rapturous feeling can overcome anybody in certain moods, as it sometimes overcame Nietzsche; but in yielding to it, besides contradicting all other moral judgments, these mystics break their difficult resolution never to judge at all.

Nietzsche, however, was entirely free from this divine impediment in morals. The courage to cling to what his soul loved—and this courage is the essence of morality—was conspicuous in him. He was a poet, a critic, a lover of form and of distinctions. Few persons have ever given such fierce importance to their personal taste. What he disliked to think of, say democracy, he condemned with the fulminations of a god; what he liked to think of, power, he seriously commanded man and nature to pursue for their single object.

What Nietzsche disparaged, then, under the name of morality was not all morality, for he had an enthusiastic master-morality of his own to impose. He was thinking only of the Christian virtues and especially of a certain Protestant and Kantian moralism with which perhaps he had been surfeited. This moralism conceived that duty was something absolute and not a method of securing whatever goods of all sorts are attainable by action. The latter is the common and the sound opinion, maintained, for instance, by Aristotle; but Nietzsche, who was not humble enough to learn very much by study, thought he was propounding a revolutionary doctrine when he put goods and evils beyond and above right and wrong: for this is all that his *Jenseits von Gut und Böse* amounts to. Whatever seemed to him admirable, beautiful, eligible, whatever was good in the sense opposed not to *böse* but to *schlecht,* Nietzsche loved with jealous affection. Hence his ire against Christianity, which he thought renounced too much. Hence his hatred of moralism, which in raising duty to the irresponsible throne of the absolute had superstitiously sacrificed half the goods of life. Nietzsche, then, far from transcending ethics, re-established it on its true foundations, which is not to say that the sketchy edifice which he planned to raise on these foundations was in a beautiful style of architecture or could stand at all.

The first principle of his ethics was that the good is power. But this word power seems to have had a great range of meanings in his mind. Sometimes it suggests animal strength and size, as in the big blonde beast; sometimes vitality, sometimes fortitude, sometimes contempt for the will of others, sometimes (and this is perhaps the meaning he chiefly intended) dominion over natural forces and over the people, that is to say, wealth and military power. It is characteristic of this whole school that it confuses the laws which are supposed to preside over the movement of things with the good results which they may involve; so Nietzsche confuses his biological insight, that all life is the assertion of some sort of power—the power to breathe, for instance—with the admiration he felt for a masterful egotism. But even if we identify life or any kind of existence with the exertion of strength, the kinds of strength exerted will be heterogeneous and not always compatible. The strength of Lucifer does not insure victory in war; it points rather to failure in a world peopled by millions of timid, pious, and democratic persons. Hence we find Nietzsche asking himself plaintively, "Why are the feeble victorious?" The fact rankled in his bosom that in the ancient world martial aristocracies had succumbed before Christianity, and in the modern world before democracy. By strength, then, he could not mean the power to survive, by being as flexible as circumstances may require. He did not refer to the strength of majorities, nor to the strength of vermin. At the same time he did not refer to moral strength, for of moral strength he had no idea.

The arts give power, but only in channels prescribed by their own principles, not by the will of untrained men. To be trained is to be tamed and harnessed, an accession of power detestable to Nietzsche. His Zarathustra had the power of dancing, also of charming serpents and eagles: no wonder that he missed the power, bestowed by goodness, of charming and guiding men; and a Terpsichorean autocrat would be hard to imagine. A man intent on algebra or on painting is not striving to rule anybody; his dominion over painting or algebra is chiefly a matter of concentration and self-forgetfulness. So dominion over the passions changes them from attempts to appropriate anything into sentiments of the mind, colouring a world which is no longer coveted. To attain such autumnal wisdom is, if you like, itself a power of feeling and a kind of strength; but it is not helpful in conquering the earth.

Nietzsche was personally more philosophical than his philosophy. His talk about power, harshness, and superb immorality was the hobby of a harmless young scholar and constitutional invalid. He did not crave in the least either wealth or empire. What he loved was solitude, nature, music, books. But his imagination, like his judgment, was captious; it could not dwell on reality, but reacted furiously against it. Accordingly, when he speaks of the will to be powerful, power is merely an eloquent word on his lips. It symbolises the escape from mediocrity. What power would be when attained and exercised remains entirely beyond his horizon. What meets us everywhere is the sense of impotence and a passionate rebellion against it.

The phrases in which Nietzsche condensed and felt his thought were brilliant, but they were seldom just. We may perhaps see the principle of his ethics better if we forget for a moment the will to be powerful and consider this: that he knew no sort of good except the beautiful, and no sort of beauty except romantic stress. He was a belated prophet of romanticism. He wrote its epitaph, in which he praised it more extravagantly than anybody, when it was alive, had had the courage to do.

Consider, for example, what he said about truth. Since men were governed solely by the will to be powerful, the truth for its own sake must be moonshine to them. They would wish to cultivate such ideas, whether true or false, as might be useful to their ambition. Nietzsche (more candid in this than some other pragmatists) confessed that truth itself did not interest him; it was ugly; the bracing atmosphere of falsehood, passion, and subjective perspectives was the better thing. Sometimes, indeed, a more wistful mood overtook him, and he wondered whether the human mind would be able to endure the light of truth. That was the great question of the future. We may agree that a mind without poetry, fiction, and subjective colouring would not be human, nor a mind at all; and that neither truth nor the knowledge of truth would have any intrinsic value if nobody cared about it for its own sake. But some men do care; and in ignoring this fact Nietzsche expresses the false and pitiful notion that we can be interested in nothing except in ourselves and our own future. I am solitary, says the romantic egotist, and sufficient unto myself. The world is my idea, new every day: what can I have to do with truth?

This impulse to turn one's back on truth, whether in contempt or in despair, has a long history. Lessing had said that he preferred the pursuit of truth to the truth itself; but if we take this seriously (as possibly it was not meant) the pursuit of truth at once changes its character. It can no longer be the pursuit of truth, truth not being wanted, but only the pursuit of some fresh idea. Whether one of these ideas or another comes nearer to the truth would be unimportant and undiscoverable. Any idea will do, so long as it is pregnant with another that may presently take its place; and as presumably error will precipitate new ideas more readily than truth, we might almost find it implied in Lessing's maxim that, as Nietzsche maintained, what is really good is neither truth nor the pursuit of truth (for you might find it, and what would you do then?), but rather a perpetual flux of errors.

This view is also implied in the very prevalent habit of regarding opinions as justified not by their object but by their date. The intellectual ignominy of believing what we believe simply because of the time and place of our birth, escapes many evolutionists. Far from trying to overcome this natural prejudice of position, they raise it into a point of pride. They declare all opinions ever held in the past to be superseded, and are apparently content that their own should be superseded to-morrow, but meantime they cover you with obloquy if you are so backward or so forward as not to agree with them to-day. They accept as inevitable the total dominion of the point of view. Each new date, even in the life of an individual thinker, is expected by them to mark a new phase of doctrine. Indeed, truth is an object which transcendental philosophy cannot envisage: the absolute ego must be satisfied with consistency. How should the truth, actual, natural, or divine, be an expression of the living will that attempts, or in their case despairs, to discover it? Yet that everything, even the truth, is an expression of the living will, is the corner-stone of this philosophy.

Consider further the spirit in which Nietzsche condemned Christianity and the Christian virtues. Many people have denounced Christianity on the ground that it was false or tyrannical, while perhaps admitting that it was comforting or had a good moral influence. Nietzsche denounced it—and in unmeasured terms—on the ground that (while, of course, as true as any other vital lie) it was mean, depressing, slavish, and plebeian. How beastly was the precept of love! Actually to love all these grotesque bipeds was degrading. A lover of the beautiful must wish almost all his neighbours out of the way. Compassion, too, was a lamentable way of assimilating oneself to evil. That contagious misery spoiled one's joy, freedom, and courage. Disease should not be nursed but cauterised; the world must be made clean.

Now there is a sort of love of mankind, a jealous love of what man might be, in this much decried maxim of unmercifulness. Nietzsche rebelled at the thought of endless wretchedness, pervasive mediocrity, crying children, domestic drudges, and pompous fools for ever. *Die Erde war zu lange schon ein Irrenhaus!* His heart was tender enough, but his imagination was impatient. When he praised cruelty, it was on the ground that art was cruel, that it made beauty out of suffering. Suffering, therefore, was good, and so was crime, which made life keener. Only crime, he said, raises a man high enough for the lightning to strike him. In the hope of sparing some obscure person a few groans or tears, would you deprive the romantic hero of so sublime a death?

Christians, too, might say they had their heroes, their saints; but what sort of eminence was that? It was produced by stifling half the passions. A sister of charity could not be an Arminius; devotion to such remedial offices spoilt the glory of life. Holiness was immoral; it was a half-suicide. *All* experience, the ideal of Faust, was what a spirited man must desire. All experience would involve, I suppose, passing through all the sensations of a murderer, a maniac, and a toad; even through those of a saint or a sister of charity. But the romantic mind despises results; it is satisfied with poses.

Consider, too, the romantic demand for a violent chiaroscuro, a demand which blossoms into a whole system of ethics. Good and evil, we are told, enhance one another, like light and shade in a picture; without evil there can be no good, so to diminish the one is to undermine the other, and the greatest and most heroic man is he who not only does most good but also most harm. In his love of mischief, in his tenderness for the adventurer who boldly inflicts injury and suffering on others and on himself, in order to cut a more thrilling and stupendous figure in his own eyes, Nietzsche gave this pernicious doctrine its frankest expression; but unfortunately it was not wholly his own. In its essence it belongs to Hegel, and under various sophistical disguises it has been adopted by all his academic followers in England and America. The arguments used to defend it are old sophisms borrowed from the Stoics, who had turned the physical doctrine of Heraclitus, that everything is a mixture of contraries, into an argument for resignation to inevitable evils and detachment from tainted goods. The Stoics, who were neither romantic nor worldly, used these sophisms in an attempt to extirpate the passions, not to justify them. They were sufficiently refuted by the excellent Plutarch where he observes that according to this logic it was requisite and necessary that Thersites should be bald in order that Achilles might have leonine hair. The absurdity is, indeed, ludicrous, if we are thinking of real things and of the goods and evils of experience; but egotists never think of that; what they always think of is the picture of those realities in their imagination. For the observer, effects of contrast do alter the values of the elements considered; and, indeed, the elements themselves, if one is very unsympathetic, may not have at all in contemplation the quality they have in experience: whence æsthetic cruelty. The respect which Hegel and Nietzsche have for those sophisms becomes intelligible when we remember what imperturbable egotists they were.

This egotism in morals is partly mystical. There is a luxurious joy in healing the smart of evil in one's mind, without needing to remove or diminish the evil in the world. The smart may be healed by nursing the conviction that evil after all is good, no matter how much of it there is or how much of it we do. In part, however, this egotism is romantic; it does not ask to be persuaded that evil, in the end, is good. It feels that evil is good in the present; it is so intense a thing to feel and so exciting a thing to do. Here we have what Nietzsche wished to bring about, a reversal of all values. To do evil is the true virtue, and to be good is the most hopeless vice. Milk is for babes; your strong man should be soaked in blood and in alcohol. We should live perilously; and as material life is the power to digest poisons, so true excellence is the power to commit all manner of crimes, and to survive.

That there is no God is proved by Nietzsche pragmatically, on the ground that belief in the existence of God would have made him uncomfortable. Not at all for the reason that might first occur to us: to imagine himself a lost soul has always been a point of pride with the romantic genius. The reason was that if there had been any gods he would have found it intolerable not to be a god himself. Poor Nietzsche! The laurels of the Almighty would not let him sleep.

It is hard to know if we should be more deceived in taking these sallies seriously or in not taking them so. On the one hand it all seems the swagger of an immature, half-playful mind, like a child that tells you he will cut your head off. The dreamy impulse, in its inception, is sincere enough, but there is no vestige of any understanding of what it proposes, of its conditions, or of its results. On the other hand these explosions are symptomatic; there stirs behind them unmistakably an elemental force. That an attitude is foolish, incoherent, disastrous, proves nothing against the depth of the instinct that inspires it. Who could be more intensely unintelligent than Luther or Rousseau? Yet the world followed them, not to turn back. The molecular forces of society, so to speak, had already undermined the systems which these men denounced. If the systems have survived it is only because the reformers, in their intellectual helplessness, could supply nothing to take their place. So Nietzsche, in his genial imbecility, betrays the shifting of great subterranean forces. What he said may be nothing, but the fact that he said it is all-important. Out of such wild intuitions, because the heart of the child was in them, the man of the future may have to build his philosophy. We should forgive Nietzsche his boyish blasphemies. He hated with clearness, if he did not know what to love.

William James

Character and Opinion in the United States: With Reminiscences of William James and Josiah Royce and Academic Life in America. New York: Charles Scribner's Sons; London: Constable and Co. Ltd.; Toronto: McLeod, 1920, 64–96. Volume eleven of the critical edition of *The Works of George Santayana.*

Character and Opinion in the United States *was one of three books that together marked, in Santayana's words, his "emancipation from official control and professional pretensions. . . . all was now a voluntary study, a satirical survey, a free reconsideration. . . . My official career had happily come to an end" (PP, 414). This significant book included as Chapter III the present selection on William James (1842–1910), who, in addition to being a giant in American intellectual life, was Santayana's teacher and then colleague at Harvard. At the time of James' death, ten years before the publication of this book, Santayana wrote to a friend, "I have hardly had the time, or the freedom of mind, to think his life and work over, and sum it up to myself—not even the part he has played in my own growth and career. I owe him more than I perhaps realize: he was all kindness, but of the sort, curiously enough, that excludes sympathy. It was a motherly sort of kindness for a humanity of his own fancy and creation. He never knew <u>me</u>" (LGS, 2:19–20).*

William James enjoyed in his youth what are called advantages: he lived among cultivated people, travelled, had teachers of various nationalities. His father was one of those somewhat obscure sages whom early America produced: mystics of independent mind, hermits in the desert of business, and heretics in the churches. They were intense individualists, full of veneration for the free souls of their children, and convinced that every one should paddle his own canoe, especially on the high seas. William James accordingly enjoyed a stimulating if slightly irregular education: he never acquired that reposeful mastery of particular authors and those safe ways of feeling and judging which are fostered in great schools and universities. In consequence he showed an almost physical horror of club sentiment and of the stifling atmosphere of all officialdom. He had a knack for drawing, and rather the temperament of the artist; but the unlovely secrets of nature and the troubles of man preoccupied him, and he chose medicine for his profession. Instead of practising, however, he turned to teaching physiology, and from that passed gradually to psychology and philosophy.

In his earlier years he retained some traces of polyglot student days at Paris, Bonn, Vienna, or Geneva; he slipped sometimes into foreign phrases, uttered in their full vernacular; and there was an occasional afterglow of Bohemia about him, in the bright stripe of a shirt or the exuberance of a tie. On points of art or medicine he retained a professional touch and an unconscious ease which he hardly acquired in metaphysics. I suspect he had heartily admired some of his masters in those other subjects, but had never seen a philosopher whom he would have cared to resemble. Of course there was nothing of the artist in William James, as the artist is sometimes conceived in England, nothing of the æsthete, nothing affected or limp. In person he was short rather than tall, erect, brisk, bearded, intensely masculine. While he shone in expression and would have wished his style to be noble if it could also be strong, he preferred in the end to be spontaneous, and to leave it at that; he tolerated slang in himself rather than primness. The rough, homely, picturesque phrase, whatever was graphic and racy, recommended itself to him; and his conversation outdid his writing in this respect. He believed in improvisation, even in thought; his lectures were not minutely prepared. Know your subject thoroughly, he used to say, and trust to luck for the rest. There was a deep sense of insecurity in him, a mixture of humility with romanticism: we were likely to be more or less wrong anyhow, but we might be wholly sincere. One moment should respect the insight of another, without trying to establish too regimental a uniformity. If you corrected yourself tartly, how could you know that the correction was not the worse mistake? All our opinions were born free and equal, all children of the Lord, and if they were not consistent that was the Lord's business, not theirs. In reality, James was consistent enough, as even Emerson (more extreme in this sort of irresponsibility) was too. Inspiration has its limits, sometimes very narrow ones. But James was not consecutive, not insistent; he turned to a subject afresh, without egotism or pedantry; he dropped his old points, sometimes very good ones; and he modestly looked for light from others, who had less light than himself.

His excursions into philosophy were accordingly in the nature of raids, and it is easy for those who are attracted by one part of his work to ignore other parts, in themselves perhaps more valuable. I think that in fact his popularity does not rest on his best achievements. His popularity rests on three somewhat incidental books, *The Will to Believe, Pragmatism,* and *The Varieties of Religious Experience,* whereas, as it seems to me, his best achievement is his *Principles of Psychology.* In this book he surveys, in a way which for him is very systematic, a subject made to his hand. In its ostensible outlook it is a treatise like any other, but what distinguishes it is the author's gift for evoking vividly the very life of the mind. This is a work of imagination; and the subject as he conceived it, which is the flux of immediate experience in men in general, requires imagination to read it at all. It is a literary subject, like autobiography or psychological fiction, and can be treated only poetically; and in this sense Shakespeare is a better psychologist than Locke or Kant. Yet this gift of imagination is not merely literary; it is not useless in divining the truths of science, and it is invaluable in throwing off prejudice and scientific shams. The fresh imagination and vitality of William James led him to break through many a false convention. He saw that experience, as we endure it, is not a mosaic of distinct sensations, nor the expression of separate hostile faculties, such as reason and the passions, or sense and the categories; it is rather a flow of mental discourse, like a dream, in which all divisions and units are vague and shifting, and the whole is continually merging together and drifting apart. It fades gradually in the rear, like the wake of a ship, and bites into the future, like the bow cutting the water. For the candid psychologist, carried bodily on this voyage of discovery, the past is but a questionable report, and the future wholly indeterminate; everything is simply what it is experienced as being.

At the same time, psychology is supposed to be a science, a claim which would tend to confine it to the natural history of man, or the study of behaviour, as is actually proposed by Auguste Comte and by some of James's own disciples, more jejune if more clear-headed than he. As matters now stand, however, psychology as a whole is not a science, but a branch of philosophy; it brings together the literary description of mental discourse and the scientific description of material life, in order to consider the relation between them, which is the nexus of human nature.

What was James's position on this crucial question? It is impossible to reply unequivocally. He approached philosophy as mankind originally approached it, without having a philosophy, and he lent himself to various hypotheses in various directions. He professed to begin his study on the assumptions of common sense, that there is a material world which the animals that live in it are able to perceive and to think about. He gave a congruous extension to this view in his theory that emotion is purely bodily sensation, and also in his habit of conceiving the mind as a total shifting sensibility. To pursue this path, however, would have led him to admit that nature was automatic and mind simply cognitive, conclusions from which every instinct in him recoiled. He preferred to believe that mind and matter had independent energies and could lend one another a hand, matter operating by motion and mind by intention. This dramatic, amphibious way of picturing causation is natural to common sense, and might be defended if it were clearly defined; but James was insensibly carried away from it by a subtle implication of his method. This implication was that experience or mental discourse not only constituted a set of substantive facts, but the only substantive facts; all else, even that material world which his psychology had postulated, could be nothing but a verbal or fantastic symbol for sensations in their experienced order. So that while nominally the door was kept open to any hypothesis regarding the conditions of the psychological flux, in truth the question was prejudged. The hypotheses, which were parts of this psychological flux, could have no object save other parts of it. That flux itself, therefore, which he could picture so vividly, was the fundamental existence. The *sense* of bounding over the waves, the *sense* of being on an adventurous voyage, was the living fact; the rest was dead reckoning. Where one's gift is, there will one's faith be also; and to this poet appearance was the only reality.

This sentiment, which always lay at the back of his mind, reached something like formal expression in his latest writings, where he sketched what he called radical empiricism. The word experience is like a shrapnel shell, and bursts into a thousand meanings. Here we must no longer think of its setting, its discoveries, or its march; to treat it radically we must abstract its immediate objects and reduce it to pure data. It is obvious (and the sequel has already proved) that experience so understood would lose its romantic signification, as a personal adventure or a response to the shocks of fortune. "Experience" would turn into a cosmic dance of absolute entities created and destroyed *in vacuo* according to universal laws, or perhaps by chance. No minds would gather this experience, and no material agencies would impose it; but the immediate objects present to any one would simply be parts of the universal fireworks, continuous with the rest, and all the parts, even if not present to anybody, would have the same status. Experience would then not at all resemble what Shakespeare reports or what James himself had described in his psychology. If it could be experienced as it flows in its entirety (which is fortunately impracticable), it would be a perpetual mathematical nightmare. Every whirling atom, every changing relation, and every incidental perspective would be a part of it. I am far from wishing to deny for a moment the scientific value of such a cosmic system, if it can be worked out; physics and mathematics seem to me to plunge far deeper than literary psychology into the groundwork of this world; but human experience is the stuff of literary psychology; we cannot reach the stuff of physics and mathematics except by arresting or even hypostatising some elements of appearance, and expanding them on an abstracted and hypothetical plane of their own. Experience, as memory and literature rehearse it, remains nearer to us than that: it is something dreamful, passionate, dramatic, and significative.

Certainly this personal human experience, expressible in literature and in talk, and no cosmic system however profound, was what James knew best and trusted most. Had he seen the developments of his radical empiricism, I cannot help thinking he would have marvelled that such logical mechanisms should have been hatched out of that egg. The principal problems and aspirations that haunted him all his life long would lose their meaning in that cosmic atmosphere. The pragmatic nature of truth, for instance, would never suggest itself in the presence of pure data; but a romantic mind soaked in agnosticism, conscious of its own habits and assuming an environment the exact structure of which can never be observed, may well convince itself that, for experience, truth is nothing but a happy use of signs—which is indeed the truth of literature. But if we once accept *any* system of the universe as literally true, the value of convenient signs to prepare us for such experience as is yet absent cannot be called truth: it is plainly nothing but a necessary inaccuracy. So, too, with the question of the survival of the human individual after death. For radical empiricism a human individual is simply a certain cycle or complex of terms, like any other natural fact; that some echoes of his mind should recur after the regular chimes have ceased, would have nothing paradoxical about it. A mathematical world is a good deal like music, with its repetitions and transpositions, and a little trill, which you might call a person, might well peep up here and there all over a vast composition. Something of that sort may be the truth of spiritualism; but it is not what the spiritualists imagine. Their whole interest lies not in the experiences they have, but in the interpretation they give to them, assigning them to troubled spirits in another world; it but both another world and a spirit are notions repugnant to a radical empiricism.

I think it is important to remember, if we are not to misunderstand William James, that his radical empiricism and pragmatism were in his own mind only methods; his doctrine, if he may be said to have had one, was agnosticism. And just because he was an agnostic (feeling instinctively that beliefs and opinions, if they had any objective beyond themselves, could never be sure they had attained it), he seemed in one sense so favourable to credulity. He was not credulous himself, far from it; he was well aware that the trust he put in people or ideas might betray him. For that very reason he was respectful and pitiful to the trustfulness of others. Doubtless they were wrong, but who were we to say so? In his own person he was ready enough to face the mystery of things, and whatever the womb of time might bring forth; but until the curtain was rung down on the last act of the drama (and it might have no last act!) he wished the intellectual cripples and the moral hunchbacks not to be jeered at; perhaps they might turn out to be the heroes of the play. Who could tell what heavenly influences might not pierce to these sensitive half-flayed creatures, which are lost on the thick-skinned, the sane, and the duly goggled? We must not suppose, however, that James meant these contrite and romantic suggestions dogmatically. The agnostic, as well as the physician and neurologist in him, was never quite eclipsed. The hope that some new revelation might come from the lowly and weak could never mean to him what it meant to the early Christians. For him it was only a right conceded to them to experiment with their special faiths; he did not expect such faiths to be discoveries of absolute fact, which everybody else might be constrained to recognise. If any one had made such a claim, and had seemed to have some chance of imposing it universally, James would have been the first to turn against him; not, of course, on the ground that it was *impossible* that such an orthodoxy should be true, but with a profound conviction that it was to be feared and distrusted. No: the degree of authority and honour to be accorded to various human faiths was a moral question, not a theoretical one. All faiths were what they were experienced as being, in their capacity of faiths; these faiths, not their objects, were the hard facts we must respect. We cannot pass, except under the illusion of the moment, to anything firmer or on a deeper level. There was accordingly no sense of security, no joy, in James's apology for personal religion. He did not really believe; he merely believed in the right of believing that you might be right if you believed.

It is this underlying agnosticism that explains an incoherence which we might find in his popular works, where the story and the moral do not seem to hang together. Professedly they are works of psychological observation; but the tendency and suasion in them seems to run to disintegrating the idea of truth, recommending belief without reason, and encouraging superstition. A psychologist who was not an agnostic would have indicated, as far as possible, whether the beliefs and experiences he was describing were instances of delusion or of rare and fine perception, or in what measure they were a mixture of both. But James—and this is what gives such romantic warmth to these writings of his—disclaims all antecedent or superior knowledge, listens to the testimony of each witness in turn, and only by accident allows us to feel that he is swayed by the eloquence and vehemence of some of them rather than of others. This method is modest, generous, and impartial; but if James intended, as I think he did, to picture the *drama* of human belief, with its risks and triumphs, the method was inadequate. Dramatists never hesitate to assume, and to let the audience perceive, who is good and who bad, who wise and who foolish, in their pieces; otherwise their work would be as impotent dramatically as scientifically. The tragedy and comedy of life lie precisely in the contrast between the illusions or passions of the characters and their true condition and fate, hidden from them at first, but evident to the author and the public. If in our diffidence and scrupulous fairness we refuse to take this judicial attitude, we shall be led to strange conclusions. The navigator, for instance, trusting his "experience" (which here, as in the case of religious people, means his imagination and his art), insists on believing that the earth is spherical; he has sailed round it. That is to say, he has seemed to himself to steer westward and westward, and has seemed to get home again. But how should he know that home is now where it was before, or that his past and present impressions of it come from the same, or from any, material object? How should he know that space is as trim and tri-dimensional as the discredited Euclidians used to say it was? If, on the contrary, my worthy aunt, trusting to her longer and less ambiguous experience of her garden, insists that the earth is flat, and observes that the theory that it is round, which is only a theory, is much less often tested and found useful than her own perception of its flatness, and that moreover that theory is pedantic, intellectualistic, and a product of academies, and a rash dogma to impose on mankind for ever and ever, it might seem that on James's principle we ought to agree with her. But no; on James's real principles we need not agree with her, nor with the navigator either. Radical empiricism, which is radical agnosticism, delivers us from so benighted a choice. For the quarrel becomes unmeaning when we remember that the earth is *both* flat and round, if it is experienced as being both. The substantive fact is not a single object on which both the perception and the theory are expected to converge; the substantive facts are the theory and the perception themselves. And we may note in passing that empiricism, when it ceases to value experience as a means of discovering external things, can give up its ancient prejudice in favour of sense as against imagination, for imagination and thought are immediate experiences as much as sensation is: they are therefore, for absolute empiricism, no less actual ingredients of reality.

In *The Varieties of Religious Experience* we find the same apologetic intention running through a vivid account of what seems for the most part (as James acknowledged) religious disease. Normal religious experience is hardly described in it. Religious experience, for the great mass of mankind, consists in simple faith in the truth and benefit of their religious traditions. But to James something so conventional and rationalistic seemed hardly experience and hardly religious; he was thinking only of irruptive visions and feelings as interpreted by the mystics who had them. These interpretations he ostensibly presents, with more or less wistful sympathy for what they were worth; but emotionally he wished to champion them. The religions that had sprung up in America spontaneously–communistic, hysterical, spiritistic, or medicinal–were despised by select and superior people. You might inquire into them, as you might go slumming, but they remained suspect and distasteful. This picking up of genteel skirts on the part of his acquaintance prompted William James to roll up his sleeves–not for a knock-out blow, but for a thorough clinical demonstration. He would tenderly vivisect the experiences in question, to show how living they were, though of course he could not guarantee, more than other surgeons do, that the patient would survive the operation. An operation that eventually kills may be technically successful, and the man may die cured; and so a description of religion that showed it to be madness might first show how real and how warm it was, so that if it perished, at least it would perish understood.

I never observed in William James any personal anxiety or enthusiasm for any of these dubious tenets. His conception even of such a thing as free-will, which he always ardently defended, remained vague; he avoided defining even what he conceived to be desirable in such matters. But he wished to protect the weak against the strong, and what he hated beyond everything was the *non possumus* of any constituted authority. Philosophy for him had a Polish constitution; so long as a single vote was cast against the majority, nothing could pass. The suspense of judgement which he had imposed on himself as a duty, became almost a necessity. I think it would have depressed him if he had had to confess that any important question was finally settled. He would still have hoped that something might turn up on the other side, and that just as the scientific hangman was about to despatch the poor convicted prisoner, an unexpected witness would ride up in hot haste, and prove him innocent. Experience seems to most of us to lead to conclusions, but empiricism has sworn never to draw them.

In the discourse on "The Energies of Men," certain physiological marvels are recorded, as if to suggest that the resources of our minds and bodies are infinite, or can be infinitely enlarged by divine grace. Yet James would not, I am sure, have accepted that inference. He would, under pressure, have drawn in his mystical horns under his scientific shell; but he was not naturalist enough to feel instinctively that the wonderful and the natural are all of a piece, and that only our degree of habituation distinguishes them. A nucleus, which we may poetically call the soul, certainly lies within us, by which our bodies and minds are generated and controlled, like an army by a government. In this nucleus, since nature in a small compass has room for anything, vast quantities of energy may well be stored up, which may be tapped on occasion, or which may serve like an electric spark to let loose energy previously existing in the grosser parts. But the absolute autocracy of this central power, or its success in imposing extraordinary trials on its subjects, is not an obvious good. Perhaps, like a democratic government, the soul is at its best when it merely collects and co-ordinates the impulses coming from the senses. The inner man is at times a tyrant, parasitical, wasteful, and voluptuous. At other times he is fanatical and mad. When he asks for and obtains violent exertions from the body, the question often is, as with the exploits of conquerors and conjurers, whether the impulse to do such prodigious things was not gratuitous, and the things nugatory. Who would wish to be a mystic? James himself, who by nature was a spirited rather than a spiritual man, had no liking for sanctimonious transcendentalists, visionaries, or ascetics; he hated minds that run thin. But he hastened to correct this manly impulse, lest it should be unjust, and forced himself to overcome his repugnance. This was made easier when the unearthly phenomenon had a healing or saving function in the everyday material world; miracle then re-established its ancient identity with medicine, and both of them were humanised. Even when this union was not attained, James was reconciled to the miracle-workers partly by his great charity, and partly by his hunter's instinct to follow a scent, for he believed discoveries to be imminent. Besides, a philosopher who is a teacher of youth is more concerned to give people a right start than a right conclusion. James fell in with the hortatory tradition of college sages; he turned his psychology, whenever he could do so honestly, to purposes of edification; and his little sermons on habit, on will, on faith, and this on the latent capacities of men, were fine and stirring, and just the sermons to preach to the young Christian soldier. He was much less sceptical in morals than in science. He seems to have felt sure that certain thoughts and hopes—those familiar to a liberal Protestantism—were every man's true friends in life. This assumption would have been hard to defend if he or those he habitually addressed had ever questioned it; yet his whole argument for voluntarily cultivating these beliefs rests on this assumption, that they are beneficent. Since, whether we will or no, we cannot escape the risk of error, and must succumb to some human or pathological bias, at least we might do so gracefully and in the form that would profit us most, by clinging to those prejudices which help us to lead what we all feel is a good life. But what is a good life? Had William James, had the people about him, had modern philosophers anywhere, any notion of that? I cannot think so. They had much experience of personal goodness, and love of it; they had standards of character and right conduct; but as to what might render human existence good, excellent, beautiful, happy, and worth having as a whole, their notions were utterly thin and barbarous. They had forgotten the Greeks, or never known them.

This argument accordingly suffers from the same weakness as the similar argument of Pascal in favour of Catholic orthodoxy. You should force yourself to believe in it, he said, because if you do so and are right you win heaven, while if you are wrong you lose nothing. What would Protestants, Mohammedans, and Hindus say to that? Those alternatives of Pascal's are not the sole nor the true alternatives; such a wager—betting on the improbable because you are offered big odds—is an unworthy parody of the real choice between wisdom and folly. There is no heaven to be won in such a spirit, and if there was, a philosopher would despise it. So William James would have us bet on immortality, or bet on our power to succeed, because if we win the wager we can live to congratulate ourselves on our true instinct, while we lose nothing if we have made a mistake; for unless you have the satisfaction of finding that you have been right, the dignity of having been right is apparently nothing. Or if the argument is rather that these beliefs, whether true or false, make life better in this world, the thing is simply false. To be boosted by an illusion is not to live better than to live in harmony with the truth; it is not nearly so safe, not nearly so sweet, and not nearly so fruitful. These refusals to part with a decayed illusion are really an infection to the mind. Believe, certainly; we cannot help believing; but believe rationally, holding what seems certain for certain, what seems probable for probable, what seems desirable for desirable, and what seems false for false.

In this matter, as usual, James had a true psychological fact and a generous instinct behind his confused moral suggestions. It is a psychological fact that men are influenced in their beliefs by their will and desires; indeed, I think we can go further and say that in its essence belief is an expression of impulse, of readiness to act. It is only peripherally, as our action is gradually adjusted to things, and our impulses to our possible or necessary action, that our ideas begin to hug the facts, and to acquire a true, if still a symbolic, significance. We do not need a will to believe; we only need a will to study the object in which we are inevitably believing. But James was thinking less of belief in what we find than of belief in what we hope for: a belief which is not at all clear and not at all necessary in the life of mortals. Like most Americans, however, only more lyrically, James felt the call of the future and the assurance that it could be made far better, totally other, than the past. The pictures that religion had painted of heaven or the millennium were not what he prized, although his Swedenborgian connection might have made him tender to them, as perhaps it did to familiar spirits. It was the moral succour offered by religion, its open spaces, the possibility of miracles *in extremis*, that must be retained. If we recoiled at the thought of being dupes (which is perhaps what nature intended us to be), were we less likely to be dupes in disbelieving these sustaining truths than in believing them? Faith was needed to bring about the reform of faith itself, as well as all other reforms.

In some cases faith in success could nerve us to bring success about, and so justify itself by its own operation. This is a thought typical of James at his worst—a worst in which there is always a good side. Here again psychological observation is used with the best intentions to hearten oneself and other people; but the fact observed is not at all understood, and a moral twist is given to it which (besides being morally questionable) almost amounts to falsifying the fact itself. Why does belief that you can jump a ditch help you to jump it? Because it is a symptom of the fact that you *could* jump it, that your legs were fit and that the ditch was two yards wide and not twenty. A rapid and just appreciation of these facts has given you your confidence, or at least has made it reasonable, manly, and prophetic; otherwise you would have been a fool and got a ducking for it. Assurance is contemptible and fatal unless it is self-knowledge. If you had been rattled you might have failed, because that would have been a symptom of the fact that you were out of gear; you would have been afraid because you trembled, as James at his best proclaimed. You would never have quailed if your system had been reacting smoothly to its opportunities, any more than you would totter and see double if you were not intoxicated. Fear is a sensation of actual nervousness and disarray, and confidence a sensation of actual readiness; they are not disembodied feelings, existing for no reason, the devil Funk and the angel Courage, one or the other of whom may come down arbitrarily into your body, and revolutionise it. That is childish mythology, which survives innocently enough as a figure of speech, until a philosopher is found to take that figure of speech seriously. Nor is the moral suggestion here less unsound. What is good is not the presumption of power, but the possession of it: a clear head, aware of its resources, not a fuddled optimism, calling up spirits from the vasty deep. Courage is not a virtue, said Socrates, unless it is also wisdom. Could anything be truer both of courage in doing and of courage in believing? But it takes tenacity, it takes *reasonable* courage, to stick to scientific insights such as this of Socrates or that of James about the emotions; it is easier to lapse into the traditional manner, to search natural philosophy for miracles and moral lessons, and in morals proper, in the reasoned expression of preference, to splash about without a philosophy.

William James shared the passions of liberalism. He belonged to the left, which, as they say in Spain, is the side of the heart, as the right is that of the liver; at any rate there was much blood and no gall in his philosophy. He was one of those elder Americans still disquieted by the ghost of tyranny, social and ecclesiastical. Even the beauties of the past troubled him; he had a puritan feeling that they were tainted. They had been cruel and frivolous, and must have suppressed far better things. But what, we may ask, might these better things be? It may do for a revolutionary politician to say: "I may not know what I want—except office—but I know what I don't want"; it will never do for a philosopher. Aversions and fears imply principles of preference, goods acknowledged; and it is the philosopher's business to make these goods explicit. Liberty is not an art, liberty must be used to bring some natural art to fruition. Shall it be simply eating and drinking and wondering what will happen next? If there is some deep and settled need in the heart of man, to give direction to his efforts, what else should a philosopher do but discover and announce what that need is?

There is a sense in which James was not a philosopher at all. He once said to me: "What a curse philosophy would be if we couldn't forget all about it!" In other words, philosophy was not to him what it has been to so many, a consolation and sanctuary in a life which would have been unsatisfying without it. It would be incongruous, therefore, to expect of him that he should build a philosophy like an edifice to go and live in for good. Philosophy to him was rather like a maze in which he happened to find himself wandering, and what he was looking for was the way out. In the presence of theories of any sort he was attentive, puzzled, suspicious, with a certain inner prompting to disregard them. He lived all his life among them, as a child lives among grown-up people; what a relief to turn from those stolid giants, with their prohibitions and exactions and tiresome talk, to another real child or a nice animal! Of course grown-up people are useful, and so James considered that theories might be; but in themselves, to live with, they were rather in the way, and at bottom our natural enemies. It was well to challenge one or another of them when you got a chance; perhaps that challenge might break some spell, transform the strange landscape, and simplify life. A theory while you were creating or using it was like a story you were telling yourself or a game you were playing; it was a warm, self-justifying thing then; but when the glow of creation or expectation was over, a theory was a phantom, like a ghost, or like the minds of other people. To all other people, even to ghosts, William James was the soul of courtesy; and he was civil to most theories as well, as to more or less interesting strangers that invaded him. Nobody ever recognised more heartily the chance that others had of being right, and the right they had to be different. Yet when it came to understanding what they meant, whether they were theories or persons, his intuition outran his patience; he made some brilliant impressionistic sketch in his fancy and called it by their name. This sketch was as often flattered as distorted, and he was at times the dupe of his desire to be appreciative and give the devil his due; he was too impulsive for exact sympathy; too subjective, too romantic, to be just. Love is very penetrating, but it penetrates to possibilities rather than to facts. The logic of opinions, as well as the exact opinions themselves, were not things James saw easily, or traced with pleasure. He liked to take things one by one, rather than to put two and two together. He was a mystic, a mystic in love with life. He was comparable to Rousseau and to Walt Whitman; he expressed a generous and tender sensibility, rebelling against sophistication, and preferring daily sights and sounds, and a vague but indomitable faith in fortune, to any settled intellectual tradition calling itself science or philosophy.

A prophet is not without honour save in his own country; and until the return wave of James's reputation reached America from Europe, his pupils and friends were hardly aware that he was such a distinguished man. Everybody liked him, and delighted in him for his generous, gullible nature and brilliant sallies. He was a sort of Irishman among the Brahmins, and seemed hardly imposing enough for a great man. They laughed at his erratic views and his undisguised limitations. Of course a conscientious professor ought to know everything he professes to know, but then, they thought, a dignified professor ought to seem to know everything. The precise theologians and panoplied idealists, who exist even in America, shook their heads. What sound philosophy, said they to themselves, could be expected from an irresponsible doctor, who was not even a college graduate, a crude empiricist, and vivisector of frogs? On the other hand, the solid men of business were not entirely reassured concerning a teacher of youth who seemed to have no system in particular—the ignorant rather demand that the learned should have a system in store, to be applied at a pinch; and they could not quite swallow a private gentleman who dabbled in hypnotism, frequented mediums, didn't talk like a book, and didn't write like a book, except like one of his own. Even his pupils, attached as they invariably were to his person, felt some doubts about the profundity of one who was so very natural, and who after some interruption during a lecture—and he said life was a series of interruptions—would slap his forehead and ask the man in the front row "What *was* I talking about?" Perhaps in the first years of his teaching he felt a little in the professor's chair as a military man might feel when obliged to read the prayers at a funeral. He probably conceived what he said more deeply than a more scholastic mind might have conceived it; yet he would have been more comfortable if some one else had said it for him. He liked to open the window, and look out for a moment. I think he was glad when the bell rang, and he could be himself again until the next day. But in the midst of this routine of the class-room the spirit would sometimes come upon him, and, leaning his head on his hand, he would let fall golden words, picturesque, fresh from the heart, full of the knowledge of good and evil. Incidentally there would crop up some humorous characterisation, some candid confession of doubt or of instinctive preference, some pungent scrap of learning; radicalisms plunging sometimes into the sub-soil of all human philosophies; and, on occasion, thoughts of simple wisdom and wistful piety, the most unfeigned and manly that anybody ever had.

Josiah Royce

Character and Opinion in the United States: With Reminiscences of William James and Josiah Royce and Academic Life in America. New York: Charles Scribner's Sons; London: Constable and Co. Ltd.; Toronto: McLeod, 1920, 97–138. Volume eleven of the critical edition of *The Works of George Santayana.*

This selection appeared as Chapter IV in Character and Opinion in the United States *but originally was part of a lecture on both William James and Josiah Royce (1855–1916). Santayana explained to a correspondent that "in filling out the paper on James and Royce I got into a terrible mess; and that one lecture has now expanded into four chapters" (LGS, 2:342). Commenting later on the published chapter Santayana wrote, "I <u>did</u> enjoy writing it, not only "maliciously" but also imaginatively, in trying to call up the complete figure and tragedy of such a man, a patient voluminous straggling mind, with a sort of childish insistence and stubbornness in fundamental matters—puzzled and muddled, and yet good and wise. . . . Of course, his friends and disciples were angry: it was so unlike an obituary notice" (LGS, 3:213–14). Royce, the leading idealist philosopher in America, had been Santayana's teacher, dissertation director, and then colleague at Harvard.*

Meantime the mantle of philosophical authority had fallen at Harvard upon other shoulders. A young Californian, Josiah Royce, had come back from Germany with a reputation for wisdom; and even without knowing that he had already produced a new proof of the existence of God, merely to look at him you would have felt that he was a philosopher; his great head seemed too heavy for his small body, and his portentous brow, crowned with thick red hair, seemed to crush the lower part of his face. "Royce," said William James of him, "has an indecent exposure of forehead." There was a suggestion about him of the benevolent ogre or the old child, in whom a preternatural sharpness of insight lurked beneath a grotesque mask. If you gave him any cue, or even without one, he could discourse broadly on any subject; you never caught him napping. Whatever the text-books and encyclopædias could tell him, he knew; and if the impression he left on your mind was vague, that was partly because, in spite of his comprehensiveness, he seemed to view everything in relation to something else that remained untold. His approach to anything was oblique; he began a long way off, perhaps with the American preface of a funny story; and when the point came in sight, it was at once enveloped again in a cloud of qualifications, in the parliamentary jargon of philosophy. The tap once turned on, out flowed the stream of systematic disquisition, one hour, two hours, three hours of it, according to demand or opportunity. The voice, too, was merciless and harsh. You felt the overworked, standardised, academic engine, creaking and thumping on at the call of duty or of habit, with no thought of sparing itself or any one else. Yet a sprightlier soul behind this performing soul seemed to watch and laugh at the process. Sometimes a merry light would twinkle in the little eyes, and a bashful smile would creep over the uncompromising mouth. A sense of the paradox, the irony, the inconclusiveness of the whole argument would pierce to the surface, like a white-cap bursting here and there on the heavy swell of the sea.

His procedure was first to gather and digest whatever the sciences or the devil might have to say. He had an evident sly pleasure in the degustation and savour of difficulties; biblical criticism, the struggle for life, the latest German theory of sexual insanity, had no terrors for him; it was all grist for the mill, and woe to any tender thing, any beauty or any illusion, that should get between that upper and that nether millstone! He seemed to say: If I were not Alexander how gladly would I be Diogenes, and if I had not a system to defend, how easily I might tell you the truth. But after the sceptic had ambled quizzically over the ground, the prophet would mount the pulpit to survey it. He would then prove that in spite of all those horrors and contradictions, or rather because of them, the universe was absolutely perfect. For behind that mocking soul in him there was yet another, a devout and heroic soul. Royce was heir to the Calvinistic tradition; piety, to his mind, consisted in trusting divine providence and justice, while emphasising the most terrifying truths about one's own depravity and the sinister holiness of God. He accordingly addressed himself, in his chief writings, to showing that all lives were parts of a single divine life in which all problems were solved and all evils justified.

It is characteristic of Royce that in his proof of something sublime, like the existence of God, his premiss should be something sad and troublesome, the existence of error. Error exists, he tells us, and common sense will readily agree, although the fact is not unquestionable, and pure mystics and pure sensualists deny it. But if error exists, Royce continues, there must be a truth from which it differs; and the existence of truth (according to the principle of idealism, that nothing can exist except for a mind that knows it) implies that some one knows the truth; but as to know the truth thoroughly, and supply the corrective to every possible error, involves omniscience, we have proved the existence of an omniscient mind or universal thought; and this is almost, if not quite, equivalent to the existence of God.

What carried Royce over the evident chasms and assumptions in this argument was his earnestness and passionate eloquence. He passed for an eminent logician, because he was dialectical and fearless in argument and delighted in the play of formal relations; he was devoted to chess, music, and mathematics; but all this show of logic was but a screen for his heart, and in his heart there was no clearness. His reasoning was not pure logic or pure observation; it was always secretly enthusiastic or malicious, and the result it arrived at had been presupposed. Here, for instance, no unprejudiced thinker, not to speak of a pure logician, would have dreamt of using the existence of error to found the being of truth upon. Error is a biological accident which may any day cease to exist, say at the extinction of the human race; whereas the being of truth or fact is involved indefeasibly and eternally in the existence of anything whatever, past, present, or future; every event of itself renders true or false any proposition that refers to it. No one would conceive of such a thing as error or suspect its presence, unless he

had already found or assumed many a truth; nor could anything be an error actually unless the truth was definite and real. All this Royce of course recognised,
and it was in some sense the heart of what he meant to assert and to prove; but it
does not need proving and hardly asserting. What needed proof was something
else, of less logical importance but far greater romantic interest, namely, that the
truth was hovering over us and about to descend into our hearts; and this Royce
was not disinclined to confuse with the being of truth, so as to bring it within the
range of logical argument. He was tormented by the suspicion that he might be
himself in the toils of error, and fervently aspired to escape from it. Error to him
was no natural, and in itself harmless, incident of finitude; it was a sort of sin, as
finitude was too. It was a part of the problem of evil; a terrible and urgent problem when your first postulate or dogma is that moral distinctions and moral experience are the substance of the world, and not merely an incident in it. The mere
being of truth, which is all a logician needs, would not help him in this wrestling
for personal salvation; as he keenly felt and often said, the truth is like the stars,
always laughing at us. Nothing would help him but *possession* of the truth, something eventual and terribly problematic. He longed to believe that all his troubles
and questions, some day and somewhere, must find their solution and quietus; if
not in his own mind, in some kindred spirit that he could, to that extent, identify
with himself. There must be not only cold truth, not even cold truth personified,
but victorious *knowledge* of the truth, breaking like a sun-burst through the clouds
of error. The nerve of his argument was not logical at all; it was a confession of
religious experience, in which the agonised consciousness of error led to a strong
imaginative conviction that the truth would be found at last.

The truth, as here conceived, meant the whole truth about everything; and
certainly, if any plausible evidence for such a conclusion could be adduced, it
would be interesting to learn that we are destined to become omniscient, or are
secretly omniscient already. Nevertheless, the aspiration of all religious minds
does not run that way. Aristotle tells us that there are many things it is better not
to know; and his sublime deity is happily ignorant of our errors and of our very
existence; more emphatically so the even sublimer deities of Plotinus and the
Indians. The omniscience which our religion attributes to God as the searcher of
hearts and the judge of conduct has a moral function rather than a logical one;
it prevents us from hiding our sins or being unrecognised in our merits; it is not
conceived to be requisite in order that it may be true that those sins or merits
have existed. Atheists admit the facts, but they are content or perhaps relieved
that they should pass unobserved. But here again Royce slipped into a romantic
equivocation which a strict logician would not have tolerated. Knowledge of the
truth, a passing psychological possession, was substituted for the truth known,
and this at the cost of rather serious ultimate confusions. It is the truth itself, the
facts in their actual relations, that honest opinion appeals to, not to another opinion or instance of knowledge; and if, in your dream of warm sympathy and public corroboration, you lay up your treasure in some instance of knowledge, which
time and doubt might corrupt, you have not laid up your treasure in heaven.
In striving to prove the being of truth, the young Royce absurdly treated it as

doubtful, setting a bad example to the pragmatists; while in striving to lend a psychological quality to this truth and turning it into a problematical instance of knowledge, he unwittingly deprived it of all authority and sublimity. To personify the truth is to care less for truth than for the corroboration and sympathy which the truth, become human, might bring to our opinions. It is to set up another thinker, ourself enlarged, to vindicate us; without considering that this second thinker would be shut up, like us, in his own opinions, and would need to look to the truth beyond him as much as we do.

To the old problem of evil Royce could only give an old answer, although he rediscovered and repeated it for himself in many ways, since it was the core of his whole system. Good, he said, is essentially the struggle with evil and the victory over it; so that if evil did not exist, good would be impossible. I do not think this answer set him at rest; he could hardly help feeling that all goods are not of that bellicose description, and that not all evils produce a healthy reaction or are swallowed up in victory; yet the fact that the most specious solution to this problem of evil left it unsolved was in its way appropriate; for if the problem had been really solved, the struggle to find a solution and the faith that there was one would come to an end; yet perhaps this faith and this struggle are themselves the supreme good. Accordingly the true solution of this problem, which we may all accept, is that no solution can ever be found.

Here is an example of the difference between the being of truth and the ultimate solution of all our problems. There is certainly a truth about evil, and in this case not an unknown truth; yet it is no solution to the "problem" which laid the indomitable Royce on the rack. If a younger son asks why he was not born before his elder brother, that question may represent an intelligible state of his feelings; but there is no answer to it, because it is a childish question. So the question why it is right that there should be any evil is itself perverse and raised by false presumptions. To an unsophisticated mortal the existence of evil presents a task, never a problem. Evil, like error, is an incident of animal life, inevitable in a crowded and unsettled world, where one spontaneous movement is likely to thwart another, and all to run up against material impossibilities. While life lasts this task is recurrent, and every creature, in proportion to the vitality and integrity of his nature, strives to remove or abate those evils of which he is sensible. When the case is urgent and he is helpless, he will cry out for divine aid; and (if he does not perish first) he will soon see this aid coming to him through some shift in the circumstances that renders his situation endurable. Positive religion takes a naturalistic view of things, and requires it. It parts company with a scientific naturalism only in accepting the authority of instinct or revelation in deciding certain questions of fact, such as immortality or miracles. It rouses itself to crush evil, without asking why evil exists. What could be more intelligible than that a deity like Jehovah, a giant inhabitant of the natural world, should be confronted with rivals, enemies, and rebellious children? What could be more intelligible than that the inertia of matter, or pure chance, or some contrary purpose, should mar the expression of any platonic idea exercising its magic influence over the world? For the Greek as for the Jew the task of morals is the same: to subdue nature as far as possible to the uses of the soul, by whatever agencies material or spiritual may be at hand; and when a limit is reached in that direction, to harden and cauterise the heart in the face of inevitable evils, opening it wide at the same time to every sweet influence that may descend to it from heaven. Never for a moment was positive religion entangled in a sophistical optimism. Never did it conceive that the most complete final deliverance and triumph would *justify* the evils which they abolished. As William James put it, in his picturesque manner, if at the last day all creation was shouting hallelujah and there remained one cockroach with an unrequited love, *that* would spoil the universal harmony; it would spoil it, he meant, in truth and for the tender philosopher, but probably not for those excited saints. James was thinking chiefly of the present and future, but the same scrupulous charity has its application to the past. To remove an evil is not to remove the fact that it has existed. The tears that have been shed were shed in bitterness, even if a remorseful hand afterwards wipes them away. To be patted on the back and given a sugar-plum does not reconcile even a child to a past injustice. And the case is much worse if we are expected to make our heaven out of the foolish and cruel pleasures of contrast, or out of the pathetic offuscation [*sic*] produced by a great relief. Such a heaven would be a lie, like the sardonic heavens of Calvin and Hegel. The existence of any evil anywhere at any time absolutely ruins a total optimism.

Nevertheless philosophers have always had a royal road to complete satisfaction. One of the purest of pleasures, which they cultivate above all others, is the pleasure of understanding. Now, as playwrights and novelists know, the intellect is no less readily or agreeably employed in understanding evil than in understanding good—more so, in fact, if in the intellectual man, besides his intelligence, there is a strain of coarseness, irony, or desire to belittle the good things others possess and he himself has missed. Sometimes the philosopher, even when above all meanness, becomes so devoted a naturalist that he is ashamed to remain a moralist, although this is what he probably was in the beginning; and where all is one vast cataract of events, he feels it would be impertinent of him to divide them censoriously into things that ought to be and things that ought not to be. He may even go one step farther. Awestruck and humbled before the universe, he may insensibly transform his understanding and admiration of it into the assertion that the existence of evil is no evil at all, but that the order of the universe is in every detail necessary and perfect, so that the mere mention of the word evil is blind and blasphemous.

This sentiment, which as much as any other deserves the name of pantheism, is often expressed incoherently and with a false afflatus; but when rationally conceived, as it was by Spinoza, it amounts to this: that good and evil are relations which things bear to the living beings they affect. In itself nothing—much less this whole mixed universe—can be either good or bad; but the universe wears the aspect of a good in so far as it feeds, delights, or otherwise fosters any creature within it. If we define the intellect as the power to see things as they are, it is clear that in so far as the philosopher is a pure intellect the universe will be a pure good to the philosopher; everything in it will give play to his exclusive passion.

Wisdom counsels us therefore to become philosophers and to concentrate our lives as much as possible in pure intelligence, that we may be led by it into the ways of peace. Not that the universe will be proved thereby to be intrinsically good (although in the heat of their intellectual egotism philosophers are sometimes betrayed into saying so), but that it will have become in that measure a good to us, and we shall be better able to live happily and freely in it. If intelligibility appears in things, it does so like beauty or use, because the mind of man, in so far as it is adapted to them, finds its just exercise in their society.

This is an ancient, shrewd, and inexpugnable position. If Royce had been able to adhere to it consistently, he would have avoided his gratuitous problem of evil without, I think, doing violence to the sanest element in his natural piety, which was joy in the hard truth, with a touch of humour and scorn in respect to mortal illusions. There was an observant and docile side to him; and as a child likes to see things work, he liked to see processions of facts marching on ironically, whatever we might say about it. This was his sense of the power of God. It attached him at first to Spinoza and later to mathematical logic. No small part of his life-long allegiance to the Absolute responded to this sentiment.

The outlook, however, was complicated and half reversed for him by the transcendental theory of knowledge which he had adopted. This theory regards all objects, including the universe, as merely terms posited by the will of the thinker, according to a definite grammar of thought native to his mind. In order that his thoughts may be addressed to any particular object, he must first choose and create it of his own accord; otherwise his opinions, not being directed upon any object in particular within his ken, cannot be either true or false, whatever picture they may frame. What anything external may happen to be, when we do not mean to speak of it, is irrelevant to our discourse. If, for instance, the real Royce were not a denizen and product of my mind—of my deeper self—I could not so much as have a wrong idea of him. The need of this initial relevance in our judgements seems to the transcendentalist to drive all possible objects into the fold of his secret thoughts, so that he has two minds, one that seeks the facts and another that already possesses or rather constitutes them.

Pantheism, when this new philosophy of knowledge is adopted, seems at first to lose its foundations. There is no longer an external universe to which to bow; no little corner left for us in the infinite where, after making the great sacrifice, we may build a safe nest. The intellect to which we had proudly reduced ourselves has lost its pre-eminence; it can no longer be called the faculty of seeing things as they are. It has become what psychological critics of intellectualism, such as William James, understand by it: a mass of human propensities to abstraction, construction, belief, or inference, by which imaginary things and truths are posited in the service of life. It is therefore on the same plane exactly as passion, music, or æsthetic taste: a mental complication which may be an index to other psychological facts connected with it genetically, but which has no valid intent, no ideal transcendence, no assertive or cognitive function. Intelligence so conceived understands nothing: it is a buzzing labour in the fancy which, by some obscure causation, helps us to live on.

To discredit the intellect, to throw off the incubus of an external reality or truth, was one of the boons which transcendentalism in its beginnings brought to the romantic soul. But although at first the sense of relief (to Fichte, for instance) was most exhilarating, the freedom achieved soon proved illusory: the terrible Absolute had been simply transplanted into the self. You were your own master, and omnipotent; but you were no less dark, hostile, and inexorable to yourself than the gods of Calvin or of Spinoza had been before. Since every detail of this mock world was your secret work, you were not only wiser but also more criminal than you knew. You were stifled, even more than formerly, in the arms of nature, in the toils of your own unaccountable character, which made your destiny. Royce never recoiled from paradox or from bitter fact; and he used to say that a mouse, when tormented and torn to pieces by a cat, was realising his own deepest will, since he had sub-consciously chosen to be a mouse in a world that should have cats in it. The mouse really, in his deeper self, wanted to be terrified, clawed, and devoured. Royce was superficially a rationalist, with no tenderness for superstition in detail and not much sympathy with civilised religions; but we see here that in his heart he was loyal to the aboriginal principle of all superstition: reverence for what hurts. He said to himself that in so far as God was the devil—as daily experience and Hegelian logic proved was largely the case—devilworship was true religion.

A protest, however, arose in his own mind against this doctrine. Strong early bonds attached him to moralism—to the opinion of the Stoics and of Kant that virtue is the only good. Yet if virtue were conceived after their manner, as a heroic and sublimated attitude of the will, of which the world hardly afforded any example, how should the whole whirligig of life be good also? How should moralism, that frowns on this wicked world, be reconciled with pantheism and optimism, that hug it to their bosom? By the ingenious if rather melodramatic notion that we should hug it with a bear's hug, that virtue consisted (as Royce often put it) in holding evil by the throat; so that the world was good because it was a good world to strangle, and if we only managed to do so, the more it deserved strangling the better world it was. But this Herculean feat must not be considered as something to accomplish once for all; the labours of Hercules must be not twelve but infinite, since his virtue consisted in performing them, and if he ever rested or was received into Olympus he would have left virtue—the only good—behind. The wickedness of the world was no reason for quitting it; on the contrary, it invited us to plunge into all its depths and live through every phase of it; virtue was severe but not squeamish. It lived by endless effort, turbid vitality, and *Sturm und Drang*. Moralism and an apology for evil could thus be reconciled and merged in the praises of tragic experience.

This had been the burden of Hegel's philosophy of life, which Royce admired and adopted. Hegel and his followers seem to be fond of imagining that they are moving in a tragedy. But because Aeschylus and Sophocles were great poets, does it follow that life would be cheap if it did not resemble their fables? The life of tragic heroes is not good; it is misguided, unnecessary, and absurd. Yet that is what romantic philosophy would condemn us to; we must all strut and roar. We must lend ourselves to the partisan earnestness of persons and nations calling their rivals villains and themselves heroes; but this earnestness will be of the histrionic German sort, made to order and transferable at short notice from one object to another, since what truly matters is not that we should achieve our ostensible aim (which Hegel contemptuously called ideal) but that we should carry on perpetually, if possible with a *crescendo,* the strenuous experience of living in a gloriously bad world, and always working to reform it, with the comforting speculative assurance that we never can succeed. We never can succeed, I mean, in rendering reform less necessary or life happier; but of course in any specific reform we may succeed half the time, thereby sowing the seeds of new and higher evils, to keep the edge of virtue keen. And in reality we, or the Absolute in us, are succeeding all the time; the play is always going on, and the play's the thing.

It was inevitable that Royce should have been at home only in this circle of Protestant and German intuitions; a more refined existence would have seemed to him to elude moral experience. Although he was born in California he had never got used to the sunshine; he had never tasted peace. His spirit was that of courage and labour. He was tender in a bashful way, as if in tenderness there was something pathological, as indeed to his sense there was, since he conceived love and loyalty to be divine obsessions refusing to be rationalised; he saw their essence in the child who clings to an old battered doll rather than accept a new and better one. Following orthodox tradition in philosophy, he insisted on seeing reason at the bottom of things as well as at the top, so that he never could understand either the root or the flower of anything. He watched the movement of events as if they were mysterious music, and instead of their causes and potentialities he tried to divine their *motif.* On current affairs his judgements were highly seasoned and laboriously wise. If anything escaped him, it was only the simplicity of what is best. His reward was that he became a prophet to a whole class of earnest, troubled people who, having discarded doctrinal religion, wished to think their life worth living when, to look at what it contained, it might not have seemed so; it reassured them to learn that a strained and joyless existence was not their unlucky lot, or a consequence of their solemn folly, but was the necessary fate of all good men and angels. Royce had always experienced and seen about him a groping, burdened, mediocre life; he had observed how fortune is continually lying in ambush for us, in order to bring good out of evil and evil out of good. In his age and country all was change, preparation, hurry, material achievement; nothing was an old and sufficient possession; nowhere, or very much in the background, any leisure, simplicity, security, or harmony. The whole scene was filled with arts and virtues which were merely useful or remedial. The most pressing arts, like war and forced labour, presuppose evil, work immense havoc, and take the place of greater possible goods. The most indispensable virtues, like courage and industry, do likewise. But these seemed in Royce's world the only honourable things, and he took them to be typical of all art and virtue—a tremendous error. It is very true, however, that in the welter of material existence no concrete thing can be good or evil in every respect; and so long as our rough arts and virtues do more good than harm we give them honourable names, such as unselfishness, patriotism, or religion; and it remains a mark of good breeding among us to practise them instinctively. But an absolute love of such forced arts and impure virtues is itself a vice; it is, as the case may be, barbarous, vain, or fanatical. It mistakes something specific–some habit or emotion which may be or may have been good in some respect, or under some circumstances the lesser of two evils–for the very principle of excellence. But good and evil, like light and shade, are ethereal; all things, events, persons, and conventional virtues are in themselves utterly valueless, save as an immaterial harmony (of which mind is an expression) plays about them on occasion, when their natures meet propitiously, and bathes them in some tint of happiness or beauty. This immaterial harmony may be made more and more perfect; the difficulties in the way of perfection, either in man, in society, or in universal nature, are physical not logical. Worship of barbarous virtue is the blackest conservatism; it shuts the gate of heaven, and surrenders existence to perpetual follies and crimes. Moralism itself is a superstition. In its abstract form it is moral, too moral; it adores the conventional conscience, or perhaps a morbid one. In its romantic form, moralism becomes barbarous and actually immoral; it obstinately craves action and stress for their own sake, experience in the gross, and a good-and-bad way of living.

Royce sometimes conceded that there might be some pure goods, music, for instance, or mathematics; but the impure moral goods were better and could not be spared. Such a concession, however, if it had been taken to heart, would have ruined his whole moral philosophy. The romanticist must maintain that *only* what is painful can be noble and *only* what is lurid bright. A taste for turbid and contrasted values would soon seem perverse when once anything perfect had been seen and loved. Would it not have been better to leave out the worst of the crimes and plagues that have heightened the tragic value of the world? But if so, why stop before we had deleted them all? We should presently be horrified at the mere thought of passions that before had been found necessary by the barbarous tragedian to keep his audience awake; and the ear at the same time would become sensitive to a thousand harmonies that had been inaudible in the hurly-burly of romanticism. The romanticist thinks he has life by virtue of his confusion and torment, whereas in truth that torment and confusion are his incipient death, and it is only the modicum of harmony he has achieved in his separate faculties that keeps him alive at all. As Aristotle taught, unmixed harmony would be intensest life. The spheres might make a sweet and perpetual music, and a happy God is at least possible.

It was not in this direction, however, that Royce broke away on occasion from his Hegelian ethics; he did so in the direction of ethical dogmatism and downright sincerity. The deepest thing in him personally was conscience, firm recognition of duty, and the democratic and American spirit of service. He could not adopt a moral bias histrionically, after the manner of Hegel or Nietzsche. To those hardened professionals any rôle was acceptable, the more commanding the better; but the good Royce was like a sensitive amateur, refusing the rôle of villain, however brilliant and necessary to the play. In contempt of his own speculative insight, or in an obedience to it which forgot it for the time being, he lost himself in his part, and felt that it was infinitely important to be cast only for the most virtuous of characters. He retained inconsistently the Jewish allegiance to a God essentially the vindicator of only one of the combatants, not in this world often the victor; he could not stomach the providential scoundrels which the bad taste of Germany, and of Carlyle and Browning, was wont to glorify. The last notable act of his life was an illustration of this, when he uttered a ringing public denunciation of the sinking of the *Lusitania*. Orthodox Hegelians might well have urged that here, if anywhere, was a plain case of the providential function of what, from a finite merely moral point of view, was an evil in order to make a higher good possible—the virtue of German self-assertion and of American self-assertion in antithesis to it, synthesised in the concrete good of war and victory, or in the perhaps more blessed good of defeat. What could be more unphilosophical and *gedankenlos* than the intrusion of mere morality into the higher idea of world-development? Was not the Universal Spirit compelled to bifurcate into just such Germans and just such Americans, in order to attain self-consciousness by hating, fighting against, and vanquishing itself? Certainly it was American duty to be angry, as it was German duty to be ruthless. The Idea liked to see its fighting-cocks at it in earnest, since that was what it had bred them for; but both were good cocks. Villains, as Hegel had observed in describing Greek tragedy, were not less self-justified than heroes; they were simply the heroes of a lower stage of culture. America and England remained at the stage of individualism; Germany had advanced to the higher stage of organisation. Perhaps this necessary war was destined, through the apparent defeat of Germany, to bring England and America up to the German level. Of course; and yet somehow, on this occasion, Royce passed over these profound considerations, which life-long habit must have brought to his lips. A Socratic demon whispered No, No in his ear; it would have been better for such things never to be. The murder of those thousand passengers was not a providential act, requisite to spread abroad a vitalising war; it was a crime to execrate altogether. It would have been better for Hegel, or whoever was responsible for it, if a millstone had been hanged about his neck and he, and not those little ones, had been drowned at the bottom of the sea. Of this terrestrial cock-pit Royce was willing to accept the agony, but not the ignominy. The other cock was a wicked bird.

This honest lapse from his logic was habitual with him at the sight of sin, and sin in his eyes was a fearful reality. His conscience spoiled the pantheistic serenity of his system; and what was worse (for he was perfectly aware of the contradiction) it added a deep, almost remorseful unrest to his hard life. What calm could there be in the double assurance that it was really right that things should be wrong, but that it was really wrong not to strive to right them? There was no conflict, he once observed, between science and religion, but the real conflict was between religion and morality. There could indeed be no conflict in his mind between faith and science, because his faith began by accepting all facts and all scientific probabilities in order to face them religiously. But there was an invincible conflict between religion as he conceived it and morality, because

morality takes sides and regards one sort of motive and one kind of result as better than another, whereas religion according to him gloried in everything, even
in the evil, as fulfilling the will of God. Of course the practice of virtue was not
excluded; it was just as needful as evil was in the scheme of the whole; but while
the effort of morality was requisite, the judgements of morality were absurd. Now
I think we may say that a man who finds himself in such a position has a divided
mind, and that while he has wrestled with the deepest questions like a young
giant, he has not won the fight. I mean, he has not seen his way to any one of
the various possibilities about the nature of things, but has remained entangled,
sincerely, nobly, and pathetically, in contrary traditions stronger than himself. In
the goodly company of philosophers he is an intrepid martyr.

In metaphysics as in morals Royce perpetually laboured the same points, yet
they never became clear; they covered a natural complexity in the facts which his
idealism could not disentangle. There was a voluminous confusion in his thought;
some clear principles and ultimate possibilities turned up in it, now presenting
one face and now another, like chips carried down a swollen stream; but the most
powerful currents were below the surface, and the whole movement was hard to
trace. He had borrowed from Hegel a way of conceiving systems of philosophy,
and also the elements of his own thought, which did not tend to clarify them. He
did not think of correcting what incoherence there might remain in any view,
and then holding it in reserve, as one of the possibilities, until facts should enable
us to decide whether it was true or not. Instead he clung to the incoherence as if it
had been the heart of the position, in order to be driven by it to some other position altogether, so that while every view seemed to be considered, criticised, and
in a measure retained (since the argument continued on the same lines, however
ill-chosen they might have been originally), yet justice was never done to it; it was
never clarified, made consistent with itself, and then accepted or rejected in view
of the evidence. Hence a vicious and perplexing suggestion that philosophies are
bred out of philosophies, not out of men in the presence of things. Hence too a
sophistical effort to find everything self-contradictory, and in some disquieting
way both true and false, as if there were not an infinite number of perfectly consistent systems which the world might have illustrated.

Consider, for instance, his chief and most puzzling contention, that all minds
are parts of one mind. It is easy, according to the meaning we give to the word
mind, to render this assertion clear and true, or clear and false, or clear and
doubtful (because touching unknown facts), or utterly absurd. It is obvious that
all minds are parts of one flux or system of experiences, as all bodies are parts
of one system of bodies. Again, if mind is identified with its objects, and people
are said to be "of one mind" when they are thinking of the same thing, it is certain that many minds are often identical in part, and they would all be identical
with portions of an omniscient mind that should perceive all that they severally
experienced. The question becomes doubtful if what we mean by oneness of
mind is unity of type; our information or plausible guesses cannot assure us how
many sorts of experience may exist, or to what extent their development (when
they develop) follows the same lines of evolution. The animals would have to

be consulted, and the other planets, and the infinite recesses of time. The strait-jacket which German idealism has provided is certainly far too narrow even for the varieties of human imagination. Finally, the assertion becomes absurd when it is understood to suggest that an actual instance of thinking, in which something, say the existence of America, is absent or denied, can be part of another actual instance of thinking in which it is present and asserted. But this whole method of treating the matter—and we might add anything that observation might warrant us in adding about multiple personalities—would leave out the problem that agitated Royce and that bewildered his readers. He wanted all minds to be one in some way which should be logically and morally necessary, and which yet, as he could not help feeling, was morally and logically impossible.

For pure transcendentalism, which was Royce's technical method, the question does not arise at all. Transcendentalism is an attitude or a point of view rather than a system. Its Absolute is thinking "as such," wherever thought may exert itself. The notion that there are separate instances of thought is excluded, because space, time, and number belong to the visionary world posited by thought, not to the function of thinking; individuals are figments of constructive fancy, as are material objects. The stress of moral being is the same wherever it may fall, and there are no finite selves, or relations between thinkers; also no infinite self, because on this principle the Absolute is not an existent being, a psychological monster, but a station or office; its essence is a task. Actual thinking is therefore never a part of the Absolute, but always the Absolute itself. Thinkers, finite or infinite, would be existing persons or masses of feelings; such things are dreamt of only. *Any* system of existences, *any* truth or matter of fact waiting to be recognised, contradicts the transcendental insight and stultifies it. The all-inclusive mind is my mind as I think, mind in its living function, and beyond that philosophy cannot go.

Royce, however, while often reasoning on this principle, was incapable of not going beyond it, or of always remembering it. He could not help believing that constructive fancy not only feigns individuals and instances of thought, but is actually seated in them. The Absolute, for instance, must be not merely the abstract subject or transcendental self in all of us (although it was that too), but an actual synthetic universal mind, the God of Aristotle and of Christian theology. Nor was it easy for Royce, a sincere soul and a friend of William James, not to be a social realist; I mean, not to admit that there are many collateral human minds, in temporal existential relations to one another, any of which may influence another, but never supplant it nor materially include it. Finite experience was not a mere element in infinite experience; it was a tragic totality in itself. I was not God looking at myself, I was myself looking for God. Yet this strain was utterly incompatible with the principles of transcendentalism; it turned philosophy into a simple anticipation of science, if not into an indulgence in literary psychology. Knowledge would then have been only faith leaping across the chasm of coexistence and guessing the presence and nature of what surrounds us by some hint of material influence or brotherly affinity. Both the credulity and the finality which such naturalism implies were offensive to Royce, and contrary to his sceptical and mystical instincts. Was there some middle course?

The audience in a theatre stand in a transcendental relation to the persons and events in the play. The performance may take place to-day and last one hour, while the fable transports us to some heroic epoch or to an age that never existed, and stretches through days and perhaps years of fancied time. Just so transcendental thinking, while actually timeless and not distributed among persons, might survey infinite time and rehearse the passions and thoughts of a thousand characters. Thought, after all, needs objects, however fictitious and ideal they may be; it could not think if it thought nothing. This indispensable world of appearance is far more interesting than the reality that evokes it; the qualities and divisions found in the appearance diversify the monotonous function of pure thinking and render it concrete. Instances of thought and particular minds may thus be introduced consistently into a transcendental system, provided they are distinguished not by their own times and places, but only by their themes. The transcendental mind would be a pure poet, with no earthly life, but living only in his works, and in the times and persons of his fable. This view, firmly and consistently held, would deserve the name of absolute idealism, which Royce liked to give to his own system. But he struggled to fuse it with social realism, with which it is radically incompatible. Particular minds and the whole process of time, for absolute idealism, are *ideas* only; they are thought of and surveyed, they never think or lapse actually. For this reason genuine idealists can speak so glibly of the mind of a nation or an age. It is just as real and unreal to them as the mind of an individual; for within the human individual they can trace unities that run through and beyond him, so that parts of him, identical with parts of other people, form units as living as himself; for it is all a web of themes, not a concourse of existences. This is the very essence and pride of idealism, that knowledge is not knowledge of the world but is the world itself, and that the units of discourse, which are interwoven and crossed units, are the only individuals in being. You may call them persons, because "person" means a mask; but you cannot call them souls. They are knots in the web of history. They are words in their context, and the only spirit in them is the sense they have for me.

Royce, however, in saying all this, also wished not to say it, and his two thick volumes on *The World and the Individual* leave their subject wrapped in utter obscurity. Perceiving the fact when he had finished, he very characteristically added a "Supplementary Essay" of a hundred more pages, in finer print, in which to come to the point. Imagine, he said, an absolutely exhaustive map of England spread out upon English soil. The map would be a part of England, yet would reproduce every feature of England, including itself; so that the map would reappear on a smaller scale within itself an infinite number of times, like a mirror reflected in a mirror. In this way we might be individuals within a larger individual, and no less actual and complete than he. Does this solve the problem? If we take the illustration as it stands, there is still only one individual in existence, the material England, all the maps being parts of its single surface; nor will it at all resemble the maps, since it will be washed by the sea and surrounded by foreign nations, and not, like the maps, by other Englands enveloping it. If, on the contrary, we equalise the status of all the members of the series, by making it infinite in both directions, then there would be no England at all, but only map within map of England. There would be no absolute mind inclusive but not included, and the Absolute would be the series as a whole, utterly different from any of its members. It would be a series while they were maps, a truth while they were minds; and if the Absolute from the beginning had been regarded as a truth only, there never would have been any difficulty in the existence of individuals under it. Moreover, if the individuals are all exactly alike, does not their exact similarity defeat the whole purpose of the speculation, which was to vindicate the equal reality of the whole and of its *limited* parts? And if each of us, living through infinite time, goes through precisely the same experiences as every one else, why this vain repetition? Is it not enough for this insatiable world to live its life once? Why not admit solipsism and be true to the transcendental method? Because of conscience and good sense? But then the infinite series of maps is useless, England is herself again, and the prospect opens before us of an infinite number of supplementary essays.

Royce sometimes felt that he might have turned his hand to other things than philosophy. He once wrote a novel, and its want of success was a silent disappointment to him. Perhaps he might have been a great musician. Complexity, repetitions, vagueness, endlessness are hardly virtues in writing or thinking, but in music they might have swelled and swelled into a real sublimity, all the more that he was patient, had a voluminous meandering memory, and loved technical devices. But rather than a musician—for he was no artist—he resembled some great-hearted mediæval peasant visited by mystical promptings, whom the monks should have adopted and allowed to browse among their theological folios; a Duns Scotus earnest and studious to a fault, not having the lightness of soul to despise those elaborate sophistries, yet minded to ferret out their secret for himself and walk by his inward light. His was a gothic and scholastic spirit, intent on devising and solving puzzles, and honouring God in systematic works, like the coral insect or the spider; eventually creating a fabric that in its homely intricacy and fulness arrested and moved the heart, the web of it was so vast, and so full of mystery and yearning.

Dewey's Naturalistic Metaphysics

Obiter Scripta: Lectures, Essays and Reviews. Edited by Justus Buchler and Benjamin Schwartz. New York: Charles Scribner's Sons; London: Constable and Co. Ltd., 1936, 213–40.

A version of this selection first appeared in The Journal of Philosophy *(22 [1925]: 673–88) as a review of John Dewey's* Experience and Nature *(Chicago: Open Court Publishing Company, 1925). It was reprinted with changes in* Obiter Scripta *and in the inaugural volume of* The Library of Living Philosophers *series,* The Philosophy of John Dewey *(edited by Paul Arthur Schilpp [Evanston and Chicago: Northwestern University Press, 1939], 243–62). Until this review, Santayana had not published on Dewey or studied him "at all attentively or completely" (LGS, 3:7), though Dewey had already published four favorable reviews of Santayana's work. Santayana had aimed to write his review "without irritating the author" (LGS, 3:243) and hoped that "it may amuse Dewey and not offend him" (LGS, 3:261), but his hope was disappointed. Dewey published a sharp response, taking his title from Santayana's charge against him. In "Half-Hearted Naturalism" (*Journal of Philosophy, 24 [1927], 57–64*), Dewey labeled Santayana's naturalism broken-backed for its seeming supernatural character. Santayana wrote to a friend, "I am sorry that Dewey should have been so much enraged by my article: I meant to be friendly and sympathetic" (LGS, 3:327).*

Here is a remarkable rereading of things with a new and difficult kind of sincerity, a near-sighted sincerity comparable in philosophy to that of contemporary painters in their painful studies. The intellect here, like the fancy there, arrests its dogmatic vision and stops short at some relational term which was invisible because it is only a vehicle in natural seeing. No wonder that these near elements, abstracted and focused in themselves, have a queer look. For my part, I am entirely persuaded of the genuineness and depth of Dewey's views, within the limits of his method and taken as he means them. He is, fortunately, not without an active band of followers who will be able to interpret and elaborate them in his own spirit. I am hardly in their case, and all I can hope to accomplish is to fix the place and character of this doctrine in relation to the points of view which I instinctively take or which seem to me, on reflection, to be most comprehensive. And I will append such conclusions as I may provisionally reach on this subject to a phrase by which Dewey himself characterizes his system: *Naturalistic Metaphysics.* In what sense is this system naturalistic? In what sense is it metaphysical? How comes it that these two characters (which to me seem contradictory) can be united in this philosophy?

Naturalism is a primary system, or rather it is not a special system at all, but the spontaneous and inevitable body of beliefs involved in animal life, beliefs

---

Review of John Dewey, *Experience and Nature.*

of which the various philosophical systems are either extensions (a supernatural environment, itself natural in its own way, being added to nature) or interpretations (as in Aristotle and Spinoza) or denials (as in idealism). Children are interested in their bodies, with which they identify themselves; they are interested in animals, adequate playmates for them, to be bullied with a pleasing risk and a touch of wonder. They are interested later in mechanical contrivances and in physical feats and adventures. This boyish universe is indefinitely extensible on its own plane; it may have heaven around it and fairyland in its interstices; it covers the whole field of possible material action to its uttermost reaches. It is the world of naturalism. On this material framework it is easy to hang all the immaterial objects, such as words, feelings, and ideas, which may be eventually distinguished in human experience. We are not compelled in naturalism, or even in materialism, to ignore immaterial things; the point is that any immaterial things which are recognized shall be regarded as names, aspects, functions, or concomitant products of those physical things among which action goes on. A naturalist may distinguish his own person or self, provided he identifies himself with his body and does not assign to his soul any fortunes, powers, or actions save those of which his body is the seat and organ. He may recognize other spirits, human, animal, or divine, provided they are all proper to natural organisms figuring in the world of action, and are the natural moral transcript, like his own feelings, of physical life in that region. Naturalism may, accordingly, find room for every sort of psychology, poetry, logic, and theology, if only they are content with their natural places. Naturalism will break down, however, so soon as words, ideas, or spirits are taken to be substantial on their own account, and powers at work prior to the existence of their organs, or independent of them. Now it is precisely such disembodied powers and immaterial functions prior to matter that are called metaphysical. Transcendentalism is not metaphysical if it remains a mere method, because then it might express the natural fact that any animal mind is its own centre and must awake in order to know anything: it becomes metaphysical when this mind is said to be absolute, single, and without material conditions. To admit anything metaphysical in this sense is evidently to abandon naturalism.

It would be hard to find a philosopher in whom naturalism, so conceived, was more inveterate than in Dewey. He is very severe against the imagination, and even the intellect, of mankind for having created figments which usurp the place and authority of the mundane sphere in which daily action goes on. The typical philosopher's fallacy, in his eyes, has been the habit of hypostatizing the conclusions to which reflection may lead, and depicting them to be prior realities–the fallacy of dogmatism. These conclusions are in reality nothing but suggestions or, as Dewey calls them, "meanings" surrounding the passing experience in which, at some juncture, a person is immersed. They may be excellent in an instrumental capacity, if by their help instinctive action can be enlarged or adjusted more accurately to absent facts; but it would be sheer idolatry to regard them as realities or powers deeper than obvious objects, producing these objects and afterwards somehow revealing themselves, just as they are, to the thoughts of metaphysicians. Here is a rude blow dealt at dogma of every sort: God, matter, Platonic ideas, active spirits, and creative logics all seem to totter on their thrones; and if the blow could be effective, the endless battle of metaphysics would have to end for lack of combatants.

Meantime there is another motive that drives Dewey to naturalism: he is the devoted spokesman of the spirit of enterprise, of experiment, of modern industry. To him, rather than to William James, might be applied the saying of the French pragmatist, Georges Sorel, that his philosophy is calculated to justify all the assumptions of American society. William James was a psychologist of the individual, preoccupied with the varieties of the human imagination and with the possible destinies of the spirit in other worlds. He was too spontaneous and rare a person to be a good mirror of any broad general movement; his Americanism, like that of Emerson, was his own and within him, and perhaps more representative of America in the past than in the future. In Dewey, on the contrary, as in current science and ethics, there is a pervasive quasi-Hegelian tendency to dissolve the individual into his social functions, as well as everything substantial or actual into something relative or transitional. For him events, situations, and histories hold all facts and all persons in solution. The master-burden of his philosophy, which lends it its national character, is a profound sympathy with the enterprise of life in all lay directions, in its technical and moral complexity, and especially in its American form, where individual initiative, although still demanded and prized, is quickly subjected to overwhelming democratic control. This, if I am not mistaken, is the heart of Dewey's pragmatism, that it is the pragmatism of the people, dumb and instinctive in them, and struggling in him to a laboured but radical expression. His pragmatism is not inspired by any wish to supply a new argument to support some old speculative dogma. Nor is he interested, like Nietzsche and Vaihinger, in a heroic pessimism, desperately living as if postulates were true which it knows to be false. He is not interested in speculation at all, balks at it, and would avoid it if he could; his inspiration is sheer fidelity to the task in hand and sympathy with the movement afoot: a deliberate and happy participation in the attitude of the American people, with its omnivorous human interests and its simplicity of purpose.

Now the philosophy by which Americans live, in contrast to the philosophies which they profess, is naturalistic. In profession they may be Fundamentalists, Catholics, or idealists, because American opinion is largely pre-American; but in their hearts and lives they are all pragmatists, and they prove it even by the spirit in which they maintain those other traditional allegiances, not out of rapt speculative sympathy, but because such allegiance seems an insurance against moral dissolution, guaranteeing social cohesion and practical success. Their real philosophy is the philosophy of enterprise. Now enterprise moves in the infinitely extensible boyish world of feats and discoveries—in the world of naturalism. The practical arts, as Dewey says, assume a mechanical unity and constancy established in the universe. Otherwise discoveries made today would not count tomorrow, inventions could not be patented, the best-laid plans might go astray, all work might be wasted, and the methods of experts could not be adjusted more and more accurately to their tasks. This postulated mechanical system must evidently include the hands and brain of the worker, which are intertwined inextricably with the work done. It must also include his mind, if his mind is to be of any practical account and to make any difference in his work. Hence the implicit American philosophy, which it is Dewey's privilege to make explicit, involves behaviourism. This doctrine is new and amazing if taken to deny the existence of thought; but on its positive side, in so far as it puts all efficient processes on one level, it has been an implication of naturalism from time immemorial. For a naturalist nothing can be substantial or efficacious in thought except its organs and instruments, such as brains, training, words, and books. Actual thought, being invisible and imponderable, eludes this sort of chase. It has always been rather ignored by materialists; but it remained for American optimists to turn their scorn of useless thought into a glad denial of its existence. This negative implication of behaviourism follows also from the commonsense view that mind and body act upon each other alternately; for when this view is carried out with empirical rigour, it corrects the speculative confusion which first suggested it. What it called mind turns out never to have been anything but a habit in matter, a way people have of acting, speaking, and writing. The actuality of spirit, mystically momentary, does not fall within the purview of this empirical inventory any more than the realm of truth, invisibly eternal. Men of affairs, who can easily tell a clever man from a fool, are behaviourists by instinct; but they may scout their own conviction when it is proposed to them by philosophers in paradoxical language. The business intellect, by the time it comes to theorizing, is a little tired. It will either trust a first impression, and bluff it out, or else it will allow comfortable traditional assurances in these hazy regions to relieve it of responsibility.

Is Dewey a behaviourist? On the positive side of the theory, he certainly is; and it is only when we interpret what he says about ideas, meanings, knowledge, or truth behaviouristically, that the sense and the force of it begin to appear. Often, indeed, he seems to jump the barrier, and to become a behaviourist in the negative sense also, denying the existence of thought: because it would be to deny its existence if we reduced it to its material manifestations. At least at one point, however, the existence of thought in its actuality and spiritual concentration is admitted plainly. Not, indeed, on the ground which to most philosophers would seem obvious and final, namely, that people sometimes do actually feel and think. This consideration might seem to Dewey irrelevant, because actual feeling and thinking are accounted for initially, on his view, by the absolute existence of the specious or conventional world: they do not need to be introduced again among its details. An impersonal transcendental spectator, though never mentioned, is always assumed; and the spectacle of nature unrolled before him may be, and strictly speaking must be, wholly observable and material. There cannot be any actual mind in experience except the experience itself. The consideration which nevertheless leads Dewey to graft something consciously actual and spiritual upon the natural world is of quite another sort. Essentially, I suspect, it flows from his choice of "events" to be his metaphysical elements (of which more presently) ; incidentally it is attached to the sympathetic study which he has made of Aristotle. Events, he thinks, have natural "endings," "culminations," or "consummations." They are not arbitrary sections made in the flux of nature, as if by geometrical planes passed across the current of a river. They are natural waves, pulsations of being, each of which, without any interruption in its material inheritance and fertility, forms a unit of a higher order. These units (if I may express the matter in my own language) fall sometimes into the realm of truth, when they are simply observable patterns or rhythms, and sometimes into the realm of spirit, as in animal perception or intent, when the complex tensions of bodily or social life generate a single sound, an actual pang, or a vivid idea. Mind at such moments possesses a hypostatic spiritual existence, over and above the whole behaviourist or pragmatic ground-work of mind: it has become conscious, or as Aristotle would say, has reached its second entelechy and become intellect in act. This hypostatic spiritual existence Dewey seems to recognize at least in æsthetic contemplation; but evidently every actual feeling or idea, however engrossed in action or however abstractly intellectual, is in the same case.

Such an admission, if taken to heart, would have leavened this whole philosophy; but Dewey makes it grudgingly, and hastens to cover it up. For instance, when he comes upon the phrase "knowledge of acquaintance,"* he says that acquaintance implies recognition and recognition familiarity; on the ground, I suppose, that people are called "acquaintances" when they bow to one another: and we are left with an uncomfortable suspicion that it is impossible to inspect anything for the first time. In another place we are told that consummations are themselves fruitful and ends are also means. Yes, but in what sense? Of course, no earthly flame is so pure as to leave no ashes, and the highest wave sinks presently into the trough of the sea; but this is true only of the substance engaged, which, having reached a culmination here, continues in its course; and the habit which it then acquired may, within limits, repeat the happy achievement, and propagate the light. One torch by material contact may kindle another torch; and if the torches are similar and the wind steady, the flames, too, may be similar and even continuous; but if any one says that the visible splendour of one moment helps to produce that of another, he does not seem ever to have seen the light. It will therefore be safer to proceed as if the realm of actual spirit had not been broached at this point, and as if the culminations recognized were only runs or nodes discoverable in nature, as in the cycle of reproduction or in sentences in discourse. The behaviourist landscape will then not be split by any spiritual lightning, and naturalism will seem to be established in its most unqualified form. Yet in this case how comes it that Dewey has a metaphysics of his own, that cosmology is absent from his system, and that every natural fact becomes in his hands so strangely unseizable and perplexing?

This question, which is the crux of the whole system, may be answered, I think, in a single phrase: *the dominance of the foreground*. In nature there is no

---

*The article originally contained here a clause stating that knowledge of acquaintance means intuition of essence. The author now remarks concerning it:

"I was wrong in thinking that 'knowledge of acquaintance' was meant to be intuition of essence. It was meant to mean knocking up against something, *personal contact*. It was only my own analysis that distinguished the spiritual from the physical 'acquaintance' involved."

foreground or background, no here, no now, no moral cathedra, no centre so really central as to reduce all other things to mere margins and mere perspectives. A foreground is by definition relative to some chosen point of view, to the station assumed in the midst of nature by some creature tethered by fortune to a particular time and place. If such a foreground becomes dominant in a philosophy naturalism is abandoned. Some local perspective or some casual interest is set up in the place of universal nature or behind it, or before it, so that all the rest of nature is reputed to be intrinsically remote or dubious or merely ideal. This dominance of the foreground has always been the source of metaphysics; and the metaphysics has varied according as the foreground has been occupied by language or fancy or logic or sceptical self-consciousness or religious rapture or moral ambition. Now the dominance of the foreground is in all Dewey's traditions: it is the soul of transcendentalism and also of empiricism; it is the soul of moralism and of that kind of religion which summons the universe to vindicate human notions of justice or to subserve the interests of mankind or of some special nation or civilization. In America the dominance of the foreground is further emphasized by the prevalent absorption in business life and in home affections, and by a general feeling that anything ancient, foreign, or theoretical cannot be of much consequence.* Pragmatism may be regarded as a synthesis of all these ways of making the foreground dominant: the most close-reefed of philosophical craft, most tightly hugging appearance, use, and relevance to practice today and here, least drawn by the lure of speculative distances. Nor would Dewey, I am sure, or any other pragmatist, ever be a naturalist instinctively or on the wings of speculative insight, like the old Ionians or the Stoics or Spinoza, or like those many mystics, Indian, Jewish, or Mohammedan, who, heartily despising the foreground, have fallen in love with the greatness of nature and have sunk speechless before the infinite. The pragmatist becomes, or seems to become, a naturalist only by accident, when as in the present age and in America the dominant foreground is monopolized by material activity; because material activity, as we have seen, involves naturalistic assumptions, and has been the teacher and the proof of naturalism since the beginning of time. But elsewhere and at other periods experience is free to offer different perspectives into which the faithful pragmatist will be drawn with equal zeal; and then pragmatic metaphysics would cease to be naturalistic and become, perhaps, theological. Naturalism in Dewey is accordingly an assumption imposed by the character of the prevalent arts; and as he is aware that he is a naturalist only to that extent and on that ground, his naturalism is half-hearted and short-winded. It is the specious kind of naturalism possible also to such idealists as Emerson, Schelling, or any Hegelian of the Left, who may scrupulously limit their survey, in its range of objects, to nature and to recorded history, and yet in their attitude may remain romantic, transcendental,

---

* I can imagine the spontaneous pragmatism of some president of a State University, if obliged to defend the study of Sanskrit before a committee of senators. "You have been told," he would say, "that Sanskrit is a dead language. Not at all: Sanskrit is Professor Smith's department, and growing. The cost is trifling, and several of our sister universities are making it a fresh requirement for the Ph.D. in classics. That, gentlemen, is what Sanskrit *is*."

piously receiving as absolute the inspiration dominating moral life in their day and country. The idealists, being self-conscious, regarded this natural scene as a landscape painted by spirit; Dewey, to whom self-consciousness is anathema, regards it as a landscape that paints itself; but it is still something phenomenal, all above board. Immediacy, which was an epistemological category, has become a physical one: natural events are conceived to be compounded of such qualities as appear to human observers, as if the character and emergence of these qualities had nothing to do with the existence, position, and organs of those observers. Nature is accordingly simply experience deployed, thoroughly specious and pictorial in texture. Its parts are not (what they are in practice and for living animal faith) substances presenting accidental appearances. They are appearances integrally woven into a panorama entirely relative to human discourse. Naturalism could not be more romantic: nature here is not a world but a story.

We have seen that the foreground, by its dominance, determines whether the empirical philosopher shall be provisionally a naturalist or shall try being something else. What now, looked at more narrowly, is the character of this foreground? Its name is Experience; but lest we should misunderstand this ambiguous word, it is necessary to keep in mind that in this system experience is impersonal. It is not, as a literary psychologist might suppose, a man's feelings and ideas forming a life-long soliloquy, his impressions of travel in this world. Nor is it, as a biologist might expect, such contact of sensitive animals with their environment as adapts them to it and teaches them to remember it. No: experience is here taken in a transcendental, or rather in a moral, sense, as something romantically absolute and practically coercive. There exists a social medium, the notorious scene of all happenings and discoveries, the sum of those current adventures in which anybody might participate. Experience is deputed to include everything to which experience might testify: it is the locus of public facts. It is therefore identical with nature, to the extent and in the aspects in which nature is disclosed to man. Death, for instance, should be set down as a fact of experience. This would not be possible if experience were something personal, unless indeed death were only a transition to another life. For so long as a man's sensations and thoughts continue, he is not dead, and when dead he has no more thoughts or sensations. But is such actual death, we may ask, the death that Dewey can have in mind? The only death open to experience is the death of others (here is a neat proof of immortality for those who like it); and death, for the pragmatist, simply *is* burial. To suppose that a train of thoughts and feelings going on in a man invisibly might at last come to an end, would be to place the fact of death in a sphere which Dewey does not recognize, namely, in the realm of truth; for it would simply be true that the man's thoughts had ceased, although neither he nor anybody else could find that fact in experience. For other people it would remain a fact assumed and credited, for him it would be a destiny that overtook him. Yet Experience, as Dewey understands it, must include such undiscoverable objects of common belief, and such a real, though unobserved, order of events. The dominant foreground which he calls Experience is accordingly filled and bounded not so much by experience as by convention. It is the social world.

How conventional this foreground is will appear even more clearly if we note the elements which are said to compose it. These are events, histories, situations, affairs. The words "affairs" and "situations," in their intentional vagueness, express very well the ethical nerve of this philosophy; for it is essentially a moral attitude or a lay religion. Life is a practical predicament; both necessity and duty compel us to do something about it, and also to think something about it, so as to know what to do. This is the categorical imperative of existence; and according to the Protestant tradition (diametrically opposed to the Indian) the spirit, in heeding its intrinsic vocation, is not alienated from earthly affairs, but on the contrary pledges itself anew to prosecute them with fidelity. Conscience and nature here exercise their suasion concurrently, since conscience merely repeats the summons to enter a field of responsibility—nature—formed by the deposit of its past labours. The most homely business, like the widest policies, may be thus transfused with a direct metaphysical inspiration; and although Dewey avoids all inflated eloquence on this theme, it is clear that his philosophy of Experience is a transcendental moralism. The other two terms, however, "events" and "histories," point to the flux of matter, although this is still gathered up and subdivided under units of discourse. "Event" is now a favourite word among philosophers who are addressed to the study of nature, but bring with them an empirical logic; and it well expresses that conjunction. An event does not involve a spectator, and does involve an environment on the same plane as the event: so far events belong directly to the flux of nature. At the same time an event is a change, and all the dialectic of change applies to the conception. Are events the crises between existence characterized in one way and existence characterized in another way? Or are events the intervals between such crises? But if these intervals, each having a somewhat different quality, were taken separately, they would not lodge in a common space or time; there would be no crises between them, no change, and (as I think would appear in the end) they themselves would have no existence. If events are to be successive, and fragments of the flux of nature, they must be changes in an abiding medium. In other words, an event, in its natural being, is a mode of substance, the transit of an essence. Moreover, natural events would have to be microscopic, because intervals containing no internal crisis, however long or even eternal they might seem sentimentally, could not be measured and would count as instants. This corollary is well fitted to remind us that nature laughs at our dialectic and goes on living in her own way. Her flux, like the flow of a river, is far more substantial than volatile, all sleepy continuity, derivation, persistence, and monotony. The most ordinary form of change in her—perhaps the only fundamental form—is motion; and it would be highly artificial to call the parts of a motion events where there are no crises and no intervals. Even night and day, unless we choose a particular point on the earth's surface for our station, are not events, since both are perpetual. It is apparently only on higher levels, genetically secondary, that nature produces events, where movement becomes rhythmical, and a culmination is followed by a breakdown and a repetition, as in animal birth and death. These secondary rhythms naturally attract the attention of a human observer, whose units of perception are all impressionistic and pictorial; he selects events from the vast continuities of nature because they go with rhythms in his own organism, with which his intuitions—the only vital culminations—are conjoined. Hence the empirical impression that nature is a series of events, although if they were mere events they could not be parts of nature, but only essences succeeding one another before vacant attention or in discourse; in other words, we should be in the mock world of psychologism.

The superficial level proper to empirical events becomes even more obvious if instead of calling them events we call them histories. The parts of nature seem events when we ignore their substance and their essence and consider only their position; anything actual is an event only, so to speak, at its margins, where it ceases to be itself. But before the parts of nature can seem to be histories, we must impose on them dramatic unities fetched from a far more derivative sphere. Histories are moral units, framed by tracing the thread of some special interest through the maze of things, units impossible to discriminate before the existence of passions and language. As there is a literary psychology which represents the mind as a mass of nameable pictures and describable sentiments, so there is a romantic metaphysics which hypostatizes history and puts it in the place of nature. "Histories" bring us back into the moral foreground where we found "situations" and "affairs." The same predicaments of daily life are viewed now in a temporal perspective, rather than as they beset us at any one moment.

That the foreground of human life is necessarily moral and practical (it is so even for artists) and that a philosophy which limits itself to clarifying moral perspectives may be a very great philosophy, has been known to the judicious since the days of Socrates. Why could not Dewey have worked out his shrewd moral and intellectual economy within the frame of naturalism, which he knows is postulated by practice, and so have brought clearness and space into the picture, without interposing any metaphysics? Because it is an axiom with him that nothing but the immediate is real. This axiom, far from being self-evident, is not even clear: for everything is "real" in some sense, and there is much doubt as to what sort of being is immediate. At first the axiom produced psychological idealism, because the proudly discoursing minds of philosophers took for granted that the immediate for each man could be only his own thoughts. Later it has been urged (and, I think, truly) that the immediate is rather any object—whether sensible or intelligible makes no difference—found lying in its own specious medium; so that immediatism is not so much subjective as closely attentive and mystically objective. Be it noted, however, that this admitted objectivity of natural things remains internal to the immediate sphere: they must never be supposed to possess an alleged substantial existence beyond experience. This experience is no longer subjective, but it is still transcendental, absolute, and groundless; indeed it has ceased to seem subjective only because it seems unconditioned; and in order to get to the bottom and to the substance of anything, we must still ask with Emerson, What is this *to me,* or with William James, What is this *experienced as.* As Dewey puts it, these facts of experience simply *are* or *are had,* and there is nothing more to say about them. Such evidence flooding immediate experience I just now called mystical, using the epithet advisedly; because in this direct possession of being there is no division of subject and object, but rapt identification of some term, intuition of some essence. Such is sheer pleasure or pain, when no source or object is assigned to it; such is æsthetic contemplation; such is pure thinking, the flash of intellectual light. This mystical paradise is indefinitely extensible, like life, and far be it from me to speak evil of it; it is there only that the innocent spirit is at home. But how should pragmatism, which is nothing if not prehensile, take root in this Eden? I am afraid pragmatism is the serpent; for there is a forbidden tree in the midst, the tree of Belief in the Eventual, the fruit of which is Care; and it is evident that our first parents must have partaken of it copiously; perhaps they fed on nothing else. Now when immediate experience is crossed by Care it suffers the most terrible illusion, for it supposes that the eventual about which it is troubled is controllable by the immediate, as by wishes, omens, or high thoughts; in other words, that the essences given in the immediate exist, generate their own presence, and may persist and rearrange themselves and so generate the future. But this is sheer superstition and trust in magic; the philosophy not of experience but of inexperience. The immediate, whether a paradise or a hell, is always specious; it is peopled by spectres which, if taken for existing and working things, are illusions; and although they are real enough, in that they have definite character and actual presence, as a dream or a pain has, their reality ends there; they are unsubstantial, volatile, leaving no ashes, and their existence, even when they appear, is imputed to them by a hidden agency, the demon of Care, and lies wholly in being perceived.

Thus immediate experience of things, far from being fundamental in nature, is only the dream which accompanies our action, as the other dreams accompany our sleep; and every naturalist knows that this waking dream is dependent for its existence, quality, intensity, and duration on obscure processes in the living body, in its interplay with its environment; processes which go back, through seeds, to the first beginnings of life on earth. Immediate experience is a consummation; and this not in æsthetic contemplation alone, but just as much in birth-pangs or the excitement of battle. All its episodes, intermittent and wildly modulated, like the sound of wind in a forest, are bound together and rendered relevant to one another only by their material causes and instruments. So tenuous is immediate experience that the behaviourist can ignore it altogether without inconvenience, substituting everywhere objects of conventional belief in their infinite material plane. The immediate is, indeed, recognized and prized only by mystics, and Dewey himself is assured of possessing it only by virtue of his social and ethical mysticism, by which the whole complex theatre of contemporary action seems to him to be given immediately: whereas to others of us (who are perhaps mystical at other points) this world of practice seems foreign, absent from our better moments, approachable even at the time of action only by animal faith and blind presumption, and compacted, when we consider its normal texture, out of human conventions, many of them variable and foolish. A pragmatist who was not an ethical or social mystic, might explore that world scientifically, as a physician, politician, or engineer, and remain throughout a pure behaviourist or materialist, without noticing immediate experience at all, or once distinguishing what was given from what was assumed or asserted. But to the mystic, if he is interested in that world, it all comes forward into the immediate; it becomes indubitable, but at the same time vague. Actual experience sucks in the world in which conventional experience, if left to dogmatize, would have supposed it was going on; and a luminous cloud of immediacy envelops everything and arrests the eye, in every direction, on a painted perspective; for if any object becomes immediate, whatever it may be, it becomes visionary. That same spiritual actuality which Dewey, in passing, scarcely recognized at the top of animal life, he now comes upon from within, and without observing its natural locus, lays at the basis of the universe. The universe, in his system, thereby appears inverted, the accidental order of discovery being everywhere substituted for the natural order of genesis; and this with grave consequences, since it is not so easy for the universe as for an individual to stand on its head.*

Consider, for instance, the empirical status of the past. The only past that ever *is* or *is had* is a specious past, the fading survival of it in the present. Now the form which things wear in the foreground, according to this philosophy, is their *real* form; and the meaning which such immediate facts may assume hangs on their use in executing some living purpose. What follows in regard to past time? That the survival or memory of it comprises all its reality, and that all the meaning of it lies in its possible relevance to actual interests. A memory may serve as a model or condition in shaping some further enterprise, or may be identified with a habit acquired by training, as when we have learned a foreign language and are ready to speak it. Past experience is accordingly real only by virtue of its vital inclusion in some present undertaking, and yesterday is *really* but a term perhaps useful in the preparation of tomorrow. The past, too, must work if it would live, and we may speak without irony of "the futurity of yesterday" in so far as yesterday has any pragmatic reality.

This result is consistent with the general principle of empirical criticism by which we are forbidden to regard God, truth, or the material cosmos as anything but home vistas. When this principle is applied to such overwhelming outer realities, it lightens the burden of those who hate external compulsions or supports; they can henceforth believe they are living in a moral universe that changes as they change, with no sky lowering over them save a portable canopy which they carry with them on their travels. But now this pleasant principle threatens the

---

* A curious reversal of the terms "natural" and "ideal" comes about as we assume that the immediate is substantial or that it is visionary. Suppose I say that "everything ideal emanates from something natural." Dewey agrees, understanding that everything remote emanates from something immediate. But what I meant was that everything immediate—sensation, for instance, or love—emanates from something biological. Not, however, (and this is another verbal snare) from the concepts of biological science, essences immediately present to the thoughts of biologists, but from the largely unknown or humanly unknowable process of animal life. I suppose we should not call some of our ideas scientific if they did not trace the movement of nature more accurately and reliably than do our random sensations or dramatic myths; they are therefore presumably truer in regard to those distributive aspects of nature which they select. But science is a part of human discourse, and necessarily poetical, like language. If literal truth were necessary (which is not the case in practice in respect to nature) it would be found only, perhaps, in literature—in the reproduction of discourse by discourse.

march of experience itself: for if my ancestors have no past existence save by working in me now, what becomes of my present being, if ever I cease to work in my descendants? Does experience today draw its whole existence from their future memories? Evidently this cannot be the doctrine proposed; and yet if it be once admitted that all the events in time are equally real and equally central, then at every point there is a by-gone past, intrinsically perfectly substantial and self-existent; a past which such memories or continuations as may be integral to life at this later moment need continue only very partially, or need recover only schematically, if at all. In that case, if I ever find it convenient to forget my ancestors, or if my descendants find it advantageous to forget me, this fact might somewhat dash their vanity or mine if we should hear of it, but cannot touch our substantial existence or the truth of our lives. Grant this, and at once the whole universe is on its feet again; and all that strange pragmatic reduction of yesterday to tomorrow, of Sanskrit to the study of Sanskrit, of truth to the value of discovering some truth, and of matter to some human notion of matter, turns out to have been a needless equivocation, by which the perspectives of life, avowedly relative, have been treated as absolute, and the dominance of the foreground has been turned from a biological accident into a metaphysical principle. And this quite wantonly: because practice, far from suggesting such a reduction, precludes it, and requires every honest workman to admit the democratic equality of the past and the future with the present, and to regard the inner processes of matter with respect and not with transcendental arrogance. The living convictions of the pragmatist himself are those involved in action, and therefore naturalistic in the dogmatic sense; action involves belief, belief judgment, and judgment dogma; so that the transcendental metaphysics and the practical naturalism of the pragmatist are in sharp contradiction, both in logic and in spirit. The one expresses his speculative egotism, the other his animal faith.

Of course, it is not Dewey nor the pragmatic school that is to blame for this equivocation; it is a general heirloom, and has infected all that criticism of scholastic dogma on which modern philosophy is founded. By expressing this critical principle more thoroughly, the pragmatists have hoped to clear the air, and perhaps ultimately may help to do so. Although I am myself a dogmatic naturalist, I think that the station assumed by Dewey, like the transcendental station generally, is always legitimate. Just as the spirit has a right to soliloquize, and to regard existence as a strange dream, so any society or nation or living interest has a right to treat the world as its field of action, and to recast the human mind, as far as possible, so as to adapt it exclusively to that public function. That is what all great religions have tried to do, and what Sparta and Carthage would have done if they had produced philosophers. Why should not America attempt it? Reason is free to change its logic, as language to change its grammar; and the critic of the life of reason may then distinguish, as far as his penetration goes, how much in any such logic or grammar is expressive of material circumstances, how much is exuberant rhetoric, how much local, and how much human. Of course, at every step such criticism rests on naturalistic dogmas; we could not understand any phase of human imagination, or even discover it, unless we found it growing in the common world of geography and commerce. In this world fiction arises, and to this world it refers. In so far as criticism can trace back the most fantastic ideas—mythology, for instance—to their natural origin, it should enlighten our sympathies, since we should all have lived in the society of those images, if we had had the same surroundings and passions; and if in their turn the ideas prevalent in our own day can be traced back to the material conditions that bred them, our judgment should be enlightened also. Controversy, when naturalism is granted, can yield to interpretation, reconciling the critical mind to convention, justifying moral diversity, and carrying the sap of life to every top-most intellectual flower. All positive transcendental insights, whether empirical, national, or moral, can thus be honoured (and disinfected) by the baldest naturalism, remaining itself international, Bohemian, and animal. The luminous fog of immediacy has a place in nature; it is a meteorological and optical effect, and often a blessing. But why should immediacy be thought to be absolute or a criterion of reality? The great error of dogmatists, in hypostatizing their conclusions into alleged preexistent facts, did not lie in believing that facts of some kind pre-existed; the error lay only in framing an inadequate view of those facts and regarding it as adequate. God and matter are not any or all the definitions which philosophers may give of them: they are the realities confronted in action, the mysterious but momentous background, which philosophers and other men mean to describe by their definitions or myths or sensible images. To hypostatize these human symbols, and identify them with matter or with God, is idolatry: but the remedy for idolatry is not iconoclasm, because the senses, too, or the heart or the pragmatic intellect, can breed only symbols. The remedy is rather to employ the symbols pragmatically, with detachment and humour, trusting in the steady dispensations of the substance beyond.

Index

Absolute, 298, 375, 376, 441, 442, 522, 523, 528, 600, 601, 602, 606, 608
Absolutism, 563, 565
Achilles, 137
Act(s), 402, 403, 448
Action(s), 20, 112, 163, 166, 174, 179, 191, 182, 183, 199, 198, 204, 205, 231, 232, 237, 163, 257, 283, 284, 286, 315, 317, 334, 337, 424, 429, 430, 432, 444, 471, 539, 573, 576, 610, 618, 620
Actuality, 146, 147
Adam, 119, 373
Adaptation(s), 151, 188
Aeschylus, 601
Aesthetic(s)
  criticism, 321
  experience, 325
  faculty, 318
  feeling, 321
  goods, 316
  instinct, 318
  life, 322
  value(s), 309, 316, 317, 318, 325
  vice, 318
  virtue, 163
  mentioned, 15, 16, 317
Aestheticism, 332
Agnosticism, 254, 587, 588, 589
Alcibiades, 128, 134, 136
Alexander, 130, 418
Allah, 389–90, 441, 442
Altruism, 428, 429
America(n)
  and Calvinism, 529, 538
  and cooperation, 542, 543, 549
  and democracy, 542
  and duty, 547–48
  education systems, 543
  and England, 542
  and Englishmen, 541
  essence of, 542–43
  and freedom, 546–47
  and the genteel tradition, 527, 533, 534, 538, 555, 563
  and good will, 528
  and government, 546, 552
  humanists, 557, 561, 562, 567, 576
  intellect, 527
  and James, 534, 535
  mind, 527, 531
  and moral absolutism, 563
  and moral integrity, 563

  and morality, 528
  opinion, 611
  orthodoxy, 548
  philosophers, 530, 531
  philosophy, xlii, 527, 538, 611, 612
  and Protestantism, xxxvi
  and religions, 543, 589
  self-assertion, 604
  society, 611
  and transcendentalism, 530, 538
  and Whitman, 534
  will, 527
  writers, 529, 534
  mentioned, 471–72, 473, 541, 543, 620
Anglo-Saxon, 543, 544, 548
Animal(s)
  and absolute truth, 153
  action, 249
  being, 67
  bodies, 14
  and consciousness, 14
  and dreams, 111, 131
  and egotism, 81, 150
  essence of, 415
  and experience, 111, 151, 551
  faith, xxxiv, xliii, xliv, 14, 21, 40, 71, 83, 85, 86, 92, 95–97, 96, 97, 101, 111, 121, 122, 126, 141, 142, 144, 146, 159, 160, 174, 177, 183, 185, 187, 257, 259, 618, 620
  and feelings, 462
  harmony, 377
  and hatred, 422
  illusion, 86
  and imagination, 154
  and impulses, 428
  instincts, 85, 437, 551–52
  and intuition, 163
  and knowledge, 92, 153, 158
  and language, 138
  life, 14, 79, 81, 85, 88, 89, 95, 100, 119, 123, 138, 146, 158, 162, 213, 234, 263, 376, 383, 550, 598, 609, 619
  and literary psychology, 104
  and mind, 68, 97, 158, 572
  and moral reality, 572
  and nature, 19, 104, 320, 551
  passions, 385
  and perception, 207
  and philosophy, 153
  and psyche, 163, 227, 263, 372, 391, 406
  and scientific psychology, 104
  and the soul, 131, 415